# Revised and Expanded

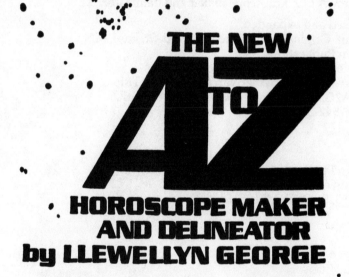

# THE NEW
# A TO Z
# HOROSCOPE MAKER
# AND DELINEATOR
# by LLEWELLYN GEORGE

Revised and Edited by Marylee Bytheriver

1994
Llewellyn Publications
St. Paul, Minnesota 55164-0383, U.S.A.

FIRST EDITION, 1910
THIRTEENTH EDITION (REVISED), 1981
Sixty-first Printing, 1994


Library of Congress Cataloging-in-Publication Data
George, Llewellyn, 1876-1954
    The new A to Z horoscope maker and delineator.

    "Revised and expanded."
    Reprint. Originally published: 13th ed. St. Paul, MN :
Llewellyn Publications, 1981.
    Includes index.
    1. Horoscopes.  I. Bytheriver, Marylee.  II. Title.
BF1728.A2G36    1986        133.5'4        83-80177
ISBN 0-87542-264-0


Llewellyn Publications
A Division of Llewellyn Worldwide, Ltd.
P.O. 64383, St. Paul, MN 55164-0383

To students of the useful arts and sciences and lovers of truth: to assist further research into the laws of nature, as interpreted by Astrology, for the benefit of all beings.

# Table of Contents

**Figures:**

# Foreword

Llewellyn George was proud to be a Leo, and throughout his life exhibited the positive Leo traits of open-heartedness, generosity, and good humor. He was born on August 17, 1876, at 4:18 AM, in Swansea, Wales. Coming to America as a young boy, he grew up in Chicago, where he was graduated from the Chicago School of Electricity in 1898. Though he was largely self-educated in the fields of philosophy and Astrology, he did complete a course at the Weltmer Institute of Suggestive Therapeutics in Nevada, Missouri.

After graduation, the 22-year old George moved to Portland, Oregon, and began to study Astrology under the tutelage of the noted Professor W. H. Chaney. There is no way of knowing what made this personable, intelligent young man turn to Astrology. At that time, there was a growing interest in all metaphysical subjects on the part of "advanced thinkers" in England and the U.S.

Earlier, Astrology had fallen into disrepute and become heavily laced with superstition and quackery, but the formation of the Theosophical Society in 1875 marked a whole new trend of interest in spiritualism, Astrology and other occult subjects. Astrology in particular gained in popularity under the pen name of Alan Leo, who wrote for the Theosophists in England, just before the turn of the century.

George soon met another young Astrology buff, L.H. Weston, and the two of them took rooms in the same boarding house. The two struggling students of the Occult arts taught Astrology classes and wrote articles for astrological periodicals. Even after West-

on moved to the eastern coast many years later, George continued
to hold great affection for him. Upon hearing of his death in 1945,
George wrote, "Professor Weston was perhaps my oldest friend. Together we did some of our best work."

In 1901 George, together with another young student of Professor Chaney's, Mrs. Ida Huley Fletcher, started the Portland School
of Astrology. Mrs. Fletcher, a handsome woman of about 50, had the
energy and enthusiasm needed to match that of the young men.
Together they rented a two-story house where Weston occupied the
entire garret and in the basement turned out *The Astrolite*. The school
took up the remaining space. Llewellyn Publishing Company was
officially launched that same year. A professional printer by this time,
George produced all of his own writings.

In 1906 George turned out his first issue of *The Moon Sign Book*,
which has been in continual publication ever since. This annual almanac
was as unique then as it is now, giving accurate, practical information
on using the Moon's cycles in gardening and other daily activities.

These bachelor years were very creative and productive for Llewellyn George. The year before he had started publishing the *Portland
School of Astrology Bulletina*, which in 1908 became the *Astrological
Bulletina*—one of George's most successful projects, running for fifty
years.

In 1910 George published his major work, the *A to Z Horoscope
Maker and Delineator*, from which this present volume stems. At this
time there were very few good Astrology textbooks. Except for transla-
tions of historical manuscripts, Alan Leo's works were the only quality
textbooks available. The *A to Z* and the *Bulletina* gained steadily in
popularity because George was able to combine a metaphysical
viewpoint with sound scientific procedures.

As a Theosophist, George advocated their approach to Astrology
as outlined by P.I.H. Naylor, in *Astrology in Historical Examination:*

[Astrology] was to be an insight into types of humanity, into
character, and into spiritual evolution of the people concerned.
The "inner meaning" of a horoscope became of much more
importance than its practical application.

Yet, as a scientist—for George considered Astrology a science—he did not let religious ideas interfere with common-sense, practical application or research methods. As he wrote to beginning students:

> Mathematically Astrology is a science, and therefore if you have made no mistake in your horoscopal calculations the results obtained will agree in a very astonishing manner with the facts as you know them.

In all, Llewellyn George wrote 17 books on Astrology and inumerable magazine articles and pamphlets. He felt teaching Astrology was a vital task and pursued it enthusiastically throughout his life. L.J. Jensen describes George's sense of mission:

> His heart and every thought was to popularize Astrology and show the world what a boon to humanity it could be. Study groups, individual reading and college courses in the subject were his dream.

Llewellyn George was also concerned with the public image of Astrology and the advancement of Astrology as a reputable profession. His small firm had a rough time in the conservative environment of Portland. Yet the adversity just threw him all the more intensely into his writing and studies. Throughout his life he was continually active in a number of professional organizations, and in 1913, he co-founded the American Astrological Society of New York, and installed A. Z. Stevenson as its first president.

In 1917, the 44-year-old George married Mignon Ruth of Tacoma, Washington. The first years were hard on the young George family, and outside agitation against George's work caused his wife to resent Astrology. Later George was saddened when she passed her prejudice on to their only child.

In 1920, seeking a more liberal environment where he could work in peace and respect, George moved with his wife and infant son to Los Angeles. He had a hard time at first, supporting his family and struggling to establish his printing plant and publishing company. During the depression years, George traveled around the country, lecturing on Astrology and Theosophy and selling his books and magazines. The popularity of Astrology increased dramatically with the advent of many who still regarded it as superstitious nonsense.

By this time George's half-brother, Griffith Ewart Abrams, had joined him. For many years, Griff served as best friend and aide-de-camp to his older brother. The plump, good-natured, lovable Lew, and the wiry, nervous, fast-talking Griff, were welcome in the homes of Astrology supporters throughout the country. George is still remembered affectionately by many of the people he met casually during this period.

Yet Llewellyn George still had time for organization work, and in 1927, he founded the National Astrological Association in Los Angeles, serving as its president for the first five years. This group was an early attempt to unify the many diverse astrological organizations throughout the country. An outgrowth of this group, the American Federation of Scientific Astrologers was formed in 1938, with its headquarters in Washington, D.C. It published a *Bulletin* and held national conventions. These two functions continue to be popular today.

By 1931, George's reputation and skill had grown to the point that the *Los Angeles Times* described him as:

> . . . a gentleman, a scholar, an astrologer, a resident of Westwood, LA. He is probably the best known astrological expert in this country, certainly the most read. He has gained international recognition during his 30 years of earnest and conscientious study and research work.

In 1939, at the age of 63, Llewellyn George was awarded the first endowment of Life Membership of the American Federation of Scientific Astrologers at their convention in New York City. From the first George was supportive of the group. Like his own National Astrological Association and later his Educational Astrology, Inc., the AFSA was founded by astrologers who were trying to disassociate themselves from "gyp artists," circus fortune-tellers and sidewalk showmen. The requirements for membership were "study, practice, experience, good citizenship and upholding the ethics of the community in which the astrologer practiced."

George formed a long-lasting personal friendship as well as a working relationship with Ernest and Catherine Grant who were active in the organization's headquarters. Upon receiving the award, George wrote to Ernest Grant:

I wish to emphasize that I sincerely appreciate the Certificate and all it implies, including the title, "Fellow of Astrology," as I consider myself a humble student feeling his way toward enlightenment among the stars.

George frequently wrote articles for the *Los Angeles Times* and other periodicals. He often made numerous predictions, and took an early stand against U.S. involvement in World War II. In 1940, Lew and Griff took a national lecture tour to try to awaken people to the probable devastation of a long war.

Yet, Llewellyn George was loyal to his adopted country. When, in 1942 an astrologer was arrested for treason, many people denounced Astrology. George wrote to Ernest Grant:

I have no sympathy for him [the traitor], but I am sorry for the slur he has brought upon the patriotic and legitimate practitioners in this profession. However, this will not really hurt Astrology, for it has withstood the ravages of time immemorial and has improved with age.

As Astrology gained in respectability and prestige during George's long career, he became increasingly optimistic and sought every opportunity to popularize and publicize Astrology. He believed that people like himself were the vanguard of the Aquarian Age, the "advance guard of an army of Truth and Peace." As he wrote in a new introduction to the *A to Z* in the early 1940's, "...Astrology is making rapid strides forward. The time has arrived for the masses as a whole to take an interest in the subject seriously and practically. Astrology has a grander, nobler, greater mission now than ever before in history."

At an age when most people have retired, Llewellyn George founded another professional organization and took on his most ambitious cause—the legalization of Astrology. On June 5, 1943, he became the first president of Educational Astrology, Inc. After finishing a five-year term, the jovial, affable George continued to serve as master of ceremonies at all their monthly public dinners.

A good friend, Mrs. Harriet K. Banes, served as vice-president to the young group. Several years earlier she and George had become charter members of the First Temple and College of Astrology in

Los Angeles. Harriet Banes served as Dean to the College from 1942 until her death in 1959. Mrs. Edna Scott, who served jointly as the vice-president of the American Federation of Scientific Astrologers and the treasurer of Educational Astrology, Inc., was also active in the First Temple.

When anti-fortune-telling laws were threatening the existence of legitimate Astrology in California, George, despite an overloaded work schedule and an ailing wife, threw himself into the fray. He became active in a committee which included prominent astrologers from all over the western coast: Lenora Conwell of the Church of Light; Edna Scott and Harriet Banes from the First Temple and College of Astrology; Ernest R. Mathison of the Church of the Cosmic Rays; L. Ada Fohl of the Hollywood School of Astrology; and Elbert Benjamine of the Astrological Brotherhood of California. (Benjamine is better known as C. C. Zain, author of the Church of Light lessons.) Together they drew up legislation designed to certify qualified astrological professionals. In January, 1943, Assemblyman Everett G. Burkhalter presented the Astrologic Law, Bill No. 1793, to the state legislature.

These many astrological organizations were riding a tide of interest in the Occult which began around the turn of the century. Along with the Theosophists and the Rosicrucians, there were a number of other metaphysically-oriented organizations which advocated and taught Astrology from a spiritual perspective.

Though he was a Theosophist, George was known for his scientific, impartial approach to Astrology. His motto was "facts, not fancies." George, like Ernest Grant and other founders of the ASFA, believed it was important for Astrology to divorce itself from any one religious philosophy. They were concerned that all legislative proposals be free from any mention of spiritual matters, and George acted as a mediator among the diverse religious perspectives on the committee.

Though this attempt to gain legal sanctions for Astrology failed, a year later George was again organizing others in his cause. As he wrote to Grant in March, 1944:

> On Sunday last I called a meeting of representatives of the Astrological Fraternity in Los Angeles to discuss a plan to propose to

the L. A. Council (via the Police Commissioners) the idea of
enacting an Ordinance [requiring] all applicants for [an Astrology]
license to pass an examination satisfactorily before being per-
mitted to practice.

Thirty years later the American Federation of Astrologers*
instituted such a plan.

Educational Astrology, Inc. hired an attorney to act as their
lobbyist, and "to get us separated from the fortune-tellers in the minds
of the Councilmen." The organization also contributed to the re-
election campaign of Assemblyman Burkhalter, so that he would
"again befriend us in Sacramento."

When this attempt also failed, George was not discouraged.
In 1945, he was again writing the AFA asking for more donations
to support the new Educational Astrology legislative plans. Though
none of his bills were ever passed, he never gave up the vision that
Astrology would someday be as respectable and controlled a profession as medicine or law.

Though Mrs. George's continued ill health prevented Lew from
traveling, he had enough to do at home. It was not unusual for him to
write until 4 or 5 AM, take a brief nap, then get up to go to work at the
print shop. During this period, he wrote Grant, " 'Life begins at forty'—
said somebody who seemed to know all about life; and I say that at 68
it is exceedingly interesting and in my special case, very, very,
strenuous!"

Llewellyn George died in 1954 at the age of 77. But his ideas
continue to be relevant today. He, perhaps more than any other
astrologer in this century, is credited with re-establishing Astrology as a
valid and workable system and removing the connotations of charlatanry
and superstition from the astrologer's trade. In 1963, the International
Congress of Astral Sciences, meeting in Santa Monica, voted Llewellyn
George "America's finest astrological writer."

In 1960, Llewellyn Publications was sold to Carl L. Weschcke
who moved the firm to his home town of St.Paul, Minnesota. There he
continues to publish the annual *Moon Sign Book* and *Astro-Calendar*
and has sold over 100,000 copies of the original edition of the *A to Z
Horoscope Maker and Delineator*.

*The American Federation of Astrologers dropped the word "Scientific" from
their name in 1945.

When I began working for Llewellyn Publications in March of 1970, one of my first jobs was to write a catalog of about 300 Astrology books. At that time it was Llewellyn's policy to distribute every book in print in English on the subject of Astrology. Up through the 1970s there were very few standard reference books available. The *A to Z Horoscope Maker and Delineator* was then, and remains today, a classic in its field.

In this revised and updated version we have streamlined the organization, eliminated some of the idiomatic language and modernized the social perspective. Occasionally we have retained such words as "delineation" or "genethiacal" which may be unfamiliar. These are fully explained in the expanded *Dictionary of Astrological Terms*. All materials essential to Llewellyn George's ideas and teachings remain complete.

The original edition of the *A to Z* was written before the discovery of Pluto in 1930. Therefore a major change in the revised edition is the inclusion of material on Pluto throughout the text. This change is especially noticeable in the interpretation section. Isabel Hickey's *Pluto or Minerva, The Choice is Yours* (Altieri Press, Bridgeport, Conn.) was used as a reference for this material.

Many years ago Llewellyn George wrote:

By conscious cooperation with natural law indicated by the solar system, conditions are created which provide opportunities for us to rise above the common illusions of life by spiritual interpretation and finer reactions.

If from these pages the reader gains but a small part of the pleasure and practical benefit the author has derived from the study of Astrology, I will feel well repaid for thus presenting the results of investigations and practice which have extended over many years.

Marylee Bytheriver, Garberville, California
November, 1980

# Basic Principles
# of
# Astrology

# Introduction

The word *Astrology* is derived from two Greek words, *astra*, a star, and *logos*, logic or reason. It literally implies the doctrine and law as shown by the stars or planets. Astrology is the science which defines the action of celestial bodies upon animate and inanimate objects, and their reaction to such influences. It is the parent of astronomy.

Originally all who studied the stars were astrologers. The antiquity of Astrology is such as to place it among the very earliest records of human learning. Later, Astrology and astronomy were one science, but the latter now may be termed a purely objective science, concerned as it is with the outer expressions of other worlds. Astrology may be considered as subjective, dealing with the influence of the life within the form and its effect upon surrounding bodies, the earth and its inhabitants in particular, and so it may be termed: *the study of life's reaction to planetary vibrations*. The making of a horoscopal figure is an astronomical process; the reading of the chart is astrological.

Astrology is taken from the records of astral phenomena and reduced to a science by observing the effects of planetary influence, commencing with the history of humans, these observations being compiled and recorded by some of the brightest intellects known, both ancient and modern. To test the reliability, its truth and the advantages it offers, requires only earnest unprejudiced investigation.

Astrology as the interpreter of nature, shows that the world is conducted according to a well-defined plan. Everything is arranged

with wonderful order, duly timed with marvelous precision and eff-
ected with unerring accuracy. Nothing happens by chance; there are
no accidents in the divine plan; and in reality there is no discord, for
nature recognizes no distinctions and works only for progress through
a refining process which sometimes destroys only to reconstruct with
improvement. As students advance in the study of Astrology they
realize that we are here for certain definite, natural purporses, each
in his or her own place according to an orderly or cosmic plan, with
opportunities to produce certain results by refining our reactions to
planetary influences.

Anyone with ordinary ability can learn much of Astrology. It is
no longer a difficult study. Nothing out of the ordinary is required to
become acquainted with it. With proper instruction and a reasonable
amount of effort one can learn to cast a horoscope and read it so that
it becomes a guide regarding changes, health, marriage, business and all
important affairs of life. The capable astrologer is a student of psychology, anatomy, biochemistry, hygiene, dietetics, agriculture, political
and domestic economy, vocational analysis and metaphysics.

However, Astrology is most readily assimilated by those who have
an inborn love of mystical subjects, and who at the same time, possess
an active sixth sense faculty, that of intuition.

If the foregoing remarks seem to relate to ponderous or mysterious subjects, do not be alarmed, for in pursuing this fascinating study
the features referred to will be gradually and easily assimilated.

Many of the world's best astrologers who are teaching and prac-
ticing today received their initial training through this study course. In
it they found a complete, accurate and practical system of Astrology
which could be employed in public practice and applied to personal
requirements.

Due to the universality of Astrology, students of the stellar science
are drawn from all races and nations and from widely varying stations
of life. The artist, the musician, the teacher, the homemaker, the
businessman—each represent different lifestyles to which astrology is
applicable and individualized.

There is not only pleasure but satisfaction and profit as well in
the knowledge which Astrology provides. Here you contact the higher
realms of nature; you become conversant with her duly timed operations; you recognize the laws of vibration which throb through the

universe, animating every object, developing attitudes, directing actions and determining environment. With those urges for expression the student is enabled to direct his or her conduct intelligently, according to the degree of knowledge and the nature of aspirations, along those paths which mean health, happiness, usefulness and progress.

Astrology asks only impartial, fair investigation on its merits and when accorded such consideration always emerges with the same respect and admiration as other subjects which are being developed along scientific lines to reveal the workings of nature and to interpret its influences.

Although Astrology has been criticized, *it has never yet been disproved by its own tenets*; on the contrary, it is continually presenting proof of its merits. These lessons supply abundant material for you to test its values satisfactorily.

**Note.** All the technical terms used in these lessons are defined in the *Astrological Dictionary*, page 555.

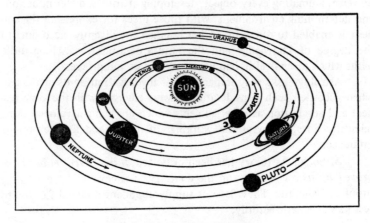

Figure 1: Our Solar System

# The Signs
# of the Zodiac

The Zodiac is a circle of space in the sky, containing the orbits of the planets. It may be imagined as a belt of space in the heavens about 15 degrees wide in which the planets travel. It is also the Sun's apparent path called the ecliptic. The zodiacal circle is divided into twelve parts; each part contains 30 degrees of space, making a total of 360 degrees in the circle. The twelve divisions are known as the *signs of the Zodiac*.

Each zodiacal sign possesses a certain specific influence and quality of its own. The revolution of the earth around the Sun, complete in one year, causes the Sun to appear to travel through the Zodiac at the rate of one sign per month, or approximately through one degree per day and its influence (according to sign and degree) determines not only the seasons but also the general nature and character of beings born at that time.

The various planets as they travel through the Zodiac also exert an influence according to their separate natures and in correspondence with the quality of each aspect which they may form, blended with the nature of the signs in which they are located. The luminaries (Sun and Moon) are classified as planets for convenience. (See: *The Planets in the Signs*, page 223.)

When erecting a chart or horoscope we draw a circle and divide it into twelve spaces. These spaces are termed *houses* and are numbered from one to twelve. The First House is that space which is located just *under* the eastern angle of the chart on the left hand side. The Twelfth House is the space just *above* the eastern angle. At the cusps (dividing lines) of these houses are written the zodiacal signs. The sign that is placed on the cusp of the First House, i.e., the line marking the eastern horizon, is called the *Rising Sign* or *Ascendant*.

To an ordinary observer the earth appears to be stationary and the signs of the Zodiac seem to revolve around it from east to west. This appearance is in reality due to the rotation of the earth from west to east. This causes a new degree of the Zodiac to appear to ascend a-bove the eastern horizon every four minutes, a complete sign every two hours and the whole twelve signs of the Zodiac in twenty-four hours. The First House is *always* the space just under the eastern horizon, regardless of which sign might be passing over that cusp.

Due to the earth's rotation on its axis, making a complete turn every twenty-four hours, a new degree of the Zodiac appears on the eastern horizon every four minutes and a new sign appears every two hours. Astrological researchers are very particular as to the time of a birth, in order to determine exactly what degree and sign were on the eastern horizon when the blessed event occurred.

"Each star has its own glory," quotes the Bible. Astrologers have determined that each of the twelve signs has its own distinctive qualities which are bestowed upon individuals according to their birthday. In fact, during the long ages in which some of the brightest minds of the world have given attention to the influence of the signs of the Zodiac, it has developed that each of the 360 degrees, constituting the zodiacal circle, has a specific influence, and in various ways they express themselves in individuals in whose life they have association through relationship at the time of birth.

At the moment of birth one of the twelve signs of the Zodiac and one degree out of the thirty degrees constituting that particular sign, are ascending on the eastern horizon and these largely determine the personality and characteristics of that individual.

It is obvious that as the earth turns one degree in four minutes, thirty degrees or one sign will appear and pass up over the horizon every two hours; while during the twenty-four hours of one day all the signs and degrees will have passed the horizon. Consequently, it would seem that during the day there would be twelve types (signs) of characters, with thirty variations (degrees) in each sign type. By this is seen one reason why humans differ, instead of being all alike, when born on the same day. To accentuate this dissimilarity among those closely related in point of time (but disassociated in point of space) we have also to consider such elements as race, caste and hereditary strain.

However, we are mainly concerned with potent astrological influences. If the earth's rotation on its axis were the only factor involved, we would have the comparatively limited number of 360 characters representing 360 zodiacal degrees differentiated (in groups of thirty) by the twelve signs. But in reality this number is augmented by the fact that during rotation on its axis in one day the earth is also transiting one degree along its orbit thereby each day giving a new variety to the types and the 360 variations, of those born in that rotation. This variety multiplies for approximately thirty days during which time the earth will have traversed thirty degrees in orbit and will then enter the next sign of the Zodiac, to repeat the daily variations with a different lot of individuals under a new month-sign. The orbit transit from one sign to another determines the type of individuality while, as before stated, the rotation on axis determines the type of personality. Thus, people born in the same Sun Sign inherently possess similar individualities but the date of the month and the time of day both operate to provide different personalities.

Astrologically the individuality is designated by the apparent zodiacal position of the Sun; personality is designated by the ascending degree and sign due to the relative axial position of the earth as indicated from any certain latitude.

*Individuality* may be considered as inherent qualities, tendencies and latent powers or those inner qualities by which the individual knows himself.

*Personality* may be regarded as the style or nature of expression which outwardly characterizes the person; that which distinguishes him and identifies him to others.

It has been said by esoteric students that your ascending sign in this birth was your Sun Sign in the preceding incarnation; what is your Sun Sign now will be your ascending sign in the next life. If your Sun Sign and your Ascendant are now the same, you are repeating that sign because you failed to it properly or fully in your previous incarnation.

To this great variety of differences manifested in human beings, other astrological factors must be reckoned. Among a few of those which make considerable difference might be mentioned: the Sun either above or below the horizon at the moment of birth; the Moon above or below; the Moon's distance from the Ascendant, the location and position of the other planets by sign and house, the latitude and longitude of the place of birth, etc. All these factors act to produce the innumerable specimens of humanity.

## Ascendant: Axial Rotation of the Earth Determines Personality

Every four minutes: a new ascending degree.

Every two hours: a new zodiacal sign.

Every twenty-four hours: twelve signs of 360°.

360 variations per day (axial) multiplied by 365 days per year (orbital) equals 131,400 variations of personality yearly.

## Sun Sign: Orbital Revolutions of the Earth Determine Individuality

Each day: approximately one degree of the Zodiac.

Each month: one sign giving the Sun the appearance of passing through one sign each month.

One year: twelve signs of 360°.

360 variations of individuality yearly.

Adding the variations produced by these earth movements, we have a total of 131,760 astrological types.

You may learn a great deal about anyone just by studying his or her Sun Sign. You may acquire additional information by studying his or her Ascendant. You may learn still more about that person when you read the influence of the planets as they were located in the different signs at the time of birth. The house positions of the planets at the time of birth will provide further revelations.

## Fate vs. Free Will

The progressive student will do well to remember that destiny properly means *whatever is possible unto us* and fate means the *outward circumstances which appear in our pathway*, to be manipulated and eventually overcome through effort and understanding. "He who would slay dragons must first learn their habits." To overcome fate you must first know your fate. Astrology points the way to that desirable information.

Astrology is not a doctrine of fatalism. It provides us with an inventory of the working materials with which we were endowed at birth in the form of tendencies, mental capacity, physical endowments and abilities; but how you use or neglect to use the tools remains within your own jurisdiction. "Wisdom puts an end to pain." Through Astrology, you learn to improve your workmanship on the wheel of life and consequently to improve your fate by complying consciously with nature's laws instead of violating them.

## Earth-centered Astrology

This system of Astrology is known as the modernized Arabian System, the oldest known but revised and adapted to present times and people. Corresponding to and harmonizing with astronomy, it is necessarily *geocentric* in its methods (*geo* meaning earth and *centric* meaning center). In other words, recognizing the earth as a center of influence and observation.

As it is difficult to realize the movement of the earth in its orbit at the rate of 1,102.8 miles per minute and as the apparent movement of the Sun seems so real, for simplicity and convenience these two bodies are transposed, that is, the earth is put in the center and the Sun seen to transit the earth's path. Thus, modern Astrology uses a geo-centric instead of heliocentric system.

Earth is a planet whose orbit lies between that of Venus and Mars. It has an axial rotation complete in 24 hours producing diurnal and nocturnal phenomena. This rotation from west to east gives the appearance of the Sun, Moon and stars rising in the east and setting in the west, while actually the reverse is true as they in reality proceed in the direction of the order of the signs, from Aries to Taurus, etc. The earth's passage through the Zodiac, in which it revolves around the Sun in approximately 365½ days, causes the sun to appear to be transiting through the signs opposite to those through which the earth courses, hence the expressions, Sun in Aries, Sun in Taurus, etc. When the Sun seems to be in Aries between March 21 and April 19, the earth is in the opposite sign, Libra, but the astrological influence and position are designated as Sun in Aries.

Placing the earth in the center of the chart also makes it easy to visualize how by turning on its axis, the signs appear to ascend on the eastern horizon and descend on the western.

## The Chart Illustrated

The chart given below illustrates the position which the houses always maintain in a horoscope; also the direction in which the signs and planets appear to move, as mentioned above. It is a conventional type of astrological diagram of the heavens (Zodiac) at a certain date, time and place.

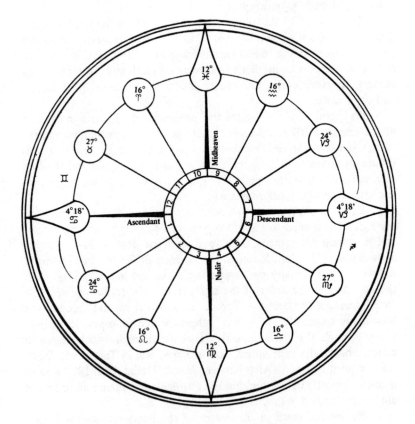

**Figure 2: The Chart Illustrated**

The outer circle shows degrees of the signs (shown in the inner circle) which are crossing over the dividing cusps of the houses. The houses are the twelve segments or spaces in which the planets' places can be recorded.

As the birthday was between August 23 and September 22, the Sun is in the zodiacal sign Virgo, so this individual's Sun Sign is Virgo.

At the time of day this person was born the zodiacal sign Cancer was on the Ascendant, of which four degrees was ascending or crossing the First House cusp.

## Longitude

> 60 seconds (") make 1 minute (')
> 60 minutes (') make 1 degree (°)
> 30 degrees (°) make 1 sign
> 12 signs (or 360°) make a complete circle—the Zodiac

**Table 1: Longitude**

## The Symbols of the Signs

| ♈ Aries | ♎ Libra |
| ♉ Taurus | ♏ Scorpio |
| ♊ Gemini | ♐ Sagittarius |
| ♋ Cancer | ♑ Capricorn |
| ♌ Leo | ♒ Aquarius |
| ♍ Virgo | ♓ Pisces |

**Table 2: The Signs**

**Note.** When placed in a chart the signs of the Zodiac always come opposite to each other as show above. Learn them in that order. In Figure 2: *The Chart Illustrated* note how the signs are placed on opposite cusps as shown in this table.

Practice making the symbols until you can make them very quickly and read them without referring to the text. Learn which signs are opposite each other. Also memorize thoroughly the names of the signs with their planetary rulers. Remember that a planet is a heavenly body, a sign is a space in the Zodiac and a house is a section of a chart.

## The Planetary Rulers

There is a corresponding vibration, a harmonious interchange as it were, between certain zodiacal signs and certain planets. To each sign is therefore assigned a planet which is termed its ruler. Venus and Mercury each rule two signs. Memorize the following table. It contains the planetary rulerships.

♂ Mars rules ♈ Aries
♀ Venus rules ♉ Taurus and ♎ Libra
☿ Mercury rules ♊ Gemini and ♍ Virgo
☽ Moon rules ♋ Cancer
☉ Sun rules ♌ Leo
♇ Pluto rules ♏ Scorpio
♃ Jupiter rules ♐ Sagittarius
♄ Saturn rules ♑ Capricorn
♅ Uranus rules ♒ Aquarius
♆ Neptune rules ♓ Pisces

**Table 3: The Signs and Their Rulers**

## Zones of the Human Body Ruled by the Zodiacal Signs

Aries rules the head and face.

Taurus rules the neck, throat and ears.

Gemini rules the hands, arms, shoulders, collar bone, lungs and nervous system.

Cancer rules the breasts and stomach.

Leo rules the heart, sides and the upper portion of the back.

Virgo rules the solar plexus and the bowels.

Libra rules the kidneys, reins, loins, ovaries and the lower back.

Scorpio rules the bladder and the sex organs.

Sagittarius rules the liver, hips and thighs.

Capricorn rules the knees.

Aquarius rules the calves and ankles.

Pisces rules the feet.

## Triplicity

The zodiacal signs are divided into four groups called triplicities, representing the four elements, fire, earth, air and water. These manifest in humanity as four specific temperaments.

### The Fire Triplicity—Aries, Leo, Sagittarius

The Fire Triplicity is represented by the choleric or bilious temperament, exhibiting a rash, feverish, easily-excited or impulsive nature with inflammatory and bilious affections, sudden illness, generally acute but usually of short duration.

The fiery signs represent the vital spirit, the bodily heat with its elements of combustion, all of which incline to activity: political, military and speculative interests.

To this triplicity of fire and spirit belong the little nature spirits called Salamanders.

### The Earth Triplicity—Taurus, Virgo, Capricorn

The Earth Triplicity is represented by the nervous temperament more especially noticed through Virgo and Capricorn, exhibiting alert, restless, worried, agitated, neurasthenic characteristics, with disposition to rheumatism and chronic disorders. The earthly signs represent the physical or temporal states all of which produce artistic, imaginative, studious and organizing tendencies.

"Little folk of the hills and vales" or Gnomes, as they are usually called, have an especial affinity for the triplicity of earth.

### The Air Triplicity—Gemini, Libra, Aquarius

The Air Triplicity is represented by the sanguine temperament, exhibiting active circulation, plump body, good complexion, genial nature, cheerful anticipation, good fellowship and general dexterity. The airy signs are said to represent the relative or connective conditions both within and without the body. For instance, Gemini rules the nervous system which connects the entire body and even neighbors, with whom the native is associated. In this airy family we find another relative not ordinarily included in that category – Sylphs.

This trigon expresses as active, scientific and industrial. It has a tendency toward illnesses arising from exhaustion or over-exertion.

### The Water Triplicity—Cancer, Scorpio, Pisces

The Water Triplicity is represented by the lymphatic temperament exhibiting as languid, anemic, pallid, weak-pulsed, lack of red corpuscles in the blood, and deficient vascular action. The watery trigone represents the mutational and propagative conditions. This triplicity is known as emotional, plastic, contemplative.

Sprites of the waters, the Undines, find their best expression through the watery signs.

### Quadrature

The zodiacal signs are also divided into three groups called quadratures, representing cardinal, fixed and mutable signs.

### The Cardinal or Movable Signs—Aries, Cancer, Libra, Capricorn

The cardinal signs may be likened to the cardinal points of a compass: Aries, east; Libra, west; Cancer, north; Capricorn, south. These signs are called cardinal signs because of the change of seasons then: Aries, spring; Cancer, summer; Libra, fall; Capricorn, winter. These changes of season are due to the Sun's apparent change of declination or in reality, to the obliquity of the Earth according to its location in its orbit.

Persons born during the time of cardinal signs are said to be versatile, adaptable and readily capable of adjusting themselves to changing conditions as they occur.

### The Fixed Signs—Taurus, Leo, Scorpio, Aquarius

The fixed signs may be likened to the middle of the season, there being three signs to every season. If the cardinal signs bring us into a change of season then the fixed signs see us firmly centered or set in those seasons.

Those born in fixed signs are more set in their ways and more fixed in their views than those born in cardinal or mutable signs. They are likely to have more continuity and be more difficult to move, change or sway. They do not so readily change their minds; are not so quick to adjust and adapt themselves.

### The Mutable, Common  or Flexed Signs—Gemini, Virgo, Sagittarius, Pisces

Mutable signs are the third or last months of the four seasons. We have all become well acquainted with the season throughout the cardinal and fixed months and in the common signs we finish up the duties which are common to such season and begin to prepare for the change in the next quarter.

Those born in mutable signs have more or less the attributes of both the cardinal and fixed signs and can adapt themselves to the natures of both those signs; consequently, to the natives of the other signs, those of mutable signs seem to be unstable.

## Classifications

**Fruitful signs**—Cancer, Scorpio, Pisces.

**Barren signs**-Aries, Gemini, Leo, Virgo, Sagittarius, Aquarius.

**Semi-fruitful signs**—Taurus, Libra, Capricorn.

**Masculine, or positive signs**—Aries, Gemini, Leo, Libra, Sagittarius, Aquarius.

**Feminine, or negative signs**—Taurus, Cancer, Virgo, Scorpio, Capricorn, Pisces.

**Northern signs**—Aries, Taurus, Gemini, Cancer, Leo, Virgo; signs in which the Sun has north declination from March 21 to September 23.

**Southern signs**—Libra, Scorpio, Sagittarius, Capricorn, Aquarius, Pisces; signs in which the Sun has south declination from September 24 to March 20.

**Signs of short ascension**—Capricorn, Aquarius, Pisces, Aries, Taurus, Gemini; these are signs which are often found intercepted in horoscopes. For places in the southern hemisphere the signs long and short must be reversed.

**Signs of long ascension**—Cancer, Leo, Virgo, Libra, Scorpio, Sagittarius; they often take longer to ascend over the horizon than the others and therefore occupy two cusps in a chart, which is due to mundane rather than zodiacal causes.

**Bi-corporeal or double-bodied signs**—Gemini, Pisces and the first half of Sagittarius; each sign is pictured as of two distinct parts: Gemini, the twins; Sagittarius, the horse and the archer; Pisces, the two fishes. They incline toward duality.

**Equinoctial signs**—Aries, Libra. They begin on the Spring equinox, March 21, and Autumnal equinox, September 23.

**Tropical signs**—Cancer, Capricorn. The points in the ecliptic in which the Sun is farthest from the Equator occur on June 22, the beginning of Cancer, at the Tropic of Cancer, and on December 22, the beginning of Capricorn, at the Tropic of Capricorn.

**Human signs**—Gemini, Virgo, Aquarius and the first part of Sagittarius.

**Bestial signs**—Aries, Taurus, Leo, Capricorn and the last half of Sagittarius.

**Signs of voice**—Gemini, Virgo, Libra, Sagittarius and Aquarius.

**Mute signs**—Cancer, Scorpio, Pisces.

## Decans

A decan or decanate consists of ten degrees or one-third of a sign, hence there are three decans in each sign, thirty-six in the Zodiac. While a planet rules its sign as a whole and especially the first decan the other two divisions of a sign each expresses a sub-influence of the nature of the planets which rule the remaining signs of the same triplicity. To illustrate: in the case of Aries, Mars rules the whole sign and the first decan; the Sun, because it rules the next sign of the fire triplicity, Leo, rules the second decan; and Jupiter, because it rules the next sign of the fire triplicity, Sagittarius, rules the third decan.

The use of the decans in Natal Astrology is applicable principally to the ascending sign. By noting which decan is on the First House cusp, we get an idea of what particular part of the sign the native is expressing. The planet ruling the decan ascending should be given attention along with the other planets which are the rulers in the Horoscope.

| Signs | 0° - 10° | 11° - 20° | 21° - 30° |
|---|---|---|---|
| Aries | Mars | Sun | Jupiter |
| Taurus | Venus | Mercury | Saturn |
| Gemini | Mercury | Venus | Uranus |
| Cancer | Moon | Pluto | Neptune |
| Leo | Sun | Jupiter | Mars |
| Virgo | Mercury | Saturn | Venus |
| Libra | Venus | Uranus | Mercury |
| Scorpio | Pluto | Neptune | Moon |
| Sagittarius | Jupiter | Mars | Sun |
| Capricorn | Saturn | Venus | Mercury |
| Aquarius | Uranus | Mercury | Venus |
| Pisces | Neptune | Moon | Pluto |

Table 4: The Decans

# The Planets

In Astrology ten of the heavenly bodies are used because of their size, proximity and influence on the earth, and its human, animal, vegetable. and mineral kingdoms. In the proper order of their speed through the Zodiac they are: ☾ the Moon, ☿ Mercury, ♀ Venus, ☉ the Sun, ♂ Mars, ♃ Jupiter, ♄ Saturn, ♅ Uranus, ♆ Neptune and ♇ Pluto.

For various reasons it is more convenient to speak of the Sun as transiting the Zodiac instead of the earth. It is simpler to imagine the earth as the center of observation and all planets revolving around it. In astronomy the Sun is the center while the earth actually revolves around the Sun in an orbit between Venus and Mars.

The Moon is a satellite of the earth and revolves about it. To an observer on the earth the Moon appears to be going through one sign after another, making the circuit in approximately 28 days.

## Nature of the Planets

The benefic planets are Jupiter and Venus; Jupiter is known as "the greater fortune" and Venus as "the lesser fortune." The influence of the Sun and Moon is considered good also.

Mars, Saturn and Uranus are known as the malefics.

Mercury, Neptune and Pluto are neutral planets—their influence is good when they are well aspected with other planets, but malefic when adversely aspected.

When you see words like "malefic," "adverse," "bad," "unfavor-

35

able," etc., bear in mind that such terms are used only for want of terminology that more fittingly describes planetary vibrations. All signs and all planets are good but our human reactions may be bad, according to our stage of development. As more people become astrologically educated, a new terminology will develop which will more definitely describe astrological influences. Later it will be shown that no planets are evil in nature, but our manifested responses may be judged as good or adverse.

## The Moon

The Moon rules the domestic and maternal interests and represents the personality as shown outwardly. Personality is what we see of a person in physical appearance, word, act, etc., which distinguishes one person from another. If the Moon is well placed in the horoscope, the person exhibits a pleasing personality; vice versa if the Moon is not. Refer to what was said in Lesson One about the sign ascending at the moment of birth and the personality.

The Moon is moist, cold, plastic, feminine and fruitful. It governs the stomach and breasts and rules liquids and common commodities.

The Moon rules reproduction, the domestic and maternal instinct, growth of plant life, publicity.

## Mercury

Mercury is related to or rules, the mind, objective sight, perception and expression and has dominion over communications, travel, barter, and trade.

Mercury is neutral, convertible, cold and moist. It governs the nervous system and intellectual perception. It rules handwriting, study, literature and journalism.

Mercury rules sight, imitation and the power to learn and convey to others what has been learned.

## Venus

Venus rules the affections (love), the sense of touch, art, pleasure, toiletries, luxury.

Venus is feminine, passive, warm, moist, fruitful and benefic. It rules the throat and veins, inclines to the finer attributes of the mind as expressed through the arts and crafts, grace, beauty, adornment, refined amusement, sympathy and compassion. It is called the "lesser fortune."

Venus rules conjugality, love, music, coquetry, entertainment and sociability.

## The Sun

The Sun rules character, individuality (that which we are), power and authority, the "top man."

The Sun is hot, dry, masculine, inflammatory and electric. It also governs the sides, back and heart. It signifies influence and high office.

The Sun rules the hope, courage, magnanimity and the aspirations. Represents rulership, honor.

## Mars

Mars rules energy, force, action, muscle, enterprise, initiative, contention, desire, the sense of taste, accidents.

Mars is hot, dry, masculine, inflammatory and malefic. It governs the head, face and muscular system. It signifies strength and activity.

Mars rules volition, work, conquest and the desires. Construction and destruction.

## Jupiter

Jupiter rules benevolence, expansion, optimism and confidence in the meaning and purpose of life.

Jupiter is hot, moist, moderate and temperate. It governs the blood, liver and thighs. It rules reason and judgment. Being a benefic, its tendency is towards opulence and success and is called the "greater fortune."

Jupiter rules promotion, growth, joviality, reasoning, calculation, philosophy.

## Saturn

Saturn rules solidification, discrimination, reserve, delay, sorrow and the sense of hearing.

Saturn is cold, hard, earthly, masculine and malefic. It governs the bones generally, knees and spleen particularly. It is grave, cautious and binding.

Saturn rules form and organization. It is contractive, cohesive, adhesive, cooling and sustaining.

## Uranus

Uranus rules inner sign (clairvoyance), intuition, surprise, adventure, ingenuity, originality and invention.

Uranus is cold, dry, airy, positive, electromagnetic, occult, extreme, spasmodic and precipitate. It governs the aura and intuitive perception and rules invention, investigation, reforms, revolution and rebellion.

## Neptune

Neptune rules feeling without physical contact (psychometry), psychism, perversion.

Neptune is cold, moist, neutral, convertible, negative and neurotic. It governs spirit perception and mediumship. It rules secret, mysterious, questionable and obscure matters, idealism and aesthetic art.

Neptune rules the psychic faculty, the sea, serums, narcotics, mystery.

## Pluto

Pluto is concerned with the underworld, poison, death and other such murky matters. It has affinity with interests related to rejuvenation, regeneration, transformation, metamorphosis; the spirit world, materializations and astral projection. It is concerned with the subconscious mind and the conscience, metabolism, chemicalization and assimilation. Also chemistry, alchemy, refining processes, poisonous fumes, lethal drugs, counterirritants like linaments and capsicum, and possibly volatile oils and vapors used for energy and power.

Pluto rules conscience, that inner prompter which helps us judge right from wrong, subconscious activities, and stern, incorruptible judges.

A distinction should be made between the different ways in which signs and planets express their energy. The signs correspond to parts of the body and by analogy, parts of the psyche. The twelve signs together represent the sum total of physical and psychological functioning. Their expression is moderated by the placement of the planets and their rulerships over the signs. Thus, a planet channels, interferes with, intensifies, concertizes, or effects in some way, according to the nature of that planet, the sign it is in and has rulership over.

## Octaves

**Venus and Neptune.** Venus, ruler of the signs Taurus and Libra, calls forth response from the finer attributes of the being, inclining to beauty, harmony, sociability, gaiety and popular music. It gives appreciation or ability for art and for producing beautiful music.

Neptune is termed the higher octave of Venus. It reveres beauty in its broader, deeper or universal aspect, in contradistinction to personal appearances. Venus may be said to represent the cultivated musician; Neptune the inspired. Venus rules the sense of touch or feeling; Neptune rules the psychometric faculty. Venus and Neptune are natural complements. Venus is exalted in Neptune's sign, Pisces.

**Mercury and Uranus.** Mercury is the ruler of the mental signs, Gemini and Virgo. Mercury rules ordinary mental processes through which one acquires knowledge by observation, perception, reading, writing, speaking, listening.

Uranus is termed a higher octave of Mercury. It rules a mental sign, Aquarius. It governs that phase of the mind which is not dependent upon the ordinary perceptive processes. Mercury represents knowledge we acquire through present conditions; Uranus represents accumulated wisdom gained through previous experiences manifesting as intuition. Mercury is the learner; Uranus is the knower. Mercury rules sight; Uranus rules clairvoyance.

**Mars and Pluto.** Mars, ruler of Aries, is concerned with physical and sexual energy. It rules the physical body, health, and outward directed energy.

Pluto is a higher octave of Mars. Pluto is concerned with energy that is directed inward for spiritual growth. Mars represents destruction and violence; Pluto represents the rebirth which follows death, and the transformative process which should accompany the violent destruction of old, irrelevant life phases.

## Planets and Occupations

The commercial world is divided into ten general divisions, each ruled by a planet in the following order:

The Moon: common employments.

Mercury: schools, intellectual affairs and publishing.
Venus: entertainment, art and social functions.
The Sun: government employment.
Mars: manufacturing, building, and munitions.
Jupiter: religious, legal and financial affairs.
Saturn: mining, farming, and cement work.
Uranus: railroads, aerial and electric industries.
Neptune: oil and fishing industries.
Pluto: waste recycling and research work.

Each division is subject to ten sub-divisions which in turn are ruled by the ten planets. Take the oil industry for example: the first division is ruled by Neptune itself and the first impression is that this industry is a vast, intricate, complicated scheme whereby the people represented by every other planet down the scale are frequently deceived and robbed and the power to do this is gained through secret intrigues, lobbying interests and other underhand and out-of-sight methods. This represents Neptune's unfavorable influence; more correctly speaking, a gross interpretation or manifestation of its influence.

The second division of the industry under consideration is ruled by Uranus, the enlightener. (Oil is used for light and power.) This planet governs the transportation facilities connected therewith. The next division is ruled by Saturn and represents the oil well diggers, drillers, pipemen, etc. Jupiter represents the numerous legal departments, the financiers and cashiers. Mars represents the agents, contractors and the construction departments. The Sun governs the various directors and high officials.

Venus, being the octave of Neptune, in this case expresses some of the latter's subtleness by extending and maintaining the influence and prosperity of the industry through social intercourse at banquets and other such functions given for the purpose of influencing various dignitaries in power to gain the desired ends. Venus, therefore, rules the social and entertaining elements connected with the enterprise. Mercury rules the clerical forces, the advertising and the press agents which it maintains. The Moon rules the teamsters and other common employees and also the masses who buy and consume the product. And Pluto represents the research of new products and the exploration of new oil deposits.

## Beyond Good and Evil

There are no *evil* planets. Certain planetary configurations produce changes in the constituents of the human body that develop into tendencies which may be classed as subnormal or abnormal amounting to specific disorders, as in the case we mentioned before of the affliction to Saturn, for instance, but of themselves no planets are evil. When a planet arrives at a point in the Zodiac where its angular relation with another planet focuses the aspect on the earth and certain people who are responsive to it find it unpleasant or disruptive, it is commonly termed evil, adverse or malign. In the course of time, as planetary vibrations are better understood, a more correct and appropriate terminology will develop.

Take the case of Saturn which has been much maligned. Saturn is often called a "malefic," yet the truth is that its vibrations are identified with contraction, cohesion and stability. What would industry do if things did not properly set or contract? What would chemistry do if things did not properly cohere and adhere? What would the business world do if there were no stability, no regular foundation principles on which to establish trade? These are the attributes of Saturn.

On the same premise, Jupiter is not benefic although generally termed fortunate. Its vibrations are identified with those things which please and gratify. Its vibrations direct the operation of growth, expansion and increase.

In the realm of physical sensation it is easy to see how the vibrations of Saturn became associated with the word malign. Its cooling, contracting, retarding, suppressing tendencies and its tissue destroying or catabolistic actions develop anxiety, apprehension, nervousness or fearfulness of impending evil.

While on the other hand, Jupiter is associated with the sensations of joviality, pleasure, generosity, relaxation, satisfaction or contentment. Its anabolistic action of tissue building promotes the attitude of safety, security, protection and plenty or the state of being fortunate.

A noted scientist once said, "Life is a constant internal adjustment to external environment." This is a statement nowhere so much appreciated as by astrologers. The "internal adjustments" mentioned are largely influenced and directed by planetary vibrations, which in turn give rise to urges, tendencies, attitudes, feelings and thoughts. The quality and intensity of thought cause our actions; actions develop environment. Hence, planetary influences are intimately associated with our feelings, thoughts and acts. So realistic is our expression of our reaction to planetary vibrations that an observant astrologer while listening to your words and noting your actions can tell just which planetary influence you are expressing at that time, that is, whether it is Saturn, Jupiter or otherwise.

Outside the world of sensation we take a different view of the action of planetary vibrations. Here we see the activity of Jupiter in the shepherd protecting his flocks, the banker guarding funds, the merchant plying foreign trade, the dean directing the extension of knowledge, the physician healing ills.

In Saturn's activities we see the forest denuded of its trees to furnish lumber, the surface of the earth scarred by mining, the decay of husks after the harvest, the storms of winter renewing and replenishing the substance of the soil in preparation for the next season's planting.

So we perceive in the activities of the planets simply nature in operation. "There is no evil, but thinking makes it so"—thinking, *not the planets!* The catabolistic action of Saturn in destroying worn out cells is vitally important in view of the fact that Jupiter is constantly engaged in the anabolistic action of cell building. Without Saturn this would soon promote plethora, while without Jupiter to rebuild, Saturn would soon cause devastation. In making observations we quickly realize that the planets are neither good nor evil. All the planets are expressing nature; we are continually reacting to their influences and it is through knowledge of Astrology we can best learn to react in finer, nobler degree.

### The Lunar Effect

It is now an established scientific fact that the Moon is a principle factor in the ebb and flow of the tides, just as the ancient astrologers taught long ago. In relation to this idea of lunar rulership of water, a remarkable simile presents itself in that seven-tenths of the earth is covered by water while the human body is also seven-tenths fluid. The fluid chemicals of the body are much more finely composed and much more tenuous than the salty waters of the sea, hence they are infinitely more susceptible to lunar influence. Lunar vibrations cause the earth to expand and contract as if taking two great breaths daily, producing the tides. Lunar aspects with other planets cause subtle changes to occur in the human body, affecting it according to the nature and significance of those aspects.

## The Symbolism of the Planets

Symbolism may be called a common language. By this is meant that certain concrete forms are employed to represent abstract ideas, which, presented to the view of one versed in the form, convey to the mind of that person a definite idea, though the spoken words for that idea will differ according to the language used. Thus the symbols for the planets used in Astrology relate certain ideas about the nature of the planets.

Essentially the symbols for all the planets contain one or more of three elements: the *circle* which denotes spirit, the *cross* which denotes matter and the *half-circle* which denotes the intellectual aspect of the soul or mind.

### Mercury ☿

Let us begin with the planet Mercury. Here we find the cross, the circle and also the half-circle, showing that Mercury represents body, soul and spirit, the threefold division of man. Hence we may deduce the fact that Mercury is pre-eminently the planet dealing with man, the thinker. It is spirit and matter with added faculty of mind. Those who have given any study to Astrology know that Mercury represents the mind, or rather the inner understanding and is that connecting link that runs through the consciousness of man all the way from matter to the highest spirit. It is the link between spirit and matter, hence we see all three symbols joined together to represent the type of energy sent out from that planetary center.

### Mars ♂

In Mars, from the symbol of the circle and the cross, we see a different form of energy working throughout nature, entering into the composition of the material and emotional bodies but not the mental, as we see no semi-circle in connection with this planetary symbol, but the cross placed above the circle showing that the Mars force works almost entirely with material conditions. Its work is to energize that side of nature which, at the present time, obscures the spiritual. For instance, the Mars force is predominant in the animal kingdom and in the merely animal man and is not directly connected with mind but with sensation. Its work with man is to spur him to action and finally knowledge comes as the result of his activities.

## Venus ♀

But after man has grown into a thinking and reasoning being and has begun to refine this wonderful Mars energy, we have what is called the reversing of the spheres of our being and then you will find the symbol of Venus with the circle above the cross, the explosive and blustering energy of Mars has become the rhythmical and harmonious force of Venus, which brings beauty, sweetness and love, and which, while it does not directly work with the mentality of man, modifies the type of mind we express. For instance, if Venus and Mercury be in conjunction, the result will be a beautiful and harmonious expression either in speaking or writing; it will be rhythmical and poetical. An overabundance of Mars force energizing a man would make him a warrior by choice, the same amount of force of the Venus-type would present us with an actor or a dancer, something which would express rhythm of motion and beauty. While the force of Mars energizing in a working man would make him a blacksmith, the same amount of Venus force would make him an artistic craftsman. We see in the Venus symbol the circle above the cross, showing that the Venus force works with the spiritual side of man and deals directly with the appreciation of beauty by the human soul.

## Saturn ♄

In Saturn we have only the cross and half-circle showing its relation to the mind in connection with matter. It has been said by some astrologers that we do not touch the higher side of Saturn, that "we do not reach Saturn above his belt." In other words, humanity at the present time can only respond to a limited range of the Saturn vibration. Saturn's special work in nature is to crystallize, to make stable, so a harmonious aspect to the planet Mercury would tend to make the mind more material, to make it one pointed and more stable, so that the ego can get better control of it and turn it to detailed study. We must always keep in mind that our relation to Saturn is purely material and if it touches our consciousness, it is only to materialize it.

## Jupiter ♃

Just the opposite is the force which emanates from the lordly planet Jupiter. Here we find the mind or the half-circle placed above the cross, revealing to us the fact that though mind and matter are still conjoined, the mind is above the purely material side of the man's nature and can expand into the plane of pure reason, for Jupiter is expansive in nature and his work is to unfold, to throw from the center outward, just as it is the nature of Saturn to draw from the circumference to the center. The type of mind dominated by Jupiter would be broad, comprehensive and benevolent. An overabundance of the Jupiter force would cause the mind to be too general to apply itself to detailed work; it would ever be dealing in glittering generalities, while the same amount of Saturn force energizing the mind would make it painfully detailed. Jupiter deals more with the etheric than with the physical brain, for it holds within itself the higher powers of the soul to a far greater degree than can be manifested through the physical brain today.

## Uranus ♅

In the symbol of Uranus we find a combination of the Mars and Moon symbols, as the half-circle is on each side of the cross and circle. This shows that while spirit is still working through material conditions it is completely controlled by mind. Not only is the symbol of the intellectual aspect of the soul (the semi-circle) on one side of the cross. but on both sides, showing the working of the higher and lower mind as one. When two or more forces work together, they produce a new force or property which was not possessed (or expressed) by either of the constituents working singly. Hence we find that in the case of Uranus a new note is struck which directly affects the superconsciousness in man. It is the great syntheisizer, and we might say that it gathers up the various aspects of intelligence symbolized by all the planets and weaves them into a synthetic whole, and from that comes the fully individualized man, the complete man, the master.

## Neptune ♆

The symbol of Neptune, showing as a trident, indicates that it is more directly related to the three-fold spirit in man and only those who have entered into a greater spiritual consciousness can come directly under its subtle and intangible influence. Negatively, this manifests mainly as psychic disturbances, which, acting through the emotional nature, produce strange physical disorders difficult to diagnose and yet more difficult to overcome. At the same time its influence produces genius of an exceptional nature.

## Pluto ♀

Various symbols have been proposed for the newest planet, Pluto. ♀ seems to have come into general usage and is used throughout this text. The symbol P is frequently used to denote Pluto in such references as the *Rosicrucian Ephemerides*. In *Die Deutsche Ephemeriden* (a German ephemeris) the symbol for Pluto is given as P̲ for some of the more recent years. (The symbol for Uranus is given as ⚸ in *Die Deutsche*.)

### Planetary Rulership, Detriment, Exaltation and Fall

You have learned that certain signs and planets are closely related in nature and in the manner of their influence. Because of this harmonious relationship, certain planets are said to rule the signs in which they best express their natural qualities. For instance, Venus is better able to express its refined, artistic, lovable characteristics when posited in the signs Libra, Taurus or Pisces, than if in Aries, Scorpio or Virgo; just as people can better express the highest and noblest qualities of their nature in an environment of understanding and love than in one of strife and discord. The sign is also said to be the "domicile" or "home" of the given planet.

As the planets are constantly transiting through the Zodiac, they are often found in signs which they do not rule. In some signs a planet may be quite powerful while in others it will be weak or debilitated. It is very necessary to understand the dignities of planets in order to determine the *strength of the ruling planets in a chart*. The home or ruling sign is the strongest position for a planet. The sign of its exaltation is the next in power but when in the sign of its detriment it becomes weak and in the sign of its fall the planet is weakest and most undesirably located.

It should be understood that the planet itself does not thus become strong or weak but that our responses to its influence are stronger or weaker.

## Home Sign and Detriment

A planet is said to be in its *detriment* when located in the sign opposite to the one which it rules. Thus: Mars rules Aries, therefore Mars is in its detriment when located in the opposite sign, which is Libra.

As you have already learned which signs the planets rule, it is now necessary to remember that their detriments are in the signs opposite to the signs they govern.

Mars rules Aries and is in its detriment in Libra.
Venus rules Taurus and is in its detriment in Scorpio.
Mercury rules Gemini and is in its detriment in Sagittarius.
The Moon rules Cancer and is in its detriment in Capricorn.
The Sun rules Leo and is in its detriment in Aquarius.
Mercury rules Virgo and is in its detriment in Pisces.
Venus rules Libra and is in its detriment in Aries.
Pluto rules Scorpio and is in its detriment in Taurus.
Jupiter rules Sagittarius and is in its detriment in Gemini.
Saturn rules Capricorn and is in its detriment in Cancer.
Uranus rules Aquarius and is in its detriment in Leo.
Neptune rules Pisces and is in its detriment in Virgo.

## The Moon's Nodes

The Moon's Nodes are not planets but points in the heavens where the Moon crosses the ecliptic from north latitude to south latitude and vice versa. They are commonly known as the "Dragon's Head" and the "Dragon's Tail." The North Node ( ☊ ) is considered benefic and the South Node ( ☋ ) is considered malefic.

## Exaltation of the Planets

A planet's *fall* is the sign opposite its *exaltation*. Thus: Mars is exalted in the sign Capricorn; its fall is in the sign opposite, which is Cancer.

The following table shows the exaltation of the planets; their fall will always be in the sign opposite to the exaltation.

The Sun is exalted in Aries and is in its fall in Libra.
The Moon is exalted in Taurus and is in its fall in Scorpio.

The North Node is exalted in Gemini and is in its fall in Sagittarius.

Jupiter is exalted in Cancer and is in its fall in Capricorn.

Neptune is exalted in Leo and is in its fall in Aquarius.

Mercury is exalted in Virgo and is in its fall in Pisces.

Saturn is exalted in Libra and is in its fall in Aries.

Uranus is exalted in Scorpio and is in its fall in Taurus.

The South Node is exalted in Sagittarius and is in its fall in Gemini.

Mars is exalted in Capricorn and is in its fall in Cancer.

Pluto and Venus are exalted in Pisces and are in their fall in Virgo.

## Exercise

In the inner ring of a horoscope blank insert the signs of the Zodiac with the planets they rule. In the circle of houses place the planets in the signs of their exaltation. In the outer most circle draw the planets in their signs of detriment and fall.

After having made a chart as directed, practice reading it in the following manner: *Mars rules Aries; its detriment is in the sign opposite, which is Libra. The Sun is exalted in Aries, its fall is in the sign opposite, which is Libra.* The second sign, Taurus, the same way: *Venus rules Taurus; its detriment is in the sign opposite, which is Scorpio. The Moon is exalted in Taurus; its fall is in the sign opposite, which is Scorpio.*

In this manner proceed around the chart.

The following diagram illustrates the foregoing. It shows the dignities, home and exaltations as well as the detriments and falls. Keep a copy of this chart handy when delineating horoscopes.

## Dignities and Debilities

The following table shows the dignity and debility of the planets in the zodiacal signs as explained above. It also indicates the exaltation degrees—that is the degrees where the dignity or debility is strongest.

**Note.** Some astrologers believe Neptune to be exalted in Cancer and in its fall in Capricorn.

| Planet | Home | Detriment | Exaltation | Fall |
|--------|------|-----------|------------|------|
| Sun | Leo | Aquarius | 19° Aries | 19° Libra |
| Moon | Cancer | Capricorn | 3° Taurus | 3° Scorpio |
| Mercury | Gemini | Sagittarius | 15° Virgo | 15° Pisces |
| | Virgo | Pisces | | |
| Venus | Taurus | Scorpio | 27° Pisces | 27° Virgo |
| | Libra | Aries | | |
| Mars | Aries | Libra | 28° Capricorn | 28° Cancer |
| Jupiter | Sagittarius | Gemini | 15° Cancer | 15° Capricorn |
| Saturn | Capricorn | Cancer | 21° Libra | 21° Aries |
| Uranus | Aquarius | Leo | Aquarius | Leo |
| | | | Scorpio | Taurus |
| Neptune | Pisces | Virgo | Leo | Aquarius |
| Pluto | Scorpio | Taurus | Pisces | Virgo |
| North Node | | | 3° Gemini | 3° Sagittarius |
| South Node | | | 3° Sagittarius | 3° Gemini |

Table 5: Dignities and Debilities

## Critical Degrees

These sensitive or critical degrees were given considerable importance by the ancients. A planet's strength or power in the horoscope is believed to be increased when in any of these degrees or within orb of 3° of the critical degree. A planet dignified by sign or house or strongly aspected receives still greater power, and one weakly placed or poorly aspected receives help from such location. Students may wish to observe these critical degree influences in horoscopes, as well as in horary charts and planets by transit over them.

## Hylegical Degrees

The Sun or Moon is "hyleg" or "the giver of life" if posited between 5° above to 25° below the Ascendant; 5° below to 25° above the cusp of the Seventh House; or between 5° below the cusp of the Ninth House to 25° below the cusp of the Eleventh House. If neither the Sun nor the Moon is in one of these places then the ascending sign and degree are hyleg. When the hyleg is afflicted by directions there is danger to life and health.

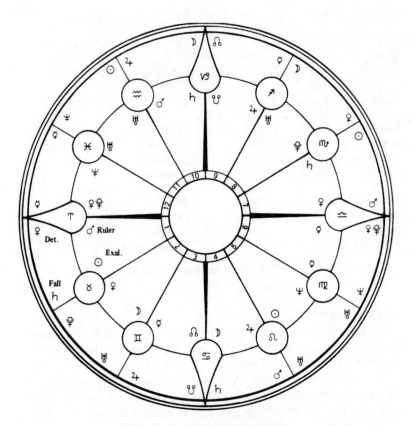

**Figure 3: Dignities and Debilities**

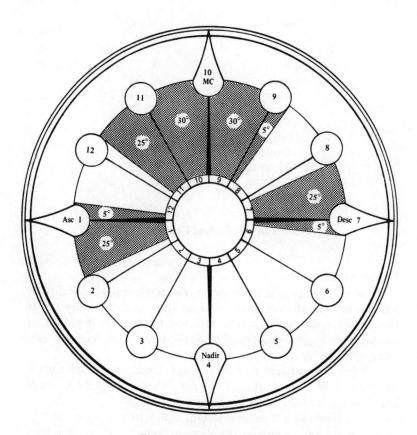

**Figure 4: Hylegical Degrees**

| Sign | Degree |
|------|--------|
| Aries | 0° 13° 26° |
| Taurus | 9° 21° |
| Gemini | 4° 17° |
| Cancer | 0° 13° 26° |
| Leo | 9° 21° |
| Virgo | 4° 17° |
| Libra | 0° 13° 26° |
| Scorpio | 9° 21° |
| Sagittarius | 4° 17° |
| Capricorn | 0° 13° 26° |
| Aquarius | 9° 21° |
| Pisces | 4° 17° |

**Table 6: Critical Degrees**

## Delineations

When a planet is at home (in its own sign), exalted, dignified by position in the chart (in angles or being the planet most elevated or nearest the midheaven) or well aspected by beneficent planets, it manifests its highest qualities, that is, the native is inclined to react wisely or favorably.

When a planet is out of dignity and debilitated by unfavorable sign position or aspects, especially by malefic planets, the lower side of its nature is more likely to be prominently manifested.

If a planet should receive a good aspect from a benefic and an adverse aspect from a malefic, the planet in question will manifest both sides of its nature—the higher and the lower—when influenced by directions and transits and in accordance with the nature of such aspects.

The delineations following will be helpful in understanding the principal expressions of each planet when dignified by sign, house position or good aspects as compared with their expressions when ill-dignified, that is, debilitated by sign, house position or adverse aspects.

## Moon

*Dignified*—Reflective, receptive, pliable, variable, refined, domestic, public, maternal, productive, adaptable.

*Debilitated*–Frivolous, passive, weak, conceited, common, nonsensical, personal, childish, changeable, luny.

## Mercury

*Dignified*–Perceptive, observant, intellectual, accomplished, clever, skillful, vigilant, adroit, fluent, lucid, expeditious, studious, concentrative, possessed of good mental ability and memory.

*Debilitated*–careless, profuse, indecisive, imitative, shiftless, desultory, embarrassed, nervous, rambling, unpoised, uninformed, forgetful, diffusive, shrewd, crafty, artful, untruthful.

## Venus

*Dignified*–Affectionate, harmonious, chaste, sympathetic, contented, cheerful, graceful, humane, compassionate, refined, companionable, artistic.

*Debilitated*–Immodest, disorderly, lewd, emotional, indolent, loud, untidy, thoughtless, gaudy, extravagant, excessive love of pleasure and ease.

## Sun

*Dignified*–Ambitious, honorable, lofty, dignified, loyal, faithful, distinguished, gallant.

*Debilitated*–Disdainful, proud, domineering, despotic, arrogant, authoritative, haughty.

## Mars

*Dignified*–Courageous, venturesome, strong, daring, aggressive, energetic, active, fearless, constructive, passionate.

*Debilitated*–Bold, contemptuous, violent, irritable, coarse, audiacious, forceful, impulsive, impatient, combative, destructive, sensual.

## Jupiter

*Dignified*–Benevolent, philanthropic, generous, truthful, honest, moral, sincere, charitable, reasonable, compassionate, impartial.

*Debilitated*–Prodigal, wasteful, extravagant, pretentious, improvident, dissipated, hypocritical, thriftless, unjust, dishonest, artificial, despotic.

## Saturn

*Dignified*—Prudent, contemplative, cautious, responsible, precise, persistent, persevering, industrious, provident, patient, economical, reserved, serious, resolute, considerate, mathematical, temperate, chaste, executive.

*Debilitated*—Skeptical, melancholic, deceitful, incompetent, exacting, avaricious, perverse, indifferent, laborious, impotent, repining, acquisitive, secretive, suspicious, fearful, slow, callous, lewd, pessimistic, unreliable.

## Uranus

*Dignified*—Original, inventive, ingenious, progressive, reformative, intuitive, socially talented, metaphysical, unique, unconventional, clairvoyant, magnetic, premonitory, constructive.

*Debilitated*—Abnormal, fantastic, extreme, roving, eccentric, abrupt, repellant, erratic, grosteque, precipitate, premature, destructive, radical.

## Neptune

*Dignified*—Psychic, inspirational, idealistic, psychometric, impressionable, mystical, spirit-perceptive, poetical, musical.

*Debilitated*—Vague, emotional, indulgent, supersensitive, deceptive, dreamy, vacillating, scheming, obsessed.

## Pluto

*Dignified*—Conscientious, purifying, regenerative, liberating, just, incorruptible.

*Debilitated*—Suspicious, destructive, decaying, vicious, sorrowful, suffering, deadly, violent.

## Ruling Planets

The planet which rules the Rising Sign in a horoscope at the moment of birth is called the Significator and its power and influence, according to the sign in which it may be located, is very important. Its tendencies according to the house in which it is posited, along with the indications as shown by the aspects it may bear with other planets, must be thoroughly considered, as well as its own inherent nature, i.e., good, evil, positive, neutral, etc. (How to find this Rising Sign in a horoscope is the subject of another lesson.)

The features outlined in the paragraphs below are guides to the determining the strength of a planet. By this you will realize the necessity of knowing the nature of planets and their rulerships and the nature of the houses of a horoscope.

Planets other than the Significator which have a ruling influence in a chart are:

1. Any planet which may be within 12° above the rising degree (cusp of the First House) or within 20° below the first cusp.

2. The planet ruling the sign in which the Sun is located at birth. This is called the Planetary Ruler.

3. The planet in the closest number of degrees of any aspect to the Sun. This is not necessarily the planet closest to the Sun.

4. The planet most elevated (nearest the Midheaven) in a map.

5. The Sun, Moon and Mercury are always considered co-rulers. When reading a horoscope pay strict attention to the rulers and co-rulers; take note of their position by zodiacal sign and houses and their aspects.

Aside from the Significator, Ruling Planet and the co-rulers, the strength of a planet may be determined as follows:

A planet is at its best when located in its own home sign, as Saturn in Capricorn, or Mercury in Gemini or Virgo. It is next best when located in the sign of its exaltation, as Sun in Aries, or Moon in Taurus. It is not so strong when in the sign of its detriment, as Venus in Scorpio or Aries. It is most weakly located when in the sign of its fall, as Mars in Cancer, or Jupiter in Capricorn.

When a planet is neither in its home sign, exaltation, detriment or fall, its strength is judged according to its position by house in the horoscope, whether angular, succedent or cadent. If angular, its strength is the same as though in home or exalted sign; if in a succedent house it is the same as though in sign of detriment; if in a cadent house it is the same as though in sign of fall.

The good or evil qualities of a planet are accentuated by the aspects it may receive from other planets.

Jupiter, for instance, in its own sign, angular and well aspected, may bring the native great good fortune, whenever well aspected by favorable directions or transits. But if in its fall, cadent or adversely aspected, it has little or no power for good and the native may suffer lack of favorable opportunities at needed times, also discredit and loss.

# The Houses

Just as we divide the ecliptic into twelve signs beginning with 0° Aries, so we divide the horoscope into twelve "houses" beginning with the ascendant, the point that was on the eastern horizon when the native was born. While the expression of the twelve signs is all-pervasive across the planet, that of the ascendant and houses is personal to the native. If we think of the signs as relating to the inherent psychic and physical anatomy, and the planets as functional modifiers of this pattern, then the houses will represent the outward environment and avenue of expression for this energy pattern. Thus, Saturn in Leo will represent a contracted heart, physically and psychologically, while a placement in the third house will indicate that it is in the area of communication that the energy expresses itself, through one's own difficulty in communicating with others, and through difficulty in communicating with the native. An afflicted planet in Scorpio will indicate retention or poisoning by waste products. If it falls in the fourth house, it may indicate faulty plumbing or food at home; in the sixth, poor eating habits.

The twelve houses reflect the meanings of the twelve signs. The first house is like Aries, the second like Taurus, etc. The houses are grouped into three categories reflecting the three Quadratures. These are *angular*, *succedent* and *cadent* (analogous to cardinal, fixed and mutable).

An *angular house* is a house situated on an angle. The angles are the four main points of the chart: the Ascendant, Descendant, Midheaven, and Nadir. The importance of these points is discussed later. Planets located in angular houses are traditionally held to be strengthened by this positioning, or "accidentally dignified." The angular houses are the First House, the Fourth House, the Seventh House and the Tenth House, corresponding to the cardinal signs.

*Succedent houses* follow after angular houses; a planet placed therein is neither strengthened or weakened. The succedent houses are the Second House, the Fifth House, the Eighth House and the Eleventh House, corresponding to the fixed signs.

*Cadent houses* follow succedent houses. Planets located therein are traditionally held to be weakened, or "accidentally debilitated," except for the natural rulers of the cadent houses: Mercury of the Third House and the Sixth House, Jupiter of the Ninth House and Neptune of the Twelfth House. These correspond to the mutable signs.

### The First House—Angular

The First House rules the personality, natural disposition and tendencies, self-interest and worldly outlook generally. The parts of the body represented are the head and face.

### The Second House—Succedent

Financial affairs, monetary prospects, gain or loss according to the nature of the planets therein and how the ruler of this house is aspected and where posited in the chart. Represents throat and ears.

### The Third House—Cadent

Brethren, short journeys, writings, studies, mental inclinations and ability. Denotes shoulders, arms, hands, lungs, collar bones and the nervous system.

### The Fourth House—Angular

Father, home, environment, domestic affairs and general condition at the close of life. The outlook regarding mines, lands, property and the result of undertakings. Rules the breast, stomach and digestive organs.

### The Fifth House—Succedent

Children, love affairs, pleasurable emotions and speculation are all ruled by the Fifth House. It also rules the heart and back.

## The Sixth House—Cadent

The Sixth House rules sickness, servants, employees, service, work, food, hygiene, clothing and small animals. Denotes the solar plexus and bowels.

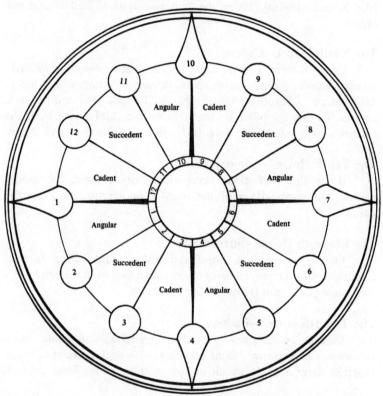

**Figure 5: The Houses**

## The Seventh House—Angular

The Seventh House rules unions, partnerships, marriage, contracts, lawsuits, open enemies, dealings with others and the public generally. Parts denoted are kidneys, ovaries and lower half of the back.

### The Eighth House—Succedent

This house rules legacies, the money or goods of others, death and all matters connected with the dead and astral experiences. Financial affairs of the partner, being the second house of the partner (the Seventh House). Rules the muscular system, bladder and sex organs.

### The Ninth House—Cadent

Long journeys, foreign countries and places remote from birth, dreams, visions, psychic experiences, education, intuition and higher development, scientific, philanthropic, philosophic and spiritual tendencies. Partner's brother or sister, being the third house from the partner's own house (the Seventh House). Signifies liver and thighs.

### The Tenth House—Angular

Rules the profession, occupation, honor, fame, promotion, mother, employer, affairs of the country or government. Rules the knees.

### The Eleventh House—Succedent

Friends, associations, hopes and wishes, indicates the financial condition of the employer, being the second house from the employer's own house (the Tenth House). Rules the ankles.

### The Twelfth House—Cadent

Unseen or unexpected troubles, restraint, limitations, exile, seclusion, secret sorrows, silent suffering, self-undoing, secret enemies, hospitals, large animals, occult or hidden side of life. Rules the feet.

**Note**: Traditional astrologers assign the father to the Fourth House and the mother to the Tenth House. Some modern astrologers reverse this order while still others assign the parent of the same sex to the Fourth House and the parent of the opposite sex to the Tenth House. In actuality, it would appear that the parent who plays the emotional, nurturing, domestic role is represented by the Fourth House and the parent who fulfills the authoritarian, financially-supportive role is ruled by the Tenth House.

# The Aspects

There is an angle between every two planets in the horoscope which is measured in degrees. When the angle produces a significant interaction between two or more planets they are said to be "in aspect." The angles which give rise to the "major aspects" are produced by dividing a circle by units of 2 and 3 (just as the zodiac is produced by such a division). These aspects are the conjunction (0°), the semi-sextile (60°), the square (90°), the trine (120°), and the opposition (180°). In order for two planets to be in aspect to each other they must be within a certain distance of the exact angle division. This is called the "orb" of the aspect and generally the planets must be within 5 to 12 degrees of a perfect aspect for the effect to be noticeable. For example, if Mars is at 19° Aquarius, and Mercury is at 21° Taurus, then the aspect is a square and the difference of 2° from the perfect angle is well within the allowable orb. The larger orbs are reserved for the Sun and Moon or conjunctions and oppositions. The smallest orbs are allowed for the "inner planets," Mercury, Venus and Mars, and the less powerful aspects.

Besides those aspects mentioned above, are the semi-sextile (30°), the semi-square (45°), the sesqui-quadrate (135°), and the quincunx (150°). These have traditionally been considered the "minor aspects," but in recent times the quincunx has gained notoriety and has shown itself to be equal to any of the "major aspects" when it is properly understood. Two other important aspects are based not on the distance between two planets by angle, but on the number of degrees above or below the ecliptic, or the declination. When two planets are the same distance above the ecliptic they are said to be "parallel." When they are the same distance on opposite sides of the ecliptic they are "contra-parallel." The former is considered like a conjunction in effect, the latter like an opposition.

Aspects are either considered "favorable" or "unfavorable" according to how harmoniously the two planets in aspect function together. The "favorable" aspects are angle relationships based on division of a circle by three. The "unfavorable" aspects are based on division by two.

Of course, from a higher perspective, one could not say that particular aspects were better or worse. It is merely a question of how these aspects are felt by the average person. It said that if it were not for the "unfortunate " aspects, humanity would not have the urge to improve itself so strongly. Some astrologers consider the "unfortunate" aspects to be the only worthwhile ones to look at in a chart.

The conjunction occurs when planets come together. This produces a blending of planetary energies which is not, in itself, "unfavorable." Only if one of the "outer " planets, Uranus, Neptune or Pluto, closely conjuncts one of the "personal" planets, Mercury, Venus or Mars, or the Moon, do we get a difficult energy. This is because some otherwise personal aspect of life is conjoined with a very impersonal and extraordinary energy. For instance, when Mercury closely aspects with Neptune, or Venus with Pluto, energy patters are produced which resist the flow of everyday life.

Squares produce a "fight" between planets, with each one wanting to control or direct the behavior of the other. There is always a feeling that something is right and something else is wrong. The expression of each planet is in conflict with the other. The way to resolve this conflict is to accept each planetary force on its own ground as a valid statement in and of itself and to allow the conflict to continue, if necessary, but without taking sides.

Oppositions indicate a "stand-off" where it is impossible for two planets to function simultaneously. There is not a "fight" here, but an inability for the two to function at the same time. When one functions it forfeits the opportunity to work with the energy of the other. For example, if the Moon and Sun are in opposition, the conscious and unconscious forces oppose each other. When one acts, the other cannot contribute any of its own merits. The way to resolve this conflict is not to choose sides, to allow each to express its own virtue, but not to forget that the missing force is equally valid in its own field of action. This is considered an "unfavorable" aspect, though it does not produce the friction and tension of the square or quincunx.

Trines harmonize the functioning of different planets so that they "sympathize" with each other. When one is called forth to work, the other can aid it. This is particularly beneficial where the nature of the planets is otherwise antagonistic, but sometimes the effect is too mild to be consciously appreciated. We more often count our woes than our blessings.

Sextiles are based on a division of three and two, and indicate a sympathetic partnership between planets which, however, may demand some conscious attunement in order to function. With trines one rests on one's laurels, but with sextiles one either uses the laurels, or doesn't get any benefit from them.

The quincunx, or inconjunct, was long considered a minor aspect but in recent years astrologers have come to consider it of substantial importance. Although the quincunx can be considered "unfortunate," it works in a way which is quite different from the square or opposition. The influence is more subtle, but often more powerful than these or any other aspects. When a quincunx occurs between planets in a horoscope the individual feels that the functions of these two planets is somehow in opposition, yet requiring synthesis. The attempts of the particular individual to harmonize these forces produce a strain which is particularly distinctive. The individual is constantly attempting to unify these forces but never quite succeeds---sort of the Sisyphus syndrome. To the person and those in proximity, the effect is frustrating, grating and abrasive, yet unless pointed out, usually the person is not conscious that the struggle is going on. He has made an assumption, on an unconscious level, that a certain action must take place. Often there is an aspirational quality to this assumption, a high ideal, or a hope, but it is the nature of this aspect that this aspiration is always based on an unconscious assumption which is presumptuous. The only solution to this problem is not to try harder at solving it consciously, but to leave it alone. There is a relaitonship between the quincunx and Virgo (150° from Aries) which teaches us that the native must bow his head in service to the two planets in aspect, and give up on a conscious solution to the situation. Virgo is the sign of service, and a true servant does not question the master.

## How The Basic Principles of Astrology Work Together

The signs are the "organs" of our physical and psychological bodies. The angles and the houses show how we identify with the energy of the signs and planets, making them a part of ourselves (the ascendant), or of our environment (the houses). The aspects show the interaction between the planets. The planets, by placement, channel the energy of the signs they occupy. By rulership they channel the energy of the signs they have affinity with. The horoscope reveals the physical and psychological body that the personality operates through. It shows how the personality relates to the environment surrounding it and to the spiritual elements which constitute its internal self, but not the spiritual character of that inner self *per se*. The components of astrology are based on the laws and truths of creation. They were placed by the Creator God in our environment to show the truths and laws of creation. We were placed in our environment to learn these things.

# Constructing
# the Horoscope

# Time Calculations

Before launching into the process of erecting a horoscope, the student should know something definite about the time factors involved. The following explanations will give an idea of the time measure distinctions and define why one sort of time, rather than another, is used in Astrology, in order that calculations may be utilized which synchronize with nature's movements.

There are four kinds of time: sidereal time, apparent time, astronomical time and mean time. But there are only two measures of time and these are called the mean scale and sidereal scale.

## Astronomical Time

Astronomical time has been measured from midnight to midnight since January 1, 1925. Prior to that date the astronomical day began at noon. The astronomical day is reckoned as twenty-four hours continuously, therefore no AM or PM is mentioned. For instance, when a civil clock shows 11:00 PM the astronomical time is 23:00. This time is measured on the mean time scale. However, it is not employed in the erection of horoscopes.

## Apparent Time

Apparent time, or apparent solar time—the word *apparent* here is understood to mean clearly perceived or perceivable, evident, obvious, actual, true, manifest. At the middle of every day at every place on earth the Sun will reach its meridian. The moment of this culmination is known as apparent noon. The interval of time between two successive apparent noons is an apparent solar day. The Sun moves daily at a rate varying between 57' 10" to 1° 11". Although the apparent solar day is a natural day, its varying duration renders it unsuitable for civil purposes; hence it is not used for clock time. As it is always longer than a sidereal day it is not used for erecting horoscopes.

## Mean Time

Because as seen by the foregoing paragraph, an apparent solar day is not of uniform duration, the idea has been conceived of using an imaginary mean Sun which is assumed to move at the uniform rate of 59' 8", this being the average motion of the apparent Sun. When this mean Sun reaches the meridian of any place it is mean noon. The interval between any two successive mean noons is always the same and is known as a mean solar day. In other words, it is simply an average apparent day, and because of its uniformity is suitable for civil time measurement. This is *clock time*, that is, *mean local clock time*. It has become known by various names such as *mean solar day*, *mean time*, *civil time*, *mean local time*. Its duration is uniformly twenty-four hours and constitutes the civil day beginning at midnight. The twelve hours before noon are called AM (*ante meridian*), and the twelve hours after mean noon are PM (*post meridian*). Where standard time is used, as in the U.S., it is necessary to reduce the standard time to terms of this mean local time for place of birth in horoscope work. As the mean solar day is always longer than a sidereal day by approximately three minutes fifty-six seconds, the mean local time of birth is always changed to terms of sidereal time for erecting horoscopes.

## Sidereal Time

Expressed in hours, minutes, and seconds at any moment, this is the angular distance of the first point of Aries from the meridian of any place. Right ascension of the meridian (RAM) is practically the same thing but is expressed in degrees and minutes, instead of hours, minutes, and seconds. Sidereal time is that shown by an astronomical clock which indicates twenty-four hours in 23:56:4.09 of mean solar time which is civil or ordinary clock time. Sidereal time therefore increases over mean time at the rate of approximately 3' 55.91" per day and is counted straight through from 0:00 hours to 24:00 hours without considering AM or PM as with civil clocks. The sidereal time at noon for any place is shown daily in the ephemeris. From the fact that sidereal time is the measurement of the angular distance of 0° Aries from the meridian of any place, it is readily seen that sidereal time is in reality astrological time; hence the mean, mean solar, civil, or ordinary clock time of birth is always converted into terms of sidereal time for horoscopal purposes.

**Note.** Refer to sidereal time in an ephemeris and note how it advances one day after another until in 365 days it has gone through the twenty-four hours and begins at 0 hours on or about March 21 each year.

Because, as before stated, sidereal time advances or increases at the rate of approximately four minutes per day, a correction to sidereal time (ST) should be made at the rate of ten seconds added to it for every hour that birth occurs after noon; but subtracted from it if born before noon.

The foregoing explanation is given for the benefit of those students who are desirous of knowing the different kinds of time in use, and which kinds are used in Astrology. Mean time and sidereal time are the principle factors. However, if at this time the student feels he does not entirely comprehend these various times he need feel no concern about the matter as the remarks are explanatory only. The instructions for using sidereal time and mean time (local clock time) are simple and they follow further along in the lesson.

## Standard Time

However, there is a factor which must be considered for all horoscope work and that is the difference between standard time and mean local time. In some cases the difference amounts to half an hour. Unless standard time is converted into mean local time (the time used astrologically) errors will occur in the signs and degrees occupying the twelve houses in a horoscope. As you have already learned that a degree of the Zodiac crosses the Midheaven every four minutes, in the half hour mentioned the discrepancy would amount to an error of 7½° which might cause the wrong sign to be placed on the Ascendant and make the chart misleading. It is well for students to spend all of the time needed to acquire thorough understanding of standard time and how to convert it into mean local time for astrological uses.

Standard time is the common clock time in use in the U.S. Except in those places which are right on the center of a standard time zone where clock time and mean local time correspond, all other places will need a correction from their clock time to mean local time. That is, when a birth is stated in clock time, that clock time must be transformed to the equivalent mean local time, which is used for erecting the horoscope.

## Time Zone Divisions

On November 18, 1883, at noon, a change was made from local to standard time; therefore, for all birth times and for all charts to be cast for any years since that date in America, calculation should be made to convert standard time back to mean local time.

America is divided into eight hour zones, each including 15° of longitude. The center of each zone is a dividing line; places east of center need something added to clock time; places west of center need something subtracted from clock time, to determine the mean local time for horoscopal purposes.

The first zone is *Atlantic Standard Time.* It extends from 52½° west longitude to 67½° west longitude. This space of 15° includes Nova Scotia, the Bermudas, the Lesser Antilles, British Guiana, and the Virgin Islands. The center of this zone is the sixtieth degree of west longitude.

The second zone is *Eastern Standard Time.* It extends from 67½° west longitude to 82½° west longitude. It includes the eastern seaboard states. The center of this division is 75° west longitude. It is five hours behind Greenwich Mean Time.

The third time zone is *Central Standard Time.* It extends from 82½° west longitude to 97½° west longitude. It includes most of the midwestern states. The center of this division is ninety degrees west longitude. It is six hours behind Greenwich Mean Time.

The fourth time zone is *Rocky Mountain Time.* It extends from 97½° west longitude to 112½° west longitude. The center of this division is 105° west longitude. It is seven hours behind Greenwich Mean Time.

The fifth time zone in the United States is *Pacific Standard Time.* It extends from 112½° west longitude to 127½° west longitude, and includes the Pacific coast states. The center of this west coast division is 120° west longitude. It is eight hours behind Greenwich Mean Time.

The sixth time zone is *Yukon Standard Time* which extends from 127½° west longitude to 141° and includes a small portion of southeastern Alaska, and the Canadian province of Yukon. Its center is 135° west longitude which is nine hours behind Greenwich Mean Time.

*Alaska-Hawaii Standard Time* (formerly Central Alaska Time and Hawaii Standard Time) extends from 141° west longitude to 157½° west longitude with the center at 150° west longitude. It includes the entire state of Hawaii, and is ten hours behind Greenwich Mean Time.

The eighth time zone discussed here is the *Bering Standard Time*. It extends from 157½° west longitude to 172½° west longitude with its center at 165° west longitude. This includes the west coast of Alaska and the Aleutian Islands, and is eleven hours behind Greenwich Mean Time.

On the center of a division, i.e., 60°, 75°, 90°, 105°, 120°, 135°, 150°, 165° west longitude, standard time and mean time are the same. Therefore, for a place exactly on one of these centers no correction is required. Use the clock time.

As one proceeds east or west of a center a difference between standard and true time occurs at the rate of four minutes for each degree of longitude, which must be added to or subtracted from your clock in order to get mean local time for erecting horoscopes.

**Note**. When it is found that the place of residence is very near the limit of a zone, i.e., near 67½°, 82½°, 97½°, 112½° west longitude, great care should be taken to ascertain what standard of time is in use at that place, i.e., what time zone. The foregoing applies to Canada.

The book *Longitudes and Latitudes in the United States* by Eugene Dernay (published by the National Astrological Library, 1975) is an invaluable aid to modern astrologers. It lists not only the longitude and latitude, but also the mean local time variation from standard time and the time differences between mean local time and Greenwich Mean Time for all communities in the U.S. with a population of 2500 or more. *Longitudes and Latitudes Throughout the World* by Eugene Dernay, published by the American Federation of Astrologers in 1948, gives similar information for cities outside the United States.

## Daylight Saving Time

It is important in horoscopal work to remember to deduct one hour from clock time when Daylight Saving Time is used.

For a complete list of the dates and times that Daylight Saving Time was in effect for all communities in the U.S. see *Time Changes in the U.S.A.* and *The 1966-1968 Supplement to Time Changes in the U.S.A.,* both by Doris Chase Doane, distributed by Professional Astrologers Inc. We quote from the forward:

"The United States and Canada observed Daylight Saving Time in 1918 and 1919, as a wartime measure. Then from February 9, 1942 until September 30, 1945, Daylight Saving Time was again observed nationwide. It was called War Time by President Franklin D. Roosevelt. These war periods have been the only times when Daylight Saving Time was observed uniformly across the nation. In 1920, a congressional act discontinued Daylight Saving Time; however, local communities began to pass ordinances to observe it anyway.

"Daylight Saving Time is the use of the time used as standard time in the next time zone to the east.

"When Daylight Saving is in effect, the clock is set one hour ahead. Then when standard time comes in again, the clock is set back one hour."

As you can see, it is extremely important to ascertain whether the recorded birth time was during Daylight Saving Time or not. It is usually observed between April and September or October, but can start as early as the middle of March and end anywhere from late August to the first of November. In certain areas when there was a power shortage, Daylight Time was observed all year.

## Retrograde Planets

The term *retrograde* is somewhat misleading as no planet is actually retrograde. It is an appearance due mainly to the position of the planet in orbit and its relation to the earth. It might be briefly defined as follows:

**Retrograde.** A backward motion which the planets appear to have due to the relation of the planets to the earth in their various positions in the Zodiac.

**Influence of retrogradation.** The planet's influence is not changed when retrograde, but the individual's response to the particular influence of that planet is different; the channel for expression of its especial qualities or characteristics is not quite as good when retrograde as when direct in motion.

In the ephemeris, where the planets' positions are recorded daily by zodiacal sign and degree, when a planet appears to begin to move backward in the order of the signs, it is usually denoted by the symbol ℞ . When it apparently turns direct in motion, it is usually indicated by D. A planet is said to be stationary when appearing to be neither moving direct nor retrograde. While the longitude is increasing between one day and the next you may know such a planet is direct in motion. When the longitude decreases between one day and the next, the planet is retrograde.

**Saturn** is retrograde for 140 days, and stationary approximately five days before and after retrogradation.

**Jupiter** is retrograde 120 days and is stationary approximately five days before and after.

**Mars** is retrograde for 80 days and is stationary two or three days before and after.

**Venus** is retrograde 42 days and is stationary approximately two days before and after.

**Mercury** is retrograde 24 days and is stationary approximately one day before and after.

**The Sun** and **Moon** are never retrograde or stationary.

We believe the influence of benefic planets is weakened when they are retrograde. The condition of retrogradation is contrary or inharmonious to the regular direction of actual movement in the Zodiac; hence, when malefic planets are retrograde their malefice is increased. Aspects to a retrograde planet fall short of their promise, and should both planets be retrograde the things indicated by the aspect would be deficient or disappointing, hence retrogradation is considered a debility.

## The Difference Between Retrograde and Direct Motion

In astronomical circles, much has been said concerning the phenomenon known as the *red shift*. It is concerned with the effects of motion on light, specifically the shift toward red found in the spectrums of light originating from bodies moving away from our vantage point at incredible speeds. The consistency of the phenomenon

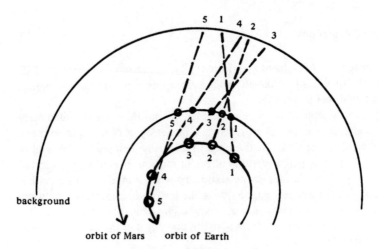

background

orbit of Mars    orbit of Earth

**Figure 6: Retrograde Motion**

provides a method for measuring those speeds. It is reasonable, therefore, to assume that the same natural laws apply to planets as well as stars.

When Venus is receding from the earth, lines are displaced toward the red end of the spectrum. When Venus is moving toward earth, lines are toward the violet end of the spectrum.

This fact of recent scientific discovery clearly shows that there is a difference in the direction of the vibrations from planets which retrograde and from those which are direct.

This recent discovery in astronomy has been known for ages in Astrology which has always taught that there is a difference in influence of a planet, determined by whether it is direct or retrograde in motion.

Note that lines in a spectrum are displaced toward the red end (Mars) of the spectrum when Venus is receding, which corresponds to a weakening of its beneficent powers when retrograde, as Mars is the antithesis of Venus. When Venus is direct we note that lines are displaced toward the violet end of the spectrum. Violet is a color which harmonizes with the nature of Venus. When a planet is direct the power of its own inherent nature is normal; when retrograde the influence is subnormal among the benefics, abnormal among the malefics.

Of course, the planets are never actually retrograde or stationary. Such apparent positions are phenomena caused by the relative positions of the earth and the planets (see Figure 6, above).

# The George Method of Horoscope Calculation

The following is Llewellyn George's original method of calculating the Ascendant, Midheaven and house cusps of a horoscope. It is important to understand the reasons behind the steps, rather than to learn calculation by rote memorization. Through this lesson, two example charts will illustrate the calculations: Chart 1. Person born January 22, 1936, 10:20 PM, Sillersville, PA., and Chart 2. Person born March 30, 1947, 9:38 AM, Red Wing, MN.

The George Method is presented here in five steps:
1. Change Standard Time to Mean Local Time
2. Correct for Daylight Saving Time or War Time
3. Convert to Sidereal Time at Birth
4. Correct for Longitude and Acceleration
5. Find the Ascendant, Midheaven and house cusps

## 1. Change Standard Time to Mean Local Time

As has been explained, America is divided into five hour zones, each including 15° of longitude. The center of each zone is a dividing line; places east of the center need something added to clock time; places west of center need something subtracted from clock time, to determine the mean local time for horoscopal purposes.

**East of Center—Add.** Add four minutes to clock time for every degree of longitude (one minute for each 15' of longitude) a place is situated east of a center of its time zone. The result is mean local time.

**West of Center—Subtract.** Subtract four minutes from clock time for every degree of longitude (one minute for each 15' of longitude) a place is situated west of a center of its time zone. The result is mean local time.

**Example 1. Person born January 22, 1936, 10:20 PM, Sillersville, PA.** Sillersville, Pennsylvania has a longitude of 75° 24' west. It is located in the Eastern Standard Time zone, the center of which is 75° west longitude. Sillersville is 24' west of the center. Twenty-four minutes are therefore multiplied by four and the result of one minute and thirty-six seconds is subtracted from the birth time to convert standard time to mean local time.

    75° 24'    (birth longitude)
    -75  00    (center of time zone)
    00  24'    (longitudinal difference)

    24         (longitudinal difference)
    x 4        (correction per degree)
    96 = 01m 36s  (correction for 24')

    10h 20m 00s =  10h 19m 60s  (standard time of birth)
                   -00  01   36  (correction)
                   10h 18m 24s  (mean local time of birth)

**Example 2. Person born March 30, 1947, 9:38 AM, Red Wing, MN.** Red Wing, Minnesota has a longitude of 92° 31' west. It is in the Central Standard Time zone, the center of which is the ninetieth longitude. Red Wing is 2° 31' west of the center. Two degrees and thirty-one minutes are therefore multiplied by four and the result of ten minutes and four seconds is subtracted from the birth time to convert standard time to mean local time.

92° 31'     (birth longitude)
-90  00     (center of time zone)
02° 31'     (longitudinal difference)


02    31    (longitudinal difference)
x 4     4   (correction per degree)
08m 124   = 02m 04s


08m  00s
+02    04
10m  04s (correction for 02° 31')


09h 38m 00s =  09h 37m 60s  (standard time of birth)
               -00  10  04  (correction)
                09h 27m 56s  (mean local time of birth)


## 2. Correct for Daylight Saving Time or War Time

One hour must be subtracted from the mean local time of birth whenever Daylight Saving Time or War Time were in effect.

In neither of these two examples was Daylight Saving Time or War Time in effect, therefore the mean local time of birth is correct.

## 3. Convert to Sidereal Time at Birth

Sidereal time is quoted in an ephemeris daily for noon any place on earth. Ordinary clock time as we use it commonly is but an artificial method of reckoning time invented to facilitate business affairs. It is therefore necessary to transform our clock time into ST (sidereal time) in order to know the true astrological time of an event, such as a birth, for horoscopal purposes.

Sidereal Time is approximately the same on the same date each year, and it may be found for any day in a geocentric ephemeris. The student is advised to study the pages of the Rosicrucian Fellowship's *Simplified Scientific Ephemeris* for January 1936 and March 1947 reproduced on the following pages in order to follow readily the examples given here.

## SIMPLIFIED SCIENTIFIC
## EPHEMERIS OF THE PLANETS' PLACES
### Calculated for Mean Noon at Greenwich
### January, 1936
### New Moon, January 24th, 7:18 A. M., in ♒ 3° 08′
### Longitude of the Planets

| Day | ☉ ♑ | | ♀ ♏ | | ☿ ♑ | | ☽ ♈ | | ♄ ♓ | | ♃ ♐ | | ♂ ♒ | | ♅ ♉ | | ♆ ♏ | | ☊ ♑ | |
|---|---|---|---|---|---|---|---|---|---|---|---|---|---|---|---|---|---|---|---|---|
| | ° | ′ | ° | ′ | ° | ′ | ° | ′ | ° | ′ | ° | ′ | ° | ′ | ° | ′ | ° | ′ | ° | ′ |
| W 1 | 9 | 55 | 27 | 32 | 22 | 39 | 8 | 08 | 5 | 59 | 11 | 46 | 19 | 46 | 1 | R35 | 16 | R44 | 12 | 54 |
| Th 2 | 10 | 56 | 28 | 43 | 24 | 15 | 22 | 17 | 6 | 04 | 11 | 58 | 20 | 33 | 1 | 35 | 16 | 43 | 12 | 51 |
| F 3 | 11 | 57 | 29 | 54 | 25 | 51 | 6 ♉ | 19 | 6 | 09 | 12 | 11 | 21 | 20 | 1 | 34 | 16 | 43 | 12 | 47 |
| S 4 | 12 | 58 | 1 ♐ | 05 | 27 | 26 | 20 | 13 | 6 | 15 | 12 | 23 | 22 | 07 | 1 | 34 | 16 | 43 | 12 | 44 |
| Su 5 | 13 | 59 | 2 | 16 | 29 | 00 | 3 ♊ | 57 | 6 | 20 | 12 | 36 | 22 | 54 | 1 | 34 | 16 | 42 | 12 | 41 |
| M 6 | 15 | 00 | 3 | 28 | 0 ♒ | 33 | 17 | 30 | 6 | 25 | 12 | 49 | 23 | 42 | 1 | 34 | 16 | 41 | 12 | 38 |
| Tu 7 | 16 | 02 | 4 | 38 | 2 | 06 | 0 ♋ | 50 | 6 | 31 | 13 | 01 | 24 | 28 | 1 | 33 | 16 | 41 | 12 | 35 |
| W 8 | 17 | 03 | 5 | 50 | 3 | 37 | 13 | 57 | 6 | 37 | 13 | 13 | 25 | 15 | 1 | 33 | 16 | 40 | 12 | 31 |
| Th 9 | 18 | 04 | 7 | 01 | 5 | 06 | 26 | 48 | 6 | 42 | 13 | 25 | 26 | 02 | 1 | 33 | 16 | 39 | 12 | 28 |
| F 10 | 19 | 05 | 8 | 13 | 6 | 32 | 9 ♌ | 25 | 6 | 48 | 13 | 37 | 26 | 49 | 1 | 33 | 16 | 39 | 12 | 25 |
| S 11 | 20 | 06 | 9 | 24 | 7 | 56 | 21 | 49 | 6 | 54 | 13 | 49 | 27 | 36 | 1 | 33 | 16 | 38 | 12 | 22 |
| Su 12 | 21 | 07 | 10 | 37 | 9 | 18 | 4 ♍ | 00 | 7 | 00 | 14 | 01 | 28 | 23 | 1 | 33 | 16 | 37 | 12 | 19 |
| M 13 | 22 | 08 | 11 | 48 | 10 | 36 | 16 | 01 | 7 | 06 | 14 | 13 | 29 | 10 | 1 | D33 | 16 | 36 | 12 | 15 |
| Tu 14 | 23 | 10 | 13 | 01 | 11 | 50 | 27 | 56 | 7 | 12 | 14 | 25 | 29 | 57 | 1 | 33 | 16 | 36 | 12 | 12 |
| W 15 | 24 | 11 | 14 | 12 | 12 | 59 | 9 ♎ | 48 | 7 | 17 | 14 | 37 | 0 ♓ | 44 | 1 | 34 | 16 | 35 | 12 | 09 |
| Th 16 | 25 | 12 | 15 | 25 | 14 | 02 | 21 | 42 | 7 | 24 | 14 | 49 | 1 | 31 | 1 | 34 | 16 | 34 | 12 | 06 |
| F 17 | 26 | 13 | 16 | 37 | 14 | 58 | 3 ♏ | 42 | 7 | 30 | 15 | 00 | 2 | 18 | 1 | 34 | 16 | 33 | 12 | 03 |
| S 18 | 27 | 14 | 17 | 49 | 15 | 48 | 15 | 53 | 7 | 36 | 15 | 12 | 3 | 04 | 1 | 34 | 16 | 32 | 11 | 59 |
| Su 19 | 28 | 15 | 19 | 01 | 16 | 29 | 28 | 19 | 7 | 42 | 15 | 24 | 3 | 51 | 1 | 35 | 16 | 31 | 11 | 56 |
| M 20 | 29 | 16 | 20 | 14 | 17 | 01 | 11 ♐ | 06 | 7 | 48 | 15 | 36 | 4 | 39 | 1 | 36 | 16 | 30 | 11 | 53 |
| Tu 21 | 0 ♒ | 17 | 21 | 26 | 17 | 23 | 24 | 14 | 7 | 54 | 15 | 47 | 5 | 25 | 1 | 36 | 16 | 29 | 11 | 50 |
| W 22 | 1 | 18 | 22 | 39 | 17 | 34 | 7 ♑ | 46 | 8 | 00 | 15 | 58 | 6 | 12 | 1 | 36 | 16 | 28 | 11 | 47 |
| Th 23 | 2 | 19 | 23 | 51 | 17 | R35 | 21 | 42 | 8 | 07 | 16 | 09 | 6 | 59 | 1 | 37 | 16 | 27 | 11 | 44 |
| F 24 | 3 | 20 | 25 | 04 | 17 | 24 | 5 ♒ | 57 | 8 | 13 | 16 | 20 | 7 | 46 | 1 | 38 | 16 | 26 | 11 | 40 |
| S 25 | 4 | 21 | 26 | 16 | 17 | 02 | 20 | 29 | 8 | 20 | 16 | 31 | 8 | 33 | 1 | 39 | 16 | 25 | 11 | 37 |
| Su 26 | 5 | 23 | 27 | 29 | 16 | 28 | 5 ♓ | 10 | 8 | 26 | 16 | 42 | 9 | 20 | 1 | 40 | 16 | 23 | 11 | 34 |
| M 27 | 6 | 24 | 28 | 42 | 15 | 44 | 19 | 52 | 8 | 33 | 16 | 53 | 10 | 07 | 1 | 40 | 16 | 22 | 11 | 31 |
| Tu 28 | 7 | 25 | 29 | 54 | 14 | 50 | 4 ♈ | 30 | 8 | 40 | 17 | 04 | 10 | 53 | 1 | 41 | 16 | 21 | 11 | 28 |
| W 29 | 8 | 26 | 1 ♑ | 07 | 13 | 48 | 18 | 57 | 8 | 46 | 17 | 15 | 11 | 40 | 1 | 42 | 16 | 20 | 11 | 24 |
| Th 30 | 9 | 26 | 2 | 20 | 12 | 40 | 3 ♉ | 10 | 8 | 53 | 17 | 25 | 12 | 27 | 1 | 43 | 16 | 19 | 11 | 21 |
| F 31 | 10 | 26 | 3 | 33 | 11 | 28 | 17 | 06 | 9 | 00 | 17 | 36 | 13 | 14 | 1 | 44 | 16 | 17 | 11 | 18 |

Pluto, Longitude, January 1, ♋ 26° 39′

Figure 7: Left Hand Page Rosicrucian Ephemeris, January 1936

SIMPLIFIED SCIENTIFIC
# EPHEMERIS OF THE PLANETS' PLACES
Calculated for Mean Noon at Greenwich—January, 1936
Full Moon, January 8th, 6:15 P. M., in ♋ 17° 18'
Total Eclipse of the Moon, January 8th, at 6:15 P. M., in ♋ 17° 18'
### Declination of the Planets

| D | S. T. (H. M. S.) | Dec ☽ (° N ') |
|---|---|---|
| 1 | 18 39 53 | 8 04 |
| 2 | 18 43 49 | 13 30 |
| 3 | 18 47 46 | 18 12 |
| 4 | 18 51 42 | 21 51 |
| 5 | 18 55 39 | 24 12 |
| 6 | 18 59 35 | 25 07 |
| 7 | 19 03 32 | 24 32 |
| 8 | 19 07 28 | 22 37 |
| 9 | 19 11 25 | 19 33 |
| 10 | 19 15 21 | 15 37 |
| 11 | 19 19 18 | 11 05 |
| 12 | 19 23 15 | 6 12 |
| 13 | 19 27 12 | 1 10 |
| 14 | 19 31 09 | 3 S 51 |
| 15 | 19 35 06 | 8 43 |
| 16 | 19 39 02 | 13 17 |
| 17 | 19 42 58 | 17 23 |
| 18 | 19 46 55 | 20 49 |
| 19 | 19 50 51 | 23 23 |
| 20 | 19 54 48 | 24 51 |
| 21 | 19 58 44 | 25 00 |
| 22 | 20 02 41 | 23 41 |
| 23 | 20 06 37 | 20 53 |
| 24 | 20 10 34 | 16 47 |
| 25 | 20 14 30 | 11 37 |
| 26 | 20 18 26 | 5 45 |
| 27 | 20 22 23 | 0 N 26 |
| 28 | 20 26 19 | 6 32 |
| 29 | 20 30 16 | 12 14 |
| 30 | 20 34 12 | 17 10 |
| 31 | 20 38 08 | 21 05 |

| D | ☉ (° S ') | ♀ (° S ') | ☿ (° S ') | ♄ (° S ') | ♃ (° S ') | ♂ (° S ') | ♅ (° N ') | ♆ (° N ') |
|---|---|---|---|---|---|---|---|---|
| 1 | 23 05 | 17 15 | 23 39 | 10 56 | 21 36 | 16 00 | 11 34 | 6 10 |
| 2 | 23 00 | 17 32 | 23 21 | 55 | 37 | 15 43 | 33 | 10 |
| 4 | 22 48 | 18 05 | 22 40 | 50 | 41 | 15 12 | 33 | 10 |
| 6 | 22 36 | 18 35 | 21 53 | 46 | 44 | 14 40 | 33 | 11 |
| 8 | 22 21 | 19 05 | 21 01 | 42 | 47 | 14 08 | 33 | 12 |
| 10 | 22 05 | 19 32 | 20 05 | 38 | 50 | 13 35 | 33 | 12 |
| 12 | 21 47 | 19 58 | 19 05 | 34 | 53 | 13 01 | 33 | 13 |
| 14 | 21 27 | 20 21 | 18 03 | 29 | 56 | 12 27 | 33 | 14 |
| 16 | 21 06 | 20 43 | 17 02 | 25 | 21 59 | 11 52 | 33 | 14 |
| 18 | 20 43 | 21 02 | 16 04 | 20 | 22 01 | 11 17 | 33 | 15 |
| 20 | 20 18 | 21 19 | 15 11 | 15 | 04 | 10 42 | 34 | 16 |
| 22 | 19 52 | 21 33 | 14 29 | 10 | 06 | 10 07 | 35 | 17 |
| 24 | 19 25 | 21 46 | 13 56 | 05 | 09 | 9 31 | 35 | 18 |
| 26 | 18 56 | 21 56 | 13 40 | 10 00 | 11 | 8 54 | 36 | 19 |
| 28 | 18 25 | 22 03 | 13 38 | 9 55 | 13 | 8 18 | 36 | 20 |
| 30 | 17 54 | 22 08 | 13 52 | 9 50 | 22 15 | 7 41 | 11 37 | 6 21 |

### Latitude of the Planets

| D | ☽ (° N ') | ♀ (° N ') | ☿ (° S ') | ♄ (° S ') | ♃ (° N ') | ♂ (° S ') | ♅ (° S ') | ♆ (° N ') |
|---|---|---|---|---|---|---|---|---|
| 1 | 5 16 | 2 26 | 2 08 | 1 45 | 0 37 | 1 09 | 0 30 | 1 00 |
| 2 | 5 13 | 2 24 | 2 06 | 45 | 37 | 1 08 | 30 | 00 |
| 4 | 4 12 | 2 21 | 2 01 | 45 | 37 | 1 07 | 30 | 00 |
| 6 | 2 16 | 2 18 | 1 53 | 44 | 37 | 1 05 | 30 | 00 |
| 8 | 0 S 06 | 2 14 | 1 43 | 44 | 37 | 1 04 | 30 | 01 |
| 10 | 2 22 | 2 10 | 1 30 | 44 | 37 | 1 03 | 30 | 01 |
| 12 | 4 07 | 2 06 | 1 13 | 44 | 37 | 1 02 | 30 | 01 |
| 14 | 5 06 | 2 01 | 0 51 | 44 | 37 | 1 01 | 30 | 01 |
| 16 | 5 12 | 1 57 | 0 25 | 44 | 37 | 1 00 | 30 | 01 |
| 18 | 4 25 | 1 52 | 0 N 03 | 44 | 37 | 0 59 | 30 | 01 |
| 20 | 2 46 | 1 47 | 0 36 | 43 | 36 | 0 57 | 29 | 01 |
| 22 | 0 27 | 1 41 | 1 11 | 43 | 36 | 0 56 | 29 | 01 |
| 24 | 2 N 04 | 1 35 | 1 47 | 43 | 36 | 0 55 | 29 | 01 |
| 26 | 4 10 | 1 30 | 2 21 | 43 | 36 | 0 54 | 29 | 01 |
| 28 | 5 11 | 1 24 | 2 52 | 43 | 36 | 0 53 | 29 | 01 |
| 30 | 4 54 | 1 18 | 3 15 | 1 43 | 0 36 | 0 51 | 0 29 | 1 01 |

Pluto. Declination. January 1. N. 22° 56'

Figure 8: Right Hand Page Rosicrucian Ephemeris, January 1936

SIMPLIFIED SCIENTIFIC
## EPHEMERIS OF THE PLANETS' PLACES
Calculated for Mean Noon at Greenwich
March, 1947
New Moon, March 22, 4:33 P.M., in ♈ 1° 12′
Longitude of the Planets

| Day | ☉ ♓ | ♀ ♑ | ☿ ♓ | ☽ ♊ | ♄ ♌ | ♃ ♏ | ♂ ♒ | ♅ ♊ | ♆ ♎ | ☊ ♊ |
|---|---|---|---|---|---|---|---|---|---|---|
| S  1 | 10 04 02 | 25 45 | 22ʀ53 | 24♊40 | 2ʀ56 | 27 18 | 27 29 | 17ᴅ46 | 10ʀ13 | 7 00 |
| S  2 | 11 04 13 | 26 53 | 22 31 | 8♋57 | 2 52 | 27 21 | 28 16 | 17 46 | 10 11 | 6 57 |
| M  3 | 12 04 22 | 28 02 | 22 02 | 23 21 | 2 50 | 27 23 | 29 04 | 17 46 | 10 10 | 6 53 |
| T  4 | 13 04 29 | 29 01 | 21 24 | 7♌51 | 2 46 | 27 25 | 29 50 | 17 47 | 10 09 | 6 50 |
| W  5 | 14 04 35 | 0♒19 | 20 40 | 22 20 | 2 44 | 27 27 | 0♓38 | 17 47 | 10 08 | 6 47 |
| T  6 | 15 04 38 | 1 29 | 19 49 | 6♍41 | 2 40 | 27 28 | 1 26 | 17 48 | 10 06 | 6 44 |
| F  7 | 16 04 40 | 2 37 | 18 55 | 20 50 | 2 38 | 27 29 | 2 12 | 17 48 | 10 04 | 6 40 |
| S  8 | 17 04 39 | 3 47 | 17 56 | 4♎39 | 2 34 | 27 31 | 3 00 | 17 49 | 10 03 | 6 37 |
| S  9 | 18 04 38 | 4 57 | 16 58 | 18 06 | 2 32 | 27 32 | 3 47 | 17 49 | 10 02 | 6 34 |
| M 10 | 19 04 33 | 6 05 | 15 58 | 1♏09 | 2 30 | 27 33 | 4 34 | 17 50 | 10 00 | 6 31 |
| T 11 | 20 03 58 | 7 15 | 14 59 | 13 49 | 2 26 | 27 33 | 5 22 | 17 50 | 9 58 | 6 27 |
| W 12 | 21 04 20 | 8 25 | 14 02 | 26 10 | 2 24 | 27 34 | 6 09 | 17 51 | 9 57 | 6 24 |
| T 13 | 22 04 16 | 9 35 | 13 10 | 8♐14 | 2 22 | 27 34 | 6 56 | 17 52 | 9 56 | 6 21 |
| F 14 | 23 04 05 | 10 44 | 12 20 | 20 09 | 2 19 | 27 34 | 7 44 | 17 53 | 9 54 | 6 18 |
| S 15 | 24 03 17 | 11 54 | 11 36 | 1♑57 | 2 17 | 27 34 | 8 30 | 17 54 | 9 52 | 6 15 |
| S 16 | 25 03 34 | 13 04 | 10 47 | 13 47 | 2 15 | 27ʀ33 | 9 18 | 17 55 | 9 51 | 6 12 |
| M 17 | 26 03 17 | 14 14 | 10 24 | 25 42 | 2 13 | 27 33 | 10 04 | 17 56 | 9 49 | 6 09 |
| T 18 | 27 03 00 | 15 24 | 9 58 | 7♒46 | 2 12 | 27 32 | 10 52 | 17 57 | 9 47 | 6 04 |
| W 19 | 28 02 40 | 16 34 | 9 37 | 20 05 | 2 10 | 27 31 | 11 38 | 17 58 | 9 45 | 6 02 |
| T 20 | 29 02 19 | 17 44 | 9 22 | 2♓39 | 2 09 | 27 30 | 12 26 | 17 59 | 9 44 | 6 00 |
| F 21 | 0♈01 56 | 18 54 | 9 15 | 15 31 | 2 07 | 27 29 | 13 14 | 18 01 | 9 42 | 5 57 |
| S 22 | 1 01 31 | 20 05 | 9ᴅ11 | 28 40 | 2 05 | 27 27 | 14 00 | 18 02 | 9 41 | 5 53 |
| S 23 | 2 01 03 | 21 15 | 9 16 | 12♈05 | 2 04 | 27 26 | 14 48 | 18 04 | 9 39 | 5 50 |
| M 24 | 3 00 34 | 22 26 | 9 36 | 25 42 | 2 03 | 27 25 | 15 34 | 18 05 | 9 37 | 5 47 |
| T 25 | 4 00 03 | 23 36 | 9 41 | 9♉30 | 2 01 | 27 23 | 16 22 | 18 06 | 9 36 | 5 43 |
| W 26 | 4 59 30 | 24 46 | 10 00 | 23 26 | 2 00 | 27 21 | 17 08 | 18 07 | 9 34 | 5 40 |
| T 27 | 5 58 53 | 25 58 | 10 25 | 7♊26 | 1 59 | 27 18 | 17 56 | 18 09 | 9 33 | 5 37 |
| F 28 | 6 58 15 | 27 08 | 10 55 | 21 31 | 1 59 | 27 16 | 18 42 | 18 11 | 9 31 | 5 34 |
| S 29 | 7 57 35 | 28 20 | 11 38 | 5♋37 | 1 58 | 27 14 | 19 30 | 18 12 | 9 29 | 5 30 |
| S 30 | 8 56 52 | 29 30 | 12 06 | 19 46 | 1 58 | 27 10 | 20 17 | 18 14 | 9 27 | 5 27 |
| M 31 | 9 56 06 | 0♓42 | 12 48 | 3♌54 | 1 58 | 27 08 | 21 03 | 18 16 | 9 26 | 5 24 |

Pluto, Longitude, March 1, 1947, ♌ 11° 30′ʀ

**Figure 9: Left Hand Page Rosicrucian Ephemeris, March 1947**

SIMPLIFIED SCIENTIFIC
## EPHEMERIS OF THE PLANETS' PLACES
Calculated for Mean Noon at Greenwich—March, 1947
Full Moon, March 7, 3:18 A.M., in ♍ 15° 42'
### Declination of the Planets

| D | S. T.<br>H.M.S. | Dec☽<br>° N ' | D | ☉<br>° S ' | ♀<br>° S ' | ☿<br>° N ' | ♄<br>° N ' | ♃<br>° S ' | ♂<br>° S ' | ♅<br>° N ' | ♆<br>° S ' |
|---|---|---|---|---|---|---|---|---|---|---|---|
| 1 | 22 33 47 | 24 53 | 1 | 7 48 | 19 33 | 0 06 | 20 08 | 18 29 | 13 23 | 22 59 | 2 37 |
| 2 | 22 37 44 | 25 49 | 3 | 7 02 | 19 15 | 0 04 | 20 09 | 18 30 | 12 50 | 22 59 | 2 36 |
| 3 | 22 41 40 | 25 01 | 5 | 6 16 | 18 55 | $0^{S}37$ | 20 11 | 18 30 | 12 17 | 22 59 | 2 35 |
| 4 | 22 45 37 | 22 33 | 7 | 5 30 | 18 34 | 1 10 | 20 12 | 18 31 | 11 43 | 22 59 | 2 34 |
| 5 | 22 49 33 | 18 40 | 9 | 4 43 | 18 10 | 1 52 | 20 14 | 18 31 | 11 09 | 22 59 | 2 33 |
| 6 | 22 53 30 | 13 42 | 11 | 3 56 | 17 44 | 2 50 | 20 15 | 18 31 | 10 34 | 22 59 | 2 31 |
| 7 | 22 57 27 | 8 05 | 13 | 3 09 | 17 16 | 3 51 | 20 16 | 18 31 | 9 59 | 22 59 | 2 30 |
| 8 | 23 01 23 | 2 11 | 15 | 2 21 | 16 46 | 4 50 | 20 17 | 18 31 | 9 24 | 23 00 | 2 29 |
|  |  |  | 17 | 1 34 | 16 15 | 5 43 | 20 18 | 18 30 | 8 48 | 23 00 | 2 28 |
|  |  |  | 19 | 0 47 | 15 41 | 6 29 | 20 19 | 18 30 | 8 12 | 23 00 | 2 26 |
| 9 | 23 05 09 | $3^{S}40$ | 21 | 0 12 | 15 05 | 7 04 | 20 20 | 18 29 | 7 36 | 23 00 | 2 25 |
| 10 | 23 09 16 | 9 12 | 23 | $0^{S}48$ | 14 29 | 7 31 | 20 21 | 18 28 | 6 59 | 23 00 | 2 24 |
| 11 | 23 13 13 | 14 13 | 25 | 1 35 | 13 49 | 7 48 | 20 21 | 18 27 | 6 13 | 23 01 | 2 22 |
| 12 | 23 17 09 | 18 30 | 27 | 2 22 | 13 09 | 7 55 | 20 22 | 18 26 | 5 46 | 23 01 | 2 21 |
| 13 | 23 21 06 | 21 56 | 29 | 3 10 | 12 28 | 7 53 | 20 22 | 18 25 | 5 08 | 23 01 | 2 19 |
| 14 | 23 25 02 | 24 22 | 31 | 3 56 | 11 44 | 7 44 | 20 22 | 18 23 | 4 31 | 23 01 | 2 18 |
| 15 | 23 28 59 | 25 42 |  |  |  |  |  |  |  |  |  |

### Latitude of the Planets

| D | ☽<br>° N ' | ♀<br>° N ' | ☿<br>° N ' | ♄<br>° N ' | ♃<br>° N ' | ♂<br>° S ' | ♅<br>° N ' | ♆<br>° N ' |
|---|---|---|---|---|---|---|---|---|
| 1 | 1 33 | 1 29 | 3 10 | 0 38 | 1 06 | 1 06 | 0 06 | 1 33 |
| 3 | 3 39 | 1 21 | 3 27 | 0 38 | 1 06 | 1 06 | 0 06 | 1 33 |
| 5 | 4 51 | 1 12 | 3 36 | 0 38 | 1 07 | 1 06 | 0 06 | 1 33 |
| 7 | 4 51 | 1 03 | 3 42 | 0 39 | 1 07 | 1 06 | 0 06 | 1 33 |
| 9 | 3 43 | 0 55 | 3 32 | 0 39 | 1 08 | 1 06 | 0 06 | 1 33 |
| 11 | 1 52 | 0 46 | 3 20 | 0 39 | 1 08 | 1 06 | 0 06 | 1 33 |
| 13 | $0^{S}15$ | 0 35 | 3 04 | 0 39 | 1 08 | 1 06 | 0 06 | 1 33 |
| 15 | 2 16 | 0 27 | 2 38 | 0 39 | 1 09 | 1 05 | 0 06 | 1 33 |
| 17 | 3 54 | 0 20 | 2 11 | 0 39 | 1 09 | 1 05 | 0 06 | 1 33 |
| 19 | 4 52 | 0 12 | 1 41 | 0 39 | 1 09 | 1 05 | 0 06 | 1 33 |
| 21 | 4 57 | 0 04 | 1 11 | 0 39 | 1 09 | 1 05 | 0 06 | 1 34 |
| 23 | 4 00 | $0^{S}08$ | 0 42 | 0 39 | 1 09 | 1 05 | 0 06 | 1 34 |
| 25 | 2 08 | 0 11 | 0 14 | 0 39 | 1 10 | 1 05 | 0 06 | 1 34 |
| 27 | $0^{N}18$ | 1 19 | $0^{S}20$ | 0 39 | 1 10 | 1 04 | 0 06 | 1 34 |
| 29 | 2 40 | 0 26 | 0 40 | 0 39 | 1 10 | 1 04 | 0 06 | 1 34 |
| 31 | 4 25 | 0 32 | 1 02 | 0 39 | 1 10 | 1 04 | 0 06 | 1 34 |

Remaining S. T. and Dec☽ entries (days 16–31):

| D | S. T.<br>H.M.S. | Dec☽<br>° N ' |
|---|---|---|
| 16 | 23 32 56 | 25 52 |
| 17 | 23 36 52 | 24 50 |
| 18 | 23 40 48 | 22 40 |
| 19 | 23 44 45 | 19 25 |
| 20 | 23 48 42 | 15 13 |
| 21 | 23 52 38 | 10 16 |
| 22 | 23 56 35 | 4 45 |
| 23 | 00 30 31 | $1^{N}05$ |
| 24 | 00 04 28 | 6 59 |
| 25 | 00 08 24 | 12 39 |
| 26 | 00 12 21 | 17 43 |
| 27 | 00 16 18 | 21 51 |
| 28 | 00 20 14 | 24 42 |
| 29 | 00 24 10 | 26 00 |
| 30 | 00 28 07 | 25 37 |
| 31 | 00 32 04 | 23 34 |

Pluto, Declination, March 1, 1947, N. 24° 01'—Latitude, N. 6° 56'

Figure 10: Right Hand Page Rosicrucian Ephemeris, March 1947

# JANUARY 1936

## LONGITUDE

| Day | Sid. Time | ☉ | ☽ | ☽ 12 Hour | Mean ☊ | True ☊ | ☿ | ♀ | ♂ | ♃ | ♄ | ♅ | ♆ | ♇ |
|---|---|---|---|---|---|---|---|---|---|---|---|---|---|---|
| | h m s | ° ′ ″ | ° ′ ″ | ° ′ ″ | ° ′ | ° ′ | ° ′ | ° ′ | ° ′ | ° ′ | ° ′ | ° ′ | ° ′ | ° ′ |
| 1 | 6 37 55 | 9♑ 24 12 | 1♈ 1 52 | 8♈ 7 52 | 12♑ 55 | 12♑ 46 | 21♑ 51 | 26♏ 56 | 19♒ 22 | 11♐ 39 | 5♓ 56 | 1♉ 35R | 16♍ 44R | 26♋ 39R |
| 2 | 6 41 52 | 10 25 22 | 15 12 48 | 22 16 22 | 12 52 | 12 46R | 23 27 | 28 7 | 20 9 | 11 52 | 6 1 | 1 35 | 16 44 | 26 38 |
| 3 | 6 45 48 | 11 26 31 | 29 18 22 | 6♉ 18 32 | 12 49 | 12 46 | 25 2 | 29 18 | 20 56 | 12 4 | 6 6 | 1 34 | 16 43 | 26 37 |
| 4 | 6 49 45 | 12 27 40 | 13♉ 16 41 | 20 12 36 | 12 46 | 12 46D | 26 38 | 0♐ 29 | 21 43 | 12 17 | 6 12 | 1 34 | 16 43 | 26 36 |
| 5 | 6 53 41 | 13 28 50 | 27 6 4 | 3♊ 56 54 | 12 42 | 12 46 | 28 12 | 1 40 | 22 30 | 12 29 | 6 17 | 1 34 | 16 42 | 26 34 |
| 6 | 6 57 38 | 14 29 59 | 10♊ 44 53 | 17 29 51 | 12 39 | 12 46 | 29 46 | 2 51 | 23 17 | 12 42 | 6 22 | 1 33 | 16 42 | 26 33 |
| 7 | 7 1 34 | 15 31 7 | 24 11 38 | 0♋ 50 4 | 12 36 | 12 46R | 1♒ 19 | 4 2 | 24 4 | 12 54 | 6 28 | 1 33 | 16 41 | 26 32 |
| 8 | 7 5 31 | 16 32 15 | 7♋ 25 1 | 13 56 23 | 12 33 | 12 46 | 2 51 | 5 14 | 24 51 | 13 6 | 6 33 | 1 33 | 16 41 | 26 30 |
| 9 | 7 9 28 | 17 33 24 | 20 24 6 | 26 48 9 | 12 30 | 12 46 | 4 21 | 6 25 | 25 38 | 13 19 | 6 39 | 1 33 | 16 40 | 26 29 |
| 10 | 7 13 24 | 18 34 32 | 3♌ 8 32 | 9♌ 25 20 | 12 27 | 12 46 | 5 49 | 7 37 | 26 25 | 13 31 | 6 45 | 1 33D | 16 39 | 26 28 |
| 11 | 7 17 21 | 19 35 39 | 15 38 40 | 21 48 42 | 12 23 | 12 45 | 7 15 | 8 49 | 27 12 | 13 43 | 6 50 | 1 33 | 16 38 | 26 26 |
| 12 | 7 21 17 | 20 36 46 | 27 55 40 | 3♍ 59 50 | 12 20 | 12 44 | 8 38 | 10 0 | 27 59 | 13 55 | 6 56 | 1 33 | 16 38 | 26 25 |
| 13 | 7 25 14 | 21 37 54 | 10♍ 1 33 | 16 1 10 | 12 17 | 12 43 | 9 57 | 11 12 | 28 46 | 14 7 | 7 2 | 1 33 | 16 37 | 26 24 |
| 14 | 7 29 10 | 22 39 1 | 21 59 9 | 27 55 55 | 12 14 | 12 41 | 11 13 | 12 24 | 29 33 | 14 19 | 7 8 | 1 33 | 16 36 | 26 23 |
| 15 | 7 33 7 | 23 40 8 | 3♎ 52 1 | 9♎ 47 57 | 12 11 | 12 40 | 12 25 | 13 36 | 0♓ 20 | 14 31 | 7 14 | 1 33 | 16 35 | 26 21 |
| 16 | 7 37 3 | 24 41 14 | 15 44 18 | 21 41 37 | 12 7 | 12 40D | 13 31 | 14 48 | 1 7 | 14 43 | 7 20 | 1 34 | 16 34 | 26 20 |
| 17 | 7 41 0 | 25 42 21 | 27 40 32 | 3♏ 41 37 | 12 4 | 12 40 | 14 31 | 16 0 | 1 54 | 14 54 | 7 26 | 1 34 | 16 34 | 26 19 |
| 18 | 7 44 57 | 26 43 27 | 9♏ 45 28 | 15 52 40 | 12 1 | 12 40 | 15 24 | 17 12 | 2 40 | 15 6 | 7 32 | 1 34 | 16 33 | 26 17 |
| 19 | 7 48 53 | 27 44 33 | 22 3 46 | 28 19 17 | 11 58 | 12 41 | 16 9 | 18 25 | 3 27 | 15 18 | 7 38 | 1 35 | 16 32 | 26 16 |
| 20 | 7 52 50 | 28 45 39 | 4♐ 39 41 | 11♐ 5 23 | 11 55 | 12 43 | 16 46 | 19 37 | 4 14 | 15 29 | 7 44 | 1 35 | 16 31 | 26 15 |
| 21 | 7 56 46 | 29 46 44 | 17 36 42 | 24 13 51 | 11 52 | 12 44 | 17 13 | 20 49 | 5 1 | 15 41 | 7 51 | 1 36 | 16 30 | 26 13 |
| 22 | 8 0 43 | 0♒ 47 49 | 0♑ 56 59 | 7♑ 46 4 | 11 48 | 12 45R | 17 30 | 22 2 | 5 48 | 15 52 | 7 57 | 1 36 | 16 29 | 26 12 |
| 23 | 8 4 39 | 1 48 53 | 14 40 59 | 21 41 28 | 11 45 | 12 45 | 17 37R | 23 14 | 6 35 | 16 3 | 8 3 | 1 37 | 16 28 | 26 11 |
| 24 | 8 8 36 | 2 49 57 | 28 47 5 | 5♒ 57 19 | 11 42 | 12 44 | 17 31 | 24 27 | 7 22 | 16 15 | 8 10 | 1 38 | 16 27 | 26 9 |
| 25 | 8 12 32 | 3 51 0 | 13♒ 11 28 | 20 28 47 | 11 39 | 12 43 | 17 15 | 25 39 | 8 9 | 16 26 | 8 16 | 1 38 | 16 25 | 26 8 |
| 26 | 8 16 29 | 4 52 2 | 27 48 23 | 5♓ 9 24 | 11 36 | 12 40 | 16 46 | 26 52 | 8 56 | 16 37 | 8 23 | 1 39 | 16 24 | 26 7 |
| 27 | 8 20 26 | 5 53 3 | 12♓ 30 54 | 19 51 59 | 11 33 | 12 37 | 16 7 | 28 5 | 9 43 | 16 48 | 8 29 | 1 40 | 16 23 | 26 5 |
| 28 | 8 24 22 | 6 54 3 | 27 11 50 | 4♈ 29 40 | 11 29 | 12 34 | 15 18 | 29 18 | 10 29 | 16 59 | 8 36 | 1 41 | 16 22 | 26 4 |
| 29 | 8 28 19 | 7 55 1 | 11♈ 44 51 | 18 56 49 | 11 26 | 12 31 | 14 20 | 0♑ 30 | 11 16 | 17 9 | 8 43 | 1 42 | 16 21 | 26 3 |
| 30 | 8 32 15 | 8 55 59 | 26 5 10 | 3♉ 9 36 | 11 23 | 12 29 | 13 15 | 1 43 | 12 3 | 17 20 | 8 49 | 1 43 | 16 19 | 26 2 |
| 31 | 8 36 12 | 9♒ 56 55 | 10♉ 9 55 | 17♉ 6 2 | 11♑ 20 | 12♑ 29D | 12♒ 5 | 2♑ 56 | 12♓ 50 | 17♐ 31 | 8♓ 56 | 1♉ 44 | 16♍ 18 | 26♋ 0 |

## DECLINATION and LATITUDE

| Day | ☉ | ☽ | | ☽ 12 Hr. | ☿ | | ♀ | | ♂ | | ♃ | | ♄ | |
|---|---|---|---|---|---|---|---|---|---|---|---|---|---|---|
| | Decl | Decl | Lat | Decl | Decl | Lat | Decl | Lat | Decl | Lat | Decl | Lat | Decl | Lat |
| 1 | 23S 7 | 5N 9 | 5N11 | 8N 4 | 23S48 | 2S 9 | 17S 6 | 2N26 | 16S 6 | 1S 9 | 21S35 | 0N37 | 10S58 | 1S45 |
| 2 | 23 2 | 10 52 | 5 17 | 13 30 | 23 30 | 2 8 | 17 23 | 2 25 | 15 51 | 1 8 | 21 37 | 0 37 | 10 56 | 1 45 |
| 3 | 22 57 | 15 58 | 5 4 | 18 12 | 23 11 | 2 6 | 17 40 | 2 24 | 15 36 | 1 8 | 21 38 | 0 37 | 10 54 | 1 45 |
| 4 | 22 52 | 20 10 | 4 33 | 21 51 | 22 51 | 2 3 | 17 57 | 2 22 | 15 20 | 1 7 | 21 40 | 0 37 | 10 52 | 1 45 |
| 5 | 22 46 | 23 12 | 3 47 | 24 12 | 22 29 | 1 60 | 18 12 | 2 21 | 15 4 | 1 7 | 21 42 | 0 37 | 10 50 | 1 45 |
| 6 | 22 39 | 24 51 | 2 48 | 25 7 | 22 6 | 1 56 | 18 28 | 2 19 | 14 48 | 1 6 | 21 43 | 0 37 | 10 48 | 1 45 |
| 7 | 22 33 | 25 0 | 1 41 | 24 32 | 21 41 | 1 51 | 18 43 | 2 17 | 14 32 | 1 5 | 21 45 | 0 37 | 10 46 | 1 44 |
| 8 | 22 25 | 23 44 | 0 30 | 22 37 | 21 15 | 1 46 | 18 58 | 2 15 | 14 16 | 1 5 | 21 46 | 0 37 | 10 43 | 1 44 |

| Day | ♅ | | ♆ | | ♇ | |
|---|---|---|---|---|---|---|
| | Decl | Lat | Decl | Lat | Decl | Lat |
| 1 | 11N34 | 0S30 | 6N10 | 1N 0 | 22N56 | 2N 8 |
| 5 | 11 33 | 0 30 | 6 11 | 1 0 | 22 57 | 2 8 |
| 9 | 11 33 | 0 30 | 6 12 | 1 1 | 22 58 | 2 9 |
| 13 | 11 33 | 0 30 | 6 13 | 1 1 | 22 60 | 2 9 |
| 17 | 11 34 | 0 30 | 6 15 | 1 1 | 23 1 | 2 9 |
| 21 | 11 34 | 0 29 | 6 16 | 1 1 | 23 2 | 2 10 |
| 25 | 11 35 | 0 29 | 6 18 | 1 1 | 23 3 | 2 10 |
| 29 | 11N37 | 0S29 | 6N20 | 1N 1 | 23N 5 | 2N10 |

Figure 11: The New American Ephemeris, January 1936

**DAILY ASPECTARIAN**

In an ephemeris for the birth year, on a line with the date of birth, in the proper month, will be found figures expressing the ST, for noon at any place on that date. This ST is usually given in hours, minutes and seconds.

**Note.** Many modern ephemerides are calculated for midnight, or 0 hour, instead of noon. *Golgge's Ephemeris* switched to midnight in 1960. The *New American Ephemeris*, by Astro Computing Service, also uses midnight as the reference point.

When using a midnight ephemeris, change the given Sidereal Time to noon equivalent by adding 12h 02m.

**Afternoon births.** When birth occurs in the afternoon, add the time of the event to the ST as given in the ephemeris for that date, and the answer will be the Sidereal Time at birth. If this sum is more than twenty-four hours (a complete astrological day), subtract twenty-four and use the remainder as the ST at birth.

**Morning births.** When the birth occurs between midnight and noon, the method of calculation is somewhat different from the one just described.

For an AM birth, first subtract the time of the event from noon (12h 00m or 11h 60m for convenience in subtracting) then subtract the remainder from the ST as given in the ephemeris for the birth date. The answer is the sidereal time at birth. In other words, subtract the interval between birth time and noon from the ST in the ephemeris for all AM births.

If the ST in the ephemeris for any date is too small to be subtracted from, add it to twenty-four hours and then subtract.

**Example 1. Person born January 22, 1936, 10:20 PM, Sillersville, PA.** The mean local time at birth is 10h 18m 24s PM which is added to the ST at noon as given for the date of birth in the ephemeris (see Figure 7). The result is more than twenty-four, so twenty-four is subtracted from it. The remainder is the sidereal time at birth.

20h 02m 41s (ST at noon)
+10  18  24  (mean local time of birth)
30h 20m 65s = 30h 21m 05s

30h 21m 05s
-24  00  00
06h 21m 05s (ST at birth)

**Example 2. Person born March 30, 1947, 9:38 AM, Red Wing, MN.** The mean local time at birth is 9h 27m 56s AM which is two hours, thirty-two minutes and four seconds before noon. Therefore, 02h 32m 04s are subtracted from the ST at noon as given for the date of birth in the ephemeris (see Figure 9). Since the ST is too small to have over two hours subtracted from it, twenty-four hours are first added to the ST. The result is the sidereal time at birth.

12h 00m 00s = 11h 59m 60s  (noon)
            -09  27  56  (mean local time of birth)
            02h 32m 04s  (interval between birth and noon)

00h 28m 07s  (ST at noon)
+24  00  00
24h 28m 07s

24h 28m 07s = 23h 88m 07s
            -02  32  04  (interval between birth and noon)
            21h 56m 03s  (ST at birth)

## 4. Correct for Longitude and Acceleration

**Correction for acceleration.** Because as stated before, sidereal time advances or increases at the rate of approximately four minutes per day, a correction to ST should be made at the rate of ten seconds added to it for every hour that birth occurs after noon, but subtract from it if born before noon.

**Example 1. Person born January 22, 1936, 10:20 PM, Sillersville, PA.** The mean local time of birth at 10h 18m 24s is afternoon. Therefore 10h 18m is multiplied by ten seconds and the result is added to the ST at birth. In this instance the seconds of the birth time are dropped because they would be too small a figure to calculate.

```
   10                18  (mean local time of birth)
  x10               x10  (correction per hour)
100s = 1m 40s  180 = 03s
```

```
  01m 40s
 +00   03
  01m 43s  (correction for 10h 18m)
```

```
  06h 21m 05s  (ST at birth)
 +00   01   43   (acceleration)
  06h 22m 48s  (corrected ST at birth)
```

**Example 2. Person born March 30, 1947, 9:38 AM, Red Wing, MN.** The mean local time at birth is 9h 27m 56s which is two hours, thirty-two minutes and four seconds before noon. Therefore, 2h 32m is multiplied by ten seconds and the result is subtracted from the ST at birth. Again, note the seconds are dropped from this calculation.

```
12h 00m 00s =  11h 59m 60s  (noon)
              -09   27   56   (mean local time of birth)
               02h 32m 04s  (interval between birth

                                   and noon)
```

```
   02                32  (interval between birth and noon)
  x10               x10  (correction per hour)
   20s              320 = 05s
```

```
  20s
 +05s
  25s  (correction for 02h 32m)
```

```
21h 56m 03s =  21h 55m 63s  (ST at birth)
              -00   00   25   (acceleration)
               21h 55m 38s  (corrected ST at birth)
```

Correction for longitude. Still another correction to sidereal time is necessary to make it exact. It is called the *correction to ST for longtude*. If birth occurred in longitude east of Greenwich subtract ten seconds from the given ST for each hour of time difference between GMT and the mean local time. If birth occurred in longitude west of Greenwich, add ten seconds to the given ST for each hour of difference between GMT and the mean local time.

Example 1. Person born January 22, 1936, 10:20 PM, Sillersville, PA. Sillersville, at 75° 24' west longitude is five hours, one minute and thirty-six seconds different in time from Greenwich Mean Time. Therefore, 05h 01m is multiplied by 10s and the result is added to the ST at birth. Again, the seconds are dropped.

```
  75                24   (birth longitude)
 x04               x04   (time difference per degree)
300m = 05h          96s = 01m 36s

05h 00m 00s
+00  01  36
05h 01m 36s (difference between mean local time and GMT)

  05                01   (time difference)
 x10               x10   (correction per hour)
 50s                10

06h 22m 48s  (ST at birth)
+00  00  50  (longitudinal correction)
06h 22m 98s = 06h 23m 38s (corrected ST at birth)
```

Example 2. Person born March 30, 1947, 9:38 AM, Red Wing, MN. Red Wing, at 92° 31' west longitude is six hours, ten minutes and four seconds different in time from Greenwich. Therefore, 06h 10m is multiplied by 10s and the result is added to the sidereal time at birth to get the sidereal time at birth corrected for longitude. Again, the seconds are dropped from this calculation.

```
    92                 31  (birth longitude)
   x04                x04  (time difference per degree)
  368m = 6h 08m  124s = 02m 04s


   06h 08m 00s
  +00   02   04
   06h 10m 04s  (difference between mean local time and GMT)


   06                 10  (time difference)
  x10                x10  (correction per hour)
   60s = 1 m         100 = 1s


   01m 00s
  +00   01
   01m 01s  (correction for 06h 10m)


   21h 55m 38s  (ST at birth)
  +00   01   01   (correction for longitude)
   21h 56m 39s  (corrected ST at birth)
```

This handy table shows the correction to ST for acceleration and longitude for parts of an hour or degree, and can be used as a short cut once the processes are understood.

```
          1 hour = 60 minutes = 10 seconds correction
                   54 minutes =  9 seconds correction
                   48 minutes =  8 seconds correction
                   42 minutes =  7 seconds correction
                   36 minutes =  6 seconds correction
  one half hour = 30 minutes =  5 seconds correction
                   24 minutes =  4 seconds correction
                   18 minutes =  3 seconds correction
                   12 minutes =  2 seconds correction
                    6 minutes =  1 second correction
```

**Table 7: Correction for Acceleration and Longitude**

It would be absurd to bother with these corrections to ST unless the birth time is known within two minutes, since in a whole day the corrections mentioned never exceed four minutes.

**Note.** Any calculations are only as accurate as the least accurate data. In horoscope work, this is usually the birth time. Birth time is often only known within fifteen to thirty minutes, and in these cases seconds are usually not used, even for the ephemeris sidereal time. It is important, however, to be accurate in all your arithmetic, and to check each step as you go along.

## 5. Find the Ascendant, Midheaven and House Cusps

**How to use the Tables of Houses.** When the sidereal time at birth has been ascertained, use it as a starting point to enter an appropriate Tables of Houses. Find the number, in hours and minutes, nearest that of the sidereal time at birth, and find the correct birth latitude. Then look up the 10, 11, 12, 1, 2, and 3 house cusps. The First House cusp is, of course, the Ascendant; the Tenth House cusp, the Midheaven. See Dalton's *Tables of Houses* reproduced on the following pages, Figures 12 and 13.

It will be noted that the Tables of Houses fill only six cusps in the chart. As you have already learned which signs are opposite each other, fill in the remaining cusps with the other six signs in their proper order, and the same number of degrees as shown in the Tables.

**Example 1. Person born January 22, 1936, 10:20 PM, Sillersville, PA.** The corrected sidereal time at birth is 06h 23m 38s, the latitude of birth is 40° 16' north. Look up the nearest ST in the Tables of Houses (Figure 12) which is 06h 21m 47s. Then look down the columns to find 40° latitude. The house cusps are:

| | | | | |
|---|---|---|---|---|
| Ascendant | 4° ♎ 21' | | Seventh House | 4° ♈ 21' |
| Second House | 0.9° ♍ = | | Eighth House | 0° ♉ 54' |
| | 0° ♏ 54' | | Ninth House | 1° ♊ 24' |
| Third House | 1° ♐ 24' | | Fourth House | 5° ♑ |
| Midheaven | 5° ♋ | | Fifth House | 8° ♒ 24' |
| Eleventh House | 8° ♌ 24' | | Sixth House | 8° ♓ 36' |
| Twelfth House | 8.6° ♍ = | | | |
| | 8° ♍ 36' | | | |

**UPPER MERIDIAN, CUSP OF 10th H.**                    19

Group column groups (H. M. S. / ARC / sign):

- **A:** SID. T. 6 17 26 · ARC 94° 21'.5 · ♋ 4°
- **B:** 6 21 47 · 95° 26'.9 · ♋ 5°
- **C:** 6 26 9 · 96° 32'.2 · ♋ 6°
- **D:** 6 30 30 · 97° 37'.4 · ♋ 7°
- **E:** 6 34 50 · 98° 42'.6 · ♋ 8°
- **F:** 6 39 11 · 99° 47'.7 · ♋ 9°

Columns per group: 11 (♌) · 12 (♍) · 1 (♎) · 2 (♏) · 3 (♐)

| H Lat | A:11 | A:12 | A:1 | A:2 | A:3 | B:11 | B:12 | B:1 | B:2 | B:3 | C:11 | C:12 | C:1 | C:2 | C:3 | D:11 | D:12 | D:1 | D:2 | D:3 | E:11 | E:12 | E:1 | E:2 | E:3 | F:11 | F:12 | F:1 | F:2 | F:3 |
|---|---|---|---|---|---|---|---|---|---|---|---|---|---|---|---|---|---|---|---|---|---|---|---|---|---|---|---|---|---|---|
| 22 | 4.7 | 5.2 | 4 3 | 3.2 | 3.4 | 5.7 | 6.2 | 5 3 | 4.2 | 4.4 | 6.8 | 7.2 | 6 4 | 5.2 | 5.4 | 7.8 | 8.3 | 7 4 | 6.2 | 6.4 | 8.8 | 9.2 | 8 5 | 7.2 | 7.4 | 9.8 | 10.2 | 9 5 | 8.2 | 8.4 |
| 23 | 8 | 3 | 4 1 | 0 | 3 | 9 | 3 | 5 1 | 0 | 3 | 9 | 4 | 6 1 | 0 | 3 | 9 | 4 | 7 1 | 0 | 3 | 9 | 3 | 8 1 | 1 | 3 | 10.0 | 4 | 9 1 | 0 | 3 |
| 24 | 5.0 | 4 | 3 59 | 2.8 | 1 | 6.0 | 4 | 4 59 | 3.9 | 1 | 7.0 | 5 | 5 58 | 4.8 | 2 | 8.0 | 5 | 6 58 | 5.9 | 1 | 9.1 | 4 | 7 58 | 6.9 | 1 | 1 | 5 | 8 57 | 7.8 | 1 |
| 25 | 1 | 5 | 3 57 | 7 | 0 | 1 | 5 | 4 57 | 7 | 0 | 1 | 6 | 5 56 | 7 | 0 | 2 | 6 | 6 55 | 7 | 0 | 2 | 5 | 7 54 | 7 | 0 | 2 | 6 | 8 53 | 7 | 0 |
| 26 | 2 | 5.7 | 3 56 | 5 | 2.8 | 2 | 6.7 | 4 54 | 5 | 3.8 | 3 | 7 | 5 53 | 5 | 4.9 | 3 | 7 | 6 51 | 5 | 5.8 | 3 | 9.7 | 7 50 | 5 | 6.8 | 3 | 10.7 | 8 48 | 5 | 7.8 |
| 27 | 4 | 8 | 3 54 | 3 | 7 | 4 | 8 | 4 52 | 3 | 7 | 4 | 8 | 5 50 | 3 | 7 | 4 | 8 | 6 48 | 3 | 7 | 4 | 8 | 7 47 | 3 | 7 | 10.4 | 8 | 8 44 | 3 | 7 |
| 28 | 5.5 | 9 | 3 52 | 1 | 5 | 6.5 | 9 | 4 50 | 1 | 5 | 7.5 | 8.0 | 5 47 | 1 | 6 | 8.5 | 9.0 | 6 45 | 1 | 5 | 9.6 | 9 | 7 43 | 1 | 5 | 5 | 6 | 9 40 | 1 | 5 |
| 29 | 6 | 6.1 | 3 50 | 0 | 4 | 7 | 7.1 | 4 47 | 0 | 4 | 7 | 1 | 5 45 | 3.9 | 4 | 7 | 1 | 6 42 | 4.9 | 4 | 7 | 10.0 | 7 39 | 5.9 | 4 | 7 | 11.0 | 8 36 | 6.9 | 4 |
| 30 | 8 | 2 | 3 48 | 1.8 | 2 | 8 | 2 | 4 45 | 2.8 | 2 | 8 | 2 | 5 42 | 8 | 2 | 8 | 2 | 6 39 | 8 | 2 | 8 | 1 | 7 35 | 7 | 2 | 8 | 1 | 8 32 | 7 | 2 |
| 31 | 9 | 3 | 3 46 | 6 | 1 | 9 | 3 | 4 43 | 6 | 1 | 9 | 3 | 5 39 | 6 | 1 | 9.0 | 3 | 6 35 | 6 | 1 | 10.0 | 3 | 7 32 | 5 | 1 | 11.0 | 3 | 8 28 | 5 | 0 |
| 32 | 6.1 | 5 | 3 44 | 4 | 1.9 | 7.1 | 5 | 4 40 | 4 | 2.9 | 8.1 | 8.4 | 5 36 | 4 | 3.9 | 1 | 4 | 6 32 | 4 | 4.9 | 1 | 4 | 7 28 | 3 | 5.9 | 1 | 4 | 8 24 | 3 | 6.9 |
| 33 | 2 | 6.6 | 3 43 | 3 | 7 | 2 | 7.6 | 4 38 | 2 | 7 | 2 | 6 | 5 33 | 2 | 7 | 2 | 9.6 | 6 29 | 2 | 7 | 2 | 10.5 | 7 24 | 1 | 7 | 2 | 11.5 | 8 20 | 1 | 7 |
| 34 | 4 | 8 | 3 41 | 1 | 6 | 4 | 7 | 4 36 | 0 | 6 | 4 | 7 | 5 31 | 0 | 6 | 4 | 7 | 6 26 | 0 | 6 | 4 | 6 | 7 21 | 4.9 | 5 | 4 | 6 | 8 15 | 5.9 | 5 |
| 35 | 5 | 9 | 3 39 | 0.9 | 4 | 5 | 9 | 4 33 | 1.9 | 4 | 5 | 8 | 5 28 | 2.8 | 4 | 9.5 | 8 | 6 22 | 3.8 | 4 | 10.5 | 7 | 7 17 | 7 | 4 | 11.5 | 7 | 8 11 | 7 | 3 |
| 36 | 7 | 7.0 | 3 37 | 7 | 2 | 7 | 8.0 | 4 31 | 7 | 2 | 7 | 9.0 | 5 25 | 6 | 2 | 7 | 9 | 6 19 | 6 | 2 | 7 | 9 | 7 13 | 5 | 2 | 7 | 8 | 8 7 | 5 | 2 |
| 37 | 9 | 2 | 3 35 | 5 | 0 | 9 | 1 | 4 29 | 5 | 0 | 9 | 1 | 5 22 | 4 | 0 | 9 | 10.1 | 6 16 | 3 | 0 | 9 | 11.0 | 7 9 | 3 | 0 | 9 | 12.0 | 8 3 | 3 | 0 |
| 38 | 7.0 | 3 | 3 33 | 3 | 0.8 | 8.0 | 3 | 4 26 | 3 | 1.8 | 9.0 | 2 | 5 19 | 2 | 2.8 | 10.0 | 2 | 6 12 | 1 | 3.8 | 11.0 | 1 | 7 5 | 1 | 4.8 | 12.0 | 1 | 7 58 | 1 | 5.8 |
| 39 | 2 | 5 | 3 31 | 1 | 7 | 2 | 4 | 4 24 | 1 | 6 | 2 | 3 | 5 16 | 0 | 6 | 2 | 3 | 6 9 | 2.9 | 6 | 2 | 2 | 7 1 | 3.9 | 6 | 2 | 2 | 7 54 | 4.9 | 6 |
| 40 | 4 | 6 | 3 29 | 29.9 | 5 | | 8.6 | 4 21 | 0.9 | 4 | 4 | 9.4 | 5 13 | 1.8 | 4 | 4 | 5 | 6 6 | 7 | 4 | 4 | 3 | 6 58 | 7 | 4 | 3 | 3 | 7 50 | 6 | 4 |
| 41 | 6 | 8 | 3 27 | 7 | 2 | 6 | 7 | 4 19 | 7 | 2 | 6 | 5 | 5 10 | 5 | 2 | 6 | 10.6 | 6 2 | 5 | 2 | 5 | 11.4 | 6 54 | 5 | 2 | 5 | 12.4 | 7 45 | 4 | 1 |
| 42 | 8 | 8.0 | 3 25 | 5 | 0 | 8 | 9 | 4 16 | 5 | 0 | 8 | 7 | 5 7 | 3 | 0 | 7 | 7 | 5 59 | 3 | 2.9 | 7 | 5 | 6 50 | 2 | 3.9 | 7 | 6 | 7 41 | 1 | 4.9 |
| 43 | 8.0 | 1 | 3 23 | 2.29.3 | | 9.0 | 9.0 | 4 14 | 3 | 0.8 | 10.0 | 8 | 5 4 | 1 | 1.8 | 9 | 9 | 5 55 | 1 | 7 | 9 | 7 | 6 46 | 0 | 7 | 9 | 7 | 7 36 | 3.9 | 7 |
| 44 | 2 | 3 | 3 21 | 0 | 6 | 2 | | 4 11 | 1 | 5 | 2 | 10.0 | 5 1 | 0.8 | 6 | 11.1 | 11.0 | 5 51 | 1.8 | 5 | 12.1 | 8 | 6 41 | 2.7 | 4 | 13.1 | 8 | 7 31 | 6 | 4 |
| 45 | 4 | 5 | 3 19 | 28.8 | 4 | 4 | 4 | 4 9 | 29.9 | 3 | 4 | 2 | 4 58 | 6 | 4 | 3 | 2 | 5 48 | 6 | 2 | 2 | 12.0 | 6 37 | 5 | 2 | 2 | 13.0 | 7 27 | 4 | 1 |
| 46 | 6 | 8.6 | 3 17 | 6 | 2 | 6 | 5 | 4 6 | 6 | 1 | 5 | 3 | 4 55 | 4 | 2 | 5 | 3 | 5 44 | 3 | 0 | 4 | 2 | 6 33 | 3 | 0 | 1 | | 7 22 | 1 | 3.9 |
| 47 | 8 | 7 | 3 15 | 4 | 0 | 8 | 7 | 4 3 | | 29.9 | 7 | 5 | 4 52 | 2 | 0 | 7 | 5 | 5 40 | 1 | 1.8 | 6 | 4 | 6 29 | 0 | 2.8 | 6 | 3 | 7 17 | 28.9 | 7 |
| 48 | 9.0 | 9 | 3 13 | 2 | 28.8 | 10.0 | 9 | 4 1 | 1 | 7 | 9 | 7 | 4 49 | 29.9 | 0.7 | 9 | 11.7 | 5 37 | 0.9 | 6 | 9 | 5 | 6 25 | 1.8 | 6 | 8 | 4 | 7 12 | 5 | 5 |
| 49 | 2 | 9.1 | 3 10 | 27.9 | 5 | 2 | 10.1 | 3 58 | 28.9 | 4 | 11.1 | 8 | 4 45 | 7 | 4 | 12.1 | 8 | 5 33 | 6 | 3 | 13.1 | 7 | 6 20 | 5 | 3 | 14.0 | 13.6 | 7 7 | 3 | 2 |
| 50 | 4 | 3 | 3 8 | 7 | 2 | 4 | 2 | 3 55 | 6 | 1 | | 11.0 | 4 42 | 4 | 1 | 3 | 9 | 5 29 | 3 | 0 | 3 | 8 | 6 16 | 2 | 0 | 2 | 7 | 7 2 | 0 | 2.9 |
| 51 | 7 | 5 | 3 6 | 4 | 27.9 | 6 | 3 | 3 52 | 4 | 28.8 | 6 | 2 | 4 39 | 1 | 29.8 | 5 | 12.0 | 5 25 | 1 | 0.7 | 5 | 13.0 | 6 11 | 0.9 | 1.7 | 4 | 8 | 6 57 | 1.7 | 6 |
| 52 | 9 | 7 | 3 4 | 2 | 6 | 9 | 5 | 3 49 | 1 | 5 | 8 | 4 | 4 35 | 28.9 | 5 | 7 | 2 | 5 21 | 29.8 | 4 | 7 | 1 | 6 6 | 6 | 4 | 6 | 9 | 6 52 | 4 | 3 |
| 53 | 10.2 | 9 | 3 1 | 0 | 3 | 11.2 | 7 | 3 46 | 27.8 | 2 | 12.1 | 6 | 4 31 | 6 | 2 | 13.0 | 4 | 5 17 | 5 | 1 | 9 | 2 | 6 2 | 3 | 1 | 9 | 14.1 | 6 47 | 1 | 0 |
| 54 | 5 | 10.1 | 2 59 | 26.7 | 0 | 5 | 9 | 3 43 | 5 | 27.9 | | 8 | 4 28 | 3 | 28.9 | 3 | 6 | 5 12 | 2 | 29.8 | 14.2 | 4 | 5 57 | 0 | 0.7 | 15.2 | 3 | 6 41 | 0.8 | 1.6 |
| 55 | 8 | 3 | 2 56 | 4 | 26.6 | 8 | 11.1 | 3 40 | 2 | 5 | 7 | 12.0 | 4 24 | 0 | 5 | 6 | 8 | 5 8 | 28.9 | 5 | 4 | 5 | 6 5 | 52.29.7 | 3 | 3 | 5 | 5 36 | 5 | 2 |
| 56 | 11.1 | 5 | 2 54 | 1 | 2 | 12.1 | 3 | 3 37 | 26.9 | 1 | 13.0 | 2 | 4 20 | 27.7 | 1 | 9 | 13.0 | 5 3 | 6 | 0 | 8 | 8 | 5 47 | 3 | 29.9 | 8 | 7 | 6 30 | 1 | 0.8 |

**Figure 12: Dalton's Tables of Houses**

| UPPER MERIDIAN, CUSP OF 10th H. | | | | | | | | | | | | | | | | | | | | | | | | | | | | | | 61 |
|---|---|---|---|---|---|---|---|---|---|---|---|---|---|---|---|---|---|---|---|---|---|---|---|---|---|---|---|---|---|---|

| SID. T. 21 49 8 }  ≃ 25° <br> ARC 327° 17'.1 | 21 53 0 } ≃ 26° <br> 328° 15'.1 | 21 56 52 } ≃ 27° <br> 329° 12'.9 | 22 0 42 } ≃ 28° <br> 330° 10'.6 | 22 4 33 } ≃ 29° <br> 331° 8'.1 | 22 8 22 } ⋂ 0° <br> 332° 5'.5 |

| H. | 11 | 12 | 1 | 2 | 3 | 11 | 12 | 1 | 2 | 3 | 11 | 12 | 1 | 2 | 3 | 11 | 12 | 1 | 2 | 3 | 11 | 12 | 1 | 2 | 3 | 11 | 12 | 1 | 2 | 3 |
|---|---|---|---|---|---|---|---|---|---|---|---|---|---|---|---|---|---|---|---|---|---|---|---|---|---|---|---|---|---|---|
| Lat. | ✕ | ♉ | ♊ | ♋ | ♋ | ✕ | ♉ | ♊ | ♋ | ♋ | ✕ | ♉ | ♊ | ♊ | ♋ | ♈ | ♉ | ♊ | ♊ | ♌ | ♈ | ♉ | ♊ | ♋ | ♌ | ♈ | ♉ | ♊ | ♋ | ♌ |
| 22 | 26.9 | 2.9 | 8 17 | 3.7 | 28.1 | 28.0 | 4.1 | 9 16 | 4.6 | 29.0 | 29.1 | 5.1 | 10 14 | 5.4 | 29.9 | 0.2 | 6.2 | 11 12 | 6.3 | 0.8 | 1.3 | 7.3 | 12 9 | 7.2 | 1.7 | 2.4 | 8.4 | 13 6 | 8.0 | 2.6 |
| 23 | 8 | 3.1 | 8 46 | 4.0 | 2 | 0 | 3 | 9 45 | 9 | 1 | 1 | 3 | 10 43 | 7 | ♋ | 2 | 5 | 11 41 | 6 | 9 | 3 | 6 | 12 38 | 5 | 8 | 4 | 7 | 13 35 | 3 | 7 |
| 24 | 8 | 3 | 9 15 | 3 | 4 | 0 | 5 | 10 14 | 5.2 | 3 | 1 | 6 | 11 12 | 6.0 | 0.2 | 2 | 7 | 12 10 | 9 | 1.0 | 3 | 8 | 13 8 | 8 | 9 | 4 | 9 | 14 4 | 6 | 8 |
| 25 | 8 | 5 | 9 46 | 6 | 5 | 0 | 7 | 10 44 | 5 | 4 | 1 | 8 | 11 43 | 4 | 3 | 2 | 9 | 12 40 | 7.2 | 2 | 3 | 8.0 | 13 38 | 8.1 | 2.1 | 4 | 9.1 | 14 35 | 9.0 | 3.0 |
| 26 | 8 | 8 | 10 17 | 5.0 | 28.6 | 0 | 9 | 11 15 | 8 | 29.5 | 1 | 6.0 | 12 13 | 7 | 4 | 2 | 7.1 | 13 11 | 6 | 3 | 3 | 3 | 14 9 | 4 | 2 | 4 | 4 | 15 6 | 3 | 1 |
| 27 | 26.8 | 4.0 | 10 48 | 3 | 8 | 27.9 | 5.1 | 11 47 | 6.2 | 7 | 29.1 | 3 | 12 45 | 7.0 | 6 | 0.2 | 4 | 13 43 | 9 | 5 | 1.3 | 5 | 14 40 | 7 | 4 | 2.5 | 6 | 15 37 | 6 | 3 |
| 28 | 8 | 2 | 11 20 | 6 | 9 | 9 | 4 | 12 19 | 5 | 8 | 1 | 5 | 13 17 | 4 | 7 | 2 | 7 | 14 15 | 8.2 | 1.6 | 3 | 8 | 15 13 | 9.1 | 5 | 5 | 9 | 16 9 | 9 | 4 |
| 29 | 8 | 5 | 11 53 | 6.0 | 29.1 | 9 | 6 | 12 52 | 8 | ♋ | 1 | 8 | 13 51 | 7 | 9 | 2 | 9 | 14 48 | 6 | 8 | 3 | 9.0 | 15 46 | 4 | 7 | 5 | 10.2 | 16 43 | 10.3 | 3.5 |
| 30 | 8 | 7 | 12 27 | 3 | 3 | 9 | 9 | 13 26 | 7.2 | 0.1 | 1 | 7.0 | 14 25 | 8.1 | 1.0 | 2 | 8.2 | 15 22 | 9 | 9 | 3 | 3 | 16 20 | 8 | 8 | 5 | 4 | 17 16 | 6 | 7 |
| 31 | 8 | 5.0 | 13 2 | 7 | 4 | 9 | 6.2 | 14 1 | 5 | 3 | 1 | 3 | 14 59 | 4 | 2 | 2 | 5 | 15 57 | 9.3 | 2.1 | 4 | 6 | 16 54 | 10.1 | 3.0 | 5 | 7 | 17 51 | 11.0 | 8 |
| 32 | 26.7 | 3 | 13 38 | 7.0 | 6 | 27.9 | 4 | 14 37 | 9 | 5 | 29.1 | 6 | 15 35 | 8 | 3 | 0.2 | 8 | 16 33 | 6 | 2 | 1.4 | 9 | 17 30 | 5 | 1 | 2.5 | 11.1 | 18 27 | 3 | 4.0 |
| 33 | 7 | 6 | 14 15 | 4 | 7 | 9 | 7 | 15 14 | 8.3 | 6 | 1 | 9 | 16 12 | 9.2 | 5 | 2 | 9.1 | 17 10 | 10.0 | 4 | 4 | 10.2 | 18 7 | 9 | 3 | 5 | 4 | 19 3 | 7 | 1 |
| 34 | 7 | 9 | 14 53 | 8 | 9 | 9 | 7.0 | 15 51 | 7 | 8 | 1 | 8.2 | 16 50 | 5 | 1.7 | 2 | 4 | 17 47 | 4 | 5 | 4 | 5 | 18 44 | 11.2 | 4 | 5 | 7 | 19 41 | 12.1 | 3 |
| 35 | 7 | 6.2 | 15 32 | 8.2 | 0.1 | 9 | 3 | 16 30 | 9.1 | 1.0 | 0. | 5 | 17 28 | 9 | 8 | 2 | 7 | 18 26 | 8 | 7 | 4 | 9 | 19 23 | 6 | 3.6 | 5 | 12.0 | 20 19 | 5 | 5 |
| 36 | 7 | 5 | 16 12 | 6 | 2 | 9 | 7 | 17 10 | 5 | 1 | 0 | 8 | 18 8 | 10.3 | 9 | 2 | 10.0 | 19 6 | 11.2 | 9 | 4 | 11.2 | 20 3 | 12.0 | 8 | 5 | 20 59 | 9 | 4.6 |
| 37 | 26.7 | 8 | 16 54 | 9.0 | 4 | 27.8 | 8.0 | 17 52 | 9 | 3 | 29.0 | 9.2 | 18 50 | 7 | 2.1 | 0.2 | 4 | 19 47 | 6 | 3.1 | 1.4 | 6 | 20 44 | 4 | 9 | 2.6 | 8 | 21 40 | 13.3 | 7 |
| 38 | 6 | 7.1 | 17 37 | 4 | 6 | 8 | 3 | 18 35 | 10.3 | 5 | 0 | 6 | 19 32 | 11.2 | 3 | 2 | 8 | 20 29 | 12.0 | 2 | 4 | 9 | 21 26 | 8 | 4.1 | 6 | 13.1 | 22 22 | 7 | 9 |
| 39 | 6 | 4 | 18 21 | 9 | 8 | 8 | 6 | 19 19 | 7 | 7 | 0 | 9 | 20 16 | 6 | 5 | 2 | 11.1 | 21 13 | 4 | 4 | 4 | 12.3 | 22 10 | 13.3 | 3 | 6 | 5 23 | 6 | 14.1 | 5.1 |
| 40 | 6 | 8 | 19 7 | 10.3 | 1.0 | 8 | 9.0 | 20 5 | 11.2 | 9 | 0 | 10.3 | 21 2 | 12.0 | 7 | 2 | 5 21 | 59 | 9 | 6 | 4 | 7 22 | 55 | 7 | 5 | 6 | 9 | 23 50 | 5 | 3 |
| 41 | 6 | 8.2 | 19 54 | 8 | 2 | 8 | 4 | 20 52 | 6 | 2.1 | 0 | 7 | 21 49 | 5 | 9 | 2 | 9 | 22 45 | 13.3 | 8 | 4 | 13.1 | 23 41 | 14.2 | 7 | 6 | 14.3 | 24 37 | 15.0 | 5 |
| 42 | 26.6 | 6.2 | 20 43 | 11.3 | 4 | 27.8 | 8 | 21 41 | 12.1 | 3 | 29.0 | 11.1 | 22 38 | 13.0 | 3 | 0.2 | 12.3 | 23 34 | 8 | 4.0 | 1.4 | 6 | 24 29 | 6 | 9 | 2.6 | 8 | 25 24 | 4 | 7 |
| 43 | 6 | 9.0 | 21 34 | 8 | 6 | 8 | 10.2 | 22 31 | 6 | 5 | 0 | 5 | 23 28 | 5 | 3 | 2 | 8 | 24 24 | 14.3 | 2 | 4 | 14.1 | 25 19 | 15.1 | 5.1 | 6 | 15.3 | 26 14 | 9 | 9 |
| 44 | 5 | 4 | 22 27 | 12.3 | 8 | 8 | 7 | 23 24 | 13.1 | 7 | 0 | 12.0 | 24 20 | 14.0 | 5 | 2 | 13.3 | 25 16 | 8 | 4 | 4 | 6 | 26 11 | 6 | 3 | 6 | 8 27 | 5 | 16.4 | 6.1 |
| 45 | 5 | 9 | 23 22 | 8 | 2.0 | 8 | 11.2 | 24 18 | 7 | 9 | 0 | 5 | 25 14 | 5 | 7 | 2 | 8 | 26 10 | 15.3 | 7 | 5 | 15.1 | 27 5 | 16.1 | 5 | 7 | 16.3 | 27 58 | 9 | 3 |
| 46 | 5 | 10.4 | 24 19 | 13.4 | 2 | 7 | 7 | 25 15 | 14.2 | 3.1 | 0 | 13.0 | 26 10 | 15.0 | 9 | 2 | 14.3 | 27 5 | 8 | 9 | 5 | 6 28 | 0 | 6 | 7 | 7 | 8 28 | 53 | 17.4 | 5 |
| 47 | 26.5 | 9.25 | 19 | 9 | 5 | 27.7 | 12.2 | 26 14 | 8 | 3 | 29.0 | 6 27 | 9 | 6 | 4.2 | 0.2 | 9 28 | 4 | 16.4 | 5.1 | 1.5 | 16.2 | 28 57 | 17.2 | 9 | 2.7 | 17.4 | 29 50 | 18.0 | 7 |
| 48 | 4 | 11.5 | 26 21 | 14.5 | 7 | 7 | 8 | 27 15 | 15.3 | 6 | 0 | 14.2 | 28 10 | 16.1 | 4 | 2 | 15.5 | 29 4 | 9 | 3 | 5 | 8 | 29 57 | 7 | 6.1 | 7 | 18.0 | 0 ⋂ 49 | ⋃ 7.0 |
| 49 | 4 | 12.1 | 27 25 | 15.1 | 3.0 | 7 | 13.4 | 28 19 | 9 | 9 | 0 | 8 | 29 13 | 7 | 7 | 2 | 16.1 | 0 ⋂ 7 | 17.5 | 5 | 5 | 17.4 | 0 59 | 18.3 | 3 | 7 | 6 | 1 51 | 19.1 | 2 |
| 50 | 4 | 8 | 28 32 | 7 | 3 | 7 | 14.1 | 29 26 | 16.5 | 4.1 | 0 | 15.5 | 0 ⋂ 19 | 17.3 | 5.0 | 2 | 8 | 1 12 | 18.1 | 8 | 5 | 18.1 | 2 4 | 9 | 6 | 8 | 19.3 | 2 55 | ∶ | 5 |
| 51 | 4 | 13.5 | 29 42 | 16.4 | 6 | 7 | 8 | 0 ⋂ 36 | 17.1 | 4 | 28.9 | 16.2 | 1 28 | 9 | 3 | 2 | 17.5 | 2 20 | 7 | 6.1 | 5 | 8 | 3 11 | 19.5 | 9 | 8 | 20.0 | 4 1 | 20.4 | 8 |
| 52 | 26.4 | 14.2 | 0 ⋂ 56 | 17.1 | 9 | 27.7 | 15.6 | 1 48 | 8 | 7 | 9 | 17.0 | 2 40 | 18.6 | 6 | 0.2 | 18.3 | 3 31 | 19.4 | 4 | 1.5 | 19.6 | 4 21 | 20.1 | 7.2 | 2.8 | 8 | 5 11 | 21.0 | 8.1 |
| 53 | 3 | 15.0 | 2 12 | 8 | 4.2 | 6 | 16.4 | 3 4 | 18.5 | 5.0 | 9 | 8 | 3 54 | 19.3 | 8 | 2 | 19.2 | 4 44 | 20.1 | 7 | 5 | 20.5 | 5 34 | 8 | 5 | 8 | 21.7 | 6 23 | 7 | 4 |
| 54 | 3 | 9 | 3 32 | 18.5 | 5 | 6 | 17.3 | 4 23 | 19.3 | 3 | 9 | 18.7 | 5 12 | 20.0 | 6.1 | 2 | 20.1 | 6 2 | 8 | 7.0 | 6 | 21.5 | 6 50 | 21.5 | 8 | 9 | 22.7 | 7 38 | 22.4 | 6 |
| 55 | 3 | 16.9 | 4 56 | 19.3 | 8 | 6 | 18.3 | 5 45 | 20.1 | 6 | 9 | 19.7 | 6 34 | 8 | 4 | 2 | 21.1 | 7 22 | 21.6 | 3 | 2 | 22.5 | 8 10 | 22.3 | 8.1 | 9 | 23.8 | 8 57 | 23.1 | 9 |
| 56 | 3 | 18.0 | 6 24 | 20.1 | 5.2 | 6 | 19.4 | 7 12 | 9 | 6.0 | 9 | 20.8 | 7 59 | 21.6 | 8 | 2 | 22.2 | 8 46 | 22.4 | 7 | 6 | 23.6 | 9 33 | 23.1 | 5 | 9 | 25.0 | 10 18 | 9 | 9.2 |

Figure 13: Dalton's Tables of Houses

Entering these cusps on a chart form, we have:

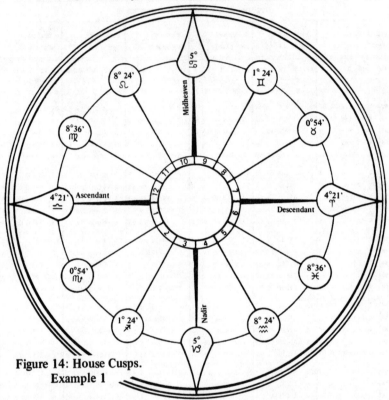

**Figure 14: House Cusps.**
**Example 1**

**Example 2. Person born March 30, 1947, 9:38 AM, Red Wing,**
**MN.** The corrected ST at birth is 21h 56m 39s, the latitude of birth is
44° 34' north. Look up the nearest ST in the Tables of Houses (Figure
13) which is 21h 56m 52s. Look up the nearest latitude, which is 45°.
The house cusps are:

| | | | |
|---|---|---|---|
| Ascendant | 25° ♊ 14' | Seventh House | 25° ♐ 14' |
| Second House | 14° ♋ 30' | Eighth House | 14° ♑ 30' |
| Third House | 3° ♌ 42' | Ninth House | 3° ♒ 42' |
| Midheaven | 27° ♒ | Fourth House | 27° ♌ |
| Eleventh House | 29° ♓ | Fifth House | 29° ♍ |
| Twelfth House | 12° ♉ 30' | Sixth House | 12° ♏ 30' |

Entering these cusps on a chart form, we have:

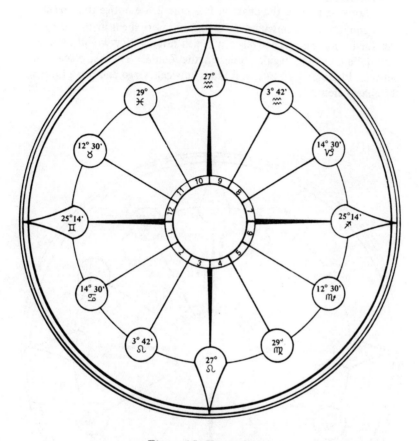

**Figure 15: House Cusps.**
**Example 2**

**Note.** Another system largely used by modern astrologers is the *Equal House System*. Essentially, the system assumes the Ascendant to be the calculation of maximum importance, with the house cusps all drawn thirty degrees from each other. For example, if the Ascendant is 20° Taurus, the cusp of the Fourth House is 20° Virgo, the cusp of the Fifth House is 20° Libra, and so on.

## Interception

Looking around the chart in Example 2, we notice that the signs Aries and Libra are missing. We therefore insert them in the Eleventh and Fifth Houses, respectively, in which houses they would naturally have fallen in their regular order in the Zodiac. That is, place Aries between Pisces and Taurus, and Libra between Virgo and Scorpio, as in the chart below:

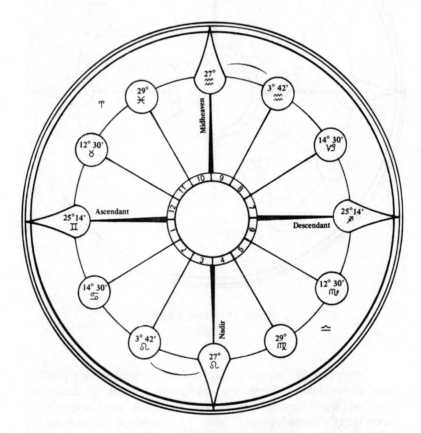

**Figure 16: Intercepted Houses.**
**Example 2**

Frequently it will appear that the Tables of Houses have skipped a sign and left it out entirely. Therefore it will be necessary to put the missing sign in the chart in the middle of the house where it would have naturally appeared in its regular order.

Its opposite sign should be treated in the same manner. It often occurs that two and sometimes four signs are thus *intercepted*, so always be cautious and look the map over carefully to see that all signs are present and in consecutive order. When you find a sign (and its opposite) extending over two cusps you will know there are intercepted signs in the chart.

Interception is caused mainly by the latitude of the country. At the equator all the signs rise in regular order, but as one proceeds north or south, an inequality in their movements occurs. Interception makes no actual difference in the nature or quality of a sign. It merely makes that house space in the chart contain more zodiacal degrees that it ordinarily would, were an additional whole sign not thus located in it. For instance, reference to the chart in Example 2 shows the Eleventh House has one degree of Pisces, thirty degrees of Aries and thirteen degrees of Taurus, or a total of forty-four degrees. We call attention to this matter in order to emphasize the need for accuracy in placing the signs and degrees on the house cusps.

## South Latitude

To erect a chart for south latitude, simply add twelve hours to the sidereal time at birth. If the sum amounts to more than subtract twenty-four and use the remainder.

Enter a Tables of Houses for the latitude desired but instead of inserting the given signs and degrees as customary for the house cusps, enter the given signs and degrees on the opposite cusps, that is, on the Fourth, Fifth, Sixth, Seventh, Eighth and Ninth House cusps. Then fill in the remaining cusps in the proper sequence.

## SUPPLEMENTARY CALCULATIONS

### Interpolation of Ascendant Longitude

When more exact work is desired, the Ascendant can be interpolated according to the rule of proportionals. This is not usually necessary for natal horoscope work however.

**1. Find the Sidereal Time Difference.** Note the sidereal times given in the Table of Houses on either side of your specific Sidereal Time. Subtract the earlier ST from the larger number to find the total amount of elapsed ST for that period. Record this in seconds of time.

**2. Find the Ascendant Difference.** Note the corresponding Ascendants, and again, subtract the smaller from the larger to find the total distance of zodiacal longitude covered by the Ascendant in that ST period. Record this in seconds of longitudinal arc.

**3. Find the Equivalent of One Second ST.** By dividing the total seconds of longitudinal arc by the total seconds of ST you will obtain the number of seconds of longitude that is equal to one second of ST.

**4. Find the ST Interval to Birth ST.** By subtracting the earlier ST from the birth ST you will get the amount of ST elapsed from the earlier recorded ST until the actual birth ST. This interval should be recorded in seconds.

**5. Find the Ascendant Interval to Birth Ascendant.** Multiply the ST interval (4) by the seconds of longitude per ST second (3) to get the ascendant interval (5).

**6. Add the Ascendant Interval to the Earlier Ascendant.** The result will be the corrected, interpolated Ascendant for the exact ST at birth.

**Example 1. Person born January 22, 1936, 10:20 PM, Sillers-ville, PA.** The corrected Sidereal Time at birth is 06h 23m 38s. Refer to Figure 12, page 90. The birth ST actually lies between 06h 21m 47s and 06h 26m 90s. The birth Ascendant therefore lies between 4° 21' Libra and 5° 13' Libra.

    1. The ST Difference:     06h 26m 09s  (later ST)
                                  −06  21    47  (earlier ST)
                                  00h 04m 22s  (ST difference) = 262s

    2. The Ascendant Difference:  05° 13'  (Libra, later Ascendant)
                                        −04  21   (Libra, earlier Ascendant)
                                        00° 52'  (Ascendant difference) =
                                                              3120"

3. The Longitudinal Equivalent of One Second ST:
   3120 ÷ 262 = 11.91 = 12"

4. ST Interval:                 06h 23m 38s (birth ST)
                               -06   21   47 (earlier ST)
                                00   01   51 (ST interval) = 111s

5. Ascendant Interval:          111s (ST interval)
                               x 12  (equivalent of one second)
                               1332  (Ascendant interval) = 22' 12"

6. Interpolated Ascendant:  04° 21' 00" (earlier Ascendant)
                                  22 12  (Ascendant interval)
                            04° 43' 12" (interpolated Ascendant)

**Example 2, Person born March 30, 1947, 9:38 AM, Red Wing, MN.** The corrected Sidereal Time at birth is 21h 56m 39s. Refer to Figure 13, page 91. The birth ST is only 13s away from the given ST of 21h 56m 52s, so interpolation would not be necessary, even for more exact work.

## Interpolation of Latitude

When more exact work is required, the latitude can be interpolated. This is not usually necessary for natal horoscope work, however.

**1. Note the Extra Latitude.** This will always be less than 1° and should be recorded in minutes.

**2. Find the Ascendant Difference.** Taking the nearest ST, note the Ascendants for latitudes on either side of the exact birth latitude.

**3. Find the Ascendant Interval.** Multiply the extra minutes of latitude (1) by the Ascendant difference (2) and divide the result by 60 to get the extra amount of zodiacal longitude covered by the Ascendant in the extra minutes of latitude. If the result is less than 60, do not divide, simply record it as seconds of longitude.

**4. Add the Ascendant Interval to the Lesser Latitude's Ascendant.** The result will be the exact Ascendant for the specific latitude of birth. If the Ascendant has been interpolated to a more exact birth ST, add the Ascendant interval to the interpolated Ascendant.

Example 1. **Person born January 22, 1936, 10:20 PM, Sillers-ville, PA.** The corrected Sidereal Time of birth is 06h 23m 38s. The birth latitude is 40° 16' N. Refer to Figure 12, page 90. Since the Ascendant difference is only 2', 16' of extra latitude would not make an appreciable difference, and interpolation would not be required even for more exact work.

Example 2. **Person born March 30, 1947, 9:38 AM, Red Wing, MN.** The corrected Sidereal Time of birth is 21h 56m 39s. The birth latitude is 44° 34' N. Refer to Figure 13, page 91.

1. Extra Latitude:           34'.

2. Ascendant Difference:     25° 14'   (Gemini, 45° latitude)
                             -24  20   (Gemini, 44° latitude)
                             00° 54'   (Ascendant difference)

3. Ascendant Interval:       34'   (extra latitude)
                             x54   (Ascendant difference)
                             1836   (Ascendant interval) = 30' 36"

4. Birth Ascendant:          24° 20' 00"   (Gemini Ascendant,
                                                  44° latitude)
                             +     30  36   (Ascendant interval)
                             24° 50' 36"   (birth Ascendant)

## Correcting the Midheaven Degree

As the Tables of Houses quote the Midheaven by sign and degree only it is sometimes necessary to correct the Midheaven to exact minute of longitude. This is not usually necessary for natal horoscope work.

**1. Find the Sidereal Time Interval.** Note the sidereal time in the Tables of Houses directly before the birth ST and subtract it from the birth ST to get the ST interval.

**2. Note Zodiacal Longitude Equivalent.** Look up the ST interval in the right hand column of Table 8: Relation of Zodiacal Longitude to Sidereal Time.

**3. Find the Corrected Midheaven.** Add the zodiacal longitude equivalent to the earlier recorded MC as found in the Tables of Houses.

1' of Long. =    4s of ST
2' of Long. =    8s of ST
3' of Long. =   12s of ST
4' of Long. =   16s of ST
5' of Long. =   20s of ST
6' of Long. =   24s of ST
7' of Long. =   28s of ST
8' of Long. =   32s of ST
9' of Long. =   36s of ST
10' of Long. =   40s of ST
11' of Long. =   44s of ST
12' of Long. =   48s of ST
13' of Long. =   52s of ST
14' of Long. =   56s of ST
15' of Long. =   60s or 1m of ST
16' of Long. =   64s or 1m   4s of ST
17' of Long. =   68s or 1m   8s of ST
18' of Long. =   72s or 1m 12s of ST
19' of Long. =   76s or 1m 16s of ST
20' of Long. =   80s or 1m 20s of ST
30' of Long. = 120s or 2m of ST
45' of Long. = 180s or 3m of ST
60' of Long. = 240s or 4m of ST

**Table 8: Relation of Zodiacal Longitude to Sidereal Time**

**Example 1. Person born January 22, 1936. 10:20 PM, Sillersville, PA.** The corrected sidereal time at birth is 06h 23m 38s. Refer to Figure 12, page 90. The MC for 06h 21m 47s is 5° Cancer.

1. ST Interval:

      06h 23m 38s  (birth ST)
      -06  21  47  (earlier ST)
      00h 01m 51s  (ST interval)

2. Zodiacal Longitude Equivalent:  1m ST = 15' long
                               +51s ST = 13' long
                                        28' long

3. Corrected MC:

        5°       (Cancer, earlier MC)
        +0 28'  (equivalent to ST interval)
        5° 28'  (Cancer, corrected MC)

Example 2. Person born March 30, 1947, 9:38 AM, Red Wing, MN. The corrected sidereal time at birth is 21h 56m 39s. This is only 13s away from a recorded ST, so correction is not needed.

# Finding the Positions of the Planets

Upon reference to the ephemeris for the date of birth, our attention will be attracted to columns which designate the planets' longitude, latitude and declination. Our work for the present deals with longitude only.

The celestial longitude of a planet is the sign and degree of the Zodiac in which it is located at a given time. The planets' zodiacal locations are calculated for the ephemeris according to the laws of astronomy for each date at either twelve o'clock (noon) or twelve o'clock (midnight) in Greenwich, England. Therefore, if a child were born in Greenwich exactly at noon or midnight, no correction is needed to the planets' places as given, but if he or she were born before or after twelve o'clock, a correction to their places as given in the ephemeris is required for the amount of their separate motions in the time between birth and twelve o'clock, which is added if the birth occurs after the ephemeris time, and subtracted if the birth occurs before the ephemeris time.

**Note.** If using an ephemeris other than the Rosicrucian ephemeris recommended, check to see if the planets' places are given for noon or midnight.

To change the planets' positions from midnight to noon, in order to use the George Method of Horoscope Calculation, simply note the recorded places at midnight of the date desired and their places the preceding midnight. One half their distance between is their place at noon of the birth date. Some of the midnight ephemerides also quote

101

the Moon's position for noon. See Figure 11, pages 82-83.

The correlation of the planets' positions is made with that of proportional logarithms, a simple mathematical tool in which representational numbers are added together to replace complicated multiplication. The method of finding the positions of the planets is presented here in three steps:

1. Find the Constant Log.
2. Calculate the Daily Motion of the Planets
3. Figure the Planets' Positions at Birth.

## 1. Find the Constant Log

The *constant log* is a number which represents the interval between the time of birth and the time for which the planets' positions are given in the Rosicrucian ephemeris (noon, Greenwich).

**Finding the Interval.** In the George Method of Horoscope Calculation, noon GMT is changed to the equivalent mean local time and called the Noon Mark. As we have learned, a difference in mean time occurs at the rate of four minutes for each degree of terrestrial longitude. In **Correction for Longitude**, page 87, we found the difference between the mean local time and GMT. This time difference is subtracted from noon for all births west of Greenwich and added to noon for all births east of Greenwich to find the Noon Mark.

Once the Noon Mark has been found it is easy to calculate the interval between the mean local time of birth (**Change Standard Time to Mean Local Time**, page 75) and the nearest Noon Mark.

**Example 1. Person born January 22, 1936, 10:20 PM, Sillersville, PA.** The time difference between Greenwich and Sillersville is 05h 01m 36s. This is subtracted from noon and a Noon Mark of 06h 58m 24s AM is found. Since the mean local time of birth (10h 18m 24s PM) is closer to the Noon Mark (6:58 AM) of January 23, the next morning, this interval is found by figuring the time between the birth and midnight and adding the Noon Mark to this. An interval of 08h 40m results.

12h 00m 00s =  11h 59m 60s  (noon)
            <u>+05  01   36  </u> (time difference)
            06h 58m 24s  (Noon Mark)

12h 00m 00s =  11h 59m 60s  (midnight)
            <u>+10  18   24  </u> (mean local time of birth)
            01h 41m 36s  (interval)

01h 41m 36s  (interval)
<u>+06  58   24  </u> (Noon Mark)
07h 99m 60s = 08h 40m 00s (interval)

**Example 2. Person born March 30, 1947, 9:38 AM, Red Wing, MN.** The time difference between Red Wing and Greenwich is 06h 10m 04s. This is subtracted from noon and a Noon Mark of 05h 49m 56s AM is found. The mean local time of birth (09h 27m 56s AM) is 03h 38m 00s after the Noon Mark.

12h 00m 00s =  11h 59m 60s  (noon)
            <u>–06  10   04  </u> (time difference)
            05h 49m 56s  (Noon Mark)

09h 27m 56s =  08h 87m 56s  (mean local time of birth)
            <u>–05  49   56  </u> (Noon Mark)
            03h 38m 00s  (interval)

The following table presents the student with a handy shortcut for figuring the Noon Mark for any place in the world. It can be a time-saver once the process is thoroughly understood.

**Table of Noon Marks—How to Use.** The Noon Mark is simply the mean local time at the place of birth when it is noon in Greenwich, England, the time for which the planets' places are figured in some standard ephemerides.

To find the Noon Mark with the aid of the tables below, find the longitude in the center column. If the birth place is to the *east* of Greenwich, read the figure in the column to the *left* of the longitude. If the birth place is to the *west* of Greenwich, read the figure in the column to the *right* of the longitude.

| E. PM | Long. | W. AM | E. PM | Long. | W. AM | E. PM | Long. | W. AM |
|---|---|---|---|---|---|---|---|---|
| 12.00 | 0 | 12.00 | 2.00 | 30 | 10.00 | 4.00 | 60 | 8.00 |
| 0.04 | 1 | 11.56 | 2.04 | 31 | 9.56 | 4.04 | 61 | 7.56 |
| 0.08 | 2 | 11.52 | 2.08 | 32 | 9.52 | 4.08 | 62 | 7.52 |
| 0.12 | 3 | 11.48 | 2.12 | 33 | 9.48 | 4.12 | 63 | 7.48 |
| 0.16 | 4 | 11.44 | 2.16 | 34 | 9.44 | 4.16 | 64 | 7.44 |
| 0.20 | 5 | 11.40 | 2.20 | 35 | 9.40 | 4.20 | 65 | 7.40 |
| 0.24 | 6 | 11.36 | 2.24 | 36 | 9.36 | 4.24 | 66 | 7.36 |
| 0.28 | 7 | 11.32 | 2.28 | 37 | 9.32 | 4.28 | 67 | 7.32 |
| 0.32 | 8 | 11.28 | 2.32 | 38 | 9.28 | 4.32 | 68 | 7.28 |
| 0.36 | 9 | 11.24 | 2.36 | 39 | 9.24 | 4.36 | 69 | 7.24 |
| 0.40 | 10 | 11.20 | 2.40 | 40 | 9.20 | 4.40 | 70 | 7.20 |
| 0.44 | 11 | 11.16 | 2.44 | 41 | 9.16 | 4.44 | 71 | 7.16 |
| 0.48 | 12 | 11.12 | 2.48 | 42 | 9.12 | 4.48 | 72 | 7.12 |
| 0.52 | 13 | 11.08 | 2.52 | 43 | 9.08 | 4.52 | 73 | 7.08 |
| 0.56 | 14 | 11.04 | 2.56 | 44 | 9.04 | 4.56 | 74 | 7.04 |
| 1.00 | 15 | 11.00 | 3.00 | 45 | 9.00 | 5.00 | 75 | 7.00 |
| 1.04 | 16 | 10.56 | 3.04 | 46 | 8.56 | 5.04 | 76 | 6.56 |
| 1.08 | 17 | 10.52 | 3.08 | 47 | 8.52 | 5.08 | 77 | 6.52 |
| 1.12 | 18 | 10.48 | 3.12 | 48 | 8.48 | 5.12 | 78 | 6.48 |
| 1.16 | 19 | 10.44 | 3.16 | 49 | 8.44 | 5.16 | 79 | 6.44 |
| 1.20 | 20 | 10.40 | 3.20 | 50 | 8.40 | 5.20 | 80 | 6.40 |
| 1.24 | 21 | 10.36 | 3.24 | 51 | 8.36 | 5.24 | 81 | 6.36 |
| 1.28 | 22 | 10.32 | 3.28 | 52 | 8.32 | 5.28 | 82 | 6.32 |
| 1.32 | 23 | 10.28 | 3.32 | 53 | 8.28 | 5.32 | 83 | 6.28 |
| 1.36 | 24 | 10.24 | 3.36 | 54 | 8.24 | 5.36 | 84 | 6.24 |
| 1.40 | 25 | 10.20 | 3.40 | 55 | 8.20 | 5.40 | 85 | 6.20 |
| 1.44 | 26 | 10.16 | 3.44 | 56 | 8.16 | 5.44 | 86 | 6.16 |
| 1.48 | 27 | 10.12 | 3.48 | 57 | 8.12 | 5.48 | 87 | 6.12 |
| 1.52 | 28 | 10.08 | 3.52 | 58 | 8.08 | 5.52 | 88 | 6.08 |
| 1.56 | 29 | 10.04 | 3.56 | 59 | 8.04 | 5.56 | 89 | 6.04 |

Table 9: Table of Noon Marks

| E. PM | Long. | W. AM | E. PM | Long. | W. AM | E. PM | Long. | W. AM |
|-------|-------|-------|-------|-------|-------|-------|-------|-------|
| 6.00  | 90    | 6.00  | 8.04  | 121   | 3.56  | 10.04 | 151   | 1.56  |
| 6.04  | 91    | 5.56  | 8.08  | 122   | 3.52  | 10.08 | 152   | 1.52  |
| 6.08  | 92    | 5.52  | 8.12  | 123   | 3.48  | 10.12 | 153   | 1.48  |
| 6.12  | 93    | 5.48  | 8.16  | 124   | 3.44  | 10.16 | 154   | 1.44  |
| 6.16  | 94    | 5.44  | 8.20  | 125   | 3.40  | 10.20 | 155   | 1.40  |
| 6.20  | 95    | 5.40  | 8.24  | 126   | 3.36  | 10.24 | 156   | 1.36  |
| 6.24  | 96    | 5.36  | 8.28  | 127   | 3.32  | 10.28 | 157   | 1.32  |
| 6.28  | 97    | 5.32  | 8.32  | 128   | 3.28  | 10.32 | 158   | 1.28  |
| 6.32  | 98    | 5.28  | 8.36  | 129   | 3.24  | 10.36 | 159   | 1.24  |
| 6.36  | 99    | 5.24  | 8.40  | 130   | 3.20  | 10.40 | 160   | 1.20  |
| 6.40  | 100   | 5.20  | 8.44  | 131   | 3.16  | 10.44 | 161   | 1.16  |
| 6.44  | 101   | 5.16  | 8.48  | 132   | 3.12  | 10.48 | 162   | 1.12  |
| 6.48  | 102   | 5.12  | 8.52  | 133   | 3.08  | 10.52 | 163   | 1.08  |
| 6.52  | 103   | 5.08  | 8.56  | 134   | 3.04  | 10.56 | 164   | 1.04  |
| 6.56  | 104   | 5.04  | 9.00  | 135   | 3.00  | 11.00 | 165   | 1.00  |
| 7.00  | 105   | 5.00  | 9.04  | 136   | 2.56  | 11.04 | 166   | 0.56  |
| 7.04  | 106   | 4.56  | 9.08  | 137   | 2.52  | 11.08 | 167   | 0.52  |
| 7.08  | 107   | 4.52  | 9.12  | 138   | 2.48  | 11.12 | 168   | 0.48  |
| 7.12  | 108   | 4.48  | 9.16  | 139   | 2.44  | 11.16 | 169   | 0.44  |
| 7.16  | 109   | 4.44  | 9.20  | 140   | 2.40  | 11.20 | 170   | 0.40  |
| 7.20  | 110   | 4.40  | 9.24  | 141   | 2.36  | 11.24 | 171   | 0.36  |
| 7.24  | 111   | 4.36  | 9.28  | 142   | 2.32  | 11.28 | 172   | 0.32  |
| 7.28  | 112   | 4.32  | 9.32  | 143   | 2.28  | 11.32 | 173   | 0.28  |
| 7.32  | 113   | 4.28  | 9.36  | 144   | 2.24  | 11.36 | 174   | 0.24  |
| 7.36  | 114   | 4.24  | 9.40  | 145   | 2.20  | 11.40 | 175   | 0.20  |
| 7.40  | 115   | 4.20  | 9.44  | 146   | 2.16  | 11.44 | 176   | 0.16  |
| 7.44  | 116   | 4.16  | 9.48  | 147   | 2.12  | 11.48 | 177   | 0.12  |
| 7.48  | 117   | 4.12  | 9.52  | 148   | 2.08  | 11.52 | 178   | 0.08  |
| 7.52  | 118   | 4.08  | 9.56  | 149   | 2.04  | 11.56 | 179   | 0.04  |
| 7.56  | 119   | 4.04  | 10.00 | 150   | 2.00  | 12.00 | 180   | 0.00  |
| 8.00  | 120   | 4.00  |       |       |       |       |       |       |

**Finding the constant log.** Tables of proportional logarithms are found in the ephemeris and are reproduced here for your convenience (Figures 17 and 18). The figures reading across the top of the page represent hours or degrees, those reading down the first column at the left side represent minutes. The interval is simply looked up in the log tables and the constant log recorded.

Degrees or Hours.

| Min | 0 | 1 | 2 | 3 | 4 | 5 | 6 | 7 | 8 | 9 | 10 | 11 | |
|---|---|---|---|---|---|---|---|---|---|---|---|---|---|
| 0 | 3.1584 | 1.3802 | 1.0792 | 9031 | 7781 | 6812 | 6021 | 5351 | 4771 | 4260 | 3802 | 3388 | 0 |
| 1 | 3.1584 | 1.3730 | 1.0756 | 9007 | 7763 | 6798 | 6009 | 5341 | 4762 | 4252 | 3795 | 3382 | 1 |
| 2 | 2.8573 | 1.3660 | 1.0720 | 8983 | 7745 | 6784 | 5997 | 5330 | 4753 | 4244 | 3788 | 3375 | 2 |
| 3 | 2.6812 | 1.3590 | 1.0685 | 8959 | 7728 | 6769 | 5985 | 5320 | 4744 | 4236 | 3780 | 3368 | 3 |
| 4 | 2.5563 | 1.3522 | 1.0649 | 8935 | 7710 | 6755 | 5973 | 5310 | 4735 | 4228 | 3773 | 3362 | 4 |
| 5 | 2.4594 | 1.3454 | 1.0614 | 8912 | 7692 | 6741 | 5961 | 5300 | 4726 | 4220 | 3766 | 3355 | 5 |
| 6 | 2.3802 | 1.3388 | 1.0580 | 8888 | 7674 | 6726 | 5949 | 5289 | 4717 | 4212 | 3759 | 3349 | 6 |
| 7 | 2.3133 | 1.3323 | 1.0546 | 8865 | 7657 | 6712 | 5937 | 5279 | 4708 | 4204 | 3752 | 3342 | 7 |
| 8 | 2.2553 | 1.3258 | 1.0511 | 8842 | 7639 | 6698 | 5925 | 5269 | 4699 | 4196 | 3745 | 3336 | 8 |
| 9 | 2.2041 | 1.3195 | 1.0478 | 8819 | 7622 | 6684 | 5913 | 5259 | 4690 | 4188 | 3737 | 3329 | 9 |
| 10 | 2.1584 | 1.3133 | 1.0444 | 8796 | 7604 | 6670 | 5902 | 5249 | 4682 | 4180 | 3730 | 3323 | 10 |
| 11 | 2.1170 | 1.3071 | 1.0411 | 8773 | 7587 | 6656 | 5890 | 5239 | 4673 | 4172 | 3723 | 3316 | 11 |
| 12 | 2.0792 | 1.3010 | 1.0378 | 8751 | 7570 | 6642 | 5878 | 5229 | 4664 | 4164 | 3716 | 3310 | 12 |
| 13 | 2.0444 | 1.2950 | 1.0345 | 8728 | 7552 | 6628 | 5866 | 5219 | 4655 | 4156 | 3709 | 3303 | 13 |
| 14 | 2.0122 | 1.2891 | 1.0313 | 8706 | 7535 | 6614 | 5855 | 5209 | 4646 | 4148 | 3702 | 3297 | 14 |
| 15 | 1.9823 | 1.2833 | 1.0280 | 8683 | 7518 | 6600 | 5843 | 5199 | 4638 | 4141 | 3695 | 3291 | 15 |
| 16 | 1.9542 | 1.2775 | 1.0248 | 8661 | 7501 | 6587 | 5832 | 5189 | 4629 | 4133 | 3688 | 3284 | 16 |
| 17 | 1.9279 | 1.2719 | 1.0216 | 8639 | 7484 | 6573 | 5820 | 5179 | 4620 | 4125 | 3681 | 3278 | 17 |
| 18 | 1.9031 | 1.2663 | 1.0185 | 8617 | 7467 | 6559 | 5809 | 5169 | 4611 | 4117 | 3674 | 3271 | 18 |
| 19 | 1.8796 | 1.2607 | 1.0153 | 8595 | 7451 | 6546 | 5797 | 5159 | 4603 | 4109 | 3667 | 3265 | 19 |
| 20 | 1.8573 | 1.2553 | 1.0122 | 8573 | 7434 | 6532 | 5786 | 5149 | 4594 | 4102 | 3660 | 3258 | 20 |
| 21 | 1.8361 | 1.2499 | 1.0091 | 8552 | 7417 | 6519 | 5774 | 5139 | 4585 | 4094 | 3653 | 3252 | 21 |
| 22 | 1.8159 | 1.2445 | 1.0061 | 8530 | 7401 | 6505 | 5763 | 5129 | 4577 | 4086 | 3646 | 3246 | 22 |
| 23 | 1.7966 | 1.2393 | 1.0030 | 8509 | 7384 | 6492 | 5752 | 5120 | 4568 | 4079 | 3639 | 3239 | 23 |
| 24 | 1.7781 | 1.2341 | 1.0000 | 8487 | 7368 | 6478 | 5740 | 5110 | 4559 | 4071 | 3632 | 3233 | 24 |
| 25 | 1.7604 | 1.2289 | 0.9970 | 8466 | 7351 | 6465 | 5729 | 5100 | 4551 | 4063 | 3625 | 3227 | 25 |
| 26 | 1.7434 | 1.2239 | 0.9940 | 8445 | 7335 | 6451 | 5718 | 5090 | 4542 | 4055 | 3618 | 3220 | 26 |
| 27 | 1.7270 | 1.2188 | 0.9910 | 8424 | 7318 | 6438 | 5706 | 5081 | 4534 | 4048 | 3611 | 3214 | 27 |
| 28 | 1.7112 | 1.2139 | 0.9881 | 8403 | 7302 | 6425 | 5695 | 5071 | 4525 | 4040 | 3604 | 3208 | 28 |
| 29 | 1.6960 | 1.2090 | 0.9852 | 8382 | 7286 | 6412 | 5684 | 5061 | 4516 | 4032 | 3597 | 3201 | 29 |
| 30 | 1.6812 | 1.2041 | 0.9823 | 8361 | 7270 | 6398 | 5673 | 5051 | 4508 | 4025 | 3590 | 3195 | 30 |
| 31 | 1.6670 | 1.1993 | 0.9794 | 8341 | 7254 | 6385 | 5662 | 5042 | 4499 | 4017 | 3583 | 3189 | 31 |
| 32 | 1.6532 | 1.1946 | 0.9765 | 8327 | 7238 | 6372 | 5651 | 5032 | 4491 | 4010 | 3576 | 3183 | 32 |
| 33 | 1.6398 | 1.1899 | 0.9737 | 8300 | 7222 | 6359 | 5640 | 5023 | 4482 | 4002 | 3570 | 3176 | 33 |
| 34 | 1.6269 | 1.1852 | 0.9708 | 8279 | 7206 | 6346 | 5629 | 5013 | 4474 | 3994 | 3563 | 3170 | 34 |
| 35 | 1.6143 | 1.1806 | 0.9680 | 8259 | 7190 | 6333 | 5618 | 5003 | 4466 | 3987 | 3556 | 3164 | 35 |
| 36 | 1.6021 | 1.1761 | 0.9652 | 8239 | 7174 | 6320 | 5607 | 4994 | 4457 | 3979 | 3549 | 3157 | 36 |
| 37 | 1.5902 | 1.1716 | 0.9625 | 8219 | 7159 | 6307 | 5596 | 4984 | 4449 | 3972 | 3542 | 3151 | 37 |
| 38 | 1.5786 | 1.1671 | 0.9597 | 8199 | 7143 | 6294 | 5585 | 4975 | 4440 | 3964 | 3535 | 3145 | 38 |
| 39 | 1.5673 | 1.1627 | 0.9570 | 8179 | 7128 | 6282 | 5574 | 4965 | 4432 | 3957 | 3529 | 3139 | 39 |
| 40 | 1.5563 | 1.1584 | 0.9542 | 8159 | 7112 | 6269 | 5563 | 4956 | 4424 | 3949 | 3522 | 3133 | 40 |
| 41 | 1.5456 | 1.1540 | 0.9515 | 8140 | 7097 | 6256 | 5552 | 4947 | 4415 | 3942 | 3515 | 3126 | 41 |
| 42 | 1.5351 | 1.1498 | 0.9488 | 8120 | 7081 | 6243 | 5541 | 4937 | 4407 | 3934 | 3508 | 3120 | 42 |
| 43 | 1.5249 | 1.1455 | 0.9462 | 8101 | 7066 | 6231 | 5531 | 4928 | 4399 | 3927 | 3501 | 3114 | 43 |
| 44 | 1.5149 | 1.1413 | 0.9435 | 8081 | 7050 | 6218 | 5520 | 4918 | 4390 | 3919 | 3495 | 3108 | 44 |
| 45 | 1.5051 | 1.1372 | 0.9409 | 8062 | 7035 | 6205 | 5509 | 4909 | 4382 | 3912 | 3488 | 3102 | 45 |
| 46 | 1.4956 | 1.1331 | 0.9383 | 8043 | 7020 | 6193 | 5498 | 4900 | 4374 | 3905 | 3481 | 3096 | 46 |
| 47 | 1.4863 | 1.1290 | 0.9356 | 8023 | 7005 | 6180 | 5488 | 4890 | 4365 | 3897 | 3475 | 3089 | 47 |
| 48 | 1.4771 | 1.1249 | 0.9330 | 8004 | 6990 | 6168 | 5477 | 4881 | 4357 | 3890 | 3468 | 3083 | 48 |
| 49 | 1.4682 | 1.1209 | 0.9305 | 7985 | 6975 | 6155 | 5466 | 4872 | 4349 | 3882 | 3461 | 3077 | 49 |
| 50 | 1.4594 | 1.1170 | 0.9279 | 7966 | 6960 | 6143 | 5456 | 4863 | 4341 | 3875 | 3454 | 3071 | 50 |
| 51 | 1.4508 | 1.1130 | 0.9254 | 7947 | 6945 | 6131 | 5445 | 4853 | 4333 | 3868 | 3448 | 3065 | 51 |
| 52 | 1.4424 | 1.1091 | 0.9228 | 7929 | 6930 | 6118 | 5435 | 4844 | 4324 | 3860 | 3441 | 3059 | 52 |
| 53 | 1.4341 | 1.1053 | 0.9203 | 7910 | 6915 | 6106 | 5424 | 4835 | 4316 | 3853 | 3434 | 3053 | 53 |
| 54 | 1.4260 | 1.1015 | 0.9178 | 7891 | 6900 | 6094 | 5414 | 4826 | 4308 | 3846 | 3428 | 3047 | 54 |
| 55 | 1.4180 | 1.0977 | 0.9153 | 7873 | 6885 | 6081 | 5403 | 4817 | 4300 | 3838 | 3421 | 3041 | 55 |
| 56 | 1.4102 | 1.0939 | 0.9128 | 7854 | 6871 | 6069 | 5393 | 4808 | 4292 | 3831 | 3415 | 3034 | 56 |
| 57 | 1.4025 | 1.0902 | 0.9104 | 7836 | 6856 | 6057 | 5382 | 4798 | 4284 | 3824 | 3408 | 3028 | 57 |
| 58 | 1.3949 | 1.0865 | 0.9079 | 7818 | 6841 | 6045 | 5372 | 4789 | 4276 | 3817 | 3401 | 3022 | 58 |
| 59 | 1.3875 | 1.0828 | 0.9055 | 7800 | 6827 | 6033 | 5361 | 4780 | 4268 | 3809 | 3395 | 3016 | 59 |

Figure 17: Table of Proportional
Logarithms

**Degrees or Hours.**

| | 12 | 13 | 14 | 15 | 16 | 17 | 18 | 19 | 20 | 21 | 22 | 23 | |
|---|---|---|---|---|---|---|---|---|---|---|---|---|---|
| 0 | 3010 | 2663 | 2341 | 2041 | 1761 | 1498 | 1249 | 1015 | 0792 | 0580 | 0378 | 0185 | 0 |
| 1 | 3004 | 2657 | 2336 | 2036 | 1756 | 1493 | 1245 | 1011 | 0788 | 0577 | 0375 | 0182 | 1 |
| 2 | 2998 | 2652 | 2330 | 2032 | 1752 | 1489 | 1241 | 1007 | 0785 | 0573 | 0371 | 0179 | 2 |
| 3 | 2992 | 2646 | 2325 | 2027 | 1747 | 1485 | 1237 | 1003 | 0781 | 0570 | 0368 | 0175 | 3 |
| 4 | 2986 | 2640 | 2320 | 2022 | 1743 | 1481 | 1233 | 0999 | 0777 | 0566 | 0364 | 0172 | 4 |
| 5 | 2980 | 2635 | 2315 | 2017 | 1738 | 1476 | 1229 | 0996 | 0774 | 0563 | 0361 | 0169 | 5 |
| 6 | 2974 | 2629 | 2310 | 2012 | 1734 | 1472 | 1225 | 0992 | 0770 | 0559 | 0358 | 0166 | 6 |
| 7 | 2968 | 2624 | 2305 | 2008 | 1729 | 1468 | 1221 | 0988 | 0766 | 0556 | 0355 | 0163 | 7 |
| 8 | 2962 | 2618 | 2300 | 2003 | 1725 | 1464 | 1217 | 0984 | 0763 | 0552 | 0352 | 0160 | 8 |
| 9 | 2956 | 2613 | 2295 | 1998 | 1720 | 1460 | 1213 | 0980 | 0759 | 0549 | 0348 | 0157 | 9 |
| 10 | 2950 | 2607 | 2289 | 1993 | 1716 | 1455 | 1209 | 0977 | 0756 | 0546 | 0345 | 0153 | 10 |
| 11 | 2944 | 2602 | 2284 | 1988 | 1711 | 1451 | 1205 | 0973 | 0752 | 0542 | 0342 | 0150 | 11 |
| 12 | 2938 | 2596 | 2279 | 1984 | 1707 | 1447 | 1201 | 0969 | 0749 | 0539 | 0339 | 0147 | 12 |
| 13 | 2933 | 2591 | 2274 | 1979 | 1702 | 1443 | 1197 | 0965 | 0745 | 0535 | 0335 | 0144 | 13 |
| 14 | 2927 | 2585 | 2269 | 1974 | 1698 | 1438 | 1193 | 0962 | 0742 | 0532 | 0332 | 0141 | 14 |
| 15 | 2921 | 2580 | 2264 | 1969 | 1694 | 1434 | 1189 | 0958 | 0738 | 0529 | 0329 | 0138 | 15 |
| 16 | 2915 | 2574 | 2259 | 1965 | 1689 | 1430 | 1185 | 0954 | 0734 | 0525 | 0326 | 0135 | 16 |
| 17 | 2909 | 2569 | 2254 | 1960 | 1685 | 1426 | 1182 | 0950 | 0731 | 0522 | 0322 | 0132 | 17 |
| 18 | 2903 | 2564 | 2249 | 1955 | 1680 | 1422 | 1178 | 0947 | 0727 | 0518 | 0319 | 0129 | 18 |
| 19 | 2897 | 2558 | 2244 | 1950 | 1676 | 1417 | 1174 | 0943 | 0724 | 0515 | 0316 | 0125 | 19 |
| 20 | 2891 | 2553 | 2239 | 1946 | 1671 | 1413 | 1170 | 0939 | 0720 | 0511 | 0313 | 0122 | 20 |
| 21 | 2885 | 2547 | 2234 | 1941 | 1667 | 1409 | 1166 | 0935 | 0717 | 0508 | 0309 | 0119 | 21 |
| 22 | 2880 | 2542 | 2229 | 1936 | 1663 | 1405 | 1162 | 0932 | 0713 | 0505 | 0306 | 0116 | 22 |
| 23 | 2874 | 2536 | 2223 | 1932 | 1658 | 1401 | 1158 | 0928 | 0709 | 0501 | 0303 | 0113 | 23 |
| 24 | 2868 | 2531 | 2218 | 1927 | 1654 | 1397 | 1154 | 0924 | 0706 | 0498 | 0300 | 0110 | 24 |
| 25 | 2862 | 2526 | 2213 | 1922 | 1649 | 1393 | 1150 | 0920 | 0702 | 0495 | 0296 | 0107 | 25 |
| 26 | 2856 | 2520 | 2208 | 1917 | 1645 | 1398 | 1146 | 0917 | 0699 | 0491 | 0293 | 0104 | 26 |
| 27 | 2850 | 2515 | 2203 | 1913 | 1640 | 1384 | 1142 | 0913 | 0695 | 0488 | 0290 | 0101 | 27 |
| 28 | 2845 | 2509 | 2198 | 1908 | 1636 | 1380 | 1138 | 0909 | 0692 | 0485 | 0287 | 0098 | 28 |
| 29 | 2839 | 2504 | 2193 | 1903 | 1632 | 1376 | 1134 | 0905 | 0688 | 0481 | 0283 | 0094 | 29 |
| 30 | 2833 | 2499 | 2188 | 1899 | 1627 | 1372 | 1130 | 0902 | 0685 | 0478 | 0280 | 0091 | 30 |
| 31 | 2827 | 2493 | 2183 | 1894 | 1623 | 1368 | 1126 | 0898 | 0681 | 0474 | 0277 | 0088 | 31 |
| 32 | 2821 | 2488 | 2178 | 1889 | 1619 | 1363 | 1123 | 0894 | 0678 | 0471 | 0274 | 0085 | 32 |
| 33 | 2816 | 2483 | 2173 | 1885 | 1614 | 1359 | 1119 | 0891 | 0674 | 0468 | 0271 | 0082 | 33 |
| 34 | 2810 | 2477 | 2168 | 1880 | 1610 | 1355 | 1115 | 0887 | 0670 | 0464 | 0267 | 0079 | 34 |
| 35 | 2804 | 2472 | 2164 | 1875 | 1605 | 1351 | 1111 | 0883 | 0667 | 0461 | 0264 | 0076 | 35 |
| 36 | 2798 | 2467 | 2159 | 1871 | 1601 | 1347 | 1107 | 0880 | 0664 | 0458 | 0261 | 0073 | 36 |
| 37 | 2793 | 2461 | 2154 | 1866 | 1597 | 1343 | 1103 | 0876 | 0660 | 0454 | 0258 | 0070 | 37 |
| 38 | 2787 | 2456 | 2149 | 1862 | 1592 | 1339 | 1099 | 0872 | 0656 | 0451 | 0255 | 0067 | 38 |
| 39 | 2781 | 2451 | 2144 | 1857 | 1588 | 1335 | 1095 | 0868 | 0653 | 0448 | 0250 | 0064 | 39 |
| 40 | 2775 | 2445 | 2139 | 1852 | 1584 | 1331 | 1092 | 0861 | 0649 | 0444 | 0248 | 0061 | 40 |
| 41 | 2770 | 2440 | 2134 | 1848 | 1579 | 1327 | 1088 | 0861 | 0646 | 0441 | 0245 | 0058 | 41 |
| 42 | 2764 | 2435 | 2129 | 1843 | 1575 | 1322 | 1084 | 0857 | 0642 | 0437 | 0242 | 0055 | 42 |
| 43 | 2758 | 2430 | 2124 | 1838 | 1571 | 1318 | 1080 | 0854 | 0639 | 0434 | 0239 | 0052 | 43 |
| 44 | 2753 | 2424 | 2119 | 1834 | 1566 | 1314 | 1076 | 0850 | 0635 | 0431 | 0235 | 0048 | 44 |
| 45 | 2747 | 2419 | 2114 | 1829 | 1562 | 1310 | 1072 | 0846 | 0632 | 0428 | 0232 | 0045 | 45 |
| 46 | 2741 | 2414 | 2109 | 1825 | 1558 | 1306 | 1068 | 0843 | 0629 | 0424 | 0229 | 0042 | 46 |
| 47 | 2736 | 2409 | 2104 | 1820 | 1553 | 1302 | 1064 | 0839 | 0625 | 0421 | 0226 | 0039 | 47 |
| 48 | 2730 | 2403 | 2099 | 1816 | 1549 | 1298 | 1061 | 0835 | 0621 | 0418 | 0223 | 0036 | 48 |
| 49 | 2724 | 2398 | 2095 | 1811 | 1545 | 1294 | 1057 | 0832 | 0618 | 0414 | 0220 | 0033 | 49 |
| 50 | 2719 | 2393 | 2090 | 1806 | 1540 | 1290 | 1053 | 0828 | 0614 | 0411 | 0216 | 0030 | 50 |
| 51 | 2713 | 2388 | 2085 | 1802 | 1536 | 1286 | 1049 | 0824 | 0611 | 0408 | 0213 | 0027 | 51 |
| 52 | 2707 | 2382 | 2080 | 1797 | 1532 | 1282 | 1045 | 0821 | 0608 | 0404 | 0210 | 0024 | 52 |
| 53 | 2702 | 2377 | 2075 | 1793 | 1528 | 1278 | 1041 | 0817 | 0604 | 0401 | 0207 | 0021 | 53 |
| 54 | 2696 | 2372 | 2070 | 1788 | 1523 | 1274 | 1037 | 0814 | 0601 | 0398 | 0204 | 0018 | 54 |
| 55 | 2691 | 2367 | 2065 | 1784 | 1519 | 1270 | 1034 | 0810 | 0597 | 0394 | 0201 | 0015 | 55 |
| 56 | 2685 | 2362 | 2061 | 1779 | 1515 | 1266 | 1030 | 0806 | 0594 | 0391 | 0197 | 0012 | 56 |
| 57 | 2679 | 2356 | 2056 | 1774 | 1510 | 1261 | 1026 | 0803 | 0590 | 0388 | 0194 | 0009 | 57 |
| 58 | 2674 | 2351 | 2051 | 1770 | 1506 | 1257 | 1022 | 0799 | 0587 | 0384 | 0191 | 0006 | 58 |
| 59 | 2668 | 2346 | 2046 | 1765 | 1502 | 1253 | 1018 | 0795 | 0583 | 0381 | 0188 | 0003 | 59 |

Figure 18: Table of Proportional
Logarithms

Example 1. Person born January 22, 1936, 10:20 PM, Sillersville, PA. We have found the interval to be 08h 40m. Locate 8 along the top column of the log tables, and 40 along the left side. Where these two columns meet, we read 4424, which is the constant log.

Example 2. Person born March 30, 1947, 9:38 AM, Red Wing, MN. We have found the interval to be 03h 38m. Locate 3 along the top column of the log tables and 38 along the left side. Where these two columns meet we read 8199, which is the constant log.

## 2. Calculate the Daily Motion of the Planets

Only the Sun, Moon, Mercury, Venus and Mars move enough in one day to make figuring their precise positions practical. The noon positions of the other planets are copied from the ephemeris onto the chart blank. The nearest Pluto position given in the ephemeris nearest the birth date is used.

To calculate a planet's position at the exact time of birth we need to know the distance the planet traveled during the twenty-four hour period in which the birth took place. For births after noon, Greenwich Mean Time, or after the Noon Mark, subtract the planet's position on the birth day from its position the next day. For births before noon, GMT, or before the Noon Mark, subtract the planet's position on the day preceding birth from its position on the birth day.

Note. These rules are reversed for retrograde planets. That is, for afternoon births, subtract the planet's position on the day after birth from its position on the birth day. For morning births, subtract the planet's position on the birth day from its position on the day preceding birth.

Example 1. Person born January 22, 1936, 10:20 PM, Sillersville, PA. The birth took place in the morning of January 23, GMT (before the Noon Mark). Therefore, the planets' positions on January 22 are subtracted from their positions on January 23. Note that Mercury is so nearly stationary during this period that its position need not be figured exactly.

02° ♒ 19'  (Sun, January 23)
-01 ♒ 18  (Sun, January 22)
01°    01'  (Sun, daily motion)

21° ♑ 42' = 20° ♑ 102'  (Moon, January 23)
                    -07 ♑ 46  (Moon, January 22)
                     13°    56'  (Moon, daily motion)

23° ♐ 51'  (Venus, January 23)
-22 ♐ 39  (Venus, January 22)
01°    12'  (Venus, daily motion)

06° ♓ 12'    06° ♓ 59'  (Mars, January 23)
              - 06° ♓ 12'  (Mars, January 22)
                00°    47'  (Mars, daily motion)

**Example 2. Person born March 30,1947, 9:38 AM, Red Wing, MN.** The birth took place in the afternoon of March 30, GMT (after the Noon Mark). Therefore, the planets' positions on March 30, are subtracted from their positions on March 31 to get their daily motion.

09° ♈ 56' 06" = 08° ♈ 115' 66"  (Sun, March 31)
                       -08 ♈ 56 52  (Sun, March 30)
                        00°    59' 14"  (Sun, daily motion)

03° ♌ 54' = 33° ♋ 54'  (Moon, March 31)
                   -19 ♋ 46  (Moon, March 30)
                    14°    08'  (Moon, daily motion)

12° ♓ 48'  (Mercury, March 31)
-12 ♓ 06  (Mercury, March 30)
00°    42'  (Mercury, daily motion)

00° ♓ 42' = 30° ♒ 42'  (Venus, March 31)
                   -29 ♒ 30  (Venus, March 30)
                    01°    12'  (Venus, daily motion)

21° ♓ 03' =  20° ♓ 63'  (Mars, March 31)
            -20 ♓ 17   (Mars, March 30)
            00°    46'  (Mars, daily motion)

## 3. Figure the Planets' Positions at Birth

First add the log of the daily motion to the constant log. The log of the daily motion is looked up in the same way the constant log was found in the log tables. Find the degrees in the top column and the minute in the left column and read the log where the two columns meet.

The log of the daily motion represents the distance the planet traveled in the twenty-four hour period during which birth took place. The constant log represents the interval between the time of birth and the time for which the planets positions are given (noon GMT, or Noon Mark, mean local time). The result of adding these two logs will represent the distance the planet traveled during that interval of time. After the result is found, it will be changed back into minutes and degrees, by finding the anti-log, so that the precise position of the planets at the time of birth can be calculated.

**Example 1. Person born January 22, 1936, 10:20 PM, Sillersville, PA.** The log of the daily motion of each of the planets is added to the constant log, 4424.

01° 01'  (Sun, daily motion)        1.3730  (log of daily motion)
                                   + 4424   (constant log)
                                    1.8154

13° 56'  (Moon, daily motion)        .2362  (log of daily motion)
                                   + 4424   (constant log)
                                     .6786

01° 12'  (Venus, daily motion)      1.3010  (log of daily motion)
                                   + 4424   (constant log)
                                    1.7434

00° 47'  (Mars, daily motion)       1.4863  (log of motion)
                                   + 4424   (constant log)
                                    1.9287

Example 2. Person born March 30, 1947, 9:38 AM, Red Wing, MN. The log of the daily motion of each of the planets is added to the constant log, 8199.

00° 59' (Sun, daily motion)        1.3875  (log of daily motion)
                                 +  8199  (constant log)
                                   2.2074

14° 08' (Moon, daily motion)        .2300  (log of daily motion)
                                 +  8199  (constant log)
                                   1.0499

00° 42' (Mercury, daily motion)  1.5351  (log of daily motion)
                                 +  8199  (constant log)
                                   2.3550

01° 12' (Venus, daily motion)      1.3010  (log of daily motion)
                                 +  8199  (constant log)
                                   2.1209

00° 46' (Mars, daily motion)       1.4956  (log of daily motion)
                                 +  8199  (constant log)
                                   2.3155

To find the anti-log of the result, locate the nearest number in the log tables and look up the column for the degrees and to the left side for the minutes. In a morning GMT, or before Noon Mark birth, the anti-log is subtracted from the positions of the planets on the date of birth. For an afternoon add the anti-log to the planets' position.

Note. For retrograde planets this rule is reversed. For morning or before Noon Mark births, add the anti-log to the planets' positions on the date of birth. For afternoon births, subtract the anti-log.

Example 1. Person born January 22, 1936, 10:20 PM, Sillersville, PA. Since the birth occurred in the morning of January 23, GMT (before the Noon Mark, mean local time), the anti-logs of the results of the foregoing addition are now subtracted from the positions of the planets on January 23.

02° ♒ 19' =   01° ♒ 79'   (Sun, January 23)
             -00      22   (anti-log of 1.8154)
             01° ♒ 57'    (Sun, time of birth)


21° ♑ 42'   (Moon, January 23)
-05     02   (anti-log of .6786)
16° ♑ 40'   (Moon, time of birth)


23° ♐ 51'   (Venus, January 23)
-00     26   (anti-log of 1.7434)
23° ♐ 25'   (Venus, time of birth)


06° ♓ 12'      06°♓ 59'   (Mars, January 23)
              -00°    17'  (anti-log of 1.9287)
              06°♓ 42'    (Mars, time of birth)


**Example 2. Person born March 30, 1947, 9:38 AM, Red Wing, MN.** Since the birth occurred in the afternoon of March 30, GMT (after the Noon Mark, mean local time), the anti-logs of the results of the foregoing addition are now added to the positions of the planets on March 30.

08° ♈ 56' 52"   (Sun, March 30)
+00     09      (anti-log of 2.2074)
08° ♈ 65' 52" = 09°    05' 52"   (Sun, time of birth)


19° ♋ 46'   (Moon, March 30)
+02     08   (anti-log of 1.0499)
21° ♋ 54'   (Moon, time of birth)


12° ♓ 06'   (Mercury, March 30)
+00     06   (anti-log of 2.3550)
12° ♓ 12'   (Mercury, time of birth)


29° ♒ 30'   (Venus, March 30)
+00     11   (anti-log of 2.1209)
29° ♒ 41'   (Venus, time of birth)

20° ♓ 17'   (Mars, March 30)
+00     07   (anti-log of 2.3155)
20° ♓ 24'   (Mars, time of birth)

## Planets—How to Enter Them in a Chart

When entering the positions of the planets, the Part of Fortune or the Moon's nodes in a chart, use the degree of the sign on the house cusps as a guide to determine where the planet is situated, whether before or after a cusp. Observe these rules:

*1. When a planet's degrees are more than the degrees of the sign on the cusp, it has already crossed over and gone beyond the imaginary cusp line.*

*2. When a planet's degrees are less than the degrees of the sign on the cusp it has not yet reached the cusp and is placed in the space preceding the cusp; if not within eight degrees of the cusp it is read in the preceding house. If within eight degrees of the cusp, it is placed in the house preceding, but is read as though already actually in the house toward which it is moving.*

The cusp of a house is the most important or sensitive part of the house.

The effect of a planet's influence is more marked or noticeable when in the same sign and degree as the cusp, although in any location in a house the planet activates the things indicated by that house and in accordance with the nature of the planet.

This strong cusp effect will be appreciated when studying the effect of transiting or progressed planets when they come to a conjunction with a cusp. As regards this cusp influence it makes no difference whether the planet reaches it by direct or retrograde motion.

When a planet is approaching the Ascendant it is read as though actually in the First House, as soon as it arrives within twelve degrees of the ascending degree if it is in the same sign as that on the Ascendant; if not, allow only eight degrees orb, and if it is more than that amount above the First House cusp, it is read as though still in the Twelfth House.

A planet is still to be considered in the First House when within twenty degrees below the ascending degree; but if also close (within eight degrees) to the Second House, it is to be considered as influencing both houses.

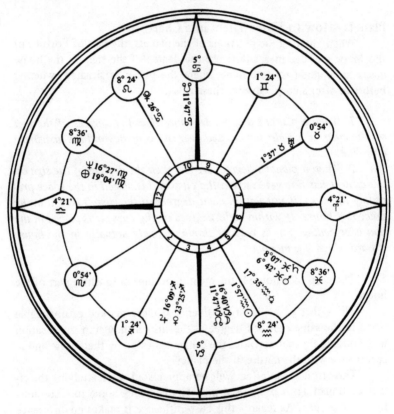

**Figure 19: Planets' Positions.
Example 1**

## SUPPLEMENTARY CALCULATIONS

### Figuring the Part of Fortune

The Part of Fortune is a zodiacal point which is equally distant from the Ascendant as the Moon is from the Sun in longitude. It ben-

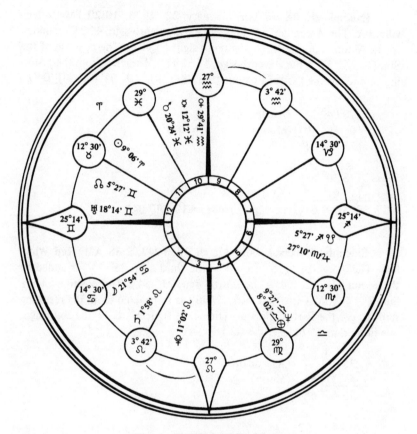

**Figure 20: Planets' Positions.
Example 2**

efits the house in which it is located at birth. The place of the Part of Fortune must be calculated from the horoscope itself.

**Rule**: Add the longitude of the Ascendant to the Moon's longitude from which sum subtract the longitude of the Sun. The remainder will be the place of the Part of Fortune.

**Example 1. Person born January 22, 1936, 10:20 PM, Sillersville, PA.** The Ascendant (4° ♎ 21' = the seventh sign, 4° 21') is added to the Moon (16° ♑ 40' = the tenth sign, 16° 40'). The position of the Sun (1° ♒ 57' = the eleventh sign, 1° 57') is subtracted from the resulting sum to get the Part of Fortune (the sixth sign, 19° 04' = 19°♍ 04').

```
    7S 04° 21'   (Ascendant)
 +10  16   40    (Moon)
  17S 20° 61'
```

```
  17S 20° 61'
 -11  01   57    (Sun)
  06S 19° 04'   (Part of Fortune) = 19°  ♍ 04'
```

**Example 2. Person born March 30, 1947, 9:38 AM, Red Wing, MN.** The Ascendant (25° ♊ 14' = the third sign, 25° 14') is added to the Moon (21° ♋ 54' = the fourth sign, 21° 54'). The position of the Sun (9° ♈ 06' = the first sign, 9° 06') is subtracted from the resulting sum, to get the Part of Fortune (the sixth sign, 37° 62' = the sixth sign, one more sign, 7° 62' = 8°♎ 02').

```
    3S 25° 14'   (Ascendant)
 +  4  21   54   (Moon)
   7S 46° 68'
```

```
   7S 46° 68'
 - 1  09   06   (Sun)
   6S 37° 62'   (Part of Fortune) = 8° ♎ 02'
```

**Note**: At the time of the New Moon the Part of Fortune is always on the Ascendant. At the time of the Full Moon, the Part of Fortune is always on the descendant of a chart made for that time.
time.

## Arabic Parts

Though the Part of Fortune is the only Arabic Part in common use today, there are a total of 32 different parts used historically. The formulas for these Arabic Parts are listed below.

### Parts Proper to the First House

*1. Part of Life.* Ascendant plus the Moon, minus the position of the New Moon or Full Moon immediately preceding birth.

*2. Part of Understanding.* Ascendant plus Mars, minus Mercury.

*3. Part of Spirit.* Ascendant plus the Sun, minus the Moon.

### Parts Proper to the Second House

*4. Part of Fortune.* Ascendant plus the Moon, minus the Sun.

*5. Part of Goods.* Ascendant plus the cusp of the Second House, minus the position of the ruler of the Second House.

### Parts Proper to the Third House

*6. Part of Brethren.* By day: Ascendant plus Jupiter, minus Saturn. By night: Ascendant plus Saturn, minus Jupiter.

*7. Part of Love of Brethren.* Ascendant plus Saturn, minus the Sun.

### Parts Proper to the Fourth House

*8. Part of the Father.* Ascendant plus the Sun, minus Saturn.

*9. Part of Fortune in Husbandry.* Ascendant plus Saturn, minus Venus.

*10. Part of Inheritances and Possessions.* Ascendant plus the Moon, minus Saturn.

### Parts Proper to the Fifth House

*11. Part of Male Children.* Ascendant plus Jupiter, minus the Moon.

*12. Part of Female Children.* Ascendant plus Venus, minus the Moon.

*13. Part of Plays.* Ascendant plus Venus, minus Mars.

### Parts Proper to the Sixth House

*14. Part of Sickness.* Ascendant plus Mars, minus Saturn.

*15. Part of Slavery and Bondage.* Ascendant plus the Moon, minus the position of the dispositor of the Moon.

*16. Part of Servants.* Ascendant plus the Moon, minus Mercury.

### Parts Proper to the Seventh House

*17. Part of Marriage.* Ascendant plus the cusp of the Seventh House, minus Venus.

*18. Part of Discord and Controversy.* Ascendant plus Jupiter, minus Mars.

### Parts Proper to the Eighth House

*19. Part of Death.* Ascendant plus the cusp of the Eighth House minus the Moon.

*20. Part of the Perilous and Most Dangerous Year.* Ascendant plus the ruler of the Eighth House, minus Saturn.

### Parts Proper to the Ninth House

*21. Part of Faith.* Ascendant plus Mercury, minus the Moon.

*22. Part of Journeys by Water.* Ascendant plus 15° Cancer minus Saturn.

*23. Part of Travels by Land.* Ascendant plus the cusp of the Ninth House, minus the ruler of the Ninth House.

### Parts Proper to the Tenth House

*24. Part of the Mother.* Ascendant plus the Moon, minus Venus.

*25. Part of Nobility and Honor.* By Day: Ascendant plus 19° Aries, minus the Sun. By night: Ascendant plus 3° Taurus, minus the Moon.

*26. Part of Sudden Advancement.* Ascendant plus the Part of Fortune, minus Saturn. (If Saturn is conjunct the Sun, substitute Jupiter).

*27. Part of Magistery and Profession.* Ascendant plus the Moon, minus Saturn.

*28. Part of Merchandise.* Ascendant plus the Part of Fortune, minus the Part of Spirit.

### Parts Proper to the Eleventh House

*29. Part of Friends.* Ascendant plus the Moon, minus Uranus.

*30. Part of Honorable Acquaintance.* By day: Ascendant plus Sun minus Earth. By night: Ascendant plus earth minus Sun.

### Parts Proper to the Twelfth House

*31. Part of Imprisonment, Sorrow and Captivity.* Ascendant plus the Part of Fortune, minus Neptune.

*32. Part of Private Enemies.* Ascendant plus the cusp of the Twelfth House, minus the ruler of the Twelfth House.

## The Moon's Nodes

The Moon's North Node: Dragon's Head or Caput Draconis.
The Moon's South Node: Dragon's Tail or Cauda Draconis.

The point in the Zodiac where a planet crosses out of the south into north latitude is called the North Node; the opposite point is the South Node. The Moon's Nodes regress about 3 minutes of arc per day, taking nineteen years to completely circle the Zodiac.

The North Node can be copied from the ephemeris, and the South Node is the opposite point.

## Planetary House Rulers

Some significance is placed on the position of the planet ruling the sign on each house cusp. This planet is called the planetary house ruler. For delineation of the house rulers see *Planetary House Rulers*, page 361.

**Example 1. Person born January 22, 1936, 10:20 PM, Sillersville,PA.**
Refer to Figure 21: Planetary House Rulers, Example 1.

Venus, ruler of the First House (Libra), is in the Third House.

Pluto, ruler of the Second House (Scorpio), is in the Tenth House.

Jupiter, ruler of the Third House (Sagittarius), is in the Third House.

Saturn, ruler of the Fourth House (Capricorn), is in the Sixth House (within 29' of the cusp).

Uranus, ruler of the Fifth House (Aquarius), is in the Eighth House.

Neptune, ruler of the Sixth House (Pisces), is in the Twelfth House, its Natural House.

Mars, ruler of the Seventh House (Aries), is in the Sixth House (within 1° 54' of the cusp).

Venus, ruler of the Eighth House (Taurus), is in the Third House.

Mercury, ruler of the Ninth House (Gemini), is in the Fifth House.

The Moon, ruler of the Tenth House (Cancer), is in the Fourth House, its Natural House.

The Sun, ruler of the Eleventh House (Leo), is in the Fifth House (within 6° 27' of the cusp).

Mercury, ruler of the Twelfth House (Virgo), is in the Fifth House.

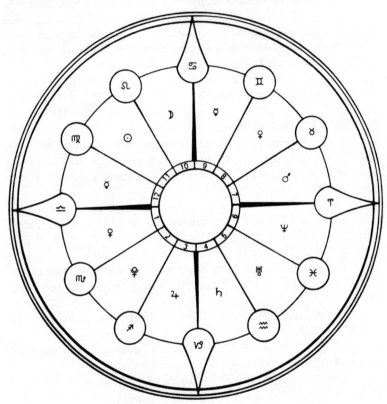

**Figure 21: Planetary House Rulers.
Example 1**

**Example 2. Person born March 30, 1947, 9:38 AM, Red Wing, MN.**
Refer to Figure 22: Planetary House Rulers, Example 2.

Mercury, ruler of the First House (Gemini), is in the Tenth House.

The Moon, ruler of the Second House (Cancer), is in the Second House, in its own sign.

The Sun, ruler of the Third House (Leo), is in the Eleventh House.

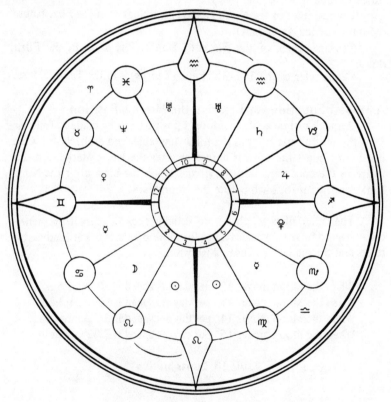

**Figure 22: Planetary House Rulers.**
**Example 2**

The Sun, ruler of the Fourth House (Leo), is in the Eleventh House.

Mercury, the ruler of the Fifth House (Virgo) is in the Tenth,

Pluto, ruler of the Sixth House (Scorpio), is in the Third House. House.

Jupiter, ruler of the Seventh House (Sagittarius), is in the Sixth House.

Saturn, ruler of the Eighth House (Capricorn), is in the Third House (within 1° 44' of the cusp).

Uranus, ruler of the Ninth House (Aquarius), is in the First House (within 7° of the Ascendant).

Neptune, ruler of the Eleventh House (Pisces), is in the Fifth House.

Venus ruler of the Twelfth House (Taurus) is in the Tenth House.

## A Mental Equation for Figuring the Moon's Position

A quick estimate of the Moon's position can be made as follows: Find the motion per hour in the following table, and multiply it by the number of hours the birth is before or after the Noon Mark. Add this figure to the ephemeris position of the Moon for birth after the Noon Mark, subtract it for birth before the Noon Mark.

The other planets' places are usually easy to correct by mental calculation similar to the above, but for more precise work it is advisable to correct the planets' places by logarithms.

When the Moon moves 12° per day its speed is 30' per hour.
When the Moon moves 13° per day its speed is 32½' per hour.
When the Moon moves 14° per day its speed is 35' per hour.
When the Moon moves 15° per day its speed is 37½' per hour.

**Table 10: Lunar Motion**

# Finding the Aspects

Aspect: An aspect is a certain angular distance between the points in the Zodiac; from one planet to another or from a planet to a point in the chart, as for instance, the Ascendant. Certain distances produce effective angles which are appropriately named. Astrology uses sixteen aspects including the conjunction and parallel.

Rule: To find whether or not a planet is in aspect with another count the number of degrees between them, refer to the table of planetary aspects and note the aspect, if any. They are not always in aspect.

## Major Aspects

✳ Sextile, complete at 60° apart. Its influence is good, its nature favorable, creative. The least powerful of the major aspects.

□ Square, complete at 90° apart. Its influence is adverse, its nature is disappointing, rejective, obstructive.

△ Trine, complete at 120° apart. Its influence is good, its nature is fortunate, constructive, harmonious. The third strongest aspect.

☍ Opposition, complete at 180° apart. Its influence is adverse, its nature separative, extreme, opposed, destructive. The second strongest aspect.

☌ Conjunction, 0° apart. Two or more planets in the same degree of longitude. The effect of this position is good or adverse according to the nature of the planets. It is unifying, binding. The strongest aspect.

|| or ℙ Parallel means equal distance from the celestial equator, north or south, or one stellar body north and the other south of it. A parallel of declination has the same effect as a conjunction. (The declinations of the planets are to be found in an ephemeris for the date of birth.)

## Minor Aspects

 ⊻ or ✕ Semi-sextile, 30° apart, slightly good, harmonizing.

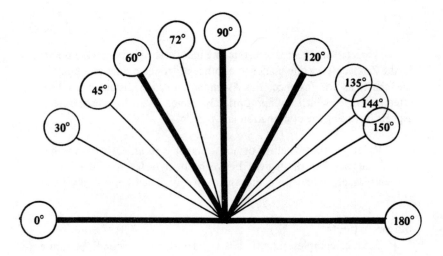

Figure 23: Aspects

∠ Semi-square, 45° apart, slightly adverse, disintegrating.

Q Quintile, 72° apart, slightly good, harmonizing.

⛢ Sesquiquadrate, 135° apart, slightly adverse, provoking.

± Bi-quintile, 144° apart, slightly good.

⊼ or ⊠ Quincunx, 150° apart, slightly adverse, indifferent, indecisive.

**Note:** Four other aspects of negligible influence on the natal chart are sometimes used in progressed charts. They are: ⅃Vigintile, 18° apart, slightly good; √ Quindecile, 24° apart, slightly good; ⊥ Decile, 36° apart, slightly good; ∓ Tredecile, 108° apart, slightly good.

Some investigators have recently advanced several new aspects which they claim are to be considered along with the other older aspects whose influences are now well known. Those proposed aspects are not included here for two reasons: They are of minor influence and they have not as yet been investigated sufficiently to warrant their inclusion.

## Parallels of Declination

**Parallel:** Equal distance from the celestial equator, north or south; or one stellar body north and the other south.

The declinations for the planets are given on the right hand pages in the Rosicrucian ephemeris, see Figures 8 and 10, pages 79 and 81.

**Note:** If you are using an ephemeris which gives the declinations for every third day or every other day be sure to make the necessary correction by subtracting the declinations of the two days on either side of the desired date. Then find the correct portion of this motion, either one-half, or one-third, or two-thirds, and add or subtract it to the declination preceding the birth date, depending on whether the declination is increasing or decreasing.

Only the declinations of the Sun and Moon are interpolated to the hour and minute of birth, it is sufficient to record the declination for the day only, for the other planets.

To find out whether or not any of the planets are parallel, compare their declinations. If you find any planets within one degree of another, they are said to be parallel. Parallels so found are recorded in the list of aspects because the effect of a parallel is similar in nature to a conjunction. Whether one planet is north and the other south, or both north or both south makes no difference.

Example 1. Person born January 22, 1936, 10:20 PM, Sillers-ville, PA. The declinations for the Sun and Moon were interpolated to get their exact birth time declination, see page 128. The declinations for the other planets (except Pluto) are given in the ephemeris and are simply copied, see Figure 8.

Moon: 22° S 40'     Moon parallel Jupiter and Pluto              ,
Sun: 19° S 47'
Mercury: 14° S 29'
Venus: 21° S 33'     Venus parallel Jupiter
Mars: 10° S 07'     Mars parallel Saturn
Jupiter: 22° S 06'     Jupiter parallel Pluto
Saturn: 10° S 10'
Uranus: 11° N 35'
Neptune: 06° N 17'
Pluto: 23° N 04'     (February 1 position)

Example 2. Person born March 30, 1947, 9:38 AM, Red Wing, MN. The declinations of the Sun and Moon were interpolated to get their exact birth time declinations, see page 128. The declinations for the other planets are given every other day. The difference in declin-ations between March 29 and March 30 is found and half of this is add-ed to the March 29 position when increasing and subtracted when de-creasing, see Figure 10.

Moon: 25° N 18'
Sun: 3° N 36'          Sun parallel Mercury
Mercury:   7° S 53' (declination March 29)
          -7° S 44' (declination March 31)
           0°    9' (motion for two days)

           ½ of 9' = 4' (daily motion)

           7° S 53'  (declination March 29)
        .     4'  (daily motion)
           7° S 49'  (declination March 30)

Venus:      12° S 28'   (declination March 29)
            -11     44   (declination March 31)
            00     44'   (motion for two days)

½ of 44' = 22' (daily motion)

            12° S 28'   (declination March 29)
            -      22   (daily motion)
            12° S 06'   (declination March 30)

Mars:       5° S 08'   (declination March 29)
            -4     31   (declination March 31)
            0     37'   (motion for two days)

½ of 37' = 18' (daily motion)

            5° S 08'   (declination March 29)
            -      18   (daily motion)
            4° S 50'   (declination March 30)

Jupiter:    18° S 25'   (declination March 29)
            -18     23   (declination March 31)
            00     02'   (motion for two days)

½ of 02' = 01' (daily motion)

            18° S 25'   (declination March 29)
            -      01   (daily motion)
            18° S 24'   (declination March 30)

Saturn: 20° N 22'
Uranus: 23° N 01'
Neptune: 2° S 19'
Pluto: 24° N 07' (April 1 position)

**Note:** When the ephemeris shows that the declination will change north to south or vice versa, between the two dates, add (instead of subtract) to find the motion for two days. Half of this is the daily motion, which is subtracted from the earlier position, if possible, and the same direction (north or south) is used. If the daily motion is larger than the earlier declination, subtract it from the daily motion and change direction (north or south).

## The Declinations of the Sun and Moon

The declinations of the planets are copied onto the chart from the ephemeris for the day of birth for future reference in calculating the parallel aspects and for progressed work. The declinations are given on the right hand pages in the Rosicrucian ephemeris, see Figures 8 and 10, pages 79 and 81. For further information on the declinations of the planets, see *Parallels of Declination*, page 125.

The declinations of the Sun and Moon change rapidly enough to require interpolation. This is done in identical manner as finding the birth time positions of the faster moving planets. The same constant log is used.

In the case of the Moon (or Sun if the daily declination is given in the ephemeris), the daily motion is found by subtracting the lesser declination from the greater using the birth date and the day after. That is, if the declination is *increasing* (as with the longitude of the planets when in direct motion), the declination for the day of birth is subtracted from the declination the day after birth. When the declination is *decreasing* (as with the longitude of the planets when retrograde in motion), the declination for the day after birth is subtracted from the declination of the birth date.

In the case of the Sun (or the Moon if the declination is only given every other day), the dates used are the birth date or day preceding and the next day for which the declination is given. The result is the motion for two days. This is then divided in half to find the daily motion. If the birth date lies between the two days for which the declination is given, the daily motion is *added* to the preceding day when or *subtracted* when *decreasing* to find the declination at noon of the birth date.

The log of the daily motion is added to the constant log, and the anti-log of the product is used to adjust the noon declination of the birth date. This is *added* when the declination is *increasing* (as in the case of direct-motion planets), and *subtracted* when *decreasing* (as in the case of retrograde planets).

**Example 1. Person born January 22, 1936, 10:20 PM, Sillers-ville, PA.** The declination of the Moon, given daily is decreasing so its position on January 23 (day after birth) is subtracted from its position on January 22 (the birth date) to find its daily motion. The log of the daily motion is added to the constant log and the anti-log of the product is subtracted from the birth date declination. The declination of the Sun is decreasing, so its position on January 24 is subtracted from its position on January 22 to find the motion for two days. Half of this is the daily motion. The log of the daily motion is added to the constant log and the anti-log of the product is subtracted from the birth date declination.

```
23° S 41'   (declination of Moon, January 22)
-20   53    (declination of Moon, January 23)
02° S 48'   (daily motion)
```

```
0.9330  (log of daily motion)
+ 4424  (constant log)
1.3754
```

```
23° S 41'   (declination of Moon, January 22)
-01   01    (anti-log of 1.3754)
22° S 40'   (declination at birth time)
```

```
19° S 52'   (declination of Sun, January 22)
-19   25    (declination of Sun, January 24)
00° S 27'   (motion for two days)
```

½ of 27' = 13' (daily motion)

```
2.0444  (log of daily motion)
+ 4424  (constant log)
2.4868
```

```
19° S 52'   (declination of Sun, January 22)
-     05    (anti-log of 2.4868)
19° S 47'   (declination at birth time)
```

Example 2. Person born March 30, 1947, 9:38 AM, Red Wing, MN. The declination of the Moon given daily, is decreasing, so its position on March 31 (day after birth) is subtracted from its position on March 30 (the birth date) to find its daily motion. The log of the daily motion is added to the constant log and the anti-log of the product is subtracted from the birth date declination. The declination of the Sun is increasing, so its position on March 29 is subtracted from its position on March 31 to find the motion for two days. Half of this is the daily motion which can be added to the March 29 declination to get the declination for noon March 30 (the birth date). The log of the daily motion is added to the constant log and the anti-log of the product is added to the birth date declination.

```
 25° N 37'   (declination of Moon, March 30)
-23    34    (declination of Moon, March 31)
 02° N 03'   (daily motion)
```

```
1.0685   (log of daily motion)
+ 8199   (constant log)
1.8884
```

```
 25° N 37'   (declination of Moon, March 30)
-      19    (anti-log of 1.8884)
 25° N 18'   (declination at birth time)
```

```
 3° N 56'   (declination of Sun, March 31)
-3    10    (declination of Sun, March 29)
 0    46    (motion for two days)
```

½ of 46' = 23' (daily motion)

```
 3° N 10'   (declination of Sun, March 29)
+     23    (daily motion)
 3° N 33'   (declination of Sun, March 30)
```

```
1.7966   (log of daily motion)
+ 8199   (constant log)
2.6165
```

3° N 33'  (declination of Sun, March 30)
+      03   (anti-log of 2.6165
3° N 36'  (declination at time of birth)

## Declinations of the Ascendant and Midheaven

Declinations of the Ascendant and Midheaven are rarely used. They can be found by noting when the Sun is in the same degree of longitude as the Ascendant and Midheaven. The corresponding declination of the Sun gives the desired figure.

## To Figure Aspects

Always go to the shortest way through the Zodiac in the chart, either forward or back, to figure an aspect.

The following diagram is a simple illustration of aspects. It is intended to help students picture mentally how aspects are formed. For convenience every aspect is shown here as exact or *partile*. (An aspect which is not exact is *platic*.) Major aspects are indicated by solid lines, minor aspects by broken lines.

A planet moving away from another, moving out of aspect, is considered *dexter;* an aspect which is forming is *sinister*. These terms apply to the faster-moving planets.

**When checking up aspects do the work in this order:**

| | |
|---|---|
| Moon to | Mercury, Venus, Sun, Mars, Jupiter, Saturn, Uranus, Neptune, Pluto |
| Mercury to | Venus, Sun, Mars, Jupiter, Saturn, Uranus, Neptune, Pluto |
| Venus to | Sun, Mars, Jupiter, Saturn, Uranus, Neptune, Pluto |
| Sun to | Mars, Jupiter, Saturn, Uranus, Neptune, Pluto |
| Mars to | Jupiter, Saturn, Uranus, Neptune, Pluto |
| Jupiter to | Saturn, Uranus, Neptune, Pluto |
| Saturn to | Uranus, Neptune, Pluto |
| Uranus to | Neptune, Pluto |
| Neptune to | Pluto |
| Pluto to | none |

**Table 11: Order of Determining Aspects**

The orb of a planet or of an aspect is its surrounding circle of influence.

Eight degrees forward and back of a planet or of a given point in the Zodiac constitutes its orb. This amount of distance in longitude applies to all the planets except the Sun and the Moon. The Sun's orb is 12° when applying to (forming) a major aspect, and its orb is 17° when leaving it (having passed the point of aspect).

The Moon's orb is 8° when approaching a major aspect, and 12° when leaving it.

Allow the full orb of a planet to form a major aspect, except the parallel which has an orb of only one degree. The minor aspects of semi-sextile, semi-square and quintile has four degree orbs, while the other minor aspects (sesquiquadrate, bi-quintile, quincunx, vigintile, quindecile, decile, tredecile) have orbs of only two degrees.

## Solar Aspects

The table below shows each aspect and the number of degrees constituting it when formed by the Sun.

| | |
|---|---|
| Semi-sextile | 26-34° apart |
| Semi-square | 41-49° apart |
| Sextile | 50-68° apart |
| Quintile | 68-76° apart |
| Square | 78-107° apart |
| Trine | 109-133° apart |
| Sesquiquadrature | 133-137° apart |
| Bi-quintile | 142-146° apart |
| Quincunx | 148-152° apart |
| Opposition | 168-197° apart |
| Conjunction | 12° approaching, 17° separating |

**Table 12: Solar Aspects**

## Lunar Aspects

The table below shows each aspect and the number of degrees constituting it when formed by the Moon.

| Semi-sextile | 26-34° apart |
|---|---|
| Semi-square | 41-49° apart |
| Sextile | 52-68° apart |
| Quintile | 68-76° apart |
| Square | 82-102° apart |
| Trine | 112-132° apart |
| Sesquiquadrature | 133-137° apart |
| Bi-quintile | 142-146° apart |
| Quincunx | 148-152° apart |
| Opposition | 172-192° apart |
| Conjunction | 8° approaching, 12° separating |

Table 13: **Lunar Aspects**

## Inter-planetary Aspects

The table below shows each aspect and number of degrees constituting it when formed between any of the eight planets.

| Semi-sextile | 26-34° apart |
|---|---|
| Semi-square | 41-49° apart |
| Sextile | 52-68° apart |
| Quintile | 68-76° apart |
| Square | 82-98° apart |
| Trine | 112-128° apart |
| Sesquiquadrature | 133-137° apart |
| Bi-quintile | 142-146° apart |
| Quincunx | 148-152° apart |
| Opposition | 172-188° apart |
| Conjunction | 8° approaching or separating |

Table 14:**Inter-planetary Aspects**

When the Moon, for instance, is traveling toward a planet in question, the sextile (∗) begins its influence when the Moon arrives at 68° distance and increases in power as the Moon draws up to the exact degree of aspect (60°), after which its power wanes as the influence diminishes until the Moon reaches 48° distance, or 12° past the actual degree of sextile aspect. However, its influence from 8° to 12° past the aspect is practically imperceptible.

**Example.** Venus in Libra 18° ( ♀18°♎︎ ), Moon in Leo 10°
( ☽ 10° ♌ ) = Moon sextile Venus beginning ( ( ☽ ✳ ♀ ). Moon 18° in
Leo ( ☽ 18°♌ ) = sextile exact ((☽✳♀ E). Moon in 30° Leo
( ☽ 30° ♌ ) = end of sextile.

When the Moon, for instance, is traveling away from a planet in
question, the sextile aspect begins to form at 52° distance, and its
influence increases in power to the 60° (exact degree of sextile) aspect.
From 60° to 72° away from the planet the power of the aspect wanes
as the influence of the separating aspect diminishes.

**Example.** Mercury 13° in Scorpio ( ☿13°♏︎ ), Moon 5° in Pisces
( ☽ 5° ♓ ) = Moon trine Mercury beginning ( ☽ ✳ ☿ ). Moon 13° in
Pisces ( ☽ 13° ♓ ) = trine exact ( ☽ ✳ ☿ E). Moon 25° Pisces
( ☽ 25° ♓ ) = end of trine.

The applying planet (the swifter moving one) comes into aspect
(forms the aspect), and that aspect begins to operate as soon as its orb
reaches the degree constituting the aspect. It remains effective until the
planet has passed out of its range or orb. The quality of this joint
influence is determined by the nature of the aspect, i.e., whether it is a
good or an adverse influence.

Suppose that Mars is approaching Jupiter. When Mars gets within
8° of the place in the Zodiac occupied by Jupiter the influence of the
conjunction begins, the strongest point being where the two planets
occupy the same degree of longitude, beyond which the influence of
the aspect decreases in power and ceases at 8° past the place of Jupiter.

**Example.** Jupiter 9° in Leo ( ♃9°♌ ), Mars 1° in Leo ( ♂1°♌ )
= Mars conjunct Jupiter forming (♂✳♃). Mars 9° Leo ( ♂9°♌ ) =
conjunction exact ( ♂✳♃ E). Mars 17° in Leo ( ♂17°♌ ) = end of
conjunction.

These rules apply to all the aspects and should be thoroughly
mastered in order that the student may determine with accuracy
whether an aspect is forming or separating. It is very important to
know whether an aspect is forming or separating. If the three foregoing
examples are studied until perfectly understood the subject of
planetary aspects becomes quite simple, and predictions may be made
more accurately. For instance, in the branch of Astrology known as
Horary Astrology it is not to be predicted that an event will occur from
an aspect that is past (separating or waning).

The influence of an aspect that is forming is more powerful than one which is separating. As the aspecting planet draws near the culminating degree the aspect grows stronger, but as soon as the culminating point is passed and the aspecting planet begins to leave the culminating degree of the aspect its power wanes, and when the planet arrives at the limit of the orb the influence of the aspect is practically imperceptible.

In the orb of aspect with the Sun or Moon the line of demarcation between the sextile and quintile seems obscure, but that is of little moment because these aspects are of the same quality, i.e., good.

It appears that the rule of 12° applying and 17° leaving an aspect, must not be too strictly adhered to, for instance: When the Sun is leaving a trine aspect and proceeding away from the aspected planet the orb of 17° added to 120° = 137°, or 2° past the sesquiquadrate aspect (135°).

Likewise, the Sun leaving sextile and drawing away from a planet: 60° + 17° = 77° or 5° past the quintile (72°).

In such cases the drop the diminishing aspect and record the next aspect as soon as the applying planet is within 2° or 4° of aspect, as the case requires.

**Note:** When finding aspects in a horoscope recollect that each sign contains 30°, and remember to count from one zodiacal sign to another, including the intercepted signs. *Not from one house to another,* as the houses seldom contain 30° evenly, especially those houses which contain an intercepted sign, for in that case the whole 30° of the intercepted sign is therein, as well as those degrees of the other sign, as shown by the cusp. Count the number of degrees between planets from sign to sign regardless of whether or not a sign may be intercepted. Interception makes no difference in figuring aspects.

## Orb of Influence Explained

Students sometimes wonder how a planet's orb of influence became known, that is, the range in degrees where an aspect begins to manifest prior to the actual or partile aspect.

One of the interesting ways in which the extent of orbs is ascertained, is by watching in an ephemeris, the approach of two planets to a conjunction and noting by newspaper reports the beginning of events which coincide with the nature of such conjunction. Observations of such phenomena began long before there were newspapers; long before printing was invented, which is of comparatively recent origin. In fact, the invention of writing was largely the result of the need to adequately record celestial phenomena with relation to seasons for planting, hunting, fishing, warnings of floods, famine, or pestilence.

Probably the reason that Jupiter has a larger orb than the other planets (excepting our satellite the Moon, and the Sun) is because it is by far the largest among those planets.

Jupiter, the "giant planet," is (excepting the Sun), the largest body in our solar system. It is more than three times as large and about three times as massive as all the other planets put together. Yet, such is the preponderating mass of our Sun that Jupiter is less than one-thousandth part of our central luminary

Another way for students to study the length or range of planetary orbs is by noting in their own horoscope the distance in degrees from an aspect when events transpire of its coinciding nature, by the movement of transiting planets.

Because the native has knowledge of planetary influences, he or she is able to discount or minimize the effects of that influence through the warning which Astrology provides.

Planetary aspects are continually occurring; usually there are a number of them in operation each day. Every aspect has its own particular influence while it also assists in making up the general tendencies in combination with the other aspects that may also be in operation.

The various aspects derive their names from the angular relations which planets form one with another in their transit through the Zodiac; the Earth in each case being the focal point of the rays. The aspects which are in operation at the time of a birth are of particular significance to that individual. Their vibrations motivate and cast the tendencies of metabolism and other bodily functions which find physical and mental expression that identify the personality, qualify the actions and largely determine the environment and experience.

The conjunction and parallel, strictly speaking, are not aspects but positions. However, for convenience they are usually referred to as aspects.

## Aspects to House Cusps

House cusps do not actually have an orb, as cusps are imaginary lines dividing the sky between the earth and the outer boundary of the zodiacal circle into twelve wedge-shaped spaces, across which the planets travel. House cusps are dependent on the exact birth time. If the time used for making a horoscope is not exact, neither are the house cusps. However, in considering the influence of an aspect that may be formed between a planet and a house cusp in a natal chart, allow the degree of orb of the planet as taught in this lesson.

## Example Form for Tabulating Aspects

This table is for recording distance between planets in a chart, what aspects result (if any), their quality, and whether applying to the degree constituting an aspect, or separating from it.

**Note.** The object of Table 15 is principally to show the student how to record aspects in a systematic and complete manner. It is sufficient for beginners to tabulate the aspects to the nearest degree; the minutes of longitude may safely be omitted.

Enter the aspects as shown in the examples below.

**Example 1.** Moon in Aries 15° ( ☽ 15° ♈ ) is 65° from Mercury in Gemini 20° ( ☿ 20° ♊ ), which equals the sextile ( ☽ ✶ ☿ ) aspect applying by 5°.

**Example 2.** Suppose Mercury is in Scorpio 18° ( ☿ 18° ♏ ), and Mars in Leo 15° ( ♂ 15° ♌ ). There are 93° between them. You record the aspect noted in the second example.

**Example 3.** Sun in Libra 10° ( ☉ 10° ♎ ), Neptune in Libra 8° ( ♆ 8° ♎ ).

# Form for Tabulating Aspects

| Planets | No. of Degs. Apart | Aspect | Nature | Applying or Separating |
|---|---|---|---|---|
| Moon from Mercury | | | | |
| Moon from Venus | | | | |
| Moon from Sun | | | | |
| Moon from Mars | | | | |
| Moon from Jupiter | | | | |
| Moon from Saturn | | | | |
| Moon from Uranus | | | | |
| Moon from Neptune | | | | |
| Moon from Pluto | | | | |
| Mercury from Venus | | | | |
| Mercury from Sun | | | | |
| Mercury from Mars | | | | |
| Mercury from Jupiter | | | | |
| Mercury from Saturn | | | | |
| Mercury from Uranus | | | | |
| Mercury from Neptune | | | | |
| Mercury from Pluto | | | | |
| Venus from Sun | | | | |
| Venus from Mars | | | | |
| Venus from Jupiter | | | | |
| Venus from Saturn | | | | |
| Venus from Uranus | | | | |
| Venus from Neptune | | | | |
| Venus from Pluto | | | | |
| Sun from Mars | | | | |
| Sun from Jupiter | | | | |
| Sun from Saturn | | | | |
| Sun from Uranus | | | | |
| Sun from Neptune | | | | |
| Sun from Pluto | | | | |
| Mars from Jupiter | | | | |
| Mars from Saturn | | | | |
| Mars from Uranus | | | | |
| Mars from Neptune | | | | |
| Mars from Pluto | | | | |
| Jupiter from Saturn | | | | |
| Jupiter from Uranus | | | | |
| Jupiter from Neptune | | | | |
| Jupiter from Pluto | | | | |
| Saturn from Uranus | | | | |
| Saturn from Neptune | | | | |
| Saturn from Pluto | | | | |
| Uranus from Neptune | | | | |
| Uranus from Pluto | | | | |
| Neptune from Pluto | | | | |

**Table 15: Form for Tabulating Aspects**

# Interpreting
# the Horoscope

# Introduction to Horoscope Interpretation

It has been observed that many who learn to erect a horoscope are all at sea when it comes to delineating it. For that reason we are here giving the George Method of Horoscope Delineation used effectively for many years by Llewellyn George and his countless followers.

The secret of horoscope delineation lies in the preparation. That is, before commencing to delineate a chart make careful preparation by compiling a *table of notes* for guidance. The more complete the memoranda, the simpler becomes the work of delineation. In the table make notes with each element to be featured. The orderly table of elements, the notes you make in connection with them, together with references to **Delineations for Horoscopes** in Part III, will enable you to modify or adjust the readings to suit the particular horoscope under consideration. Once more, let us impress the student with the fact that the secret of success in delineation lies largely in the preparation.

## STUDYING THE HOROSCOPE

Begin to study the chart by reading the influences of the Sun according to the zodiacal sign in which it may be located.

Read the delineation of the influence of the ascending sign.

Read the influence of the Moon according to sign.

Read the influence of Mercury according to sign.

Read the influence of the Significator and other co-rulers according to the signs in which they may be located.

Read the aspects to the Significator and to the co-rulers. Keep in mind whether or not the planets in question are in their home sign. exaltation, detriment, or fall, and regulate the delineations accordingly.

By this time you will have gained a fair idea of the power of each planet in the chart, and keeping that in view proceed to read the planets according to their positions in the chart houses, being careful to adjust the delineations as conditions require, which will not be difficult when you are familiar with the nature of the *planets, signs, aspects,* and *houses.* Remember that no science or art can be mastered in a short time, but the elements having been learned, their correct application brings accurate results. After the chart has been studied as outlined above, prepare to write a delineation.

## Features of the Horoscope

The features are usually taken in this order:

Individuality
Personality
Finances
Mentality
Journeys
Home Life
Pleasure
Children
Health
Marriage-Partnerships
Legacies
Death
Voyages
Education and the Higher Mind
Occupation
Honors
Friends
Restrictions

To gather data for each feature refer to Delineations for Horoscopes into the various delineations and make notes that appropriately relate to it.

**House Cusps.** The matter of house cusps cannot be confined to set rules, as the dividing line between the houses is a mundane thing; in reality there are not dividing lines in the heavens. In fact, it should be treated as a psychological influence and has a close relation to the entire chart. When the Sun has reached 28° of a sign its influence is mainly in the next sign. By way of example, if the Sun is in 28° of Virgo, we use Mercury as the ruling planet, although the characteristics of Libra would be very noticeable in that person's make-up.

**Physical description.** This is derived from the combined influences of the ascending sign, planet ruling the Ascendant and the sign in which it is here located, together with its principle aspects and the planets which may be in the Ascendant. This combination is usually so difficult to delineate correctly that the average student had best omit it.

## Individuality

Read the description of the sign occupied by the Sun. Read the house occupied by the Sun. Note which house the Sun rules in the chart and read its influence. Note which cusp Leo occupied, as the Sun is the ruler of that particular house.

Make notes on the influence of the major aspects to the Sun.

## Personality

Read the influence of the Ascendant.

Read the sign occupied by the planet which rules the sign on the cusp of the First House.

Read the major aspects to that planet. If any planets are in the First House read their influence by house and sign.

Read the influence of the Moon by sign, house and principle aspects.

**Note.** In compiling notes you may at first experience difficulty in defining individuality and personality. Remember that *individuality,* as indicated by the Sun Sign, consists of inherent tendencies, capabilities, and abilities, or those inner qualities by which the individual knows himself. The *personality* may be considered as the outward expressions which characterize the person; that which distinguishes him or her and identifies him or her to others, as indicated by the Rising Sign.

## Finances
Note which sign occupies the cusp of the Second House. Read its influence and that of its ruling planet by sign and house and its principle aspects.

Should any planet occupy the Second House, read its influence by sign and house it occupies, then by sign and house it rules in the chart.

## Mentality
Note the sign which occupies the cusp of the Third House. Read its influence and that of its ruling planet by sign and house and its principle aspects.

Should any planet occupy the Third House, read its influence by the sign and house it occupies, then by the sign and house it rules in the chart.

The mental rulers are the Sun, Moon, and Mercury, although all of the planets have an influence on the mind, especially the ruler of the Ascendant, and the rulers of the Third and the Ninth Houses. Also Saturn and Uranus if in aspect to the mental rulers. Read their delineations according to the aspects they form. Uranus rules the intuition.

## Journeys
Note which sign occupies the cusp of the Third House. Read its influence and that of its ruling planet by sign and house and its principle aspects. The Third House relates to short trips and short journeys.

Should any planet occupy the Third House, read its influence by the sign and house it occupies, then by the sign and house it rules in the chart.

## Home Life
Note which sign occupies the cusp of the Fourth House. Read its influence and that of its ruling planet by sign and house and its principle aspects. The Fourth House relates to father, property, environment and home life.

Should any planet occupy the Fourth House, read its influence by the sign and house it occupies, then by the sign and house it rules in the chart.

## Pleasures

Note which sign occupies the cusp of the Fifth House. Read its influence and that of its ruling planet by sign and house and its principle aspects. The Fifth House relates to pleasure, sports, speculation and love affairs.

Should any planet occupy the Fifth House, read its influence by the sign and house it occupies, then by the sign and house it rules in the chart.

## Children

Note which sign occupies the cusp of the Fifth House. Read its influence and that of its ruling planet by sign and house and its principle aspects.

Should any planet occupy the Fifth House, read its influence by the sign and house it occupies, then by the sign and house it rules in the chart.

The nature of the sign occupied by the Moon, and its aspects, are to be considered carefully in this question.

The Moon in Cancer, Scorpio, Pisces, or Taurus makes the native fruitful and if in good aspect to Jupiter or Venus it usually give a large family. The Moon angular (in the First, Fourth, Seventh or Tenth House) increases the number of children. The Moon, Jupiter or Venus in the Fifth or Eleventh House is a favorable testimony for children. The Sun in the Fifth House is a fruitful sign, and well aspected by the Moon or Venus is a testimony for producing many children or children of exceptional physical appearance.

Consider the Fifth and Eleventh House (the Eleventh House because it is the fifth one of the partner). Fruitful signs covering these cusps are favorable and increase the number of children.

A fruitful sign ascending or the Sun in a fruitful sign is favorable for children.

Barren signs on the cusps of the First, Fifth or Eleventh House or the Sun in a barren sign, decrease fertility and lessen the chances for having offspring.

The Moon in Aries, Leo or Sagittarius, or afflicted by Uranus, Saturn, Mars, or the Sun lessens the chance for any children also.

Uranus, Saturn, Mars or the Sun in the Fifth or Eleventh House denies children or destroys them, according to the nature of the sign, the aspects and the dignity of the planet.

Mercury and Neptune depend upon the aspects received and the nature of the sign occupied.

When the testimony is for children and the cusp of the Fifth House is covered by a feminine sign and its ruler a feminine planet, most of the children will be girls.

When the sign and its ruler are masculine, most of the offspring will be boys.

The Fifth House shows the first child; the Seventh House the second child; the Ninth House the third child; the Eleventh House the fourth; the First House the fifth child; the Third House the sixth child; the Fifth House the seventh child and so on around the circle. By children is meant not alone those who live to be born and reared, but all conceptions.

If the Fifth House shows children and the Eleventh House denies them, or vice versa, some will live and some will die.

If malefic influences the Seventh House the second child may die, and so on. If the ruler of one of these houses is heavily afflicted there is danger of losing that child.

## Health

Note which sign occupies the cusp of the Sixth House. Read its influence and that of its ruling planet by sign and house and its principle aspects.

Should any planet occupy the Sixth House, read its influence by the sign and house it occupies, then by the sign and house it rules in the chart.

In speaking for health, look to the Sun for a male, and to the Moon for a female.

Sun in good aspect to the Moon, Mars or Jupiter is favorable testimony for health and a strong constitution with an abundance of vitality, especially if the Sun is in the First House.

Sun or Moon in the Sixth House is not good for health; Uranus there indicates peculiar and complex disorders, although there should be a chance of recovery by employing methods harmonizing with the nature of Uranus, such as electric, magnetic, mesmeric treatments, etc.

Oriental positions of the planets signify short, sudden, sharp attacks of sickness, but occidental positions produce serious, long, lingering sickness and chronic diseases.

**Note.** The chart is divided into two halves, the western, or *occidental* half is that which begins at the Tenth House cusp, includes the Ascendant, ending with the Fourth House cusp. The *oriental*, or eastern half, begins with the Fourth House cusp and ends at the Midheaven.

Remember to look to the Moon and its aspects when judging the health of a female. If the Moon is in adverse aspect to Venus, it weakens and deranges the constitution, and indicates annoying periodical sickness.

The particular physical ailments to which one is liable are judged by the Ascendant and by the signs occupied by the malefic planets, especially if any of them afflict the Sun or Moon; also judge by the sign which the Sun or Moon is in when so afflicted.

## Marriage—Partnerships

Note which sign occupies the cusp of the Seventh House. Read its influence and that of its ruling planet by sign and house and its principle aspects.

Should any planet occupy the Seventh House, read its influence by the sign and house it occupies, then by the sign and house it rules in the chart.

Moon and Venus rule attractions in a male chart; Sun and Mars in a female chart.

If the Moon and Venus (or the Sun and Mars in a female chart) are strong and free from affliction especially by Saturn, the native has an early attraction.

The Sun or Moon in the Fifth or Seventh House and aspected to several planets causes an early attraction.

Fruitful signs on the cusps of the Fifth and Seventh Houses are favorable for an early union.

When Saturn afflicts Sun or Moon it delays marriage and should these planets be weak and Saturn strong, and barren signs on the cusps of the First and Fifth Houses, the native is not likely to marry.

If the Sun or Moon applies to more than one aspect it signifies more than one union; two aspects, two unions; three aspects; three unions, etc.

Astrology shows the union of affections regardless of whether the unions are made legal or not according to the laws of the land.

If the Sun or Moon be in Gemini, Sagittarius or Pisces, more than one union is denoted.

If Saturn afflicts the Sun or Moon, death of the partner is signified, or coldness develops between them.

In a female chart, if the Sun is afflicted by Uranus she is liable to go astray. Saturn afflicting the Sun, the husband is likely to be miserly, gloomy, crude, unfortunate and somewhat sickly. Mars afflicting the Sun, the husband may be hot-tempered, coarse, and harsh; Venus afflicting the Sun, a passionate partner. Moon afflicting the Sun, a changeable partner. Jupiter afflicting the Sun indicates a partner liable to financial losses.

In a male chart when the Moon aspects Uranus men cohabit with married women; if Venus aspects Uranus they cohabit with single females. In either chart, male or female, if Uranus, Neptune, or Saturn be in either the First, Fifth, or Seventh House it is seldom that the native leads an entirely chaste life.

Jupiter or Venus in the Seventh House gives domestic felicity and comfort; well aspected, gain by marriage.

The Sun or Moon in the Seventh House is favorable but much depends upon the aspects and the dignity by sign.

The Moon (in a male chart) afflicted by Uranus, Saturn or Mars indicates heavy misfortune for the wife through accident, sickness, or operation and danger of her demise. The Sun (in a female chart) afflicted in a like manner affects the husband.

Neptune in affliction with Venus indicates deception in courtship and marriage. Uranus in adverse aspect with Venus indicates mistrust, separation, and danger of scandals. Saturn in adverse aspect with Venus indicates delays, trouble, sorrow, and disappointment. Mars in adverse aspect with Venus indicates suspicion and irritability. Very little happiness, comfort or prosperity is experienced if Uranus, Saturn, or Mars occupy the Seventh House (unless they be well dignified and aspected) and if they are afflicted therein the union will prove a very unfortunate event.

## Legacies

Note which sign occupies the cusp of the Eighth House. Read its influence and that of its ruling planet by sign and house and its principle aspects. The Eighth House rules legacies, bequests, money received through insurance, and matters connected with the goods or property of the dead.

Should any planet occupy the Eighth House, read its influence by the sign and house it occupies, then by the sign and house it rules in the chart.

## Death

Note which sign occupies the cusp of the Eighth House. Read its influence and that of its ruling planet by sign and house and its principle aspects.

Should any planet occupy the Eighth House, read its influence by the sign and house it occupies, then by the sign and house it rules in the chart.

The time or date of death is a difficult thing to ascertain definitely, and even if known it is seldom wise to announce it, but the kind of death is often signified by the Sun, Moon, ruler of the Ascendant, Sixth and Eighth Houses.

If these planets are afflicted by malefics in the oriental half of the chart, violent or sudden death is denoted.

Occidental planets and aspects point more to death by sickeness. The lights afflicted and the malefics elevated above them show violent death. Sun or Moon in conjunction with Mars in the First, Sixth, Eighth, or Tenth House indicates sudden death, especially if Uranus or Saturn add a testimony of affliction. Death is usually caused by a combination of aspects.

Neptune indicates a mysterious death by gas, drowning, drugs or poisons. Uranus shows strange deaths, usually sudden and unexpected, through inventions, electricity, lightning, railroads, vehicles, explosions, travel, or suicide.

Saturn denotes colds, consumption, dropsy, spleen disorder and chronic diseases. Jupiter shows death by liver troubles, blood disorders, apoplexy, or inflammation of the lungs.

Mars indicates fevers, smallpox, bladder troubles, erysipelas, burst blood vessels, hemorrhage, miscarriage, abortion, strangury, cuts, burns, scalds, and wounds. Death is usually the result of a short, sudden attack of sickness.

The Sun shows heart troubles, fevers, or constitutional weakness.

Venus shows kidney or functional derangement.

Mercury indicates brain, nervous or intestinal disorders.

The Moon inclines to stomach troubles, public death, by drowning, etc., according to the aspects.

It is generally a good policy not to attempt to tell people how or when they are likely to die.

## Voyages

Note which sign occupies the cusp of the Ninth House. Read its influence and that of its ruling planet by sign and house and its principle aspects. The Ninth House relates to long journeys, voyages, foreign countries, foreign affairs, foreigners and all places remote from that of birth regardless of whether actually under another flag. To persons born in the U.S., Alaska or the Philippines would be foreign places. Judgment must be exercised on such questions as these, for circumstances alter cases. Distance does not make it a foreign affair, but circumstances, conditions, and new elements and activities do so.

Should any planet occupy the Ninth House, read its influence by the sign and house it occupies, then by the sign and house it rules in the chart.

## Education and the Higher Mind

Note the sign which occupies the cusp of the Ninth House. Read its influence and that of its ruling planet by sign and house and its principle aspects. The Ninth House relates to higher education, academic achievement, invention and scientific attainments.

Should any planet occupy the Ninth House, read its influence by the sign and house it occupies, then by the sign and house it rules in the chart.

## Occupation

Note the signs which occupy the cusps of the Tenth House and the Sixth House. Read their influence and that of their ruling planets by sign and house and their principle aspects.

It is difficult to designate the exact occupation for several reasons. Some persons have no choice in the matter, their parents having decided their work for them, and they follow their parents' will, ofttimes in direct opposition to their own desires. In this respect the Tenth House may be regarded as designating the ideal or self-chosen occupation, and the Sixth House, work, service, drudgery carried on under dislike, distaste, protest, or force of circumstances. On the other hand, many choose a line of work not because of any particular liking for it, but for monetary gain, thereby bringing their occupation largely under the rule of the Second House.

Any planet in the Tenth House will show in what direction the natural desires may lead, by blending the nature of the planet with the nature of the sign it occupies and the aspect which it may behold.

The nature of the planet and the quality of its aspects will determine the benefits or difficulties of the occupation. It is necessary also to note the strongest planet in the nativity by house, sign and aspect.

With most of the planets in the map below the earth, or weak, or mostly in common signs, the native should be in the employ of others. If above the earth, strong or well aspected, the native may be the employer of others. If the majority of planets are in Air Signs, a profession should be chosen, but if in the Earth Signs, a business would be best.

The Sun and its aspects are very important in this matter.

Mercury in conjunction with the Sun inclines to success in bookkeeping, accounting, clerking, secretarial and literary work.

Venus in good aspect to the Sun inclines to success as a jeweler, musician, artist, actor, photographer, etc.

The Sun in good aspect to Mars inclines to success in military affairs, work with iron and steel, dentist, barber, butcher, surgeon, chemist or agent. In good aspect to Jupiter, inclines to success as a lawyer, clergyman, physician, banker, judge or senator; in good aspect to Saturn, inclines to success in mining, agriculture, real estate, property, lead, coal or other minerals; in good aspect to Uranus, inclines to success in public or governmental positions or as an engineer, electrician, inventor, astrologer, also as a reporter on a progressive paper; in good aspect to Neptune, inclines to success as a druggist, oil dealer, detective, speculator, or success in some occult, inspirational or unusual pursuit.

Moon in good aspect to the Sun, inclines to success with the general public in liquids, common commodities, hawker, cabman, expressman, policeman, oysterman, laundryman, dairyman, milkman, sailor, fisherman, or traveler.

If many planets are in one sign, things signified by the sign and by the house they occupy will attract attention, but whether it will be fortunate or not depends upon the nature of the combination and the aspects.

The most success will come through things indicated by the planet best aspected and in connection with the sign and house it occupies in the chart.

The Sun and Moon in good aspect; Business and employment come readily and benefit through them; the adverse aspect of the Sun and Moon has a reverse effect.

Moon afflicting Saturn: Likely to lose in business through financial slumps and depression and when out of employment have a hard time getting started again.

The Sun and Moon in good aspect are very favorable for employment and business, denoting rapid advancement; Sun afflicting Mars, disagreement with employers and danger of accidents.

## Honors

Note the sign which occupies the cusp of the Tenth House. Read its influence and that of its ruling planet by sign and house and its principle aspects. The Tenth House rules honors, fame, and affairs of the country or government.

Should any planet occupy the Tenth House, read its influence by the sign and house it occupies, then by the sign and house it rules in the chart.

## Friends

Note the sign which occupies the cusp of the Eleventh House. Read its influence and that of its ruling planet by sign and house and its principle aspects. The Eleventh House rules friends and also hopes and wishes.

Should any planet occupy the Eleventh House, read its influence by the sign and house it occupies, then by the sign and house it rules in the chart.

## Restrictions

Note the sign which occupies the cusp of the Twelfth House. Read its influence and that of its ruling planet by sign and house and its principle aspects. The Twelfth House relates to unseen or unexpected troubles, secret enmities, secret sorrows, self-undoing, jails, hospitals, and the secret or occult side of life.

Should any planet occupy the Twelfth House, read its influence by the sign and house it occupies, then by the sign and house it rules in the chart.

Some can read a chart more readily than others, but anyone who desires to do so can acquire the knack, on the same principle as acquiring musical ability; i.e., the elements having been learned, practice brings proficiency. The same rule applies to Astrology inasmuch as the elements having been mastered, their correct application brings accurate results. After the system has been learned the quickest way to further development and understanding along these lines is through casting and reading horoscopes.

## TWINS

Astrologers are often asked questions about twins. Why, for instance, if astrology is to be considered valid, do twins born at approximately the same time differ in appearance and character? One would expect identical twins to be identical in personality, and yet often they are not. The famous Siamese twins, Chang and Eng, had strikingly different personalities. One was a teetotaler and the other drank to excess, causing the premature death of both. Astrology can often provide clues to why twins are the way they are.

In studying this question it must be held in mind that there are two kinds of twins—those which are genetically identical, or maternal twins, and those which are not, were conceived separately, but were delivered on the same date, or fraternal twins.

By way of illustration let us consider a case which came under the observation of Llewellyn George—a very unusual case and one very difficult to explain satisfactorily except by means of Astrology. Mr. George spent twenty years in the city where these twins were born and had the opportunity of watching their development from birth to maturity.

The case surely proved interesting because, although born but four minutes apart, the boy and girl grew to manifest very dissimilar characteristics in addition to being quite different in appearance.

Llewellyn George was well acquainted with the prospective father and urged him to secure the exact time of each birth. He said "each" birth because about six months previously when there were indications of a family increase, he asked about the matter and a horary chart made for the time of the query clearly indicated that his wife was pregnant, and because Mercury and Venus were in the same degree of Gemini in the Eleventh House, it was easy to predict twins; a boy and a girl. Mercury in Gemini, masculine; while Venus furnished the feminine indication. The Moon being in a position which designated months, the number of degrees and minutes required for it to make an aspect to the two planets told of the week in which the births would occur; a calculation which subsequently proved correct.

To those not versed in horoscopy these correspondences seem astounding, but to the practitioner they are not unusual for he expects that the testimonies rendered by celestial phenomena coincide exactly with the facts, events or conditions.

The eventful day arrived. The clock time was carefully recorded for each birth and after the proper adjustment was made between the standard clock time and mean time for that longitude, it was found that they were born just as the sign on the Ascendant was changing. The boy was born when the last degree of Virgo was ascending while the girl was born four minutes later with the beginning of Libra rising.

The planetary significator of the boy was Mercury; that of the girl, Venus. In childhood the boy was shy and retiring; the girl enjoyed and readily made friendships. In youth the boy was quiet, studious and frugal; the girl was sociable, dressy and extravagant. He was dark and slender; she was fair and plump. The youth became a messenger, then a clerk, then owner of a grocery store. Note that Mercury indicates messengers and clerks, while Virgo indicates foodstuffs. The girl took music lessons, became a milliner and dressmaker; all Venus occupations. In fact, they were just as different as could be, and as they should be, according to Astrology, being born with different signs ascending though only four minutes apart.

Another case which came under the observation of Llewellyn George was of twins who looked as alike as two peas. These two young men were the bane of their friends, with their practical jokes of substituting for each other. No one could tell which was which. They confided in Mr. George that one often went out with the other's girl just for a lark, until the young ladies were in despair and perplexity. Not only did they look alike but their habits were the same; they dressed alike, wore each other's clothes, had the same likes and dislikes, were ill at the same time, they worked in the same store, and the women they were in love with were sisters.

With all these similar traits it would naturally be supposed that they were born at very nearly the same time. But strange to say, they were not. Yet Astrology, better than anything else, logically accounts for the facts. They were born in the month of Gemini, symbolized by the Twins and of that sign they were typical specimens as individuals. They were born one whole hour apart but at a time when the sign of Gemini was on the Ascendant at each birth.

Perhaps it might be argued that in large hospitals where births are occurring every few minutes, children born nearly at the same time do not always resemble each other, although some have the same sign rising.

In such instances it should be remembered that although born at the same place and at nearly the same time, coition and conception took place at different times and at different places, with gestation in entirely different environments; therefore the subject of twins must be considered further in relation to the pre-natal epoch, also to heredity, environment, and other factors involving physiological and psychological principles. Even so, cases of "astrological twins" are well-known. The best example was recorded in Raphael's *Manual of Astrology* (London, 1828). This was the case of George the Third, King of England, and Samuel Hennings, an Ironmonger. Both were born at the same time and at almost the same location. Although born into entirely different social settings, the careers of each were parallel. When George the Third ascended to the throne in October 1760, Hennings went into business for himself as an ironmonger. Both were married on September 8, 1761, and both died at nearly the same time on Jan. 28, 1820.

# The Signs

## ARIES

### Classifications
Fire triplicity, cardinal quadrature. Hot, dry, masculine, positive. Short ascension, equinoctial, eastern. Inflammatory, choleric, sterile, violent, bestial, intemperate, mental-motive.

### Planets
**Ruler:** Mars. **Detriment:** Venus, being a lustful sign. **Exaltation:** The Sun. **Fall:** Saturn.

### General Description
Aries is the first, or head sign, of the Zodiac and is known to have influence on the head and face. The Sun enters this sign on or about March 21 each year, constituting the Vernal Ingress. While it is in this eastern sign we celebrate Easter.

### Symbols
Aries has been represented by the cock, denoting boastful or fighting qualities but is more generally symbolized by the ram, being in nature rash, hardy, springy, lascivious, and combative. Aries represents the "gate of gold on the east," therefore called an oriental sign, denoting the beginning of right ascension (RA) or the oriental first Right Ascension Midheaven (RAM).

## Biblical Correspondences

The Gospel says, "I have exalted thee, O Father," and in this sign the Sun is exalted, particularly in the nineteenth degree. In the New Testament it probably answers to Mark. **Archangel**: Malchidial. **Angel**: Sharhiel. **Apostle**: Matthias. **Tribe of Israel**: Gad. **Prophet**: Malachi.

## Stellar Symbols

Stars in the Aries constellation are Shedar, Ruckbah and Dat al Cursa. The first decan is Cassiopeia. Cetus, a monster constellation to the south of the ecliptic, represents the second decan. Perseus represents the third decan or constellation.

## Anatomical Correspondences

**Bones**: Skull and face, except perhaps the nasal bones, which may be co-ruled by Scorpio. **Muscles**: The muscles used in eating, talking, smiling and in making other expressions; the superficial muscles under the scalp; the deep muscles in the mouth; and the other muscles in the head. **Arteries**: Temporal and internal Carotids (those carrying blood to the head). **Vein**: Cephalic (coming from the right arm).

## Health

Morbid action is shown through various kinds of eruptive maladies affecting the head and face: pimples, ringworm, headaches, migraine, encephalitis, smallpox, and perhaps harelip. Worry, anxiety, excitement or anger produce overstrain of the brain and tend to upset the general health. Aries people require plenty of rest and sleep, peaceful and harmonious surroundings. They should partake freely of vegetables and brain food, avoiding stimulants and partaking lightly of meat. Herbs belonging to this sign are mustard, eye-bright, bay and others of pungent nature.

## Desirable Characteristics

Enterprising, action, ambition, courage, ardor, industry, generosity, pioneering, practicality, constructive, leadership.

## Undesirable Characteristics

Belligerence, headstrong, excitability, audaciousness, impatience, irresolution, imprudence, insubordination, quarrelsomeness, foolhardiness, selfishness, disregard, jealousy.

## Associations
Ash-Lesh, (flaming star), Tuesday, Smith, Samael, Headen, Sang (herb), Taleh (sacrificial lamb), Ramah (exalted place), Ramesis (the best in the land of Egypt), Ramadan (Muslim feast in spring), Benjamin, Rachael, Amroo.

## Locations
Sandy, hilly, dry or rather barren places; places where sheep are kept; lime or brick kilns, fireplaces, ceilings, plaster, tool houses, forges; prominent corner buildings facing east, east corner rooms.

# TAURUS

## Classifications
Earth triplicity, fixed quadrature. Cold most, feminine, negative. Short ascension, eastern. Semi-fruitful, bestial, melancholy.

## Planets
**Ruler**: Venus. **Detriment**: Mars, which is not at ease in the home of Venus. **Exaltation**: The Moon, particularly the third degree. **Fall**: Uranus.

## General Description
Taurus is the second sign of the Zodiac, the Sun beginning its apparent yearly transit through it on or about April 20. It is the middle, or fixed sign, of the spring quarter.

Taurus suggests energy, reserve force, endurance and stability. An energy devoted to stable things ensures a firm foundation and an enduring structure.

## Symbols
Taurus is symbolized by a bull with unusual horns on head and toes, appearing in a rage, crouched to rush forward with fierce energy; representing a stubborn and tenacious nature.

Taurus is one of the four fixed sign comprising the Cherubim.

It was the original Bull, or Baal, of the Assyrian religious rites, sometimes referred to as "The Sacred Bull" or "The Golden Calf," emblematic of the period a few thousand years ago when the solar system was precessing through that constellation. Our May Day festival with its may pole and garlands are remains of the ancient Egyptian festival celebrating the entrance of the Sun into Taurus.

### Biblical Correspondences

**Prophet**: The Gospel apparently alludes to Haggai as the prophet. **Archangel**: Asmodeus. **Angel**: Araziel. **Disciple**: Thaddeus. **Tribe of Israel**: Ephraim in Hebraic mythology refers to the sign of Taurus.

### Stellar Symbols

In the first decan of the Taurus constellation is Orion, to the south of the ecliptic but very beautiful, Amos and Homer. Rigel and Bellatrix are other stars there also. The second decan shows the constellation Eridanus. Auriga is the third constellation associated with this sign.

In Taurus are the Pleiades, a cluster of seven stars whose "sweet influences" are referred to with the band of Orion.

### Anatomical Correspondences

The sign is said to include under its domain the neck, throat, ears, pharynx, eustachian tubes, tonsils, upper portion of the esophagus, palate, thyroid gland and vocal chords. **Bones**: cervical vertebrae in the neck. **Muscles**: Those in the front and back of the neck enabling movement of the head. **Arteries**: External carotids and basilar artery. **Veins**: Jugulars in the neck and the veins of the thyroid gland.

### Health

Morbid action manifests as sore throat, glandular swellings in the neck, croup, mumps, goiter, abscess, suffocation, strangulation, apoplexy. By reflex action from Leo and Scorpio the heart may be affected, also the excretory system, giving rise to piles, fistulas or bladder trouble.

Fattening foods should be used in moderation as this sign usually increases the appetite, tends to obesity and to fondness of ease. Moderate and regular exercise is essential as well as moderation in food and drink. Because of failure to observe these essentials, rheumatism is prevalent among Taureans. Herbs belonging to this sign are ground-ivy, deadly night-shade and vervain.

## Desirable Characteristics

Trustworthiness, steadfastness, perseverance, endurance, persistence, composure, self-reliance, constructive, practicality, humor, kindness, sympathy, magnetism, care, fearlessness.

## Undesirable Characteristics

Stubbornness, domineering, exacting, obstructive, stolid, brusque, dogmatic, conceit, self-centeredness, covetous, lazy. It is said that their accusers are seldom forgiven and that they retain the memory of an injury for a long time.

## Associations

This second sign is akin to the Second House with its relation to money, finances and movable effects of extrinsic value. Astarte, Ataur, (Arabian name for Taurus), Mineves, Aleph, Reem (an animal resembling the bull but fiercer), Aurochs (similar to Reem), Unicorn Hunter, Capella (a star), Atlas.

## Locations

Banks, cash boxes, money drawers, jewelry boxes; stables for cows, dairies; places where farming implements are kept or sold; pastures, feeding places; wheat or corn fields. In the house it represents the middle rooms or places in the middle of the block. Also round things such as castors. rings, money, etc. Shoes, leather, purses; garlands, may-poles, canes, altars, all places where property or food are stored, e.g., refrigerators, cellars.

# GEMINI

## Classifications

Air triplicity, mutable of flexed quadrature. Moist, masculine, positive. Short ascension, northern. Barren, sanguine, double-bodied, dual, human, violent.

### Planets

Ruler: Mercury. Detriment: Jupiter. Exaltation: The Moon's North Node. Fall: The Moon's South Node.

### General Description

The Sun enters this sign on or about May 21 and apparently transits through it by June 20.

Gemini inclines to tall, upright body, long arms and hands; feet short; a quick walker with swinging arms, open hands, fingers spread apart slightly; piercing eye, quick sight; keen mentality.

### Symbols

Gemini is symbolized by the twins, the portals, a monkey. The monkey is associated with Gemini by the Chinese; they depict it as the three graces symbolized by the three little monkeys with hands over eyes, ears and mouth. Gemini is also related by the Aryans or ancient Hindus to Buddha or Krishna. The twins are sometimes Castor and Pollux, Eros and Anteros, Gog and Magog, Romulus and Remus. Sometimes pictured as a man and woman walking hand in hand, perhaps Adam and Eve. In the Babylonian calendar they are the "Two Gods of the Door."

### Biblical Correspondences

Gemini is biblically referred to as Cain and Abel, and as Simeon and Levi. Archangel: Ambriel. Angel: Sarayel. Prophet: Zachariah. Disciple: Simeon. Tribe of Israel: Manasseh.

### Stellar Symbols

In the first decan south of the ecliptic is Lepus, *the hare*. The stars in Sirius, *the great dog,* which is the second decan, are Mirzam *the ruler*, Muliphen, *leader*, Wasen, *shining* and Adhara, *glorious*. The third decan also shows a wolf or dog (canis minor) somewhat smaller and behind the first one. Procyon and Al Gomeize, two prominent stars are in this constellation.

### Anatomical Correspondences

Gemini rules the nervous system by which all parts of the body are brought into communication, giving it sensation and flexibility.

Through respiration furnishes the two lungs with water from the air which normally bathes them and oxygen which they pass into the blood. **Bones**: Upper ribs, collarbones, shoulder blades and bones in upper arms, forearms, wrists and hands. **Veins**: Those coming from shoulders, arms, lungs and rib cage. **Arteries**: Those carrying blood to the lungs, rib cage area, shoulders and arms.

## Health

Nervous disorders are liable through worry, anxiety, mental overstrain, restlessness and excessive activity. The lungs, shoulders, arms and hands are subject to affections and accidents. Tubercular tendencies or disorders of the respiratory organs may develop. Gemini indicates such disorders as asthma, bronchitis, pleurisy, pneumonia.

This mentally-motivated sign requires attention to proper breathing, light out-of-doors exercises and walking with long, deliberate steps. The chest and lung area should be given protection and rubbing. Particular care should be given to diet; cereals and nerve foods being essential.

## Desirable Characteristics

Intelligence, expressiveness, eloquence, idealism, studiousness, inquiring mind, ambition, resourcefulness, dexterity, courage, tolerance, responsiveness, generosity, sympathy, temperance, breadth, liberalism.

## Undesirable Characteristics

Restlessness, variation, verbosity, effusiveness, trickiness, shiftness, diffusion, diffidence, waywardness, improvidence, impulsiveness, exaggeration, theory, lack of concentration.

## Associations

Thaumin, (Hebrew name for Gemini meaning united), Anubis, Hermes, Messia, messenger or wandering teacher.

The third sign of the Zodiac has things in common with the Third House, in that they both indicate letters, communications, messengers, news, inquiries, information, rumors, newspapers, magazines, neighbors, relatives, short journeys, lecturing, debating, teaching, advertising, clerical work, reporting, story-writing, merchandising, printing, education.

## Locations

Where hay or straw are kept, granaries; coffers or chests with doors; pillared buildings, doorways, walls, wainscoting, upper back rooms, bookcases; hills and mountains of barren nature; things made or sold in pairs as salt and pepper shakers, etc.

# CANCER

## Classifications

Water triplicity, cardinal quadrature. Cold, moist, feminine, negative. Long ascension, solstitial, tropical, northern. Fruitful, maternal; domestic, mute, phlegmatic.

## Planets

**Ruler**: The Moon. **Detriment**: Saturn. **Exaltation**: Jupiter, especially the fifteenth degree. **Fall**: Mars.

## General Description

The Sun enters Cancer on or about June 21 and apparently transits through the sign by July 22. Reference to any ephemeris will show that the Sun apparently reaches its highest point or north declination (23° 27') and remains in it for three days, apparently standing still, after which it slowly starts, crablike, backward toward its south declination. The middle day of the three mentioned is therefore the longest day of the year.

Cancer is said to be receptive, transforming, metamorphic, nurturing, fructifying, but lacking in vitality.

## Symbols

The crab represents possession and retention; it carries its house on its back. The symbol is drawn from the breasts, emblematic of motherhood, to nurture, cherish, to ripen, to carry, to bear. Although it has land-travel facilities, the crab is a creature born of water. The Egyptians represented this sign with the scarab.

## Biblical Correspondences

In the Gospel, Issachar is likened to a strong ass which at one time was the symbol of Cancer. **Archangel**: Muriel. **Angel**: Pakiel. **Prophet**: It is said that Cancer refers to the prophet Amos. **Disciple**: John. **Tribe of Israel**: Issachar.

## Stellar Symbols

Within the constellation Cancer is Praespe, *the manager*. The first decan is modernly called Ursa Minor, or Little Bear. It contains the pole star. Ursa Major, or Great Bear (the big dipper) is the second decan. The third decan is Argo, *the heavenly ship*, whose main star is Canopus.

## Anatomical Correspondences

Cancer has dominion over that zone of the body containing the breasts, chest, stomach and therefore related to the pancreas and thoraic duct. **Bones**: The breast bone, the ribs which are nearest to the stomach. **Muscles**: Intercostals (those between the ribs) and diaphragm (those used in breathing). **Arteries**: Diaphragmatic; those serving the stomach. **Veins**: Mammary, gastric, gastro-epiploric, diaphragmatic.

## Health

The stomach being the principle source of affection, it is essential that foods taken into it be pure, undefiled or which will not cause fermentation. Foods should be well cooked, stimulants avoided. Especial care is required when the Moon is transiting through Cancer or Capricorn. Guard against colds or chills; avoid imagining diseases; avoid worrying about finances. Frequent changes of scenery are beneficial.

## Desirable Characteristics

Patience, tenacity, conscientiousness, economy, domesticity, maternity, kindness, devotion, versatility, sociability, adaptability, sympathy, patriotism.

## Undesirable Characteristics

Timorousness, variation, vanity, fancy, imagination, untruthfulness, changeability, sentimentality, touchiness, grasping, pride, disorderliness, resentment, indolence.

## Associations

May, mother, holy water, Arthur.

## Locations

Lakes, rivers, brooks, etc.; place where rushes or vegetables grow; homes, stalls, sheepfolds; taverns, public houses; wash houses, kitchens, water tanks; cellars, corner houses facing north.

# LEO

## Classifications

Fire triplicity, fixed quadrature. Hot , dry, masculine, positive. Long ascension, northern. Choleric, barren, bestial, commanding, fortunate, feral, broken, strong, bitter.

## Planets

**Ruler**: The Sun. **Detriment**: The recalcitrant Uranus who will bow to no king. **Exaltation**: The inspirational Neptune. **Fall**: Uranus.

## General Description

The Sun enters Leo on July 22. It is universally symbolized by a lion, whose nature it represents. It symbolizes the fervid heat of July and August when the Sun has attained its greatest power. It represents the type of electric, fiery mind whose expression is often destructive, whose energy is often rapacious and daring, kingly, commanding yet generous.

## Symbols

Leo is represented by the ancients as the Nemean Lion, which leaped down from the skies and was killed by Hercules. Leo is the emblem of violence and fury in the hierglyphic writings. In the ancient maps the lion is shown just above Hydra, the great dragon, with his claws about to rend the serpent.

Feasts and sacrifices formerly celebrated during the Sun's transit in Leo in honor of the Sun, were termed Leonitica, while the priests who performed the rites were called Leones. Among the Persians these celebrations were called Mithra.

## Biblical Correspondences

**Archangel**: Verchiel. **Angel**: Sharatiel. **Prophet**: Leo is said to correspond to the prophet Hosea. **Apostle:** Peter. **Tribe of Israel:** Judah. Leo, the Lion is one of the beasts of the cherubim. Jacob assigned this sign to the tribe of Judah and the subsequent warlike and victorious energy of the tribe proved the allocation correct. Samson represents the Sun in Leo. Michael is the archangel of the Sun.

## Stellar Symbols

Regel, or Regulus, is a mighty fixed star in the heart of the Lion (now about 29° Leo). Hydra forms the first decan. The second decan is Crater, *the cup*. Corvus, *the raven*, constitutes the third decan. The fixed star Algorab is in this constellation.

## Anatomical Correspondences

The heart, indicative of vital power, ardency, interchange and generation, as well as the spinal marrow, nerves and fiber, are represented by Leo. **Bones:** Dorsal vertebrae. **Muscles:** Those of the back and around shoulder blades. **Arteries:** Aorta (coming out of the heart), anterior and posterior coronary. **Veins:** Coronaries.

## Health

Physical disorders of Leo manifest in the various forms of heart disease, palpitation, fevers, spinal meningitis; heat exhaustion, sunstroke, pestilence and inflammations.

As this is a vital and motive sign ruling the heart, temperate living is essential. Harmony, order and moderation in all things should be cultivated; excitement and haste curtailed. Heating and stimulating foods or beverages should be avoided but nutritious blood-building food is necessary.

## Desirable Characteristics

Loyalty, outspokenness, ardor, kindness, tolerance, generosity, philanthropy, inspiration, magnetism, inspiration, hope, chivalry, industry, fearlessness, magnanimity, idealism, sincerity, hospitality, intuition, comprehension.

## Undesirable Characteristics

Arrogance, dictatorial manner, overbearing, condescension, impetuousness, pomposity, dominance, sensitivity, promiscuity, gullibility, fussiness, striking, hot-headedness.

## Associations

Adam, Abraham, David, Esau, Israel, Hercules, Judy, Osiris, Leonis, Richard the Lion-Hearted, Alphard, Lea or Lee. Its colors are orange, yellow, flaxen and golden. Gold watches, rings, amber, gold coins.

## Locations

High, round-topped hills, places inhabited by wild beasts, deserts, forests; hard, stony, gravelly ways or hills; castles, forts, theatres, playgrounds, dance halls; places for sports, gambling, speculation; formal social functions; fireplaces, ovens, solariums.

# VIRGO

## Classifications

Earth triplicity, mutable or flexed quadrature. Cold, dry, feminine, negative. Long ascension, western. Melancholy, barren, nocturnal, scientific, human, maternal.

## Planets

**Ruler**: Mercury. **Detriment**: Neptune. **Exaltation**: Mercury. **Fall**: Venus.

## General Description

The Sun appears to transit Virgo between August 23 and September 22. Virgo is known to have a bearing on matters pertaining to sickness, hygiene, clothing, food, cereals, employees, servants, service, work, and domestic animals.

## Symbols

In some ancient Zodiacs, this sign was symbolized as a virgin lying prostrate; in one hand she holds a "spica" (see wheat) and in the other a "branch" (often referred to as a bough, sprout, plant, root tree, stem, rod).

Mercury the ruler, is a messenger, Messiah, A-Rab, or wandering teacher.

## Biblical Correspondences

Virgo, bearing the sheaf, was called "the house of corn" or Bethlehem and is sometimes related to Joseph. **Archangel**: Hamaliel. **Angel**: Shelathiel. **Disciple**: Andrew. **Tribe of Israel**: Nephtali.

## Stellar Symbols

Virgo, the constellation, rises at midnight, December 25. In the first decan of Virgo, is Coma; the second decan is Centaurus, *the despised* or *the pierced.* The principal stars in it are Bungula and Agena. Bootes, is the third decan of this constellation. Prominent fixed stars in the constellation and near the ecliptic, are Caphir, *an atonement offering,* and Spica, *seed.*

## Anatomical Correspondences

Virgo's domain is the bowels or abdomen. It is chiefly associated with the duodenum, peritoneum. **Muscles**: Rectal and abdominal. **Arteries**: Those serving the digestive system, particularly the intestines. **Veins**: The intestinal veins.

## Health

Virgo indicates disorders pertaining to the bowel and abdominal functions, such as colic, cholera, peritonitis, constipation, malnutrition and affections of the intestinal regions. Virgo affects the nervous system considerably. Virgo people benefit by paying attention to diet, hygiene, sanitation and mental poise. Hypochondria is characteristic of this sign, while absorption, assimilation, selection and utilization are Virgo functions.

Diet is an important factor to Virgo people. Meals should be regular and food well masticated. Foods, especially cereals, which regulate the bowels properly should be chosen. It is said that a vegetarian diet, well proportioned is favorable. Strong drinks or condiments should be avoided.

## Desirable Characteristics

Thoughtfulness, action, seriousness, conciseness, discretion, sensitivity, intuition, efficiency, caution, intelligence, perception, contemplation, domesticity, prudence, providence, industry, methodicalness, thrift.

### Undesirable Characteristics

Calculation, mercenary, selfishness, anxiety, worry, irritability, apprehension, discontent, secretiveness, criticism, skepticism, cold, unresponsiveness, inconsistency, indecisions, quick temper, timidity, lack of self-confidence.

### Associations

Astrea, Athene, Beth, Bess, Bula, Elizabeth, Celeste, Stella, Adorah, Virgin, Eve, Madonna, Paris, Notre Dame, Gene.

In Mundane Astrology the sixth sign has special reference to public health, general conditions of working people and of poultry and domestic animals. It also indicates matters relating to municipal or national service, army or navy, departments or labor, horticulture, agriculture, agrostology, medicinal herbs, prophylactics, Red Cross, humane, relief societies.

### Locations

Gardens, cornfields, granaries, pantries, restaurants; places where fruit and vegetables are kept and where hay, wheat, barley, cheese or butter are stored; places where books, papers, maps, charts, planes or medicines are kept.

# LIBRA

### Classifications

Air triplicity, cardinal quadrature. Hot, moist, masculine, positive. Long ascension, equinoctial, western. Semi-fruitful, humane, scientific, sanguine.

### Planets

**Ruler**: Venus. **Detriment**: Mars. **Exaltation**: Saturn. **Fall**: Sun.

### General Description

The Sun appears to enter Libra September 23 and to transit this sign until October 22. Libra is a crossing place or meeting place of the ecliptic and equator, the autumnal equinox. The Sun passes over from north to south declination at the first point of Libra and on that date the day and night are of equal length—they weigh evenly, are balanced.

## Symbols

It is symbolized by the apparently commonplace scales, but the arms of that tilting beam react out into eternities. The position of the attached bowls, which a feather's weight may change, indicates the destinies of ages, the fortunes of empires, the estates of immortality. The equipoise of the beam marks the adjustment of mighty feuds internal and external.

## Biblical Correspondences

**Archangel**: Zuriel. **Angel**: Chedquiel. **Disciple**: Bartholomew. **Apostle**: Luke. **Tribe of Israel**: Asher.

## Stellar Symbols

Two stars formerly in Libra: Zuben al Genubi, *insufficient price* and Zuben al Schemali, *the full price*. Hydra, *the serpent*, extends through the meridian of this sign also. On the south of this sign is the first decan, Crucis, or crux, meaning *cross*; on the north of Libra is the third decan, Corona Borealis, *the crown*. Between these two and close to Libra was what is now called Lupus, *the wolf*.

## Anatomical Correspondences

Libra rules the lumbar region in general and the kidneys in particular. Its zone of influence includes the loins, ovaries and the substance of the kidneys. Libra represents equipoise, distillation, sublimation and filtration. **Bones**: Lumbar vertebrae, just below the ribs. **Muscles**: Those of the lower back and top of pelvic bone. **Arteries**: Those going to the kidneys and lower back. **Veins**: Those coming from the kidneys and lower back.

## Health

Libra disturbances manifest through Bright's disease, nephritis, suppression of urine, neuralgia of kidneys, weak lower back, etc. Pains in the lower part of the back are symptoms which should be given attention. A well balanced diet between acid and starchy foods is necessary. Plenty of fresh air, harmonious surroundings and mild exercises are essential. Attention should be given to proper diet, especially concerning liquid foods, as the kidneys are the chief organs affected.

## Desirable Characteristics

Thoughtfulness, impartiality, unprejudice, conciliation, foresight, justice, grace, modesty, decorum, refinement, art, adaptability, persuasiveness, affection, peace, cheerfulness, sympathy, forgiveness, generosity, idealism, tact, balance.

## Undesirable Characteristics

Indecision, uncertainty, extremism, recklessness, hesitance, susceptibility, impressionability, illusion, punctilious, pedanticism, vanity, aloofness, shirking, carelessness, vascillation.

## Associations

Justice, Justine, Zuben, Ruben, Corona, Sura, Luke, Harpocrates, Charles, beam, cross, scale, weights, measures, pianos, tables, upholstered furniture.

It is said that Libra people usually make good buyers for large concerns, having good discrimination and intuition regarding what to buy that can be sold readily, especially in seasonable goods and quickly moving items such as novelties, fancy goods, perfumes, apparel, jewels. They are also good as court attaches, bailiffs, clerks, justices.

## Locations

Places near wind-mills, straggling barns; where wood is cut or piled; saw-pits; harbor for ships, where boats are made or launched; tops of mountains, mounds or hills; trees; ground where hunting or hawking is practiced; golf links, sandy or gravelly places; tops of buildings with cupolas or domes; closets, guest chambers; tops of dressers, wardrobes, jewel cases.


# SCORPIO

## Classifications

Water triplicity, fixed quadrature. Cold, feminine, negative. Long ascension, nocturnal, western. Fruitful, phlegmatic, reproductive, violent, mute.

## Planets

**Ruler**: Mars was the traditional ruler of Scorpio, but when Pluto was discovered in 1930 it proved to have a great affinity for this sign. However, there is still some controversy over the correct rulership, with some astrologers claiming that Pluto is the ruler of Aries, Mars of Scorpio. **Detriment**: Venus. **Exaltation**: in the ancient tables of disguises and debilities Scorpio was left blank as to exaltation. No planet was exalted in Scorpio, but modern astrologers assign it as the exaltation of Uranus. **Fall**: The Moon.

## General Description

The Sun appears to transit this sign yearly between October 23 and November 21.

## Symbols

Scorpio is symbolized by a scorpion or sometimes by a snake or eagle. Scorpio in Arabic and Syriac is Al Akrab, meaning *wounding, conflict, war*. In Coptic it is Isidis: *attack of the enemy*. In the Hebrew Zodiac, Scorpio was ascribed to Dan. The banner of the tribe of Israel was originally a scorpion, but afterwards an eagle.

## Biblical Correspondences

**Archangel**: Barkiel. **Angel**: Saitziel. **Disciples**: Judas Iscariot is the disciple indicated by Scorpio. Philip is also assigned here. **Tribe of Israel**: Dan. The cherubim had the head of a bull (Taurus), the head of a lion (Leo) and the head of an eagle (Scorpio), as well as a human head (Aquarius).

## Stellar Symbols

In the three decans, or side pieces—the parts outside the Zodiac in the constellations which in older days corresponded with the longitude of the sign—we see pictured in the star map the serpent, Ophiuchus and above, Hercules and the three-headed dog of hell, Cerberus. Beneath all these is the scorpion. The bright star in the Hercules constellation is Ras el Gethi, meaning *head of him who bruises*. The star in the knee means, *the branch kneeling*.

## Anatomical Correspondences

Scorpio is concerned with both the reproductive and destructive processes, procreation and readaptation, exercising special influence over the generative organs. The parts of the body coming within its zone are: bladder, ureters, pelvis of the kidney, urethra, prostrate gland, groin, rectum, colon, nostrils and sense of smell. Scorpio is responsible both for producing the subtle scents of sexual excitation, and picking them up. **Bones:** The pelvic and pubic bones. **Muscles:** Those governing the openings of the bladder, rectum and urethra. **Arteries:** Those serving the pelvic region. **Veins:** Those serving the reproductive organs.

## Health

Physical disorders manifest as rupture, fistulas, piles, afflictions associated with the generative organs, including injuries to the groin.

## Desirable Characteristics

Energy, action, positiveness, fearlessness, tenacity, penetration, thoughtfulness, optimism, pleasantness, eloquency, devotion, patience, ambition.

## Undesirable Characteristics

Severity, callousness, causticity, sarcasm, suspicion, destruction, vindictiveness, dogmatism, shrewdness, parsimoniousness, tyranny, passion.

## Associations

Isidis, Frons, Antares, Shiloh, Lesuth, Judas.

Scorpio indicates success in positions requiring patience, perseverance and concentration and produces good surgeons, chemists, detectives, researchers and in lines where courage, strength and personal effort are necessary.

## Locations

Low gardens, vineyards; muddy, sluggish streams; ill smelling ponds, peat bogs, quagmires; slaughterhouses, meat markets, operation rooms; lavatories, sinks, drains, cesspools; places where junk or old iron is stored; garbage dumps, compost heaps; tanneries, incinerating plants, chemical laboratories, crematories.

# SAGITTARIUS

## Classifications
Fire triplicity, mutable of flexed quadrature. Hot, dry, masculine, positive. Long ascension, southern. Choleric, double doubled, motive, bilious.

## Planets
**Ruler:** Jupiter. **Detriment:** Mercury. **Exaltation:** The south node of the Moon. **Fall:** The north node of the Moon.

## General Description
The Sun appears to transit this sign between November 22 and December 21, yearly.

## Symbols
Sagittarius is pictured as half man, half horse, the man an archer with bow and arrow: a Centaur or Centaurion. The symbol of Sagittarius is pictured by a sharp instrument like an arrow or spear; an armed horseman or warrior represents this fiery sign. The Greeks called him Chieron.

## Biblical Correspondences
**Archangel:** Adnachiel. **Angel:** Samequiel. **Prophet:** Zephaniah. **Apostle:** James, son of Zebedee. **Tribe of Israel:** Benjamin.

## Stellar Symbols
The first decan, or side piece, of the constellation of Sagittarius was Lyra, *the harp*, the oldest of stringed musical instruments, the invention of which the ancients ascribed to the gods. The harp connects the archer with superior joy, delight, gladness and praiseworthy action, all typical of the characteristics of the advanced sons of Jove as we know them today. Vega, meaning *victory*, the brightest star in the northern skies was in Lyra.

The second decan of Sagittarius was Ara, called by the Arabs, Al Mugamra, *the completing*. In the third decan we see Draco, *the dragon*. Its chief star, once the pole star (four to six thousand years ago) had several names as Al Waid, *who is to be destroyed*, Thuban, *the subtile*,

Al Dib, *the reptile*. Other stars in Draco are Etanin, *long serpent*; Grumain, *the deceiver*; El Athik, *the fraudful*; El Asieh, *the humbled*; Gianser, *the punished enemy*.

## Anatomical Correspondences

Sagittarius rules the sacrum, the sciatic nerve which proceeds down from it, ennervating the upper and back parts of the legs, the hips and the thighs. Tradition gives it rulership over the liver, although Virgo and Cancer are probably more influential here. **Bones**: The sacrum and tibia. **Muscles**: Thigh muscles, buttocks. **Arteries**: Those serving the thighs and buttocks. **Veins**: Those serving the thighs and buttocks.

## Health

Sagittarians are susceptible to felons, whitlow, abscesses, supera- tion, septic inflammations, as well as injuries through horses and falls. Being opposite to Gemini, the sign Sagittarius also is given to affection denoted by that sign, i.e. lung and nerve trouble. Disease may also manifest as enteric disorders, sciatia, rheumatism, gout, dislocations of the hip joint, feverish ailments, blood disorders, cuts and wounds and volitional disturbances.

This sign has a tendency to over-activity; therefore moderation and deliberate action are essential when ailing. The great open spaces is their sphere; the out-of-doors with sports, physical exercises and hiking. Its herb is pimpernal.

## Desirable Characteristics

Sincerity, honesty, frankness, justice, generosity, foresightedness, prophecy, perseverance, dependability, buoyancy, geniality, joviality, hope, logical, charitability.

## Undesirable Characteristics

Boisterousness, over-confidence, rashness, changeableness, blunt- ness, brusqueness, aggression, defiance, uncompromising, prodigality, independence, speculation, sportiveness.

## Associations

Jove, Jehovah, Vega, Terebellum, St. George, Swift, horseman, victory, obelisk, Oedipus, Leviathan, Victor.

## Locations

Highest places in the land, hills, ground that rises higher than the surrounding country; the topmost room in a house; places near fire or where it has been; stables for war horses or racers; also long, slim pointed things as arrows, spears, swords, etc. Incense burners, harps, race horses.

# CAPRICORN

## Classifications

Earth triplicity, cardinal quadrature. Cold, dry, feminine, negative. Short ascension, solstitial, southern. Tropical, melancholy, quadrupetal, serving.

## Planets

**Ruler:** The much maligned Saturn. **Detriment:** The Moon. **Exaltation:** Mars. **Fall:** Jupiter.

## General Description

The Sun apparently transits Capricorn between December 22 and January 19. From the astronomical standpoint the Sun is seen to come yearly to the lower part of the great cross at the winter solstice in Capricorn, reaching its lowest point in southern declination (23° 27') called *the grave* on December 22, remaining in that degree for three days, after which on December 25 it ascends out of the grave like a new birth or a resurrection.

## Symbols

Capricorn in modern Astrology is symbolized by a goat, but in ancient uranographies it was portrayed as half goat, with the tail of a fish. In early religious history the goat was a sacrificial animal. The Philistines connected Dagon, the half-fish god with Capricornus. The Babylonians connected the half-fish god, Oannes, with Capricornus.

## Biblical Correspondences

**Archangel:** Hanael. **Angel:** Saritiel. **Prophet:** Nathum. **Disciples:** Simon Peter and Thomas. **Tribe of Israel:** Zebulon. Capricorn is related to Nephtali, the son of Jacob.

## Stellar Symbols

The first decan of Capricorn is Sagitta, a heavenly arrow speeding to its aim. The second decan shows Aquila, *the pierced and falling eagle*. Its principal star is Al Tair meaning *the wounded*. The third decan to this sign is a beautiful cluster of stars named Delphinus or Dolphin, a vigorous fish springing upward.

## Anatomical Correspondences

The two words, *catabolism* and *metamorphosis*, adequately describe decay, death and rebirth, attributes of Capricorn, which also signifies contraction, limitation, dry epidermis, nucleolation, induration. The joints come under Capricorn's influence, particularly those of the knee and the patella bone, as well as the bony structure or skeleton generally, as indicated by Saturn. **Muscles:** The muscles of the knee. **Nerves:** Those in the knees. **Artery:** Those in the knees. **Veins:** Those running through the knees.

## Health

As Capricorn governs the epidermis, morbid action registers in skin diseases such as eczema, impetigo, pruritus; falls, bruises and dislocations are indicated, also hysterics, rheumatism and colds. Because of the tendency of this sign toward depression, melancholia, despondency, discontent, worry and nervousness, special attention should be given to transcending these tendencies. Cheerful company and comfortable, congenial surroundings are helpful. Heating and stimulating foods are usually required as well as those which are laxative. A fair amount of physical exercise is beneficial. Its herb is dock.

## Desirable Characteristics

Dignity, prudence, caution, reverence, practicality, thoughtfulness, particularity, diplomacy, profundity, positiveness, magnetism, ambition, organization, concentration, service.

## Undesirable Characteristics

Nervousness, limitation, conceit, jealousy, selfishness, discontention, capriciousness, suspicious, authoritativeness, gloominess, depression, avarice, impatience.

## Associations

Messiah, mediator, atoner, sexton, set, stone, priest, winters, Calvary, Golgotha, St.Peter, Simon Peter, church, Vatican, religion, cross, gates, groves, Janus, Naphtali (son of Jacob), Pan, Bacchus, Father Time, King Winter, Jack Frost, Dionysius, caper, Adolph.

Things ruled by Capricorn are: ice chests; leather for harness, belts, shoes; logs, old trees; coffins, ashes, stones, tile, cement, lime brick; ice, snow, frost; brimstone, rock salt; goats; bones, skeletons, knees, horns; quince, hemlock.

## Locations

Jails, cells, vaults, sepulchres, tombs, etc.; mangers, goat pens, corrals, etc.; thorny or barren ground; cellars, deep pits; frozen places, fallow ground, dungeons, convents, old churches, caves; thick, dark forests.

# AQUARIUS

## Classifications

Air triplicity, fixed quadrature. Moist, masculine, positive. Short ascension, southern. Sanguine, human, scientific, electric, serving, eloquent, intuitive.

## Planets

**Ruler:** Uranus. **Detriment:** The Sun. **Exaltation:** Uranus. **Fall:** Neptune.

## General Description

The Sun appears to transit through this sign between January 20 and February 18.

## Symbols

Aquarius is symbolized by the man emptying a waterpot. It is noticeable that in some of the Zodiacs he holds a rod, branch or wand in one uplifted hand. In some of the older Zodiacs Aquarius is pictured as a woman. This is interesting in connection with the prevailing thought that this is the woman's age or era. Always associated with Aquarius is the urn, or the cupbearer. The Hebrew name for Aquarius was Delphi or *water urn* signifying a pouring out or baptism, related to atonement. The waters poured by the heavenly man are the waters of life, the beneficence of fresh, sparkling water to parched mankind on earth.

## Biblical Correspondence

This is one of the four fixed signs constituting the Cherubim mentioned in the scriptures (Taurus, Leo, Scorpio and Aquarius). It is believed that it corresponds with Jacob's son, Reuben. It is also associated with John the Baptist. **Archangel**: Cambiel. **Angel**: Tzakmiqiel. **Prophet**: Habukkuk. **Disciple**: Matthew. **Tribe of Israel**: Reuben.

## Stellar Symbols

The first decan was the Southern Fish, Pisces Australis; the second decan, Pegasus, a great horse rushing forward with huge wings at his shoulders. The stars in the constellation are Markab, *the returning;* Scheat, *he who goeth and returneth;* Enif, *the branch;* Al Genib, *who carries;* Homan, *the waters;* Matar, *who causeth plenteous overflow.* The third decan is that of a beautiful swan, which, though injured, circles and mounts the Milky way; it lies in the midst of the great Galactic Stream of nebulous stars. The principal stars in its form a beautiful cross. Its brightest stars are Deneb, *The Lord Judge to come;* Azel, *who goes and returns;* Fafoge, *glorious;* Sadr, *who returns in a circle;* Adige, *flying swiftly;* Arided, *he shall come down.*

## Anatomical Correspondences

Aquarius rules the coccyx at the base of the spine, the calves and ankles, and the cones and rods in the eye. **Bones**: Coccyx, lower leg bones and shins. **Muscle**. Calf muscles, those in the ankles and shins. **Arteries**: Those in the lower leg. **Veins**: Those in the lower leg.

## Health

Aquarius inclines to falls, sprained, broken or swollen ankles, anemia, spasmodic and nervous diseases, blood poisoning, hay fever, heart weakness, cramps.

As Aquarius has much to do with the water in the bloodstream, the blood should be kept in good condition and any sign of impurity gives prompt remedial attention. Fresh air, good water, with plenty of vegetables and fruit are necessary, as well as music and harmonious surroundings. Brain and blood building foods are required, but stimulants and fat or greasy foods should be avoided. The eyes should be given proper care. Its herb is Dragonwort.

## Desirable Characteristics

Leadership, truthfulness, science, sincerity, earnestness, humane, co-operativeness, sociability, service, consideration, unbiasedness, patience, steadiness, invention, philosophy, intuition, pleasantness, progression, cosmopolitan.

## Undesirable Characteristics

Unnecessary radicalism, mental fanaticism, emphasizes ideas over feelings or non-rational subjective material, political extremism, derives enjoyment from shocking people, gullibility where social injustice is involved.

## Associations

Cup, water pot, Delee, Ganymede, fountain, Pacha, chief, Cygnus, smoke, steam, rain, ferries, bridges, railways, roundhouses, cars, airplanes, gas, motors, telephones, radios, electricity, wool, hair.

## Locations

Hilly and uneven places where rivulets run, near springs or conduits; vineyards; roofs of houses, eaves; highways, railroad crossings, stop signs; broadcasting stations, power lines, electric power houses, uranium mines, garages.

# PISCES

## Classifications

Water triplicity, mutable or flexed quadrature. Cold, moist, feminine, negative. Short ascension, eastern. Fruitful, lympatic, serving, psychic, emotional, inspirational, bi-corporal.

## Planets
**Ruler:** Neptune. **Detriment:** Mercury. **Exaltation:** Venus, Neptune's octave. **Fall:** Mercury.

## General Description
The Sun appears to transit Pisces between February 19 and Marh 20 annually.

## Symbols
Pisces is pictured by two fishes, one headed toward the north, the other parallel with the path of the Sun. They are some distance apart but bound together with the undulating band which falls upon the neck of Cetus the whale, and under the leg of the Lamb.

## Biblical Correspondences
**Archangel:** Amnitziel. **Angel:** Barchiel. **Prophet:** Joel. **Disciple:** The younger James. **Tribe of Israel:** Simeon. Ephraim, the son of Israel is associated with Pisces.

## Stellar Symbols
The first decan is the constellation named The Band. The second decan is the constellation Cepheus, the figure of the kind seated in repose in the attitude of power with one foot on the pole star; in one hand he holds aloft a sceptre, in the other he grasps the bands. The star on his right shoulder is Al Deramin, *quickly returning*; in the girdle is Al Phirk, *the redeemer*; in the left knee, the Shepherd. The north fish reaches right over into the third decan Andromeda, a woman in chains which are broken.

## Anatomical Correspondences
The feet and the toes come under the domain of Pisces, particularly the soles. Also the lymphatic system, all the extremities in general (for instance, the fingers, the tip of the nose and ears), the duodenum and the caecum. The Pisces-Virgo axis rules peristaltic action as well. **Bones:** Those in the feet and toes. **Muscles:** The muscles governing the movement of the feet and toes. **Arteries:** Those in the feet and the extremities. **Veins:** Those in the feet and the extremities.

## Health

Physical disturbances manifest through deformities of the feet and toes, bunions, gout, discharges, dropsy, glandular softening, lung trouble, bowel troubles; danger through contagious diseases and by the use of drugs.

As the recuperative power may be weak, attention to the rules of hygiene, dietand sanitation is necessary. There may be a tendency to take too much liquid; stimulating beverages should be avoided. It is said that the dandelion is very beneficial because of its tonic effect.

## Desirable Characteristics

Inspiration, idealism, concentration, hospitality, service, peace, refinement, purity, perception, psychometry, order, method.

## Undesirable Characteristics

Negativism, diffidence, dreaminess, lethargy, carelessness, indolence, indecisiveness, easy-going, improvidence, apologetic, submissiveness, variation, self-depreciation, inferiority complex, timidity, sensitiveness, self-pity, loyalty, criticism.

## Associations

Nuno, Picot, Okda, holy water, fish nets, boats, aquariums, submarines, deep sea divers.

## Locations

Oceans, fishing places, fish ponds, canneries; grounds overflowed with water, damp, wet, boggy places; places formerly under water; oil fields, oil tanks; spiritualistic churches, seances.

# Ascendants

The following delineations of the effect of Ascending Signs are for the signs alone without any planet in the First House. If any planet be therein it will modify these testimonies. A fortunate planet will increase the good and diminish the adverse qualities; vice versa if the planet be malefic.

The physical descriptions denoted by the Sign Ascending may be termed the ideal or normal, which may be expected from each sign. In actual practice, however, it will be observed that they frequently vary from the normal in some respects. The variations are mainly due to the effect of the sign in which is located the planet ruling the Ascending Sign; whether it be in one of similar or contrary nature; the nature of the planets strongly aspecting that significator, etc. Racial characteristics, hereditary peculiarities, early training, environment, occupational traits and geographical influences, all have some effect in molding the physiognomy.

The planet ruling the hour of birth also has considerable effect on the physical and mental make-up of a native.

## ARIES ASCENDING

### Personality

Those who are born at a time when the sign Aries is rising are at their best when they can guide, control and govern themselves or others, as they have the ability to plan and map out the future and lay out modes of action. They are lovers of independence, fond of their own way and happy only in activity and command. The desire is to be at the head of things and leaders in thought and action. They are enterprising and ambitious, quite versatile and usually rather headstrong and impulsive; forceful and determined in effort and expressive in speech; intense when interested, vehement when excited. Somewhat inclined to be fiery or quick-tempered and ready to resent abuse or imposition and although liable to go to extremes through indignation, they do not hold a grudge for any great length of time. They admire scientific thought and are quite philosophical; do not become discouraged easily as they possess a sharp, penetrating will power. They do best in vocations requiring quick action, decision, executive or mechanical ability and responsibility. Motive temperament. The planetary significator is Mars.

## Physical Appearance

Middle stature or rather above it, spare body, long face and neck, ruddy complexion, head broad at the temples and narrow at the chin, thin features, mark or scar on head or temples; bushy eyebrows, sharp sight, eyes gray to grayish brown; rough or wiry hair but sometimes fine in youth, varying in color from dark to sandy, sometimes going bald at the temples, sandy whiskers.

## Mental Tendencies

Ambition, activity, energy, courage, enterprise, impulsiveness, ardor, combativeness and ingenuity.

## TAURUS ASCENDING

### Personality

A self-reliant, persistent nature capable of working hard and long in order to accomplish their purposes. Gentle while unprovoked, but "mad as a bull" when really angered and when opposed are stubborn and unyielding. Usually quiet, dogmatic and somewhat secretive or reserved concerning their affairs. They have a great deal of endurance, latent power and energy; are practical and have organizing ability; usually sincere, reliable and trustworthy. They are fond of pleasure and love beauty in nature, art, music and literature; are influenced greatly by sympathy. Possessing a magnetic quality, they are able to benefit those who are irritable or nervous. They are careful, steady and able to carry to completion the projects they undertake. Have the ability to earn money for others and are good at all executive work. Matters connected with the earth and its products succeed under their supervision; vital temperament. The planetary significator is Venus.

## Physical Appearance

In stature short to middle height inclined to plumpness and often stoop-shouldered; square face and square build of body, short, strong neck, full forehead, nose, lips, cheeks and mouth; heavy jaw; dark eyes; hair wavy, dark and sometimes curling; round and prominent eyes; hands plump, short and broad.

## Mental Tendencies

Persevering, constant, conservative, determined, obstinate, proud and ambitious of power, yet sociable, affectionate and loving, but can also be very unreasonable, prejudiced and stubborn as a bull. When angry will not stop at anything. Usually slow, but good, steady worker. The undeveloped types are sometimes very indolent and sensual.

## GEMINI ASCENDING

### Personality

Ambitious, aspiring, curious and given to inquiry, investigation and experimenting; also apt, dexterous, active and capable of engaging in two or more pursuits at the same time. The nature is sympathetic and sensitive, the mind is intuitional, perceptive and imaginative, also quite idealistic and fond of all mental recreation. There is a liking for pleasure, adventure, science and educational pursuits. At times restless, anxious, high-strung and diffusive, mentally timid, indecisive, irritable and excitable. Love change and diversity and must be constantly busy to be happy, because inactivity creates impatience. As a rule Geminis are very clever as they are progressive, inventive, mechanical, ingenious and possess inherent conversational and literary ability. They do best in occupations where there is variety of activity, where the mind and hands can be engaged in several different things. The literary and educational world is their best outlet. Mental temperament. The planetary significator is Mercury.

### Physical Appearance

Tall, slender, erect but lithe figure; quick, active walk; long arms and fingers; thin features, long face, nose and chin; sanguine complexion; hazel or gray eyes; quick sight; dark hair, usually brown.

### Mental Tendencies

Quick at learning, fond of reading and writing, inquisitive, capable of acquiring a good education; dexterous, lively, ingenious, quick-witted; inclination and admiration for music, drawing, painting, languages, dancing, travel and invention. Sometimes shy or retiring, good disposition, humane. Nervous and restless.

## CANCER ASCENDING

### Personality

Changeable, sensitive and retiring disposition with many changes and ups and downs of position and occupation. They have a fertile imagination, are somewhat sentimental, sympathetic and talkative. Fond of home and family; have a tenacious memory, especially for family or historical events; industrious, frugal, economical and anxious to acquire the goods of life. Fear of ridicule or criticism makes them discreet, diplomatic and conventional. They appreciate approbation and are easily encouraged by kindness. The emotions are strong and they delight in beautiful scenery and in romantic or strange experiences and adventures. They have psychic and mediumistic faculty, are very conscientious, receptive to new ideas and have the ability to adapt themselves to environment. They are adapted to pursuits of a fluctuating nature, such as catering to public needs and desires. Vital temperament. The planetary significator is the Moon.

### Physical Appearance

Not usually above average height, tendency to stoutness, sometimes an awkward or heavy gait; round face, full cheeks, tendency to double chin, short nose sometimes prominent at the tip; gray or light blue eyes, pale complexion, wide chest, hands and feet small; uses crab-like positions and motions of the arms.

## Mental Tendencies

Fond of novelty, change and traveling, yet usually attached to relatives and home, inclined to public life. Desirous of possessions, cautious, prudent, careful with money yet often imposed upon; sympathetic and changeful. As a rule some psychic or occult faculty manifests.

# LEO ASCENDING

## Personality

Good-natured, philosophical, generous, kind-hearted, noble disposition. Leo natives are frank, free, outspoken, independent, impulsive, forceful and demonstrative in manner. Their nature is electric and inspiring. They have great hope, faith and fortitude; are energetic and lavish in the expenditure of energy and vitality when their sympathy or interest is aroused. In affection they are ardent, sincere and passionate. They are philanthropic, charitable, loyal, aspiring, conscientious, adaptable, inventive and intuitive; are imperious and fond of power and command; usually popular and leaders in their social sphere. They are generally good-tempered, though high-strung and quick to anger, yet are very forgiving and do not hold a grudge for long; high ideals. They receive and grant favors readily and are usually fortunate in the long run. They succeed best where they have authority or hold some high or responsible position in managing or executive departments. Motive temperament. The significator is the Sun.

## Physical Appearance

Broad shoulders, large bones and muscles, tall, upper part of body better formed than the lower, thin waist, prominent knees, upright carriage; hair soft and wavy, usually light in color with tendency to baldness; head full-sized and round, gray eyes, ruddy or florid complexion.

## Mental Tendencies

Ambitious, generous, honorable, frank, warm-hearted, self-confident, fearless, impulsive, determined persevering and conscientious; fond of power and distinction; liking for art, cheerful, optimistic disposition.

# VIRGO ASCENDING

## Personality

Modest, conservative, thoughtful, contemplative and industrious. Virgos have a desire for wealth but require extra effort to save money; are very active, not easily contented and learn readily and quickly; have good endurance and do not show their age. Of a speculative turn and often give way to worry and over-anxiety; are sensitive to surroundings and to the conditions of others. They are quite discriminative and careful of details. Cautious regarding their own interests and will not neglect the interests of others, being diplomatic, tactful and shrewd. They are prudent, economical, practical and usually act with forethought. The Virgo native should avoid drugs and animal foods as much as possible, and study hygiene in connection with diet to maintain health. Commercial and business affairs and matters connected with the earth and its products succeed under their careful supervision. Usually mental-motive temperament. The planetary significator is Mercury.

## Physical Appearance

Average height or a little above, moderately plump, well formed; oval face, dark hair, eyes and complexion; straight nose; active walk.

## Mental Tendencies

Fond of learning, active mind, good mental abilities, critical, thoughtful, methodical, ingenious; sometimes rather undecided but usually precise though nervous and lacking self-confidence.

# LIBRA ASCENDING

## Personality

Love justice, neatness and order, peace and harmony and are usually very courteous, pleasant and agreeable persons; although quick in anger, are easily appeased. They are fond of beauty in all forms: in nature, art, music, literature, etc., and can enter with zest into refined and cultural pleasures and amusements and greatly enjoy the company and society of brave, happy, sunny and mirthful people. They are affectionate, sympathetic, kind generous and compassionate; idealistic, artistic, adaptable, constructive, intuitive, impressionable and inspirational. They admire modesty and refinement; are ambitious but dislike unclean work and all discord. The best outlet for their talents is in the professions and they have ability for lines requiring good taste, artistic touch and fine finish. Mental-vital temperament. The planetary significator is Venus.

### Physical Appearance

Well-formed body, tall, slender in youth but tendency to stoutness in middle age; hair, smooth, brown to black, blue or brown eyes, Grecian nose, round or oval face, features regular, often have dimples, good-looking, youthful appearance, good complexion.

### Mental Tendencies

Good mental abilities, keen sense of perception with foresight and good comparison, imaginative or artistic, good-natured, hopeful, cheerful, genial, humane, just, orderly; usually amorous, loving but changeful, fond of society and amusements. Like to go places and do things, be in style or up-to-date. Fond of fine clothes and jewelry.

## SCORPIO ASCENDING

### Personality

Reserved, tenacious, determined and secretive, somewhat inclined to be suspicious or skeptical and stingingly sarcastic. They are quick-witted, quick in speech and action, alert, forceful and positive. They are often blunt, brusque and seemingly fond of contest; nevertheless they make staunch and splendid friends. They possess grit and enterprise that will enable them to reach high attainments. They accomplish their purposes by subtlety and strength of will, or by force if necessary. They have mechanical skill and much constructive (or destructive) ability.

They enjoy travel, are fond of investigating mysteries and things occult. Although appreciating luxury, can be very frugal and economical. They are natural detectives, sheriffs, bailiffs, chemists, surgeons and contractors and gifted in accomplishing things requiring muscular skill or aggressive enterprise. Motive-vital temperament. The planetary significator is Pluto.

## Physical Appearance

Average height or slightly below, tendency to stoutness or at least full form, often square type of face and build of body; thick, dark hair curling or wavy, sometimes crimpy or frizzy; prominent brows and perceptive faculties, aquiline or Jewish type of nose and profile, dusky complexion.

## Mental Tendencies

Quick, keen, shrewd, critical, penetrating mind and keen judgment. Strong will and determination; self-reliant, bold, fixed views. A subtle mind hard to influence, not easily imposed upon, willful, courageous, energetic and active when interested but at other times indolent. Sarcastic or impulsive and very angry when provoked. Frequently interested in some form of Occult or chemical research and fond of mystery. Some are very practical, matter-of-fact, executive, good businessmen, contractors, etc. They make good officers, naval men, workers with or dealers in liquids. Inclination to surgery or some practical scientific research or pursuit.

# SAGITTARIUS ASCENDING

## Personality

Inclined to be jovial, bright, hopeful, generous and charitable. Love liberty and freedom, are very independent, dislike a matter and will allow no one to order or drive them about but are usually good-humored and honorable. In disposition, frank, fearless, impulsive, demonstrative, outspoken, nervously energetic, ambitious, sincere and quick to arrive at conclusions. They are sympathetic and loving, possess good calculation and foresight, are intuitive and prophetic and, although often appearing blunt or abrupt, they rarely miss the mark in their deductions. At times they are restless, over-anxious and high-strung. They respect religious customs, enjoy outdoor sports, are fond of animals and interested in travel, law, medicine and philosophy. In the professions or commercial world Sagittarians are generally aggressive, progressive and aspiring, quick to see and take advantage of opportunities and to consummate business arrangements definitely. In speech they go straight to the point and aim directly at the mark. They like wholesale, big business and large financial undertakings. Motive-mental temperament. The planetary significator is Jupiter.

## Physical Appearance

Tall, slender, well-made figure inclined to stoop; generally long or oval face, rounded forehead, expressive blue or hazel eyes, clear complexion, hair brown or chestnut inclining to baldness especially near the temples; tendency to stamp or scrape the feet.

## Mental Tendencies

Generous, good-hearted, good-tempered, just, frank, free, cheerful, charitable and friendly; active and enterprising; sympathetic, humane and somewhat impulsive. Inclination for philosophy, law, medicine or religion; fond of traveling, voyaging and out-of-door sports and exercises.

# CAPRICORN ASCENDING

## Personality

Serious, quiet, thoughtful, contemplative nature, possessing dignity and self-esteem enough to look well after their interests. They are cautious, prudent, economical and practical and usually act only after due premeditation. They are ambitious and persevering and can work hard and long without becoming discouraged. Capable of much endeavor where opportunity is afforded, especially in business. They possess organizing ability and being determined and persistent, also cautious and calculating, of profound thought and concentrative ability, they are able to plan and carry out schemes of considerable magnitude. They are not demonstrative in feeling and do not readily show their sympathy; they prefer ideas to words and acts to promises. They are industrious, self-reliant and thrifty; respect religion, are given to investigation, interested in theology and become very profound in any subject or science undertaken. If Saturn, the significator, is much afflicted in the horoscope, they meet with many delays and disappointments and are inclined to give way too readily to adverse circumstances; also restricted by poor health. Otherwise they do well in matters connected with the earth and its products and with large corporations and public utility concerns. Motive or motive-mental temperament.

## Physical Appearance

Stature average to short; generally defective walk and liability to rheumatism in the joints or marks and scars about the knees; sometimes thin and bony; prominent features usually long and thin; long or prominent nose, thin neck, long chin, hair dark or black, not over plentiful, thin beard; usually not very handsome.

## Mental Tendencies

Self-willed, strong in purpose, ambitious, reserved, pensive and secretive. In disposition quiet, cold, sometimes despondent, much mental ingenuity and fertility, changeable, capricious, conniving and determined. A great desire for wealth, power, position and tendency to look out for themselves. Ability for managing and organizing. They succeed by perseverance and forceful, steady action, rather than by spasmodic effort.

# AQUARIUS ASCENDING

## Personality

Determined, quiet, patient, unobstrusive and faithful nature as a rule. Aquarians are philosophical, very humanitarian and usually refined; fond of art, music, scenery and literature. In disposition reasonable, thoughtful, discriminative. Have good memory, are clear reasoners and very capable of dealing with facts. Everything in the mental world appeals to them and they are sincere and practical, fond of honor and dignity, active in reforms, progressive in ideas and possess a sympathetic, good-hearted, pleasant, generous nature. Have strong likes and dislikes, usually sociable and of large acquaintance; intuitive, fond of Occult research; peculiar, radical or eccentric in some ways. They succeed in pursuits where steady application of mind and concentration of thought are necessary or where sociability and friends are required. They have inventive genius and literary ability. Mental-motive temperament. Uranus is the planetary significator.

## Physical Appearance

Middle stature, full or square build of figure, strong, well-formed, tendency to stoutness in middle age; good, clear complexion, oval or long, fleshy face; hair varies from light to dark, flaxen, brown, etc.; usually good-looking, friendly countenance.

## Mental Tendencies

Intelligent, good memory and reasoning faculty, very capable of dealing with facts; possess good concentration and appreciate knowledge. Kind, humane, self-controlled, constant, persevering, happy disposition; ingenious, inventive, sometimes incline to psychic or socialistic matters; love for humanizing influences, pursuits and occupations; often become physicians; have many friends.

## PISCES ASCENDING

## Personality

Kind, loving, trustful, confiding, sympathetic nature. The disposition is courteous, affable, hospitable and methodical. Pisces are idealistic, imaginative, impressionable, emotional, mediumistic, receptive and quiet. Apt in detail and orderly in manner. Quick to observe deficiencies in others or lack of completeness in anything. They are usually lacking in confidence and self-esteem, are modest and timid and hesitate about putting themselves forward. At times they are inclined to be over-anxious and become disheartened, indecisive and lacking in life and energy. Capable of developing fine psychometric, telepathic, intuitive and inspirational faculty. They love music, scenery and animals and usually succeed in occupations that require industry, discretion and power to make the best of circumstances and in any employment that brings some kind of change or where attention to details and completeness is necessary. Vital temperament. The planetary significator is Neptune.

## Physical Appearance

Middle to short stature with short limbs, inclining to corpulence especially in later years; full or fleshy face, pale complexion, tendency to double chin; full eyes, wide mouth, plentiful hair, dark brown to black, small hands and feet.

## Mental Tendencies

Quick in understanding, inspirational, versatile, easy-going, good-natured, uncertain, changeful, psychically receptive, emotional and fond of music; passionate, affectionate, charitable; sometimes reserved, secretive or mysterious in their way of doing things.

# The Planets

It is interesting to note that in everyday affairs we unconsciously employ astrological terms, as all words are originally the attempt to communicate in definite terms human urges or reactions to planetary influences.

In this chapter Llewellyn George carefully listed a number of words chosen for their relation to the planets. Only the more commonly used words were allocated, therefore the list is by no means complete and is subject to amplification. The words are arranged in alphabetical order under three headings: Characteristics, Occupations and Other. The sagacious student will find among these key words many which may be used effectively in horoscope delineations.

## THE MOON

People ruled by the Moon are usually sensitive, emotional and domesticated, possessing a love for home and kindred. They usually are posted regarding the family tree, are very patriotic and have a good memory for events in history. They are interested in public conditions of some sort or other. They are very sympathetic and the women are easily led to tears. Having a fertile imagination and being also very conscientious, they meet with many ups and downs in life. They are quite receptive or mediumistic and frequently possess musical talent. They like water and natural beauty and should never live for long in a dry, barren place.

When undeveloped, that is, unenlightened, they may be either too "easy-going" and given to self-gratification and over-indulgence in eating, drinking or pleasure, or are too changeable, negative and uncertain.

In Astrology we refer to the Moon as being cold, moist, feminine, fruitful and convertible in character; that is, being fortunate or unfortunate according to its position and aspects in the horoscope.

It rules public or common commodities such as groceries, liquids, etc., that pertain to the domestic side of life. Monday is the day of the Moon; metal: silver.

The Moon exerts considerable influence over the general or ordinary and common affairs of daily life. It makes a complete transit of the Zodiac every 27 days, 7 hours and 43 minutes. In other words, it makes one complete revolution through the horoscope of every individual in that length of time. As it passes through the various houses and forms the different aspects to the planets' places at birth, it produces conditions, events, feelings and states of mind or health accordingly. As no two horoscopes are exactly alike, the Moon's monthly transit produces all manner of varying conditions.

## Characteristics

Adaptable, agreeable
Beaming
Changeable
Domestic, dreamy
Emotional
Feminine, frivolous, fruitful
Generative
Inconsistent
Maternal, mobile, moist, moody
Nocturnal
Pale, passive, peaceful
Queer, quiet
Rambling, receptive, restless
Serene
Tender, timid
Vacillating, vulgar
Weak

## Occupations
Baker
Caterer, cook
Fisherman
Gardener, grocer
Janitor
Laundry-worker
Maritime worker, midwife, milk deliverer
Navigator, nurse
Obstetrician
Restaurant worker
Scrubber, security guard
Waiter, washer

## Other
Baby, baptize, bathroom, boat, breasts
Cabbage, canal, cheese, china, conception, crescent, crying
Dock, duck
Eel, evening
Faint, family, fermentation, fish
Geese, glass, groceries
Harbor, hen, home, hotel
Infant
Juice
Kitchen
Lady, lake, lighthouse, liquid, luncheon
Mammal, melon, menses, milk, month, mother, mushroom
Night, nutrition
Omen, owl, oyster
Phantom, plastic, pond, the public
Queen
Rabbit, reflector, restaurant, river
Saloon, shellfish, silver, sleep, snail, stomach
Tides, turtle
Umbilical
Voyage
Wake, water, willow, womb, women
Youngster

## MERCURY

In Astrology the influence of the planet Mercury is known to be variable, convertible, neutral and dualistic. That is, it expresses a nature in accordance with the character of the planet which it aspects: benefic when with fortunate planets or when in favorable aspect, and malefic otherwise.

Mercury has particular influence over the nervous system, bowels, hands, arms, shoulders, collar-bone, tongue, sense of sight, perception, understanding, interpretation and expression.

Persons who respond to Mercury as a ruling planet are active-minded, quick to discern, eager to acquire knowledge, fond of investigation, inquiry, research, exploration and are usually much given to reading. If Mercury is well placed in the horoscope at birth they are fully capable of maintaining any position where adaptability, dexterity, perception, skill, quick wit, imagination and good memory are required. They usually conduct their work in an orderly, methodical, systematic and handy manner, being adept at simplifying arrangements.

But when Mercury is ill placed at birth and afflicted the native has the same inclinations as those just mentioned but not the expert power of execution and they carry out ideas rather than create them.

When Mercury is afflicted it inclines to excessive nervous activity both of body and mind, and unless controlled by will power the tendency is to worry, haste and irritability, which inclines to mistakes, forgetfulness and controversy.

The influence of the afflicted Mercury may be much improved by cultivating continuity, concentration, deliberation and patience.

Among the ancients, Mercury was known as Thoth, Hermes and the Messenger of the Gods. Its speed in orbit is approximately 95,000 miles per hour. It was usually portrayed as a youth, flying with wings at his heels, bearing a caduceus made of olive wood about which were twined two serpents, the rod being surmounted with a pair of wings. This symbol well represents the essential qualities of the planet: duality, speed and wisdom. It is noticed that Mercurial people have a youthful appearance.

### Characteristics
Adroit, alert, analytical

Cheating, clever, critical, cunning
Debating, dexterous, diplomatic
Eloquent
Fanciful, forgetful
Glib
Handy
Imaginative, inconsistent, ingenious, intellectual
Juvenile
Literate
Meddling, mediating, memorizing, mental
Neurotic
Perceiving, persuasive, perverting, petty
Restless
Sensitive, shifting, shrewd, skillful, speedy, stammering, subtle
Talkative, thinking, trembling
Understanding
Variable, versatile
Witty
Youthful

## Occupations

Accountant, advertiser, architect, astronomer
Bookkeeper
Child monitor, clerk
Distributor
Educator
Graphologist, grocer
Handyman
Interviewer, interpreter
Journalist
Lecturer, linguist
Mail carrier, merchant, messenger
Orator
Printer, publisher
Reporter
Secretary, storekeeper
Teacher, tennis player, translator, typist
Writer

## Other

Account, acoustics, agreement, ant, arm, autograph
Bargain, book, bowels, brothers
Cereal, communication
Diary, diet, double
Education, errand, essay
Fingers, fox
Greyhound
Hare, herald, hound, hygiene
Illusions, imagination, imbecile, information, inquiry
Journal, journey, juggle
Kernel, kin
Language, lilac, literature
Mail, merchandise, mimicry, mischief, monkey
Neighbors, nerves, newspaper, number
Observation, opinion
Pair, paper, parrot, parsley, pen, perjury
Question
Record, relate, rumor
School, shoulders, sisters, squirrel
Telegram, theory, thermometer, thought, tongue, travel, twin
Wednesday, wheat, words
Youth

# VENUS

Venus is fruitful and productive, and is called a feminine planet as she governs the gentler and more refined attributes. Men and women ruled by this planet are noticeably kind or sociable.

When well aspected in a chart Venus endows the native with a pleasant or handsome countenance, symmetrical form and graceful manners. Inclines to harmony, and as she rules the sense of touch, favors art, music and decoration. By their pleasing personality the subjects of Venus are natural peacemakers; their refined natures soften the ruffled feelings of friends and convert anger to pleasure. As Venus is the promoter of pleasure these people are splendid entertainers and excellent hosts.

When adversely aspected in the horoscope of birth she bestows less beauty and the native is apt to cultivate the social and pleasure-giving tendencites to an extent which is detrimental to other interests, for when living too much on the personal plane the real, or finer, attributes are submerged and the emotions dominate.

When afflicted Venus produces unsatisfactory domestic conditions, anxiety in love, difficulty with friends or through finances. She rules the skin, throat, veins, ovaries and internal generative organs, and these are adversely affected by over-indulgence in amusements, eating and drinking.

Venus aids the faculties of comparison and perception as related to order, form, size, weight, color, tune and time. Also acts on conjugality, amorousness, friendship, mirthfulness and agreeableness. On the days when Venus is well aspected by the Moon or other planets, the activities of those faculties are accentuated and manifest the best of which the native is then capable, according to the moral status or soul unfoldment, and they are conversely affected in the same manner when Venus is afflicted by transit or by directions in the progressed horoscope.

Venus is feminine in nature. She rules the sense of touch and has much to do with the disposition. She inclines to all that appertains to the higher attributes of the mind: music, singing, poetry, painting, drama and all refined amusements and adornment. She is beneficial and fruitful and expresses through the character of an individual by generosity, good humor and love. Colors are all the pastel shades and especially the clear blue of turquoise; some also give to Venus the clear red of crimson. Metal: copper.

## Characteristics

Affectionate, amiable, amorous, artistic
Beautiful, benign
Calm, cheerful, clean, compassionate, courteous
Delicate, dissolute
Elegant, erotic
Feminine, flirting, foundling, frivolous, fruitful
Genteel, gentle, graceful
Immaculate, immodest, immoral, indolent, indulgent
Kind

Laughing, lazy, lenient, lewd, loving, luxurious
Mirthful, modest
Normal, nourishing
Peaceful, pleasing, plump, poetical
Queenly
Refined, rejoicing
Sensual, sociable, soothing, sympathetic
Tame, tender
Untidy
Warm
Yielding

## Occupations

Artist
Beautician
Dancer, dramatist, dressmaker
Entertainer
Florist
Gardener
Haberdasher, hotel keeper, horticulturist
Jeweler
Milliner, musician
Opera singer
Tailor, theatre worker
Vocalist

## Other

Adolescent, adultery, amusement, approval
Balm, bedroom, bridal
Calf, candy, caress, clothing, club, copper, courtship
Deer, dimple, dining, dolphin, dove, drama, dude
Embellishment, emerald, engagement
Fair, Friday, furnishings
Garden, gem, gown
Honeymoon, hussy
Jewelry
Lady, leisure, loins, luxury
Marriage, maiden, matinee, myrtle

Neck, negligee, nosegay
Orchestra, ovaries
Party, partridge, peach, perfume, picnic, plum
Quinsy
Rose
Sapphire, sheik, society, sofa, song, swan
Thanks, throat, tint
Unify, upholstery
Vacation, vineyard, violet
Wardrobe, warm, wedding, wine
Yarrow

# THE SUN

The Sun apparently passes through all the signs of the Zodiac in one year, leaving one sign and entering the next about the 21st day of each month. The Sun is always on the ecliptic, therefore, void of latitude. It rules the sign Leo and has but one sign for its home.

If not hampered by unfavorable aspects from other planets, and dignified by position in the horoscope, the Sun bestows a nature which is ambitious, proud, (but seldom admitting it) magnanimous, frank, generous, humane, firm and honorable. Leo natives aspire to positions of rulership and by their earnest nature inspire others with a respect for their abilities, so they usually attain positions of trust, responsibility and honor where they are perfectly at home and capable of practical execution to a very satisfactory degree.

But when the Sun at birth is unfavorably aspected and otherwise undignified the native is inclined to be too forceful, lordly, domineering, positive, arrogant and extravagant, inclining, also, to sickness of a feverish, inflammatory nature, eye afflictions and heart disorders, as well as losses of position, credit or esteem due to impulsiveness.

All the adverse testimonies, particularly those owing their origins to the mind and physical condition can be corrected and greatly improved by studying psychology and by taking a deep interest in advanced thought, subjects with a view to unfolding latent qualities, developing self-control and harmonizing the environmental conditions. The early morning sunshine should be sought, the heat of day avoided. When making conscious effort along constructive lines, Leo people will find frequent exercise conducive to inspiration, vigor and harmony. Many important events will occur on Sundays.

The Sun by nature is hot, dry, masculine and life-giving. It has much to do with health and the vital principle. It has dominion over the individual progress and social success. It rules positions of rank and title and high office generally. In the human anatomy it governs the sides, back, heart, right eye of the male and left eye of the female.

## Characteristics
Absurd, ambitious, ardent, arrogant, authoritarian
Boastful, bombastic, brilliant
Candid, charitable, commanding, condescending
Dignified, disdainful, dry
Egotistical, energetic
Famous
Gaudy
Haughty, healing, honorable, hot
Illustrious, imperialistic, inflammatory, influential
Kind
Loyal, luminous
Magnanimous, majestic
Omniscient, optimistic
Prominent, proud
Radiant
Scrupulous, stimulating, sumptuous
Vigorous, virile
Warm, wasteful
Zealous

## Occupations
Actor
Biologist
Healing professions
Leader
Park attendant, playground director
Supervisor
Theatre worker

**Other**

    Ablaze, alive, amber, animation
    Ballroom, boss
    Cardiac, central, circle, coliseum, conscience, cooperation
    Daylight, desert, dictator, diurnal
    Elevate, exalt
    Faith, flame, flaxen, fire, frankincense
    Game, gift, glow, gold, grand, grant
    Halo, health, heart, heat, helium, honor, hope
    Joy, juniper
    King, kingdom
    Light, lion, living
    Mansion, mid-day, marigold, monarch, myrrh
    Noon, nucleus
    Orange
    Palace, peacock, president, prince
    Quality, queen
    Radiation, rank, recuperation, respect, rosemary, ruler
    Salamander, spirit, starfish, sunburn, Sunday, sunstroke
    Theatre, throne
    Walnut

# MARS

Mars is significant of energy, the form that energy assumes depending upon its position, aspects and location in the horoscope. Manifests as hot, dry and masculine and has much to do with the ambitions, desires and animal nature.

People ruled by Mars are noticeably ambitious, positive and fond of leadership. Being quite inventive and mechanical they become good designers, builders and managers and usually make their way to the front in whatever they undertake.

Being averse to the dictatorship of others and unhappy in subordinate positions, they usually find the best outlet for their special abilities when in business for themselves or in positions where they can direct the work of others.

On the undeveloped plane they are the cruel boss, the domineering husband or wife. But when intelligently enlightened and spiritually inclined they are excellent healers and teachers and may be found at the foremost of movements for the advancement of public welfare.

Mars has a two-year cycle, and every 15 years Mars reaches its least distance from the earth, i.e., about 36,000,000 miles, when it shines with a splendor like that of beautiful Venus.

Mars rules strength, force and courage. Its manifestation is con-structive or destructive, according to the nature of the aspect and what use an individual makes of the vibrations as compared to his desires, the nature or quality of effort and degree of his understanding.

Anatomically considered, Mars governs the external sex organs, muscular system, head, face, left ear, sense of taste and the bladder, and these parts are the most readily affected with disease when the health has been abused or neglected. Mars predisposes one to injuries through accidents and hurts by cuts, burns, scalds, surgery, firearms, etc., and to feverish or inflammatory complaints. Metals governed by Mars are iron and steel.

## Characteristics

Abusive, aggressive, angry, antagonistic
Bellicose, boastful, bold, brave
Caustic, combative, compelling, courageous
Daring, defiant, destructive, disruptive, dreadful
Energetic, exciting
Feverish, fiery, forceful, furious
Headstrong, hostile
Impulsive, industrious, inflammable, invincible
Keen
Loud, lusty
Muscular
Obscene, obstinate, oppressive
Poignant, positive
Quarrelsome, quick
Reckless, resentful, resourceful, ribald, rough
Sensual, sharp, stimulating
Turbulent
Uncouth, urgent

Valiant, victorious
Willful

## Occupations
Athlete
Barber, bootlegger, builder, butcher
Carpenter, construction worker
Dentist, designer
Engineer, executive
Firefighter, foundry worker
Garbage collector, guard, gunner
Jailer
Locksmith, lumberjack
Machinist, manager, mechanic
Police officer, prizefighter
Saw-filer, salesperson, steel worker, soldier, surgeon
Wrestler

## Other
Accident, action, arena, armor, army
Battle, bile, bladder, burn
Cannon, cayenne, chimney, contagion, crime, crow
Danger, dart
Eagle
Fever, file, forge, friction
Gamecock, guns
Hardware, hawk, house
Iron, implement
Junk
Knife
Lamb
Measles, missile, motion, mustard
Nail, navy, needle
Onion, operation
Panther, puncture
Radish, ram, rape, rash, razor, red, regiment, rifle
Scar, scorpion, steel
Thistle, tiger, torture, Tuesday, turbine

Violence, vivisection
War, weapon, wolf

# JUPITER

The typical Jupiter native is usually termed jovial owing to the fact that Jupiter gives such characteristics as sociability, hope, benevolence, veneration, compassion, justice, honesty, spirituality, also well developed faculties of proportion, calculation and location. The Jupiter person is usually quick to hit the mark, as his symbol is The Archer, and they love out-of-doors exercises; in fact, he requires considerable such recreation if he would overcome uneasiness and develop poise.

In the business world they become interested in large popular enterprises. Science and medicine, insurance and commercial traveling, often engage their attention, also affairs of philanthropic, charitable, religious or benevolent import, as well as other matters in the professional world.

Jupiter is termed "the greater fortune," and indeed, he seems well named, for, unless Jupiter is ill placed in the horoscope, he bestows a that sign, who are usually fitted for positions of dignity, trust or power in business and social circles. Having a logical, broad mind, considerable self-possession, self-confidence and determination, they usually inspire confidence and attain responsible positions.

If Jupiter is not dignified or if adversely aspected in the horoscope it causes restlessness and uncertainty, giving liability to losses through midjudgment, unfortunate speculation, investments and trusts.

Jupiter in nature is said to be warm, moist, sanguine, temperate, social, expansive, masculine and moderate. Has dominion over the blood, liver, veins, arteries and thighs. Rules higher education and philosophic reasoning. If in a person's birth chart Jupiter is unafflicted, the native will be a good, sound and correct reasoner, whereas, if it is ill-dignified or badly aspected, will often exhibit poor, uncertain and unreliable judgment.

## Characteristics
Abundant, affluent, ample, auspicious
Benevolent, big

Careless, charitable, comfortable, correct, costly
Dull
Erroneous, excessive, expansive, expensive, exorbitant, extravagant
Formal, flourishing
Gluttonous
Hazardous, honest, hospitable, huge, humorous
Illicit, immense, indulgent
Jovial, judicious, just
Lavish, lucrative
Magnificent
Noble
Peaceful, philanthropic, philosophical, professional
Rational, reckless, religious, respectable, rich
Sporting, successful
Tactful, temperate, thriftless, truthful
Unimpeachable
Valuable
Wholesome

## Occupations

Academician, ambassador, appraiser, archer
Banker, barrister, broker
Cashier
Diplomat
Financier
Gambler, golfer
Hunter
Judge, jockey
Lawyer
Minister
Physician
Scholar

## Other

Abscess, apoplexy, aristocrat
Bishop, blood, boil, bond
Ceremony, collegiate, customary
Default, development, disburse

Finances
Gambling, goodwill, growth
Hale, ham, heir, hips
Income, inherit, insurance, interest
Jubilee, judgment, jury
Knowledge
Legacy, legal, leisure, litigation, liver
Maximum, millionaire
Official, opportune, ordain
Precious, profit, prosperity
Quality, quantity
Race horse, ransom, right, rubber
Shares, smell, success, supply, surplus, stocks
Tallow, thigh, thunder, Thursday, tin, tour, treasury, truth
Value, voyage
Wager, wart, wealth, whale, winnings

# SATURN

The influence of Saturn is commonly called evil, and in this respect it is much maligned, as in reality there is no evil, since all things work together for good ultimately. Saturn acts as a deterrent and because it brings denial and necessity into some lives, has been considered an oppressor, a Satan. "He that filleth with pride will suffer a fall," for Saturn will bring him to his knees, humble his nature, and by means of restrictions, limitations and adversities, will cause the individual to ponder, study and seek to find the source of woe, that in the future it may be overcome. Thus, while Saturn is a destroyer (of false ideals), it is also a redeemer, in that it brings the mind to a state of introspection and stimulates effort toward perfection and victory.

Persons born with Saturn well placed and aspected in their horoscope have a serious and practical nature; they are wisely economical, prudent, conservative, executive and profound, being good organizers and managers. Their special ability depends upon which planet most strongly and favorably aspects Saturn in the chart.

Saturn children are extremely sensitive, but they hide their feelings and emotions under a mask of reserve. If frequently censured they withdraw from association and their progress and development are much delayed.

When adversely aspected in a chart, Saturn does indeed seem to produce a train of adversities, for delays, restrictions, disappointments and sorrow are plentiful and usually these lead to misery, poverty and ill-health.

Saturn governs the knees, teeth, spleen and bones, and these parts are most readily afflicted when any inharmony prevails. At his influence is cold and dry, heat and moisture are the antidotes. For the native of Saturn, critical and important years are those in which Saturn will transit in adverse aspect to his radical place, that is, between the years 14 to 15, 21 to 22, 29 to 30, 36 to 37, 44 to 45, 51 to 52, 59 to 60, etc. Avoid new undertakings during these periods, rest as much as possible, seek the society of cheerful people and live in a light, airy, new place. Persistent metaphysical treatment, cheerful associates and environment will do much to overcome the adverse effects of Saturn's influence.

## Characteristics

Afraid, aged, apprehensive, ascetic, astringent, austere
Bitter
Calculating, callous, chronic, cold, conservative, contemplative
Deficient, depressed, discrete, doleful, dry
Earthly, economical
Faithful, firm, frigid
Glum, grasping, grievous
Haggard, harsh, heavy
Immovable, inscrutable, introspective
Jealous
Laborious
Malevolent, materialistic, methodical, miserly, morose
Needy, nonchalant
Obnoxious, old
Patient, poor, practical, prudent, punctual
Querulous, quiet
Realistic, retarded
Scrupulous, secretive, sober, sordid, sour, stiff, stoic, suspicious
Taciturn, tardy, tense, thin, tight, tired, tranquil

Vested
Weary

## Occupations

Cement worker, coal miner
Farmer, framer
Hearse driver
Leather worker
Mason
Priest, prison worker
Refrigeration worker
Tanner, timekeeper
Undertaker

## Other

Acoustic, adhesive, agriculture, ash, astringent, atrophy
Ballast, bankrupt, basic, bones, brick
Calendar, carbon, cave, clock, coal, continuity, crystallization
Debt, decay, delay, destroy, doom, drudge
Emaciation, embargo, envy, ephemeris
Failure, famine, fear, firm, foundation, frigid, funeral
Garter, gather, glue, goat, gravel
Harness, hate, heap, hearing, hearse, heavy, hireling
Ice, inert, inside
Jackass, join, junction
Keep, kill, knees, knot
Labor, lack, land, late, leather, lime, limitation
Matrix, mines, misfortune, monument, morgue, mortgage, mum
Necessity, no, nunnery
Paralysis, past, permanence, pottery, prison
Quarry, quit
Ranch, rheumatism, rocks, ruin
Sedative, sepulchre, skeleton, soot, space, spleen
Taint, tan, tar, task, teeth, terror, threadbare
Underneath, uphold, urn
Valley, vault, vow
Wall, wedge, wintry, woe
Yeoman, yesterday, yoke

# URANUS

Those who are born during that period of the year ruled by Uranus, or who have Uranus strongly posited in their horoscope, are usually attracted to some form of Occult research; in fact, they are reformers and pioneers in advanced lines of thought. It often makes one appear odd, eccentric or peculiar and said to be living ahead of their time. It attracts one to such subjects as astrology, phrenology, occultism, mesmerism, magnetic healing, telepathy, electricity, inventions, Free Masonry, etc; it predisposes to the antiquated, curious, new, odd and everything out of the ordinary.

When Uranus is well aspected by other planets in the nativity, it endows the native with strong intuitive tendencies, giving also metaphysical and inventive ability. With keen foresight they can predict the outcome of business or the results of action quickly and with considerable accuracy in a manner not dependent upon the reasoning process, but by *knowing*. They have strong and constructive imagination and can see a way to improve upon almost everything. Their premonition and intuition guide them in the path of progress and freedom.

When Uranus is adversely aspected in the horoscope it gives all the aforementioned intuitive activity and inventive genius, but it inclines to make one overforceful, abrupt, brusque, erratic, willful, sarcastic and easily offended and the native is liable to accidents through explosions, electricity or vehicles of transportation. All the mental malformations can be improved and accidents avoided by those who firmly unite effort with aspiration. Great aid in this matter may be obtained by finding the dates on which Uranus is adversely aspected and care then taken to maintain poise and self-control and to avoid risks with the things which Uranus rules.

The planet Uranus makes a complete transit of the zodiacal circle every 84 years. It requires about seven years for Uranus to pass through each sign.

The nature of Uranus is cold, dry, airy, positive, magnetic, strange, Occult and malefic. It inclines to acts without premeditation. It governs the faculties of curiosity, invention and investigation and all things of a curious or wonderful nature; modernistic art. It rules the ankles and the intuitive intellect. Its metals are platinum, aluminum, uranium, radium, and also has dominion over wireless and radio-active elements.

## Characteristics

Abnormal, abrupt, acute, adventurous, antiquarian, audacious
Bizarre, brusque
Clairvoyant, communistic, contrary, cooperative
Defiant, dire, disruptive, drastic
Electric, erratic, explosive
Fanatic
Garish, grotesque
Humanitarian
Illegitimate, incompatible, ingenious
Kinetic
Lawless, liberal
Magnetic, meddlesome, modern
Nonconformist
Original
Paradoxical, peculiar, premature
Quaint
Radical, raving, rejecting, roving
Spasmodic, spectacular
Telepathic, turbulent
Uncertain, unconventional
Vibrant
Whimsical

## Occupations

Astrologer, auto mechanic
Broadcaster
Distributor, dynamiter
Electrician
Humanitarian
Inventor
Lineman
Metaphysician, motorman
Telegrapher, tractor driver
X-ray technician
Zoo keeper

## Other

> Abortion, air, alarm, ankles, aura
> Battery, bicycle, bomb, brotherhood
> Colonize, commoner, crisis, cyclone
> Detour, disaster, divorce
> Earthquake, electronics, emancipation
> Firecracker, flying, freedom, freelance
> Garage, gases, generator
> Hangar, hobo
> Illegal
> Kilowatt
> Liberty, lightning
> Magnetic, microscope, mutiny
> Outlaw
> Panic, pioneer, prodigy
> Quest
> Radioactive, revolt
> Satire, separation, shock
> Tantrums, telescope, tornado, trespass
> Uranium
> Vapor
> Whim, whirlwind
> Zealot, zigzag

# NEPTUNE

The influence of Neptune upon humankind is that of a mediumistic order and those who are responsive to the vibrations of this mysterious planet are often subject to queer and indefinable feelings, sensations and emotions.

At times it produces negative states in which the subject takes on the influence of surrounding conditions either consciously or unconsciously and acts or feels, for the time being, in harmony with the nature of persons contacted.

When this planet is well aspected in a horoscope, the native is endowed with aspiration and correct premonitions and is apparently often directed to do just the right thing, or to be in just the right place at opportune times.

Such persons are frequently clairvoyant and have feelings about things which should be carefully analyzed as Neptune gives psychometric faculty which can be developed to so fine an order that its subjects can give truly interesting facts through the sense of touch and feeling, when handling an article for that purpose. They can also very correctly interpret dreams if they make a careful study of that subject. It usually bestows some artistic gift, which is susceptible to high development.

In fact, briefly stated, Neptune represents inspiration, psychometry, mediumship and inner feeling, as Venus, its octave, rules touch or outer feeling. It rules things or conditions of a mysterious, hidden nature, such as seances, "silence" meetings or affairs of a secret order. Its influence is considered neutral, because the character of its expression is dependent upon the quality of the aspects made with other planets and its position in sign and house of the horoscope. It represents the feet in the human organism, but in its esoteric sense it governs the very base of understanding and knowledge of things as they are and not as they seem to be.

When Neptune is found adversely located and aspected in a chart, it leads to over-receptivity, inertness and states too negative and passive, which result in various ills or defects of character, allowing weakness to temptations when strength and resistance are most needed. The emotions seem to predominate, which, if allowed to run into extremes, produce unnatural appetites, changefulness, uncertainty, indolence, vague imagination, intrigues and confusion, bringing troubles through schemes, plots, deception and secret enmities.

When well aspected Neptune bestows some gift, but when afflicted it gives some weakness which should be discovered early in life and properly transmuted. With Neptune afflicted, the native, being quickly affected by the environment mentally and physically, should investigate the philosophy of all things mysterious before trying the phenomena.

The planet Neptune seems to be in a nebulous state and its influence appears to be more psychic than physical or material. It represents spirit feeling, sensing or inner perception. It governs the receptive faculties. Its nature is neutral and spiritual (not necessarily from a religious standpoint). It is not known to rule any metal, mineral or other material substance as do the other planets, but is related to gas, drugs, chemicals and anesthetics. It is dualistic in character; on the one hand it may represent chaos, and on the other, fine spiritual insight. It has affinity for oil, liquids, beverages, tobacco and the sea; impressionistic art.

## Characteristics
Abstract, adaptable, assuming
Beguiling, bewildering
Cataleptic, counterfeit
Distraught, dreamy, doubtful
Elusive, emotional, exceptional, exotic
Fanciful, formidable
Gullible, glamorous
Hysterical
Idealistic, imaginative, indulgent
Limpid
Mediumistic, mysterious
Naive, nebulous, nude
Obscure
Poetical, psychic
Questionable
Receptive
Scheming, spiritual
Toxic, tranquil
Uncanny, undulating
Vacillating, vague, visionary
Weird, whimsical

## Occupations
Alchemist
Bootlegger
Diver
Irrigation worker
Marine, medium
Oil fields worker
Poet, psychic
Sea farer, sorcerer, submariner
Yogi

**Other**
>Alcohol, alibi, astral
>Bath, beach, bribery, bogus
>Camouflage, coma, communism, confusion, conspiracy
>Defile, delusion, dike, dive, dope
>Engulf, ether, evade
>Fantasy, fiddle, film
>Gasoline, gelatin, graft
>Hallucination, harem, hydraulics, hypodermic
>Incense, irrigate, intrigue
>Kelp, kerosene
>Liquid, lure
>Moron, morphine
>Narcotic, nautical, nymph
>Obsession, ocean, oil, opiate
>Poison, pool, pretence, prophecy
>Quack
>Rendezvous
>Scandal, seclusion, seduce, seer, siren, swim
>Tangle, tea, trance, tobacco
>Utopia
>Vapor
>Wade, waves, wet
>Yacht, yeast

# PLUTO

At the time of the writing of the original edition of the *A to Z* in 1910, Pluto had not yet been discovered. After its discovery in 1930 Llewellyn George made revisions in his text to accommodate this new planet, relying heavily upon classical mythology.

In mythology Pluto was the god of the outer regions, the ruler of the dead. In no sense was he depicted as a tempter or seducer of mankind, like the devil of Christian theology. Pluto was certainly depicted as stern and pitless, but he was only so in discharge of his duty as custodian of the dead.

Pluto is called masculine, stern, somewhat inscrutable, not itself malignant but dealing with high potencies; invoked by or responsive to music, especially the kind of music called "jazz."

Pluto rules the underworld, the subconscious workings of the body, the fluxing influences, the contest between acid and alkali; the fusing actions; burning out of dross material; all those processes whose transmuting actions tend to regenerate the body; to sustain, repair, renew or perpetuate it through the burning up and casting out of dead material—from death to life. It also rules conscience, that inner prompter which helps us judge right from wrong, subconscious activities, the underworld, stern, incorruptible judges. Its keywords are: regeneration, levitation, transformation, materialization, metamorphosis, transfiguration.

The good aspects to Pluto favor the discovery of error, detection of injustice. Revitalizing ideas and incidents which tend to promote health, preserve life and encourage freer expression of the subconscious activities are probably due to Pluto's vibrations.

The adverse aspects to Pluto incline to inversion of its better qualities, low morality, lack of conscience, indecency, disrespect of law, underworld proclivities.

## Characteristics

Anonymous
Betraying
Callous, corrupt, covert
Defiant, degenerate, depraved, destroyer
Enigmatic
Fiendish, foul
Grave, guilty
Indifferent, insatiable, inscrutible, immoral, immortal
Lawless
Nefarious
Obscene, odious, outrageous
Passionate, putrid
Rotting
Sadistic, sardonic, severe, sexual, sinister, subnormal
Taciturn, terrible, terse
Unscrupulous, ungodly, unknown
Vindictive

Wasteful, wicked

## Occupations
Gunner
Psychoanalyst

## Other
Abyss, atlas, ambush, amnesia, atom bomb
Brimstone
Chasm, conscience, covert, crematory, criminal
Defiance, demon, dice
Erase, evolution
Felon, fumigate
Hag, holocaust, hoodlum
Kidnap
Loot, lust
Magic, marsh, menace, monster
Null
Pollute, purgatory
Racketeer, recuperation, regimentation, reproduction
Scavenger, sewer, siren, spoil, steel, swamp
Transformer
Underworld
Vampire, vanish, vermin, victim, virus

# The Planets in the Signs

## THE MOON

### The Moon in Aries

Strong imagining faculty, positive, forceful, masterful, independent, self-reliant, courageous and practical. Enthusiastic in whatever line is of interest at that time; changeable, restless, uneasy and dislikes to be ordered about or held to any one line. Generally quick-tempered, inclined to be persistent, impulsive and aggressive. Imbued with activity, energy, enterprise, originality and inventive ability. Fond of traveling and of original and independent ventures. Will attempt to hew out a path of their own and apt to be at the head of some undertaking or in some way prominent in their sphere of influence. If afflicted, some danger of drowning and trouble through women, changes of occupation and position. Indicates aches or pains in the head.

### The Moon in Taurus (Exaltation)

This bestows a courteous and affable disposition inclined to friendship, love and marriage. Determined, and not to be thwarted in their aims. The nature is conservative and resists forced changes or outside influences. Hopeful, ambitious and desirous of excelling. Good hearted, sympathies easily aroused. Tends to the acquisition of friends, possessions, houses and lands. Favors occupations connected with the

223

earth and its products and all dealings in such things; success in chemistry or hygiene, in business and in places near the water; sometimes assistance in a financial or business way through the opposite sex. Intuitive and as a rule has good judgment.

## The Moon in Gemini

This location of the Moon gives the subject an agreeable, warm-hearted, sympathetic, humane, progressive and ingenious nature, with the capacity of being very reserved in some matters, such as personal or domestic matters, but fluent concerning local or national affairs. Strengthens and enlivens the intellect, inclines to literature and gains pleasure from books or scientific pursuits. Gives an active body and a versatile, receptive mind, responsive to new ideas and capable of following artistic, literary, or professional occupations.

Dislikes quarreling and warfare. Subject to many changes and some journeys. Through lack of caution, discretion or prudence apt to be drawn into embarrassing or difficult positions.

## The Moon in Cancer (Home)

This indicates one whose desire is to work along lines of least resistance; friendly, sociable and domestic in manner and usually much attached to his home; feeling and emotion are active and usually for good. Somewhat changeable, influenced greatly by the surroundings and is sensitive to outside influences; in other words, senses conditions psychically (consciously or unconsciously).

The native is kind and agreeable to all, sympathetic and humane. Sometimes allows imposition without an act of resentment; sometimes is elected to posts of honor. Good, conscientious, sensitive, superior nature; hard struggles, great obstacles, voyages. Loves traveling, also home; attraction to the mother. It favors dealing with the public in liquids, chemistry, catering, shipping and a residence near the water. Fond of the occult, antique and curious things, family history, and history in general, patriotism and cooking.

There is some ability for acting and expressing the thoughts or emotions of others, and usually for poetry or music. The Moon in this sign heightens sensitivity to all things of a feeling nature.

## The Moon in Leo

This makes one ambitious, self-confident, self-reliant, loyal, honorable, generous in money matters, high-minded, magnanimous, candid and warm-hearted; a persevering, lively and penetrating mind; organizing ability; generally a leader among his associates; popular with the opposite sex; sincere love; fond of home and honor; particular in dress and very orderly in conduct. It favors intuition and genius and gives a free-hearted nature with a love for pleasure, music, art, sports.

This location of the Moon has a tendency to uplift the native, mentally and socially, and place him in positions of trust, respect and responsibility or in control or management of enterprises.

## The Moon in Virgo

Good mental ability, receptive mind, good memory and ability to learn easily; capable of following some intellectual pursuit. Fondness for science in general and things occult. Often has clairvoyant, psychometric or intuitive faculty. The native is usually quiet, unostentatious and unpretentious, though talented and quietly ambitious, preferring to earn his way through merit of mental ability; fertile imagination, fondness for change, travel and investigation.

Although somewhat reserved, has many friends, especially of the opposite sex; usually has secret sorrows through marriage. Trouble with stomach and bowels until proper discretion is observed in diet.

There is likelihood of many short journeys and changes. This location favors a variety of occupations in literature or as teacher, secretary, bookkeeper, clerk, messenger, traveler, chemist, druggist, confectioner; sometimes success with the earth and its products, but more especially when the subject has an earthly sign rising at birth, or the planet ruling the Ascendant is in an earth sign.

This location of the Moon makes a good, trustworthy servant, and the native is usually fortunate through those who serve under him, unless a malefic be in the Sixth House.

## The Moon in Libra

This location of the Moon, taken alone, favors or inclines to unions, partnerships and general popularity. Fond of pleasure, society

and amusements and the company of young people. The native is affectionate, good-natured, agreeable, courteous, warm-hearted, affable,
mirthful, inclined to love and marriage; kind in manner and makes
friends easily. Liking for fine clothes, adornment, luxury, approbation
and all refining and harmonious influences.

The life is considerably affected by other people and the Libran
usually prefers to work in association with another.

Appreciation for music, painting, scenery and all the fine arts
generally; considerable skill and ingenuity along these lines if Mercury
is in good aspect.

### The Moon in Scorpio (Fall)

Inclines to vigorous activity. The native has enterprise, will, determination, practical ability; is firm and self-confident enough to push
forward and gain success in undertakings and take care of his own;
somewhat abrupt and impulsive. It gives a fondness for pleasure,
comfort and desire to satisfy the tastes. The nature is energetic, forceful, independent, masterful, aggressive, courageous and positive; will
not tolerate imposition, nor be swerved from his purpose by opposition,
yet will often sacrifice a great deal in return for kindness; sometimes
quick-tempered. It inclines to interest in the Occult or mysterious in
nature, and, if there are any conforming aspects, will advocate and assist
in carrying out revolutionary changes, employing sarcasm or satire.

Taken alone the location signifies attachments or attractions
and difficulties with the opposite sex and inharmony in the marriage
state. Dangers through voyages. To women, it inclines to dangerous
childbirth.

### The Moon in Sagittarius

Shows the native to be generous, benevolent, humanitarian, charitable, kind-hearted, sociable, good-humored, jovial, sometimes quickly
angered but forgiving, of ready promise, hopeful, frank and free; shows
love of beauty, harmony and sports.

Usually has a quick, restless and unsettled manner, either in
mind or body, and often both. Inclines to travel or change the place
of residence frequently; active, never averse to physical exercise, a

quick walker and worker; fond of children, pets and sports; some inclination for the investigation of religion, philosophy, law, commerce and foreign affairs generally. A natural teacher; very philosophical and often has something of the prophet in his nature, usually being correct in judgment regarding the outcome of movements or enterprises. Ingenious, talented and has ability for science.

This location of the Moon tends to bring one out before the public in some manner and he may assist in carrying on great religious, educational or political reforms. Benefits through women. It is somewhat significant of inheritance if Sagittarius occupies the cusp of the Eighth House.

### The Moon in Capricorn (Detriment)

Tends to bring one before the public in some manner, but whether beneficially or otherwise depends upon the other indications in the chart.

If the Moon is well aspected at birth, especially by the Sun, may attract attention as a prominent and respectable person. If the environment has been good it may manifest as rulership, generalship and administrative ability.

If the mental rulers (the Sun, Moon, Mercury and rulers of the Third and Ninth House cusps), were afflicted and the early training neglected it gives a vague, indeterminate mind, lack of creative energy although ambitious; misfortune through women and lax control of the appetites. Usually has enemies whether merited or not, and some drawback or difficulty attached to the occupation or reputation of the native. If the aspects in the chart are generally good it indicates honors and prominence; the native has ability to interest others and inspire confidence; a good organizer and welfare worker.

This location is also indicative of care and caution in money matters. The nature is often too cold and calculating and at times too regardless of the feelings of others.

### The Moon in Aquarius

Active, intuitional, agreeable, friendly and courteous disposition. The native is sociable and sympathetic in manner; broad, humane, independent and somewhat unconventional. Gives liking for the strange and curious with an inclination for subjects that are unusual, original or eccentric; inventive ability.

It tends to political, educational and scientific work, interest in astrology, occult matters generally, secret societies, etc. It gives a good faculty for image-making; mental sensitiveness; sorrow and changes occasioned by friends.

Troubles through women and liability to sorrow and wandering life, if badly aspected.

### The Moon in Pisces

Kind, benevolent, quiet, retiring, sympathetic, fond of luxury, comfort, diversity, change, beauty and harmony. Meets with many misfortunes and obstacles which tend to make the native feel irresolute, inert, downhearted and easily discouraged at times. It gives a taste for reading and keen perception of romance, having a powerful and fruitful imagination. As speaker, writer or composer he is copious, fluent, earnest and very correct in details.

Inconstancy is indicated in the love affairs; generally has a hard time saving money. If the Sun also is in a water sign or a water sign ascending the native is likely to grow corpulent.

With the Moon in this location, the native is often very receptive, mediumistic or inspirational and responsive to psychic conditions generally. Suffers both physically and mentally through adverse environment, uncongenial surroundings and misunderstanding.


# MERCURY


### Mercury in Aries

Impulsive and fiery, quick in thought and speech, good in repartee or argument and often contentious, antagonistic and disputative; expressive, earnest and demonstrative; apt to enlarge or exaggerate unconsciously, but is liberal, inventive, unique, interesting and clever.

Fond of reading, writing, literature and literary people. Inclined to enter quickly into projects and given to change of opinions. The faults are want of mental continuity, lack of order and method, and general restlessness, although a friendly aspect from Saturn will largely correct these and give much more stability.

### Mercury in Taurus

Pleasant and happy disposition, fond of the opposite sex, pleasure, recreation, music, art and intellectual or refined amusement. Very practical and determined mind, especially where mental development is concerned. Good reasoning and judgment, persevering and somewhat obstinate; however, discreet and diplomatic although of fixed opinions and strong likes and dislikes; desirous of acquiring money, possessions and an established income.

### Mercury in Gemini (Home)

Quick, ingenious, clever, inventive and resourceful mind. Sympathetic, unbiased, very seldom prejudiced, usually good-humored and generous. Perceptive, observing, shrewd and executive in detail; good orator, lawyer or business man. Informed on topics of the day.

Fond of travel, change, novelty, speculation, reading, literature, science and the acquisition of knowledge, especially of the Occult.

### Mercury in Cancer

Diplomatic, tactful, discreet, faithful and good-natured. The intellect is clear and reasonable with retentive powers. Readily adapt themselves to surrounding conditions and capable of changing their opinions quickly; sociable disposition. Fond of pleasure, picnics and family reunions.

Very impressionable and sensitive. Easily influenced by kindness and encouraged by approbation.

The mind is somewhat restless and requires an abundance of material for reflection. Usually spiritually inclined and interested in psychic investigation. Appreciation for the poetry of motion or of rhyme and music; liking for journeys by water and public entertainment. Gives the ability to mentally understand, verbalize and communicate the personal emotions.

## Mercury in Leo

Denotes an ambitious, confident, persistent, determined, lofty mind, fiery, quick-tempered. Kind-hearted and sympathetic; dignified and aspiring; intuitive intellect and high, noble ideals; will seldom stoop to low action. Positive mentality and governing, controlling or organizing ability. Will-power of progressive and expansive development; concentration. Fond of children, pets, music, singing, drama, fine arts, sports, pleasures; tendency to self-indulgence. Danger through drugs, etc., which affect the heart action.

## Mercury in Virgo (Home and exaltation)

Good intellect: comprehensive, cautious, prudent, discriminative, practical, versatile, inventive, intuitive, perceptive and possesses ability for study and memorizing. Power of persuasion; a good scholar or linguist; fluency as a writer, well informed, capable in detail, sequence and expression; innate love for mystery or for occult investigation.

Quiet or somewhat serious nature but at times critical and skeptical; must see, know and understand thoroughly before convinced. Taste for mathematics or literature; capable of undertakings that require ability, planning and dexterity. Interest in hygiene, prophylactics, nursing, healing or chemistry.

## Mercury in Libra

A refined, good and broad mind; quiet, just, tender, dispassionate disposition; fond of comparison, capable of judgment and reason. Taste for mental pursuits, often musical, splendid natural abilities, aptitude for delicate mathematical work or invention. Very favorable location for all intellectual development. Good for club, fraternal, or social welfare work.

## Mercury in Scorpio

A bold and somewhat obstinate, sarcastic, forceful, positive and reckless nature, but ingenious, keen, shrewd and desirous of gaining knowledge and mental ability. Often has troublesome friends, relatives and neighbors; fond of the opposite sex and partial to company and pleasure-seeking; many disappointments. Fond of occult and mystical subjects and the different "ologies" and "isms"; very careful of personal interests; somewhat critical, curious, suspicious and mistrustful. Mesmeric ability, suggestive mental healing qualities, mental resourcefulness, fertility and practical utility.

## Mercury in Sagittarius (Detriment)

The nature is ambitious, sincere, just, generous, very independent and often rebellious, with some tendency towards rashness or impulse.

The mind becomes prophetic, wise and philosophical, inclining to freedom of thought and speech. Very active mentally or physically, somewhat changeable but progressive. Appreciation for the beautiful in nature, fond of change and travel, also of home and family; likes authority, also likes sports and animals. Inclination toward mental development through philosophy, religion, science, law or medicine.

## Mercury in Capricorn

Acute, sharp, penetrating, tactful, curious, diplomatic and critical. Somewhat suspicious, peevish, fickle, discontented or restless. Careful, economical and painstaking, especially towards perfecting the intellect. Constantly busy about something. Interest and ability for literature, science, chemistry, philosophy and the occult. Influenced only through kindness. Serious, thoughtful, contemplative and practical nature. Observant, discriminating; organizing ability. Many generals and military strategists have benefited from this placement of Mercury.

## Mercury in Aquarius

The mind is refined, comprehensive, critical, original, penetrative, observing and keen in judgment of human nature, possessing good reasoning and concentrative powers. Makes acquaintances readily.

Fondness for science generally, also the occult and metaphysical. Apt in study, mathematics, invention, business methods, political or lodge work.

Great readers, deep thinkers, sociable and kind; expounders of humanitarian principles. Delight in discussing ideas, original thought and mental stimulation. Often seek the company of intellectual, unusual or elderly persons.

### Mercury in Pisces (Detriment and fall)

The intellect gains in knowledge not so much by deep and profound application to study, as by intuitive perception. Possesses an understanding not acquired from books; knows things in a peculiar manner; rarely at a loss to explain any condition and are often called "walking encyclopedias."

The mind is imaginative, impressionable and quickly adapted to the requirements of the moment; possesses great absorptive capacity and the power to memorize. Tends to psychic or mediumistic qualities but attended with some danger or inconvenience through over-receptivity in nature. Fond of pleasure, recreation and travel, especially on the water. Numerous abilities, often changes employment, good judge of human nature. Analytical, diplomatic, cautious, just, good-humored, versatile, ingenious and dexterous. Interest in hygiene, prophlactics, nursing, healing, hospitals.

## VENUS

### Venus in Aries (Detriment)

Fondness for travel, music, painting, sculpture, decorative art, singing, poetry, romance, theatres, entertainment and all genteel muscular and mental recreation.

The nature is ardent, affectionate, demonstrative, generous in the bestowal of affection, fond of love and admiration, warm-hearted, passionate and attracted to friends of the opposite sex.

This location of Venus inclines to popularity, many friends and, if other testimonies in the chart warrant, an early or hasty marriage. However, there are usually many inharmonies in the marital relation. The disposition is charitable and the feeling and sympathies quickly respond to appeals for worthy assistance; free and generous in gifts and expenditures.

### Venus in Taurus

This location of Venus endows the native with deep feelings and lasting emotions; an affectionate and faithful love nature. Precise, careful and correct with regard to form and custom in connection with pleasure, sociability and friendship. Fixed and stable in feelings, decided and tenacious in opinions. Fond of money for the pleasure and comfort it brings and generous with it in that respect.

Venus in Taurus is generally favorable for money and possessions gained by the native's personal efforts in business or profession and by the occupations of Venus. If other testimonies in the chart warrant, it assists to gain by legacy, partnership or marriage. The location inclines to marriage, but it is sometimes delayed.

## Venus in Gemini

The native may find pleasure and profit from travel and Mercurial pursuits. Money is gained from more than one source; several occupations. If Mercury is in good aspect, or the education complete, much can be accomplished through writings, speaking, music, art and drama. This location of Venus tends to refine the feelings and intellect, giving clear ideas, intuition, originality, inventive ability, good humor, friendliness, sociability and keen appreciation for all light, airy, mental recreations.

Dual love affairs, inconstancy or tendency to flirt, likelihood of several love affairs, one with a relative; many loving friends. Venus in Gemini inclines to marriage, and if other testimonies in the chart permit, more than one union.

If unafflicted, much good-will between brethren, cousins and neighbors. Spiritual tendencies of a progressive or mystical nature.

## Venus in Cancer

This location gives love of home, domestic attractions, strong affection for the mother. The nature is sympathetic, kind-hearted, loving, receptive, imaginative and quickly responsive to the emotions. Several love affairs, secret attractions, union with one of Occult tendencies or with considerable difference in age.

Venus in Cancer is not wholly fortunate for marriage, as it indicates obstacles, either on account of parents, money or occupation; unforeseen difficulties. Friendships among inferiors and connection with some obscure, unpopular or plebian occupation.

Ability in Occult arts, psychic research and in matters connected with the unseen world; love for mystical religion. Gain by matters associated with water, refreshments and, if other indications in the chart show it, gain through houses, land or parents. Mediumistic gifts.

### Venus in Leo
The nature is sympathetic, charitable, kind-hearted, free and generous. Earnest, sincere and ardent in affection. The native is attracted to the opposite sex, fond of social display, pleasure, friends, entertainment and amusements of all sorts. There may be real talent for something signified by Venus: music, poetry, singing, acting, art, etc.

Gain through young people, superiors, those of good position and social standing. If other testimonies in the chart warrant, the native will gain by judicious investment, speculation, inheritance and by occupations connected with pleasure.

### Venus in Virgo (Fall)
Venus in Virgo has a tendency to endow the native with a quiet nature and a deep sympathy seldom expressed. Some delay and disappointment in love, secret or dual attachments, union with one of a different station, possibly an employee, invalid or a doctor.

Money is gained through servants or subordinates or by the native himself occupying such positions; gain by matters connected with drugs, medicine, nursing, food, farming, gardening and through vocations associated with the earthly elements. If other testimonies in the chart permit, gain by careful speculation, investment and through the partner.

### Venus in Libra (Home)
Contributes to kindness, sympathy, pure and refined affections and rich love nature. It conduces to marriage, friendships, sociability, popularity, a fruitful union and talented offspring.

Venus in Libra gives a love for fine arts, music, poetry, singing, painting, drama, opera and all refined, cultured amusements and social functions.

Preference for friends and associates among philosophical people and those of good social standing, also affection for cousins or relatives.

The native may earn money through the things signified by Venus, and, if other testimonies in the chart permit, will gain through marriage and partnership.

## Venus in Scorpio (Detriment)

The native is free, generous and even lavish in expenditures. Money may be earned through the watery elements, catering to the tastes or by matters connected with the dead and, if other testimonies in the chart warrant, gain by gifts, legacy, partnership or marriage, but there will be some delay or trouble in connection with them.

This location of Venus increases the passions and emotions and gives a love of sensation, luxury and pleasure; ardent in love, demonstrative in affection. It attracts to the opposite sex and brings trouble, disappointment, delay or loss in courtship or marriage. Sorrow through disagreement or jealousy, attacks upon the honor, death of partner.

Trouble or failure in social affairs; friends with mystical or occult tendencies, also friendships with some of doubtful repute. If Venus is much afflicted, liable to death by poison or by suicide due to unhappy alliances.

## Venus in Sagittarius

This location of Venus refines the nature, making the native light-hearted, impressionable, intuitive, imaginative, prophetic, generous and of loyal intentions, fond of beauty, fine arts, traveling, voyaging, romance, animals, and all out-of-door sports and amusements. It inclines to charity, benevolence and justice; to religion of a mystical or spiritual nature; to respect for literary and intellectual work, philosophies, philanthrophy and all lines leading to harmony and involving the higher attributes of the mind.

Money may be gained from two sources and through things signified by the sign Sagittarius, also through horses, shipping, traveling, sports, etc., and if other testimonies in the chart agree, through speculation, investment, legacy and partnership.

The love nature is susceptible and attracted to the opposite sex. This location inclines to more than one union and affection for a foreigner or one from a considerable distance. Gives many friends, some of good position and social standing. Friendship with partner's relatives and friends among educators, scientists, ministers and mariners.

## Venus in Capricorn

This location tends to uplift the native and place him in positions of trust, responsibility, authority and profit, giving the favor of employers, superiors and elders.

It inclines to business, commerce, banking, investments, stocks, shares and executive positions which bring contact with many, also to affairs connected with the earthly elements. It conduces to social and business popularity, friends of high standing with gain and advancement through them.

The love nature is ambitious, diplomatic and careful of honor. Marriage is usually for convenience or for social purposes. There is disappointment in love, domestic unhappiness, coldness or indifference on the part of the partner. If other testimonies in the chart agree, marriage is delayed for reasons arising out of age, parents, money or occupation. Either the native or the partner is likely to be older, more serious, calculating, wealthy, or of a different position in life, or hold a different and maybe an indifferent attitude.

If Venus is afflicted here it gives liability to business treachery through associates; loss and trouble through alliances with inferiors or those of doubtful repute.

## Venus in Aquarius

This location of Venus gives fondness for pleasure and social life. The native makes friends easily and readily forms acquaintances with strangers. Friends among inferiors and also with those of wealth and refinement.

The nature is intuitive, philosophical, generous, reserved in opinions and sincere in convictions; liking and ability for fine arts and all cultured and intellectual pursuits. Fond of romance and pleasure, friends among the opposite sex, faithful and earnest in affection, secret alliances, remarkable or strange, sudden and unexpected experiences or events in love, union with one of Uranian nature; possibly marriage in middle life or later years, and to one of different age.

Indicates gain financially through friends, societies and public enterprises. If other testimonies in the chart agree, it signifies gain through partnership, association, companies and firms, also through speculation, investment and inheritance. Many hopes and wishes realized.

### Venus in Pisces (Exaltation)

Venus in Pisces bestows a nature that is charitable, philanthropic, easily moved to sympathy, inclined to relieve suffering and to assist the weak or afflicted; interested in work connected with institutions. The native is compassionate, sensitive, psychic, mediumistic, emotional, idealistic and inspirational.

Fond of all things beautiful: poetry, music, painting and fine arts generally. Cheerful, genial, hospitable, fond of society and friendly intercourse; desirous of peace, ease, comfort and luxury; at times indolent.

Money is gained through friends, charity, gifts, Venusian occupations, or through obscure, subordinate or plebian pursuit. There is apt to be more than one marriage and the native may be careless or fickle in matters of affection. Attraction to an inferior; secret alliance. If Venus is much afflicted here the native may have a hard time gaining money, or if he possesses it will lose heavily through fraud, deception and unscrupulous methods and maybe by his own action. Difficulty, detriment and loss through intrigue; obstacles, delays and trouble in marriage.

## THE SUN

Occasionally the Sun may enter the sign a day earlier or later than the dates quoted in this chapter. If a person is born on one of the dates given as the change from one sign to another it becomes necessary to note carefully the Sun's place given in the birth year ephemeris to determine whether or not it had changed signs at the time of birth. An ancient rule was to the effect that when a planet reached the twenty-eighth degree it began to influence the next sign.

The planet which rules the sign the Sun occupies at birth is known as a *ruling planet* and throughout life the aspects of the ruling planet, whether by transit or by progression, are important factors in producing events and changing conditions.

### The Sun in Aries—March 21 - April 19 (Exaltation)

In Aries the Sun gives much mental energy and quick wit. Natives of this sign are natural leaders, more or less headstrong or impulsive, ambitious, full of enterprise and new ideas. They do not like to be under the direction of a master and are inclined to be fiery and quick-tempered, quick to resent abuse or imposition but forgiving and do not hold a grudge long. Their great love of freedom and justice, coupled with their enthusiasm and self-will, makes them liable to go to extremes through indignation, hasty speech or lack of discretion. They possess penetrating will-power, are persistent, determined and not easily discouraged. Are philosophical by nature, admire scientific thought and are at their best when at the head of things, such as director, instructor, superintendent or manager.

Mars is the planetary ruler of the sign Aries.

### The Sun in Taurus—April 20 - May 20

In Taurus the Sun makes the native self-reliant, determined, persistent, stable, firm, careful and cautious. Taurians fear pain. They seem patient and will wait a long time for their plans to mature; gentle when unprovoked but furious when angered and then headstrong and unyielding; secretive and reserved with latent energy and mental power; practical and constructive. Lovers of nature, art, music, literature and amusement. Are usually capable of becoming psychics, mediums and healers. Make good public servants, officials and splendid executive workers.

Venus is the planetary ruler of the sign Taurus.

### The Sun in Gemini—May 21 - June 20

In Gemini the Sun makes the native sympathetic, kind-hearted, affectionate, fond of home and children and easily influenced by kindness, at times to his detriment. Is sensitive, intuitional, idealistic. Fond of science and as a rule studious and usually endowed with great imaginative ability. Possesses an active mind and can be relied upon to act quickly in emergency. Is an experimenter and investigator, quick reasoner, generally a good writer; likes to be busy and can engage in two or more occupations at once but must be allowed to work in his own way. Changeful, inquiring, doubtful nature, hard to understand but versatile, alert, dexterous and skillful. Is ambitious, aspiring and loves change and diversity.

Mercury is the planetary ruler of the sign Gemini.

### The Sun in Cancer—June 21 - July 22

In Cancer the Sun gives a quiet, reserved, retiring, sensitive disposition, yet inclined to publicity. Versatile, changeable; with many ups and downs, changes of occupation and position but desires to stick to his own course. Possesses a fertile imagination and dramatic ability, loves nature, adventure and strange experiences. Is mediumistic, receptive and influenced greatly by surroundings. Industrious, prudent, frugal and very conscientious. Has a retentive memory. Loves approbation, sympathy and kindness; fears ridicule. Fruitful and reproductive.

The Moon is the planetary ruler of the sign Cancer.

### The Sun in Leo—July 23 - August 22 (Home)

In Leo the Sun gives an active mind, good nature, generosity, many friends. Is a natural leader, ambitious, independent, determined, persistent, industrious, honest and very conscientious; philosophical, philanthropic. Quickly angered but quickly appeased. Has a sunny disposition, is frank, outspoken, candid, forceful and greatly appreciates affection in which he is usually ardent and sincere. Magnetic, intuitive and inventive; fond of children, sports, drama, honors and high office.

The Sun is the planetary ruler of the sign Leo.

### The Sun in Virgo—August 23 - September 22

In Virgo the Sun makes the native modest, thoughtful, serious, contemplative and industrious with desire to refine the mind and acquire knowledge. Learns quickly, is philosophical, a good reasoner and usually has a good command of language. It gives good endurance, reserve force, quick recuperation and as a rule Virgos do not show their age. Quick-tempered but not a fighter, as Virgo prefers arbitration. Loves order, beauty, art and literature. Not easily discouraged or kept down, although somewhat given to worry. Is idealistic yet practical, frugal yet speculative, ingenious, careful, cautious and usually endowed with good forethought. Very active and seldom contented long at a time. Desires wealth but not able, as a rule, to acquire wealth easily. Interested in hygiene, diet and labor conditions.

Mercury is the planetary ruler of the sign Virgo.

### The Sun in Libra—September 23 - October 22 (Fall)

In Libra the Sun gives love of justice, peace and harmony. The native is courteous, pleasant, agreeable and as a rule even tempered, affectionate, sympathetic and sensitive to surroundings and conditions of friends. Is a natural peacemaker, just, kind, amiable and generous. Modest, neat, particular; loves art, refined pleasure and amusements; artistic and dislikes unclean work. Is intuitive and has objective foresight. Usually marries young and generally more than once.

Venus is the planetary ruler of the sign Libra.

### The Sun in Scorpio—October 23 - November 21

In Scorpio the Sun gives strong characteristics and shrewd, keen judgment. The Scorpio native is critical, suspicious, skeptical but enterprising, reserved, tenacious, determined and secretive. Fond of luxuries but economical and calculating; restless, energetic, fond of travel, especially on water, and admires grandeur in nature. Attends to own affairs in business but in matters of duty may make trouble for others. In speech plain, blunt, sarcastic and forceful; in politics or law very aggressive. At best, original, scientific, sagacious, daring and creative, capable of much success through bold enterprise. Fine engineers, contractors, surgeons, chemists, detectives and sheriffs are born in this sign.

Pluto is the planetary ruler of the sign Scorpio.

### The Sun in Sagittarius—November 22 - December 21

In Sagittarius the Sun gives a jovial, bright, hopeful, generous and charitable nature: self-reliant, active, enterprising, frank, outspoken, honest, ambitious, persevering and not easily discouraged. Loves liberty, freedom and out-of-doors sports; dislikes a master and will not be driven. Generally has a strong will and is sincere, honorable, earnest, aspiring, energetic and what he says goes right to the mark. Shows reverence for philosophy and science, has good calculation and foresight and is usually prophetic as to the outcome of movements or enterprises.

Jupiter is the planetary ruler of the sign Sagittarius.

## The Sun in Capricorn—December 22 - January 19

In Capricorn the Sun gives a quiet, thoughtful, serious nature, deep mind and good reasoning ability; generally practical, economical and given to investigation. Capricorns act with dignity and self-esteem, are somewhat particular, ambitious and persevering; never entirely discouraged although often disappointed; thorough and hard workers. Careful, cautious, frugal, and make the most of opportunities. Usually meet with some heavy obstacles in the path of desires and progress, yet by dint of persistent, patient and concentrated effort often butt their way through and triumph over circumstances.

Saturn is the planetary ruler of the sign Capricorn.

## The Sun in Aquarius—January 20 - February 18 (Detriment)

In Aquarius the Sun gives a quiet, patient, determined, unobtrusive and faithful nature, as a rule. The Aquarian is refined, pleasant, friendly, generous, charitable, dignified and humanitarian; fond of art, music, scenery and literature; cautious, steady, intelligent, intuitive, discriminative, concentrative, studious, thoughtful and philosophical. Good reasoner, practical as well as theoretical; strong likes and dislikes and often with very radical and advanced ideas; is cheerful, sincere and honest, easily influenced by kindness, slow to anger but will not be driven; loves liberty and is fond of Occult research.

Uranus is the planetary ruler of the sign Aquarius.

## The Sun in Pisces—February 19 - March 20

In Pisces the Sun generally gives a kind and loving nature, confiding, honest, amiable, sympathetic and especially kind to defenseless animals and people in distress. There is sometimes a sense of blessedness, or of being protected by the forces of nature, which either the native or those around him sense. Neat, particular and a lover of order and completeness; modest, often timid and lacking self-confidence. As a rule, Pisceans and industrious, methodical and logical in their processes; idealistic, imaginative, inspirational; often gifted with mediumistic faculty and usually fond of secret, occult of psychic investigation. The Pisces is retiring and humble.

Neptune is the planetary ruler of the sign Pisces.

# MARS

### Mars in Aries (Home)

Gives force, positivity, self-assurance, combativeness, activity, industry, enterprise, originality and mechanical ability.

The native is enthusiastic, electric and inspiring.

Philosophic and idealistic in spirit and so frank and free that he usually meets with poor success in concealing anything. Very independent and often acts hastily and forcefully on impulse.

Possesses a keen sense of enjoyment, a love for sport, pleasure and adventure. Has a strong dislike for all bonds, limitations and restrictions, preferring to be free to explore and pioneer into all new lines of thought and activity.

Self-interest is strong and the native will usually push his affairs forward with very little outside encouragement, sometimes without any and in the face of discouragement. Mars in Aries increases the vitality but makes the native subject to danger by fire, surgical operations, fevers, inflammatory and mental complaints, accidents, wounds and scalds.

If Mars is afflicted it gives hasty temper and trouble through the head, face and eyes. It usually gives a mark or scar of some kind on head or face.

### Mars in Taurus

Gives practical qualities, quiet ambition, quick wit and foresight, good executive power, ability to organize and direct: a good manager capable of carrying plans and ideas into practical materialization. Not usually deterred, nonplussed or thwarted by obstacles; works determinedly and persistently where self-interests are concerned, gaining the desired end through tact, diplomacy and sheer strength of internal force or confidence. This location of Mars indicates good earning powers, free expenditures and pleasure as well as gain through the occupation.

If Mars is unafflicted the native usually handles much money and gains by legacy. But if Mars is afflicted the native will be liable to loss of money, property and slumps in finances. The temper, during the period of affliction, is hasty and violent, native is irritable, acquisitive, and when angry he is "mad as a bull" and quite apt to act "bull-headed". This position of Mars also indicates powerful opponents and legal difficulties, loss of legacy, unfavorable unions, some scandal and monetary difficulties.

In either case this location inclines to marriage, but trouble through it and also through the opposite sex.

## Mars in Gemini

Sharpens the insight and perception, giving acute, keen, quick intellect; mentally combative and forceful, plain-spoken; desire for educational attainments; active and nimble.

If Mars is well aspected the native can write or speak well and is fond of reading, lectures, travel, science, law or chemistry. Possesses a mind that is mechanical, inventive and ingenious. In manner is practical, apt, quick to make deductions and to arrive at conclusions.

If Mars is afflicted, often disagreeable and forceful in speech, satirical, fault-finding and critical. Trouble through neighbors, relatives and inferiors, also through writings, letters, education and traveling; difficulty, estrangement or separation from brothers or sisters. The mind is restless, indecisive and lacking in concentration. Pains in the lungs and injuries to hands, arms, shoulders and collar bone.

Mars in Gemini tends to more than one union, to two attachments at the same time or affection for a relative.

## Mars in Cancer (Fall)

Makes the native bold, fearless, ambitious and industrious, with sudden outbursts of temper and irritable tendencies; when offended, likely to nurse ill-feeling for a considerable time; fond of luxury and somewhat sensuous.

The subject is original, independent and rebels against authority. Gives fitness for medicine or surgery, gain through enterprising business journeys and voyages, public concerns and through physical effort. Somewhat changeable and lacking in continuity. Possesses some domestic tastes and liking for occult, mystical, psychical and metaphysical subjects.

If Mars is afflicted, it indicates early death of mother, separation from or disagreement with her; trouble in home life and a discontented marriage partner; many worries, annoyances, sorrows and changes of residence. Trouble through lands, property and inheritance; accidents to home, such as fire, storms, earthquakes, theft, etc.; danger through the watery elements; many difficulties at close of life unless poise and harmony have been developed. Indisposition through the stomach and some trouble concerning the sight.

## Mars in Leo

The native is candid, free, fearless, independent, enterprising, honest and very conscientious. He is active, industrious and capable of rising to positions of responsibility, trust, authority, management and control. During good "directions" to Mars, success and good fortune through public appointments, government affairs, gain by speculation, investment, keen judgment in stock exchange matters, insurance and industrial concerns and through those in high rank. Sociable, fond of company, friendship and esteem; warm-hearted, ardent in affection, love and pleasure; often hasty and impulsive in love and sometimes too unrestrained in the emotions and passions. At times very forceful, positive, militant, aggressive or defiant in manner, strong in argument and likely to arouse opposition and open enmity; but very magnanimous, generous, philosophical, reasonable; enthusiastic, broad, liberal, possessing a keen sense of justice and a determined will and does not hold a grudge for long. Fondness for strenuous sports, adventure, risky enterprises, hazardous occupations and for occult phenomena.

If Mars is afflicted it threatens disappointment and sorrow in love, death of a loved one, separation or some irregularity in the union, death of a child. Trouble through superiors and also through inferiors; loss through speculation. Peculiar ailments of an inflammatory or tumorous character, difficulty through accidents and fires and trouble with sides and back. A responsive nature, amorous, forceful, bold and contemptuous of danger, quick in anger, though idealistic and fond of hazardous or strenuous pursuits.

## Mars in Virgo

Makes the native quite original and interested in bold and scientific enterprises in which he is usually successful, yet he has many struggles of a peculiar nature as this location of Mars puts difficulties in the way of the ambitions and desires for power and fame, helping to bring reversal, downfall, obstacles and continual annoyance or opposition.

It favors profit through trading in common things and foreign produce and general business enterprises. The native is a good worker in employ but usually follows his own will quietly, being mentally very active, quick-witted, shrewd and somewhat acquisitive; tactful and discriminative; possesses reserve force and energy. Mars in Virgo adapts one for science and is somewhat related to medicine, surgery, chemistry, pharmacy, hygiene, healing and food products. It gives power to resist disease by study of hygiene and care in diet but the nervous system and bowels are likely to suffer from complaints brought on or aggravated by Mars. There are also apt to be numerous ties, unions with inferiors, death of friends and helpers or parting from them through quarrels or misunderstanding.

If Mars is afflicted in the horoscope it will, at times, make one quite irritable, hasty, proud, obstinate, reserved, secretive and revengeful. Suffers from loss of friends, servants, subordinates, co-workers and false associations. Liability to accidents and sickness from overwork and trouble through labor difficulties and strikes.

## Mars in Libra (Detriment)

Promotes development of the faculties of perception and observation. Gives clear vision, refined tastes, idealistic temperament and intuitive mind of a speculative nature. The native is enterprising and often placed in a position where he rules others. Love of sciences in general and fond of refined occupations, business or professional. This location of Mars is good for a lawyer or surgeon. It also indicates many friends among scientific, philosophic, religious, legal or business people. In the business world the native meets with trouble through competitors but survives enemies. Trouble also comes through other people; he meets with rivalry, opposition, enmity and criticism both open and secret. Troubles and sadness concerning deaths and losses of those related to the family circle.

Mars in this location inclines to an ardent, rash, impulsive or passionate love. The opposite sex usually is a great attraction and exercises much control over the native. He is apt to become detrimentally entangled through the affections, causing much suffering, grief or trouble. Other testimonies concurring, it causes an early marriage and quarrels with the partner. Usually, however, a disappointment in love delays marriage.

The experiences gathered through business, marriage, etc., lead the native, in later years, to a still higher education and unfoldment which produces fine judgment. Mars in Libra is a testimony for off-spring and they are usually endowed with superior intellect.

If Mars is afflicted, particularly by Uranus, there are many separations, broken ties and difficulties between native and partner, friends, associates and relatives.

## Mars in Scorpio

This gives a practical nature with the capacity to work hard and accomplish much. There is good executive power, mechanical and inventive ability. In character the native is firm, positive, determined and forceful, with matter-of-fact manner and a seemingly cold or unconscious disregard for the feelings of others. Somewhat selfish, rash, revengeful and passionate. The mind is acute, sharp, keen and diplomatic; native is quick and capable in government office, in secret missions and work of a peculiar nature in connection with the regular employment or with confederates or associates. This location is favorable for a chemist, surgeon, assayer or any other profession or occupation which involves the use of liquids and tools. The native usually enters into projects with intensity of purpose and action, his motto being, "Produce results." Fondness for hazardous enterprises, liable to accidents and a sudden or violent end. Liking to investigate things mysterious and at some time likely to become engaged in psychical research. There is likelihood of gain by marriage; romantic courtship experiences; long journeys and voyages.

If Mars is much afflicted in Scorpio, it tends to express as unsociable, ungrateful, quarrelsome, revengeful, overbearing and selfish, with scant regard for the rights of others. Trouble through employees, severe illness, accidents and operations.

## Mars in Sagittarius

Makes the native free, frank, generous, enthusiastic, ambitious and at times impulsive in speech and action. The mind is active and although fond of argument is usually good humored, original and independent in thought, morally and mentally brave, daring and fearless of the opinions of others; firm, fixed and positive in his ideas and frequently at variance with accepted opinions. Fond of travel and adventure;

favorable results from investigation of the Occult, particularly where the inspirational, prophetic and intuitional tendencies are concerned. This location gives good mechanical ability, foresight and ingenuity; also good for lawyers and surgeons, evangelists and explorers. It gives a love of pleasure, especially strenuous sports and athletics carried on out of doors. Conduces to a liking for military tactics and if the chance offers will hold military and naval positions. If Mars is not afflicted it signifies gain through marriage, associates, legacy and social means; likelihood of more than one union and concern regarding health of others in the domestic circle.

If Mars is afflicted it signifies danger through journeys and traveling, possible loss of legacy and loss through legal decisions; unfavorable employment and some risk therein. Liable to trouble through too much risk, over-estimation, miscalculation or exaggeration. Not favorable for brothers, sisters, cousins and neighbors; disagreement with them, or one or more will die. Difficulty with religious persons or through religious or skeptical and unorthodox ideas and beliefs. In the early part of life the native is likely to be indisposed and at the close meets with dual experiences.

## Mars in Capricorn (Exaltation)

Gives courage, self-reliance and assurance, a nature that is brave, bold and not at all averse to adventure and excitement; often is very heroic. Due to disregard of danger may meet with accidents, expecially to lower limbs. Is ambitious, enterprising, industrious and acquisitive. Capable of much responsibility and endeavor; possesses good executive and organizing ability. Desire for public life and in lines allowing plenty of scope for action. Being energetic and willing to assume responsibility, attains positions of authority and prominence; friends among powerful people and Occult students.

In acquiring education the intellect is slow but is sure in the assimilation of knowledge. The mind is subtle and gains much by intuition. There is some speculative tendency or liking for risks and a desire to acquire wealth. The native becomes a lover of duty, has good business ability, gains through commerce and science, also through industrious employees, travel, foreign affairs and products of the earth. Honor and fame in profession; a successful sales-manager, general manager, agent or real estate broker. Marriage produces an important change in life, greatly affects the close of life and may bring gain socially. There is likely to be an early affair of the affections with an inferior or an elderly person.

If Mars is afflicted it indicates difficulties through friends and acquaintances; conflict with people in authority, superiors and those of high rank. The native at times is irritable, quick in temper and passion. He may arouse rivalry, opposition and criticism and is likely to suffer in honor and credit. This is rather an unfortunate location of Mars for a parent (probably the father) as there may be a disagreement or separation between the native and a parent or between the parents themselves or one of them may die prematurely.

## Mars in Aquarius

Makes a good reasoner who usually takes some unique, original and unlooked for point from which to reason. As a speaker he is a ready debater, forcible and convincing; he sums up facts and arguments clearly and often arrives at conclusions quickly. He is intellectual, prudent, quick-witted and scientific. There is some impulsiveness in manner and speech and at times he is rash, head-strong and abrupt. The native is humanitarian and interested in reforms for public good. He is fond of literature and philosophy, Occult studies and science generally. Mars in Aquarius makes one ambitious, enterprising and independent. His opinions may be fixed and not readily changed by others; when he makes a change it is usually a complete one and undergone quite suddenly or abruptly. The native is original and unique in many things, inventive and fond of machinery, electrical and aerial matters. This is a good location of Mars for medicine or surgery, hospital, philanthropic or welfare work. Makes a good director and responsible official in connection with public companies or in governmental, municipal and fraternal office. Gains by the professions, and financial success comes through public work. He is sincere and has refined tastes; makes friends readily through merit and ability.

If Mars is afflicted it indicates that at times the native is apt to be too independent, abrupt and blunt in speech and manner; apt to act hastily without realizing the consequences. This is likely to result in separation from friends and associates and suffering through opposition and hostility. Trouble occurs in connection with firms, companies, associates, societies and partners. It is thought also to indicate the death of a friend, estrangement from one or suffering through a false friend and early death of a parent or separation from them. The native may be rough and ready, faithful in affections and capable in an emergency.

## Mars in Pisces

The native is generous and free with money, yet anxious to accumulate wealth; somewhat timid or cautious but if angered or aroused becomes bold and audacious. In nature the person is sympathetic, receptive, affectionate and sensitive to imposition. Sometimes the native is quiet and retiring, easily depressed and gloomy, somewhat prone to indolence, vacillation, irresolution or indecision and too open to the influence of others, while at other times he accomplishes much quietly. Is desirous of popularity although may not gain much of it; endeavors to avoid conflicts and tries valiantly to surmount difficulties and misfortunes. Apt in details and successful in ordinary occupations and with the middle class of people, also with pursuits in connection with public or private institutions. Mars in Pisces gives ability as a detective, inspector, jailer, warden, hospital worker, sailor, marine engineer, fisherman, hotel keeper and in occupations requiring uniform. Friends among powerful people; help and gain financially from friends.

There may be some tendency to dissipation or passion, or overstimulated emotions, and danger through water and liquids generally; from drowning, scalding, poisons, food in liquid form, also through gas, anaesthetics and opiates. This location of Mars also tends to disappointment in love, to two attachments and delay in marriage. Accidents and trouble to the feet.

If Mars is afflicted it shows that the native will meet with many heavy misfortunes and difficulties; will suffer from secret enmity in various forms, such as theft, scandal, slander, false accusations, etc., whether deserving it or not. When Mars in Pisces is poorly aspected, one may suffer through overindulgence in any consciousness-altering substance, especially through drugs or drink. There may be a violent tendency or memory lapses while under the influence. This placement gives the subconscious more expression. One may become involved in trouble through lack of candor, truthfulness and honesty and this may be due either directly or indirectly to one's own fault. This placement indicates many changes in plans, views, disposition and occupation.

# JUPITER

## Jupiter in Aries

Usually signifies a progressive person, ambitious, aspiring, generous, candid, high-minded, ardent, philosophical and reasonable. Success is largely due to personal merits and through domestic relationship, social standing and influential friends. The native is capable of holding positions of responsibility, government offices, etc., and where he has authority over others; military honors. He usually changes his pursuit sometime in life and has two occupations. Strong liking for literature, science, study, philosophy, traveling and all that appertains to cultivation of mind. Shipping, voyaging, horses, sports and out-of-door exercises attract the attention. Usually respected and generally fortunate; a pioneer, in a way, and ambitious of advancement. An advocate of new ideas for improvement and whatever the religious views may be, is sincere, earnest and progressive therein. This location tends to benefit and gain through intellectual friends and acquaintances, shipping, travel, law, religious associates, children, young people, foreign securities, speculation and insurance.

## Jupiter in Taurus

Jupiter in Taurus gives love of justice. The nature is affectionate and generous, peaceful, reserved and firm. Has great love for home and not much given to change. Seldom travels except for definite purposes such as relate to health, business or learning.

A patron of philanthropic movements and philosophy; fixed in religion and views generally.

This location is favorable for benefit through the opposite sex, sociability, church, philosophy and matters connected with the higher attributes of the mind. Also for the things signified by the sign Taurus and ninth house affairs. If other testimonies in the chart permit, it tends to gain through gifts and legacies, investments, speculation, children, young people, marriage and partnership. If Jupiter is afflicted there will be losses through these things.

## Jupiter in Gemini (Detriment)

Gives a nature which expresses sympathy, charity, benevolence and humanitarian tendencies. The disposition is friendly, courteous, truthful and trustworthy. Fond of novelty, traveling and mental recreation. The tendency is to intellectual development. The mind is lofty and aspiring and although at times there seems to be restlessness and feelings of uncertainty or changeability, yet there is good comparison or mathematical faculty; also ability for literature, Occult investigation, psychic unfoldment and prophecy. It indicates the possibility of an attraction to a relative or some one closely associated and two marriages. There may be some difficulty in marriage through relatives, writings or travel. It inclines to success in literature, benefits through inventions, with large corporations, mail order business and publishing. If afflicted, sudden difficulties or opponents; unprofitable or unpopular professions; differences or separation from relatives; trouble through publishing or publications.

## Jupiter in Cancer (Exaltation)

The native is ambitious, enterprising, good-humored, humane, charitable, benevolent, sympathetic, kind and sociable; popular among his fellows, with friends among inferiors and also among those of good position. It tends to an intellectual view of life, intuition, useful imagination and fondness for all fine arts and cultured amusements; patriotic, interested in public welfare and investigation in the occult and psychic fields. It shows a fondness for home and mother, also for voyages and travels for pleasure, health or learning. It inclines to gain in public work through mental ability and if other testimonies in the chart agree, through investment, inheritance, property or marriage. A peaceful, honorable end abroad or far from the place of birth.

## Jupiter in Leo

Makes the native good-natured, noble and lofty-minded, magnanimous, loyal, courteous, generous, compassionate, benevolent and prudent. This location strengthens the constitution, increases the vitality and favors birth of children. The love nature is deep, sincere and honest; the subject is endowed with wisdom, good judgment and will power, capable of holding positions of trust and responsibility. Enjoys prestige, honors, grandeur and great undertakings. The mind is intuitive, diplomatic and inclined to higher sciences, philosophy, fine arts, religion and culture generally. Favors government employ and positions of prominence. Gain through judicious investment and speculations. Benefit through long journeys especially in connection with sports, education or diplomatic affairs.

## Jupiter in Virgo

This increases the mental inclination in all directions toward an intellectual or even somewhat materialistic view of things. The nature is cautious, not easily imposed upon, discreet, prudent and discrimina- tive and therefore the native has ability for practical scientific and philosophical investigation and study, the mind being analytical, criti- cal and matter-of-fact, possessed of wisdom, knowledge, honesty and ability for the study of natural laws. Careful in choice of acquain- tances, friendships among occult students. Rises above his sphere in life, has foreign associations and travel due to business. Marriage is in some way peculiar and possibly to a social inferior. If well aspected or unafflicted, success in business or professional pursuits; gain by em- ployees, literature, investment, commercial and speculative dealings. It tends to the occupations of Virgo and Sagittarius. If afflicted, loss and trouble through these things and disturbances of the blood, liver, bowels and hips; lack of application, method and concentration.

## Jupiter in Libra

The disposition is mild and temperate, sincere, earnest, kind, soc- iable and obliging. The native is conscientious, compassionate, imagin- ative and perceptive; loves peace, justice, mercy and harmony. Chari- table, philanthropic, fond of travel, music, art and all intellectual and cultured entertainment. Benefit from the opposite sex, powerful friends and through those who are scientific, philosophical or spiritual. If well aspected or unafflicted, gain through commerce, employees, science, medicine, law, professional associations, public institutions, theatres, hospitals, asylums, etc.; a happy marriage, fruitful union and good children; honors and esteem. If afflicted, trouble through legal difficul- ties, open enmity and opposition and through treachery from women, friends or associates.

## Jupiter in Scorpio

This gives powerful will, deep emotions, ardor, enthusiasm, per- severance, ambition and generosity. The mind is active, resolute, self-confident, fruitful, subtle, analytical, lofty, proud, aggressive, both constructive and destructive; fond of chemical and mechanical experiments or occult and psychical research and all things of a mysterious nature. Association with governmental officials or connection with the government; power among associates and societies; professional secrets and information affecting the honor of others; friendships of a peculiar nature or open to criticism; intrigues with superiors; long voyages and strange adventures abroad. If well aspected or unafflicted, gain through occupations of Scorpio, by litigation, arbitration, death of partner, legacy and public investments. If afflicted, jealous and powerful enemies; loss through questionable or unsound speculation and securities, etc.; death of child, danger, misfortune and liability to death through water and voyages; danger through social or political connections; liability to suffer from hereditary diseases, blood poisoning or heart disease. Liability to quarrels and litigation; difficulty with those engaged in law, science, religion or medicine.

## Jupiter in Sagittarius (Home)

The native is endowed with a courteous, affable, tolerant, humorous, kind, generous, sympathetic, loyal and noble nature. The mind is broad, just, liberal, merciful, compassionate, humanitarian, sincere, prophetic and philosophical. Jupiter in Sagittarius tends to good fortune and general success. The native is usually successful in his enterprises, often receives honors and is a leader among his associates. It is favorable for matters connected with sports, horses, shipping, literature and learned, scientific, philosophic or religious bodies. If other testimonies in the chart concur, it tends to gain through speculation, marriage, legacy and voyages. If afflicted, troublesome social affairs, difficulty through sports and loss by speculation or gambling.

## Jupiter in Capricorn

A mind that is serious, deliberate, thoughtful and ingenious. The nature is constructive, capable, creative with organizing ability. Is ambitious and attains some degree of popularity, power, credit and esteem. Tends to economy, frugality and the acquirement of practical education, taking part in the advancement of scientific, philosophic or spiritual knowledge, industrial or political economics. It inclines to general success in occupation, especially where the native is in authority over others or engaged in some public or governmental career. The tendency is to gain through commercial or foreign affairs and if other testimonies in the chart concur, gain through money or legacy from father or superiors. It is said to indicate a long journey or voyage and that the marriage is affected by the parents, also that the native is concerned with the sorrows and misfortunes of friends. If afflicted, it manifests as parsimony or inactivity; an unorthodox nature; trouble, difficulty and obstacles in occupation; some discredit.

### Jupiter in Aquarius

Makes the native cheerful, good-humored, obliging, just, merciful, compassionate, sympathetic, philanthropic and congenial, disliking discord and inharmony. The mind is prophetic, intuitive, genteel, refined, liberal, broad, philosophic, humanitarian and given to the investigation of new thought, social, spiritualistic and reform subjects. Inclines to fondness for and pursual of out-of-the-ordinary, Occult, curious and mystical studies. Jupiter in Aquarius gives original, independent and progressive views; often indifferent to the ordinary affairs of life; favors development of the higher attributes of mind through hygiene, philosophy, science, literature, music, classical and ancient arts. It gives pleasure and benefit through good and sincere friends who are gained by personal influence. Pleasure and interest in congressional activites, public institutions and public work. Gain and benefit through profession and, if in good aspect to ruler of Eleventh House, gain in employment with societies and associations or the government. Psychic and Occult experiences; peculiar conditions and experience brought about by associates and friends. Acquaintances among foreigners and political executives.

### Jupiter in Pisces

Gives strong ideality, interest in all philanthropic affairs; increases the emotions and imagination generally, adding to the intuition, spiritual perception and psychic impressions. The native receives benefit from pursual of investigation along lines of occult and psychical research in general and will experience some remarkable phenomena and prophetic dreams or visions. The native is studious, hospitable, quiet, unassuming, sociable, kind, charitable, fond of animals, sympathetic, always ready to help the sick and unfortunate and possessed of many good talents. It disposes somewhat to traveling, especially by water. It inclines to honors, gain, favors and high occupations through associations, companies, friends, mining and shipping affairs and institutions such as hospitals, sanitariums, laboratories, etc. If afflicted, loss through speculation and deception. The native is liable to become at times too unambitious, changeable, overly fond of ease and pleasure, indolent, inert, inactive or restless, unsettled, undecided and easily influenced.

# SATURN

## Saturn in Aries (Fall)

Resolute, determined, ambitious for success. Prosperity through industry and perseverance. Contemplative, good reasoning faculties, easily angered, not at all averse to argument and contentious when opposed. At times reserved and acquisitive. Jealous partner and probability of difficulties through marriage. Obstacles and troubles in first half of life.

## Saturn in Taurus

Thoughtful, kind, quiet but sometimes quick-tempered, stubborn, resentful and not easily appeased. Economical, prudent, diplomatic and somewhat reserved over personal affairs, especially finances. Fondness for botany, horticulture or stock breeding. Sorrow and loss through relatives; unfortunate domestic experiences; gain through thrift, economy and judicious investment.

## Saturn in Gemini

An observant, ingenious nature. Ability for scientific occupation in connection with literature, mathematics, etc. Adaptable and resourceful. Trouble and sorrow through relatives. Unfortunate legal affairs. Liable to false accusation, restraint or limitation through some of the kindred or neighbors. Interest in current and advanced thought, ability for profound intellectual attainments.

## Saturn in Cancer (Detriment)

Dissatisfied feelings causing many changes of residence and pursuits. Changeable moods; somewhat fretful, discontented or jealous.

Domestic troubles; anxiety and sorrow through attachments, parents, home and children. Affected psychically by adverse conditions surrounding others. Pleasure through occult investigation and psychic sources; interest in domestic economy and public welfare. An industrious partner. Difficulties toward the close of life unless the native endeavors to develop and apply his highest qualities.

### Saturn in Leo

Generous but quick-tempered, cautious yet bold in spirit, determined, ambitious and strong-willed. Spiritual tendencies. Troubles and secret enmity through inferiors. At times receptive to psychic conditions, consciously or unconsciously, which affect the health. Danger through accidents and overwork or over-exertion. Sorrows through love affairs and children.

### Saturn in Virgo

Reserved, discreet, cautious, prudent, frugal, serious, quiet and intuitive. Somewhat worried, anxious, doubtful or mistrustful. At times very gloomy, depressed and easily discouraged. Inclination for investigation of the mysterious; fond of the Occult and profound or scientific studies. Gain by careful investment. Troubles and misfortunes through marriage and partnerships; difficulties, struggles, obstacles and sorrows in first half of life. Liability to mental disease, headaches and bowel weakness. Troubles in employment and through servants.

### Saturn in Libra (Exaltation)

Refined tastes, respect and fondness for science, intellectual tendencies; somewhat given to debate or controversy. Generally has open or female enmities, sorrow through loss of one of deep attachment; separations, broken contracts and domestic difficulties; troubles and opposition in employment. Often Saturn raises one to high position only to drop the native into severe disgrace or misfortune later. As it tends toward the necessary mental qualities, this is a good location for lawyers, doctors and scientific men generally. In a female chart it often bestows great beauty of the brunette type. Tends to delay marriage and to produce coldness on the part of partner.

Sometimes the life is stimulated by an adversary, or through a difficult partnership.

### Saturn in Scorpio

Sudden resolutions, violent temper, passionate, self-willed, acquisitive, jealous, independent, resourceful and cautious; shrewd mind rather than profoundly intellectual. Sorrow through love affairs, secret alliances, intrigues or domestic difficulties. Psychic ability and fondness for Occult investigations, chemistry or geology. Success through persistence and cleverness after many difficulties, obstacles and trials especially if necessary attention is given to development along the higher lines.

### Saturn in Sagittarius

Frank, fearless, philosophical, kind and obliging; humanitarian views and ever ready to assist in the advancement and promotion of domestic conditions or political economy. Occult tendencies, intuitive understanding, prophetic insight with regard to future welfare or scientific development. Opposition, antagonism or reproof and censure hurt deeply and by resenting such the native often prevents his own elevation or honors, or makes it difficult to attain desired position; otherwise, it gives the power to create his own dignity through merit of ability. Trouble through public affairs, honor and reputation. Sagittarians often engage in more than one occupation; gain by careful and judicious investment. Danger of nervous breakdown at close of life unless effort is made to safeguard the health by building up the system.

### Saturn in Capricorn (Home)

Makes the native melancholic, serious, apprehensive, cautious, suspicious, discontented and acquisitive; deep thinker, good reasoner and grave or reserved in demeanor. Ambitious, very anxious to rise in life and through tact, diplomacy or persistence generally succeeds. Liable to inferior attachments, unreliable friendships, sorrow through marriage and domestic affairs; chronic ailments and possibility of some mental affliction through worry, dissatisfaction, restricted pleasure and recreation or repression. Success followed by failures.

### Saturn in Aquarius

A courteous, affable disposition; a thoughtful, well-disposed, humane, grave, reserved, serious nature. Penetrating intellect, good reasoner and deep thinker; deliberate in action and very impressive in speech when interested; sociable, friendly and usually unresentful. Generally become quite profound in what they undertake in the arts and sciences, refining the mind through study, observation and experience. As a rule, gain good financial prospects through employment or profession by practical application, quiet determination and faithfulness. Form many acquaintances and some romantic or lasting tie. The latter years are usually more fortunate than the beginning of life.

## Saturn in Pisces

If afflicted, the subject suffers loss, hindrance, delays, deception, slander and discredit through friends and acquaintances and meets with many sorrows and disappointments in life, most of which he bears secretly and attempts to present the best side of things.

Circumstances often decide his mode of procedure and compel the native to cope with lines of action entirely unexpected and undesired. He often reaches positions of honor or dignity but has difficulty in maintaining them

Misfortune, hard luck and disaster usually mark attachments or unfavorable ties are formed which severely handicap, retard or sadden life. Sorrow, romance and tragedy are elements which accompany the affectional experiences. The sympathetic and emotional nature is strong and the native is himself often the cause of his misfortune and difficulty; desire is prominent but hope, firmness and continuity need developing.

The native is ingenious and aspiring but lacks sufficient application, opportunities and favorable conditions; The health is often adversely affected by psychic conditions, colds and troubles through the feet, consumptive tendencies and lingering illnesses. Regards money only as a means of acquiring the necessities of life and often seeks relief, understanding and success through an investigation of psychic and occult affairs which usually causes retirement and seclusion, the enlightenment proving somewhat beneficial

Good aspects to Saturn in Pisces tend to mitigate the severe testimonies and assist the native to improve himself through steady, persistent effort and by means of psychical and occult research or large institutions. It gives practical execution, deep intuition, perception and some mediumistic qualities.

# URANUS

## Uranus in Aries

Note: Uranus was in Aries approximately 1844-1851 and 1927-1935.

This location of Uranus gives a love for independence and freedom, positiveness, force and impulse. It increases the mental vigor, producing activity, energy, resource, originative and inventive ability. Fond of machinery, electrical devices, and possesses mechanical ingenuity. Likes travel and often changes the residence. At times is abrupt, brusque, blunt or radical in manner, disregarding tact and self-control; often impulsive in speech without intending to be so. Disputes and estrangements are frequent. Interest in children from a mental or intellectual standpoint.

## Uranus in Taurus (Fall)

Note: Uranus was in Taurus about 1850-1859 and 1934-1942.

Makes the native determined and headstrong, but when confronted with obstacles can usually extricate himself with resource and ingenuity. The native is naturally intuitive and can become an adept in occultism. It is a slightly evil location for marriage, causing jealousy on the part of the partner.

It causes ups and downs in financial affairs and some sudden losses. If well aspected, it signifies gain through partnership, marriage, associations, inventions and original enterprise.

## Uranus in Gemini

Note: Uranus was in Gemini about 1858-1866 and 1941-1949.

Endows the native with versatility, and indicates some eccentricity in friendship and in expression. It increases mental power through originality, intuition and ingenuity. The native loves science and invention, and favors new ideas, reforms and out-of-the-ordinary subjects.

It is a favorable location for the study of electricity, aerodynamics, astrology, metaphysics, mesmerism, etc. Liking for travel and friends among literary and scientific people. Telepathic or clairvoyant faculty.

If Uranus is afflicted: Liable to estrangement from brethren, cousins, neighbors, and some trouble in education, examinations, letters and journeys; unfavorable criticism.

## Uranus in Cancer

Note: Uranus was in Cancer about 1865-1872 and 1948-1956.

Gives mediumistic ability, the feelings and emotions being sensitive and easily touched; at times this makes the native eccentric, cranky, restless, impatient, peculiar or radical.

Some domestic troubles or estrangement, although the native loves home and children. Loss and difficulty through the dwelling, land or property. Stomach troubles. The native is patriotic, loves traveling and is original in ideas and in expression. Interest in municipal or legislative activities.

## Uranus in Leo (Detriment and fall)

Note: Uranus was in Leo about 1871-1878 and 1955-1962.

A mentality which is extremely industrious in its aspirations, yet the native may be physically disposed to great moderation. It makes the person, at times, headstrong, fiery, forceful and eccentric, displaying a disregard for conventionality, a somewhat rebellious disposition and often incurs the disfavor of others. Cannot tolerate being ordered about or contradicted. Great love for freedom, independence and for daring or exciting adventures; strange aversions and attractions. Odd experiences in connection with the affections and in love affairs, and some danger of sorrow or estrangement therein. Obstacles in the home life in youth and loss or difficulty in some way through the father. Some hindrance and annoyance in social affairs and through children, and probably sudden loss of a child.

If Uranus is well aspected it indicates occult ability, success with electricity, machinery and inventions, and is good for a public or professional career of unique or distinctive nature.

## Uranus in Virgo

Note: Uranus was in Virgo about 1878-1885 and 1961-1969.

The mind is subtle, independent and original. The native is quiet, eccentric, stubborn, fond of curiosities and science generally, especially the occult in which he meets with great success. It makes a good mechanic or teacher and gives success in employment of others, especially in connection with electricity, electronics, dietetics, chemistry, metaphysics, or science.

It increases the intellectual ability and the desire for healthful comforts, also to make the most of the productive capacity in manu-facturing and other enterprises in which the native is likely to have interest.

If well aspected it denotes gain through public occupations associ-ated with the government or municipality.

If afflicted, it indicates many difficulties, disappointed ambitions, trouble through employees, or through employment, and restrictions connected with the occupation. Strange or sudden bodily afflictions.

## Uranus in Libra

Note: Uranus was in Libra about 1800-1807, 1884-1891 and 1968-1974.

Makes the native a good reasoner, fond of traveling, eccentric, ambitious, quick-tempered, restless and the possessor of good imagina-tion, taste, intuition and aesthetic faculties. This location favors scientific, artistic, literary or judicial professions, gives telepathic and inventive ability and much personal magnetism. Interest in aerial affairs.

Sometimes it leads to a hasty engagement or marriage but brings danger of separation, estrangement, divorce or death of partner. Unless well aspected it is not good here for partnership. If afflicted, it is likely through some peculiarity of manner, to produce lack of sympathy or affection, also to arouse enmity, rivalry, opposition, criticism. Indicates broken friendships and trouble through schemes, politics and strange actions of partner.

## Uranus in Scorpio (Exaltation)

Note: Uranus was in Scorpio about 1807-1813, 1890-1898 and 1974-1981.

Gives the native strength of mind, will, determination, persistence, power of concentration and a spirit which cannot be broken by resistance.

At times the native is bold, stubborn, sharp-spoken, shrewd, acute, reserved, secretive, aggressive, forceful and rebellious; frequently at variance with other people and with accepted opinions. Uranus in Scorpio intensifies the activity toward self-advancement and personal gain. It gives a love for things mechanical and an inventive nature. There is mesmeric power, ability for practical occultism, industrial chemistry and drugless healing methods.

If Uranus is afflicted there is danger of sudden accidents, falls, wounds by firearms, explosions, electrical devices, and trouble on water.

## Uranus in Sagittarius

Note: Uranus was in Sagittarius about 1814-1820 and 1897-1904.

This location of Uranus increases the imagination and inventiveness; it favors dreams, visions, intuition, premonition and traveling.

The native loves science in general and takes an interest in all passing events of a scientific nature, especially inventions connected with locomotion and all means of travel.

Uranus here assists other influences that may be present in the chart to develop the higher side of the mind in almost any line where wide cultivation and higher education or understanding give scope. The native is progressive, daring, adventuresome, generous and extremely fond of liberty of action and speech; enthusiastic in beliefs and undertakings which are not always orthodox or altogether free from risk or danger.

If much afflicted, strange difficulties arise through these things and possibly some trouble through the partner's relatives and through religious or scientific people; also through foreign affairs and journeys.

## Uranus in Capricorn

Note: Uranus was in Capricorn about 1820-1828 and 1904-1912.

Gives good reasoning faculties and generally a profound, penetrating mind. It disturbs the seriousness, reserve and conservatism of the sign Capricorn; assists in intensifying the ambition, perseverance, executive ability and independence. It tends toward bold enterprise and radical departures from established systems or accustomed methods, initiating innovations of progressive nature. Foresight, intuition, business hunches and the faculty of prevision often help the native to anticipate public trends, conditions or needs. Unique or original undertakings, and progressive or equitable attitude toward patrons or employees. It is a good location for success in governmental or public occupations; or those connected with special lines like electricity, manufacturing, machinery, radio and transportation; also municipal offices, positions of power, authority or responsibility.

There are times, when Uranus is disturbed by transits and directions, that the native feels restless, uneasy and acts eccentric, radical, stubborn or headstrong.

If Uranus is afflicted, it indicates some family discord or trouble in early life, loss of father, separation or estrangement from him, opposition from those of authority, reversals or difficulty in occupation; incurs the disfavor of superiors and severe public criticism.

## Uranus in Aquarius (Home and exaltation)

Note: Uranus was in Aquarius about 1828-1836 and 1912-1920.

Uranus in Aquarius increases the mental ability, giving originality, ingenuity, resourcefulness, inventiveness, comprehensiveness, strong intuition and imagination.

The native is peculiar and eccentric in beliefs, fond of novelty, science and unusual pursuits, possessing great love of freedom. The disposition is pleasant, humanitarian, sociable, obliging and gains many friends some of whom are very peculiar or engaged in extraordinary occupations. The native usually succeeds in anything of a scientific or mechanical nature, also in association with others and in public life, municipal offices, large companies, railroads, radio, airway concerns; fraternal societies and social movements.

## Uranus in Pisces

Note: Uranus was in Pisces about 1836-1844 and 1919-1928.

Gives a peculiar nature, fond of all Occult investigations, mysteries and psychical research.

It usually endows the native with some Occult faculty and expresses in dreams, visions and strange experiences.

It gives far-seeing but not always on the brightest side of things; friends among Occultists and those connected with public and private institutions. May be capable of originating formulas for medication or commercial chemistry or inventing useful methods of treatment.

If afflicted, it brings trouble, difficulty, estrangement from friends and public, lack of sociability or sympathy; opposition, hostility, criticism and scandal coupled with unexpected misfortune and reversals.

## NEPTUNE

## Neptune in Aries

Note: Neptune was in Aries about 1861-1875.

If well aspected, the native will take leading parts in mystical or secret societies and push forward popularity of psychic research.

It intensifies the feelings, emotions and senses, softening or elevating the disposition through sympathy, benevolence, spirit perception or inner understanding.

It gives a love of traveling, also some mystical experiences and original ideas with regard to religious or spiritual matters and naturopathic methods. It confers vivid impulses toward the correction of human ills or conditions, the reform of existing institutions and an incentive toward a national, political or public career.

If afflicted, it gives peculiar feelings, aversions, premonitions and usually inclines to some habit for the gratification of the senses, such as smoking or excessive use of stimulants.

## Neptune in Taurus

**Note**: Neptune was in Taurus about 1874-1889.

If well aspected, it assists other testimonies in the chart for financial gain, especially through speculation, business and secret or private organizations.

It gives a love for occultism, the old, curious and mystical; in fact, it increases the aesthetic taste and adds a spiritual touch to the nature.

It denotes enthusiasm in beliefs, a companionable disposition, usually patient and good-humored and although rather quick in temper, soft-hearted. A favorable location for friendship and marriage. It contributes an active desire to disseminate scientific knowledge, simplifying it as far as possible and popularizing the truth. It gives an insight to natural and psychic phenomena and a desire to undo the doctrines of materialism. Bestows a nature which senses mental achievements, seeing human progress years in advance of the times.

In business or profession it seeks to simplify methods for practical application. The native is likely to be seclusive and lack certainty or persistence in acquiring the common pleasures of life and to disregard the conventional or business trend of the present.

If afflicted, it adds to the sensuality and increases the alimentativeness and desire for stimulants. It tends to negative and psychical states, receptivity without executiveness and a decided inclination toward imagination, mysticism and luxury.

## Neptune in Gemini

Note: Neptune was in Gemini about 1887-1902.

Well aspected, increases the mental sensitivity, giving imagination, impressions, musical taste, prophetic and symbolic dreams. It gives great linguistic or conversational capacity and an interest in the drama, poetry, philosophy and occultism.

It tends to sympathy and geniality. Favorable for quick perception, science, mathematics, invention or anything requiring mechanical ingenuity or fine handiwork.

If afflicted, it inclines to excessive geniality and romantic friendships, mental restlessness or diffusion, likelihood of complications or misunderstanding with brethen, cousins or neighbors and difficulty or anxiety through too great mental receptivity. Deception in promises or agreements; misunderstanding of reports or rumors.

## Neptune in Cancer

Note: Neptune was in Cancer about 1901-1916.

Well aspected, adds delicacy, refinement and idealism to the spiritual faculties. Increases strength of imagination, adds power to the impressions and intensifies the emotions. It conduces to love of nature and natural science, love of home and domestic comforts, although likely to bring some important changes in residence and some peculiar or mysterious experience or development therein. It gives sympathy (especially for the mother), inspiration and psychic or mediumistic faculty. Fondness for traveling, especially by water.

If afflicted, gives a highly impressionable and sensitive nature; restlessness, discontent and strong desire for change are prominent. Indisposition through stomach and by receptive, passive or negative states and inner nervousness or anxiety. Some complications or peculiar conditions in connection with home or domestic affairs.

## Neptune in Leo (Exaltation)

Note: Neptune was in Leo about 1914-1929.

If well aspected, indicates an ambitious, quiet, dignified, benevolent and warm-hearted disposition; much sympathy, charity and generosity coupled with intuitive foresight.

The higher emotions are intensified giving keen and accurate interpretation of human feelings. It bestows a high quality to the faculties of mind as expressed in spirituality and conscientiousness.

Fond of refined sports, pleasure, society and of the fine arts such as poetry, music, painting, the opera and drama. Peculiar sensations or feelings; mysterious or unconventional conditions arise through matters of affection; likely to suffer severe heartache through disappointment relating to the affections.

If afflicted, likely to give too much love of pleasure and trouble of some kind through allowing the senses, feelings and emotions to sway the reason; also difficulty through too lavish expenditure of energy, impulsive sympathy and generosity.

## Neptune in Virgo (Detriment)

Note: Neptune was in Virgo about 1928-1943.

If well aspected, gives an intellectual trend to the spiritual faculties; a rather reserved nature, capable in mathematics and profound in the investigation of psychical phenomena; mediumistic tendency.

It adds gentleness, constancy and patience to the disposition. The native may be unusual in some way and entertain peculiar ideas with regard to medication, hygiene, diet and labor conditions.

It inclines to gain through employment in clerical work, pharmacy, chemistry, nursing, etc. Love of flowers; herbs, shrubs, fish and small animals.

If afflicted, it tends to selfishness and deceit and indicates danger through the use of drugs, medicine, beverages and trouble with the bowels.

## Neptune in Libra

Note: Neptune was in Libra about 1942-1957.

If well aspected, adds tenderness and compassion to the nature, increasing the imagination and giving poetical, musical and artistic appreciations It tends to general popularity, love, friendship and marriage. It gives a love of science, especially the Occult, interest in magic and motion pictures, social and economic equity.

If afflicted, may give too much sympathetic emotion, easily moved to tears, too great an attraction toward the opposite sex. Mysterious conditions arise out of unions and associations with others.

## Neptune in Scorpio

Note: Neptune was in Scorpio about 1955-1970.

If well aspected, intensifies the feeling and emotions and gives greater scope to the inventive ability; adds a love for secret arts such as chemistry and also for the recondite sciences. To the nature it lends persistence, reserve, secrecy and quick temper. It also tends to practical mediumistic or Occult experiences and assists any other testimonies in the chart for gain by legacy.

If afflicted, likely to lead to too great a love for sensation, luxury of beverages and may often be given to slander or rebuke and loss of legacy through treachery.

## Neptune in Sagittarius

Note: Neptune was in Sagittarius about 1806-1820 and will be from 1970-1984.

If well aspected, it adds reverence, reason, determination and ambition to the nature. It gives a love for traveling and much of it. It denotes farsightedness, dreams, visions, inspiration and mystical experiences. Prophetic insight with regard to business, art, science, religion, foreign affairs, literature and psychic research.

If afflicted, likely to give too great a love for change and travel and over-sensitive emotions; vague, indefinite feelings such as strange and annoying dreams or visions and psychical states; afflictions in foreign lands; trouble through religious or political sentiments.

## Neptune in Capricorn

Note: Neptune will enter Capricorn in 1985. It was here about 1820-1834.

If well aspected, strong faith and good reasoning powers; peculiar or psychic business insight; careful and cautious but fearless when convinced. Indicates seriousness or spells of depression and also trouble or sorror in family affairs during youth, especially in connection with the father. It gives interest in psychical affairs and profit through art, music, large business enterprises and public and private institutions.

If afflicted, it will tend to make the nature somewhat indefinite and secretive. May indicate peculiar family relations and cause complications or scandal in business.

### Neptune in Aquarius (Fall)
Note: Neptune will enter Aquarius about 2000. It was here about 1834-1848.

If well aspected, increases the intuition and inner perception, gives love of nature, friendship, popularity and sociability. The native is independent and original in religious and scientific views. Interest in social welfare, clubs and congressional activities. Expansive, progressive, sympathetic and humane.

If afflicted, the native is likely to be too independant and eccentric. Apt to suffer from disappointment in love and scandal with regard to social and marital affairs. Involved in the difficulties of friends.

### Neptune in Pisces (Home)
Note: Neptune was in Pisces about 1847-1862.

If well aspected, it lends dignity to the nature and gives ability for quiet, serious, profound thought and contemplation. It is good for the inspirational faculty and intensifies the mediumistic and psychical qualities, usually conferring some occult ability and fondness for the investigation of mysticism and the recondite sciences.

The native is usually broad-minded, sympathetic, domestic and charitable. Benefits through help and charity both given and received. It gives a love for travel especially by water and gain through occupations connected with shipping, etc.

If afflicted, the native is likely to suffer in health from psychic conditions and meet with losses and ill luck through thwarted schemes and often by unaccountable circumstances.

## PLUTO

Because Pluto spends from 12 to 30 years in one sign its effects are felt on the collective unconscious which is noticeable in generations and civilizations rather than in individuals.

### Pluto in Aries
Note: Pluto was in Aries about 1822-1851.

Revolutionary ideas in political, social, scientific and economic fields. Inventiveness and eccentric thought patterns. Pioneering geographically and socially.

## Pluto in Taurus (Detriment)

Note: Pluto was in Taurus about 1851-1882.

Financial applications of new discoveries. Improved standards of living including agrarian reform, colonial expansion and commercial application of natural resources. Favors new inventions in building, industry and finances.

## Pluto in Gemini

Note: Pluto was in Gemini 1881-1912.

Inventions in the fields of communications, transportation, and electronics. Favors psychoanalytical investigations, abolition of censorship and rapid development of dialects and colloquial patterns of speech.

## Pluto in Cancer

Note: Pluto was in Cancer about 1912-1938.

Disruption of homes and families; rise in dictatorships, chauvinism, nationalism, racism. Inventions of labor savings devices, especially in Home-making fields and child care. Disruption of customs and traditions. Improved methods of family planning and new family roles.

## Pluto in Leo

Note: Pluto was in Leo about 1938-1957.

Increased leisure and emphasis on recreation, entertainment and the growth of the electronics entertainment media industry. Inventions in governmental systems and increased centralization of administration and information.

## Pluto in Virgo (Fall)

Note: Pluto was in Virgo about 1957-1971.

Emphasis on work related fields of automation, computerization, and specialization. Movement toward free trade and unrestricted flow of goods and services. Inventions in the health sciences, public sanitation, preventive medicine and pharmacy. Environmental, nutritional and ecological concerns.

## Pluto in Libra

Note: Pluto will be in Libra 1971-1984.

Redefinition of marriage and sexual codes and customs; new sex roles. Sweeping legal decisions and revisions of legal codes. Original inventions in artistic media and new standards of beauty.

### Pluto in Scorpio (Home)
Note: Pluto will be in Scorpio 1984-1995. Increased military conflicts coupled with armament inventions and possible biological warfare. Psychic research facilitates Occult breakthrough and possible extraterrestrial communication. Improved methods of birth control and increased longevity.

### Pluto in Sagittarius
Note: Pluto enters Sagittarius in 1995. Increased long distance travel effects a global familiarity with diverse ethnic cultures and a diffusion of national and racial distinctions. Religious revival. Inventions in education and publishing fields.

### Pluto in Capricorn
Note: Pluto was in Capricorn about 1762-1777. Rebellion against authority and disruption of political patterns. Improved methods of governmental administration and organization. Emphasis on work ethic and social position.

### Pluto in Aquarius
Note: Pluto was in Aquarius about 1777-1799. Astronomical and electrical discoveries. Humanitarian reform and rise of abolition movement. Increased suffrage and concern for common man. Advent of many social movements.

### Pluto in Pisces (Exaltation)
Note: Pluto was in Pisces about 1799-1822. Emphasis on mystical phenomenon, mesmerism, hidden motives and dream analysis. Romantic interest in fine arts, music, religion and philosophy. Improved methods of dealing with mentally deranged or retarded people and inventions in nursing and care of homeless, aged or diseased persons.

# The Planets in the Houses

These interpretations are for the planets by their positions in the houses only, unaspected, unless otherwise stated. If a planet is aspected, it's delineation by house will be subject to a modification. Consequently, before taking the following interpretations literally, note the sign placement, the aspects to the planet, any dignity or debility, and modify the reading accordingly.

The nature of conflicts which will be experienced in the area of life represented by the house can be determined by the planet tenanting the house, the rulership of the house, and aspects to the planet. The placement of the afflicting planet will give the area of life which is in conflict with the house in question. The nature of the planets and signs involved will give an idea of the psychological and physical energies involved, while the aspect will show the type of tension in the conflict.

When the planet in a house is well aspected, and the ruler of the house is not afflicted, the area of life represented by the house can be easily expressed. Positive aspects to the planet in question will show what other resources of the life are in harmony with the particular house involved. If the planet in the house is well aspected, but the ruler of the house is afflicted, to be difficult with the tension will more likely be between the native and the environment, rather than within oneself. Vice versa, if it is the other way around.

As you consider more and more factors, make sure to differentiate them, understand where they fit in, then join them together into a succinct statement.

271

## THE FIRST HOUSE

### The Moon in the First House

Change in fortune, residence, occupation and employment; sensitive, intuitive and receptive mind; fruitful imagination and nature; ambition, activity and an inclination for public life; refined, ingenious, observant and considerate.

In a common or cardinal sign it denotes flexibility, inconstancy, often timidity and great desire for change or roaming. In the fixed signs the nature is firmer, less changeable and more contented if employed in some ordinary or popular occupation connected with the general public.

The tendency in the First House is to elevate the native in life and bring benefits and advantages from the public through social life in which the domestic interests largely enter. Dream and astral experiences.

The Moon is an important influence in a woman's horoscope, as she rules the periodical functions and shows health or illness according to the aspects.

Afflicted in a watery sign, shows danger from water and liquids.

### Mercury in the First House

Mercury is neutral, sexless and convertible, its nature being such that it absorbs much of the character of the planets with which it comes in contact or aspect; consequently, close attention must be paid to the sign it occupies in addition to the aspect it receives, thus: Mercury assisted by the Moon is good for commissions; by Venus, good for music, singing, art; in favorable connection with the Sun, good for business and responsible positions; in good aspect to Mars, mechanical and constructive ability; if Jupiter assist, a good theologian; Saturn, a good statistician; Uranus, an originator and inventor; Neptune, foresight, prophecy, power for psychometrizing and clair-audience.

Mercury gives adaptability, fertility of resource, an inquiring mind always on the alert for new information, quick comprehension; fondness for literature, writing or speaking and for books, reading and learning.

Perceptive, studious, logical, sharp, persuasive and expressive; fertile imagination. Many changes, journeys, spells of restlessness and anxiety. Quick in speech, thought and action.

## Venus in the First House

Denotes an amiable, trustful, cheerful, sympathetic and affectionate disposition, responsive to the love and emotional side of the nature. Fond of company, enjoyment, society and likes to make others in the environment happy. It gives an appreciation of art and beauty and a fondness for pleasure, music, singing, drama, opera. It shows a refined, generous, just nature, one who is usually much admired by the opposite sex.

The nature is fruitful. The tendency of this position is towards good fortune. If in aspect to Mars, the native marries early. If in adverse aspect to Saturn, it delays marriage.

Bad aspects to Mars, Saturn, Uranus or Neptune indicate much discord and trouble in married life; afflicting Jupiter, much generosity, free and careless with money, yet fortunate in getting it.

Note carefully the influence or nature of the sign Venus occupies: Taurus, Gemini, Libra, Aquarius and Pisces are the best for this position. The nature of Venus is feminine, so look to her aspects and note the tendencies. Inspiration for art comes from Neptune, but it requires a good aspect of Venus to manifest it as Venus governs touch. This planet rules the groins, kidneys and ovaries; also the throat, chin and cheeks.

## The Sun in the First House

Frank, free, generous, outspoken; ambitious, proud, firm and stable; humane; strong, moral nature; quick perception and constructive faculty which bestows a certain appearance of dignity and strength that impresses others. It gives an independent, combative and defensive ambition, coupled with hope, confidence, love of power and authority that results in the native rising above his sphere in life and into positions of trust, influence and responsibility. It strengthens the constitution and adds to the vitality. Tends to honor and general success, advancement and good will of superiors. Lofty motives.

If afflicted by Mars, Saturn or Uranus, it indicates heavy, sharp attacks of sickness; i.e., fevers, inflammation and eye afflictions; also losses and reversals through impulsiveness.

Sun rules vitality and indicates the strength of constitution.

When afflicted, especially by Saturn, the recuperative power is not good.

### Mars in the First House (Natural House)

Ambitious, confident, enterprising, aspiring, skillful and assertive. Usually create a great deal of their own fate by impulse and strong desire nature. Have good, practical, executive ability; love of liberty and independence; free, audacious, courageous, combative and positive, scorning defeat and reckless of danger. Somewhat fiery, amorous, aggressive and defensive; at times rash, headstrong, forceful and impatient.

A great deal depends upon the sign Mars occupies.

By nature Mars is masculine, both constructive and destructive; usually causes a mark or scar about the head or face and one on that part of the body represented by the sign occupied.

Danger of cuts, burns, scalds, falls, bruises and other accidents. Look to the aspects carefully. A good aspect to Saturn is very beneficial to Mars.

Mars rules the muscular system and urino-genital organs, feverish and inflammatory troubles.

### Jupiter in the First House

Optimistic spirit; cheerful, hopeful, jovial disposition; generous, faithful, just, prudent and noble nature; sincere, humane, courteous and amiable; pleasant manners.

The influence of Jupiter is always more or less fortunate. It gives executive ability, power and dignity and fits the native for leading positions in social, educational and business circles.

Its tendency is toward good reasoning, a logical, broad mind, self-possession, confidence and determination.

If unafflicted, it indicates one of high standing, such as bankers, judges, doctors, lawyers, professors, theologians and government officals. Business connected with shipping, long-distance transit, wholesale business or commerce on a large scale. When afflicted: clerk, assistant, clothier, draper, cashier, etc. Note carefully the sign Jupiter occupies and the aspects for judging wealth, station and ability.

Jupiter as related to the body brings on disease resulting from impure blood, plethora, gout, liver complaints, excessive stoutness, varicose veins, etc., according to the sign occupied; super-abundant action of parts when afflicted by Mars or Sun, or defective action when afflicted by Saturn.

## Saturn in the First House

When well placed by sign and aspect it denotes thoughtfulness and consideration for the welfare of others; contemplation, discretion, prudence, system, diligence, economy, respect and careful attention to affairs generally.

The disposition is calm, serious, grave. The desire is to attain prominence as the result of merit and to that end they labor with method, industry, perseverance and steadiness, rarely entering into any project that is not premeditated and planned. Progress and success may be slow but is sure to bring good reputation, honor and credit through persistence, practical ability, worldly wisdom and continual effort.

When weak or afflicted it indicates liability to colds and trouble to that part of the body ruled by the sign it is in. Bruises to the head. The nature is faithful, chaste, reserved; thoughtful, mistrustful, subtle, acquisitive, penetrative and careful of personal affairs; secretive and given to periods of gloom and discontent.

Loss and misfortune through negligence, habits, lack of opportunity or fateful events and delays.

It also indicates many sorrows and disappointments, sometimes poverty and an uphill road generally.

Saturn rules the bones, teeth, right ear, knees and spleen. Gives liability to suffer from colds, chills and poor circulation, also through constipation, rheumatism, stone, gravel, obstructed growth; usually they are deficient in Phosphate of Calcium.

## Uranus in the First House

Uranus signifies originality of thought, independence of mind, inventive genius, intuition, intellectual and metaphysical ability. It inclines to the Occult, the antiquated, curious, new and the odd; in fact to everything out of the ordinary.

It attracts toward such subjects as astrology, occultism, mesmerism, hypnotism, spiritualism, psychic research, drugless healing, telepathy, psychism, Free Masonry, inventions, electricity.

It makes one appear odd, peculiar, eccentric and many years

ahead of the time.

It is significant of many changes in residence and occupation and is usually not good here for marriage, bringing about peculiar, unfortunate conditions, difficulties and separations.

It is Uranus manifesting which makes one independent and revolutionary, apt to change the mind and position radically and suddenly, forming his own opinions regardless of what others may think of them. Estrangement from parents and kindred.

Uranus stands for freedom, equality, progress and its natives can always see how conditions may be improved even when they are good enough in the opinion of others. They are nearly always on the opposite side to things that are popular, formal or limited, preferring expansion and upheaval, and therefore take the side of the unpopular in public movements, studies, sciences, religion, etc. They are often called cranks, but invariably their cranky notions become accepted facts after a time. They are usually forceful, not particularly quarrelsome or antagonistic, but are vigorous in the cause of the oppressed. They are not at all opposed to discussion or debate and seldom become angry in it; detest limitations and cannot stand control or dictation.

Uranus rules the originating or creating faculties: phrenologically expressed, the faculties of comparison and causality, without which there can be no invention or science.

Although Uranus gives originality and individuality of thought, and one may be fairly running over with good ideas, unless Mercury assists, he cannot utter them satisfactorily. Mercury gives the ability to learn, understand, interpret, expound and express.

The enlightened Uranian gives all the freedom possible to those around him, knowing that his liberty is increased correspondingly. However, just how fine the native will manifest or interpret the ray from Uranus depends upon the quality of the *aspects* to it in the birth chart.

Uranus afflicted shows quickness of mind, mental impulsiveness, originality, independence and self-will. Makes the native changeful, impulsive, abrupt, erratic, eccentric, willful, brusque, sarcastic, critical and easily offended. Gives inventive genius.

It gives ability to develop thought-reading and transference, clairvoyance, crystal-gazing, etc.

Danger through lightning, electricity and hurts by machinery, inventions, engines, explosives and vehicles of travel. Gives an interest in all Occult affairs; rules the aura and the personal magnetism; strange happenings.

## Neptune in the First House

The influence of this planet is always more or less mediumistic and the native will either consciously or unconsciously take on the conditions of the surroundings and of those with whom he comes in contact. Being a neutral planet, it depends upon *aspects* for the manner in which it will manifest.

It represents inspiration, trance, dreams, weird feelings, thoughts and experiences; romance and emotion; visionary or idealistic trend of mind.

When well aspected it gives good inspiration and spirit perception. It denotes far-seeing, ability to estimate quickly and accurately. It attracts one to peculiar people, psychic centers and mysterious, strange places.

It gives ability to cultivate psychometry, clair-audience and mediumship.

It exalts the artistic tastes, giving a love for beauty in form, color and sound. It is also related to matters connected with the sea, water and liquids in general, also mediumship and spiritualism. When it is weak or afflicted it seems to open an avenue of temptation that appeals to the passional, sense-loving and emotional side of the nature, bringing uncertainty and confusion through instability, indolence or lack of energy. Danger through plots, schemes, enmities and deception.

Although it indicates inspiration, enthusiasm and perception, yet it denotes a receptivity to psychic conditions that might run to extremes, allowing the feelings to get the upper hand of the judgment. Tendency to excitability, changefulness, morbid imagination, strange or unnatural appetites, intrigues, acts of indiscretion, deception, presumption, love of luxury; wandering disposition, many journeys, changes, ups and downs. Being readily affected both mentally and physically by the psychic conditions of the environment, individuals with Neptune in this house should investigate the philosophy of all things mysterious rather than the phenomena.

There are times when people who are strongly influenced by Neptune should have nothing to do whatever with any Occult phenomena, seances, drugs, medicines, gases, etc.; on the other hand, there are days when they should strive to develop their Occult faculties. These times are when other planets come into aspect with Neptune, particularly the Moon.

## Pluto in the First House

This position can give a lack of self-confidence to the point of self-abuse and neglect of appearance if Pluto is in detriment, debility or poorly aspected; or an unrealistically high opinion of self and an over-estimation of one's ability if Pluto is in good aspect or dignified.

Periods of identity crisis and self-doubt according to the transiting aspects. The native is governed by subconscious drives which he cannot control—whether for good or bad depends on the aspects and sign position of Pluto. The drive for personal power is strong and often manifests in devious or underhanded ways.

This position bestows an aura of mystery due to the secretiveness of the native. The native thinks himself utterly unique and is often a loner, exile or iconoclast; he has a sense of exclusiveness and isolation.

The native is subject to bodily violence, often self-inflicted or unwittingly brought about by himself. He has a tendency to get involved over his head and forms associations with persons of a tough, mean or low nature, to his own misfortune.

This native projects varying images of himself to different people because his personality is not stable and undergoes violent, drastic changes, according to the transiting aspects.

## THE SECOND HOUSE

### The Moon in the Second House

Gain by employment through public affairs and occupations, by dealing with liquids, commodities and the wants of the common people generally. Money obtained through females or the mother, or matters related to the domestic life. Good for things ruled by the Moon and the sign it occupies.

If well aspected, it is favorable for financial success, although somewhat variable, since the source of profit will usually be some fluctuating commodity, or the whim of the public or the mass mind.

## Mercury in the Second House

Denotes gain by letters, writings, speaking, traveling, teaching, clerical occupations, commissions and ordinary business and commercial affairs generally; also through study, advertising, distributing, stationery, books, etc. Gain through any occupation corresponding to the nature of the planet in closest good aspect.

## Venus in the Second House (Natural House)

By fortuitous circumstances, good will and favors from others, money usually comes readily. It may be gained through artistic pursuits, music pleasure, social affairs, friendships, societies, marriage, jewelry, millinery, hotels, confectionery and wearing apparel. A good deal of money is spent on adornment, luxuries, pleasure, friends and social interests; nevertheless, they acquire it.

## The Sun in the Second House

Money obtained by industrious effort and through the father and superiors; gain by affairs of government or through holding official appointments or other responsible positions. Benefit through superiors and persons of rank. The nature of the occupations depends much upon what sign the Sun occupies. The native is inclined to generosity in money matters, social intercourse, pleasure, luxury and sports.

## Mars in the Second House

Good earning powers but usually extravagant, over-generous or careless regarding the accumulation of wealth, and money runs quickly through the fingers.

It denotes gain by the native's own energy, activity, skill and strength; by stock farming, iron, steel, chemicals, timber, business enterprise as agent, salesman or promoter.

When well aspected to the ruler of the Eighth House it denotes money by legacy; to ruler of the Seventh House, by marriage.

If Mars is afflicted, heavy losses, expenditures or extravagance and trouble, strife and contention over finances.

## Jupiter in the Second House

Increases the chances for success, wealth and general prosperity. It has to do with government and responsible business affairs and tends to gain through law, insurance, banking, religion, science, education, literature and travel. Money acquired through things indicated by the house which Jupiter rules in the chart and by the sign it occupies.

### Saturn in the Second House

Saturn, unless well aspected, tends to make an uphill struggle and much work for little gain. The person may see many opportunities but is seldom in a position to take advantage of them.

At times things run along apparently well and smoothly and then take a turn and go persistently wrong or suffer delay; lack of money. With this position of Saturn, one should become thoroughly acquainted with the directions operating in the chart to avoid failures and to increase chances for success in land, property, produce, mines, storage, investments, coal, lead, building, labor, etc.

When well aspected or favorably located by sign: prudent financial ability, thrift, economy and solid, conservative investments bring steady but slow returns. Gains by father or employer.

### Uranus in the Second House

Many changes in fortune; financial affairs very uncertain; ups and downs. Uranus has affinity for unique occupations, affairs and employment of all kinds, especially those of a curious or mental character and which require great ingenuity.

Gain through inventions, mechanisms, railroads, electrical affairs, Occultism, Astrology, extraordinary composition and sometimes music, especially when well aspected with Venus. Money is gained through friends, associations or the government.

### Neptune in the Second House

Neptune gives liability of financial affairs becoming much involved and loss through fraud and schemes.

Neptune rules hospitals, asylums, institutions, secret service, the sea and its various industries, navigation, baths, public establishments, spiritualism, mediumship, mystical and secret societies. If well aspected the native will gain through these things, afflicted, will lose by them.

### Pluto in the Second House

Changes in financial position affect the personality of the native

and can cause emotional trauma. Much worry and anxiety over monetary affairs. Ability to change financial situation.

Possible gain or loss of money due to the death of a benefactor,
an inheritance or legacy; look to the aspects, sign position and planets
in the Eighth House for further indications.

Fields for successful financial enterprises include: any industry
which recycles waste or converts nonuseable items into useable ones;
industry which affects chemical change on raw materials; fields involved
in combating pollution; sanitation, hygiene, garbage collection; all
occupations dealing with death — funeral director, mortician, casket
salesman, undertaker, grave digger, hearse driver, etc.; occupations
involved in manufacturing organic fertilizers, and compost; all professions
delving into psychological motives; detective work of all kinds, including
medical research and geological exploration.

Poorly aspected Pluto: associations with gangsters and criminal
activity due to greed and materialistic motives. Gambling and speculation can bring sudden wealth but unexpected losses always follow.
Over-possessive of physical possessions as well as relationships. Self
indulgence in physical pleasures can affect the health. Gross appetites.


# THE THIRD HOUSE

## The Moon in the Third House

Many changes of pursuit and occupation; desire for publicity of
some sort; curious, active and inquisitive mind ever alert for new information and generally possessing a fund of knowledge regarding public
conditions and new material for thought and action.

Usually there is not sufficient continuity; unfinished education or
accomplishments. An unfavorable position for peace of mind, if afflicted.

Well aspected: Good for learning and mental attainments along
popular lines. Short studies of domestic science or social welfare and
short journeys prove beneficial.

## Mercury in the Third House (Natural House)

Many short journeys, much activity and writing.

The mind inclines to investigate whatever tends to enlightenment:

to increase the consciousness and broaden the understanding; fond of reading, study, speaking, teaching, lectures, literature, new thought, science, news.

The mentality is quick and perceptive and usually interested in or anxious regarding relatives and neighbors.

When Mercury is afflicted the native is inclined to excessive worry or anxiety. It is said that the mind reacts on the bowels which is likely true enough, as Mercury represents both, ruling Gemini and Virgo. Trouble through letters, promises, agreements or reports.

When well aspected: successful travels, mental development, accomplishments and gain through Third House affairs.

### Venus in the Third House

The mental quality is good. Strong inclination and liking for fine arts, music, singing, opera, paintings, light literature and all that tends to uplift or refine the mind and give pleasure. The mind is cheerful, fruitful, optimistic, bright and desirous of peace. It denotes favorable relatives or neighbors and aid or gain through them.

It is a good position for pleasure trips or pleasure and gain through journeys and successful travels, in fact, it is good for all things ruled by the Third House. Pleasant correspondence, many social acquaintances.

### The Sun in the Third House

It is good for all things ruled by this house. It tends to respect, good will and benefit from relatives and neighbors; successful travels for business and pleasure.

The mind is resourceful, creative, magnanimous and ambitious of success and honor through mental qualifications; the desire is to up-life, enlighten, benefit and assist others mentally. Afflicted: trouble with some of the kindred or neighbors and through proud, haughty states of mind. Discredit through letters, promises, agreements or false reports.

### Mars in the Third House

Liability to danger and accidents by journeys, trouble through travel, relatives, neighbors, writings and litigation. The mind is alert, energetic, keen, forceful, combative and likely to get out of control easily. The native is quick and prompt in speech and possesses executive power in literary or educational directions. At some time may be troubled with brain fever or deliriousness and if Mars is afflicted by Saturn, Uranus or Neptune, shows thought of suicide or violent tendencies.

The best sign for Mars in this house is Capricorn and the best aspects are the good ones to Saturn or Mercury, although a good one to Uranus will give genius in some line and inventive ability.

## Jupiter in the Third House

Gain in all things ruled by this house. The mind is optimistic, philosophical, refined, cheerful and sympathetic. Kind, thoughtful, just and considerate in all matters of correspondence, publication or exchange of thought; sincere, earnest, courteous, sociable and reasonable in speech and writing. Capable of adapting himself to conventionalities of thought prevalent and popular. Benefits through education, literature, publishing, traveling, brethren and neighbors.

## Saturn in the Third House

Trouble, loss, disappointment, annoyance, hindrance and delays in connection with education, writings, relatives, neighbors, traveling and changes. Coldness between brethren or sorrow through their demise.

The tendency of the mind is toward gloom, caution, acquisitiveness, worry, restlessness, anxiety and misgiving, especially in youth. The mental condition improves with age and is much better in later life, becoming more contemplative, thoughtful and capable of concentration on serious or profound subjects.

If Saturn is ill-aspected or afflicted by the Sun, Moon or Mercury, the melancholy expression is liable to run into extremes, despondency, morbid tendencies or mental afflictions.

When well aspected it denotes responsibility, tact, diplomacy, thought power, steady thinking, concentration and mental control, orderly reasoning; philosophic mind with ability for profound studies or writings.

## Uranus in the Third House

Denotes estrangements from kindred and neighbors and strange experiences through them; sudden and unexpected news, journeys and changes, odd happenings, meetings, adventures and occurrences through travels. The native is peculiar or eccentric in some things, but usually intellectual and possesses ability to develop clairvoyant, clairaudient or telepathic faculty in addition to magnetic healing. The mind is curious, inventive, ingenious, unconventional and fond of the Occult, mystical, new, extraordinary, profound, ancient or unpopular studies, social and mental reforms; intuitive perception and understanding with regard to things Occult. If Uranus is afflicted by Saturn or Mars, it shows danger of accidents, wrecks or explosions on journeys, through vehicles of travel or treachery on the part of relatives or neighbors.

## Neptune in the Third House

Denotes psychological faculties, spiritual perception; fruitful, inventive mind, given to the investigation of spirit phenomena and matters pertaining to the Occult or mysterious; inspirational ideas.

Produces weird feelings or experiences. Signifies journeys, peculiar difficulties with relatives, schemes, plots, deceit, etc. Changes in name: nick-name, nom de plume or alias.

If Neptune is weak or badly aspected it disturbs the mind with hallucinations, morbid fancies, imbecility, weak intellect or depraved tastes.

When well aspected it gives artistic taste or appreciation of an exalted order through a peculiar blending of the feelings and intuition and ability to contact the artistic realm inspirationally; possibility of independent or automatic writings.

## Pluto in the Third House

Denotes a tendency to morbid thoughts and dwelling on death, decay and excrement. Preoccupied with the seamy, sinister and sordid side of life.

Mind liable to moodiness and brooding if poorly aspected. Depressions and negative thinking. Many changes of mind and second thoughts about decisions.

Well aspected: inspiration from unlikely sources, finds beauty in the common place and can use normally neglected articles. Ideas about recycling and conversion of waste products. Insights on death and the meaning of life, and desire to uncover the secrets of the universe.

Very opinionated. Holds on to ideas despite contradictory evidence and pressure from others, yet has the ability to uncover hidden motives and evaluate situations and people accurately in depth.

This position indicates the need to talk, write or express artistically the native's emotional state and thus providing a therapeutic release.

## THE FOURTH HOUSE
### The Moon in the Fourth House (Natural House)

Well placed or aspected, it shows gain and benefit through the parents, home and domestic life; favors from the opposite sex; some chance of inheritance. Publicity or popularity through the parents; many changes in residence and fluctuation in affairs toward the close of life. If well dignified here it shows ultimate rise to success and independence through possessions, property, lands, farms or orchards.

If Saturn afflicts the Moon much disappointment will be encountered in desired success; in fact, great difficulty to keep from poverty and sorrow due largely to family affairs. Afflictions by Mars, Sun or Mercury denote loss by theft, fraud or deception. Jupiter adverse: denotes lack of opportunities and limitations through environment. Uranus adverse: sudden changes; difficulties with home affairs; estrangements from or loss of parents, probably the mother; loss through unexpected reversals and changes. Neptune adverse: mystery or complications concerning home affairs and property.

### Mercury in the Fourth House

Inconstancy in affairs generally; change of residence through matters connected with business. Often the subject has no fixed abode; many traveling men have this position.

Worry and anxiety regarding disturbance in home affairs.

Good position for proprietors of private schools or other stationary places where literary or clerical work is carried on, such as land, mine and real estate agencies, registry offices, newspaper offices, libraries, publishers, etc., or for business carried on in the home.

In bad aspect to Uranus: unexpected difficulties and disturbances toward the close of life or sudden end.

Saturn adverse: denotes loss through deception, fraud and theft.

Mars adverse: loss through imposition, controversy or fire.

Sun, Moon or Jupiter adverse: lack of opportunity or limitations and numerous losses.

Uranus in good aspect: unexpected gain in possessions; occult investigation and enlightenment before the close of life.

Saturn or Jupiter in good aspect: steadier, more satisfied and studious; inclines to success, opportunities and inheritance.

Sun, Moon or Venus in good aspect: activity, popularity and success before the close of life.

## Venus in the Fourth House

Indicative of favorable domestic affairs and happiness through the parents; love of home and country. Chance of gain by inheritance, parents, houses or property and investment; peaceful, comfortable conditions at the close of life. Sun, Moon or Jupiter in good aspect is exceedingly fortunate, bringing general affairs to a successful issue.

In good aspect to Uranus or Saturn: success in old age. Benefit by pension or legacy.

The adverse aspects of Sun, Moon, Mercury or Jupiter are not particularly evil but affect the finances through extravagance or misjudgment.

Mars adverse: difficulty through generosity, carelessness or extravagance toward the close of life.

Saturn, Uranus or Neptune adverse: sudden, peculiar losses, disappointments and sorrows toward the end of life.

## The Sun in the Fourth House

A chance of honor in declining years, successful ambitions, hopes and wishes realized. Good for houses, land, property and occupations connected with them. Gain or chance of inheritance by or through the parents; fortunate heredity.

In good aspect to Moon, Venus, Jupiter, Saturn or Uranus: gain through property or inheritance, financial success. To Neptune, it inclines to secrecy or investigation of Occult or spiritual affairs; some psychic experiences in the home.

If afflicted: obstacles, limitations, troubles and sorrows through the parents and home life; liability to loss and difficulty by living beyond the means or through heavy obligations. Weakens the constitution at the close of life.

The native will be content at home and amid family, and may become the stability of same, or greatly respected in the home.

## Mars in the Fourth House

Domestic unpleasantness and much misunderstanding, inharmony or quarrels in the home life, especially if Mercury afflicts. Losses by theft, fire and accidents in the dwelling place; early death of parent. Many difficulties, disappointments and obstacles. Physical indisposition caused by bad digestion and acid condition. Liability to trouble over property, loss through speculations in property, lands and mines. If Neptune, Uranus or Saturn afflict: mental distress, suicide or liability to sudden end by accident; unfortunate in the place of birth. The good aspects give much energy, force, activity and enterprise in the acquisition of possessions.

## Jupiter in the Fourth House

Tends to satisfactory, comfortable and peaceful domestic affairs; successful home life and family surroundings; gain and favor through parents; benefit through land and possessions; good position and success toward the close of life.

If unafflicted: a fortunate, easy life; success at the place of birth, successful termination to business enterprises and affairs generally.

Jupiter afflicted gives trouble through the parents or their affairs, and extravagance; hereditary limitations.

Sun or Moon adverse: liability to sudden heart trouble or apoplexy. Mars adverse: danger of loss by fire.

Mercury adverse: danger of lawsuits over property or inheritance and if both afflict the ruler of the fourth, law with or through the parents. Mars or Saturn in good aspect: a religious or satisfactory end. Uranus favorable: Occult tendencies, long life. The luminaries favorable: overcomes many adverse testimonies in the chart and shows a rise in life to opulence and popularity.

## Saturn in the Fourth House

Difficulties and trouble through property, inheritance or mines. Sorrow through parents, probably separation from the father either physically or emotionally. Acquisitiveness. Unsatisfactory domestic or home life. Much work, heavy responsibilities and great difficulty in achieving ambitions. Unfortunate in the place of birth. Seclusiveness at the close of life. If well-aspected: acquisition of property; gain through produce or mining.

## Uranus in the Fourth House

Unsettled residence; many changes; a checkered career. Unfortunate in place of birth. Estrangements from parents; domestic troubles and family affairs. Exceptional domestic experiences. Loss of inheritance, if one is expected. Many ups and downs and tastes of poverty through peculiar circumstances.

Mars or Saturn adverse: danger of violence; liability to accidents in the home. Neptune adverse: threatens loss through theft, fraud and deception, by accident, flood or action of the elements. Jupiter adverse: loss through impulsiveness or misjudgment, law, storms or by lightning.

## Neptune in the Fourth House

Changes of residence. Voyages. Peculiar domestic and family affairs, some secrets or mystery regarding the home life; schemes, fraud and misunderstanding, afflicting the parents in some way, affects the native. Much depends on the aspects. The luminaries in affliction denote weakened vitality and poor health. Mercury adverse: peculiar nervous disorders in later life. Abides in unusual or peculiar conditions. Neptune is neutral; consequently, good aspects would show benefits through property and parents, according to the nature of the aspects.

## Pluto in the Fourth House

Unsettled conditions in the home; many changes of residence. Possible secret in native's background or heredity; hereditary or sex-linked disease likely.

The end of life will be difficult with a long, lingering illness or gradual decline. This can be demoralizing if Pluto is poorly aspected or debilitated, or can serve to prepare the native spiritually for death if Pluto is well aspected.

Death of the mother greatly affects the native's mental condition, perhaps even causing emotional problems or trauma. Incest, sexual attraction to a relative, or marriage to a family member possible. Intense feelings for family often kept secret.

Difficult childhood can cause psychological problems later in life. Home and childhood very important to the native.

If adversely aspected, this position indicates selfishness and overprotectiveness.

# THE FIFTH HOUSE

## The Moon in the Fifth House

Public success in connections with places of amusement, playgrounds, bathing resorts, or with children and young people; fondness for pleasure and the society of children and the opposite sex. Strong tendencies toward speculation or games of chance. Much activity and change in all enterprise; changeable affections (except in fixed signs) yet the heart may be given to one who least deserves it and thus the affection changes to aversion, coldness or indifference.

It is indicative of a child who achieves fame and popularity, if well aspected; also that the native will in some manner be closely connected or drawn to a child or young person. Several offspring. (If Moon is in a fruitful sign.) If Neptune is in good aspect, may adopt a child.

If the Moon is afflicted it brings loss through speculations and danger or sorrow and trouble through love, children and morals.

## Mercury in the Fifth House

Refines the pleasures and makes them more mental than muscular, more of the mind than of the senses, and is good for occupations connected with entertainment, schools or travel.

This position denotes worry, anxiety and sorrow through objects of affection, children and their affairs.

A good aspect of Saturn or Jupiter much improves the position and brings success and gain through these things and also through speculation or investment. Luminaries favorable: indicates success in connection with traveling for public amusement and with children. Mars, Uranus or Neptune adverse: denotes troublesome love affairs, scandal, separations, divorce, lawsuits. Losses through speculation.

## Venus in the Fifth House

A fruitful union and beautiful children who may be endowed with artistic or musical ability; happiness, comfort and gain through offspring, which are usually or mostly girls.

This position denotes gain and success through love affairs, friendships, etc., ability to entertain others and enjoy success through all manner of social intercourse, pleasure and amusement.

It indicates gain through speculation, investment and general enterprise, also through theaters, singing, music, painting, children, schools, playgrounds, parks or summer resorts.

If Venus is much afflicted, it gives liability of injury to the health through over-indulgence in pleasurable gratification. Saturn adverse: sorrow and disappointment through love, speculation, children. Mars, Uranus or Neptune adverse: trouble and danger through the opposite sex, and careless, rash, indiscriminate or unconventional bestowal of affection.

### The Sun in the Fifth House (Natural House)

Honorable and successful attachments. Gain through speculation, investment, enterprise, children, pleasure and places of amusements. Small family. This position often denies children and inclines to difficult or dangerous child-birth. However this depends on the nature of the sign on the Fifth House cusp, whether barren or not, etc. If the Sun is afflicted here it causes loss through speculation, troubles and jealousy in courtship, and sorrow through love, pleasure and pride; trouble with children.

### Mars in the Fifth House

Pleasure through the strenuous sports, athletics, muscular exercise. Impulsive, rash and unfortunate attractions towards the opposite sex. Sensual emotions or over-ardent affections, and too much indulgence in pleasure and amusement results in physical, financial and social loss; danger of accident to first child. In a woman's horoscope this position shows difficult and dangerous childbirth. Loss by speculation, gaming, extravagance, pleasure and excess of feeling. Trouble with or through children.

Neptune, Uranus, Saturn, Jupiter, Sun, Moon or Venus adverse: threatens danger of ruin or disgrace through the opposite sex; loss through risky speculation.

Well aspected: gain through occupations and enterprise connected with pleasure and investment corresponding to the nature of Mars.

### Jupiter in the Fifth House

Good and dutiful children, who will be a help and comfort to the native. Success, happiness and gain through love affairs and the opposite sex. Pleasure, success and gain in connection with places of amusement, theaters, social functions, schools. A good position for gain through speculation, investment and financial enterprise, more especially if Mars or Sun is in good aspect. For a female it usually denotes attraction to professional men, wholesale merchants, or those in good financial or social position. Increases the number of children and is fortunate for them. If Jupiter is afflicted the good influences are modified, giving the same desires but trouble, losses and obstacles, according to the nature of the afflicting planet and house occupied.

## Saturn in the Fifth House

Denotes disappointments, delays, hindrance and sorrow in connection with love affairs; attraction to those who are older or more serious in disposition. For a female it usually denotes an attachment to an elderly gentleman or widower or to one of religious nature. Loss of child, troubles and unhappiness through children.

Loss by speculation, investment and games of chance.

Danger from animals while on pleasure. Danger of drowning if Saturn is in Scorpio, and of heart trouble if in Leo. If Saturn is well aspected by either Sun or Moon and not otherwise afflicted, it is a good position for investment in lands, mines and property and such things which Saturn governs. If afflicted by Sun, Moon or Jupiter, take no speculative chances of any kind.

## Uranus in the Fifth House

Unconventional ideas with regard to sex union; strange, romantic, inconstant, secret or impulsive love affairs. Social vexation, scandal.

Loss of first child through some sudden or extraordinary manner or separation, anxiety and trouble through children; difficulty through child birth. Difficulties in domestic life and love attachments. Loss through speculation, risks, chances. Liking for odd, new, daring pleasures or unusual places of amusement.

## Neptune in the Fifth House

Strange and peculiar experiences in connection with the feelings, emotions and affections; abnormal conditions relating to sex matters. Sensuous pleasures, seduction. If afflicted it denotes trouble, faithlessness or confusion and sorrow in love affairs and loss through lax control of the desires and appetites; losses in speculation through deceit or treachery. If well aspected the native will be assisted in self-development by a fortunate association with one of the opposite sex; gain by investment in oil, shipping and such things as Neptune rules.

### Pluto in the Fifth House

Compulsive gambler, usually in secret. If well aspected: can mean sudden wealth through gambling. Likes unusual, esoteric amusements and entertainments. Likes unconventional or perverted sexual relations. Inclines to secret love affairs. Much emphasis placed on sex.

Disappointments from children; illegitimate children, or baby given up for adoption. Factors surrounding the birth of a child cause anxiety or emotional instability later in life. Children unusual in some way.

Emotions often kept secret; relationships with people for reasons other than those given. Gives parties and entertains for ulterior reasons. Social climber. Arrogant and self-centered.

Finds emotional release in physical exercise and sex.

## THE SIXTH HOUSE

In this section, pertaining to the Sixth House, no intention is made to indicate remedies in an advisory capacity. Bodily indisposition, as well as mental disturbance, should be remedied as soon as possible. Health is important to efficiency and happiness and should not be neglected. Therefore, when indisposed, it is wise to seek the aid of those who are trained in the art of healing and by whatever method of treatment seems best, strive to re-establish physical and mental equilibrium.

### The Moon in the Sixth House

Uncertain health, especially in a woman's horoscope; much sickness and danger in infancy. Desire to serve the public in some professional capacity. The subject has better ability and opportunity of getting good results from serving others than from others serving him. Many changes among servants or employees. Success in domestic service or in catering to public desire for necessities, food stuffs, drinks, etc.

Good aspects to the Moon help the health and indicate success with small animals, servants and through some subordinate position connected with the occupations ruled by the sign the Moon occupies. Moon afflicted gives poor success with employees, treachery and dishonesty among them; poor success with small animals, poultry, etc.; weakness in the part of the body ruled by the sign the Moon occupies.

Afflicted in a common sign: danger from lung trouble and chronic diseases. Fixed sign: bronchitis, gravel or stone. Cardinal sign: nervous derangements and stomach trouble.

Moon afflicted by Mercury: indigestion, aches in head and teeth, bowel troubles.

Moon afflicted by Venus: functional or skin trouble.

Moon afflicted by Mars: inflammatory complaints.

Moon afflicted by Jupiter: liver and blood trouble.

Moon afflicted by Saturn: chronic disease, poor circulation.

Moon afflicted by Sun, Uranus or Neptune: weak vitality, indigestion, indisposition through psychic conditions.

## Mercury in the Sixth House (Natural House)

Many small vexations through servants; journeys on account of health. Good position for the study of hygiene, medicine or chemistry. Gain in subordinate positions, through writings, clerical work and Mercurial affairs generally.

Active mentality, but liable to become overstrung or impaired through anxiety, worry or overwork, causing dyspepsia or a tendency to become easily affected by the surrounding conditions.

Any afflictions to Mercury here are unfavorable to the health through the mentality and nervous system.

Afflicted by Uranus: liable to abnormal mental states; suicidal tendencies due to illness.

Afflicted by Saturn: danger of serious illness through despondency or worry.

Afflicted by Mars: mental derangement or excitability; surgical operations.

Afflicted by Sun, Moon or Neptune: fevers, stomach trouble; indisposition through psychic conditions.

## Venus in the Sixth House

Favorable to health, but common sense and discretion should be exercised to keep from excesses of all kinds, especially with regard to eating and drinking. Gain in the employ of others. It is favorable for success and benefits through servants, hygiene, medicine, nursing, and by clothing, small animals, poultry, etc. People with Venus here often take up work for the pleasure it gives them and the interest it creates. Love for pets, fine clothes and adornments. If afflicted it shows trouble to the health through indulgences, and to that part of the body ruled by the sign Venus is in or by the afflicting planet; skin diseases, kidney or ovarian trouble. Health usually improves after marriage.

### The Sun in the Sixth House

This is a cadent house; therefore the Sun, ruler of vitality, placed here is not a very good position for health, as it may slightly weaken the constitution. If afflicted by Neptune, Uranus or Saturn, the recuperative power is not good, and it indicates a great deal of indisposition, liability to contagious diseases and danger from epidemics.

When the Sun is well aspected the native seems to understand intuitively how to safeguard the health and in that way avoids illness.

Any aspect of Mars strengthens the constitution. A good aspect of Mars, Jupiter or Venus would show success and gain through servants and service rendered; success, promotion and fortunate conditions in employments that benefit others, such as healing, chemistry, hospital work, etc. In fact, the Sun well dignified or aspected here indicates that the native can do great work in relieving the sufferings of humanity.

Sun afflicted in a fixed sign: tonsillitis, bronchitis, asthma, diphtheria, gravel, heart trouble, weak back, sides and nervous disorders; organic troubles. Afflicted in a common sign: chronic diseases; troubles with respiratory organs, liver complaints. Afflicted in a cardinal sign: nervousness, weak chest and stomach, rheumatism. Also liable to some permanent injury; functional derangements.

### Mars in the Sixth House

Disputes, quarrels, losses and theft through servants or employees and much difficulty and annoyance by their taking liberties and advantage of the native. The native is usually an active, energetic and enthusiastic worker and liable to overdo himself, especially in others' employ.

Mars rules the tastes and this position of Mars tends to impair or injure the health and cause suffering through excesses, acts of indiscretion, carelessness, extravagance and by accident.

Its position here is usually significant of incision with steel to that part of the body ruled by the sign it is in; surgical operations.

Mars afflicted: inflammation or accidents to that part of the body ruled by the sign occupied; difficulty in employ; danger, loss and trouble through employees, animals, poultry, pets.

Mars gives a tendency to inflammatory complaints in the bowels and troubles in that part of the body represented by the sign occupied in about the same manner as does the Sun when in the Sixth House and in a like sign. (See Sun in the Sixth House.)

Saturn adverse: danger of death due to operations and injuries by animals.

Uranus adverse: danger of fatal accident or suicide.

Neptune adverse: danger of foul play, accidental poisoning, etc.

## Jupiter in the Sixth House

Gives health, but if indisposed the subject receives kind treatment, good attention and many comforts; in fact, is likely to gain through sickness. The native's care and presence would be beneficial and healing to others in distress.

If the person should become a physician, likely to be successful financially and with the patients.

Gain and profit through employment, especially in high circles; also through servants and inferiors, and through religious, philanthropic and social tendencies. Success with domestic animals, poultry, etc. If afflicted the health will suffer from over-indulgence or intemperance in diet; difficulty with the chest, bowels, liver, blood and digestive organs.

## Saturn in the Sixth House

Denotes much sickness through exposure and circumstances over which the subject has little control: neglect, privation, sorrow, disappointment. Many lost opportunities through the state of health. Troubles according to the nature of the sign Saturn occupies; somewhat similar to Mars in the Sixth House.

Not a good position for employment or success with servants or inferiors, denoting loss and trouble through them.

Ill success and loss with small animals, etc.

Afflicted by Uranus: incurable diseases.

Afflicted by Mars: dangerous illness, accidents and operations.

Afflicted by Sun, Moon or Neptune: chronic ill health, poor circulation and recuperation, colds, rheumatism, psychic and heavy ills. Notice the part of the body represented by the sign of the Sixth House cusp.

Saturn denotes poor digestion, constipation, obstruction, poor circulation, debility. When ill, seek the services of a doctor and accept the benefit of such aid by whatever method best suits the case: medicinal, surgical, mechanical, dietary, color, light, etc.

If Saturn is dignified or well aspected it denotes benefit through laborious or sedentary occupations; mining, masonry, sculpture, cement work, plastering, plowing, excavating, etc.

## Uranus in the Sixth House

Trouble through peculiar nervous disorders; neurosis. Sickness which is puzzling or not well understood. If much afflicted the sicknesses are strange or incurable; liability to mental derangement; danger of illness through the employment and sudden events. Not a good indice for success, harmony and happiness in employment, service, or with servants, employees, poultry, and similar lines.

Treatment by electricity, radium, hypnotism, etc., is apt to prove detrimental if Uranus is afflicted, but beneficial if well aspected, and a careful study of the diet and environment should be made.

Uranus rules the aura and sometimes the native is very sensitive to environmental conditions and should refrain from eating when tired, nervous, excited or angry.

If Uranus is well aspected here it may bring some unexpected or unique opportunity to perform exceptional service and obtain good results. Uranus well placed may give success as a metaphysician, mesmerist or electrician; and through Occult, electric or drugless treatments.

## Neptune in the Sixth House

Threatens some chronic, incurable disease, atrophy, inertia, wasting sickness, some inherited or psychopathic tendencies. Danger of some deformity through illness. If much afflicted it shows severe sickness and trouble from gratifying the tastes or desires, especially if afflicted by Mars. Should carefully avoid narcotics and opiates and if any medicine is taken use only the simplest kind. Neptune rules the mediumistic faculty and this house rules clothing, food, etc.; consequently, the native should not take food into the stomach received from a sick person or one of undesirable habits, nor should any apparel be worn once used by another. Use only the freshest and purest food obtainable and little or no animal matter.

Generally no success with poultry and other things ruled by this house. Theft, schemes, plots, deceit, or loss and difficulty through employees.

This position of Neptune may keep the native in seclusion, retirement or servitude. If well aspected the native has ability to develop fine psychometrizing powers, especially for sensing surrounding conditions. He should always pay attention to his own intuition in regard to food, clothing, environment. Neptune people need to exercise great care regarding the physical condition and habits of their associates or of those whom they engage to treat them. Being very receptive they absorb what others are throwing off and often this proves detrimental rather than beneficial, although the intentions may be good. People who indulge in tobacco, liquors, or who engage in vivisection or cruelty in any form, should not be allowed to treat the body of an indisposed Neptune person. Kindly suggestions, verbal and mental, and natural methods, seem best for them.

## Pluto in the Sixth House

Interest in the welfare of servants, pets, all people and animals dependent upon the native. Often unusual ideas and practices in employment and high turnover of employees or jobs. Problems at work cause physical upset.

Health very dependent on emotional state. Tendency to blood disorders. Health variable and nature of illness often difficult to diagnose and treat. Prone to unusual, rare diseases, and susceptible to esoteric treatments. Sensitive to faith healing and psychic healing. Health also dependent on healthy sex life.

If well aspected, this is a powerful position for a healer. The native has the intuitional ability to diagnose and cure the true cause of others' illnesses.

If poorly aspected: over-critical, picky, fussy, difficult to please; sometimes obsessed with these characteristics.

## THE SEVENTH HOUSE

### The Moon in the Seventh House

In a female chart it indicates a union with one whose affections are variable, fond of change and travel, of unsettled nature and engaged in public work. If well aspected it favors an early marriage, partnership, public favor, popularity and social success, also money or property by marriage. Unless the Moon is well aspected and located this is not a favorable position as it indicates death of partner, public opposition, unpopularity, female enmity, trouble and loss through litigation; changeful relations with the opposite sex and with partner and associates.

If the Moon is well aspected to the ruler of the First House it helps to offset the adverse testimonies and manify the good ones. In bad aspect to Mars: discord, discontent, hasty speech and action; enmities, assaults.

Saturn adverse: disappointment, loss and sorrows through unions. Uranus adverse: separation, estrangement, peculiar experience in connection with the unions; unexpected enmities or attacks.

Mercury adverse: matrimonial and business worries.

If the Moon is applying to any aspect of Uranus the native is likely to marry suddenly and meet another to whom affection is given afterwards. Taken alone: inclines to journeys and removals (especially when in a movable sign) in the interests of business for others.

### Mercury in Seventh House

The native usually carries on Mercurial pursuits in partnership or association with others and is fortunate or otherwise thereby, according to the aspects.

Unsettled married life; many inharmonies; the partner is quick in thought and action and if Mercury is afflicted, sarcastic, untruthful and hasty tempered; if well aspected, shrewd, active, clever and progressive. The partner is usually younger and oftentimes is an employee or is related in some way. Marriage is generally the result of writings or traveling and is more of the mind than of the senses or emotions. If Mercury is much afflicted: many small strifes, worries, vexations through writings, speech, contracts, traveling, legal affairs, and business dealings with others.

## Venus in the Seventh House (Natural House)

With marriage come social and financial pleasures. The native usually marries early and enjoys much happiness; love of offspring; successful partnerships; peaceful termination to strifes and success in public relations.

If badly aspected it shows delay and sorrow in marriage; probably a dissipated partner; loss through litigation and partnerships.

## The Sun in the Seventh House

If well aspected, success and rise in life after or through marriage; a proud but magnanimous, warm-hearted partner, firm and lasting attachment, happiness. Good for partnership and general popularity, especially with business people and superiors.

Difficulties averted by arbitration or mutual consent; gain through business, contracts and associations.

If afflicted: delays, opposition, disappointment, loss, etc., according to the nature of the aspecting planet.

## Mars in the Seventh House

If afflicted: impetuous in love, an early or rash love affair or union, possible separation through excessive demonstration of affections and combative or forceful nature of partner. Death of partner; troublesome opponents.

In a female chart: danger of sudden death of husband or severe accident to him. If Mars be in Cancer or Pisces he is apt to be worthless through dissipating habits.

In a male chart: The partner is industrious but assertive, positive or masculine.

Loss through litigation or partnership; business enemies; much strife, sometimes resulting in violence; criticism and opposition are frequently met. When Mars is well aspected or located by sign much of the above is modified; the native may marry a Mars person and benefit thereby.

## Jupiter in the Seventh House

If well aspected: success, gain and happiness through marriage, the partner being faithful and good.

The partner is usually of good social and financial standing;

usually older, more patient, profound or religious than the native. Success in partnership and in dealing cooperatively with others; friends and popularity with and through business people; gain through litigation or legal affairs. Jupiter is weak in Virgo and Capricorn.

If afflicted by Uranus or Mars: loss through litigation.

Saturn or luminaries adverse: marriage is delayed or indicates marriage to an unfortunate person, or to a widow or widower.

### Saturn in the Seventh House

Well aspected or in Libra: gives a sincere, prudent, faithful and well-disposed partner, or union with one older and more serious than the native, not demonstrative or emotional, but stable in affections, possessing property or children.

If afflicted: grief, sorrow, death or enduring coldness on the part of the partner, who may be of Saturn disposition and habit, according to the sign and aspects.

Ruin by contracts and partnerships, persistent opponents, litigation, business enmities and treachery. Marriage about the age of twenty-eight or after, incompatibility with the marriage partner.

### Uranus in the Seventh House

Well aspected: union with one of genius, intuition, ability or an unusual character.

A romantic, sudden, impulsive, secret or irregular union with likelihood of inharmonious results.

If afflicted: hasty or impulsive union or attachment followed by unhappy results; misunderstanding, separation, estrangement, scandal or death of partner.

Loss through strangers, partnerships, law, contracts, opponents, willfulness, opposition, open enemies and public contests. Unexpected opposition. Conflict with municipal or federal authorities.

### Neptune in the Seventh House

Threatens domestic troubles, jealousy, scandal, death of partner, or marriage to a deformed or deceptive person; much sickness; peculiar affairs. Not a good position for partnership and public dealing unless well aspected. When afflicted: some mystery, confusion and deceit in connection with unions. Two engagements or marriages.

### Pluto in the Seventh House

Pluto in this house indicates difficulty with relationships. The native intellectually understands and desires a close relationship but, because of circumstances or through the wrong choice of partners, is unable to consummate an intimate, fulfilling relationship. If poorly aspected: the native is bound to a relationship that is meaningless, but freedom is denied. If well aspected: the native's partnership is dissolved, and he learns a valuable lesson which can be applied to the next relationship. This position generally indicates a series of partnerships.

This is a good position for working with law and the legal system, and with the public, particularly indirectly as through the courts. Energy is used in dealing with others as a group, such as a corporation, or other collective bargaining unit. This work may sublimate unhappy personal relationships.

## THE EIGHTH HOUSE

### The Moon in the Eighth House

Well aspected: gain in the public affairs and finance through the business or marriage partner and the mother; gain by inheritance or goods of the dead, probably through mother's connections; natural death.

Taken alone: ability to develop latent Occult tendencies for practical results; astral plane experiences.

In a female chart it tends to increase the number of children, but signifies the death of some, especially if afflicted.

The native's mother is likely to die early; in a male chart also the wife.

If afflicted: unsettled fortunes after marriage; death of a public nature, accident, drowning, etc.

Neptune adverse: death by treachery, drugs or water, or by obscure or infectious complaint.

Uranus adverse: extraordinary, peculiar, sudden or accidental death.

Saturn adverse: demise through slow or chronic disorder.

Mars adverse: violent or sudden demise.

Sun adverse: weak vitality and serious sickness, but death usually in the presence of others.

Venus adverse: urinary troubles.

Mercury adverse: stomach, bowel or lung trouble.

### Mercury in the Eighth House

In a female chart: trouble, quarrels, dissension and difficulties with the partner regarding money; worry in connection with the financial affairs of partners and others.

The native inquires into Occult subjects, literature, lectures and meetings regarding the continuity of life. The mind is conscious and active at time of death.

Death of brother, sister, cousin, employee or neighbor causes much grief and mental anguish. A journey on account of death.

If afflicted, indicates liability to brain or nervous disorders, which in some way are related to death.

### Venus in the Eighth House

Gain in financial affairs through marriage or partnership. Gain by legacy or through goods and affairs concerning the dead. Denotes a natural, peaceful or easy demise.

If afflicted death may be caused by pursuit of pleasure; kidney, bladder or functional derangement; death of marriage partner, loss, grief and disappointment in love.

### The Sun in the Eighth House

Steady fortunes after marriage; gain by marriage, partnership or inheritance. Fame often comes at death which should have come before, or the end may be due to self-sacrifice or heroic deed. The Sun in this position tends to increase vitality and prolong life.

The foregoing is to be considered when the Sun is well aspected.

Taken alone: about the forty-fifth year may be a critical period. Death may be due to heart affliction or constitutional weakness, due to some honorable event or there are honors connected with passing. The tendency is to gain through death and through the partner, who is apt to be over-generous and extravagant.

If afflicted: likelihood of premature, sudden or violent end; the father may expire before the native; in a woman's chart the husband may die first; vice versa, in a male's chart. Sharp attacks of sickness during transits and directions afflicting the Sun, bring danger of death.

## Mars in the Eighth House

Trouble regarding financial affairs after marriage; the partner is usually extravagant and spends the money of the native if allowed to do so. Difficulties concerning legacies or property of deceased persons. Death usually comes quickly as the result of short sickness, shock or accident.

If afflicted: liability to violent or sudden death, loss or legacy, financial loss through partner. If Mars is in a water sign, danger of death by drowning; if in air sign, mental afflictions or aerial accidents; in a fire sign, by fire, accident or violence; in an earth sign, heavy sickness, inflammatory complaints; if Mars is ruler of the Fourth House or afflicts Jupiter, danger of loss by fire and theft.

## Jupiter in the Eighth House

If unafflicted: marriage brings prosperity; the partner is or will be well off financially. Gain by legacy, affairs of the dead and through occupations denoted by this house and sign; also through the handling of other people's money.

Success in the investigation of the Occult, happy dreams, natural and peaceful death.

If afflicted: denotes heart trouble and danger of blood poisoning, foul growths or consumption.

## Saturn in the Eighth House

The marriage partner is apt to be poor, financial difficulties after marriage, no gain through business partnership or legacy, delay and disappointments with regard to goods of the dead. Restrictions due to lack of capital.

If well aspected: moderates all the above and denotes long life; death from natural causes.

If afflicted or weak: lingering or slow death resulting from some chronic ailment; distressing dreams although not always remembered; death of the father.

If Saturn is in a water sign, danger of drowning. When afflicting Mars, Uranus or Neptune, danger of fatal accidents.

## Uranus in the Eighth House

Well aspected: sudden and unexpected benefits and gains through the marriage or business partner and inventions.

Taken alone: difficulties in financial affairs after marriage, sudden losses through partner and through the financial losses of others, trouble through legacy; sudden, unexpected or peculiar death; interest in occult affairs and subjects dealing with the continuity of life; peculiar psychic, dream and astral experiences.

If afflicted: worry and annoyance regarding legacies or goods of the dead; unexpected conditions arising in connection with deaths and through financial affairs.

Liability of death through some extraordinary or sudden event; violence, heart disease, epilepsy, paralysis or some uncommon nervous disorder; by electrical devices, explosion, or vehicles.

### Neptune in the Eighth House

Well aspected: ability to enter upon spirit planes and gain knowledge through the experience; gains in peculiar manner through others and possibly through the partner.

Strange psychical and dream experiences; desire to investigate spiritualism and other mystical subjects; peculiar death. Danger of death on water. Danger through poisons, opiates and anesthetics.

If afflicted: trouble in money matters after marriage, loss through complicated money affairs of others; fraud and deceit regarding legacy; partner is usually careless in money matters. Nightmares, strange dreams, weird feelings, trance conditions, astral experiences. Peculiar death.

### Pluto in the Eighth House (Natural House)

Pluto in this house indicates an interest in or preoccupation with death and all aspects of the passage from this world into the next. It usually indicates a strong life force; but if afflicted this force is dissipated through degeneracy and base sensuality. If well aspected this force is directed to the higher planes of spirituality.

This position is favorable for extra-sensory and higher consciousness experiences. The native has psychic abilities which may manifest in many levels: astral projection, dreams, mediumship, healing abilities, etc. Clairvoyance likely.

The native is apt to be financially independent, because of a legacy, inheritance, or lucky streak. If poorly aspected: he uses others for his own gain. If well aspected: he receives unexpected and unasked for bequests.

# THE NINTH HOUSE

## The Moon in the Ninth House

Well aspected: an ingenious mind; inventive, progressive, penetrative, reflective, fond of investigation; gives a love for traveling and indicates benefit or improvement through change. Keen imagination and high ideals. Interested in inventions of a public nature, especially modes and means of travel and learning. Benefits through relatives by marriage.

Taken alone: signifies voyages, life in foreign lands; legal or clerical inclinations; keen, romantic, fanciful and idealistic mind.

Remarkable dream or psychic experiences. Fond of change, diversity and novelty. Publicity of some sort regarding science, religion, philosophy, traveling or mysticism.

Sun adverse: over-enthusiastic in religion or unorthodox, probably both, at some time. Saturn adverse: sorrow and difficulty through religion, travel, publications and partner's relatives. Uranus adverse: romantic, eccentric, fond of adventure; liberal religion.

## Mercury in the Ninth House

Well aspected: a keen, clever, ingenious, studious mind; literary ability, taste for art, science and all higher educational or enlightening subjects; love of knowledge. Success in journeys, clerical or legal affairs and publishing.

Taken alone: a busy, active mind; danger of legal worries; taste for reading, science, literary pursuits and every form of knowledge. Desire for life in foreign countries or travels to and knowledge of distant places. Mercury in a movable sign is a sure indication of travels. In an air sign, interest in aerial affairs.

Afflicted: tendency to worry and scatter the forces by engaging in numerous activities instead of concentrating on one thing until completed; too much doubt, not enough decision; difficulties with clerical or legal affairs; fruitless and troublesome journeys.

## Venus in the Ninth House

Kind, sympathetic, helpful, gentle disposition and cultured intellect; philosophical, optimistic; appreciation for every form of mental improvement. Fond of fine arts, music, operas, high-class literature, lectures, social intercourse and literary persons. Favorable for social and domestic welfare interests.

Benefits from relatives by marriage, pleasant journeys, success abroad. Venus here will modify many adverse testimonies regarding mental qualities and helps the native to avoid trouble.

Indicates marriage abroad, or to a foreigner, or to one of a spiritual, scientific, literary or artistic disposition.

If Venus is the highest planet in the map it is a splendid position, denoting honors, success, good marriage and good fortune generally. If Venus is afflicted it gives longing, high ideals and desires hard to materialize and disappointments through their unattainment.

### The Sun in the Ninth House

Success or honors in connection with church, universities or law, also through travel and social intercourse; desire to investigate science and philosophy to find truths worthy of giving out to benefit others. Dignity or success abroad, or residence in foreign countries; faithful, earnest, sincere, consistent and constant in religious beliefs whether orthodox or liberal.

Ambitious, firm, self-reliant and confident. Taste for fine arts, music, science, literature and intellectual development.

Mars or Uranus afflicting: extreme, enthusiastic or peculiar in religious beliefs; trouble in foreign countries, also with legal affairs and partner's relatives; accidents in travel.

Jupiter adverse: unsuccessful in legal or clerical affairs. Trouble in foreign lands and through educational affairs or publishing.

Saturn adverse: hindrance through perversity, pride, etc.; unsuccessful in clerical or legal affairs. Losses in foreign lands.

Jupiter favorable; success and honors through popular reasoning, in science, religion, literature or philosophy; a good counselor; favor of partner's relatives; international recognition or honors.

Saturn favorable: love of justice, ability for profound or responsible undertakings; philosophical.

Mars favorable: patriotic, courageous and vigorous in defense of justice.

### Mars in the Ninth House

Much strife, generally through legal or relgious matters; danger of violence in foreign places; trouble through journeys and spouse's relatives; distressful dreams or fancies.

Enthusiasm or impulse in religion or philosophy; liberality and freedom of thought; forceful in beliefs.

If afflicted: forceful, fanatical, irregular or skeptical ideas regarding religious matters; preconceived or early religious teachings are overthrown; many troubles, litigation, disputes; danger while traveling, disagreement with some of the relatives, changes in religion or indifference.

Well aspected: active in defense of his rights; successful in law; enterprising in self-development.

## Jupiter in the Ninth House (Natural House)

Well aspected: good intuition, clear foresight; success and honors in religious, collegiate, legal, philosophic or philanthropic affairs; favorable for travel and success abroad; prophetic faculty and prophetic dreams; peaceful, logical and optimistic disposition; international interests.

Mars adverse: danger of shipwreck, fire or accident on journeys; liable to go to extremes in religious matters or trouble through them.

Uranus adverse: unexpected loss, difficulties and experiences through journeys, religion, law, philosophy, relatives.

Mars or Uranus favorable: inclination toward occult philosophy, higher science, originality of thought, invention and means of travel.

## Saturn in the Ninth House

Well aspected: the mental attitude is scientific and philosophical; the nature is studious and meditative, given to the investigation of law, geology, mineralogy, metaphysics, psychic and occult subjects generally.

Sun in good aspect: denotes a very faithful, devotional or religious spirit. Interest in geology, archeology or political economy.

Taken alone or afflicted: trouble in foreign lands, dangerous voyages (especially if in a water sign); loss through legal affairs, troubles through relatives by marriage; self-deception, lack of comprehension of the profound or higher sciences or philosophies, likelihood of religious bigotry and mental afflictions.

Mars adverse: perverse mind, danger of mental derangement or accidents in travel. Narrow religious ideas may be the cause of friction and conflict.

### Uranus in the Ninth House

Trouble in foreign lands or through relatives by marriage; peculiar, unexpected, adventurous, dangerous voyages; taste for philosophy, occult, metaphysical or unusual knowledge.

Original, inventive, peculiar, eccentric or reformative and progressive ideas. Desirous of traveling and investigating. Prophetic intuitive faculty and sometimes engaged in antiquarian, Uranian or aerial research.

### Neptune in the Ninth House

Clairvoyant or other psychic faculties; a highly inspirational nature; strange dreams, feelings and experiences. Astral experiences.

Psychic studies or investigation of spiritualism, psychic phenomena and philosophy. Voyages if in a movable or water sign.

If afflicted: distressful dreams; ominous forebodings; trouble through travels; legal involvements; complicated affairs with wife's relatives. Adverse psychical experiences; impressionable and simulative nature.

### Pluto in the Ninth House

Pluto here indicates that the native's religious and philosophical ideas will undergo drastic change during his life. A complete religious conversion is likely and he may repudiate his former beliefs, often violently. The native is drawn to emotional and sensual religious rites, and undergoes the ecstasy of religious inspiration, visions, or communion with otherworldly beings.

When well aspected the native is eloquent and persuasive in defending his beliefs; when poorly aspected, he is violent and quarrelsome; a fanatic. In either case the native believes that his religion is the only true one, and thinks that everyone should convert to his beliefs.

Contacts with foreign cultures and ideas confuse and disturb the native and cause an unsought-after questioning of his basic beliefs.

The religious ideas may embrace occultism and sex magic, and may either deteriorate into obsession and perversion, or may become purified of emotional content and reborn. The native may even be psychically preyed upon by living or disincarnate personalities who claim spiritual powers or knowledge.

# THE TENTH HOUSE

## The Moon in the Tenth House

Inclines to public life, changes in business, occupation and employment, instability of position and popularity, rise in life followed by reversal or downfall. Voyages in connection with business, if in a cardinal sign.

Women influence the position in some way according to the aspects; strong attraction to mother. If well aspected by Sun, Venus or Jupiter: favors success, popularity and prosperity. Indicates carefulness in money matters and usually gain in property and possessions. Public business; catering to the masses.

Mars adverse: public scandal, notoriety or discredit, obstacles in business. Take alone, it gives ability and tendencies to employment of a changing nature, such as shipping, voyaging, traveling, dealing in public commodities, novelties, etc.; affairs connected with common people generally, also with things ruled by the sign occupied.

## Mercury in the Tenth House

The honors and success in business or occupation depend upon the sign and aspects, Mercury being neutral.

Good position for public service or for holding responsible positions under superiors.

The vocational tendencies and abilities may be seen by delineating the planet in most powerful aspect to Mercury, as though the planet in question were actually in the tenth house, thus:

Uranus most strongly aspecting: novelists, reporters, lecturers, teachers, travelers, electricians, railroad employees, occult professions generally, psychologists, dealers in occult literature, antiquities, inventions.

Taken alone, it gives a taste for literature; several professions, occupations or undertakings; mercantile work, commissions, agencies. If in an air sign, retentive memory and fluent speech, used effectively in business activities. If much afflicted by Mars or Saturn: a restless nature, subtle and deceptive; impulsive speech or untruthfulness; trouble in business or failure.

Signifies an active, able, penetrating, adaptable mind used resourcefully in business.

## Venus in the Tenth House

This position favors honors, popularity and friendships; the native has merit and ability, possesses an agreeable and pleasant manner; usually marries above the station in life and enjoys success in dealings with women.

Generally well disposed and of good moral stamina, dislikes quarreling or trouble of any sort and delights in all that is social, pleasant and harmonious.

It favors gain through the parents (probably the mother), general prosperity and artistic or musical pursuits.

This position is fortunate for parents and home life or for the occupations of Venus and those designated by the sign she occupies. Preference for business that is beautifying, harmonizing, comforting or entertaining.

If well aspected by Sun, Jupiter or Moon, the subject meets with social distinction, honors and financial success, and the favor, good will and support of those in good position, government officers, superiors and responsible persons, especially along social or entertainment lines.

When afflicted indicates limitations, and the native suffers lack of opportunities to manifest his abilities or may occupy a lowly position in high-class undertakings.

The occupations of Venus are those which deal with artistic, refined and entertainment matters; all business directly connected with females; adornment, jewelry, finery, luxury, beauty, amusement.

If in good aspect with Mercury it makes fine musicians, artists, painters, speakers, writers, librarians, speculators, actors, singers, stage directors, band or choir masters, bailiffs and other political officers, secretaries, printers, decorators, housekeepers, carpenters, druggists, confectioners, dyers, and good character readers; public work in professions which require considerable traveling or which take one into contact with many people; influential posts; positions or trust and refinement.

The nature of the profession depends largely upon the nature of the sign in which Venus is located.

## The Sun in the Tenth House

Well aspected: honor and success, distinction, authority, independence, prosperity, high patronage and favor of those in power and good position. The position usually indicates good birth and favorable parental influences.

The native's success is generally steady in whatever business, profession or occupation he adopts; positions of trust, responsibility, honor or governmental office; good vitality; high moral standards; favorable environment.

If afflicted: love of power; dignity, pride, opposition, reversals. Although the Sun in the Tenth House is always beneficial in some respect, yet great difficulties will be met according to the nature of the affliction.

## Mars in the Tenth House

Unless Mars is in the sign Capricorn, impulse and feeling are likely to predominate, reason and intellectuality often being overridden by the passional or forceful side of the nature.

The native meets with much turmoil and strife through excessive ambition, independence, domination or force and aggressiveness.

A spirit of freedom and desire for conquest spur the subject on, at times to his detriment. It is significant of extravagance or extremes in some form. Scandal, discredit and disrepute, whether deserved or not. Death of parents or disagreement with them.

The native has plenty of courage, energy, enterprise and force, and is consequently capable of being in business for himself, but will succeed best in the occupations corresponding to the nature of Mars and the planet which best aspects Mars.

Well aspected: gain and promotion through business acumen, salesmanship, bravery and industrial pursuits; benefit through the father and also by legacy.

Mercury in good aspect indicates the engineer, carver, sculptor, draughtsman, designer, athlete, mechanic, soldier, sailor, officer, dentist, surgeon, surgical instrument maker, hardware dealer and all lines where courage or daring is necessary, or where skill is combined with muscular energy and the use of tools, such as iron or steel instruments and machinery.

If Mercury afflicts: mason, laborer, iron worker, tanner, cattleman, butcher; bath, lavatory or laundry attendant; worker in metal and where there is an element of risk and danger. Saturn adverse: laborious employments and likelihood of failure in business.

## Jupiter in the Tenth House

Usually indicates good birth, help from relatives or those in high position. The native has good moral standards and will occupy secure influential or important positions at some period.

Gain through the occupation, marriage, sports and public or political office.

This is a good position for rise in life, honors, favor of superiors, public appointments, dignities, esteem, good will, social, political and financial success.

Uranus adverse: reversals of fortune, difficulties.

Saturn adverse: downfalls, obstacles, losses.

Luminaries adverse: difficulty in social life and through changes and travel; unfavorable publicity.

Mercury favorable: good judge, minister, ambassador, philosopher, banker, merchant, government official, town councilor, stock broker, trustee, etc., and is good for positions of distinction, honor, responsibility, trust and social welfare.

If Mercury afflicts: minor or laborious government offices, bank clerk, clothier, upholsterer, draper, provision dealer or catering to the public; liability to loss or discredit through dishonesty.

## Saturn in the Tenth House (Natural House)

A great deal depends upon the sign and aspects. When well aspected: ambition for power and advancement; the native rises above his sphere in life by steady, persevering industry.

When afflicted by aspect or weak by sign: rise and success is followed by downfall or adversity. The subject is usually persistent and has ability, but lacks opportunities and meets with obstacles, delay, dull periods and disappointment. In business, financial ruin is threatened; in professional life, dishonor and failures, whether deserved or not; in political matters, defeat. Public affairs fail and bring loss and discredit. These take place during adverse transits and directions. If the native has a good situation he had best keep it and not branch out into new undertakings which entail heavy liabilities or great responsibility.

Mercury in good aspect helps to improve the conditions and denotes government officials, land surveyors and dealers, managers, organizers, solicitors, stationers, binders, lawyers, scientists, geologists, architects, contractors, builders, mining engineers, coal dealers and other employments where care and skill, patience or organized and concentrated efforts are required; diplomatic occupations. If Mercury afflicts: miner, printer, bookbinder, bricklayer, coal handler, grocer, gardener; general and practical work connected with the earth and its products; country preacher, notary public, night watchman, etc.

## Uranus in the Tenth House

A strange and eventful career; many important changes of position and credit.

Originality is a marked feature. The native is unique in that he originates new lines of activity for himself, follows uncommon lines of thought and employment and establishes customs and codes of his own, apart and opposite to the conventional.

All effort is made for freedom and to undo and overthrow all bonds of limitation. Very independent, erratic, eccentric and unconventional. Difficulties with employers; opposition from public functionaries or governmental bodies. Threatens discredit and reverses, extraordinary experiences in public or business career.

In a common sign: two simultaneous occupations are indicated. Estrangement from parents and kindred, unless good planets occupy the fourth house, not necessarily through trouble unless parental ruler afflicts.

In good aspect to Mercury, fits the native to reconstruct the old, undertake new and improved methods, create new professions, new plans of work and follow uncommon pursuits; investigator, explorer, reformer, teacher, inventor, flier, metaphysician, electrician, astrologer, psychologist.

If Mercury afflicts: novelist, reporter, hypnotist, occult student, antiquarian, dealer in curiosities and antiquities, lineman, dynamo tender, engineer, motorman, employee having to do with transit and mechanism, people of peculiar genius, and extraordinary or hazardous employment.

## Neptune in the Tenth House

A highly inspirational nature, capable of attaining honor or position through some unique achievement. Professional people become municipal officers of sanitary, hygiene, health or hospital boards. A chance of honor in some artistic or scientific field. The subject becomes interested in the mysterious nature and seeks to arrange deductions for practical application.

This position endangers the life of one of the parents while the native is yet young, but if well aspected may bring inheritance from a parent or gain through some pursuit connected with psychism, liquids, health springs, hospitals or sanitariums. Taken alone, it signifies all occupations where mystery, secrecy, inspiration, a nom-de-plume or title are employed; the sea and the various industries connected with it; secret service; inspirational writing; singer, actor, musician, artist, medium, psychic, diver, fisherman.

Being a neutral planet, the occupation indicated depends on the planet in closest or strongest aspect.

Neptune here in the sign Taurus, trine to Mercury, gives an active desire and ability to simplify science, to popularize it as far as possible and present it in the most reasonable and practical manner. Also to investigate and carry on Occult, philosophical and spiritual philosophies of life. Useful inspirational ideas; unique distinction.

If unfavorably aspected it indicates a strange and peculiar career, some disgrace or scandal whether deserved or not; peculiar circumstances, separation from the parents, unfortunate business or professional complications.

If Neptune is well aspected it reverses the unfavorable indications and the native gains through mediumistic or spiritual friends.

### Pluto in the Tenth House

Strong drive for power and public recognition. If poorly aspected, this drive is fed by greed, ruthlessness, and utter selfishness. If well aspected, the native desires power in order to help others, or to fulfill some obligation. In either case there is a tendency to believe the ends justify the means and to use other people for his own gain.

## THE ELEVENTH HOUSE

### The Moon in the Eleventh House

Large circle of acquaintances, unreliable friends, few lasting attachments, unless in a fixed sign and well aspected; success in dealing with children and young people.

Well aspected: gain through acquaintances and hopes realized; good for social life and popularity; friends among celebrities.

If afflicted, especially by Mars or Uranus: troubles, sorrows and losses through friends, disappointing friendships; sudden changes among friends and separation from them. Saturn adverse: sorrow, loss and delay or limitations occasioned by friends or through legislative enactments.

## Mercury in the Eleventh House

Gain and happiness through friends who desire to forward the interests of the native; social success and popularity.

Favors from women, socially inclined; friends are usually of an artistic nature; fruitful marriage.

Saturn adverse: unfortunate friends whose advice, if followed, leads to trouble, loss and scandal; disappointments and delays in hopes and wishes. Mars adverse: possibility of trouble through excess of pleasure with friends. Uranus or Neptune adverse: unreliable, eccentric or seductive friends.

## Venus in the Eleventh House

Gain and happiness through friends who desire to forward the interests of the native; social success and popularity.

Favors from women, socially inclined; friends are usually of an artistic nature; fruitful marriage.

Saturn adverse: unfortunate friends whose advice, if followed, leads to trouble, loss and scandal; disappointments and delays in hopes and wishes. Mars adverse: possibility of trouble through excess of pleasure with friends. Uranus or Neptune adverse: unreliable, eccentric or seductive friends.

## The Sun in the Eleventh House

Definite and lofty ambitions and desires; respect for dignitaries or superiors and those of loyal mind, honesty of purpose, self-respect, dignity, worth. Association with those of power and good position; gain in reputation, honors and esteem through friendships; successful, ambitious, well regulated hopes; firm, honorable and constant friends; social success.

### Mars in the Eleventh House

Disagreement with acquaintances, some social unpopularity, contention, alienation and deaths among friends and troubles with others in social life; few real friends; friendships are likely to lead the subject into trouble through impulse or some form of extravagance.

Saturn or Mercury in affliction: violation of friendship or treachery among friends.

Jupiter or Sun adverse: difficulty through wrong advice, law troubles, financial losses, rash men, etc.

Venus or Moon adverse: over-indulgence with friends.

Uranus adverse: disaster, extraordinary events and attachments; trouble with legislators.

Neptune adverse: losses and unfortunate complications through unreliable friends.

### Jupiter in the Eleventh House

True and fortunate friends; associations with prominent persons, legislators, senators, judges, bankers, doctors, professors; gain through acquaintances of good position; social success, popularity and credit. Ambitions are often attained and hopes brought to a successful issue due to the instrumentality of powerful or influential friends.

In a cardinal sign: executive ability, progress.

In a fixed sign: jealousy or pride among friends.

In a common sign: scientific or religious friends.

### Saturn in the Eleventh House

If Saturn is exalted or well aspected: few friends; gain through acquaintances who are older, profound, scientific or serious.

Taken alone or afflicted: false and deceitful friends, or unfortunate acquaintances by whom the subject is liable to care, sorrow, loss and ruin, especially if in a cardinal sign. Friends among the lowly, ill or unfortunate.

In a fixed sign: delay and hindrance through friends.

In a common sign: hopes are likely to be unachieved and ambitions often frustrated; sorrow through friends.

### Uranus in the Eleventh House (Natural House)

This is the natural house of Uranus but whether his presence therein will benefit the native or not depends upon the aspects. Well aspected: friends among Occult or peculiar people, unusual or extraordinary acquaintances, geniuses, inventors, writers, government executives, etc. Unexpected benefits from friends; progressive hopes and wishes. Taken alone or afflicted: peculiar or remarkable friendship, eccentric of unreliable acquaintances; sudden, unexpected estrangements, impulsive attachments often ending in coldness; peculiar hopes and wishes, strange and romantic attachments. Radicalism and humanitarianism are not uncommon. The native has strong ideals.


## Neptune in the Eleventh House

If adversely aspected: unfavorable attachments, unsatisfactory friendships, strange and unaccountable attractions and associates, seductive friends and alliances, treachery among supposed friends, unreliable advisors and losses and troubles thereby; complications among friends.

If Neptune is well aspected it reverses these indications, and gives friends among mystics, psychics, poets, musicians, swimmers, yachtsmen, nightclub workers. Gain through mediumistic or spiritual friends.

## Pluto in the Eleventh House

With Pluto in this position great care must be taken in the choice of friends, as the native is easily led and influenced by others. He is a natural leader but the people he leads seem an accidental combination. If well aspected: he uses his magnetic personality to lead others in a social welfare, humanitarian, or charitable cause. If poorly aspected: he becomes an underworld gang leader, a criminal egging others to do his dirty work for him.

There are likely to be sudden breaks with friends and associates, and people enter and leave the native's life unexpectedly. He is apt, at the height of his power, to abandon his goals and set out in an entirely different direction.

He is fiercely loyal to the cause and people of the moment, and demands the same sacrificing loyalty from his acquaintances. He is ruthless in pursuing his goals and his expectations are often unrealistically high. Demanding a lot from himself and others, he inspires either great admiration or intense hatred from those around him.

## THE TWELFTH HOUSE

### The Moon in the Twelfth House

Love of mystery, occultism, secret arts or romance. Liability of the senses dominating the reason, causing indiscreet love affairs, sorrow and loss thereby.

Hindrance and limitations are prominent, but benefit is indicated in out-of-sight work, in occupations which require seclusion rather than publicity, in hospitals, institutions or in isolated positions, in remote, quiet, obscure places. Voyages. Mystery.

If the Moon is not in Scorpio or Capricorn and well aspected, it shows development and progress, particularly through the Occult.

Well aspected: success with large animals; ability for Occult arts.

Afflicted: lacks firmness and stability and is led into acts of indiscretion, resulting in worry, trouble, secrets and female enmity. Liability to restraint, enforced retirement or sickness in a hospital; fanciful fears.

### Mercury in the Twelfth House

Fond of investigating occultism, chemistry, medicine or secret arts and of risks and adventures of a secret or dangerous nature; of unusual lines of thought generally. Love of mystery; petty worries and annoyances; many small enmities, frequently caused by writings or scandalous reports. The subject possesses ability but lacks power or opportunities to manifest. Well aspected: tends to success ultimately. Benefit through rest, quietude and seclusion.

### Venus in the Twelfth House

Inclines to romance and adventure; love of the mysterious in nature, for investigating the secret arts, medicine, chemistry; pleasure and success with horses and other animals.

Gain by an obscure or plebeian occupation, also benefit through charitable or public institutions; enjoys peaceful or voluntary seclusion.

Secret love affairs or intrigues leading to enmity of women; an early union (especially if Mars is in aspect), affection for another after marriage and if Saturn afflicts, separation or divorce and sorrow or disappointment through the opposite sex.

Scorpio, Capricorn or Cancer are the worst signs for Venus here, giving too great love for physical and emotional pleasures; detrimental to the native because of excess.

## The Sun in the Twelfth House

Occult and psychic tendencies, uncommon tastes and inclinations. Success over enemies and success in medicine, chemistry, Occult affairs, in some quiet, secure, obscure or unpopular occupation, or in connection with hospitals, prisons or other institutions; seclusion. Life in places far from birth. Help and charity received when needed.

If in a water sign: strong mediumistic faculty.

Well aspected: self-sacrificing, enduring and rises out of seclusion, obscurity or difficulties by his own efforts after the first third of life has passed.

Afflicted: sorrow and misfortune through things indicated by the sign occupied; inflammatory conditions.

## Mars in the Twelfth House

Danger of injury, slander, scandal, loss of reputation or treachery from enemies or misplaced affection; grave trouble through impulse, lack of frankness or candor; liability to imprisonment.

Unfortunate adventures, secret enemies, danger of injury through large animals and burglars; death in seclusion or restraint. The partner is subject to feverish complaints.

If Mars is in Libra or Pisces it denotes poverty or limitations and privation.

Saturn adverse: injuries or imprisonment, illness requiring hospital service; labor troubles.

Jupiter adverse: financial and social ruin.

Luminaries adverse: distressful circumstances.

The good aspects of the Sun and Venus or the sign Capricorn here improve this position of Mars.

## Jupiter in the Twelfth House

Success in medicine, chemistry or Occult studies; respect for ancient wisdom and teachings; success through asylums, hospitals or public institutions, through benevolence and philanthropy, in places remote from birth, in quiet places and with animals; charity given or received;

the native readily helps others.

The subject prevails over enemies. They become friends and he eventually gains through them; reversals followed by success.

Peculiar experience in connection with the affections, religious, collegiate, political or foreign affairs, which, however, may result in ultimate benefit.

Aid from friends and others quietly or secretly; success about the middle part of life.

## Saturn in the Twelfth House

Well aspected: success in seclusion or in quiet or laborious occupations.

Unaspected: secret enemies who work for the native's downfall; losses and bruises through animals. The nature is acquisitive, reserved and inclined to solitude; desires to work secretly, unobserved, and live peacefully or alone. Secret sorrows, fear and disappointment; liability to false accusations and even imprisonment or confinement.

Uranus adverse: unexpected or strange enmities, disgrace, loss of credit and honor; labor troubles.

Mars adverse: danger of violence, robbers or suicide.

Mercury adverse: mental disorders, hallucinations, severe sickness; loss by theft.

Luminaries adverse: tendency to despondency, melancholia; sorrow through death of loved ones.

## Uranus in the Twelfth House

Estrangement from one's native state or kindred; difficulties with animals; secret, romantic, mysterious affairs and attractions; occult investigations; psychic and mystical experiences.

Afflicted: eccentric, peculiar, violent tendencies; threatens disgrace and troubles from psychic and occult sources; mysterious and unexpected misfortunes; restraint in public institutions; strange and unexpected enmities; eccentric people perplex and annoy by underhanded actions. Sudden illness.

Well aspected: success through occult affairs, institutions and extraordinary, secret or out-of-sign avocations.

### Neptune in the Twelfth House (Natural House)

Well aspected: success in mediumship, psychical research and Occult investigations; through secret, secluded and quiet methods, detective work or laboratory research; benefit through large institutions.

Afflicted: danger from psychic sources and through deception, schemes, fraud, secret enemies, scandal, disgrace and secret sorrows. Vague or weird apprehensions. Sickness necessitating hospitalization.

### Pluto in the Twelfth House

The native is a private person, close and secretive about his true feelings. His natural desires are to help others and to give himself utterly to service to mankind. However, if Pluto is poorly aspected, all efforts to this end are thwarted, and the native ends up requiring more help than giving it. If well aspected, the service can have a therapeutic role in aiding the native to find himself while working for others.

There is a tendency to let others take advantage of his sympathies and the native suffers when not able to have enough time to himself. This can lead to self-pity and depression. The native must combat blaming himself for the problems of others, and to avoid involving himself in problems which do not affect him.

# Interpreting the Aspects

Not every one with a preponderance of good aspects is successful in life; some may be too easily satisfied or contented. Nor does every one with a preponderance of inharmonious aspects achieve success through stimulating effort; they may be too easily irritated and develop obstacles in their path through enmities, injuries, etc.

So it will be seen that aspects are the modifying influence in a horoscope. Unless aspects are properly computed the necessary modifications cannot be read and the delineations not properly made. The influence of a planet in a house is qualified by the aspects it beholds.

Much of the skill and art in reading horoscopes depends upon the correct recording of aspects and knowledge of their influence. The first requisite is the ability to calculate and collect the facts about aspects. Although this text gives the influence of each planetary aspect, the saying of Ptolemy should be observed: *Judgment must be regulated by thyself, as well as by the science.*

Consider the different applications of the same aspect in several cases as a person in the penitentiary, or lying ill in a hospital; a youth off on his or her vacation; a person in charge of a flourishing business; a person chiefly concerned with his or her family of children.

A physician does not diagnose until he is familiar with the history of the case; likewise an astrologer should not render judgment until he is familiar with his client's station in life, his condition and activities, in order that he may properly anticipate the nature of the person's response to the vibratory action of an aspect. To do this correctly he

323

must have made no mistake about the aspect.

In fact, the aspect must first be diagnosed along these lines:

1. Quality of aspect, good or adverse.
2. Platic (wide orb) or partile (exact aspect).
3. Forming or separating.
4. Is the aspecting planet sinister or dexter? How many degrees away from the aspected planet is the one which is doing the aspecting? How many degrees plus or minus the exact aspect?
5. Is the aspecting planet angular, succedent or cadent?
6. Is the aspecting planet in a cardinal, fixed or mutable sign?
7. Is the aspecting planet in a fruitful or barren sign?
8. Is the aspecting planet a so-called benefic or malefic?
9. What house of the horoscope does the aspecting planet occupy?
10. Does the aspecting planet have any other aspect at the same time? If so, compare them and decide whether one accentuates or modifies the other.
11. What is the nature of the aspected planet, malefic or benefic?
12. What house does the aspected planet occupy? Is it elevated above the aspecting planet, or below it in the chart?
13. Is either of these planets in its sign of dignity or debility?
14. Is either of them retrograde?

The most important of these questions are: 1. What is the nature of the aspect? and 2. Is it applying or separating?

## Combined Influences of Houses, Aspects and Planets

The influence and effect of planets in a horoscope depend largely upon their aspects, and an aspect, favorable or unfavorable, to any planet will alter its indications in the chart as judged without an aspect. The reading given for a planet in a house must be modifed or arranged to coincide with the aspects to the planet in order to delineate a horoscope correctly.

For example: Mercury in the Third House unaspected gives mental perception, mental activity; learns much by observation; ability in matters of speaking, writings or commissions.

Mercury in the Third House well aspected, for instance by Jupiter, gives a jovial mind with very good judgment. Ability for collegiate studies, inclination to medicine, law or philosophy. Success in writings, travel and professional matters. Gain through brethren and neighbors.

Mercury in the Third House afflicted, for instance by Mars, gives clever, sharp, shrewd, active mind. Quick tempered, sarcastic, resentful, impatient, impulsive, and forceful in speech. Difficulty through writings and trouble with brethren and neighbors. Careless with facts and hasty in drawing conclusions.

Thus it is essential not only to render judgment on a planet in a house according to the quality of its aspect but also by nature of planet with which it is aspected.

As a planet often has more than one aspect it is sometimes necessary to make a combination judgment, especially where one aspect is good and the other adverse. Saturn in the Second House in good aspect to Jupiter and in evil aspect to Venus would show success where property, land and investment were concerned but loss through women or excess of pleasure.

## THE PLANETARY ASPECTS OF THE MOON

### The Moon in Favorable Aspect to Mercury

Indicates that the native is quick in wit, perceptive, ingenious, comprehensive, reasonable; has splendid mental abilities, keen and penetrating, productive, versatile, expressive, fluent and copious in speech or writing. If any of the air signs ascend it gives admirable elocution and ability to acquire languages with ease.

The mind responds readily to new ideas and is fond of change and variety; optimism, imagination and intuition are increased, also mental sympathy, receptivity and adaptability. Fond of art, music, pleasure, literature and journeys.

### The Moon in Unfavorable Aspect to Mercury

Anxiety, worry, quick, sharp, turbulent and sarcastic states of mind. Impressionable, mutable, imaginative, indecisive, speculative and over-sensitive. Tendency to change, not enough continuity, fixity, firmness and stability of mental attitudes. Poor memory for dates and facts in history. Nevertheless, dexterous, ingenious or clever, and possesses many good qualities.

Temporary derangements of the health through the nervous system, stomach or bowels. Unsuccessful or unpopular writing; public criticism. Business losses, litigation.

## The Moon in Favorable Aspect to Venus

Good-natured, kind and cheerful; neat and tasteful in dress and pleasing in manners; fondness for the beautiful in nature, music and all things artistic; taste for pleasure, light literature, drama and public functions; fruitful nature, good intellect.

Gentle, refined, agreeable, affectionate and attractive; sociable, maternal and sympathetic.

Endowed with respect and company of the opposite sex; enjoys sociability, friends and general popularity. General public or business success through engaging personality and cheerfulness.

Profitable employment in connection with the common classes. Assistance or approval of parents.

This aspect is favorable for money and possessions, for Second, Fourth and Seventh House affairs, and the things ruled by the house which Venus occupies. It tends to success and frugality.

Gain through catering to public tastes and necessities in confectioneries, bakeries, restaurants, hotels, boarding houses, etc.; also through dealing in houses, lands and the fruits of the earth.

## The Moon in Unfavorable Aspect to Venus

It indicates over-indulgence in pleasures, a tendency to carelessness in habits and manners; changeful affections, usually amorous; losses and difficulty in connection with money, property and possessions, or in business pursuits.

Trouble in partnerships, love or marriage; disapproval of parents or may suffer unpopularity, slander and scandal, whether deserved or not.

To a female it threatens ill health periodically.

## The Moon in Favorable Aspect to the Sun

Sincerity, energy, will, loyalty, ambition and adaptability. Strengthens the constitution of both male and female; indicates success in life, rapid promotion, prosperity and assistance from influential persons; seldom has difficulty in obtaining employment and usually receives a good salary. Gain through speculation, investment, enterprise and responsibility. With a good aspect of Jupiter also, it indicates the accumulation of great wealth and fortunate, congenial marriage.

The exact conjunction of Sun and Moon is often adverse, especially when at the same time in ill aspect to the malefics, the nature of which will signify the difficulty, but of itself the conjunction is apt to make the native mutable, inert, indifferent, lethargic, sensitive, volatile, irresolute, self-centered but harmless, and may experience a lowering of vitality every month when the conjunction occurs.

## The Moon in Unfavorable Aspect to the Sun

Ambitious, venturesome, egotistical, irresolute, sensitive, compelling and immoderate.

Difficulty in financial affairs, accumulating money, or in obtaining and keeping employment; loss by speculation, ill health, inferiors, disappointment and over-confidence; misfortune or poor success with those of high position; weak constitution, and if Saturn be in affliction, long and serious sickness; difficulty through women.

## The Moon in Favorable Aspect to Mars

The subject is ambitious, energetic, firm, brave, ardent and resolute.

This aspect in the chart tends to offset many testimonies regarding sickness or weakness. It gives strength to the whole system, muscular and circulatory; increases the activity, force and vitality. It is a good aspect for those whose work requires strength for occupations carried on out of doors.

Success and promotion through resourcefulness and enterprise in business, personal affairs or employments of responsibility and publicity. Results are largely accomplished through quick action, energetic, common sense methods and hard work which inspire confidence and trust from others.

If any testimony of legacy is shown this aspect strengthens it and brings benefit, possibly through mother's connections.

It is good for things ruled by the house the Moon occupies, also for Fourth House affairs, property, timber, commodities, etc.

## The Moon in Unfavorable Aspect to Mars

Brave but headstrong; inclined to acts and words which are indiscreet or rash, causing regret, humiliation and sorrow.

The temper is quick, resulting in disputes, strife and difficulties. Self-confident, egotistic, domineering, daring and venturesome. The desire is for freedom and liberty of expression; obstacles and opposition or lack of opportunities cause fits of passion. Apt to suffer from disregard of regulations, carelessness of consequences, through appetites, sex impulse and through scandal, criticism and enmity.

An unfortunate aspect for domestic happiness; indicates loss of legacy, sorrow through mother, difficulty over property and in dwelling place, loss through partnership and theft. Not favorable for health showing liability of trouble to the sex organs, head, eyes, breast and stomach, sometimes causing indigestion and nervousness. Danger through excitement, fevers, operations, accidents, ruptured blood vessels, fire and water. The native should avoid low, swampy or stagnant districts and beware of danger on water. In a female's horoscope it threatens ill health, annoying periods and many difficulties.

### The Moon in Favorable Aspect to Jupiter

Increases the imagination, intuition and appreciation for beauty; indicates clear, sound and usually correct judgment and reasoning. Strengthens the vitality, fertility and resourcefulness. Inclines to honesty, justice, benevolence, compassion, sympathy, friendliness and sociability. Jovial, generous, humane, hopeful and popular.

Success in literature and general affairs, especially those things ruled by the houses these planets occupy, and also the Fourth and Ninth Houses, if they are unafflicted. This is one of the good aspects that assist in the acquisition of possessions, happiness in marriage and good health. Gain and development through the occult, spiritual and educational affairs and publishing; also through mother and family, especially if the Tenth and Fourth Houses are unafflicted.

### The Moon in Unfavorable Aspect to Jupiter

Unfortunate for speculations, games of chance and risky ventures. Loss through misplaced confidence, loans, deception, dishonesty, excess, lack of candor, concealment of motives, irresolution, wrong judgment, either of self or by others.

Trouble through changes and voyages; likelihood of slander and false accusations. Severe illness, misunderstanding or separation from the mother. Rather an adverse aspect for health generally, giving liability to derangement of the stomach and liver, blood disorders and tumorous growths. An unfortunate aspect for health in a woman's chart.

## The Moon in Favorable Aspect to Saturn

Denotes a thoughtful, conservative, prudent, sober and contemplative mind; not much given to gaiety, but provident, careful and attentive to business and affairs generally.

Popularity, credit, respect, esteem; diplomatic, self-reliant; systematizing, organizing and constructive ability; accomplishes most by subtlety, tact and method rather than by force.

Favorable aspect for occupation, public advancement and attainment to positions of trust and responsibility through persistent effort; approval or benefit through parents, friends, elders and employers.

Gain in business and by such things as Saturn rules: mines, lands and produce. If Jupiter is also in favorable aspect it leads to the acquisition of great wealth. If the Sun is in good aspect it denotes rise in life to very prominent and distinguished position through perseverance.

## The Moon in Unfavorable Aspect to Saturn

Indicates that the person is poor, or loses his money and becomes so, and has a hard struggle to make both ends meet.

He is earnest and ambitious, but his plans do not materialize as expected; a hard worker but generally receives little gain; usually fails in business though careful and persevering; unlooked for obstacles, delays, disappointments, rebuffs and reversals constantly arise, coupled with lack of opportunities and unfavorable circumstances at the critical or needed times.

It is an unfortunate aspect for marriage, yet if the planets are in common signs, usually marries more than once.

A bad aspect for speculation and such things as Saturn rules by nature, also by sign and house it occupies in the chart.

The native meets with persecution, slander or scandal; disapproval of seniors, parents or employers; difficulties and sorrows through parents, property and possessions. Sorrow through death of young people and mother.

Temporary derangements of the health, colds, falls and accidents.

The native should refrain from strong physics and employ healthful exercises.

This aspect affects the disposition, causing the subject to become somewhat selfish, subtle, careful of his own interests, given to periods of worry, anxiety, doubt, mistrust in self, gloom and despondency. A good aspect of Sun, Jupiter, Mars or Venus will help to offset the severity of the above.

### The Moon in Favorable Aspect to Uranus

The native is active, firm, enterprising and scientific. Fond of friendship and the opposite sex.

Success and gain through the occult, and through original, inventive and progressive people.

The aspect tends to awaken the imaging faculties, quickens the thought and intuition, leads the mind into original lines and gives interest in new methods, inventions, curiosities, etc., giving mesmeric and psychic faculty; good for healing and telepathy. Benefit through business and novelties. A good aspect for an electric expert or worker.

Inclination for and benefit through astrology.

Advantageous changes and removals. Favors traveling and if either planet be in the Third or Ninth House, many journies. If in the Fourth House, many changes of residence.

### The Moon in Unfavorable Aspect to Uranus

Unfortunate changes, journeys and removals.

Impulsive, sarcastic, abrupt, peculiar, electric and independent; danger on or near the water; trouble through the opposite sex, difficulties, annoyance and possibly separations; troubles through Occult affairs and unreliable friends.

Not good for health, tending to upset the stomach and digestion, causing mental disturbance of different kinds, sudden or peculiar changes in feelings, emotions, likes and dislikes.

Restless, active mind, ever desirous of new scenes, new working material and surroundings; cannot stand limitations. It usually produces extremes and reversals.

### The Moon in Favorable Aspect to Neptune

Inclines to success in things ruled by Neptune and as indicated by the sign and house it occupies; good for boating, swimming, shipping, dealing in liquids, choice food stuffs, canned goods, delicacies and things calculated to please the tastes of the public.

Strong inspirational and imaging faculty; mediumistic qualities; fond of investigating Spiritualism, psychism and the mysterious in nature, or some form of the Occult. Would make a good psychometrist, having active emotions and impressionability. If Venus or Mercury is also in good aspect it shows inspiration for art, music, singing, writing, speaking or acting.

## The Moon in Unfavorable Aspect to Neptune

Threatens fraud, deception or slander; difficulties through things ruled by the house Neptune occupies; misfortune through the opposite sex, delays or obstacles in regard to marriage in a male chart; desire to gratify the tastes which leads to injury of the health, especially if either is in a water sign.

Strong inspirational, psychic, emotional and imaging faculty; subtle feelings, quick impressions and eccentric, undefined or inexplainable acts. It attracts to peculiar people, exquisite tastes, luxuries, odd colors, odors and Bohemianism or unconventionality.

Impulse is liable to predominate over reason, or through over-enthusiasm the feelings may get the upper hand of judgment, leading to acts of indiscretion. Quick response to environmental influences. It affects the nervous or mental health through bodily disorder. (Notice the signs they occupy.)

In mutable signs it affects the brain and nervous system; in fixed signs, the glandular and secretory processes; in the cardinal signs, the circulatory and absorptive systems.

## The Moon in Favorable Aspect to Pluto

The native is resilient to change, able always to make the best of circumstances. He is emotionally sensitive, and able to influence others subtly.

The conjunction cannot be considered a favorable aspect in this case, since the Moon is in its fall in Scorpio. Moodiness and depression may appear, due to vulnerability to strong emotional drives. The individual will be psychologically keyed into powerful interpersonal emotional interactions at an unconscious level.

### The Moon in Unfavorable Aspect to Pluto

The native is subject to severe emotional trauma, but internalizes this, so that intense feelings may erupt violently from time to time. Lack of self-control or self-discipline. Over-sensitive and lacks emotional discrimination. The native is usually prejudiced, because the rational facility is weakened.


## THE PLANETARY ASPECTS OF MERCURY

Mercury can never be more than 28° away from the Sun in either dexter or sinister position. Therefore, Mercury can only form the following aspects to the Sun: conjunction, parallel, and within two degrees of a semi-sextile.

Venus can never be more than 48° away from the Sun in either dexter or sinister position. Therefore, if Mercury were 28° away from the Sun on one side, and Venus 48° away on the other, the extent of their possible distance is 76°. Mercury can only form the following aspects to Venus: conjunction, parallel, semi-sextile, semi-square, sextile, and quintile, all of which are considered good except the semi-square.

### Mercury in Favorable Aspect to Venus

The mind is intuitive, cheerful, merry, witty, mirthful, good tempered and hopeful. This aspect gives a sociable, friendly nature, amiability and general popularity, especially with the opposite sex. Fondness for pleasure, refined entertainment and recreation, also for all the fine arts and sciences or anything requiring finish, touch, daintiness, color and culture. It tends to mental pleasures, harmony and mirth.

It favors gain in money, property and possessions.

Indicates marriage, friendships and associations.

Oftentimes it indicates that the native has two attachments, two marriages, partnerships, or marriage to some one of kin.

It is good for employment and money earned by the wits, speaking, writing, art, manual dexterity, entertainment. Neat, artistic touch.

If Mercury is more prominent than Venus, Third and Sixth House (Mercurial) affairs are favored; i.e., gain through mental accomplishments, writing, speaking, designing, short journeys; clerking, advertising, publishing, science, commercial affairs, commissions, kindred, neighbors, business, literary and professional people.

When Venus is more prominent, it favors pleasure and profit through talents, accomplishments, refinement and good taste; all things luxurious, pleasurable and beautiful; music, singing, poetry, painting, art, theaters; dealing with women and children, doctors, nursing; also in confectionery, stationery, jewelry, fancy work, millinery, dressmaking. Fortunate for things ruled by the house Venus occupies.

## Mercury in Unfavorable Aspect to Venus

The only adverse aspect they form is semi-square. This aspect is not very malignant or important. It gives fondness or desire for all the aforementioned, but not so much ability for their execution, and some minor obstacles and hindrance in Venus and Mercury affairs.

## Mercury and the Sun

Mercury never moves more than 28° away from the Sun and is best when more than 8° in advance of that luminary. Under the latter influence the native will be ambitious, aspiring, quick-witted, intuitive, thoughtful, intelligent, ingenious, adaptable, studious, observant and capable. Good business ability; learns with facility and ease.

If Mercury is in Pisces the mind should receive careful but gentle training. In Scorpio it tends to make fine physicians or surgeons. Mercury in exact conjunction with the Sun is not considered favorable for the best reasoning and business judgment, unless located in a favorable or scientific sign, or in good aspect to other planets.

## Mercury in Favorable Aspect to Mars

Makes the native quick, lively, bright, alert, witty, humorous, satirical, constructive, ingenious, practical, skillful, dexterous and businesslike.

Enthusiastic, fluent, animated and magnetic when interested. It shows a great deal of energy, activity, force and enterprise; splendid mental abilities.

Inclination or ability for drawing, music, carving, designing, chemistry, medicine, engineering, surveying and science; inclines toward investigation and application of new practical methods in commerce and industry, mechanics, literature or business.

It favors association with or development through literary, educational or professional people and those connected with the practical sciences.

### Mercury in Unfavorable Aspect to Mars

Good intellectual powers; the mind is acute, shrewd, clever and sharp. The disposition is impulsive, forceful, quick-tempered, sarcastic, argumentative, resentful and impatient; the mind is fired with desires, but has not enough continuity, the aspect being separative rather than unifying.

The subject possesses great mental activity and is therefore liable to brain troubles through over-work, excitement or lack of suitable opportunity for expression of his particular ability, which results in irritability and periods of weariness or exhaustion, and disorganization of the stomach and digestive organs.

Apt to create enmity, opposition and disagreements through sharp, critical statements or impulsive actions. Likely to meet with difficulty through relatives, superiors, servants and neighbors. Losses through theft, risky enterprises, correspondence, contracts, litigation, carelessness with facts, hasty conclusions and criticism.

Danger through traveling, tools, machinery, instruments and electrical contrivances; also drugs, operations, wounds from insects, reptiles and small animals.

This aspect indicates difficulties, obstacles and disorganization through things ruled by the signs and houses occupied by Mars especially. Trouble through neuralgia, headaches, accidents. The aspect is worse from water signs, usually showing tendency to drink and other ruinous habits.

### Mercury in Favorable Aspect to Jupiter

Inclines to general success in life through the houses they occupy, especially if unafflicted. Denotes a broad, philosophical mind with ability to think clearly, deeply and seriously, and to develop good judgment through comparison and learning; capability for collegiate studies.

The mind is versatile, vigorous and creative, combining conscientiousness with hope, good cheer, good nature, contentment and joviality.

The disposition is generous, kind, candid, humane, honest, sincere, liberal and fruitful. Indicates beneficial changes, journies; inspirational ideas, thoughts and conclusions.

Success with literature, accomplishments, science and in professional lines. Good aspect for mail order, governmental, law or church affairs. To Occult students it is good for visions, psychic and inspirational experiences, independent and automatic writing.

With Mercury in an air sign it gives discrimination, discernment, understanding, knowledge, appreciation, perception, compassion, sympathy and forbearance.

## Mercury in Unfavorable Aspect to Jupiter

Obstacles and difficulties arise regarding matters ruled by the houses they occupy, Mercury more particularly, through unfinished education or accomplishments.

It shows liability to deceit or poor judgment leading to changes, journeys; unreliable ideas, wily thoughts, dissension, disagreements and sometimes legal troubles. Misfortune and difficulty through investments, speculation, contracts, agreements (especially verbal), writings, church affiliations, social affairs, foreign and financial matters.

Liable to suffer from scandal, slander or false reports, and accidents in travel.

The mind is active, keen, alert and impressionable, but not sufficiently steady or confident. Unfavorable changes, travels and letters. It tends to weakness in the parts of the body ruled by the signs occupied by Mercury and Jupiter.

## Mercury in Favorable Aspect to Saturn

Good intellectual abilities: memory, order, method, reasoning and judgment. The mind is contemplative, substantial, practical, studious and fond of science generally.

Success with teaching hygiene, or as a physician, mental healer, or in any capacity with large corporations, especially railroads, mining, produce and commission concerns.

Gain through tact, diplomacy, caution and perseverance.

The aspect inclines to the study of geology or mineralogy. It favors travel in connection with business; some association or business with father or brethren, probably both; may gain some prominence through societies, church, or established concerns, as agent, secretary, representative.

If Mercury be in First, Third or Ninth House it is very good for scientific or intellectual pursuits, writings, publishings, lecturing, traveling.

Denotes strength of will, steady persistence and determination; good memory, strong, sensible, practical and sound judgment. The native has ability for politics, public appointments, official positions of all kinds, large public undertakings, brokerage, speculative, commercial or financial affairs, and business where much prudence, caution and sobriety of judgment are required. Mercury in conjunction with Saturn (if not otherwise afflicted) gives a very comprehensive and profound mind, capable of achieving much in whatever direction it is turned.

## Mercury in Unfavorable Aspect to Saturn

The subject has great ambitions and desires for activity, success and mastery in lines coming under the Third, Sixth and Tenth House affairs, but his efforts are attended with delay, disappointments, obstacles and limitations, and in some cases he meets with criticism and opposition, open or secret, and his efforts are frequently thwarted and hindered or his plans overthrown.

Encounters difficulty in acquiring an education and in all matters pertaining to books and studies.

The retentive or memorizing faculty needs developing even though memory of events is strong.

The aspect signifies great sorrow through death of brethren or father, probably both, or their ill health, separation or estrangement from them, although not necessarily through quarrels, but more as the result of circumstances.

Trouble is occasioned through slander, false reports, forged letters or documents, unfriendly writings, delayed and misunderstood letters, and the subject may himself cause difficulty through these things. The effect on the nature is to make one sarcastic, bitter, impulsive and somewhat dissembling with periods of gloom, pessimism or exasperation, grave anxiety, worry, constant disturbance of the mind, errors of judgment caused by fear, circumstances, lack of initiative, procrastination and continuous restriction of actions. This leads the mind to meditate and endeavor to discover the reason for these undesirable manifestations, and from this attitude one may be prone to seek recourse in the study of Occult subjects and spiritual philosophy, and thus improve his responses to the aspect.

If either planet be in or rule the Third or Ninth House it gives an inclination for science and Occult learning, which considerably improves the reactions to this aspect, but still there is liability to loss through failures, theft, fraud and deception; difficulty or loss in employment or through lack of employment, poor health often interfering; troubles through neighbors, servants, societies, associations, messengers, travelers, and by things ruled by the sign and house occupied. This is a bad aspect for the teeth, causing decay; also causes slow or poor circulation or digestion, bowel afflictions, weakness, obstructions and constipation. People with this aspect and annoyed with these latter troubles should avoid strong drinks or highly seasoned food.

## Mercury in Favorable Aspect to Uranus

Intuitive perception, inventive ability, original and eccentric nature. Fond of old and curious things, Occult science, Astrology and advanced thought generally.

Gain through invention, originality, speculation and unique enterprises. If either be in the First, Third or Ninth House, or is ruler thereof, it promotes success in literature and the ability to become a great scholar, excelling in the arts and sciences; fine comprehension.

Good character reader; successful in connection with electrical affairs as salesman, telegrapher, bookkeeper, stockkeeper, etc., for electrical, aerial or transportation companies. Much ingenuity and unique enterprise.

Successful advertiser, publisher, writer, inventor, researcher or explorer.

## Mercury in Unfavorable Aspect to Uranus

Active mentality; impulsive, irregular and sarcastic turns of mind; very observant, ingenious and critical; unsuccessful in literary pursuits; public criticism probably through the press; difficulty through societies, friends and kindred. Skeptical and peculiar; a reformer's spirit and extreme or radical ideas; constant desire for new fields or modes of action; sudden and unexpected adverse changes and removals. Restless, dissatisfied, discontented, daring, audacious, defiant, adventurous. Subject to accidents, especially in travel.

## Mercury in Favorable Aspect to Neptune

Fertile imagination; practical, quick, sensitive and resourceful mind; versatility of genius; receptivity to new ideas and methods. Gives ability to develop mediumistic and psychic qualities, clairvoyance, psychometry, crystal gazing, automatic writing, trance and inspirational speaking.

The native is attracted to psychic centers and people, spiritual investigations, unconventional healing and hygienic methods or hydrotherapy, and success with same. It gives visions of prophetic dreams.

The Third and Ninth Houses are the best for the above.

Improves mental receptivity, psychic understanding and adaptability. Occult experiences.

It favors matters relating to liquids, chemicals, oils, drugs, beverages, canned goods, fish, the sea, hospitals and private institutions.

If Venus also is in good aspect, the subject will have remarkable faculty for music, poetry, art, literature; inspiration.

## Mercury in Unfavorable Aspect to Neptune

Conducive to an interest in all of the above, but attended with unreliability, obstacles and misfortune.

The memory is apt to be poor, the mind vacillating and somewhat unpractical, affected by spells or periods of mental aberration, abstraction, lack of concentration, absentmindedness, dreaminess, or irresolution. It tends to nervousness, sensitiveness, restlessness, changes, and liability to trouble through slander, deception, imitation, fraud, intrigue, bribery. Danger through drugs and poisons.

Difficulties through changefulness, unexplainable psychic conditions, lack of cautious self-control and the liability to be led by the impulses, sensations, appetites, emotions, sympathy, and by the ideas, thoughts and advice of others, resulting in nervous, restless excitability, which exhausts the vital processes. The native should benefit through study of dietetics.

## Mercury in Favorable Aspect to Pluto

Mental flexibility; the lack of fixed ideas allows the native to easily size up a new situation and change his tactics to meet the changing reality. Strong suggestive personality, able to persuade and even dominate others mentally. Analytical mind penetrates through the obvious searching out the causes of things. Sees connections between externally unrelated objects, ideas, and feelings.

In the conjunction there is a possibility of self-centeredness, and using the power to subtly control others for his own benefit.

### Mercury in Unfavorable Aspect to Pluto

Snap judgments made; ideas are grasped quickly but the native shows impatience with others who do not think in the same manner. Skepticism and cynicism may turn into fanaticism, and obsession. Mental turmoil causes physical disorders. An inner restlessness may drive the native to obsessive search for new knowledge and Occult information. Preoccupation with death.

## THE PLANETARY ASPECTS OF VENUS

As Venus is never more than 48° away from the Sun, only the aspects which can be formed are as follows: conjunction, parallel, semi-sextile, and semi-square.

### Venus in Good Aspect to the Sun

Fondness for company and hospitality, delighting in sociability, pleasure, ease, luxury, comfort and places of entertainment.

The nature is generous, warm-hearted, sympathetic, courteous, amiable, kind, affectionate, impressionable and cheerful.

The aspect is fruitful and creative, good for gaining money through business, profession, speculation or public occupation; it shows popularity and promotion in employment, and preferment in social affairs. Liking for music, opera, the fine arts generally, and some ability along these lines.

The conjunction leads to warm attraction, love affairs and marriage, even when there are adverse testimonies denying union.

### Venus in Unfavorable Aspect to the Sun

As Venus is never more than 48° from the Sun, the "combust"

and semi-square are the only adverse aspects Venus can form to Sol.

Neither is a very important aspect of itself, but at times may make the native extravagant, overfond of pleasure and luxury, amorous and mutable in the affections.

Some delay or misfortune in love affairs and in dealing with the opposite sex. Loss through speculation and extravagance, or carelessness.

### Venus in Favorable Aspect to Mars

Fond of pleasure, adventure and the opposite sex; aspiring, ambitious, confident, amorous, affectionate and demonstrative.

Gain through enterprise, pleasure, sport, practical artistic ability, music and matters requiring artistic and mechanical skill.

It is a good aspect for money, not for saving it (that requires a good aspect for Saturn, acquisitiveness) but for getting it, earning it through energy, activity, ingenuity, responsibility and business instinct, and through things ruled by the house Venus occupies and rules. The native is free and generous in money matters, a cheerful spender; in business, for advertisement, show and display; in social life, for pleasure, adornment, music and entertainment.

If the chart shows any indications for inheritance this aspect strengthens it. The aspect also shows social popularity and indicates marriage either early or suddenly.

### Venus in Unfavorable Aspect to Mars

Very fond of pleasure; impulsive and amorous; difficulty through excesses and the opposite sex.

Loss through over-liberal tendencies or carelessness and extravagance; also through fires, partnerships and too freely entering business or speculative enterprises.

At times the social popularity or standing will be adversely affected; danger through dishonesty or loss; opposition through friends or jealousy, separation and enmity. Trouble through marriage and partnerships.

If Venus or Mars be in a water sign, the tendency is to gratify the tastes and pleasurable emotions in dissipating habits.

### Venus in Favorable Aspect to Jupiter

Strengthens the imagination, ideality and poetical side of the nature, giving a keen appreciation for beauty in form, color, sound and touch. High motives, ambitions and aspirations.

It gives social and general popularity, preferment, esteem and respect.

Inclines to acts of charity and sympathy. The nature becomes generous, kind, thoughtful, amiable, loving, sociable, hospitable, philanthropic, liberal, talented, good-humored and optimistic; fond of pleasure and elegant, dainty and costly surroundings.

Gain through refinement, accomplishments, social intercourse, traveling, foreign affairs, influential person, companies, associations and corporations. A good indication of fortunate events, love and marriage; favors success, gain and general good fortune. Generally is associated with wealth and culture, and handles considerable money or other valuable assets.

Fortunate for things governed by the houses they occupy and also those houses which they rule in the nativity.

## Venus in Unfavorable Aspect to Jupiter

Strong desire for grace, refinement, talent, beauty and luxury, but forced to be content with these to an ordinary or limited extent and satisfied with the best show or substitute possible.

Unless other testimonies offset this, it is not a good aspect for the accumulation of money, as a great deal is spent for appearances in dress, ornaments, luxury; inclines to easy good nature and fondness for pleasure, producing lack of accurate business instinct, resulting in loss through carelessness, fraud, deception, desertion, separation, prosecution, speculation, and unsound investments or securities. Difficulty in love and marriage through faithlessness or misrepresentation. Liable to overdo in the gratification of desires for pleasure and amusements; apt to be overliberal, extravagant and amorous. Blood or skin disorders; loss through floods.

## Venus in Favorable Aspect to Saturn

Sympathetic, modest, prudent, chaste, frugal and sincere. It favors success in courtship and marriage and steady attachment to partner and family. Faithfulness in love and friendship.

The tendency is toward thrift, economy and accumulation of money. It endows the native with capacity for business: tact, method and system, and ability to make the most of opportunities. Much good luck, good will and many presents.

Gain through elders, superiors in position and by investments, associations, banking, lands and solid, secure methods.

### Venus in Unfavorable Aspect to Saturn

Disappointment and trouble in courtship and marriage or partnership; censure, unpopularity, disapproval, interference, reversals, or misfortunes through elders, parents or relatives. Danger through deception, avariciousness, sensuality, jealousy and theft.

Sorrows and difficulties through the opposite sex; marriage probably delayed until the twenty-eighth year or after; trouble through difference in age, social or pecuniary affairs or illness.

Diplomatic nature; liability to business losses; also through speculations, investments, lands, mines, companies, banks, drought, depressions or epidemics; loss of accounts or salary.

### Venus in Favorable Aspect to Uranus

Fondness, desire and ability for the fine arts, leaning toward new or extraordinary conceptions, radical and progressive departures from the usual interpretation of art.

Attractive, magnetic personality that gains many friends and acquaintances and good fortune or success through them. A fortunate business aspect.

Bright, quick, intuitive, inspirational mentality.

Benefit and gain through fraternal, social and progressive societies.

Success through such things as Venus and Uranus rule; gain by peculiar or unexpected circumstances and through strangers; favorite with the opposite sex. Friends among artists, inventors, congressman and extraordinary persons.

### Venus in Unfavorable Aspect to Uranus

Trouble and jealousy through courtship and marriage; difficulty through the opposite sex. Unconventional; liable to hasty, impulsive marriage leading to divorce.

The mind is imaginative, curious, alert and hastily influenced by unrestrained feelings, which make the native liable to be led astray; troubles by broken promises and scandal; separations, estrangements and difficulty with friends. Losses through sudden and unexpected circumstances. An unfortunate aspect for matters connected with the opposite sex. Loss through unreliable friends, associates or partners, and through risky ventures.

## Venus in Favorable Aspect to Neptune

Inclines to fondness for art, music, singing, drama, and beauty in all forms. This aspect has a tendency toward benefit and pleasure through friends, associations and acquaintances.

The feelings quickly respond to kindness, sympathy, love and appreciation. Inspirational, ardent and attracted to the opposite sex. Good aspect for benefit through mystical interests and success in speculation or as an actor if either be in the fifth house, especially in connection with the cinema.

It is a fortunate aspect for making money out of large combines, trusts or institutions; also for matters related to shipping, liquids and amusement resorts, especially at places by water.

## Venus in Unfavorable Aspect to Neptune

Disappointments, complications, deceit and danger of scandal in love or marriage; instability and liability of fraud and deception on the part of the partner, especially if either planet be in the Fifth, Seventh or Twelfth House.

Strong desires, with probability of injury and danger through catering to the gratification of the tastes, or through lack of proper emotional expression.

Caution should be observed with diet and beverages. There may be danger from ptomaine poisoning through wrong food combinations or impure substances.

Guard against loss and theft, misplaced confidence and secret organizations and affairs. Beware of financial loss through schemes, trusts, cliques or rackets.

## Venus in Favorable Aspect to Pluto

A loving personality, always able to see the best in people. Strong emotional attachment for the underdog; empathy for other's problems. Understanding nature. A strong and loyal friend, though the relationship may change many times.

In the conjunction, the sexual element is more emphasized. Intense love or lust, and strong procreative drive.

### Venus in Unfavorable Aspect to Pluto

Jealousy and possessiveness enters relationships; ultimately causing loneliness in the native. A strong sex drive can lead to uncontrolled lust and immoderate behavior. Relationships are full of conflict. The native often loses friends without understanding the reason why. The native feels emotionally insecure and fears the inability to love, or be loved.

# THE PLANETARY ASPECTS OF THE SUN

### The Sun in Favorable Aspect to Mars

Tends to strengthen the constitution and give energy, vitality, determination, enterprise, vigor, animation, confidence and courage.

The nature is frank, outspoken, assertive, aggressive, ambitious, venturesome, progressive and generous.

The native has ability to command and control; gives power of leadership through intensity of purpose, enthusiasm, activity, faith and strength of will.

Capacity for games and sports where strength and muscular exertion are depended upon. If Mars or the Sun is in an air sign, powerful intellect and much will force. If either planet is angular it denotes great executive power and leadership.

The native has quick perception and possesses practical, constructive and engineering ability; meets with favor, promotion and cooperation.

### The Sun in Unfavorable Aspect to Mars

Many ups and downs and obstacles in the path of the desires. Impulse, pride and anger cause many difficulties; deaths, separations, litigation and enmities; hasty, fiery temper, though not lasting; ambition, love of enterprise but not enough continuity of application, confidence, faith and patience.

Outspoken, assertive, aggressive, combative, defensive, impulsive, forceful, overbearing, destructive, self-willed, headstrong, audacious and sensual. Loses the esteem of superiors and those in high position.

Danger through impulsive action, assaults, quarrels, accidents, fires, fevers, inflammatory complaints, surgical operations, short, sudden, sharp attacks of sickness; cuts, burns, scalds.

If Mars is in Capricorn or the Sun dignified it lessens the tendency to rashness, etc.

## The Sun in Favorable Aspect to Jupiter

This increases the chances for success and rise in life; even with bad aspects from other planets it still indicates some good fortune, because it tends toward a far-seeing, broad outlook and sound judgment.

The native is honorable, humane, benevolent, sympathetic, kind, philanthropic, charitable, generous, sincere, frank, candid, hopeful, social, genial, popular, executive, reliable, honest and fond of sports.

Indicates influential friends and assistance or benefit through them. Inclines somewhat to religion or spiritual investigation. Appreciation of social life and its functions with a desire for the good opinion and favor of those in good position. The subject is usually "correct" with regard to fashion and customs and careful not to overstep the limits of good form.

Inclines to good health and abundant vitality. With a female, this aspect assists to a successful love or marriage.

Fortunate for those things ruled by the houses these planets occupy, especially Jupiter. If Uranus also be in good aspect, it signifies gain and the acquisition of wealth through railroads, inventions, governmental office, speculation, investment, banks, large theatrical enterprises, sports, transportation, publishing, and things electrical and political.

If Saturn assists: gain through investment and solid financial deals, government affairs, inheritance or gold mines.

Mars also in good aspect: although not detrimental to the acquisition of wealth, is not good for the saving of it on account of generosity and lavishness. It favors industrial success. Venus in good aspect: gain through refinement, pleasure, music, entertainment and general good luck. Mercury in good aspect: gain through science, art, traveling, writings and publishing. Moon in good aspect: gain through dealing with the public and possibly through shipping and public utility concerns.

### The Sun in Unfavorable Aspect to Jupiter

Threatens business and financial loss through investments, speculations, loans, errors, miscalculations, etc.

Danger of difficulty through wrong advice, extravagance, legal or social affairs. A good aspect of the Moon will help to modify these financial testimonies, but, in any event, it shows ill luck, probably through misjudgment, false "securities," pride, lack of careful reasoning or forethought.

The tendency at times is to be bombasic, irritable, haughty, egotistical, mistrustful, fond of display, pleasure and comfort.

In a woman's horoscope, it indicates a good but somewhat unlucky husband.

There is tendency toward Sun and Jupiter diseases during the latter part of life and weakened vitality.

### The Sun in Favorable Aspect to Saturn

This aspect is such that it aids general success and rise in life through the native's own efforts and meritorious qualities, and the ability to concentrate, appraise, organize and coordinate the efforts toward a definite objective.

Makes the native sincere, considerate, conservative, methodical, responsible, discreet, discriminative, serious, confident and capable of sustained effort.

The personality is strong and not easily affected by the opinions or protests of others; the mentality is contemplative and practical, authoritative and capable of organization. If assisted by any other good aspect, it tends to gain and success through lands, mines, investments and industrial enterprises.

If the Moon is in good aspect, the native gains municipal or other political honors and appointments.

### The Sun in Unfavorable Aspect to Saturn

Indicates derangements of the health, the nature of the illness threatened can be seen by the signs which the Sun and Saturn occupy. It is bad for business affairs, especially of the kind signified by the two planets.

Obstacles, limitations, hindrance and delays, cause disappointments, sorrows and losses. The ambitions are thwarted, sometimes the native seems to be getting along splendidly, success seems close and sure, but suddenly inevitable conditions and reverses arise, resulting in downfall and loss. The native incurs opposition, enmity, jealousy and public disfavor.

All of these things indicate a tendency to become unsympathetic, careless of the feelings of others, selfish, pessimistic, skeptical, or disinterested in social and economic welfare.

It indicates death of the father, disagreement or separation from him; enmity or disfavor of superiors, employers or those of high position; unfortunate marital affairs.

In a woman's horoscope this aspect signifies a denial of marriage or delay. Also indicates death of the husband or marriage to a widower. These marriages are seldom happy ones, the husband usually being domineering, exacting, selfish, or inclined to illness and misfortune.

If Saturn is in a water sign, the partner is liable to be given to drink or other dissolute habits.

## The Sun in Favorable Aspect to Uranus

Denotes talent, perception, intuition, independence, originality and enterprise. It indicates success through invention, public or governmental employ. Also a good aspect for connection with societies, associations or brotherhoods; research, exploration, adventure, transportation, aerial and electrical matters.

Tends to preserve the health in old age and lengthens life. Friends among government executives and extraordinary persons.

Benefit through the Occult; from metaphysical, electric or magnetic healing; by strangers, elderly people or occultists. (Many successful public astrologers have this aspect.)

It excites to strong attachments and generally to an early union. Interest in fraternities, reforms and progressive movements.

## The Sun in Unfavorable Aspect to Uranus

Unfortunate for marriage, causing disharmony, separation, broken vows and ties generally. Tends to make one impulsive, rash, spasmodic, erratic, radical and unconventional; inclined to leap before looking; precipitate, fond of risky ventures, enterprises and romance. It is worse in a woman's horoscope, indicating danger of scandal, disgrace and unlucky unions.

Denotes a quick, intuitive, perceptive and original mind, always alert for change, liberty, freedom, novelty and new opportunities.

It gives interest in occult affairs, but denotes liability to losses and danger through unreliable friends, disasters, calamities, enmity, opposition, love affairs, partnerships, strangers, societies, intrigue, estrangement, independence and impulsiveness. It tends to upset the health and indicates accidents, possibly through engines, inventions, vehicles, airplanes, explosions, storms, and things electrical. A good aspect from other planets helps to modify these extreme indications.

## The Sun in Favorable Aspect to Neptune

Gives an inspirational nature, and an inclination for philosophy, religion, science, psychic research, photography, motion pictures. Interest in modern sanitation, hygiene, natureopathy, sun bathing, swimming, yachting, motor-boat racing, etc. If Mercury be near the Ascendant, angular or in good aspect to these planets the native is usually inspirational in speaking or writing and can develop considerable musical skill, especially in connection with stringed instruments.

The tendency of the aspect is to refine the feelings and emotions, giving a keen appreciation for the beauties of nature and art or music in its highest forms; love of refined pleasures, concerts, yachting, sojourning at the beach, traveling and all fine luxury or elegance. The native is sympathetic, kind and generous and usually benefits through mystical and spiritual subjects.

## The Sun in Unfavorable Aspect to Neptune

Signifies that the person is liable to be the victim of fraud, and also scandal, whether deserved or not; unstable or involved affairs generally; unfortunate for the things signified by the house which Neptune occupies.

Creates desires for mysticism, romance, gratification of abnormal tastes and inclines in some way to lax morality, Bohemianism and seductive alliances.

The native is usually mediumistic and subject to weird dreams, feelings and desires. It usually indicates peculiar or irregular love affairs, some difficulty with or through children, and loss through speculation, gaming or deception concerning securities and investments.

Inclined to suffer from illness requiring hospitalization, and which is difficult to diagnose; from psychic conditions, fraud, enmity and conspiracy. It is wise in such cases to study the philosophy of all things mysterious or Occult rather than the phenomena.

## The Sun in Favorable Aspect to Pluto

This native has a very strong personality and a marked influence over others. He is able to easily discard old habits, ideas, and possessions which hinder him in attaining his goals. These he usually attains, on strength of will if nothing else. The native fights for what he believes or wants, and welcomes new conflicts.

In the conjunction the power drive may be overwhelming and there is a tendency to use this power selfishly.

## The Sun in Unfavorable Aspect to Pluto

The native is egotistical, domineering, possessive, and above all ruthless. He will do anything to achieve his goals, and has complete disregard for his fellow man. The native lacks an ethical system, and can be bought for a price, though usually he is the one who does the buying.

## THE PLANETARY ASPECTS OF MARS

### Mars in Favorable Aspect to Jupiter

Frank, free, generous, straightforward, just, active, ambitious, enterprising, self-reliant, original and constructive. Any course of action decided on is entered into with vim, confidence, determination and practical execution. A good manager or leader; capable of creating enthusiasm and action in others. Liberal concepts, broad views, capable of large and responsible undertakings, especially in wholesale, industrial and commercial affairs. Always ready to help those who are willing to help themselves. If the chart shows indications of legacy this aspect tends to strengthen it.

Fond of all legitimate sport, travel, exploration, mechanical, professional and industrial activities. Gain by personal industry, enterprise and the exercise of good judgment.

Fortunate for those things ruled by the house which Jupiter occupies.

### Mars in Unfavorable Aspect to Jupiter

Indicates excessive or impulsive generosity; careless regarding the accumulation of money and apt to suffer from the dishonesty of others.

Difficulty through and with religion, religious or political people. Loss through speculation and games of chance.

Suffers from indiscretion, dishonesty, deceit, treachery, broken contracts, desertion, misrepresentation and quarrels.

Often the subject is directly or indirectly the cause of misfortune through hasty judgment, impulsive action, extravagance, dissipation or through carelessness, overconfidence, miscalculation, anger.

Dangerous or difficult journeys, trouble in foreign places and through legal affairs.

Feverish complaints, blood and liver disorders; danger and loss through fires and accidents, and if Uranus is adverse, through lightning, electricity, floods or explosions.

### Mars in Favorable Aspect to Saturn

Confident, ambitious, determined, energetic, desirous of leading and ruling, a pioneering nature. Courageous, self-reliant, daring, somewhat overbearing and forceful, reckless of danger or defeat, capable of obtaining marked results through concentrated or sustained action. Reserve force, muscular endurance, strong bones; active mentality, capability, vigilance, skill in execution. Rises to prominence or power but usually attended by danger of some kind; would make a good military, state or city official; also practical lawyer, civil and mining engineer, surveyor, construction contractor, manufacturer, farmer, etc. Favorable aspect for legacy from father.

### Mars in Unfavorable Aspect to Saturn

The mind and senses act in confliction, causing discord, selfishness, quick temper, violence; rash, hasty, impulsive acts; deception, resentment, cruel, hard or revengeful feelings when opposed.

Trouble with parts of the body denoted by the signs occupied by the afflicted planets. Feverish complaints, wounds, falls and accidents; danger of violence through enemies, reptiles, animals, riots, strikes, uprisings, revolutions, accident, war or state. Notoriety, reversals, criticism, opposition, enmity, scandal, discredit; obstacles and difficulty in occupation, danger of loss and failure in business.

An unfortunate aspect for parents, denoting death, separation or disputes; bad for legacies; difficulties with companies, partnerships or in marriage. Liable to imprisonment.

If either planet is well aspected and well located by sign, much of the above is mitigated, but notice the houses which they occupy, as they indicate trouble for the things ruled thereby.

## Mars in Favorable Aspect to Uranus

The subject comes before the public in some capacity through the talents. The mind is very alert, quick to act and inventive; the nature is positive, self-confident, enterprising, original, expressive, energetic, impulsive, ambitious, resourceful and practical; possesses practical business intuition, talent and intellectuality. When once a course of action has been decided upon, it is followed with a good deal of originality or independence and determination, which is difficult to thwart or turn aside, for the subject generally gets his own way; he is usually generous and has Occult sympathies.

Gain through invention, electrical engineering, construction, transportation, or industrial research, unique achievements, municipal employ, government positions, progressive professional pursuits, psychology, psychoanalysis, suggestive therapeutics, metaphysics, Astrology. Also through travel, exploration, investigation, the antique and curious generally.

## Mars in Unfavorable Aspect to Uranus

The subject has most of the aforementioned traits and qualities, but is somewhat over-forceful, restless and unsettled; hasty and erroneous in judgment, quick in opposition, resentful, irritable, erratic, radical, imprudent, defiant, odd, eccentric, ungovernable, rebellious, fanciful, excitable, enigmatical. Sometimes violent or revolutionary, seeking to throw off all bonds of limitation, restraint, custom and conventionality.

An unfortunate aspect for affairs ruled by the signs and houses occupied. Danger of imprisonment and liability to violence, accidents, wounds and trouble through firearms, explosions, lightning, fire, wrecks, machinery, vehicles of transportation and electrical devices.

It denotes sudden and unfortunate events which upset prearranged affairs, reversals of plans and changes in objectives.

### Mars in Favorable Aspect to Neptune

Gives a fondness for curiosities and travel, for occult and metaphysical subjects. Favors marine activities and aquatic sports.

Increases the generosity, emotions and enthusiasm, and the liking for mysticism, romance, adventure.

A good aspect for those connected with the water or with liquids, beverages, oils, drugs, chemicals, anesthetics, hospitals, sanitariums, or the sea, and with the Occult in a practical way.

### Mars in Unfavorable Aspect to Neptune

Gives a fondness for curiosities and travel; inclines to self-indulgence and feelings of self-sufficiency.

Liable to trouble arising from relations with the opposite sex, also through scandal. Somewhat vague, indefinite or mysterious, obscure and secretive. Danger of loss and accident on or by water or liquids; through poisons, drugs or habits; also through thieves and acts of Nature. Trouble through duplicity, deception, fraud, imitation, racketeering, bribery, false accusation, arrest. To psychic persons it gives liability to distraction or obsession (possession) and produces derangements, hallucinations and strange ideas. If Mars or Neptune is well aspected or otherwise dignified, these testimonies are considerably modified.

### Mars in Favorable Aspect to Pluto

The native has a forceful personality; he shows great ambition, the capacity for hard work, is self-confident, and courageous. He is able to achieve his aims through energetic and unpredicted attack. Enjoys competition.

In the conjunction the animal self is strong and ruthlessness can be a problem. Impulsive.

### Mars in Unfavorable Aspect to Pluto

The capacity for violence lies just beneath the surface and often overwhelms the native. Lack of purpose causes inner turbulence and restlessness which may lead to irrational acts. The native has trouble controlling his impulses, and has difficulty living in a structured society. Sadistic tendencies. The native should learn to *carefully* analyze his reasons for taking actions of any sort.

## THE PLANETARY ASPECTS OF JUPITER

The aspects between the slower-moving planets will be within orbs for a long time, and so have less individual influence. The conjunction and opposition between Jupiter and Saturn recur every 21 years; between Jupiter and Uranus every 14 years; between Jupiter and Neptune about every 13 years; and between Jupiter and Pluto about every 12 years.

### Jupiter in Favorable Aspect to Saturn

A fortunate aspect for those affairs, occupations and pursuits ruled by these planets and for things ruled by the houses and signs which they occupy, especially Jupiter.

Good mental ability, capacity for deep or collegiate learnings, strength of character and power to overcome obstacles; serious, profound, philosophical or scientific; succeeds in favor of elders and those of good position generally. Power of review, appraisal, comparison, concentration, synthesis and arbitration. This aspect strengthens the credit and reputation; gives justice, contemplation, meditation and practical benevolence; indicates sincerity, honor, esteem, honesty, thrift and general prosperity.

Practical financial and executive ability; good judgment. Gain through father, friends, long journeys, investment, religion, science, publications, societies, companies, associations and political offices; also through religious, medical or scientific institutions. If the planets are in angles or cardinal signs, he acquits himself worthily wherever located and his work is of a beneficent and public nature.

Favorable for money and possessions, gain through the father and by legacy if the fourth and eighth houses are unafflicted. If in fixed signs, they endow power for conducting affairs of great weight and importance.

The trine and sextile are better than the conjunction.

### Jupiter in Unfavorable Aspect to Saturn

Losses through litigation, trustees, banks, etc. An unfortunate aspect for money success in business or occupation; threatens trouble, pecuniary or otherwise, through the father, neighbors, companies; downfall or setback by loss of money, property and credit; through miscalculation, poor judgment or speculations; trouble in connection with education and travel. Impressionable, indecisive, and mistrustful; not sufficient hope, confidence and self-will; inclined to give into circumstances and environments too readily; possibly through ill health. Danger of opposition, limitations, enmity and treachery; subject to charity, or imprisonment. Difficulty through or on account of dishonesty and misrepresentation; danger through floods, earthquakes, epidemics.

## Jupiter in Favorable Aspect to Uranus

A fortunate aspect for the things indicated by the two planets and especially in connection with the sign and house occupied by Jupiter.

It denotes broad scope of mind and originality of thought with interesting, surprising or unique logic and manner of reasoning. It is an indication of benefit through legacy and general success; gain through Uranus occupations or studies, fraternal societies, foreign travel, means of communcation, transportation and learning, law, higher science, philosophy, publishing, religious or educational movements, research, exploration, invention, speculation, political office or government.

The nature is just, refined, sociable, humanitarian and progressive; intuitive, prophetic and usually correct in foresight.

## Jupiter in Unfavorable Aspect to Uranus

The tendencies are the same as the above, but attended by unexpected difficulties, obstacles and limitations.

Loss through impulse, unwise judgment and imprudent action, risky ventures, unpremeditated acts.

Through unfortunate decisions, changes and events the subject is hindered and delayed, or denied the achievement of his highest ambitions.

Troubles and losses by litigation; annoyance and difficulty over inheritance or property.

It threatens sudden, unexpected and heavy losses by acts of nature, through friends, governmental or legal decrees, misinformation, wrong advice, misjudgment.

## Jupiter in Favorable Aspect to Neptune

Improves the artistic and poetic qualities; refines the imagination and strengthens the social, philanthropic and emotional side of the nature. Denotes honor, benevolence, courtesy, candor and sympathy. Favors traveling, psychic experiences, remarkable dreams and visions. The subject is inspirational and given to the investigation of psychism from a religious or scientific standpoint. Becomes popular and successful in secret or mystical societies. Beneficial for matters relating to the sea, hospitals, sanitariums, clubs or pleasure resorts.

## Jupiter in Unfavorable Aspect to Neptune

Difficulties and troubles trough the aforementioned affairs and things indicated by the house occupied by Neptune.

Losses through speculation, fraud and treachery; secret sorrows. Peculiar religious benefits, emotional disturbances, uncertain health, danger from deceit and dishonesty, trouble through water, liquids, drugs, oils, chemicals or beverages. Danger at sea or pleasure resorts.

## Jupiter in Favorable Aspect to Pluto

The person is optimistic, always able to see the positive side of things. This makes him a natural leader who is generous, cheerful, and caring. He can subtly influence others for their own good, and has the ability to see beyond the superficial and get to the core of things. His wit is light and subtle, and he is always able to make a funny joke to lighten an otherwise tense situation. The native may be spiritually oriented.

In the conjunction the leadership aspect is heightened and the native often achieves fame and recognition.

## Jupiter in Unfavorable Aspect to Pluto

The individual has unrealistic expectations and dissipates a lot of energy on unobtainable or inappropriate goals. His self opinion fluctuates from over-confidence to inadequacy. Inferiority feelings may be compensated by overbearing attitude and the tendency to try to force others to conform to his will. He has the power to lead but without the charm and popularity of the favorable aspects. Dogmatic, destructive.

There will be difficulty or inability to conjoin spiritual insight and training with emotional drives and ambitions. The emotional needs will be expressed contrary to confidence in spiritual realities, while the latter will not be available to assist in difficulties arising from the former.

# THE PLANETARY ASPECTS OF SATURN

These aspects are long-lasting, and infrequently occurring. The conjunction and opposition between Saturn and Uranus are exact every 91 years; between Saturn and Neptune about every 35 years. The aspects between Saturn and Pluto occur so rarely and last so long that they are only relevant when one of the planets is dignified due to house or sign position, rulership, or by aspect.

## Saturn in Favorable Aspect to Uranus

Increases the strength of mind, giving thoughtfulness, seriousness, ability to plan, control, systematize and organize, and adds concentration, intuition, perception, penetration. Tends to success in undertakings due to resourcefulness, practical foresight, fixity of purpose and determination. Inclines to interest in Occult affairs and some occult faculty, such as telepathy or mental healing, and success through them. If the aspected planets are well placed, it favors success in investment with or through large enterprises connected with the railroads, steam or electric, or in dealing with aluminum, platinum, lead, coal and inventions; also through large, solid public institutions. If one or both of the luminaries are in good aspect also, it tends to conserve the vitality and prolong life.

## Saturn in Unfavorable Aspect to Uranus

The tendencies and desires are the same as before mentioned, but the subject has not the capacity and ability to direct the forces to the same successful results and meets with general misfortune through things mentioned and indicated by the houses these planets occupy.

This aspect has an injurious effect on the health at some time, weakening the parts of the body denoted by the signs occupied, especially by Saturn, producing a heavy, complicated and serious sickness, either long drawn out or else incurable. Liability to accidents by falls, falling objects, collisions, acts of nature, riots or uprisings and disregard for the rights or feelings of others.

Mentally it gives singular, imaginative, eccentric and peculiar attitudes, sudden temper, impulsive, aggressive acts. Radical or destructive tendencies.

In a very weak or adverse chart, may invert the abilities and become thoroughly bad, treacherous, violent, or the aspect may manifest indolence, idleness, with an improvident nature, satisfied only in catering to the tastes and emotions. Disrespect for laws.

## Saturn in Favorable Aspect to Neptune

Gives inspirational ideas, intuition, concentration, clairaudience, depth and clearness of thought and favorably affects those feelings which tend toward the mystical, weird and psychic. Interest in industrial chemistry, oil, refining, mineral waters, refrigeration, preserving or fishing.

Good-hearted; deep sympathies. Success and benefit through the Occult, advanced studies, investigation and self-development; also through serious and elderly people, unusual occupations connected with liquids, oils, or the sea. When well placed it favors success and benefit through property, investments, shares, stocks and legacies.

## Saturn in Unfavorable Aspect to Neptune

Loss and difficulty through plots, treachery and failures, improperly timed activities, insufficient action, misinformation, misunderstanding, confusion or lack of co-ordination. Distressful psychic conditions. Complicated financial affairs; loss through speculation and difficulty through things indicated by the houses these planets occupy. Weird feelings. Liable to scandal, discredit, disrepute, criticism. Doubtful tastes, improper diet, inadequate health measures and accidents are apt to require hospitalization.

## Saturn in Favorable Aspect to Pluto

Serious, hard-working, reliable natives with a capacity for great self-denial and self-discipline. Frugal, moderate, patient.

The conjunction produces a native more serious, and austere. Periods of despondency.

## Saturn in Unfavorable Aspect to Pluto

As with other negative Pluto aspects: jealousy, lust, dominance. The native strives for personal power and may withdraw himself from normal human contacts in order to achieve this aim. Destructive tendencies. Frustrated drives. Dishonesty regarding emotional interactions. Miscalculations of desire.

## THE PLANETARY ASPECTS OF URANUS

The aspects between Uranus, Neptune and Pluto affect a whole generation and are only personally relevant to the native when one of the
planets is dignified due to house or sign position, rulership, or by
aspects. The conjunction and opposition between Uranus and Neptune
occur about every 171 years. The conjunction last occurred in 1820 in
Sagittarius and will next occur in 1991. The last trine was within orb
on and off 1937-47 when Uranus was in Taurus and Gemini and
Neptune in Virgo and Libra. An opposition between these two planets
(Uranus in Capricorn, Neptune in Cancer) occurred off and on between
1905 and 1913; a square (Uranus in Cancer and Neptune in Libra) on
and off between 1951 and 1958.

Uranus was conjunct Pluto in Virgo in 1965; it was square Pluto
in cardinal signs (Aries and Cancer respectively) from 1930 to 1935.
The opposition between Uranus in Sagittarius and Pluto in Gemini
occurred around the turn of the century.

### Uranus in Favorable Aspect to Neptune

Gives intuitive understanding, unaccountable attractions and
aversions, peculiar attraction to psychic centers, curious feelings,
impressions and inspirations.

Liking for journeys, curiosities,exploration, experiments, investigation, secret missions and adventure.

Interest in Occult affairs and mystical or secret societies, metaphysics, mental healing, transcendentalism and new thought. The aspect
indicates interest in unusual subjects, occupations and experiences. The
native will have success in the development of any occult faculty he
may possess and will also benefit through these things and through
Occult people. Inspirational ideas will present themselves and also some
marvelous psychic experiences. Favorable for matters relating to the
sea, large institutions and federal affairs.

### Uranus in Unfavorable Aspect to Neptune

This is not a very serious affliction; it gives the same quick, keen
intuition and faculty for the curious, with attraction for and desire to
investigate the mysterious and things occult, but indicates obstacles,
difficulties and danger in following extremes in the foregoing. The

person is subject to psychic conditions, consciously or unconsciously, therefore, may be influenced by surroundings and environment to his detriment. Many inexpressible moods and emotions will be felt, such as from trance, ecstasy and bliss to vague, semi-hysterical states. Subtle attractions and revulsions. Should exercise great discrimination in choice of friend, confidante or confrere.

### Uranus in Favorable Aspect to Pluto
The native possesses great originality, intuition, and understanding. It favors scientific and metaphysical studies.

The conjunction gives a more rebellious native.

### Uranus in Unfavorable Aspect to Pluto
An intellectual approach to the mysterious aspects of life. Original and inventive.


## THE PLANETARY ASPECTS OF NEPTUNE

During this century Neptune and Pluto have only made one major aspect: the sextile. This gives a high spiritual consciousness and sense of justice.

# Planetary House Rulers

The planet ruling the sign on a house cusp moderates the expression of that sign according to its placement and aspects. The house placement of the planet, delineated below, gives the environment which the planet expresses itself through. Thus, the house the planet rules will be the avenue of expression for the activities of the house the planet is in.

In former times, delineations such as these were used principally for Horary Astrology, but if understood and used correctly they may bring to light many points in the birth horoscope which might otherwise remain unnoticed. What follows are suggestions only as to the possible effect of the natural house rulers posited in other houses, regardless of aspects. The influence of aspects to each house ruler should be considered as a qualifying factor.

A planet is considered in a house as soon as it approaches within eight degrees of the cusp. This is true of all the houses except the Ascendant as when a planet has arrived within twelve degrees of the ascending degree it is read as though in the first house, more especially if it be in the same sign.

## THE RULER OF THE FIRST HOUSE

### When Posited in the First House

Bestows power to create conditions and own dignity; power over enemies. Well aspected: a long fortunate life, good health, harmony, triumph over difficulties. Judge the contrary is afflicted or combust.

### When Posited in the Second House

Much work and time given to the effort to obtain money. Benefit through industrious activity. If weak or afflicted: losses and wants.

### When Posited in the Third House

Mental development, voluntary short journeys; association and affairs with breathren or kindred; opportunities delayed. Afflicted: restrictions on education; troublesome relatives, journeys and writings.

### When Posited in the Fourth House

Gain through lands, mines, inheritance and possessions; home connections and affairs with the father. Success late in life; Occult investigations. Afflicted: difficulties through the above and demise in home land.

### When Posited in the Fifth House

Delight in pleasure, amusements, sports, speculation and children, with tendency to success through these. Afflicted: losses through the above, few children and difficulty through them.

### When Posited in the Sixth House

A good healer; gain through humanitarianism, food, clothing, employees, and small animals. Afflicted by the luminaries: much sickness and a short life. If afflicted by Mars: a surgical operation on the part of the body ruled by the sign on the cusp. Fondness for pets, small animals and work.

### When Posited in the Seventh House

Partnerships and close association with others; fondness for the opposite sex. Afflicted: tendency to act in opposition to own best interests; loss and trouble with the law, unions and open enemies. Marital unhappiness.

### When Posited in the Eighth House

Concern over affairs of the dead and with money of the partner and the finances of others. Death through irregularity; Occult experiences; mediumistic. Afflicted: disappointment over a legacy, trouble in financial matters. The luminaries adverse: tends to shorten the life.

## When Posited in the Ninth House

Long journeys, religious or psychic experiences; liking for science, invention, law, philosophy and all matters connected with the higher mind; prophetic dreams or visions; gain through the partner's relatives. Afflicted: trouble with foreigners and religious, legal or educational affairs; fruitless and dangerous voyages. Experiences in foreign lands.

## When Posited in the Tenth House

Merit, honor, preferment and success; rises to high social and professional position. Afflicted: incites to displeasure of superiors or those in power; suffers indignities, limitations and because of rights withheld; liable to slander and dishonor; loss of parents or trouble by them.

## When Posited in the Eleventh House

Large circle of friends, assistance to and from them; much pleasure in life; hopes and wishes often attained; gain by success of employer. Afflicted: friends are a detriment; hopes often defeated.

## When Posited in the Twelfth House

Fear of imprisonment; secret unhappiness; enmities; native; native is often the cause of his own undoing; gain and benefit through understanding of the Occult. Afflicted: imprisonment or restraint unless in its own sign; secret sorrows, suffering and misfortune. Well aspected: gain through Occult affairs and secret missions. Success in middle life.


# THE RULER OF THE SECOND HOUSE

## When Posited in the First House

Money comes readily. Afflicted: obstacles and difficulties through money which may be hard to accumulate.

## When Posited in the Second House

Money through personal ingenuity and industry. Naturally interested in financial affairs. Afflicted: much work for little gain; heavy losses.

### When Posited in the Third House

Gain through education, writing, brethren, neighbors and short journeys. Afflicted. losses through these things.

### When Posited in the Fourth House

Estate or benefit through parents; gain through household goods, lands or mines. Afflicted: loss by investment in property or mines.

### When Posited in the Fifth House

Gain by speculation, investment, pleasure, entertainment, young people and children. If afflicted: loss and trouble by such.

### When Posited in the Sixth House

Gain through inferiors, small animals, poultry, etc., or by humanitarianism, hygiene and services rendered. Fondness for pets and animals. Afflicted: losses through sickness.

### When Posited in the Seventh House

Gain by marriage, contracts, business and dealing with others, especially the opposite sex. If afflicted: trouble in unions and through open enemies, competition and theft.

### When Posited in the Eighth House

Gain by legacy and goods of the dead or through money of the partner. Afflicted: loss of legacy, loss of money through the financial losses of others, such as bank failures, etc.

### When Posited in the Ninth House

Gain by books, trading at sea, long journeys, philosophy, religion, science and the partner's kindred. If afflicted, loss through these.

### When Posited in the Tenth House

Gain by occupation, profession, merchandising, government, the partner's parents. Afflicted: financial loss through the mother or employer.

### When Posited in the Eleventh House

Gain or loss by friends and accidental fortune.

### When Posited in the Twelfth House

Gain by affairs of secret nature, through hospitals, sanitariums, Occult investigations and by large animals.

## THE RULER OF THE THIRD HOUSE

### When Posited in the First House

Journeys and removals; concern with affairs of brethren and neighbors, writings, learning and accomplishments.

### When Posited in the Second House

Money through educational affairs, short journeys, writings, music, etc. Afflicted: trouble with kindred over money matters.

### When Posited in the Third House

Benefits through learning, accomplishments, writings, short journeys and brethren.

### When Posited in the Fourth House

Traveling and writing in connection with home affairs and property. Afflicted: trouble with brethren over same.

### When Posited in the Fifth House

Pleasure journeys; mental pleasures through children, brethren, reading, study, accomplishments and travel to pleasure resorts.

### When Posited in the Sixth House

Sickness or injury through journeys; difficulty through brethren; interest in study and methods of healing or social economy.

### When Posited in the Seventh House

Marriage as a result of journeys, writing, or to one's kin. Afflicted: the union will be unfortunate. Danger of robbery while traveling.

### When Posited in the Eighth House

Sickness and death of brethren; journeys on account of trouble, false accusations, or trouble on account of death or bequests.

### When Posited in the Ninth House
Long journeys; gain through philosophy, publishing and science; brethren are likely to journey to foreign parts and marry.

### When Posited in the Tenth House
Professional or honorable journeys and gain through them; honors or renown through writings or other accomplishments. Journeys with the mother. If afflicted: the native's brethren cause mental anguish.

### When Posited in the Eleventh House
Friends through journeys or vice versa; fortunate conditions through brethren. Correspondence with friends. Hopes and wishes accomplished through progressive studies.

### When Posited in the Twelfth House
Great sorrow through brethren; secret suffering; Occult learning; seclusion or estrangement from brethren or kindred and difficulty through some of them. Danger of enmities and imprisonment while traveling.

## THE RULER OF THE FOURTH HOUSE

### When Posited in the First House
Fortunate inheritance; gain through land, property or parentage. Interest in domestic science.

### When Posited in the Second House
Gains by deals in land and property and by the estate or condition of the parents.

### When Posited in the Third House
Gain through brethren; if afflicted, the father is put to sorrow or difficulty by one of them. May reside and travel with relatives.

### When Posited in the Fourth House
Gain in property and through old people or antiquities; assistance of the father. Benefit and profit in the place of birth. Loss through

storms, floods.

### When Posited in the Fifth House
Gain and pleasure by father's good fortune; possessions descend to children. May reside near a school, public park, playground or theater.

### When Posited in the Sixth House
Loss of possessions through sickness, servants or small animals. Well aspected: gain through sickness, service, etc. May build his own house, etc.

### When Posited in the Seventh House
Property by marriage; gain by land and the opposite sex generally. Afflicted: loss of property through marriage or partnerships.

### When Posited in the Eighth House
Gain by legacy or estate. Afflicted: death of father, danger to mother during pregnancy; loss of property inheritance.

### When Posited in the Ninth House
Gain in possessions through science, religion, long journeys and wife's relatives. Afflicted: loss of foreign property.

### When Posited in the Tenth House
Gain in possessions by trade, profession, public or government work, or by the wise use of the resources of the earth and manipulation of natural resources.

### When Posited in the Eleventh House
Hopes come to good conclusions; gain through friends. Many hopes and wishes attained in old age.

### When Posited in the Twelfth House
The native's health is considerably affected by the parents taking a long journey; he suffers sorrow through one of them; loss of possessions through treachery. End of life in seclusion or devoted to the study of Occult subjects.

# THE RULER OF THE FIFTH HOUSE

### When Posited in the First House
A propensity to pleasure through gaming and children. Many love affairs.

### When Posited in the Second House
Gain through investment, pleasure and children. The native's children gain in possessions which he enjoys. Afflicted; his possessions are diminished by speculation, pleasure or young people.

### When Posited in the Third House
Journeys with or through children or young people. Pleasure through some of the kindred. Liking for travel, sports, drama and adventure.

### When Posited in the Fourth House
Estate or possessions through discovery, gaming or parents in latter part of life. Well aspected: the native's children profit through gifts from their grandfather. Love of home.

### When Posited in the Fifth House
Much pleasure; love affairs and adventures; speculations or investments; prosperous children and pleasure through them.

### When Posited in the Sixth House
Sickness among children. Money through careful speculation or by children's earnings. Pleasure in hygienic methods, through pets and hobbies.

### When Posited in the Seventh House
Pleasure, close association or understanding with the partner, but discord with children. Loss by theft. If afflicted: trouble and loss through love affairs.

### When Posited in the Eighth House
Suffers through children who may die before the native. Loss through speculations or gaming.

### When Posited in the Ninth House

Dutiful children who travel and give pleasure and learning to the native. Offspring become preachers, scientists or explorers. Pleasure in foreign lands.

### When Posited in the Tenth House

Honorable children; renown in speculation, business enterprise or in the theatrical world. Well aspected: pleasure or honor through wife's father or through own mother.

### When Posited in the Eleventh House

Great attachment between the native and his children; friends through them; happy conclusions to hopes and wishes; friends through speculation or pleasure and among legislators, ambassadors and sportsmen.

### When Posited in the Twelfth House

Children cause secret sorrow; speculations cause ruin; pleasure through investigation of things of mysterious or research nature. If afflicted: danger of imprisonment through gaming.


## THE RULER OF THE SIXTH HOUSE

### When Posited in the First House

Sickness through irregularity or lax attention to laws of hygiene. Fondness for pets. Afflicted: servants and small animals prove troublesome or unprofitable.

### When Posited in the Second House

Losses and limitations financially through sickness, servants, animals. Well aspected: money through service, employees, healing and small animals.

### When Posited in the Third House

Sickness of some of the brethren or kindred; journeys on account of sickness and vice versa. Interest in studies and methods of healing and industrial economy. Likelihood of mental disturbance when sick.

### When Posited in the Fourth House

Sickness of father through changes and worry; sickness of the native through anxiety and troublesome home or domestic affairs. Trouble through servants in the home.

### When Posited in the Fifth House

Enjoyment of health-promoting ideas or activities. If afflicted, illness by over-indulgence in pleasure or sports. Concern for children's health.

### When Posited in the Sixth House

Some severe illness. If well aspected: usually has good health; success in service and with employees, poultry, medicine, healing or social service.

### When Posited in the Seventh House

Quarrels with servants, employees, or physicians, who insinuate themselves into inappropriate relationships to the native. Over-concern with the health or activities of the partner.

### When Posited in the Eighth House

Dangerous illness; death of servants, animals, poultry, etc. Financial rewards for faithful service.

### When Posited in the Ninth House

Sickness abroad, at sea or while traveling; illness of partner's relatives; danger through over-study. Work in connection with foreign affairs or universities.

### When Posited in the Tenth House

Sickness through dishonor; sorrow or affliction on account of mother or wife's father. Well aspected: honors through service and healing or through municipal or national activities.

### When Posited in the Eleventh House

Sickness among friends and family. Hopes depend too much upon acquaintances. Interest in legislative activities, political and social welfare.

### When Posited in the Twelfth House

Imprisonment or private enemies through servants, animals or methods of healing. Sickness or work in some large institution. Work of secret or mysterious nature. Interest in archaeology or submarine life.

## THE RULER OF THE SEVENTH HOUSE

### When Posited in the First House

Public enemies, unions, partnership, love of opposite sex and benefit through them. Connection with processes of the law.

### When Posited in the Second House

Gain by marriage. Afflicted: loss of money through unions; partnerships, contracts, lawsuits, public enemies. Loss through opposite sex; death of partner and public enemies.

### When Posited in the Third House

Enmities with some of the brethren or neighbors; marriage with someone of kin or to a neighbor; difficulty through writings or contracts. Legal or religious disputes, trouble on short journeys.

### When Posited in the Fourth House

Marriage into a well-established family, possibly with land or accumulated family interests. A happy married life unless afflicted, in which case, a stultifying marriage which limits the expression of the native. When afflicted, litigation over property, or robbery of household goods is also possible.

### When Posited in the Fifth House

The native marries one younger than himself and enjoys much pleasure thereby, but has troubles and enmities with children. Loss by speculation or gaming.

### When Posited in the Sixth House

The native marries below his station mentally or socially, has a sickly partner and evilly-disposed employees. Trouble over small animals.

### When Posited in the Seventh House

Success in lawsuits, marriage in good family; a prepossessing partner, but likely one who grows cold or proves untrue or hostile.

### When Posited in the Eighth House

Money or property by marriage; death of partner; some inheritance but difficulty over it. If afflicted: loss of money through marriage and partnerships.

### When Posited in the Ninth House

Marriage to a foreigner; gain by partner's relatives. Partner journeys to foreign lands. Afflicted: contentions with religious people.

### When Posited in the Tenth House

An honorable partner beneficial to the professional career. Afflicted: trouble by rivals through some office, honor, or employment. Public disgrace or scandal through a union or enemy.

### When Posited in the Eleventh House

Friends become public opponents or enemies. Marriage to a widow or widower with children, but liable to trouble through them.

### When Posited in the Twelfth House

Unhappy marriage, secret sorrows, jealousy, vexation, sickness. Partner or opponents cause imprisonment or fear it. Danger of death at the hands of enemies if the ruler of the Eighth House afflicts.

## THE RULER OF THE EIGHTH HOUSE

### When Posited in the First House

Legacies and money through affairs and matters connected with the deceased; assists in the accumulation of money and business of others. Afflicted: trouble through the above and through the losses of others; death by irregularity.

### When Posited in the Second House

Gain in finance by the money of the partner and money of

others. Fortunate in collecting debts. Gain through the deceased. If afflicted: loss and trouble through all such matters.

## When Posited in the Third House

Danger of death on short journeys. Unfortunate brethren and death of same. Investigation regarding death and the continuity of life. Psychic and mysterious experiences.

## When Posited in the Fourth House

Gain in property through the deceased, probably by the death of parents. The native dies at home unless this planet is in conjunction with the ruler of the Ninth House, then abroad. Afflicted: death of parents, danger through falls and falling buildings, floods and storms. Trouble over inheritance, land and property.

## When Posited in the Fifth House

Unfortunate children or death of some. Danger through excessive pleasures, speculation, children and their affairs.

## When Posited in the Sixth House

Dangerous sickness. Death of pets, small animals or servants. Loss of money earned by employment and through those in whose keeping it may be.

## When Posited in the Seventh House

A rich partner or one to whom money comes unexpectedly. Affliction: death of partner and public enemies. Danger of death by violence, suicide, accident or war.

## When Posited in the Eighth House

Gain by the dead; a natural death; a comfortably fixed partner. Interest in matters relating to future life. Spiritualistic experiences.

## When Posited in the Ninth House

The partner has trouble with relatives over money matters. Death in a distant land. Danger of death by drowning or while on voyages. Well aspected: The native has a positive philosophy towards death; seeing it as an adventure.

### When Posited in the Tenth House

Death of mother and employers. Danger of violent death probably through discharge of government order or through war. Business through matters connected with the dead. Well aspected: rise to high position through an inheritance. Other persons will gain or lose money by him, according to the planet's aspects.

### When Posited in the Eleventh House

Death among friends. Well aspected: gain and legacies through friends.

### When Posited in the Twelfth House

Difficulty over inheritance. Death of secret or private enemies. Great sorrow, fear or anxiety concerning death or imprisonment. Death while in an institution. If afflicted by the ruler of the Seventh House: death or imprisonment through enemies.

## THE RULER OF THE NINTH HOUSE

### When Posited in the First House

Long journeys, learning, wisdom, prudence; fortunate with strangers, foreigners, partner's relatives and voyages. Interest in science, invention, law, philosophy or political economy.

### When Posited in the Second House

Money gained by foreign merchants or the sea, science, learning, publications, travel, invention or banking.

### When Posited in the Third House

Journeys and removals on account of beliefs and convictions. Learning, accomplishments and progress through research, travel, investigations, explorations, travel or writings.

### When Posited in the Fourth House

Ecclesiastical or scientific inheritance. Possessions through partner's relatives. Travel on account of family affairs or partner's mother. Journeys home to die.

### When Posited in the Fifth House

Liberal or unconventional ideas in regard to union. Free living. Child by strange consort, journey on account of children. Pleasure journeys. Takes pleasure in science, philosophy, voyages, air flights, sports, foreign investments, or speculation.

### When Posited in the Sixth House

Sickness through traveling or vice versa. Study of hygiene, medicine, healing, etc. Difficulty through work in foreign lands, or in connection with exporting.

### When Posited in the Seventh House

Public enemies through religious, scientific, or seafaring people. Marriage to a stranger of education or refinement whose relatives may be opposed to the native.

### When Posited in the Eighth House

Persecution regarding religious, scientific, or educational convictions, also through publications. Gain by long journeys concerning legacies or goods of deceased persons. Death of partner's kindred. Psychic experiences.

### When Posited in the Ninth House

Traveling for education, scientific or religious purposes. Prophetic dreams. Many fine qualities. Splendid possibilities through culture and development.

### When Posited in the Tenth House

If a benefic: honor, credit, and esteem through science, literature or travel. Success in foreign affairs. The reverse if a malefic unless well aspected.

### When Posited in the Eleventh House

Suffering on account of religious or other convictions. Fortunate for making friendships on voyages and friends among foreigners and in foreign countries. The native will have acquaintances among travelers, scientists, and legislators. Spiritual benefit will come from friends and organizations.

### When Posited in the Twelfth House

Difficulty and sorrow through religion, science, journeys. If a writer or inventor, has a hard time to complete his work and get it to the public. In middle or latter part of life seeks seclusion for development, Occult learning, etc., and takes long journeys for same.


## THE RULER OF THE TENTH HOUSE

### When Posited in the First House

Preferment and dignities, honors through merit, success through industrious effort, high ambitions, gain through mother and governmental office.

### When Posited in the Second House

Gain in money by industry, through trade, profession or government office.

### When Posited in the Third House

Respect among kindred and neighbors. Gain in honors and advancement through partner's relatives. Honors through short journeys, writing and accomplishments; business trips, governmental commissions.


### When Posited in the Fourth House

Gain and honors through parentage, lands and property, success at close of life. Interest in reclamations, colonization, cooperative movements, horticulture, mining, architecture or archaeology.

### When Posited in the Fifth House

The native's children suffer from sickness, but rise to honors. Gain and honors through speculation, pleasures, young people, sports or the stage.

### When Posited in the Sixth House

Modest worldly position, gain and honors through service, employment, the practice of healing or army and navy affairs. Good relationship with employees or those in one's care.

### When Posited in the Seventh House

Gain through lawsuits and dealing with the public generally. Honors and reputation assisted by honorable marriage and partnerships in responsible concerns.

### When Posited in the Eighth House

Gain and honors in handling the estate and money of others, also through lawsuits, legacies, inheritance, insurance, etc., of deceased persons.

### When Posited in the Ninth House

Honorable voyages, professional journeys; honors through learning writing, publishing, research or philosophy. A religious or intellectual mother with many fine qualities.

### When Posited in the Tenth House

Gain and honors through profession, honorary office, or government employ. Success aided by mother's care, training and efforts.

### When Posited in the Eleventh House

Eminent friends among legislators and those in high governmental or professional positions; an honorable fortune. The native is helpful to his associates and others. Ambitious ideals.

### When Posited in the Twelfth House

Loss of office or honor, dignity, etc., through business associates who become secret enemies. Unfortunate environments and conditions. Professional secrets. Difficulty in employment. Limitations relieved by the study of recondite sciences or metaphysics.

## THE RULER OF THE ELEVENTH HOUSE

### When Posited in the First House

The native meets with real friends and supporters; can overcome enemies and obstacles through the support of acquaintances. Many hopes are attained; fortunate actions. If afflicted: makes a irritable friend.

### When Posited in the Second House

Business and money by means of friends and acquaintances, through legislative interests or through development of his own creations.

### When Posited in the Third House

Friendship among kindred and neighbors; friends through writings and journies.

### When Posited in the Fourth House

Inheritance through friends; fortunate in property. Love for father. Friends reside in the home.

### When Posited in the Fifth House

Much happiness and pleasure in life through children, friends, and beneficial circumstances.

### When Posited in the Sixth House

Friends among working people and those in army, navy, or air service; concerned with sickness among friends; faithful servants. Interest in social welfare.

### When Posited in the Seventh House

A loving partner with desirable friendships and social connections. Success in lawsuits.

### When Posited in the Eighth House

Death of friends; gifts or legacies from friends. An easy demise.

### When Posited in the Ninth House

Gain and success through long journeys. Friendships through travel and learning. Friends among educators, ministers, writers, explorers, inventors.

### When Posited in the Tenth House

Friendship among those of good position. Gain and honors through those of high standing in social, business or governmental circles.

### When Posited in the Eleventh House

Many friends and beneficial acquaintances; well defined hopes and wishes; friends among unique, ingenious, original or radical people.

### When Posited in the Twelfth House

Deceitful friends who may cause much suffering. Sorrowful friends. Good friendships among Occult people. Pleasure in peaceful, quiet, harmonious or secluded places.

## THE RULER OF THE TWELFTH HOUSE

### When Posited in the First House

Animosities difficult to overcome; heavy troubles; secret sorrows; limitations; all are lightened, however, by Occult or New Thought studies. Danger of imprisonment or disablement requiring hospitalization.

### When Posited in the Second House

Gain through secrecy and the Occult, also through large animals, if well aspected. Afflicted: loss of money through enemies and generally unfortunate conditions.

### When Posited in the Third House

Disappointment, sorrow, and trouble through friends or neighbors. Troublesome short journeys and writings; Occult learning.

### When Posited in the Fourth House

Loss or great difficulty through involved property. Trouble through father or wife's mother. Secret suffering, restrictions or limitations at end of life.

### When Posited in the Fifth House

Secret sorrows and difficulty through love, speculation, children or gaming.

### When Posited in the Sixth House

Difficulty, trouble, and loss through small animals; trouble through employees. Limitations on account of sickness.

## When Posited in the Seventh House

Trouble through deceit and treachery concerning unions, partner-ships, contracts and lawsuits. Sickness, discord and opposition of partner; trouble through women generally.

## When Posited in the Eighth House

An unsatisfactory end, many misfortunes, secret enemies die, troubles over inheritance.

## When Posited in the Ninth House

Well aspected: love of seclusion for the purpose of study; monastic life. Great interest in spiritual and occult matters. Afflicted: loss through travel, lonely studies, or feeling of separation because of religious ideas, or persecution.

## When Posited in the Tenth House

Liability to disgrace, discredit and persecution from superiors, government, or those in office above the native which is likely to result in a long journey or retirement and seclusion. Governmental employ in the interest of large institutions. Sorrow through the mother or trouble with partner's parents.

## When Posited in the Eleventh House

Unfortunate undertakings; peculiar hopes; great disappointments and obstacles; deceitful friends and losses through advice of acquain-tances.

## When Posited in the Twelfth House

Occult abilities, powerless enemies, secret investigations, fondness for animals. Limitations, afflictions, and adversities prove to be blessings in disguise by developing inner growth and understanding.

# The Part of Fortune and the Moon's Nodes

## THE PART OF FORTUNE

The Part of Fortune represents worldly success as indicated by the house and sign it occupied in the nativity.

It has been said that is is influenced only by conjunctions and its house position, but in the experience of Llewellyn George a number of cases where directional aspects both good and adverse to the Part of Fortune directly affected matters ruled by the house it occupied.

### When Posited in the First House

Portends gain and happiness by the native's own industry, especially if Jupiter or Venus are favorably aspected. Saturn or Mars unfavorable to it lessen its benign significance.

### When Posited in the Second House

Happiness and gain through property, and profit by employment and business. Protection and promotion through business friendships.

### When Posited in the Third House

Profitable journeys; gain through intellectual affairs; also by means of amiable and honest kindred.

### When Posited in the Fourth House

Gain through property, treasure or other hidden things and

381

products of the earth, minerals, metals, etc. Aids any other testimony for gain by inheritance; stable patrimony.

## When Posited in the Fifth House

If afflicted: shows much loss and damage to the native through pleasure and speculation; crosses and losses in his estate by means of children. If well aspected: gain through fortunate investments and children, young people and ambassadors. A goodly portion of pleasure in life and prosperity for the offspring.

## When Posited in the Sixth House

It denotes happy and prosperous uncles and aunts who may benefit the native. It gives gain in employ and by means of those whom the native may hire, also profit by small animals, and other things ruled by this house.

## When Posited in the Seventh House

Inclines to success in dealings with others and in marriage or partnerships: gain through bargains, contracts and dealings with others; victory over enemies and gain in conquest. If afflicted: produces the contrary.

## When Posited in the Eighth House

If unafflicted: signifies gain by inheritance; gain by means of those deceased, also through the use of other people's money. Interest in psychology.

## When Posited in the Ninth House

Inclines to long journeys; success pertaining to churches or educational properties and by means of foreigners, invention, or books.

## When Posited in the Tenth House

Favorable circumstances and lucky events assist the native to rise to honor in his sphere, also by means of business assets.

## When Posited in the Eleventh House

Pleasure and gain through friends in good position, realization of hopes and wishes.

### When Posited in the Twelfth House

Afflicted: property losses through the wiles of secret enemies. Unafflicted: gains from unexpected sources. Well aspected: gain from quiet and secret sources; accumulation of possessions develops with age.

## THE MOON'S NODES

Some writers believe that the Moon's Nodes have no influence in Astrology, and need not be used. But Llewellyn George observed many cases where the influence of the Nodes was marked.

It requires nineteen years, according to its motion of approximately three minutes per day, for the Moon's Node to complete the circle of the twelve signs. It is very interesting to observe the effects of the Node's influence in nativities, as they transit to a conjunction with the various planets in the chart. This frequently corresponds with important conditions and circumstances that cannot be accounted for in any other way.

### When Posited in the First House

**North Node:** Inclines to honors, wealth and favors through religious, educational or scientific affairs. It adds power to the personality and gives opportunity for self-expression.

**South Node:** Inclines to tribulations, loss and scandals; endangers the face and eyes and is one testimony of a short life.

### When Posited in the Second House

**North Node:** Removes want and bestows affluence; fortunate heredity or gain by legacy and gifts; gain by science and learning; increases the possessions.

**South Node:** Inclines to misfortune in finances, indebtedness, loss and damage to estate; sorrow, fears and worry concerning money matters.

### When Posited in the Third House

**North Node:** Adds quality to the mentality and is conducive to interest in spiritual or educational matters and gives preferment in such; gains through brethren, neighbors, and journeys, writing or publishing.

**South Node**: Mental anxiety, trouble with brethren and neighbors; unprofitable journeys.

## When Posited in the Fourth House

**North Node**: Augurs gain by means of property and in somewhat unexpected manners; fortunate in discovery or in findings. Ancestry noble, long-lived, and trustworthy.

**South Node**: Loss or confusion with land and buildings; waste of patrimony; jeopardizes the esteem and credit; turmoil in the lives of ancestors; family discord.

## When Posited in the Fifth House

**North Node**: Frees the native from many troubles, calamities and dangers. It is favorable for children who live long and are fortunate. The native gains some public employment or office and is fond of civil recreation, pleasure and sports.

**South Node**: Denies children or else portends their destruction suddenly or violently; inclines them to adversity while they live and makes them cross or disobedient to the native. Excessive or irregular pleasures produce much harm.

## When Posited in the Sixth House

**North Node**: Favors the health and strengthens the body. Faithful and honest employees; gain through service; fortunate by means of father's kindred and by small animals.

**South Node**: The native suffers because of various physical afflictions. Is crossed and deceived by servants and suffers loss through small animals. Danger of illness through bites by insects, reptiles or animals.

## When Posited in the Seventh House

**North Node**: Lessens the number of enemies, increases profit through dealings with others and portends delight and gain through others whose influence may benefit the native. It is a testimony for a wise and wealthy partner.

**South Node**: Many oppressors, calumnies raised by enemies or competitors, contention and difficulty with partner, but it also portends the death or destruction of enemies.

## When Posited in the Eighth House
**North Node**: Promotes health and is conducive to longevity; testimony for gifts and legacies and gain by those deceased.

**South Node**: Loss of goods through deception; sudden or violent death.

## When Posited in the Ninth House
**North Node**: Improves the mental qualities and gives success in educational, legal or religious studies; favorable for voyages and foreign affairs; true dreams and prophetic intuition.

**South Node**: Afflicts the faculty of faith and portends miserable or unfortunate voyages; curious dreams, unreliable premonitions; trouble and danger of imprisonment in foreign lands.

## When Posited in the Tenth House
**North Node**: Native achieves honors, credit and high position by merit of industry and ability.

**South Node**: Loss of position through deception, treachery and adverse public conditions such as sudden depressions, changes or failures.

## When Posited in the Eleventh House
**North Node**: Meritorious friendships, acquaintances assist in the realization of hopes and wishes.

**South Node**: Undesirable associations, loss of opportunities and frustration of hopes; wrong advice and false friends.

## When Posited in the Twelfth House
**North Node**: Gain by secret methods or in seclusion; success in Occultism.

**South Node**: Frequently harassed by the machinations of secret enemies; liability to imprisonment or restraint and restrictions unfavorable to health; inclines to self-undoing.

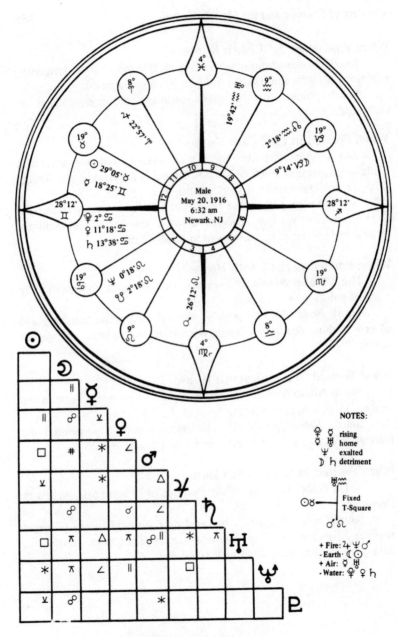

**Figure 24: Example Chart 3**

# Example of Horoscope Interpretation

To illustrate the George Method of delineating a horoscope the two charts and interpretations below will present ideas of how to choose the salient points and combine the influences of the planets in the houses with their principle aspects. It is suggested that the student follow the delineation of the charts closely.

## EXAMPLE CHART 3

Male, born May 20, 1916, Newark, NJ, 6:32 AM, Mean Local Time.

### Individuality

*Sun in Taurus.* The native is endowed with an inherent love of nature, art, music, amusement and harmony. This individual is self-reliant, determined, persistent, careful and cautious.

**Note:** The student will note that the Sun is located on the cusp of Taurus and Gemini (29° ♉ ). Modern astrologers teach that a blend of the signs occurs in this area of the Zodiac.

*Sun in the Twelfth House.* Uncommon tastes and inclinations, occult or psychic interests. Enjoys working in seclusion and is attracted to medicine, chemistry or occult pursuits. Favors quiet, obscure or unpopular occupations especially in connection with hospitals or other large institutions. He is self-sacrificing and enduring, rises out of obscurity or difficulties by his own efforts, but meets many delays, obstacles and hindrances.

*Sun sextile Neptune (⊙⚹♆).* This gives him an inspirational nature and tendency toward philosophy, religion, chemistry or science. He is sympathetic, kind, generous. Inclined to refined pleasure, concerts, yachting. Enjoys dining, luxury and elegance. Psychic experiences.

*Sun ruler of the Third House.* (Similar to Sun in the Third House). This gives him mental tendency which is creative, resourceful, magnanimous and ambitious of success or honor through merit of ability. The desire is to uplift, enlighten, benefit and assist others mentally.

*Neptune ruler of the Tenth House.* (Similar to Neptune in the Tenth House.) Strange or peculiar career; disgrace or scandal whether deserved or not: Jupiter is square to Neptune (♃□♆). Chance of honor in some artistic or scientific field. A highly inspirational nature. Capable of achievement thereby acquiring a *nom-de-plume* or title.

## Personality

*Gemini ascending.* This tends to make one ambitious and aspiring, given to inquiry, investigation, experiment and the acquisition of knowledge. Gemini rising makes a person apt, dexterous, active, perceptive and, because it is a dual sign, it inclines to interest in two or more subjects at the same time. The nature is sympathetic and sensitive; the mind is intuitive, imaginative, idealistic and fond of mental pursuits. Gemini indicates that at times the native will be restless, nervous, anxious, high-strung, diffusive, indecisive, irritable and excitable. Change and diversity are required as monotonous tasks or inactivity cause impatience and unhappiness. Gemini gives the capacity to become very clever, inventive and ingenious. It bestows conversational and literary ability. The literary and educational world is your best outlet. There is a liking for pleasure, travel, adventure, study, science, research and educational pursuits.

*Mercury in Gemini.* Gives the native a quick, active, keen, alert, sharp, shrewd, penetrating mind. Good business ability, executive in detail, fond of travel, change, novelty, speculation, and neighborly intercourse.

*Mercury conjunct the First House cusp.* Adaptability, fertility of resource, persuasive, expressive. Many changes, short journeys. Interest in neighbors, relatives, libraries and the dissemination of information.

*Mercury sextile Mars (☿□♂).* Strengthens the mental powers and makes the native bright, witty, satirical, enthusiastic, animated, fluent, enterprising and executive. It gives inclination for drawing, designing, sculpture, chemistry, engineering and mechanical construction.

*Mercury sextile Jupiter (☿ ⚹ ♃).* Inclines to success in life through literary and professional pursuits. It favors the study of theology, philosophy, law, medicine and science. This aspect broadens the mind, giving the ability to think deeply, logically, with good comparison and judgment. It inclines to good humor, joviality, congeniality. It makes the mind versatile, vigorous and creative, combining conscientiousness, hope and good cheer with a nature that is generous, kind, humane, sincere, honest and charitable.

*Mercury trine Uranus (☿ △ ♅).* Fondness for investigation along original and out-of-the-ordinary lines. This gives fine comprehension, intuitive perception, inventive ability.

*Pluto on the Ascendant.* Not much has yet been uncovered regarding the influence of Pluto but it seems to give interest in the mysterious, or undercover matters, life after death, etc. In this case Pluto has the support of semi-sextile with the Sun (☉⚺♇), a sextile to Jupiter (♃ ⚹♇) and a semi-sextile with Neptune (♆ ⚺ ♇), which means that this person may gain information from, or be assisted by, such matters.

*Venus on the Ascendant.* The planet ruling the Sun Sign is always a siginficant factor in a horoscope according to its aspects, house position and the sign it occupies. In this case the planet is Venus. It is just coming into orb of aspect (conjunction) with the second cusp still having some influence in the Ascendant. Venus in the First House usually adds cheer to the life but in this chart it is opposed to the Moon ( ☽ ☍ ♀) and conjunct Saturn ( ♀ ☌ ♄). This brings sadness through disappointment in love affairs (Venus is ruler of the Fifth House) and sorrow through death (Venus ruler of the Twelfth House, Saturn ruler of the Eighth House). These factors will make themselves felt the more keenly as Venus is in Cancer, a maternal or family sign, promoting desire for comfortable home life but the thwarted pleasures are apt to bring periods of despondency.

*Venus parallel Neptune (♀ ∥ ♆).* Good aspect. The parallel should be considered with the major aspects. This accentuates the liking for music, art, drama, beauty and pleasure. It accentuates the feelings and emotional nature; inclines to interest in occult subjects and obscure matters, chemical research, etc.

*Moon in Capricorn.* Because Capricorn is a cardinal sign and has an inherent Tenth House influence, the Moon located in it tends to some sort of publicity or notoriety, usually somewhat unfavorable, due to the Moon being in its detriment in Capricorn. In this case its detrimental influence is accentuated by its opposition to Venus (☾ ☍ ♀) and Saturn (☾ ☍ ♄). Its position in the Seventh House indicates that the difficulties will mainly be of marital nature.

*Moon parallel Mercury (☾ ∥ ☿).* Good aspect. This tends to favor mental perception, making the mind active, keen, alert, observing and practical. He will be versatile, expressive, fluent and copious in speech and writing.

## Finances

*Saturn conjunct the Second House cusp.* Same as Saturn in the Second House. Saturn in opposition to the Moon (☾ ∥ ♄), ruler of the Second House, is an unfavorable indication concerning monetary affairs. It denotes delay, hindrance, disappointments and losses through lack of money. It indicates danger of severe losses through dealings with others, partners, matters relating to land and products of the earth. As Saturn is conjunct the ruler of the Fifth House (♀ ☌ ♄) speculations and games of chance would also be a source of loss. As the Fifth House rules love affairs there may also be monetary loss through such or through lawsuits ( ♀ ☌ ♄ ) resulting from Fifth House matters.

*Neptune in the Second House.* Neptune is in adverse aspect with Jupiter (♃⚹♆) posited in the Eleventh House, which indicates loss through fraud, plots, schemes or treachery, the failure of banks or bursting of speculative bubbles. Danger of loss through advice of friends or by entrusting money to them. Danger of loss through lawsuits concerning business enterprises: Jupiter ruler of the Seventh House, Neptune ruler of the Tenth House. Business partnerships had best be avoided, also financial transactions with friends.

*Sun sextile Neptune (☉⚹♆).* Sun is in the Twelfth House and is ruler of the Third House, indicating that money may be gained by obscure and patient endeavor through writing, science, large institutions and matters relating to the sea.

*Neptune in Leo.* Neptune is ruler of the Tenth House, that of professions or government appointments but should the native try to run for political office his opponents would be likely to win while he would find the venture very costly: Jupiter ruler of the house of opponents (the Seventh House) in adverse aspect to Neptune ($2_+\square\,\Psi$). Taken alone, Neptune in Leo in the Second House denotes gain by turning his skill to matters of pleasure, sport, music, art, poetry, painting, opera, drama or healing institutions.

It is not likely he will be able to acquire any great amount of monetary wealth; what he does acquire he will earn and be in danger of losing if used speculatively. His wealth is in the mental realm—his rewards in what he achieves, discovers and disseminates for the benefit of the world.

## Mentality

*Mars in the Third House.* Signifies an ambitious, active mind desirous of acquiring knowledge and finding it necessary to take frequent trips in connection with duties. As Mars is semi-square Saturn ($\vec{O}\pi\,h$) it will be a good idea to carry accident policies, because this aspect tends to accidents in travel.

*Mars trine Jupiter ($\vec{O}\triangle 2_+$).* Interest in literary occupations especially those relating to sports, law, congressional affairs, fraternal societies, theatres, schools, colleges, universities and foreign affairs. Mars ruling the Sixth House will give him interest in labor movements, construction, engineering, hygiene, chemistry and community affairs, all of which will cause him to travel considerably but not excessively, as Mars is in a fixed sign, Leo.

## Health

*Mars is ruler of the Sixth House:* The Sixth House is the house of sickness; Mars is in Leo, a sign of its own triplicity (fire); it is therefore favorably located by sign and although cadent by house, it is in good aspect with Mercury ($\breve{Q}*\vec{O}$), ruler of the house of the life and health (the First House). Mars is also in good aspect with Jupiter ($\vec{O}\triangle 2_+$). These are all favorable indications of a strong constitution and general good health. When ailing he should seek the haunts of the lion (Leo), the woods and hills, and yet avoid excessively strenuous exercise. Mars is in semi-square with Saturn ($\vec{O}\pi\,h$), denoting feverish complaints, danger through over-exertion and accidents.

*Venus on Ascendant.* Venus is in the House of Health. (The Sixth

House is the house of sickness.) Ordinarily this would be a favorable
position but in this case Venus is in conjunction with Saturn ( ♀♂ ♄ )
both in the sign Cancer ruling the stomach, while they are opposed by
the Moon ( ☾♂ ♀, ♄     ). Venus rules the throat, kidneys and spleen;
Saturn rules knees and veins; hence all these parts are likely to be
affected at times. Physical indisposition is apt to be felt on the days in
each month when the Moon transits to adverse aspects with the places
held by itself, Venus or Saturn at birth; also when the Sun by annual
transit forms such aspects. Also when progressed planets form such
aspects. During the period of such adverse aspects great care should be
given to diet in order to minimize rather than aggravate the irritation.

### Marriage—Partnerships

*Moon opposition Venus ( ☾ ♂ ♀ ).* The first aspect formed by the
Moon after birth is an opposition to Venus ( ☾♂♀ ); Venus is in the
sign Cancer symbolically describing the mate. The opposition aspect
denotes trouble, disappointment, disapproval of parents and likelihood
of scandal. Venus is in conjunction with Saturn ( ♀♂ ♄ ) which
accentuates the troubles and also tends to delay marriage.

*Moon opposition Saturn ( ☾♂♄ ).* This is the second and last aspect formed by the Moon. It denotes the second marriage, which is
likely to be more unsatisfactory than the first.

Venus rules the Fifth and Twelfth Houses of love and sorrow. The
Moon rules the Second House, house of money—marriages are apt to be
costly experiences. Moon is in the Seventh House, therefore marriage
involves lawsuits. Saturn rules the Eighth House, house of death; Moon
opposition Saturn ( ☾♂♄ ) indicates second wife would die before the
native. These oppositions also disfavor business partnerships.

**Note.** Ordinarily the indications concerning demise had best be
omitted for ethical or psychological reasons.

### Education and the Higher Mind

*Aquarius on the ninth cusp.* On the cusp of the Ninth House of
this horoscope is Aquarius, an air, fixed, occult, progressive, scientific,
humane sign; and in this sign and house Uranus is located. This is an
indice for the development of the higher mind and for scientific
capacity. Uranus here indicates good intuition, fine foresight, prophetic
ability and inclines to research, explorations and unusual pursuits.

*Mercury trine Uranus ( ☿ △ ♅ ).* Makes the native original, inventive, progressive, philosophical, interested in literature, languages and foreign affairs. This aspect portends voyages to foreign lands on extraordinary missions, usually embarked suddenly and under curious circumstances. However, as Mars has a waning opposition to Uranus ( ♂ ☍ ♅ ), great caution should be exercised on journeys to avoid accidents; especially is there danger for him on airplane trips or in countries ruled by Uranus, such as Russia.

*The Part of Fortune and Moon's North Node near the cusp of the Ninth House.* These indicate benefits in all of the matters previously named as belonging to the Ninth House and they also lessen the danger and severity of accidents.

*Jupiter sextile Uranus ( ♃ ✳ ♅ ).* This indicates the academic type of mind as to capacity but carries it far beyond conventional bounds. It favors interest in international law, political economy, higher science, philosophy, educational movements and Uranian interests: a brilliant, logical and humanitarian mind.

## Occupation

*Gemini rising.* Gemini, an intellectual sign, is on the Ascendant; Mercury, the natural ruler of the mind, is in its own sign and angular; Mercury is sextile Mars ( ☿ ✳ ♂ ) which is ruler of the house of work (Sixth House). These all denote splendid mental capacity with practical and executive ability.

*Mercury sextile Jupiter ( ☿ ✳ ♃ ).* Gives ability for writing, law, political appointments, philosophy, medicine and academic pursuits. Mercury in good aspect to Uranus ( ☿ □ ♅ ) favors astrophysics, electrical research and investigations in biochemistry, astronomy, astrology, etc.

*Mars trine Jupiter ( ♂ △ ♃ ).* Gives ability for surgery, chemistry, engineering, army and navy posts, positions of responsibility on large commercial boats or transatlantic liners.

Professional and scientific careers are strongly indicated. The native is versatile and will engage in numerous occupations. To whatever lines he turns attention he will be original and creative. His work will be commended both at home and abroad. Mercury being the ruler of home (the Fourth House) and land, and Uranus in the Ninth House indicating foreign lands.

## Friends

*Jupiter sextile Uranus (♃*⚏).* Rich and powerful friends, acquaintance with legislators and promonent people who hold important commercial, professional and social positions. Many hopes and wishes as to intellectual progress are attained through the influence of powerful friends. Jupiter trine Mars (♂*♃) indicates the friends will be helpful to the native's work and literary career.

*Jupiter square Neptune (♃□♆).* This aspect indicates financial loss through acting upon the advice of friends in monetary affairs, through entrusting money to friends, also by handling the money of friends and he may cause friends to lose money by his advice.

Friends can and will aid him best in literary, educational and scientific matters and in publishing.

## Synthesis

Here is a person endowed with remarkable mental ability. His health will be variable; illness caused by stomach, kidneys and poor circulation. However, his constitution can be strengthened by proper physical exercise to balance his active mentality. He is apt to live long and usefully, personality and his projects improving with the years.

This person's chief sorrows will come through love affairs, marriages and the passing of loved ones. Chief troubles will arise through monetary affairs. He needs to learn the value, use and control of money in order to avoid loss through imposition, misplaced confidence and speculations.

His life should be devoted to research, invention, science, literature, reforms and political economy.


# EXAMPLE CHART 4

W.H. Chaney, born January 13, 1821, Chesterville, Massachusetts, 11:32 PM, Mean Local Time. This is the horoscope of Professor Chaney, inserted here in appreciation of his valiant service to Astrology; one of the brave pioneers of astrological work in the United States. The following is a condensed delineation of his natal horoscope.

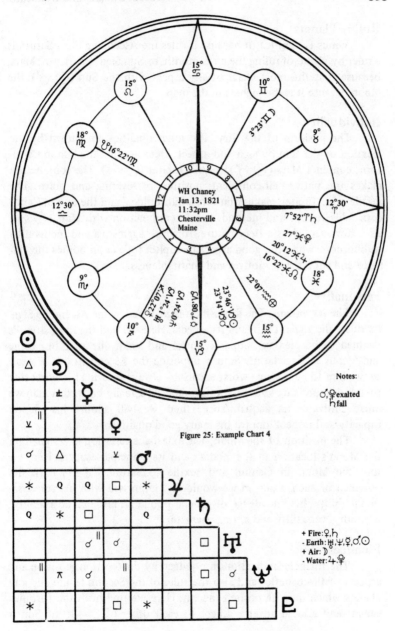

Figure 25: Example Chart 4

Notes:

♂,♀ exalted
♄ fall

+ Fire: ♀,♄
− Earth: ♅,Ψ,☿,♂,☉
+ Air: ☽
− Water: ♃,♇

## Ruling Planets

Venus is significator because it rules the Ascending Sign. Saturn is a ruler by virtue of ruling the birth month, or Sun Sign, Capricorn; Mars, because it is the most exact of any aspect with the Sun ($\odot \, \sigma \, \sigma$); the Moon because it is the highest in the map.

## Individuality

**The position of the Sun.** The inner qualities are shown by the location of the Sun by sign and aspect. Here we find the Sun in Capricorn, conjunct Mars ($\odot \, \sigma \, \sigma$), sextile Jupiter ($\odot \, * \, 2\!\!\!+$). The conjunction makes the native self-confident, positive, persevering and brave. The sextile with Jupiter makes him very philosophical and the Sun in Capricorn adds reserve and method. Sun in conjunction with Mars ($\odot \, \sigma \, \sigma$) also, however, gives a fiery nature, forceful, aggressive and inclined to stubbornness, while the good aspect to Jupiter ($\sigma \, \sigma \, 2\!\!\!+$) modifies the violence and adds higher motives and charitableness.

## Personality

**The Ascendant.** The disposition is governed by the Ascending Sign, its ruler, the signs it is in and its aspects. Here we find the disposition is inclined to be pleasant, amiable, jovial and kind, due to Libra rising and Venus in Sagittarius. Saturn opposing the Ascendant ($\hbar \, \sigma^o$ Asc.) shows him to be his own worst enemy by always showing his worst side first and impressing strangers unfavorably. To really know this man we must cultivate his acquaintance; then we will admire his mental capacity and respect him for his many good qualities.

**The position of the Moon.** The external expression is designed by the Moon's location in the Zodiac and its principle aspects. Here we find the Moon in Gemini and sextile to Saturn ( $\mathbb{C} * \hbar$ ). In the presence of such a person we would feel impressed with his conversational ability, his knowledge of general public affairs, practical ability, ingenuity, versatility and strong character.

## Finances

The financial indications are judged by the location, position and aspects of the benefics and also the ruler of the Second House and any planets which may be posited therein. Here we find both the fortunes cadent and also in adverse aspect to each other ( $\varphi \, \square \, 2\!\!\!+$); the Sun is afflicted by Mars ($\odot \sigma \sigma'$) and the Moon is going cadent in a common sign, all of which is very unfavorable for acquiring money. To make the indications still worse we see Saturn opposing the Ascendant ( $\hbar \, \mathcal{P}$ Asc.), which gives long periods of adversity; Mars, the ruler of the Second House, in conjunction with Sun ($\odot \sigma \sigma'$) and sextile Jupiter ($\odot \sigma \, 2\!\!+$), shows ability to earn money by dint of hard effort in professional service, but it is spent as soon as earned. There are no testimonies for wealth or accumulation of property. The ruler of the First House, Venus, in the Third House shows the native's mind to be taken up with study and science in which he is highly proficient, especially in the occult.

## Mentality

The mental quality and tendencies are denoted by Mercury and the sign in which it may be located, the Ascendant and aspects to the ascending degree; also the Moon and its sign and aspects and any planets which may be in the Third House. Libra governing the Ascendant gives perception, comparison, order and harmony. Venus, its ruler, posited in the Third House, gives good mental quality of fruitful or abundant nature with a love for cultural arts, such as literature, science, etc. Mercury in Capricorn adds calculation, caution and depth to the mind and serious contemplation. Its adverse aspect to Saturn ($\varphi \square \hbar$), however, indicates discontent, sarcasm and worry. Moon in the scientific sign, Gemini and in orb of conjunction with the Ninth House cusp inclines the mind to religion, law and science, adds also perception and ability for expression. Uranus in the Third House conjunct Neptune ( $\mathbb{H} \sigma \psi$) gives much mental originality, unique ideas, inventive and increase the faculty and ability for study of occult science.

## Children

Barren signs on the cusps of the Fifth and Eleventh Houses and the rulers thereof not in fruitful signs, the Moon not in a fruitful sign, the Ascendant not in a fruitful sign, its ruler not in a fruitful sign, and no fruitful planets in the Fifth or Eleventh Houses, are indications of no children.

## Health

Health and sickness are determined by the ascendant, its ruler, their aspects, and any planets therein; likewise consider the Sixth House. The signs and houses occupied by the malefics also indicate parts of the body affected and particularly so if the malefics are affected by aspect or debility. In this chart Libra on the Ascendant shows that the native would at some time be affected by kidney complaint, especially as Venus is adverse to Jupiter ( ♀□♃ ) in the Sixth House. Saturn in Aries would give tendency to colds in the head and near-sightedness, deafness, headaches, etc.; its square to Mercury ( ☿□♄ ) would cause decay of the teeth and bowel trouble, and the latter planet being in Capricorn gives a tendency to rheumatism and stiffened joints, especially the knees. Uranus and Neptune in the Third House would affect the sight, likewise the Sun afflicted ( ☉♂♂ ) in an angle. (His eyesight entirely failed in later years.) Mars and the Sun in Capricorn incline toward accidents to the knees and being in the Fourth house, indicates spells of stomach disorder. However, while this conjunction ( ☉♂♂ ) is conducive to feverish complaints it should be remembered that any aspect of the Sun to Mars strengthens the constitution and increases the vitality to throw off and overcome illness. Although the Sun is not hyleg, yet the afflictions of Mercury, Mars, and the Sun in the Fourth House show the latter part of life to be beset with many troubles. The goods aspects to Jupiter ( ☉ , ♂ ) show that in sickness he would be benefited by neighbors and would never be entirely without comforts.

## Marriage—Partnerships

Marriage in the horoscope of a male is judged by the Moon principally, with Venus as a co-indicator. Here we find Venus, the ruler of the Ascendant, parallel with and applying to a semi-sextile to Mars ( ♀∥♂ , ⊼♂   ) ruler of the Seventh House, thus showing that the native is inclined to partnerships and unions. The Moon in Gemini, sextile to the cusp of the Seventh House, shows more than one union, especially as it is in favorable aspect to Saturn ( ☽ ✳ ♄ ). However, Saturn is in adverse aspect to Mercury ( ☿ □ ♄ ) and it rules the House of Sorrow (the Twelfth House) which indicates the death of the first wife. Saturn afflicting the Seventh House, while also afflicting the Ascending degree ( ♄ ♂ Asc.), testifies against harmony or good results, although marriage may help him in publishing, etc., as Saturn is in good aspect to the Moon ( ♄ ✳ ☽ ) on the cusp of the Ninth House.

Venus applying to a conjunction with Uranus ( ♀□♅ ) indicates separations and divorce.

## Occupation

Business or profession is governed by the Tenth House, its ruler and aspects and any planets which may be posited therein. In this horoscope we have no planet in the Tenth House, so we look to the ruler thereof, which is the Moon, located in the scientific sign Gemini and in conjunction with the cusp of the Ninth House, also a scientific house. This would indicate a traveler, sailor, publisher, preacher, lawyer, scientist. Venus, ruler of the Ascendant, inclines the mind to art, or artistic application of intellectual matters; to sports and literary efforts relating to sports, adventure or travel. Jupiter, ruler of the Third House, in the Sixth House, shows professional service and it indicates that professional occupations would be more to his liking and more fortunate than business or a trade. The Moon, ruler of the Tenth House, shows his vocation would bring him a great deal of publicity.

## Synthesis

We have here a strong, forceful character, a man who never forgets a wrong and always appreciates a kindness. His early environment will be restrictive but his thirst for knowledge will result in high intellectual attainments and he will render the scientific-occult public valuable service. Marital and legal difficulties will interrupt his progress and he should avoid such matters as much as possible and concentrate upon his financial affairs, thereby conserving his forces, physically and materially, to withstand the adversities of his later days.

We have now illustrated the method of delineating a chart and shown in their logical order the points generally of most interest. In regular practice we would proceed to look up the influence of all the aspects, all the planets by sign, all the planets by house, and the rulers of all the houses as they are posited in the various houses of the chart. Study of the nativity does not end here as transiting planets, shown in the current ephemeris, are traversing through different houses in the natal chart and constantly forming aspects with planets in the radix thus bringing up new events, new conditions, new states of being and as the student watches these, he or she will realize, at times with awe, the stupendous working order of the laws of nature.

Further research is made by means of a yearly chart or progressed horoscope in which the monthly aspects of the Moon indicate the trend of affairs and mutual aspects between the planets designate the quality of the year as a whole, whether the lesson to be learned will be through pleasures or limitations. These points are fully covered in the following section, **Advanced Techniques**.

## STUDENT EXERCISE: MAKE YOUR OWN CHART

Make your horoscope following the directions given in *Part 2. Constructing the Horoscope*, sections titled *The George Method of Horoscope Calculation*, *Finding the Positions of the Planets*, and *Finding the Aspects*, pages 75-123.

Take plenty of time on this study. Work out one point at a time and do it thoroughly and completely. When delineating your own chart do not read it simply from what you know of yourself, but hold fast to the principles and procedure already outlined.

In the preceding chapters and lessons you acquired information of the various elements constituting a horoscope. You learned of the the tendencies bestowed by the signs, of how the planets bestir those tendencies into characteristic action and how their indications are modified according to the house occupied, by dignity or debility and especially their aspects. You learned what matters are embraced in each of the twelve houses of a chart; how the zodiacal signs add their special influence to the house and planet. In *The Secret of Horoscope Reading* you were shown how to correlate these elements practically, prepatory to delineating a chart.

If you find it difficult to compile the notes turn back to the preceding chapters and study everything related to the influences and indications employed in horoscope reading, as before mentioned.

No instructor or book can give the student the ability to synthesize but the proper procedure can be outlined to develop this needed faculty. The art of synthesis is like good judgment or intuition: it cannot be handed from one to another; it is *a growth within the person,* an expansion of knowledge, as a result of careful study of authentic texts, assimilation of the information thus acquired and application of the principles thus learned.

# Advanced Techniques

Progressions,
Transits,
Estimate Charts,
Rectification and
Locality Charts

# The Progressed Chart

Having learned to make the natal chart correctly, students will find it easy to erect the progressed chart. The rule simply stated is: Count forward in the birth year ephemeris, beginning with the day *after* the birth day, one day for each year to the year of age required. Call the date thus found *the progressed birth date* and from it make a chart in the usual way, using the same birth time (hour and minute) and the same Tables of Houses used for erecting the natal chart. The complete rule, with examples; and the various details associated with the making of a progressed horoscope are given further on in this lesson. However, before proceeding with the calculations required in a progressed chart, let us first discuss some of its salient features. The insight and understanding, thereby acquired, will not only simplify the necessary final efforts, but considerably increase our appreciation of the value of the various features embraced in the work. The student who undertakes this progressed horoscope lesson will very likely find it necessary to read and re-read it a number of times in order to form a general idea of the process, its purpose and application to life.

The horoscope of birth and the progressed chart may be likened to a book of information: The index shows what the volume contains and the chapters give the details. The birth chart is like an index and the progressed chart like a chapter, and as the book contains only what is indexed, so from a progressed chart must be read *only* that which is indicated at birth.

From the location in the Zodiac, the aspects and the positions in the horoscope held by the planets at birth, an influence is exerted throughout the whole life. This fact can easily be discerned by watching the transit of a planet over the place held by one of the planets in the nativity (or over the cusp of a house in a natal chart), although the planet itself has moved away from the original place in the natal chart.

The reason for the permanent influence of the planets is that they are as one writer says, ". . . inherent in the very structure of the physical body. All atoms and molecules of the physical plane and all material combinations, whether solid, liquid, gas or ether, are classified in terms of planets and signs. The physical body has been built up of these combinations, and it forms a highly complex whole, which exactly corresponds in composition to the stellar positions (locations and aspects) at birth and responds to their vibrations. The horoscope, therefore, is registered in the body itself and lasts as long as life endures."

While the birth map may be regarded as permanent because it represents the structure and composition of the body (the physical vehicle and individuality), so may a system of progression be considered valid because it represents the changes taking place in the living being within the limits imposed at birth.

The twelve zodiacal signs rise and set in the twenty-four hours of a day. The planets continually traveling through the Zodiac change their relations one to another and also the places they held at birth. For instance, if the Sun was posited in $1°$ of a sign at birth and Jupiter was in $20°$ of the same sign, the Sun would arrive at that degree held by Jupiter nineteen days after birth.

**Note:** With regard to the conjunction just used as an example: Jupiter being a benefic and the conjunction a good one, the effects would be very favorable but if Jupiter had been heavily afflicted at birth, good results would not occur.

The changes among the signs and planets after birth are classed under two heads:

**First.** The rotation of the Earth on its axis apparently causes the signs to move at a rate of approximately $1°$ every four minutes; so in the course of twenty-four hours, the whole Zodiac of $360°$ has apparently crossed over the horizon of every point on the Earth. In that twenty-four hours the Earth has also moved forward in its orbit $1°$ and by so doing it consumes approximately four minutes of time more than twenty-four hours. Reference to the Sidereal Time column in an ephemeris shows that it advances about four minutes per day in accordance with the Earth's daily orbital progress of 1°. This motion causes the Midheaven to move forward 1° per day. Therefore, as in astrological calculations one day equals one year, it is likewise called "one degree (on the Midheaven) per year." The natal chart therefore progresses at the rate of a day for a year and the Midheaven progresses 1° per year.

The Midheaven progresses uniformly at the rate of 1° per day but this is not true of the other house cusps, due mainly to inequality in the shape of the earth, except at the equator. Therefore, each day counted forward to represent one year of life changes the Midheaven 1° each day. The other cusps change in their proper sequence as indicated by the Table of Houses.

The original places of the planets in the natal chart are changed by this sign motion but not their longitudinal places. For instance, if a planet was in conjunction with the cusp of the First House at birth, every four minutes (every year) it would be carried up 1° into the Twelfth House and its distance from the horizon and meridian would change—the planet just mentioned would be exerting a Twelfth House influence and would sooner or later form aspects of sextile, semi-square, semi-sextile, conjunction, etc., with the degree constituting the Midheaven or cusp of the Tenth House at birth.

**Second.** The second change which takes place is caused by the actual movement of the planets in the Zodiac. In this way a planet may move away from the location in the Zodiac held at birth and form new aspects to other planets and also aspects to its own original place.

The measure of time for the progressed chart is *one day for each year of life*, i.e., the aspects formed during the first day indicates the events of the first year of life; the second day the second year of life and so on. The elements taken into account by *direction* are the places of the Sun, the Moon, planets and house cusps. The Ascendant and Midheaven are of more importance than the other cusps. Any of these points may progress to an aspect with any other or progress to an aspect with its own place in the birth chart.

We use the word *position* for place in the chart and the word *location* for place in the Zodiac.

The word *radix* means root or beginning and as after the birth the signs and planets all move away from the places occupied in the birth chart and because they all move at different rates of speed, they form new aspects at different times, not only to the various places in the birth chart but also among themselves as they advance. A distinction must therefore be made between any planet or cusp as it exists in the map for birth and the same one as it is placed after having moved away from the place of birth.

The word *radix* is used to designate planets or cusps in the birth chart and the term *progressed* for places and conditions in the progressed chart.

Such a directional aspect as the one previously mentioned, ($\odot \, \sigma \, 4$) would be registered in this way: progressed Sun conjunct Jupiter radix (P$\odot \sigma 4$R) meaning that the Sun by its progressed motion had come to a conjunction with the place held by Jupiter in the birth chart. This distinction is important when tabulating the aspects and it also determines in which chart to look for the planets involved and to note the house occupied by them.

Jupiter would also have moved away from its radical place and as the Sun moves faster than Jupiter, it would in a few days (years) catch up to Jupiter and form another conjunction. This second conjunction, due to the progressed motion of both planets, is termed a *progressed mutual aspect* and would be written thus: progressed Sun conjunct Jupiter progressed (P$\odot \sigma 4$P).

Thus, it will be seen in *The Progressed Aspects*, page 435, that the directional aspects are divided into two general classes. First, *directions from progressed planets or cusps to radical planets or cusps* (Lunar Progressed Aspects and Progressed Aspects to Radix). Second, *directions from progressed planets or cusps to progressed planets or cusps* (Progressed Mutual Aspects).

## EFFECTS OF CHANGE OF RESIDENCE
## ON THE PROGRESSED HOROSCOPE

Now and then a student inquires whether it is proper to make the progressed chart from Tables of Houses for the native's present place of abode instead of for the place of birth.

It is not practical to substitute house cusps of the present abode for those of the place of birth, because the further away the native has moved the larger the number of degrees difference it would make on the house cusps. Making the chart for the latitude of the present residence changes the lunar aspects to house cusps by several months, whereas, in reality the person may be but a few hours time difference removed from his place of birth.

Using the radical latitude (that of the birth place) even when the native has moved, makes a difference of only a few hours in the timing of the aspects; i.e., the difference in time between the place of birth and the present residence. The time would be earlier or later according to whether the native had moved east or west of the birthplace. This difference of a few hours is of slight importance when one considers that it is a very difficult matter to set a particular day for the operation of a progressed aspect, especially those whose influence lasts a month or more. Aspects such as the progressed Moon conjunct the radical Ascendant (P$\mathbb{C}$ ♂ Asc.R), or the progressed Sun sextile the radical Midheaven (P☉∗MC R) begin to exert an effect from four to eight weeks prior to the actual completion of the aspect by the Moon or many months by the Sun.

The progressed chart requires the natural progress of the house cusps, just as it does the planets. At the moment of birth the planets have house positions according to the latitude of the birthplace. At the first independent indrawn breath of the babe, the prevailing vibrations cast or set the tendencies of the body according to those house positions, as well as by the aspects and the signs occupied by the planets. Those particular house positions of the planets at that time are time markers of when certain conditions will appear in the life of that individual.

Thus, if Saturn is 3° below the ascending degree, its position in relation to the Ascendant denotes that when the Ascendant has advanced 3° it will be in conjunction with the place of Saturn (P Asc. ♂ ♄ R). Due to the planetary rays affecting that particular latitude at that birth time certain forces were timed for manifestation and those times can only be correctly calculated by the use of the original latitude from which the native received his original cast.

Although it is not practical to substitute house cusps of the present abode for those of the place of birth, it may be well to use the cusps made for the present residence as a supplement for investigation (assuming that the native has moved from the birth latitude), to see whether or not in such a chart the indications to cusps in any way coincide or conflict with the testimonies indicated by house cusps of the original progressed chart latitude. (See *The Locality Chart*, page 523.)

In other words, moving from the original latitude does not change or negate the indications as timed or measured from birth but a change of residence may create other conditions which tend to accentuate or modify those which are denoted by the original birthplace latitude.

# Constructing the Progressed Chart

## FINDING THE PROGRESSED BIRTHDATE

To erect a progressed chart, refer to an ephemeris for the date and year of birth and count each day after birth as one year in life, i.e., a chart made for the first day after birth would show (by planets, positions, aspects, etc.) the conditions that operate between one-year and two-years-old. A chart cast for the second day after birth would show the conditions for the twelve months following the second birthday, etc.

### Examples

Throughout this lesson two example charts will be used to illustrate the calculations: *Chart 1*, Person born January 22, 1936, 10:20 PM, Sillersville, PA., and *Chart 2*. Person born March 30, 1947, 9:38 AM, Red Wing, MN. These are the two charts used in Part 1 describing the George Method of Horoscope calculation.

**Example 1. Person born January 22, 1936, 10:20 pm, Sillersville, PA**. If a progressed chart is to be erected for the year 1978, the birth year is subtracted from 1978 giving the remainder of 42. This is equivalent to 42 days after birth. Forty-two is then added to the birth date, January 22, giving the progressed birth date of March 4, 1936 (Remember, 1936 is a leap year.) Thus, a chart erected for 10:20 PM, March 4, 1936, corrected for the longitude and latitude of Sillersville, PA., will represent the year January 22, 1978 to January 22, 1979.

SIMPLIFIED SCIENTIFIC
## EPHEMERIS OF THE PLANETS' PLACES
Calculated for Mean Noon at Greenwich

### March, 1936

New Moon, March 23rd, 4:13 A. M., in ♈ 2° 22'
Longitude of the Planets

| Day | ☉ ♓ | ♀ ♒ | ☿ ♒ | ☽ ♊ | ♄ ♓ | ♃ ♐ | ♂ ♈ | ♅ ♉ | ♆ ♍ | ☊ ♑ |
|---|---|---|---|---|---|---|---|---|---|---|
| | ° ′ | ° ′ | ° ′ | ° ′ | ° ′ | ° ′ | ° ′ | ° ′ | ° ′ | ′ |
| Su 1 | 10 45 | 10 13 | 14 17 | 24 20 | 12 34 | 22 02 | 6 24 | 2 38 | 15R32 | 9 43 |
| M 2 | 11 45 | 11 26 | 15 28 | 7 ♋17 | 12 42 | 22 08 | 7 09 | 2 41 | 15 30 | 9 40 |
| Tu 3 | 12 45 | 12 40 | 16 41 | 19 57 | 12 49 | 22 14 | 7 55 | 2 43 | 15 29 | 9 37 |
| W 4 | 13 45 | 13 54 | 17 56 | 2 ♌24 | 12 56 | 22 21 | 8 41 | 2 45 | 15 27 | 9 33 |
| Th 5 | 14 45 | 15 07 | 19 13 | 14 41 | 13 04 | 22 27 | 9 26 | 2 48 | 15 25 | 9 30 |
| F 6 | 15 45 | 16 21 | 20 31 | 26 50 | 13 11 | 22 34 | 10 12 | 2 50 | 15 23 | 9 27 |
| S 7 | 16 45 | 17 35 | 21 51 | 8 ♍53 | 13 18 | 22 39 | 10 58 | 2 53 | 15 22 | 9 24 |
| Su 8 | 17 45 | 18 48 | 23 12 | 20 51 | 13 26 | 22 46 | 11 43 | 2 56 | 15 20 | 9 21 |
| M 9 | 18 45 | 20 02 | 24 35 | 2 ♎46 | 13 33 | 22 51 | 12 29 | 2 58 | 15 18 | 9 17 |
| Tu 10 | 19 45 | 21 16 | 25 59 | 14 38 | 13 40 | 22 57 | 13 14 | 3 01 | 15 17 | 9 14 |
| W 11 | 20 45 | 22 29 | 27 25 | 26 30 | 13 48 | 23 02 | 14 00 | 3 04 | 15 15 | 9 11 |
| Th 12 | 21 45 | 23 43 | 28 52 | 8 ♏24 | 13 55 | 23 08 | 14 45 | 3 07 | 15 14 | 9 08 |
| F 13 | 22 45 | 24 57 | 0 ♓20 | 20 23 | 14 02 | 23 13 | 15 30 | 3 10 | 15 12 | 9 05 |
| S 14 | 23 45 | 26 10 | 1 50 | 2 ♐29 | 14 10 | 23 18 | 16 16 | 3 12 | 15 10 | 9 02 |
| Su 15 | 24 44 | 27 24 | 3 21 | 14 48 | 14 17 | 23 23 | 17 01 | 3 15 | 15 08 | 8 58 |
| M 16 | 25 44 | 28 38 | 4 53 | 27 24 | 14 24 | 23 27 | 17 46 | 3 18 | 15 07 | 8 55 |
| Tu 17 | 26 44 | 29 52 | 6 27 | 10 ♑22 | 14 31 | 23 32 | 18 31 | 3 21 | 15 05 | 8 52 |
| W 18 | 27 44 | 1 ♓05 | 8 02 | 23 46 | 14 38 | 23 36 | 19 16 | 3 24 | 15 04 | 8 49 |
| Th 19 | 28 43 | 2 19 | 9 38 | 7 ♒39 | 14 46 | 23 40 | 20 01 | 3 27 | 15 02 | 8 46 |
| F 20 | 29 43 | 3 33 | 11 15 | 22 02 | 14 53 | 23 44 | 20 46 | 3 30 | 15 01 | 8 42 |
| S 21 | 0 ♈42 | 4 47 | 12 54 | 6 ♓51 | 15 00 | 23 48 | 21 31 | 3 33 | 14 59 | 8 39 |
| Su 22 | 1 42 | 6 00 | 14 34 | 22 01 | 15 07 | 23 52 | 22 16 | 3 36 | 14 57 | 8 36 |
| M 23 | 2 42 | 7 14 | 16 15 | 7 ♈20 | 15 14 | 23 55 | 23 01 | 3 39 | 14 56 | 8 33 |
| Tu 24 | 3 41 | 8 28 | 17 58 | 22 39 | 15 22 | 23 59 | 23 46 | 3 42 | 14 54 | 8 30 |
| W 25 | 4 41 | 9 42 | 19 42 | 7 ♉45 | 15 29 | 24 02 | 24 31 | 3 45 | 14 53 | 8 27 |
| Th 26 | 5 40 | 10 56 | 21 27 | 22 29 | 15 36 | 24 05 | 25 16 | 3 48 | 14 51 | 8 23 |
| F 27 | 6 39 | 12 09 | 23 13 | 6 ♊46 | 15 43 | 24 08 | 26 00 | 3 51 | 14 50 | 8 20 |
| S 28 | 7 39 | 13 23 | 25 01 | 20 35 | 15 50 | 24 10 | 26 45 | 3 55 | 14 48 | 8 17 |
| Su 29 | 8 38 | 14 37 | 26 50 | 3 ♋55 | 15 57 | 24 12 | 27 30 | 3 58 | 14 47 | 8 14 |
| M 30 | 9 36 | 15 51 | 28 41 | 18 51 | 16 04 | 24 14 | 28 14 | 4 01 | 14 45 | 8 11 |
| Tu 31 | 10 36 | 17 04 | 0 ♈33 | 29 27 | 16 11 | 24 16 | 28 57 | 4 04 | 14 44 | 8 07 |

Pluto. Longitude, March 1, ♋ 25° 30'

Figure 26: Left Hand Page Rosicrucian Ephemeris, March 1936

## EPHEMERIS OF THE PLANETS' PLACES
Calculated for Mean Noon at Greenwich—March, 1936
Full Moon, March 8th, 5:13 A. M., in ♍ 17° 28'

### Declination of the Planets

| D | S. T. | Dec ☽ | D | ⊙ | ♀ | ☿ | ♄ | ♃ | ♂ | ♅ | ♆ |
|---|---|---|---|---|---|---|---|---|---|---|---|
| | H. M. S. | ° N ' | | ° S ' | ° S ' | ° S ' | ° S ' | ° S ' | ° N ' | ° N ' | ° N ' |
| 1 | 22 36 37 | 24 47 | 1 | 7 32 | 18 00 | 17 17 | 8 26 | 22 36 | 2 05 | 11 57 | 6 39 |
| 2 | 22 40 23 | 23 35 | 2 | 7 09 | 17 42 | 17 04 | 23 | 36 | 2 24 | 58 | 40 |
| 3 | 22 44 20 | 21 11 | 4 | 6 23 | 17 06 | 16 34 | 18 | 37 | 3 01 | 11 59 | 41 |
| 4 | 22 48 16 | 17 49 | 6 | 5 37 | 16 28 | 15 59 | 12 | 38 | 3 38 | 12 01 | 43 |
| 5 | 22 52 13 | 13 44 | 8 | 4 50 | 15 47 | 15 18 | 07 | 38 | 4 15 | 03 | 44 |
| 6 | 22 56 09 | 9 09 | 10 | 4 03 | 15 06 | 14 32 | 8 01 | 39 | 4 52 | 05 | 46 |
| | | | 12 | 3 15 | 14 22 | 13 41 | 7 56 | 40 | 5 28 | 07 | 47 |
| 7 | 23 00 05 | 4 16 | 14 | 2 28 | 13 37 | 12 15 | 50 | 40 | 6 05 | 09 | 48 |
| 8 | 23 04 02 | 0 S 44 | 16 | 1 40 | 12 51 | 11 44 | 45 | 41 | 6 40 | 11 | 49 |
| 9 | 23 07 59 | 5 40 | 18 | 0 54 | 12 02 | 10 38 | 39 | 41 | 7 16 | 13 | 50 |
| 10 | 23 11 56 | 10 23 | 20 | 0 07 | 11 13 | 9 28 | 34 | 41 | 7 51 | 15 | 52 |
| 11 | 23 15 52 | 14 43 | 22 | 0 N 40 | 10 22 | 8 12 | 28 | 42 | 8 26 | 17 | 53 |
| 12 | 23 19 49 | 18 29 | 24 | 1 27 | 9 31 | 6 51 | 23 | 42 | 9 01 | 19 | 54 |
| 13 | 23 23 45 | 21 31 | 26 | 2 15 | 8 38 | 5 26 | 18 | 42 | 9 35 | 21 | 55 |
| | | | 28 | 3 01 | 7 44 | 3 57 | 12 | 42 | 10 09 | 24 | 57 |
| 14 | 23 27 42 | 23 38 | 30 | 3 48 | 6 50 | 2 24 | 7 07 | 22 43 | 10 41 | 12 26 | 6 58 |
| 15 | 23 31 38 | 24 40 | | | | | | | | | |
| 16 | 23 35 35 | 24 28 | | | | | | | | | |

### Latitude of the Planets

| D | S. T. | Dec ☽ | D | ☽ | ♀ | ☿ | ♄ | ♃ | ♂ | ♅ | ♆ |
|---|---|---|---|---|---|---|---|---|---|---|---|
| 17 | 23 39 31 | 22 57 | | ° N ' | ° S ' | ° S ' | ° S ' | ° N ' | ° S ' | ° S ' | ° N ' |
| 18 | 23 43 28 | 20 07 | 1 | 1 28 | 0 18 | 0 46 | 1 43 | 0 36 | 0 30 | 0 28 | 1 02 |
| 19 | 23 47 24 | 16 03 | 2 | 0 20 | 0 22 | 0 54 | 43 | 36 | 0 29 | 28 | 02 |
| 20 | 23 51 20 | 10 56 | 4 | 1 S 52 | 0 27 | 1 09 | 43 | 37 | 0 27 | 28 | 02 |
| 21 | 23 55 17 | 5 03 | 6 | 3 38 | 0 33 | 1 23 | 43 | 37 | 0 26 | 28 | 02 |
| 22 | 23 59 14 | 1 N 14 | 8 | 4 44 | 0 38 | 1 36 | 44 | 37 | 0 24 | 28 | 02 |
| 23 | 0 03 11 | 7 30 | 10 | 5 00 | 0 43 | 1 46 | 44 | 37 | 0 23 | 28 | 02 |
| 24 | 0 07 07 | 13 19 | 12 | 4 24 | 0 48 | 1 56 | 44 | 37 | 0 22 | 28 | 02 |
| 25 | 0 11 03 | 18 14 | 14 | 3 02 | 0 53 | 2 04 | 44 | 37 | 0 21 | 28 | 02 |
| 26 | 0 15 00 | 21 53 | 16 | 1 03 | 0 57 | 2 10 | 44 | 37 | 0 19 | 28 | 02 |
| 27 | 0 18 57 | 24 02 | 18 | 1 N 16 | 1 01 | 2 15 | 44 | 37 | 0 18 | 28 | 02 |
| | | | 20 | 3 25 | 1 05 | 2 17 | 44 | 37 | 0 17 | 28 | 02 |
| 28 | 0 22 54 | 24 38 | 22 | 4 47 | 0 59 | 2 17 | 45 | 37 | 0 15 | 28 | 02 |
| 29 | 0 26 50 | 23 45 | 24 | 4 51 | 1 12 | 2 16 | 45 | 37 | 0 14 | 28 | 02 |
| 30 | 0 30 47 | 21 37 | 26 | 3 36 | 1 16 | 2 14 | 45 | 37 | 0 13 | 28 | 02 |
| 31 | 0 34 43 | 18 29 | 28 | 1 31 | 1 18 | 2 09 | 45 | 37 | 0 11 | 28 | 02 |
| | | | 30 | 0 S 46 | 1 21 | 2 02 | 1 45 | 0 37 | 0 10 | 0 28 | 1 02 |

Pluto, Declination, March 1, N. 23° 12'

Figure 27: Right Hand Page Rosicrucian Ephemeris, March 1936

New Moon, April 21, 4:18 A.M., in ♉ 0° 15'
Longitude of the Planets

| Day | ☉ ♈ | ♀ ♓ | ☿ ♓ | ☽ ♌ | ♄ ♌ | ♃ ♏ | ♂ ♓ | ♅ ♊ | ♆ ♎ | ☊ ♊ |
|---|---|---|---|---|---|---|---|---|---|---|
| T 1 | 10 55 19 | 1 52 | 13 34 | 18♌00 | 1ʀ57 | 27ʀ04 | 21 51 | 18 18 | 9ʀ24 | 5 21 |
| W 2 | 11 54 28 | 3 04 | 14 22 | 2♍02 | 1 57 | 27 01 | 22 37 | 18 19 | 9 23 | 5 18 |
| T 3 | 12 53 37 | 4 14 | 15 14 | 15 55 | 1 57 | 26 57 | 23 25 | 18 21 | 9 21 | 5 15 |
| F 4 | 13 52 42 | 5 26 | 16 09 | 29 37 | 1 57 | 26 53 | 24 11 | 18 23 | 9 19 | 5 12 |
| S 5 | 14 51 46 | 6 36 | 17 07 | 13♎05 | 1 57 | 26 49 | 24 59 | 18 25 | 9 17 | 5 09 |
| S 6 | 15 50 47 | 7 48 | 18 08 | 26 14 | 1ᴅ58 | 26 45 | 25 45 | 18 27 | 9 16 | 5 06 |
| M 7 | 16 49 47 | 8 58 | 19 11 | 9♏06 | 1 58 | 26 41 | 26 31 | 18 29 | 9 14 | 5 02 |
| T 8 | 17 48 45 | 10 10 | 20 18 | 21 40 | 1 59 | 26 36 | 27 19 | 18 31 | 9 13 | 4 59 |
| W 9 | 18 47 40 | 11 21 | 21 26 | 3♐58 | 1 59 | 26 32 | 28 05 | 18 33 | 9 11 | 4 55 |
| T 10 | 19 46 35 | 12 32 | 22 37 | 16 02 | 2 00 | 26 28 | 28 52 | 18 36 | 9 09 | 4 52 |
| F 11 | 20 45 26 | 13 44 | 23 50 | 27 57 | 2 01 | 26 22 | 29 39 | 18 38 | 9 07 | 4 49 |
| S 12 | 21 44 17 | 14 56 | 25 06 | 9♑47 | 2 02 | 26 18 | 0♈25 | 18 40 | 9 06 | 4 46 |
| S 13 | 22 43 06 | 16 07 | 26 23 | 21 38 | 2 03 | 26 12 | 1 12 | 18 42 | 9 05 | 4 43 |
| M 14 | 23 41 53 | 17 18 | 27 42 | 3♒34 | 2 04 | 26 07 | 1 59 | 18 44 | 9 03 | 4 40 |
| T 15 | 24 40 38 | 18 30 | 29 03 | 15 40 | 2 05 | 26 02 | 2 45 | 18 47 | 9 01 | 4 36 |
| W 16 | 25 39 21 | 19 42 | 0♈27 | 28 01 | 2 06 | 25 56 | 3 31 | 18 49 | 8 59 | 4 33 |
| T 17 | 26 38 04 | 20 53 | 1 52 | 10♓40 | 2 07 | 25 50 | 4 18 | 18 52 | 8 58 | 4 30 |
| F 18 | 27 36 43 | 22 04 | 3 19 | 23 41 | 2 09 | 25 44 | 5 05 | 18 54 | 8 57 | 4 27 |
| S 19 | 28 35 22 | 23 16 | 4 47 | 7♈02 | 2 10 | 25 38 | 5 51 | 18 56 | 8 55 | 4 24 |
| S 20 | 29 33 58 | 24 28 | 6 17 | 20 44 | 2 12 | 25 32 | 6 37 | 19 00 | 8 53 | 4 20 |
| M 21 | 0♉32 32 | 25 40 | 7 50 | 4♉44 | 2 14 | 25 25 | 7 23 | 19 02 | 8 52 | 4 17 |
| T 22 | 1 31 05 | 26 51 | 9 25 | 18 57 | 2 16 | 25 19 | 8 10 | 19 04 | 8 51 | 4 14 |
| W 23 | 2 29 36 | 28 03 | 11 00 | 3♊19 | 2 18 | 25 13 | 8 56 | 19 08 | 8 49 | 4 11 |
| T 24 | 3 28 05 | 29 15 | 12 47 | 17 45 | 2 20 | 25 07 | 9 42 | 19 10 | 8 47 | 4 08 |
| F 25 | 4 26 31 | 0♈26 | 14 17 | 2♋10 | 2 22 | 25 00 | 10 29 | 19 13 | 8 46 | 4 05 |
| S 26 | 5 24 55 | 1 38 | 15 58 | 16 31 | 2 25 | 24 53 | 11 15 | 19 16 | 8 45 | 4 01 |
| S 27 | 6 23 17 | 2 49 | 17 51 | 0♌44 | 2 28 | 24 47 | 12 01 | 19 18 | 8 43 | 3 58 |
| M 28 | 7 21 38 | 4 02 | 19 25 | 14 48 | 2 30 | 24 39 | 12 47 | 19 22 | 8 42 | 3 55 |
| T 29 | 8 19 55 | 5 14 | 21 11 | 28 42 | 2 33 | 24 32 | 13 33 | 19 24 | 8 41 | 3 51 |
| W 30 | 9 19 12 | 6 26 | 23 05 | 12♍24 | 2 36 | 24 25 | 14 19 | 19 26 | 8 39 | 3 49 |

Pluto, Longitude, April 1, 1947, ♌ 11° 02'ʀ

Figure 28: Left Hand Page Rosicrucian Ephemeris, April 1947

## EPHEMERIS OF THE PLANETS' PLACES
Calculated for Mean Noon at Greenwich—April. 1947
Full Moon, April 5, 3:29 P.M., in ♎ 15° 00'
### Declination of the Planets

| D | S. T. | D☊☋ | D | ⊙ | ♀ | ☿ | ♄ | ♃ | ♂ | ♅ | ♆ |
|---|---|---|---|---|---|---|---|---|---|---|---|
| | H.M.S. | ° N ' | | ° N ' | ° S ' | ° S ' | ° N ' | ° S ' | ° S ' | ° N ' | ° S ' |
| 1 | 00 36 00 | 20 06 | 1 | 4 19 | 11 22 | 7 36 | 20 22 | 18 23 | 4 12 23 02 | 2 18 |
| 2 | 00 39 57 | 15 31 | 3 | 5 06 | 10 37 | 7 13 | 20 22 | 18 21 | 3 35 23 02 | 2 17 |
| 3 | 00 43 54 | 10 09 | 5 | 5 51 | 9 50 | 6 44 | 20 22 | 18 19 | 2 58 23 02 | 2 15 |
| 4 | 00 47 50 | 4 22 | 7 | 6 36 | 9 02 | 6 09 | 20 22 | 18 17 | 2 19 23 03 | 2 14 |
| 5 | 00 51 46 | 1 S 32 | 9 | 7 22 | 8 13 | 5 27 | 20 22 | 18 15 | 1 43 23 03 | 2 13 |
| | | | 11 | 8 06 | 7 24 | 4 38 | 20 22 | 18 12 | 1 04 23 03 | 2 11 |
| 6 | 00 55 43 | 7 15 | 13 | 8 50 | 6 32 | 3 44 | 20 22 | 18 10 | 0 27 23 04 | 2 10 |
| 7 | 00 59 40 | 12 32 | 15 | 9 34 | 5 41 | 2 45 | 20 21 | 18 07 | 0 S 10 23 04 | 2 09 |
| 8 | 1 03 36 | 17 11 | 17 | 10 17 | 4 49 | 1 40 | 20 21 | 18 05 | 0 48 23 05 | 2 08 |
| 9 | 1 07 32 | 21 01 | 19 | 10 58 | 3 56 | 0 40 | 20 20 | 18 02 | 1 26 23 05 | 2 06 |
| 10 | 1 11 29 | 23 51 | 21 | 11 40 | 3 02 | 0 N 41 | 20 19 | 17 59 | 2 02 23 05 | 2 05 |
| 11 | 1 17 26 | 25 36 | 23 | 12 21 | 2 09 | 1 59 | 20 18 | 17 56 | 2 40 23 06 | 2 04 |
| 12 | 1 19 22 | 26 10 | 25 | 13 00 | 1 13 | 3 21 | 20 17 | 17 53 | 3 17 23 06 | 2 03 |
| | | | 27 | 13 39 | 0 19 | 4 46 | 20 16 | 17 49 | 3 54 23 07 | 2 02 |
| 13 | 1 23 19 | 25 32 | 29 | 14 18 | 0 N 35 | 6 14 | 20 15 | 17 46 | 4 29 23 07 | 2 01 |
| 14 | 1 27 16 | 23 44 | | | | | | | | |
| 15 | 1 31 12 | 20 51 | | | | | | | | |
| 16 | 1 35 08 | 17 00 | | | | | | | | |
| 17 | 1 39 05 | 12 19 | | | | | | | | |
| 18 | 1 43 02 | 6 58 | | | | | | | | |
| 19 | 1 46 58 | 1 09 | | | | | | | | |
| 20 | 1 50 55 | 4 N 52 | | | | | | | | |
| 21 | 1 54 51 | 10 48 | | | | | | | | |
| 22 | 1 58 48 | 16 16 | | | | | | | | |
| 23 | 2 02 45 | 20 53 | | | | | | | | |
| 24 | 2 06 41 | 24 14 | | | | | | | | |
| 25 | 2 10 37 | 26 00 | | | | | | | | |
| 26 | 2 14 34 | 26 01 | | | | | | | | |
| 27 | 2 18 31 | 24 20 | | | | | | | | |
| 28 | 2 22 27 | 21 09 | | | | | | | | |
| 29 | 2 26 23 | 16 49 | | | | | | | | |
| 30 | 2 30 21 | 11 40 | | | | | | | | |

### Latitude of the Planets

| D | D | ♀ | ☿ | ♄ | ♃ | ♂ | ♅ | ♆ |
|---|---|---|---|---|---|---|---|---|
| | ° N ' | ° S ' | ° S ' | ° N ' | ° N ' | ° S ' | ° N ' | ° N ' |
| 1 | 4 54 | 0 36 | 1 13 | 0 39 | 1 10 | 1 03 | 0 06 | 1 34 |
| 3 | 4 59 | 0 42 | 1 31 | 0 39 | 1 10 | 1 03 | 0 06 | 1 34 |
| 5 | 3 57 | 0 48 | 1 46 | 0 40 | 1 11 | 1 02 | 0 06 | 1 34 |
| 7 | 2 07 | 0 54 | 2 01 | 0 40 | 1 11 | 1 02 | 0 03 | 1 34 |
| 9 | 0 S 04 | 1 00 | 2 13 | 0 40 | 1 11 | 1 01 | 0 06 | 1 34 |
| 11 | 2 10 | 1 05 | 2 23 | 0 40 | 1 11 | 1 01 | 0 06 | 1 34 |
| 13 | 3 53 | 1 10 | 2 31 | 0 40 | 1 11 | 1 01 | 0 06 | 1 34 |
| 15 | 4 56 | 1 14 | 2 36 | 0 40 | 1 11 | 1 00 | 0 06 | 1 34 |
| 17 | 5 08 | 1 19 | 2 38 | 0 40 | 1 11 | 0 59 | 0 06 | 1 34 |
| 19 | 4 18 | 1 23 | 2 40 | 0 40 | 1 11 | 0 59 | 0 06 | 1 34 |
| 21 | 2 27 | 1 27 | 2 38 | 0 40 | 1 12 | 0 58 | 0 06 | 1 34 |
| 23 | 0 N 03 | 1 30 | 2 34 | 0 40 | 1 12 | 0 58 | 0 06 | 1 34 |
| 25 | 2 34 | 1 33 | 2 29 | 0 40 | 1 12 | 0 57 | 0 06 | 1 34 |
| 27 | 4 26 | 1 35 | 2 22 | 0 40 | 1 12 | 0 56 | 0 06 | 1 33 |
| 29 | 5 13 | 1 38 | 2 16 | 0 40 | 1 12 | 0 56 | 0 06 | 1 33 |

Pluto, Declination, April 1, 1947, N. 24° 07'—Latitude. N. 6° 56'

Figure 29: Right Hand Page Rosicrucian Ephemeris, April 1947

| 26 | UPPER MERIDIAN, CUSP OF 10th H. |
|---|---|

| | SID.T. 8 57 52 / ASC 184° 27'.9 } Ω 12° | | | | | 9 1 53 / 185° 28'.1 } Ω 13° | | | | | 9 5 53 / 186° 28'.2 } Ω 14° | | | | | 9 9 52 / 187° 28'.0 } Ω 15° | | | | | 9 13 51 / 188° 27'.7 } Ω 16° | | | | | 9 17 49 / 189° 27'.3 } Ω 17° | | | | |
|---|---|---|---|---|---|---|---|---|---|---|---|---|---|---|---|---|---|---|---|---|---|---|---|---|---|---|---|---|---|---|
| Lat. | 11 ♍ | 12 ♎ | 1 ♏ | 2 ♐ | 3 ♑ | 11 | 12 | 1 | 2 | 3 | 11 | 12 | 1 | 2 | 3 | 11 | 12 | 1 | 2 | 3 | 11 | 12 | 1 | 2 | 3 | 11 | 12 | 1 | 2 | 3 |
| 22 | 14.1 | 14.1 | 10 40 | 9.9 | 10.3 | 15.1 | 15.1 | 11 33 | 10.8 | 11.2 | 16.2 | 16.0 | 12 27 | 11.7 | 12.1 | 17.2 | 17.0 | 13 20 | 12.6 | 13.1 | 18.2 | 17.9 | 14 13 | 13.5 | 14.0 | 19.2 | 18.9 | 15 6 | 14.3 | 14.9 |
| 23 | 2 | 0 | 10 23 | 6 | 1 | 2 | 0 | 11 16 | 5 | 0 | 2 | 15.9 | 12 9 | 4 | 0 | 2 | 16.9 | 13 3 | 3 | 12.9 | 2 | 9 | 13 55 | 2 | 13.8 | 2 | 8 | 14 48 | 0 | 8 |
| 24 | 2 | 0 | 10 6 | 3 | 9.9 | 2 | 14.9 | 10 59 | 2 | 10.9 | 2 | 9 | 11 52 | 1 | 11.8 | 2 | 8 | 12 45 | 0 | 8 | 3 | 8 | 13 37 | 12.9 | 7 | 3 | 7 | 14 30 | 13.7 | 6 |
| 25 | 3 | 13.9 | 9 49 | 0 | 8 | 3 | 8 | 10 42 | 9.9 | 7 | 3 | 8 | 11 34 | 10.8 | 7 | 3 | 8 | 12 27 | 11.7 | 6 | 3 | 7 | 13 19 | 6 | 5 | 3 | 6 | 14 11 | 4 | 5 |
| 26 | 3 | 8 | 9 32 | 8.7 | 6 | 3 | 7 | 10 25 | 6 | 6 | 3 | 7 | 11 17 | 5 | 5 | 3 | 7 | 12 9 | 4 | 4 | 3 | 17.6 | 13 1 | 3 | 4 | 3 | 5 | 13 52 | 1 | 3 |
| 27 | 14.4 | 7 | 9 15 | 4 | 4 | 15.4 | 7 | 10 7 | 3 | 4 | 16.4 | 15.6 | 10 59 | 2 | 3 | 17.4 | 16.6 | 11 51 | 1 | 3 | 18.4 | 5 | 12 42 | 0 | 2 | 19.3 | 18.4 | 13 34 | 12.8 | 1 |
| 28 | 4 | 7 | 8 58 | 1 | 3 | 4 | 14.6 | 9 50 | 0 | 2 | 4 | 5 | 10 41 | 9.9 | 1 | 4 | 5 | 11 33 | 10.8 | 1 | 4 | 4 | 12 24 | 11.6 | 0 | 4 | 3 | 13 15 | 5 | 13.9 |
| 29 | 5 | 13.6 | 8 40 | 7.8 | 1 | 5 | 5 | 9 32 | 8.7 | 0 | 5 | 4 | 10 23 | 6 | 0 | 4 | 4 | 11 14 | 4 | 11.9 | 4 | 3 | 12 5 | 3 | 12.8 | 4 | 2 | 12 56 | 2 | 8 |
| 30 | 5 | 5 | 8 23 | 5 | 8.9 | 5 | 4 | 9 14 | 4 | 9.8 | 5 | 3 | 10 5 | 2 | 10.8 | 5 | 3 | 10 56 | 1 | 7 | 5 | 17.2 | 11 47 | 0 | 7 | 5 | 1 | 12 37 | 11.9 | 6 |
| 31 | 14.6 | 4 | 8 5 | 2 | 7 | 15.6 | 3 | 8 56 | 0 | 7 | 5 | 15.3 | 9 47 | 8.9 | 6 | 5 | 16.2 | 10 37 | 9.8 | 5 | 5 | 1 | 11 28 | 10.7 | 5 | 5 | 19.5 | 12 18 | 6 | 4 |
| 32 | 6 | 3 | 7 48 | 6.8 | 6 | 6 | 14.3 | 8 38 | 7.7 | 5 | 16.6 | 2 | 9 28 | 6 | 4 | 17.6 | 1 | 10 19 | 5 | 3 | 18.6 | 0 | 11 8 | 3 | 3 | 5 | 17.9 | 11 58 | 2 | 2 |
| 33 | 7 | 13.3 | 7 30 | 5 | 3 | 7 | 2 | 8 20 | 4 | 3 | 6 | 1 | 9 10 | 3 | 2 | 6 | 0 | 10 0 | 1 | 1 | 6 | 16.9 | 10 49 | 0 | 1 | 6 | 8 | 11 39 | 10.9 | 0 |
| 34 | 7 | 2 | 7 12 | 2 | 1 | 7 | 1 | 8 1 | 0 | 1 | 7 | 0 | 8 51 | 7.9 | 0 | 6 | 15.9 | 9 40 | 8.8 | 10.9 | 6 | 8 | 10 30 | 9.7 | 11.9 | 6 | 7 | 11 19 | 5 | 12.8 |
| 35 | 14.8 | 1 | 6 53 | 5.8 | 7.9 | 15.8 | 0 | 7 43 | 6.7 | 8.9 | 7 | 14.9 | 8 32 | 5 | 9.8 | 7 | 8 | 9 21 | 4 | 7 | 7 | 7 | 10 10 | 3 | 7 | 19.6 | 6 | 10 59 | 1 | 6 |
| 36 | 8 | 0 | 6 35 | 5 | 7 | 8 | 13.9 | 7 24 | 3 | 7 | 7 | 16.8 | 8 13 | 2 | 6 | 7 | 7 | 9 1 | 0 | 5 | 7 | 6 | 9 50 | 8.9 | 5 | 7 | 5 | 10 38 | 9.8 | 4 |
| 37 | 9 | 12.9 | 6 16 | 1 | 5 | 8 | 9 | 7 5 | 0 | 5 | 8 | 7 | 7 53 | 6.8 | 4 | 17.8 | 6 | 8 42 | 7.7 | 3 | 18.8 | 5 | 9 30 | 5 | 2 | 17.3 | 10 18 | 4 | 2 | |
| 38 | 9 | 8 | 5 57 | 4.7 | 3 | 9 | 7 | 6 46 | 5.7 | 2 | 9 | 6 | 6 34 | 4 | 2 | 8 | 5 | 8 22 | 3 | 1 | 8 | 16.4 | 9 9 | 1 | 0 | 8 | 2 | 9 57 | 0 | 0 |
| 39 | 15.0 | 7 | 5 38 | 3 | 1 | 16.0 | 6 | 6 26 | 3 | 0 | 9 | 5 | 7 14 | 0 | 8.9 | 9 | 15.4 | 8 1 | 6.9 | 9.9 | 8 | 2 | 8 48 | 7.7 | 10.8 | 19.8 | 1 | 9 36 | 8.6 | 11.7 |
| 40 | 1 | 7 | 5 19 | 0 | 6.8 | 0 | 5 | 6 4 | 4.9 | 7.8 | 17.0 | 14.4 | 6 53 | 5.6 | 7 | 9 | 3 | 7 40 | 6 | 6 | 9 | 1 | 8 27 | 3 | 5 | 8 | 0 | 9 15 | 2 | 5 |
| 41 | 1 | 12.6 | 4 59 | 3.5 | 6 | 1 | 13.4 | 5 46 | 5 | 5 | 0 | 3 | 6 33 | 2 | 4 | 18.0 | 1 | 7 20 | 2 | 4 | 9 | 0 | 8 6 | 6.9 | 3 | 9 | 16.9 | 8 53 | 7.8 | 2 |
| 42 | 2 | 5 | 4 39 | 1 | 3 | 1 | 3 | 5 26 | 1 | 2 | 0 | 2 | 6 12 | 4.8 | 2 | 0 | 0 | 6 59 | 5.7 | 1 | 19.0 | 15.9 | 7 45 | 5 | 0 | 9 | 7 | 8 31 | 4 | 0 |
| 43 | 15.2 | 4 | 4 19 | 2.7 | 0 | 2 | 2 | 5 6 | 3.7 | 0 | 1 | 1 | 5 51 | 4 | 7.9 | 1 | 14.9 | 6 37 | 3 | 8.8 | 0 | 8 | 7 23 | 1 | 9.8 | 20.0 | 6 | 8 9 | 6.9 | 10.7 |
| 44 | 3 | 3 | 3 59 | 3 | 5.8 | 16.2 | 1 | 4 45 | 2 | 6.7 | 17.1 | 0 | 5 30 | 3.9 | 6 | 1 | 8 | 6 16 | 4.8 | 5 | 0 | 7 | 7 1 | 5.6 | 5 | 0 | 5 | 7 46 | 5 | 4 |
| 45 | 3 | 12.3 | 3 38 | 1.8 | 5 | 3 | 0 | 4 23 | 2.8 | 4 | 2 | 13.9 | 5 9 | 5 | 3 | 1 | 7 | 5 54 | 3 | 2 | 1 | 6 | 6 38 | 1 | 2 | 0 | 16.4 | 7 23 | 0 | 1 |
| 46 | 4 | 2 | 3 17 | 4 | 2 | 3 | 12.9 | 4 2 | 3 | 1 | 2 | 8 | 4 47 | 0 | 0 | 18.2 | 6 | 5 31 | 3.9 | 7.9 | 1 | 15.5 | 6 15 | 4.7 | 8.9 | 1 | 3 | 7 0 | 5.5 | 9.8 |
| 47 | 15.4 | 1 | 2 55 | 0.9 | 4.8 | 4 | 9 | 3 39 | 1.8 | 5.8 | 3 | 7 | 4 24 | 2.5 | 6.7 | 2 | 5 | 5 8 | 4 | 6 | 19.2 | 4 | 5 52 | .2 | 6 | 1 | 2 | 6 36 | 0 | 5 |
| 48 | 5 | 0 | 2 34 | 5 | 5 | 16.4 | 8 | 3 18 | 3 | 4 | 17.3 | 6 | 4 1 | 1 | 4 | 3 | 14.4 | 4 45 | 0 | 3 | 2 | 2 | 5 28 | 3.8 | 2 | 20.1 | 0 | 6 12 | 4.6 | 2 |
| 49 | 5 | 11.9 | 2 11 | 0 | 2 | 5 | 7 | 2 55 | 0.8 | 1 | 4 | 5 | 3 38 | 1.6 | 0 | 3 | 3 | 4 21 | 2.5 | 6.9 | 3 | 1 | 5 4 | 3 | 7.9 | 21.5 | 9 | 5 47 | 1 | 8.9 |
| 50 | 6 | 7 | 1 49 | 29.5 | 3.8 | 5 | 5 | 2 32 | 3 | 4.7 | 4 | 13.3 | 3 14 | 1 | 5.6 | 4 | 1 | 3 57 | 1.9 | 6 | 3 | 14.9 | 4 39 | 2.7 | 5 | 2 | 7 | 5 22 | 3.5 | 5 |
| 51 | 15.7 | 6 | 1 26 | 0 | 4 | 6 | 12.4 | 2 8 | 29.8 | 3 | 5 | 2 | 2 50 | 0.6 | 3 | 18.4 | 0 | 3 32 | 3 | 2 | 4 | 8 | 4 14 | 1 | 1 | 3 | 6 | 4 56 | 2.9 | 1 |
| 52 | 8 | 5 | 1 22 | 28.4 | 0 | 16.7 | 3 | 1 44 | 2 | 1 ♍ | 17.5 | 1 | 2 25 | 0 | 4.9 | 5 | 13.9 | 3 7 | 0.7 | 5.8 | 19.4 | 7 | 3 48 | 1.5 | 6.7 | 20.3 | 5 | 4 30 | 3 | 7.6 |
| 53 | 8 | 11.4 | 0 38 | 27.8 | 2.6 | 7 | 2 | 1 19 | 28.6 | 5 | 6 | 0 | 2 0 | 29.4 | 4 | 5 | 8 | 2 41 | 1 | 4 | 5 | 6 | 3 22 | 0.9 | 3 | 4 | 15.4 | 4 3 | 1.7 | 2 |
| 54 | 9 | 3 | 0 13 | 2 | 1 | 8 | 1 | 0 54 | 0 | 0 | 7 | 12.9 | 1 34 | 28.8 | 3.9 | 6 | 7 | 2 15 | 29.5 | 4.9 | 5 | 14.4 | 2 55 | 3 | 5.8 | 4 | 2 | 3 35 | 1 | 6.7 |
| 55 | 16.0 | 1 | 29 48 | 26.6 | 1.6 | 9 | 11.9 | 0 28 | 27.4 | 2.5 | 8 | 7 | 1 8 | 1 | 4 | 7 | 5 | 1 48 | 28.9 | 4 | 6 | 2 | 2 27 | 29.7 | 3 | 5 | 0 | 3 7 | 0.4 | 2 |
| 56 | 1 | 0 | 29 22 | 0 | 0 | 17.0 | ♈ 0 | 2 26.7 | 0 | | 9 | 6 | 0 41 | 27.4 | 2.9 | 7 | 3 | 1 20 | 2 | 3.8 | 6 | 0 | 1 59 | 0 | 4.7 | 5 | 14.8 | 2 38 | 29.7 | 5.6 |

Figure 30: Dalton's Tables of Houses

| | UPPER MERIDIAN, CUSP OF 10th H. | | 67 |
|---|---|---|---|

| SID. T. | 23 52 40 } )( 28° | 23 56 20 } )( 29° | 24 0 0 } ♈ 0° |
|---|---|---|---|
| ARC | 358° 9'.9 | 359° 8'.0 | 360° 0'.0 |

| H. | 11 | 12 | 1 | 2 | 3 | 11 | 12 | 1 | 2 | 3 | 11 | 12 | 1 | 2 | 3 |
|---|---|---|---|---|---|---|---|---|---|---|---|---|---|---|---|
| Lat. | ♉ | ♊ | ♋ | ♌ | ♌ | ♉ | ♊ | ♋ | ♌ | ♌ | ♉ | ♊ | ♋ | ♌ | ♌ |
| 22 | 2.0 | 6.1 | 7 29 | 1.5 | 27.6 | 3.0 | 7.0 | 8 19 | 2.3 | 28.5 | 4.0 | 7.9 | 9 8 | 3.2 | 29.4 |
| 23 | 1 | 4 | 7 57 | 8 | 7 | 1 | 3 | 8 46 | 6 | 6 | 1 | 8.2 | 9 35 | 4 | 5 |
| 24 | 2 | 7 | 8 25 | 2.0 | 8 | 2 | 6 | 9 14 | 8 | 7 | 2 | 6 | 10 3 | 7 | 6 |
| 25 | 3 | 7.1 | 8 53 | 3 | 9 | 3 | 8.0 | 9 42 | 3.1 | 8 | 3 | 9 | 10 31 | 9 | 7 |
| 26 | 4 | 4 | 9 22 | 5 | 28.0 | 4 | 3 | 10 10 | 4 | 9 | 4 | 9.2 | 10 59 | 4.2 | 29.8 |
| 27 | 2.5 | 7 | 9 51 | 8 | 1 | 3.5 | 6 | 10 39 | 6 | 29.0 | 4.5 | 6 | 11 27 | 5 | 8 |
| 28 | 6 | 8.1 | 10 20 | 3.1 | 2 | 6 | 9.0 | 11 9 | 9 | 0 | 6 | 9 | 11 56 | 7 | 9 |
| 29 | 7 | 4 | 10 50 | 4 | 3 | 7 | 3 | 11 38 | 4.2 | 1 | 7 | 10.2 | 12 26 | 5.0 | ♍ |
| 30 | 8 | 7 | 11 20 | 7 | 3 | 8 | 7 | 12 8 | 5 | 2 | 8 | 6 | 12 56 | 3 | 0.1 |
| 31 | 9 | 9.1 | 11 51 | 9 | 28.4 | 4.0 | 10.0 | 12 39 | 8 | 29.3 | 9 | 11.0 | 13 26 | 6 | 2 |
| 32 | 3.1 | 5 | 12 23 | 4.2 | 5 | 1 | 4 | 13 10 | 5.0 | 4 | 5.0 | 3 | 13 57 | 8 | 3 |
| 33 | 2 | 9 | 12 55 | 5 | 6 | 2 | 8 | 13 42 | 3 | 5 | 2 | 7 | 14 29 | 6.1 | 4 |
| 34 | 3 | 10.3 | 13 27 | 8 | 7 | 4 | 11.2 | 14 15 | 6 | 6 | 3 | 12.1 | 15 1 | 4 | 5 |
| 35 | 5 | 7 | 14 1 | 5.1 | 9 | 4.5 | 6 | 14 47 | 9 | 29.7 | 4 | 5 | 15 34 | 7 | 0.6 |
| 36 | 3.6 | 11.1 | 14 34 | 5 | 29.0 | 7 | 12.1 | 15 21 | 6.2 | 8 | 5.6 | 13.0 | 16 8 | 7.0 | 7 |
| 37 | 8 | 6 | 15 9 | 8 | 1 | 8 | 5 | 15 55 | 6 | 9 | 7 | 4 | 16 42 | 3 | 8 |
| 38 | 9 | 12.1 | 15 44 | 6.1 | 2 | 5.0 | 13.0 | 16 30 | 9 | ♍ 0.1 | 9 | 9 | 17 16 | 7 | 9 |
| 39 | 4.0 | 5 | 16 20 | 4 | 3 | 1 | 5 | 17 6 | 7.2 | 2 | 6.1 | 14.4 | 17 52 | 8.0 | 1.0 |
| 40 | 1 | 13.0 | 16 57 | 7 | 4 | 2 | 14.0 | 17 43 | 5 | 3 | 3 | 9 | 18 28 | 3 | 1 |
| 41 | 3 | 6 | 17 35 | 7.0 | 29.5 | 4 | 5 | 18 20 | 9 | 4 | 4 | 15.4 | 19 5 | 7 | 2 |
| 42 | 5 | 14.1 | 18 13 | 4 | 7 | 6 | 15.0 | 18 58 | 8.3 | 0.5 | 6 | 9 | 19 43 | 9.0 | 4 |
| 43 | 7 | 7 | 18 53 | 7 | 8 | 8 | 6 | 19 38 | 6 | 6 | 8 | 16.5 | 20 22 | 3 | 5 |
| 44 | 9 | 15.3 | 19 33 | 8.1 | 9 | 6.0 | 16.2 | 20 18 | 9.0 | 8 | 7.0 | 17.1 | 21 1 | 6 | 1.6 |
| 45 | 5.1 | 9 | 20 15 | 5 | ♍ | 2 | 8 | 20 59 | 4 | 9 | 2 | 7 | 21 42 | 10.0 | 7 |
| 46 | 2 | 16.5 | 20 57 | 9 | 0.1 | 4 | 17.4 | 21 41 | 7 | 1.0 | 5 | 18.3 | 22 24 | 4 | 8 |
| 47 | 4 | 17.2 | 21 41 | 9.3 | 2 | 5 | 18.1 | 22 24 | 10.1 | 1 | 7 | 19.0 | 23 7 | 8 | 9 |
| 48 | 6 | 9 | 22 26 | 7 | 4 | 7 | 8 | 23 8 | 5 | 2 | 9 | 7 | 23 51 | 11.2 | 2.1 |
| 49 | 8 | 18.6 | 23 12 | 10.1 | 5 | 9 | 19.5 | 23 54 | 9 | 4 | 8 | 20.4 | 24 36 | 6 | 2 |
| 50 | 6.0 | 19.4 | 24 0 | 5 | 7 | 7.1 | 20.3 | 24 41 | 11.3 | 1.5 | 3 | 21.2 | 25 22 | 12.0 | 3 |
| 51 | 3 | 20.2 | 24 49 | 9 | 9 | 4 | 21.1 | 25 30 | 7 | 7 | 6 | 22.0 | 26 10 | 4 | 4 |
| 52 | 6 | 21.1 | 25 39 | 11.4 | 1.1 | 7 | 22.0 | 26 20 | 12.1 | 9 | 9 | 9 | 26 59 | 8 | 6 |
| 53 | 9 | 22.0 | 26 31 | 9 | 2 | 8.0 | 9 | 27 11 | 6 | 2.0 | 9.2 | 23.8 | 27 50 | 13.3 | 8 |
| 54 | 7.2 | 23.0 | 27 25 | 12.4 | 4 | 3 | 23.9 | 28 4 | 13.1 | 1 | 5 | 24.8 | 28 43 | 8 | 3.0 |
| 55 | 5 | 24.0 | 28 20 | 9 | 5 | 6 | 24.9 | 28 59 | 6 | 3 | 8 | 25.8 | 29 37 | 14.3 | 1 |
| 56 | 8 | 25.1 | 29 18 | 13.4 | 7 | 9 | 26.0 | 29 55 | 14.1 | 5 | 10.1 | 27.0 | ♌ 0 32 | 8 | 3 |

Figure 31: Dalton's Tables of Houses

| Day Mo. | Jan. | Feb. | March | April | May | June | July | Aug. | Sept. | Oct. | Nov. | Dec. |
|---|---|---|---|---|---|---|---|---|---|---|---|---|
| 1 | 1 | 32 | 60 | 91 | 121 | 152 | 182 | 213 | 244 | 274 | 305 | 335 |
| 2 | 2 | 33 | 61 | 92 | 122 | 153 | 183 | 214 | 245 | 275 | 306 | 336 |
| 3 | 3 | 34 | 62 | 93 | 123 | 154 | 184 | 215 | 246 | 276 | 307 | 337 |
| 4 | 4 | 35 | 63 | 94 | 124 | 155 | 185 | 216 | 247 | 277 | 308 | 338 |
| 5 | 5 | 36 | 64 | 95 | 125 | 156 | 186 | 217 | 248 | 278 | 309 | 339 |
| 6 | 6 | 37 | 65 | 96 | 126 | 157 | 187 | 218 | 249 | 279 | 310 | 340 |
| 7 | 7 | 38 | 66 | 97 | 127 | 158 | 188 | 219 | 250 | 280 | 311 | 341 |
| 8 | 8 | 39 | 67 | 98 | 128 | 159 | 189 | 220 | 251 | 281 | 312 | 342 |
| 9 | 9 | 40 | 68 | 99 | 129 | 160 | 190 | 221 | 252 | 282 | 313 | 343 |
| 10 | 10 | 41 | 69 | 100 | 130 | 161 | 191 | 222 | 253 | 283 | 314 | 344 |
| 11 | 11 | 42 | 70 | 101 | 131 | 162 | 192 | 223 | 254 | 284 | 315 | 345 |
| 12 | 12 | 43 | 71 | 102 | 132 | 163 | 193 | 224 | 255 | 285 | 316 | 346 |
| 13 | 13 | 44 | 72 | 103 | 133 | 164 | 194 | 225 | 256 | 286 | 317 | 347 |
| 14 | 14 | 45 | 73 | 104 | 134 | 165 | 195 | 226 | 257 | 287 | 318 | 348 |
| 15 | 15 | 46 | 74 | 105 | 135 | 166 | 196 | 227 | 258 | 288 | 319 | 349 |
| 16 | 16 | 47 | 75 | 106 | 136 | 167 | 197 | 228 | 259 | 289 | 320 | 350 |
| 17 | 17 | 48 | 76 | 107 | 137 | 168 | 198 | 229 | 260 | 290 | 321 | 351 |
| 18 | 18 | 49 | 77 | 108 | 138 | 169 | 199 | 230 | 261 | 291 | 322 | 352 |
| 19 | 19 | 50 | 78 | 109 | 139 | 170 | 200 | 231 | 262 | 292 | 323 | 353 |
| 20 | 20 | 51 | 79 | 110 | 140 | 171 | 201 | 232 | 263 | 293 | 324 | 354 |
| 21 | 21 | 52 | 80 | 111 | 141 | 172 | 202 | 233 | 264 | 294 | 325 | 355 |
| 22 | 22 | 53 | 81 | 112 | 142 | 173 | 203 | 234 | 265 | 295 | 326 | 356 |
| 23 | 23 | 54 | 82 | 113 | 143 | 174 | 204 | 235 | 266 | 296 | 327 | 357 |
| 24 | 24 | 55 | 83 | 114 | 144 | 175 | 205 | 236 | 267 | 297 | 328 | 358 |
| 25 | 25 | 56 | 84 | 115 | 145 | 176 | 206 | 237 | 268 | 298 | 329 | 359 |
| 26 | 26 | 57 | 85 | 116 | 146 | 177 | 207 | 238 | 269 | 299 | 330 | 360 |
| 27 | 27 | 58 | 86 | 117 | 147 | 178 | 208 | 239 | 270 | 300 | 331 | 361 |
| 28 | 28 | 59 | 87 | 118 | 148 | 179 | 209 | 240 | 271 | 301 | 332 | 362 |
| 29 | 29 |  | 88 | 119 | 149 | 180 | 210 | 241 | 272 | 302 | 333 | 363 |
| 30 | 30 |  | 89 | 120 | 150 | 181 | 211 | 242 | 273 | 303 | 334 | 364 |
| 31 | 31 |  | 90 |  | 151 |  | 212 | 243 |  | 304 |  | 365 |

**Table 16: Days Between
Two Dates**

| Day Mo. | Jan. | Feb. | March | April | May | June | July | Aug. | Sept. | Oct. | Nov. | Dec. |
|---|---|---|---|---|---|---|---|---|---|---|---|---|
| 1 | 366 | 397 | 425 | 456 | 486 | 517 | 547 | 578 | 609 | 639 | 670 | 700 |
| 2 | 367 | 398 | 426 | 457 | 487 | 518 | 548 | 579 | 610 | 640 | 671 | 701 |
| 3 | 368 | 399 | 427 | 458 | 488 | 519 | 549 | 580 | 611 | 641 | 672 | 702 |
| 4 | 369 | 400 | 428 | 459 | 489 | 520 | 550 | 581 | 612 | 642 | 673 | 703 |
| 5 | 370 | 401 | 429 | 460 | 490 | 521 | 551 | 582 | 613 | 643 | 674 | 704 |
| 6 | 371 | 402 | 430 | 461 | 491 | 522 | 552 | 583 | 614 | 644 | 675 | 705 |
| 7 | 372 | 403 | 431 | 462 | 492 | 523 | 553 | 584 | 615 | 645 | 676 | 706 |
| 8 | 373 | 404 | 432 | 463 | 493 | 524 | 554 | 585 | 616 | 646 | 677 | 707 |
| 9 | 374 | 405 | 433 | 464 | 494 | 525 | 555 | 586 | 617 | 647 | 678 | 708 |
| 10 | 375 | 406 | 434 | 465 | 495 | 526 | 556 | 587 | 618 | 648 | 679 | 709 |
| 11 | 376 | 407 | 435 | 466 | 496 | 527 | 557 | 588 | 619 | 649 | 680 | 710 |
| 12 | 377 | 408 | 436 | 467 | 497 | 528 | 558 | 589 | 620 | 650 | 681 | 711 |
| 13 | 378 | 409 | 437 | 468 | 498 | 529 | 559 | 590 | 621 | 651 | 682 | 712 |
| 14 | 379 | 410 | 438 | 469 | 499 | 530 | 560 | 591 | 622 | 652 | 683 | 713 |
| 15 | 380 | 411 | 439 | 470 | 500 | 531 | 561 | 592 | 623 | 653 | 684 | 714 |
| 16 | 381 | 412 | 440 | 471 | 501 | 532 | 562 | 593 | 624 | 654 | 685 | 715 |
| 17 | 382 | 413 | 441 | 472 | 502 | 533 | 563 | 594 | 625 | 655 | 686 | 716 |
| 18 | 383 | 414 | 442 | 473 | 503 | 534 | 564 | 595 | 626 | 656 | 687 | 717 |
| 19 | 384 | 415 | 443 | 474 | 504 | 535 | 565 | 596 | 627 | 657 | 688 | 718 |
| 20 | 385 | 416 | 444 | 475 | 505 | 536 | 566 | 597 | 628 | 658 | 689 | 719 |
| 21 | 386 | 417 | 445 | 476 | 506 | 537 | 567 | 598 | 629 | 659 | 690 | 720 |
| 22 | 387 | 418 | 446 | 477 | 507 | 538 | 568 | 599 | 630 | 660 | 691 | 721 |
| 23 | 388 | 419 | 447 | 478 | 508 | 539 | 569 | 600 | 631 | 661 | 692 | 722 |
| 24 | 389 | 420 | 448 | 479 | 509 | 540 | 570 | 601 | 632 | 662 | 693 | 723 |
| 25 | 390 | 421 | 449 | 480 | 510 | 541 | 571 | 602 | 633 | 663 | 694 | 724 |
| 26 | 391 | 422 | 450 | 481 | 511 | 542 | 572 | 603 | 634 | 664 | 695 | 725 |
| 27 | 392 | 423 | 451 | 482 | 512 | 543 | 573 | 604 | 635 | 665 | 696 | 726 |
| 28 | 393 | 424 | 452 | 483 | 513 | 544 | 574 | 605 | 636 | 666 | 697 | 727 |
| 29 | 394 | | 453 | 484 | 514 | 545 | 575 | 606 | 637 | 667 | 698 | 728 |
| 30 | 395 | | 454 | 485 | 515 | 546 | 576 | 607 | 638 | 668 | 699 | 729 |
| 31 | 396 | | 455 | | 516 | | 577 | 608 | | 669 | | 730 |

1976   (year for which chart is desired)
-1936   (birth year)
   40

January 22, 1936   (birth date)
+           40
March   4, 1936   (progressed birth date for 1976)

**Example 2. Person born March 30, 1947, 9:38 am, Red Wing, MN.**
If a progressed chart is to be erected for the year 1976, the birth year is
subtracted from 1976 giving the remainder of 29. This is equivalent to
29 days after birth. Twenty-nine is then added to the birth date, March
30, giving us the progressed birth date of April 28, 1947. Thus, a chart
erected for 9:38 am, April 28, 1947, corrected for the longitude and
latitude of Red Wing, MN., will represent the year March 30, 1976 to
March 30, 1977.

1976   (year for which chart is desired)
-1947   (birth year)
   40

March 30, 1947   (birth date)
+         29
April 28, 1947   (progressed birth date for 1976)

### Table of Days Between Two Dates
The table on pages 416-17 is very handy for finding the date representing the progressed year. For example, in Chart 1, January 22 is
day number 22. Adding 42 we get day number 64 minus one for leap
year, is day number 63 or March 4. In Chart 2, March 30 is day number
89. Adding 29 we get day number 118, or April 28.

## CALCULATING THE PROGRESSED HOROSCOPE

After finding the progressed birth date, we proceed with the calculations
just as for any other horoscope. We will review here the George Method
of Horoscope Calculation. For more details see the section with that

title beginning on page 75.

## 1. Change Standard Time to Mean Local Time

It will be remembered that in order to obtain the mean local time of birth we must add four minutes for every degree of longitude the birth is east of the center of a zone and subtract four minutes for every degree of longitude the birth is west of the center of a time zone. The time zones are given in *Time Zone Divisions*, page 70.

**Example 1. Person born January 22, 1936, 10:20 pm, Sillersville, PA**—progressed birth date March 4, 1936. We have already found that the birthplace, with a longitude of 75° 24; is 24' west of the center of the Eastern Standard Time Zone, necessitating a correction of 01m 36s which is subtracted from the birth time.

```
10h 20m 00s =  10h 19m 60s  (standard time of birth)
              -00  01  36   (correction)
               10h 18m 24s  (mean local time of birth)
```

**Example 2. Person born March 30, 1947, 9:38 am, Red Wing, MN.** —progressed birth date April 28, 1947. We have already found that the birth place, with a longitude of 92° 31', is 02° 31' west of the center of the Central Standard Time Zone, necessitating a correction of 10m 04s, which is subtracted from the birth time.

```
09h 38m 00s =  09h 37m 60s  (standard time of birth)
              -00  10  04   (correction)
               09h 27m 56s  (mean local time of birth)
```

## 2. Correct for Daylight Savings Time or War Time

Since neither Daylight Savings Time nor War Time was in effect *at the time of birth* no correction is necessary.

## 3. Convert to Sidereal Time at Birth

It will be remembered that in order to obtain the Sidereal Time at birth we must add the time of birth to the ST given in the ephemeris for noon of the birth date for afternoon births and subtract the interval between the birth and noon for morning births. (See note on page 68 for using a midnight ephemeris.)

**Example 1. Person born January 22, 1936, 10:20 PM, Sillersville, PA**—progressed birthdate March 4, 1936. The mean local time (10h 18m 24s) is added to the ST at noon March 4, 1936 (22h 48m 16s). See Figure 19. Twenty-four is subtracted from the remainder because it is larger than 24.

> 22h 48m 16s  (ST at noon)
> +10  18   24   (mean local time at birth)
>  32h 66m 40s = 33h 06m 40s

> 33h 06m 40s
> -24
>  09h 63m 40s  (ST at birth)

**Example 2. Person born March 30, 1947, 9:38 AM, Red Wing, MN.**—progressed birth date April 28, 1947. The mean local time of birth (09h 27m 56s) is 02h 32m 04s before noon, so this interval must be subtracted from the ST at noon April 28, 1947 (02h 22m 27s). See Figure 29. Twenty-four is added to the ST to enable the subtraction.

> 26h 22m 27s =  25h 82m 27s  (ST at noon)
>                -02  32   04   (interval between birth and noon)
>                 23h 50m 23s  (ST at birth)

## 4. Correct for Longitude and Acceleration

To correct for acceleration ten seconds must be added to the ST at birth for every hour it occurs after noon or subtracted from it for every hour it occurs before noon. To correct for longitude subtract ten seconds for every hour of time difference between GMT and the mean local time for births east of Greenwich, add this correction for births west of Greenwich.

**Example 1. Person born January 22, 1936, 10:20 PM, Sillersville, PA**—progressed birthdate March 4, 1936. A correction for acceleration of 01m 43s is added to the ST at birth along with a longitudinal correction of 50s.

09h 06m 40s  (ST at birth)
<u>+    01   43   </u>(acceleration)
09h 07m 83s = 09h 08m 23s (corrected ST at birth)

09h 08m 23s
<u>+         50   </u>(longitudinal correction)
09h 08m 73s = 09h 09m 13s (corrected ST at birth)

**Example 2. Person born March 30, 1947, 9:38 AM, Red Wing, MN.–progressed birth date April 28, 1947.** A correction for acceleration of 25s for the interval between birth and noon of 02h 32m 04s is subtracted from the ST at birth and a longitudinal correction of 01m 01s is added.

23h 50m 23s =  23h 49m 83s  (ST at birth)
<u>-          25s  </u>(acceleration)
23h 49m 58s  (corrected ST at birth)

23h 49m 58s
<u>+   01   01   </u>(longitudinal correction)
23h 50m 59s  (corrected ST at birth)

## 5. Find the Ascendant, Midheaven and House Cusps

Using the Tables of Houses as described in *How to Use the Tables of Houses*, page 84, we now look up the corrected ST at birth and enter the house cusps in a blank chart form. Remember to watch for intercepted houses.

**Example 1. Person born January 22, 1936, 10:20 pm, Sillersville, PA.–progressed birthdate March 4, 1936.** Looking up the ST of 09h 09m 13s (the nearest ST is 09h 09m 52s , see Figure 30) for the latitude of 40° we find:

Ascendant–7°♏40'                     Seventh House–7° ♉ 40'
Second House–6.6° ♐ =            Eighth House–6° ♊ 36'
                 6° ♐ 36'              Ninth House–9°♋ 36'
Third House–9.6°♑ =               Fourth House–15°♒
                 9°♑ 36'              Fifth House–17° ♓ 54'
Midheaven–15°♌                    Sixth House–15° ♈ 18'
Eleventh House–17.9°♍ =        Twelfth House–15.3° ♎ =
                 17°♍ 54                        15°♎ 18'

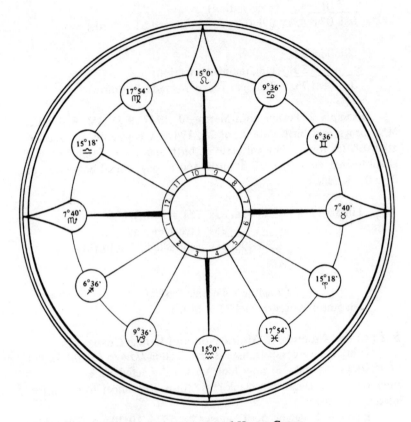

Figure 32: Progressed House Cusps.
Example 1

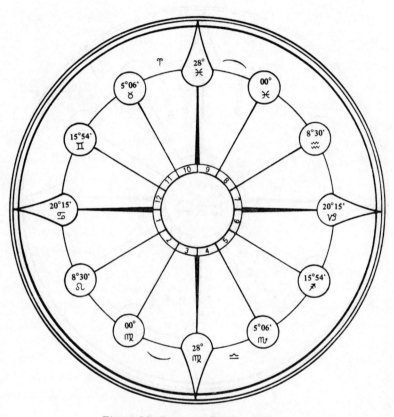

Figure 33: Progressed House Cusps.
Example 2

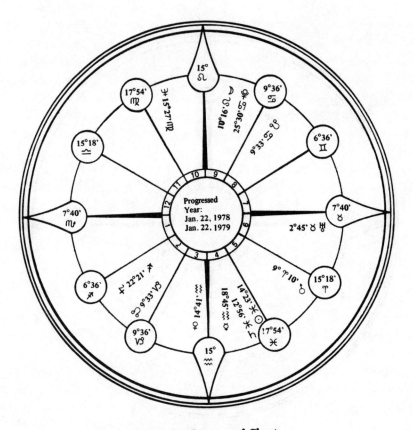

**Figure 34: Progressed Chart.**
**Example 1**

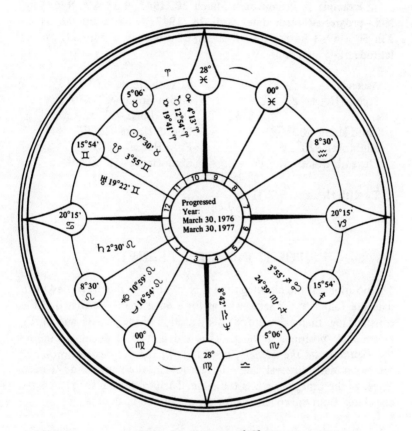

Figure 35: Progressed Chart.
Example 2

Example 2. Person born March 30, 1947, 9:38 AM, Red Wing, MN.–progressed birth date April 28, 1947. Looking up the ST of 23h 50m 59s (the nearest ST is 23h 52m 40s, see Figure 32) for the latitude of 45° we find:

Ascendant–20° ♋ 15             Seventh House–20° ♑ 15'
Second House–8.5° ♌ =           Eighth House–8° ♒ 30'
            8° ♌ 30'             Ninth House–00° ♓
Third House–00° ♍               Fourth House–28° ♍
Midheaven ·28° ♓                Fifth House–5° ♏ 06'
Eleventh House–5.1° ♉ =         Sixth House–15° ♐ 54'
            5° ♉ 06'
Twelfth House–15.9° ♊ =
            15° ♊ 54'

## POSITIONING THE PLANETS

The positions of the planets at the time of birth on the progressed birth date are found in the same way as for a natal chart. We first find the constant log, then calculate the daily motion of the planets and finally figure their positions at birth. This is described in detail in *Finding the Positions of the Planets*, page 101. In the progressed horoscope the Noon Mark, interval and constant log are the same as in the natal chart, as the time of birth is the same. The positions of the planets are calculated from the ephemeris for the progressed birth date.

Example 1. Person born January 22, 1936, 10:20 pm, Sillersville, PA.–progressed birth date March 4, 1936. The Noon Mark has been found to be 06h 58m 24s, the interval 08h 40m 00s, and the constant log to be 4424. See pages 102-105.

The planets' position on March 4, 1936 are subtracted from their positions on March 5, 1936, giving us their daily motion. The log of the daily motion is added to the constant log and since the birth occurred before the Noon Mark mean local time, the anti-log of the result is then subtracted from the planets' positions on March 5.

The Sun:   14°♓45'  (March 5)
         –13 ♓ 45  (March 4)
         01°   00'  (daily motion)

         1.3802      (log of daily motion)
        + 4424      (constant log)
         1.8826      (result)

        14°♓45'  (March 5)
       –      22  (anti-log of result)
       14° ♓ 23'  (position at time of birth)

Moon:      14°♌41'  (March 5)
         –02 ♌ 24  (March 4)
         12°   15'  (daily motion)

         .2900      (log of daily motion)
       + 4424      (constant log)
         .7333      (result)

        14°♌41'  (March 5)
      – 4     25  (anti-log of result)
      10°♌16'  (position at time of birth)

Mercury:  19°♒13'  (March 5)
        –17 ♒ 56  (March 4)
        01°   17'  (daily motion)

        1.2719      (log of daily motion)
       + 4424      (constant log)
        1.7143      (result)

      19°♒13'  (March 5)
     –      28  (anti-log of result)
     18°♒45'  (position at time of birth)

Venus:      15°♒07'  (March 5)
            -13 ♒54   (March 4)
            01°    13'  (daily motion)

            1.2950     (log of daily motion)
            + 4424     (constant log)
            1.7374     (result)

            15°♒07'  (March 5)
            -       05   (anti-log of result)
            14°    41'  (position at time of birth)

Mars:       09° ♈ 26'  (March 5)
            -08 ♈ 41   (March 4)
            00°    45'  (daily motion)

            1.5051     (log of daily motion)
            + 4424     (constant log)
            1.9475     (result)

            09° ♈ 26'  (March 5)
            -       16   (anti-log of result)
            09° ♈ 10'  (position at time of birth

**Example 2. Person born March 30, 1947, 9:38 am, Red Wing, MN. —progressed birthdate April 28, 1947.** The Noon Mark has been found to be 05h 49m 56s, the interval 03h 38m 00s, and the constant log to be 8199. See pages 105-107.

The planets' positions on April 28, 1947 are subtracted from their positions on April 29, 1947, giving us their daily motion. The log of the daily motion is added to the constant log and since the birth occurred after the Noon Mark local time, the anti-log of the result is then added to the planets' positions on April 28.

The Sun:   08° ♉ 19' 55"  (April 29)
           -07 ♉ 21 38    (April 28)
           00°    58' 17"  (daily motion)

1.3949     (log of daily motion)  
+ 8199     (constant log)  
2.2148  

07° ♉ 21' 38"  (April 28)  
+ 0    09 00   (anti-log of result)  
07° ♉ 30' 38"  (position at time of birth)  

Moon:   28°♌ 42'  (April 29)  
        -14    48   (April 28)  
        13°    54'  (daily motion)  

   .2372     (log of daily motion)  
+ 8199     (constant log)  
1.0571  

14°♌ 48'  (April 28)  
+02    06  (anti-log of result)  
16°♌ 54'  (position at time of birth)  

Mercury:  21° ♈ 11'  (April 29)  
         -19    25   (April 28)  
         01°    46'  (daily motion)  

1.1331     (log of daily motion)  
+ 8199     (constant log)  
1.9530  

19°♈ 25'  (April 28)  
+     16  (anti-log of result)  
19° ♈ 41'  (position at time of birth)  

Venus:   05° ♈ 14'  (April 29)  
        -04 ♈ 02  (April 28)  
        01°    12'  (daily motion)

$$
\begin{array}{ll}
1.3010 & \text{(log of daily motion)} \\
+\ 8199 & \text{(constant log)} \\
\hline
2.1209 & \text{(result)}
\end{array}
$$

$$
\begin{array}{ll}
04°\ \Upsilon\ 02' & \text{(April 28)} \\
+\qquad 11 & \text{(anti-log of result)} \\
\hline
04°\ \Upsilon\ 13' & \text{(position at time of birth)}
\end{array}
$$

Mars:
$$
\begin{array}{ll}
13°\ \Upsilon\ 33' & \text{(April 29)} \\
-12\ \ \Upsilon\ 47 & \text{(April 28)} \\
\hline
00°\ \Upsilon\ 46' & \text{(daily motion)}
\end{array}
$$

$$
\begin{array}{ll}
1.4956 & \text{(log of daily motion)} \\
+\ 8199 & \text{(constant log)} \\
\hline
2.3155 & \text{(result)}
\end{array}
$$

$$
\begin{array}{ll}
12°\ \Upsilon\ 47' & \text{(April 28)} \\
+\qquad 07 & \text{(anti-log of result)} \\
\hline
12°\ \Upsilon\ 54' & \text{(position at time of birth)}
\end{array}
$$

## Entering the Planets in the Chart

Only the Sun, Moon, Mercury, Venus and Mars move fast enough to make figuring their precise positions practical. The noon positions of the other planets are copied from the ephemeris onto the chart blank. The Pluto position nearest the progressed birth date is used. All the planets are drawn in the progressed chart exactly the same as in the natal chart as shown in Figures 34 and 35, examples of the progressed chart.

## The Moon's Nodes

The motion of the Moon's Nodes is retrograde at the rate of about three minutes of longitude per day. The Nodes are of some value in Natal Astrology and are useful in the horary branch. They can be copied from the ephemeris and entered in the chart. See: *The Moon's Nodes*, page 383.

## The Part of Fortune

For the rule of calculating the Part of Fortune, see: *The Part of Fortune*, page 381. As shown in the method of computing its place, its position depends partly on the location of the Moon and, as the Moon in the progressed chart is constantly moving forward and travels about thirteen degrees during the year, it follows that the place of the Part of Fortune in the progressed chart would likewise be constantly changing. Due to this there is likelihood of error in placing it, so it may be omitted, if preferred. In fact, like the Moon's Nodes, many astrologers do not use it at all, except in Horary Astrology. We mention these points in order to aid those who desire to make practical research into the matter. In Llewellyn George's own experience he found these factors important and deserving of serious attention.

## The Declination of the Sun and Moon

As in the natal chart, the declinations of the Sun and Moon must be interpolated to the exact birth time. This is done in the same manner as finding the birth time positions of the faster moving planets and is described in detail in *The Declinations of the Sun and Moon*, page 128. The daily motion is found, its log is added to the constant log and the product added (if declination is increasing) or subtracted (if declination is decreasing) to the progressed birth date declination.

**Example 1. Person born January 22, 1936, 10:20 pm, Sillersville, PA.—progressed birthdate, March 4, 1936.** The daily motion of the declination of the Moon is found; its log is added to the constant log, and the product is subtracted from the progressed birth date declination because it is decreasing. The Sun's declination is given every other day, so its motion for two days is found. Half of this is the daily motion. The log of the daily motion is added to the constant log and their product subtracted from the progressed birth date declination.

```
17° N 49'  (declination of Moon, March 4)
-13    44  (declination of Moon, March 5)
04°    05' (daily motion)


  7692   (log of daily motion)
+ 4424   (constant log)
1.2116
```

17° N 49'    (declination of Moon, March 4)
- 1      28    (anti-log of 1.2116)
16° N 21'    (declination at birth time)


6° S 23'    (declination of Sun, March 4)
- 5      37    (declination of Sun, March 6)
0     46'    (motion for two days)

½ of 46' = 23' (daily motion)

1.7966  (log of daily motion)
+   4424   (constant log)
2.2390


6° S 23'    (declination of Sun, March 4)
-          09    (anti-log of 2.2390)
6° S 14'    (declination at birth time)

**Example 2. Person born March 30, 1947, 9:38 am, Red Wing, MN. --progressed birthdate, April 28, 1947.** The daily motion of the declination of the Moon is found; its log is added to the constant log, and the product is subtracted from the progressed birthdate declination because it is decreasing. The Sun's declination is given every other day, so its motion for two days is found. Half of this is the daily motion which can be added to the April 27 declination to get the declination for noon on April 28 (the progressed birthdate). The log of the daily motion is added to the constant log and the anti-log of the product is added to the progressed birthdate declination, because the declination is increasing.

21° N 09'    (declination of Moon, April 28)
-16      49    (declination of Moon, April 29)
04°      20    (daily motion)

7434  (log of daily motion)
+   8199   (constant log)
1.5633

21° N 09'   (declination of Moon, April 28)
-       39   (anti-log of 1.5633)
20° N 30'   (declination at birth time)


14° N 18'   (declination of Sun, April 29)
-13    39   (declination of Sun, April 27)
00    39'   (motion for two days)

½ of 39' = 19' (daily motion)


13° N 39'   (declination of Sun, April 27)
+      19   (daily motion)
13° N 58'   (declination of Sun, April 28)


1.8796   (log of daily motion)
+  8199  (constant log)
2.6995


13° N 58'   (declination of Sun, April 27)
+      03   (anti-log of 2.6995)
14° N 01'   (declination at birth time)

# The Progressed Aspects

When interpreting the progressed horoscope there are six basic considerations:

*1. Aspects between the Progressed Moon and both radical and progressed planets and cusps, which will be discussed separately in this lesson (Lunar Progressed Aspects).*

*2. Directions from progressed planets or cusps to progressed planets or cusps (Progressed Mutual Aspects).*

*3. Directions from progressed planets or cusps to radical planets or cusps (Progressed Aspects to Radix).*

*4. Parallel Aspects, covered in Lesson Four.*

*5. Transits over progressed aspects to radix, covered in Lesson Five.*

*6. Transits over progressed mutual aspects, also covered in Lesson Five.*

Unless systematic tabulation of aspects is made some important aspect may be overlooked, so the student is advised to lay out six columns for the six above-mentioned categories and figure the aspects in groups.

A very good plan is to make a chart of the progressed horoscope, then to take the progressed planets one by one and enter them into the birth chart, with colored ink for distinction and note it from their progressed places in the Zodiac they form any aspect to the planets as they were at birth, allowing 2° orb to make an aspect. Only the aspects which are forming are to be tabulated for delineation.

## THE PROGRESSED MOON

The motion of the Moon is approximately 13° per day (per year by progression), consequently it will require about 2½ years to progress through a sign of the Zodiac. Thus in approximately twenty-eight years it will progress completely around the circle and return to the place it originally held at birth.

The Moon's aspects formed as it progresses from house to house through both the natal and progressed charts is very important and indicates most of the conditions and events encountered in life. This will be appreciated by noting its various influences as indicated by the houses it traverses, all of which are accentuated in accordance with the aspects which the Moon may form. In fact, in the course of its apparent twenty-eight year circle of the signs and houses, it will form every possible aspect in the natal chart and practically every possible aspect in the progressed chart. One of the main features connected with progressed horoscope work is to record the monthly place of the progressing Moon and tabulate the month and year of the various aspects which it will meet.

### Calculating the Motion of the Progressed Moon

To find the motion of the Moon on the progressed birth date count the number of degrees and minutes of longitude it will travel between its given place on the progressed birth day and its given place on the next day. Then change this amount of the Moon's motion from degrees and minutes to all minutes by multiplying the degrees by 60 and adding the minutes to this product. Then divide the total by 12 to determine the rate the Moon will move forward in the Zodiac through the chart in each of the twelve months during the progressed year. By adding this amount of the Moon's monthly motion twelve times to the place of the Moon at the birth hour on the progressed birth date, it will show in what degrees the Moon will be each month during the coming twelve months.

The average motion of the Moon is about 13° (varying from 12° to 15°) which is equal to 1° 05' of longitude per month by progression. The Moon's motion is calculated using the progressed birth date (noon positions in the ephemeris are adequate). Use the following steps.

**Example 1. Person born January 22, 1936, 10:20 pm, Sillersville, PA—progressed birth date March 4, 1936.** The Moon's position on the progressed birth date at noon (2° 24') is subtracted from its position on the next day (14° 41') to find its daily motion; see Figure 26. This motion is converted to all minutes by multiplying the degrees by 60 and adding the minutes to the product. The result of 737' represents the Moon's progressed motion during the year January 22, 1978 to January 22, 1979. This is then divided by 12 to get the progressed motion during any one month.

14° ♌41'   (position day after progressed birth date)
- 2 ♌24   (position progressed birth date)
12°   17'   (daily motion)

12° 17' = 737' (number of minutes in daily motion)

737 ÷ 12 = 61' 5/12" = 1° 01' 25" (progressed daily motion)

**Example 2. Person born March 30, 1947, 9:38 am, Red Wing, MN. —progressed birthdate April 28, 1947.** The Moon's position on the progressed birth date at noon (14° 48') is subtracted from its position on the next day (28° 42') to find its daily motion.see Figure 28. This motion is converted to all minutes by multiplying the degrees by 60 and adding the minutes to the product. The result of 834 represents the Moon's progressed motion during the year March 30, 1976 to March 30, 1977. This is then divided by 12 to get the progressed motion during any one month.

28° ♌42'   (position day after progressed birth date)
-14 ♌48   (position progressed birth date)
13°   54'   (daily motion)

13° 54' = 834' (number of minutes in daily motion)

834' ÷ 12 = 69' 6/12 = 1° 09' 30" (progressed monthly motion)

Add the monthly motion twelve times to the Moon's place on the progressed birthdate at the birth hour.

Example 1. Person born January 22, 1936, 10:20 pm, Sillersville, PA.–progressed birthdate March 4, 1936.

Position of Moon by progression, January 22, 1978
(actual position, March 4, 1936, birth):          10° ♌ 15' 00"
                                                  + 1      01 25
February 22, 1978:    11° ♌ 16' 25"
                    + 1      01 25
March 22, 1978:    12° ♌ 17' 50"
                 + 1      01 25
April 22, 1978:    13°  ♌ 19' 15"
               + 1      01 25
May 22, 1978:    14° ♌ 20' 40"
             + 1      01 25
June 22, 1978:    15° ♌ 22' 05"
              + 1      01 25
July 22, 1978:    16° ♌ 23' 30"
              + 1      01 25
August 22, 1978:    17° ♌ 24' 55"
                + 1      01 25
September 22, 1978:    18° ♌ 26' 20"
                   + 1      01 25
October 22, 1978:    19° ♌ 27' 45"
                 + 1      01 25
November 22, 1978:    20°  ♌ 29' 10"
                  + 1      01 25
December 22, 1978:    21° ♌ 30' 35"
                  + 1      01 25
January 22, 1979:    22° ♌ 32' 00"

Example 2. Person born March 30, 1947, 9:38 am, Red Wing, MN. –progressed birthdate April 28, 1947.

Position of Moon by progression, March 30, 1976
(actual position, April 28, 1947, birth hour):   16° ♌ 54' 00"
                                              + 1    09 30
April 30, 1976:   18° ♌ 03' 30"
                                              + 1    09 30
May 30, 1976:   19° ♌ 13' 00"
                                              + 1    09 30
June 30, 1976:   20° ♌ 22' 30"
                                              + 1    09 30
July 30, 1976:   21° ♌ 32' 00"
                                              + 1    09 30
August 30, 1976:   22° ♌ 41' 30"
                                              + 1    09 30
September 30, 1976:   23° ♌ 52' 00"
                                              + 1    09 30
October 30, 1976:   25° ♌ 01' 30"
                                              + 1    09 30
November 30, 1976:   26° ♌ 11' 00"
                                              + 1    09 30
December 30, 1976:   27° ♌ 20' 30"
                                              + 1    09 30
January 30, 1977:   28° ♌ 30' 00"
                                              + 1    09 30
February 28, 1977:   29° ♌ 39' 30"
                                              + 1    09 30
March 30, 1977:   00° ♍ 49' 00"

## Lunar Progressed Aspects

After compiling a table of the Moon's position each month throughout the progressed year, you are ready to record the aspects made by the Moon in its monthly motion.

These are termed *lunar aspects* and are very important. By working in the foregoing manner, you may readily see in which month during the year an aspect will become complete and thus prepare to improve or offset its effects according to its nature, whether good or adverse.

Remember that an aspect by this progressive direction has an orb of only 2° for the major aspects and an orb of 1° for the minor aspects. All aspects whether major or minor should be recorded but their influ-

ence is to be judged relative to their power and their indications in the
radix. For instance, if the progressed Moon formed an adverse aspect
with Venus, do not predict something adverse unless they were in
adverse aspect at birth, although it would not be a good month to press
matters relating to courtship and marriage or other things governed by
Venus.

The other planets move so slowly by direction that it is not necessary to find their monthly motion, as with the Moon.

The lunar progressed aspects require the closest attention because
they refer to whatever the Moon signifies by the house it then occupies
and the house it rules in the progressed chart, as well as the house it
occupied and ruled in radix, in addition to the house it may be working
through in the radix when placed in it from the progressed chart.

Enter these aspects under column 1. *Lunar Progressed Aspects.*

## Calculating the Time a Lunar Progressed Aspect Becomes Partile

In connection with aspects between the progressed Moon and
natal planets, the following example illustrates a method of calculating
the date and time when the influence reaches its maximum or peak, or
in other words, the date and time the aspect becomes partile.

**Note.** The resultant time of day derived through the use of the
following methods must be approximate and not exact, due to various
technical factors involving slight irregularity in motion of the planets,
etc., which for the sake of simplicity are omitted. However, the
variation is slight and so will rarely cause your answer to vary more
than a few minutes in time and therefore for practical purposes may be
considered correct.

**Example. Person born October 11, 1937, 4:00 AM, Los Angeles,
California.**

*Progressed birth date:* November 10, 1937, representing the
native's thirtieth year, October 11, 1967 to October 11, 1968.

*Question:* When will the progressed Moon reach an exact trine to
the natal Sun?

*Datum:*

Progressed Moon (November 10, 1937, 4:00 AM) 7°≈27' 16".
Natal Sun (October 11, 1937, 4:00 AM) 17°≏45' 09".

Progressed lunar motion–12° 24' 40" per day, representing one year.

# 1. Calculate the Distance the Planet must Travel to Partile

The progressed Moon will be in exact trine to the natal Sun when it reaches 17° ≈ 45'09". A distance of 10° 17' 53".

    17° 45' 09"  (position of exact aspect)
    <u>- 7  27  16   </u>  (position on progressed birth date)
    10° 17' 53"  (distance needed to travel)

# 2. Calculate the Time Needed to Cover that Distance

Since the position of the natal Sun is fixed, we need only calculate the time needed for the Moon to move the needed, distance. This is done by using logarithms to find out what portion of the Moon's daily motion is needed to bring it to the proper place.

    .3674  (log of distance 10° 17' 53")
    <u>-.2862</u>  (log of daily motion 12° 24' 40")
    .0812  (log of proportional distance)

.0812 = 19h 55m (time needed to cover the distance)

# 3. Calculate the Equivalent Time in the Current Calendar

The Moon must travel 19h 55m after the progressed birth date (November 10, 1937, 4:00 AM) for the aspect to become exact. This must be translated into time in the current calendar–the amount of time past the current birth date (October 11, 1967, 4:00 am)–with the aid of the following table.

| | | |
|---|---|---|
| 24 hours, 1 day | = | 1 year by progression |
| 2 hours motion | = | 1 month by progression (30 days) |
| 1 hour motion | = | ½ month by progression (15 days) |
| 4 minutes motion | = | 1 day by progression (24 hours) |
| 1 minute motion | = | 6 hours by progression (¼ day) |
| 10 seconds motion | = | 1 hour by progression |
| 1 second motion | = | 6 minutes by progression |

Table 17: Time Key

19 hours = 9½ months by progression (9 months 15 days)
55 minutes = 13¾ days by progression (13 days 18 hours)
October 11, 1967, 4:00 AM + 9 months 28 days 18 hours =
August 8, 1968, 10:00 PM.

The progressed Moon will form an exact trine to the natal Sun on August 8, 1968, at 10:00 PM.


# PROGRESSED ASPECTS

## Progressed Mutual Aspects

Upon completion of the progressed chart, the aspects are calcu-lated and tabulated exactly as in the natal chart as explained in *Finding the Aspects*, page 123. These are entered under column 2.*Progressed Mutual Aspects*.


## Progressed Aspects to Radix

After all the aspects have been noted between the planets in the progressed chart, insert the progressed planets in the birth chart with colored ink or pencil for distinction and note if they form any aspect with the radical planets (their place at birth). Pay particular attention to the aspects which may be formed by the Moon and Sun. *Solar aspects are very important.*

*It makes no difference in the nature of an aspect whether it is found in the radix or in the progressed chart; the square will always be adverse, the sextile always good, etc.*

A progressed or directional aspect is technically due to operate when the aspect is exactly complete, but the transit of a planet over the place of a directional aspect which is still forming (within a degree or so) may excite it into action prematurely, as it were. Enter these aspects in column 3.*Progressed Aspects to Radix*.


## Aspects to House Cusps

The aspects formed by any of the planets to the degree consti-tuting the cusp of a house are important, provided the exact time of birth was used, in which case the degrees on the house cusps would be correct. If only an approximate birth time was used, the degrees on house cusps would be only approximately correct and consequently it would be uncertain when a planet would reach conjunction with the actual degree ruling the cusp.

Jupiter or Venus conjunct, trine or sextile to the Midheaven (sign and degree of the Tenth House cusp) is a very fortunate indication for business affairs, honors, etc.; but the amount of good they will bring depends upon their power for good in the radix. If either planet is heavily afflicted in the radix, is cadent and in debility, its power for good by direction is correspondingly weakened.

The influence of minor aspects to house cusps are hard to detect. Of the major aspects the conjunction is most important. As the orb of influence is but $2°$ for a planet or a cusp by progression, if the time of birth is not accurately known and if the chart is erected for an approximate time of birth, the house cusp degrees may not be correct, consequently, in such cases it is useless to figure aspects of planets to cusps. However, a few hours of difference (exact birth time unknown) would not appreciably affect the aspects of planets one with another, except the Moon.

Any of the planets coming to a conjunction, parallel, opposition, trine, square, sextile, etc., with the sign and degree on the cusp of a house will bring an influence to bear according to the nature of the house and in proportion to the planet's powers in the radix by essential dignity, aspect, location and position. The conjunction, however, is of most importance.

For instance, suppose Mars by its progressive motion comes to a conjunction with the cusp of the Fourth House in either radix or progressed chart, it would bring trouble, controversy, loss and difficulty with regard to property, father and domestic affairs. And if Mars were much afflicted at birth it would make the evil so much worse; whereas if it had been well aspected and dignified at birth the evil would be much lessened. And so on in like manner with the other planets and the other cusps. The conjunction of a planet to a cusp is more important than the aspects to it, i.e., sextile, square, trine, etc. The more a planet is afflicted in the radix the more adverse is the nature which it carries with it by progression. The same rule holds both ways, the more a planet is dignified and well aspected in the radix the more beneficent is the nature which it carries with it by progression. The influence of minor aspects to cusps is almost imperceptible. Aspects to cusps should be within $2°$, forming. Aspects past (separating) do not count, that is, as the conditions they represent have already passed, they are not to be tabulated.

Aspects to cusps of houses either radix or progressed need not be considered unless the birth time is known to be correct, or corrected by a system of rectification, as a difference of every four minutes changes the cusps 1°, while a difference of every four minutes or so does not perceptibly change the planets' locations in the Zodiac; therefore pay most attention to aspects and planets.

## Calculating the Time a Progressed Mutual Aspect Becomes Partile

In connection with progressed mutual aspects, the following examples illustrates a method of calculating the time when the aspect becomes exact. The same method may be used for calculating the time an aspect between two transiting planets becomes partile. See note under Calculating the Time a Lunar Progressed Aspect Becomes Partile, page 440.

**Example. Person born October 11, 1937, 4:00 AM, Los Angeles, California.**

*Progressed birthdate:* November 28, 1937, representing the native's forty-eighth year, October 11, 1985 to October 11, 1986.

*Question:* When will the progressed Moon reach an exact sextile to the progressed Mercury?

*Datum:*

Progressed Moon (November 28,1937, 4:00 AM)—16° ≏ 55'16".

Progressed Mercury (November 28, 1937, 4:00 AM)—22° ♐ 09'.

Progressed Lunar motion—12° 11' 15" per day, representing one year.

Progressed motion of Mercury—1° 28' per day, representing one year.

## Calculate the Distance the Planet must Travel to Partile

The progressed Moon will be sextile progressed Mercury when it reaches 22° 09'. A distance of 5° 13' 44".

```
  22° 09' 00"   (position of exact aspect)
 -16  55  16    (position of progressed birth date)
   5° 13' 44"   (distance needed to travel)
```

## 2. Calculate the Time Needed to Cover that Distance

Since both the Moon and Mercury are moving, the Moon's relative motion is first calculated. Then logarithms are used to find out what portion of the Moon's daily motion is needed to bring it to the proper place.

$$12° \ 11' \ 15" \quad \text{(Moon's daily motion)}$$
$$\underline{- \ 1 \ \ 28 \ \ 00} \quad \text{(Mercury's daily motion)}$$
$$10° \ 43' \ 15" \quad \text{(Moon's relative motion)}$$

$$.6614 \quad \text{(log of distance } 5° \ 13' \ 44')$$
$$\underline{-.3501} \quad \text{(log of relative lunar motion } 10° \ 43' \ 15")$$
$$.3113 \quad \text{(log of proportional distance)}$$

.3113 = 11h 43m (time needed to cover the distance)

## 3. Calculate the Equivalent Time in the Current Calendar

The Moon must travel 11h 43m after the progressed birth date (November 28, 1937, 4:00 am) for the aspect to become exact. This must translated into time in the current calendar—the amount of time past the current birth date (October 11, 1985, 4:00 AM)—with the aid of Table 17: Time Key, page 441.

11 hours = 5½ months by progression (5 months 15 days)

43 minutes = 10¾ days by progression (10 days 18 hours)

October 11, 1984, 4:00 AM + 5 months 25 days 18 hours = April 7, 1986, 9:00 AM.

The progressed Moon will form an exact sextile to the progressed Mercury on April 7, 1986, at 9:00 AM.

## EFFECTS OF ASPECTS BY DIRECTION

Lunar aspects are very important as they show many of the common events of minor importance and at the same time many serious events, especially when one directional aspect is followed closely by another. Often a series of evil lunar directions cause severe or even fatal sickness if they occur at the same time as a bad transit or an adverse solar direction. Generally a lunar direction has its full effect within two weeks of the time when the aspect is complete but under some of the favorable aspects affecting business affairs the native will have from six weeks to two months of good conditions while the aspect is forming and separating.

The following delineations have reference to all aspects, whether formed in the radix, in the progressed chart or between one planet in the radix and the other in the progressed chart. The interpretations are general indications only and subject to modification according to the strength of the aspect, that is, whether major or minor, position of planets in chart, whether angular, succedent or cadent, the strength by dignity or weakness by debility according to the sign occupied and also according to the planet's power and influence in the birth chart.

## Planets in the Houses

The meaning of the houses in the progressed chart is the same as in the radical chart.

When a planet is in the **First House**, or is ruler of the First House (radix or progressed), the aspects formed by direction refer to health and personal affairs.

When a planet is in the **Second House**, or is the ruler of the Second House (radix or progressed), the aspects formed by direction refer to money matters.

When a planet is in the **Third House**, or is the ruler of the Third House (radix or progressed), the aspects formed by direction refer to brethren, neighbors, short journeys, writings.

When a planet is in the **Fourth House**, or is the ruler of the Fourth House (radix or progressed), the aspects formed by direction refer to parents, property, domestic affairs, father.

When a planet is in the **Fifth House**, or is the ruler of the Fifth House (radix or progressed), the aspects formed by direction refer to speculation, pleasure, love affairs, children.

When a planet is in the **Sixth House**, or is the ruler of the Sixth House (radix or progressed), the aspects formed by direction refer to sickness, employees and employment, small animals, food, medicines, clothing.

When a planet is in the **Seventh House**, or is the ruler of the Seventh House (radix or progressed), the aspects formed by direction refer to marriage, partners opponents, opposition, lawsuits.

When a planet is in the **Eighth House**, or is the ruler of the Eighth House (radix or progressed), the aspects formed by direction refer to deaths, legacy, gain through money of others.

When a planet is in the **Ninth House**, or is the ruler of the Ninth House (radix or progressed), the aspects formed by direction refer to long journeys, voyages, visions, dreams, psychic experiences.

When a planet is in the **Tenth House**, or is the ruler of the Tenth House (radix or progressed), the aspects formed by direction refer to business affairs, occupation, profession or mother.

When a planet is in the **Eleventh House**, or is the ruler of the Eleventh House (radix or progressed), the aspects formed by direction refer to friends.

When a planet is in the **Twelfth House**, or ruler of the Twelfth House (radix or progressed), the aspects formed by direction refer to restraint, limitations, difficulty, sorrow.

# Progressed Parallels

The next step is to work up the declinations to find whether any parallels are formed during this progressed year. Two planets or cusps are parallel when they are equal distant from the celestial equator, north or south; or one north and the other south.

The declinations for the planet are given on the right-hand pages of the Rosicrucian Ephemeris; see Figures 8, 10, 27 and 29. When using an ephemeris which only gives the declinations every other, or every third day, interpolate according to the directions given in *Parallels of Declination*, page 125. Beginners need not try to reduce the declination of the planets (except Sun and Moon) to the hour and minute of birth, as it is sufficient to record it for the day only.

To find out whether or not any of the planets are parallel, compare their declinations. If you find any planet within one degree of another, they are parallel. Whether north or south or one north and the other south is immaterial, for if they are equi-distant from the celestial equator they are parallel.

Parallels may be found not only between planets as they were located at birth but also as they may progress and come to the degree of another planet's declination in the radix or in the progressed chart.

## LUNAR DECLINATION

As the Moon is likely to move several degrees in declination any day

449

(equal to a year in progression), it is liable to form several parallels in the course of such a period. The influence of a parallel is likely to begin when within one degree of being complete but is most apt to operate when the parallel is exact.

The calculation and tabulation of declinations for the progressed chart are identical in method to those of the radix but we go one step further when the Moon is concerned. The Moon's declination is treated similarly to its progress in longitude month by month in order to ascertain whether it will come into parallel with the declination of any planet in either the natal or progressed charts during that year. When it does come into a parallel the effects are similar to a conjunction between the same planets and should be delineated in the same terms as a conjunction.

## Calculating the Monthly Lunar Progressed Declination

To find the Moon's declination each month in the progressed year, proceed as follows: count for number of degrees and minutes it will travel between its given place on the progressed birth date and its given place on the next day. Then change this amount of the Moon's motion from degrees and minutes to all minutes by multiplying the degrees by 60 and adding the minutes to this product. Then divide the total by 12 to determine the rate the Moon will move in declination in each of the twelve months during the progressed year. By adding this amount of the Moon's monthly motion twelve times to the declination of the Moon on the progressed birth date at time of birth when the declination is increasing, but subtracting when the declination is decreasing, we will find in what degree of declination the Moon will be each month during the coming twelve months.

Note. When the motion of the Moon in declination is less than one degree for any year (as will sometimes be the case) multiply the given minutes by 60, thus reducing the motion to seconds. Divide the seconds by 12 to get the number of seconds of declination the Moon moves per month. Divide the seconds by 60 to transform the figure to minutes and seconds of motion in declination and then add or subtract this amount from the Moon's declination on the progressed birth date, according to whether the Moon is increasing or decreasing in declination.

**Example 1. Person born January 22, 1936, 10:20 PM, Sillersville, PA—progressed birth date March 4, 1936.** The Moon's declination on the day after the progressed birth date (13° N 44') is subtracted from its declination on the progressed birth date (17° N 49') to find its daily motion; see Figure 27. This motion is converted to all minutes by multiplying the degrees by 60 and adding the minutes to the product. The result of 245' represents the Moon's progressed motion of declination during the year January 22, 1978 to January 22, 1979. This is then divided by 12 to get the progressed motion of declination during any one month.

> 17° N 49'  (declination progressed birth date)
> <u>-13      44 </u> (declination day after progressed birth date)
>  04°     05'  (daily motion)

4° 05' = 245' (number of minutes in daily motion)

245 ÷ 12 = 20' 5/12" = 20' 25" (progressed monthly motion of declination)

**Example 2. Person born March 30, 1947, 9:38 AM, Red Wing, MN—progressed birth date April 28, 1947.** The Moon's declination on the day after the progressed birth date (16° N 49') is subtracted from its declination on the progressed birth date (21° N 09') to find its daily motion; see Figure 29. This motion is converted to all minutes by multiplying the degrees by 60 and adding the minutes to the product. The result of 260' represents the Moon's progressed motion of declination during the year March 30, 1976 to March 30, 1977. This is then divided by 12 to get the progressed motion of declination during a month.

> 21° N 09'  (declination progressed birth date)
> <u>-16      49 </u> (declination day after progressed birth date)
>  04°     20'  (daily motion)

4° 20' = 260' (number of minutes in daily motion)

260' ÷ 12 = 21' 8/12" = 21' 40" (progressed monthly motion of declination)

*Add* the monthly motion twelve times to the Moon's declination on the progressed birth date at time of birth when the declination is *increasing*; *subtract* the monthly motion twelve times from the Moon's declination on the progressed birth date when the declination is *decreasing*.

**Example 1. Person born January 22, 1936, 10:20 PM, Sillersville, PA—progressed birth date March 4, 1936.**

Declination of the Moon by progression, January 22, 1978
(actual position, March 4, 1936):               16° N 21' 00"
                                              -        20 25
                          February 22, 1978:   16° N 00' 35"
                                              -        20 25
                             March 22, 1978:   15° N 40' 10"
                                              -        20 25
                             April 22, 1978:   15° N 19' 45"
                                              -        20 25
                               May 22, 1978:   14° N 59' 20"
                                              -        20 25
                              June 22, 1978:   14° N 38' 55"
                                              -        20 25
                              July 22, 1978:   14° N  18' 30"
                                              -        20 25
                            August 22, 1978:   13° N 58' 05"
                                              -        20 25
                         September 22, 1978:   13° N 37' 40"
                                              -        20 25
                           October 22, 1978:   13° N 17' 15"
                                              -        20 25
                          November 22, 1978:   12° N 56' 50"
                                              -        20 25
                          December 22, 1978:   12° N 36' 25"
                                              -        20 25
                            January 22, 1979:   12° N 16' 00"

Example 2. Person born March 30, 1947, 9:38 AM, Red Wing,
MN—progressed birth date April 28, 1947.

Declination of the Moon by progression, March 30, 1976
(actual position, April 28, 1947):           20° N 30' 00"
                                          -      21 40
                April 30, 1976:   20° N 08' 20"
                                          -      21 40
                 May 30, 1976:   19° N 46' 40"
                                          -      21 40
                June 30, 1976:   19° N 25' 00"
                                          -      21 40
                 July 30, 1976:   19° N 03' 20"
                                          -      21 40
              August 30, 1976:   18° N 41' 40"
                                          -      21 40
           September 30, 1976:   18° N 20' 00"
                                          -      21 40
             October 30, 1976:   17° N 58' 20"
                                          -      21 40
            November 30, 1976:   17° N 36' 40"
                                          -      21 40
            December 30, 1976:   17° N 15' 00"
                                          -      21 40
             January 30, 1977:   16° N 53' 20"
                                          -      21 40
            February 28, 1977:   16° N 31' 40"
                                          -      21 40
               March 30, 1977:   16° N 10' 00"

Note. When the ephemeris shows that the declinations will change
from north to south or from south to north, between the two dates,
add (instead of subtracting) to find the daily motion. Then from its
place on the progressed birth date subtract the monthly motion until it
is reduced as small as possible, after which add the monthly motion for
the remainder of the year.

## DECLINATIONS OF THE PLANETS

The declinations of the planets are found in the progressed chart in exactly the same way as in the natal chart. This is described in detail in *Parallels of Declination*, page 125.

The declinations are copied from the ephemeris for the year in which the chart was erected. When the declinations are given every other day and the necessary day falls between the two days, find the *motion for two days* by subtracting the smaller number from the larger. Half of the motion for two days is *added* to the earlier date if the declination is *increasing* or *subtracted* if the declination is *decreasing*.

Example 1. **Person born January 22, 1936, 10:20 PM, Sillersville, PA—progressed birthdate March 4, 1936.** The declinations of the Sun and Moon were interpolated to get their exact progressed birth time declinations; see page 431. The declinations for the other planets are copied from the ephemeris; see Figure 27.

Moon: 16° N 21'         Moon parallel Mercury and Venus
Sun: 6° S 14'           Sun parallel Neptune
Mercury: 16° S 34'      Mercury parallel Venus
Venus: 17° S 06'
Mars: 3° N 01'
Jupiter: 22° S 37'      Jupiter parallel Pluto
Saturn: 8° S 18'
Uranus: 11° N 59'
Neptune: 6° N 41'
Pluto: 23° N 12' (March 1 position)

Example 2. **Person born March 30, 1947, 9:38 AM, Red Wing, MN—progressed birthdate, April 28, 1947.** The declinations of the Sun and Moon were interpolated to get their exact progressed birth time declinations; see page 431. The declinations of the other planets are given every other day. The difference in declinations between April 27 and 29 is found and half of this is added to the April 27 position when increasing and subtracted when decreasing. Note that in the case of Venus the declination changes directions between the two dates. These are added together to get the motion for two days. Half of this is then the daily motion. Since this is larger than the first position that is subtracted from the daily motion and the direction changed to get the progressed birth date declination.

Moon: 20° N 30'
Sun: 14° N 01'

Mercury: April 27: 4° N 46'
April 29: 6° 14'

April 28: 5° N 30'

Venus: 0° S 19'   (April 27 declination)
+0   N 35'  (April 29 declination)
54'  (motion for two days)

½ of 54' = 27' (daily motion)

0°   27'   (daily motion)
-0   S 19'   (April 27 declination)
0° N 08'   (April 28 declination)

Mars: April 27: 3° N 54'
April 29: 4° N 29'

April 28: 4° N 11'

Jupiter:  April 27: 17° S 47'   Neptune: 2° S 02'
Saturn: 20° N 16'          Pluto: 24° N 04' (May 1 position)
Uranus: 23° N 07'

## DECLINATIONS OF HOUSE CUSPS

The cusp of a house (sign and degree) has the same declination as the Sun when in that sign and degree.

Using the ephemeris for the same year for which the chart was erected or, in the case of the progressed chart, the year the chart represents, find when the Sun is in the same sign and degree as the house cusp in question and note its declination. This will be the approximate declination of the house cusp.

The declinations for the cusps of the First House (Ascendant), Second and Third Houses and for the Tenth House (Midheaven), Eleventh and Twelfth Houses are looked up in this manner. The opposite houses have the opposite declination; that is, the same number of degrees and minutes but north instead of south, or south instead of north.

**Note.** The declinations of the cusps are not to be used except when the time of birth is known to be absolutely correct or proved so by a reliable system of rectification. Every four minutes of time changes the cusps one degree in longitude and consequently the declination changes also.

**Example 1. Person born January 22, 1936, 10:20 pm, Sillersville, PA.–progressed birthdate March 4, 1936.** Looking up the Sun's position in a 1936 ephemeris note when it has the same sign and degree as the cusps of the birth chart houses. Use the Sun's declination for the declination of the house cusps. Use a 1976 ephemeris for the progressed house cusp. Interpolate in the same manner as when finding the declinations of the planets where necessary.

| *House* | *Cusp* | *Date of Sun's same position* | *Declination* |
|---------|--------|-------------------------------|---------------|
| **Natal chart:** | | | |
| Ascendant | 4°♎21' | Sept. 27 | 1° S 40' |
| Second House | 0°♏54' | Oct. 24 | 11° S 47' |
| Third House | 1°♐24' | Nov. 23 | 20° S 26' |
| Midheaven | 5°♋ | June 26 | 23° N 21' |
| Eleventh House | 8°♌24' | July 31 | 18° N 20' |
| Twelfth House | 8°♍36' | Sept. 1 | 8° N 21' |

Their opposite cusps:

| | | | |
|---|---|---|---|
| Seventh House | 4° ♈ 21' | | 1° N 40' |
| Eighth House | 0° ♉ 54' | | 11° N 47' |
| Ninth House | 1° ♊ 24' | | 20° N 26' |
| Fourth House | 5° ♑ | | 23° S 21' |
| Fifth House | 8° ♒ 24 | | 18° S 20' |
| Sixth House | 8° ♓ 36' | | 8° S 21' |

**Progressed chart:**

| | | | |
|---|---|---|---|
| Ascendant | 7° ♍ 40' | Oct. 31 | 14° S 05' |
| Second House | 6° ♐ 36' | Nov. 29 | 21° S 25' |
| Third House | 9° ♑ 36' | Dec. 31 | 23° S 05' |
| Midheaven | 15° ♌ | Aug. 7 | 16° N 20' |
| Eleventh House | 17° ♍ 54' | Sept. 10 | 4° N 47' |
| Twelfth House | 15° ♎ 18' | Oct. 8 | 6° S 02' |

Their opposite cusps:

| | | | |
|---|---|---|---|
| Seventh House | 7° ♉ 40' | | 14° N 05' |
| Eighth House | 6° ♊ 36' | | 21° N 25' |
| Ninth House | 9° ♋ 36' | | 23° N 05' |
| Fourth House | 15° ♒ | | 16° S 20' |
| Fifth House | 17° ♓ 54' | | 4° S 47' |
| Sixth House | 15° ♈ 18' | | 6° N 02' |

**Example 2. Person born March 30, 1947, 9:38 am, Red Wing, MN. —progressed birthdate, April 28, 1947.** Looking up the Sun's position in a 1947 ephemeris note when it has the same sign and degree as the cusps of the birth chart houses. Use the Sun's declination for the declination of the house cusps. Use a 1976 ephemeris for the progressed house cusps. Interpolate in the same manner as when finding the declinations of the planets where necessary.

| House | Cusp | Date of Sun's same position | Declination |
|-------|------|------------------------------|-------------|

**Natal chart:**

| House | Cusp | Date of Sun's same position | Declination |
|-------|------|------------------------------|-------------|
| Ascendant | 25° ♊ 14' | June 17 | 23° N 22' |
| Second House | 14° ♋ 30' | June 28 | 22° N 45' |
| Third House | 3° ♌ 42' | July 27 | 19° N 34' |
| Midheaven | 27° ♒ | Feb. 16 | 12° S 32' |
| Eleventh House | 29° ♓ | Mar. 20 | 0° S 30' |
| Twelfth House | 12° ♉ 30' | May 3 | 15° N 25' |

**Their opposite cusps:**

| House | Cusp | | Declination |
|-------|------|--|-------------|
| Seventh House | 25° ♐ 14' | | 23° S 22' |
| Eighth House | 14° ♑ 30' | | 22° S 45' |
| Ninth House | 3° ♒ 42' | | 19° S 34' |
| Fourth House | 27° ♌ | | 12° N 32' |
| Fifth House | 29° ♍ | | 0° N 30' |
| Sixth House | 12° ♍ 30' | | 15° S 25' |

**Progressed chart:**

| House | Cusp | Date of Sun's same position | Declination |
|-------|------|------------------------------|-------------|
| Ascendant | 20° ♋ 15' | July 12 | 21° N 55' |
| Second House | 8° ♌ 30' | July 31 | 18° N 08' |
| Third House | 00° ♍ | Aug. 23 | 11° N 28' |
| Midheaven | 28° ♓ | Mar. 18. | 0° S 47' |
| Eleventh House | 5° ♉ 06' | Apr. 25 | 13° N 13' |
| Twelfth House | 15° ♊ 54' | June 6 | 22° N 42' |

**Their opposite cusps:**

| House | Cusp | | Declination |
|-------|------|--|-------------|
| Seventh House | 20° ♑ 15' | | 21° S 55' |
| Eighth House | 8° ♒ 30' | | 18° S 08' |
| Ninth House | 00° ♓ | | 11° S 28' |
| Fourth House | 28° ♍ | | 0° N 47' |
| Fifth House | 5° ♏ 06' | | 13° S 13' |
| Sixth House | 15° ♐ 54' | | 22° S 42' |

It will be noticed, that the declination of one cusp is the same as on the opposite cusp. Therefore, when a planet comes to a parallel of one cusp it is also parallel with the opposite cusp but it affects that house more which it on the same side of the equator as itself by north or south declination.

Unless the Tables of Houses for the exact latitude of birthplace were used in erecting the chart and birth time known to be exact, it is useless and perhaps misleading also to attempt to use cusp declinations. For this reason, it is extremely difficult to get the declinations absolutely exact and hence to state just when an event would occur, indicated by an oncoming parallel; except to state it in terms of a certain month or year.

However, a parallel usually takes about a year to complete (excepting those of the Moon) and while the parallel is on, it influences matters connected with that house. For example, Saturn parallel cusp of the Second House (♄‖2nd Hs) which would depress finances and prevent the native from accumulating an over-supply of money that year at least. If other directions for financial reserves were shown, this parallel would indicate heavy financial stringency when the aspect was on or when a planet in transit came to a parallel with this afflicted cusp.

## COMPARISONS AND CONSIDERATIONS

### Lunar Declination

After having made the column of figures showing the Moon's degree of declination each month, compare its declination each month with the degrees of declination of the other planets in both the radix and the progressed charts to ascertain in which months the parallel aspects will be formed that year. It is quite possible that in some years there will be no parallels in operation.

The most important parallels are those which may be formed by the Moon in its monthly motion or place in progress. Parallels among the other planets bear an influence upon the whole year.

### Declinations of the Planets and House Cusps

When you have found all the declinations arrange them in two columns: one for the radix and the other for the progressed chart, on one sheet of paper for convenience in comparing them for checking off parallels. Do not compare declinations of house cusps with each other. Compare planet's declinations with the declinations of cusps to find parallels.

Remember that when a planet is parallel with a cusp it is also parallel with the opposite cusp but its influence is on the house which is in the same direction (north or south) of declination as the planet.

Four types of comparisons are made:

*1. Compare the progressed planets' declination with those of the radix but do not compare a major planet's progressed declination with its radical declination.*

*2. Compare the progressed planets' declination with each other; see examples on pages 454 and 455.*

*3. Compare the progressed planets' declinations with the house cusp declinations in both the radix and progressed charts.*

*4. Compare the Moon's declination each month with the declinations of the radical and progressed planets and cusps, as described in the above paragraph.*

A planet is in influence of parallel with another planet as soon as within one degree, regardless of whether both are north or south, or one north and the other south.

When a planet appears to be within parallel of another or with a cusp, examine the ephemeris and your figures carefully to see whether the parallel is forming, or has already been formed and is separating or past. In the latter case we do not tabulate it. Record only those which are applying or forming. Observe whether a planet's declination is increasing or decreasing in order to determine if it is approaching or separating from a parallel.

Some near parallels are never actually completed or not for many years, because of the slow motion in declination. Take, for instance, the case of a progressed Neptune (16° N 52') parallel a radical Venus (17° N 13'), ♆P‖♀R. The difference between them is but 21' of declination but reference to the ephemeris for several years in advance reveals the fact that Neptune will never reach the exact declination of Venus in this native's lifetime. However, as there is always an orb of parallel between them, the effect of the parallel will be active when some planet by transit comes to a point between these two declinations and by *translation* unites Neptune and Venus by parallel of declination. The parallel of these two planets is not particularly important. We deal with it here as an illustration.

It is not absolutely necessary to work out exactly what day or date the parallel falls due, because its influence extends over an uncertain period, varying according to its motion in declination and it may begin to exert a perceptible effect several weeks before the birth date to several weeks after. Some declinations change so slowly that when a parallel begins, by orb, it may be many days (years by progress) before it becomes partile and therefore shows up in as many years' progressed charts.

Parallels seem to affect conditions which the native will find it necessary to meet and these conditions are accompanied by events, more or less radical, according to the native's plane of progress or state of consciousness.

For instance, the Moon parallel Mars ( ☾ ‖ ♂ ) would produce a feverish, passionate, rash disposition in an undeveloped type living on the purely physical plane, which would lead to accidents and quarrels. While to an advanced, refined being this same parallel would produce added energy resulting in constructive activity. In the one case the influence is apparently evil, in the other the effects are good, the difference being not in the planets but in the state of understanding of the being through which the influences operate. In other words, the sort of reactions which an individual makes to an aspect largely determines the results of the influence. Some people make a bad aspect worse by the way they think and act. Others greatly modify an adverse aspect by their intelligent response to planetary influence.

# Transits

The transit of a planet is its passage by ephemeral motion in any year as shown by the ephemeris. Thus a transiting planet may pass over an important place in either radix or progressed chart; or form aspects to those points.

Transits are particularly important in two ways.

**First**. When a transiting planet forms an aspect of similar nature with a planet it aspected at birth. For instance, if Jupiter were sextile Saturn at birth, the transit of Jupiter to any good aspects with Saturn would be very beneficial, while the effect of an adverse aspect of transiting Jupiter would almost be nil.

**Second**. When a transiting planet comes into aspect with progressed planets which are forming an aspect, it will set off (precipitate) their influences before the date when they would act of themselves. In cases where the progressed aspected planets are separating from an aspect, a transiting planet coming into aspect with them may prolong or revive the influence. Such transits afford the means of predicting events very close, sometimes to the very day by noting the date when the transit aspect is exact.

## Orb of Influence

**Note**. Transiting aspects must be forming. The orb of a transiting planet is 8°, except the Sun whose orb is 12°.

*Current year* means the year in life which the progressed chart represents. In the examples previously given in this lesson the progressed chart was desired for 1976. In Example 1, the chart was made for March 4, 1936 representing the year January 22, 1976 to January 22, 1977. In example 2, the chart was made for April 28, 1947 representing the year March 30, 1976 to March 30, 1977.

Transits of planets as shown in an ephemeris for 1976-77 are those which would be considered in their relation to planets in the natal and progressed charts.

For instance, suppose that Saturn by its progressed motion is close to forming a conjunction with Uranus in the birth chart, and that Mars by transit during the coming year would cross over Saturn's progressed place. It would then excite into action the conjunction between Saturn and Uranus, whereas without such excitement it would have been a year or two, maybe (according to the number of degrees apart), before the conjunction would become complete and operate of itself.

Therefore, if you find a direction aspect forming look carefully through the current year ephemeris and see when the Sun or any of the planets (the major planets more especially) will cross over the critical points (or form aspects thereto) and thus learn the date when the effects will be felt.

It is considered that the Sun, Moon, Mars, Jupiter, Saturn, Uranus, and Pluto, in particular, passing in aspect by direction or transit to the places of the planets at birth, or passing their own radical places, or passing the progressed places of the planets, are very important and bring about events, especially if the planets were in an aspect of similar quality at birth. Mercury, Venus and Neptune are important also, but to a lesser extent.

Transits over the places of planets in a natal chart or forming aspects with them are very effective and likewise so in the progressed chart.

A directional aspect does not manifest continually throughout the year. Its influence may be accelerated or diminished according to the transits. This action of transits (exciting the progressed aspects) provides material for very interesting study. The student will soon learn that it is also a valuable feature connected with the progressed horoscope indications. Owing to the fact that it requires some detail work it is generally neglected. But it should never be neglected. It is not a difficult matter to understand and the student is urged to study this matter carefully because of its importance.

### Lunar Transits

The Moon completes a transit through the circle of twelve signs in one month. In the course of its transit the Moon forms every possible aspect to all planets and cusps in the natal chart and progressed charts. It is interesting and valuable to note its place in the current ephemeris each day and from its given place see what aspects it forms for that day in the natal and progressed charts. It is sometimes amazing to see how events, conditions or moods correspond to the aspects formed. Take note of the house in the chart occupied by the transiting Moon from day to day, as the house positions determine largely what things will be affected by the aspects.

## EFFECTS OF TRANSITS

There is little difference between the effect of a transit and the same aspect by direction, the difference being rather in the time of duration than difference in influence; although because aspects by direction last longer than those by transit, the latter may seem different.

For example, Saturn conjunct the cusp of the Sixth House *by direction* (P ♄ 6th Hs R) might last over a year, during which time, unless offset by other testimonies, it would likely produce physical disability, obstructions, limitations, and restricted action, which might result in serious illness. While the *transit* of Saturn over the cusp of the Sixth House or over a planet in the Sixth House might cause a severe cold or an attack of the flu, but comparatively speaking, its effects would soon pass. If the nativity indicated much ill health, the native would likely suffer frequent spells of indisposition during the whole period of its passage through the Sixth House, which is the House of Sickness, and the person would feel especially indisposed on the days when the Moon (as shown in the current ephemeris) passed through this house and over Saturn therein.

In a *progressed chart* the effect of a transit over the degree of the Midheaven, Ascendant or any planet is more effective than an aspect thereto.

In a *natal chart* transits by either conjunction or aspect are noticeable, the major aspects more particularly than the minor.

To study the effect of transits, learn the effect of aspects by direction, but modify the delineations because of the shorter duration, and never predict something from a transit which is not promised by some configuration at birth. If a person has a good horoscope for health, finance, or marriage, there is no use predicting trouble because of a malefic transiting through the First, Second, or Seventh Houses, because nothing more than slight annoyances are likely to occur.

## Declinations

When looking up transits, the declinations of the transitor should not be overlooked, for when it compares with declination of any planet or cusp in the horoscope it constitutes a parallel and has an effect like a conjunction.

## Duration of Influence

The duration of the effects of transits depends upon two things.

**First.** Note which planet is doing the transiting, for each planet moves through the Zodiac at its own rate of motion, the Moon being the swiftest, and Pluto the slowest (see table below).

**Second.** Does the transitor turn retrograde before it gets out of orb of aspect with the transited? Frequently a transiting planet reaches a certain point, turns retrograde and recrosses that point; then turning direct in motion, crosses it for the third time, thus affecting that place or planet much longer than usual. Look in the current ephemeris and count how many days it requires the transitor in question to traverse 8° preceding the exact aspect. After the aspect is complete, the effect quickly diminishes, unless the transitor becomes retrograde and goes

The Moon transits the 12 signs in 27 days, 7 hours, 43 minutes.
The Sun transits the 12 signs in approximately 1 year.
Mercury transits the 12 signs in approximately 1 year.
Venus transits the 12 signs in approximately 1 year.
Mars transits the 12 signs in approximately 22 months.
Jupiter transits the 12 signs in approximately 12 years.
Saturn transits the 12 signs in approximately 29½ years.
Uranus transits the 12 signs in approximately 84 years.
Neptune transits the 12 signs in approximately 165 years.
Pluto transits the 12 signs in approximately 248 years.

**Table 18: Geocentric Period of Planetary Transits**

back over the aspect.

It takes Neptune several years to form and complete an aspect, while Venus or Mercury would cover the same amount of longitude in a few days. During a period of good direction the potency of good transits is enhanced and the adverse transits diminished in influence.

## Tabulating Aspects

Look in a current ephemeris and take note of the various planetary positions, then compare their ephemeral places with radix planets to see if any aspects are formed. Note the date in the ephemeris when the transiting planet begins the aspect (allowing an orb of 8° applying, 12° for the Sun) and the date when the aspect is complete (exact). This will show the length of the period of influence.

In every month the transits of *Neptune, Uranus, Saturn, Jupiter*, and *Mars* should be noted to see if any of them cross over the planets in the radix, or form major aspects to some planets in the progressed chart which are themselves in aspect. In that case, the transit sets the progressed aspect into activity during the period of the transit. But generally speaking, the transits through the radix are the most important.

The transit of the *Sun* through the radix is important. The good and adverse aspects which it forms to radical planets indicate the favorable and unfavorable solar periods in each year. The Sun moves forward about one degree each day, hence, it is twelve days applying to an aspect. Do not seriously consider the minor aspects.

The transits of *Mercury* and *Venus* are not very important unless they are ruling planets. They concern the minor details of life, when considered as transits, yet in the lives of people who are concerned mostly with ordinary matters these two are quite important. In the lives of those who are concerned with larger things, business and public affairs, the larger planets are more important.

The transit of the native's *ruling planets* (one ruling the birth month and the one which rules the ascending sign at birth) are very important. The aspects formed by rulers in transit, which coincide with aspects they held at birth, are very powerful compared with other aspects they may form. For instance, if Mars is a ruling planet and was in opposition to Jupiter at birth, then the adverse transits of Mars to the radix Jupiter would be very strong, while its good aspects to Jupiter would bring but little benefit.

Transits to the *Part of Fortune* and the *Moon's nodes* should also be observed, especially the conjunction.

**An Easy Way to Find Transits.** From the birth chart make a table for permanent use, showing for each planet the degree of the Zodiac which is in exact opposition, conjunction, sextile, square, and trine. Then look in a current ephemeris and note when any planet will pass through the degrees you have recorded. In that way you will know the dates when your radix is affected by transiting planets and thus be enabled to prepare yourself according to whether the aspect formed is good or adverse.

Those who wish to be very exact can amplify their table, or aspect reference sheet, by finding also the points of minor aspects and it is then useful to watch aspects from planets in the progressed chart, as affecting the points of aspect in the radix. Once the table is made it is good for all time.

## Transits in Relation to the Natal Chart

The influence of transits should be judged according to their radical indications, i.e., if a planet is in adverse aspect to another at birth its adverse aspects to that planet by transit are of more significance than its good aspects. In other words, its adverse aspects being in accord with the original indication would stir up corresponding conditions. Whereas its good aspects, being contrary to the original indications, would not have the power to produce any particular or noticeable advantages.

Aspects by transit which coincide with the original indication will act directly upon the native and in his affairs. Aspects which do not coincide will act indirectly: not upon the native and his own affairs but more upon other people whom he is contacting during such transit. All aspects operate in some manner, but whether directly on the native or on others about him depends upon the original indications between the two planets in question.

If the planets are in adverse aspect at birth the good aspect by transit is not likely to bring the native any particular benefit but he will see others benefiting in a manner coinciding with the nature of this aspect as related to its transiting house and sign.

**Example.** If the aspecting planet is transiting through the Seventh

House in the sign of Scorpio, forming a *good* aspect to the radical Moon
with which it was in *adverse* aspect at birth, it might benefit his partner
or his wife. If he happened to be engaged in a lawsuit at that time it
would benefit the opponent and if the Moon at birth ruled the Third
House and was posited in the Eleventh House, then that good transit
would also benefit his brothers, sisters, neighbors, and his friends.

On the other hand, if that *good* transit concerned planets that had
been in *good* aspect at birth, then the native would benefit directly
through the matters and people mentioned above and might also be in
a position to help them.

# LUNATIONS

The New Moon (lunation) is commonly used in mundane astrology to determine the trend of world or large scale events. It has been
found that the positions and aspects of the planets at this time indicate general trends on a global level.

**Does the monthly New Moon affect individuals?**

Some New Moons (lunations) are very important, depending
upon whether or not the luminaries at their conjunction form any
important aspects to planets in the individual's nativity. When the
lunation occurs in a favorable place in the horoscope and in good aspect to some of the radical planets it betokens that the month, summed
up in a general way, will be fortunate, especially if no strongly malignant aspects testify otherwise, but even then such lunation will tend to
mitigate the evil. The contrary is to be judged when the lunation occurs
in adverse aspect to planets in the radix, the evil being magnified
should the lunation be an eclipse. The New Moon may be applied to the
progressed horoscope in like manner.

The results of a lunation (good or adverse) are determined by the
combined influences of the house in which it occurs, the houses occupied by planets aspected by the lunation, and the houses these planets
rule.

As the lunation, or New Moon, is virtually a transit, the sign and
degree of its occurrence each month in the Zodiac should be correlated
to both the natal and progressed charts.

## FAVORABLE DAYS

Favorable and unfavorable days are indicated by the dates when the Moon (as shown by its place in the current ephemeris) crosses over or aspects important places in the nativity. This is the main technique used in "Sun Sign" Astrology.

The Moon's aspects are the most important factor of all in determining the *daily* events in one's life. Observing students will soon learn how to apply these to their own horoscope, as the lunar transits are all of monthly occurrence.

Look in the current ephemeris at the Moon's longitude on the first of the month. Find that place in your own natal chart, then note what aspects it will form to your radical planets during the day considering that it will move forward in the Zodiac about thirteen degrees in the next twenty-four hours.

The Moon's place as listed in the ephemeris is its position at the time of the *Noon Mark* of the place where you now reside. After Noon Mark, the Moon will advance at the rate of about one degree every two hours.

For example, Sillersville, PA with a longitude of 75° 24' has a Noon Mark of 6:58:24 am; and Red Wing, MN with a longitude of 92° 31' has a Noon Mark of 5:49:56 am. The Noon Mark is the equivalent of noon in Greenwich, England, and is the time for which the planet's position in the ephemeris are calculated.

### Aspects Formed by the Moon's Transit

For specific delineations, see: *Planetary Aspects by Transit*, page 513. The good transits of the Moon will be more powerful in the months when there is a favorable transit of some other planet operating at the same time or during a period of a favorable lunation.
some other planet operating at the same time, or during a period of a favorable lunation.

The Moon's favorable transits will be much weaker in the months when the Moon is adversely aspected by its progressed position. The Moon's good monthly transit aspect to a planet will avail little if in the same month the progressed Moon is adversely afflicting that particular planet, and especially so if the previous lunation occurred unfavorably in the horoscope.

### The Moon's Transit Through the Houses

The advantage of knowing the Moon's place and aspects as connected with your natal chart, lies in the fact that it has much dominion over general daily affairs. Its influence is important because it goes entirely around your chart each month, through each house, and forms every aspect to all the planets. Look in the current ephemeris and note its place, then find that place in your chart. When you see the Moon forming an aspect, judge its effect, and decide in advance what course of action is in keeping with the indications.

The house through which the transiting Moon is passing the natal chart is important, as it helps to color the aspect with the nature of things ruled by that house. See *The Transiting Moon through the Houses*, page 509.

It is presumed that you are thoroughly familiar with the characteristics of the zodiacal signs and the influences of the planets, as well as the things signified by the houses. This knowledge should enable you to interpret correctly the influence of the aspects formed by the daily transits of the Moon in your natal chart. In this matter, it should be remembered that you are to use the current ephemeris and not the birth or progressed year ephemeris.

If you will make it a point to note the Moon's daily positions and aspects in your natal chart day by day, regularly for a few months, you will soon learn what to expect of each aspect as it occurs. This will be found of inestimable value in helping to determine the best course of action, especially on days when important business matters should be transacted.

## SOLAR PERIODS

As the Sun in its apparent daily motion transits through the Zodiac it moves away from the place it held on your birthday, passing through one sign each month and at the end of a year returning to the place of your birthday.

In the sixth month from your birthday the Sun comes into opposition of your zodiacal sign of birth and its own place in your nativity, and tends to produce a trying time generally. Not a good time to make any important move or ask favors. In the third and ninth months it forms a square to your sign which is also an unfavorable period.

### Your Adverse Solar Periods Each Year

From 78 to 95 days after birthday.
From 168 to 185 days after birthday.
From 258 to 275 days after birthday.

### Your Good Solar Periods Each Year

From 48 to 65 days after birthday.
From 108 to 125 days after birthday.
From 228 to 245 days after birthday.
From 288 to 305 days after birthday.

### Table 19: Good and Adverse Solar Periods

In the four good periods aim to extend your interests and advance your business. Your good days in these good periods are apt to be more favorable than at other times, while your adverse days are usually less severe. Likewise, your adverse days during your adverse solar periods are apt to be more so than usual, while the good days are less favorable.

## Eclipses

**Are eclipses effective only in natal charts, or do they also affect the progressed chart?** Eclipses affect that chart most in which they form the strongest aspects. Generally speaking, the natal chart is more responsive to New Moons, eclipses, and transits than the progressed horoscope. For instance, if an eclipse occurred in such a sign and degree that it formed no aspects in either natal or progressed charts, its influence would be felt through its house position in the natal chart more than by its house position in the progressed horoscope.

A New Moon, eclipse, or transit may cause an aspect forming in the progressed chart to be set off prematurely if they come into a like aspect with that formed by the planets. However, there is really nothing premature in nature. If the eclipse, New Moon, or transiting planet should form an aspect contrary to a progressed aspect in process of forming it would tend to retard the latter or modify its influence during the time the transit, New Moon, or eclipse would be effectively in operation.

# Example Progressed Horoscope

The progressed horoscope is a chart made for any year after birth, in which one may see what conditions are to affect the native during those twelve months according to the aspects which will come into operation.

Each day after the birthday is equal to one year. In the ephemeris begin with the day after the birthday and count forward as many days (equal to the same number of years) to the year desired for the progressed horoscope. Having arrived at the desired date, make a chart as though you were born on this day, using the same birth time and Tables of Houses for birth place.

When the planets are properly inserted in the chart you are ready to figure the aspects between the planets, but remember that in a progressed horoscope we consider only the aspects which are applying or forming and allow an orb of only $2°$ because planets in their motion by direction require a year or more to move $1°$, according to their rate of motion, with the exception of the Moon, which moves forward about $1°$ per month.

The influences in a progressed chart are discerned principally from aspects. If the aspects are all good, the native will have a very successful year, and vice versa. Planets crossing over the cusps of houses portend conditions according to the nature of the planet and the things ruled by such house.

The Moon, on account of its swifter motion, requires more consideration than the other planets, because during a progressed year it will move forward $12°$-$15°$ and is therefore likely to form several

473

aspects.

After noting all the aspects the Moon will form in its journey through the twelve months refer to the radix (birth chart) to see if the progressing Moon will form any aspects to planets therein during the twelve months. When an aspect is formed, mark it beside the month and day in which it falls due, as before noted, as the Moon by its direction or progressed motion produces effects whenever it comes to aspects of planets in either the radix or progressed chart. As this is true of all the planets by progression, we must look from each one in the progressed to each one in the radix and note any aspects which may be formed between them, as well as the aspects they may form to their own radical places. Remember to record only those aspects which are forming within 2°.

The effect of an aspect is the same whether it is formed in the radix or in the progressed chart. The nature of the influence is determined by the nature of the aspect—whether good or adverse. The conditions and events produced are indicated by the houses and signs occupied by the aspecting planets as well as by the houses they rule.

The declinations of planets in the progressed chart should be compared with the declinations of planets in the radix. When two planets have the same degree of declination they are parallel, the effect of a parallel being the same as the effect of a conjunction. Parallels sometimes have an effect for more than a year and often tend to modify or accentuate the influence of other aspects, especially of the progressed Moon. For a detailed discussion see: *Parallels of Declination*, page 128.

After all the aspects have been calculated as directed above, it is well to summarize their effects briefly, especially those of the Moon, from month to month, being careful to modify or accentuate its influence according to the presence or absence of parallels or aspects between the major planets, among which those of the Sun are most important. Be very careful not to predict anything that is not promised by some testimony in the radix. For instance, if the progressed Moon is coming to a conjunction with the radical Venus do not predict marriage if the radix denies marriage.

When the progressed chart has been erected, look in an ephemeris for the calendar year which the progressed chart represents and tracing the movement (transit) of the major planets month by month, make note if they come into conjunction with any of the progressed chart planets. Tabulate the date when any conjunctions occur and look up the meaning in your textbook. Also note if any transiting planet forms a major aspect to any of the progressed chart planets, and tabulate the date when such an aspect occurs.

All the applications of transiting planets (in current year ephemeris just mentioned) should be made to the natal chart also. When making these tabulations record them in two lists headed *Transits to the natal chart* and *Transits to the progressed chart*.

As the effects of transiting planets are important, although they are not in operation as long as progressed directional aspects, it will be well worthwhile to trace and record systematically the transits of the major planets, Sun, Mars, Jupiter, Saturn, Uranus, Neptune, and Pluto.

## EXAMPLE CHART 5

On the next few pages will be an example of the delineation of a progressed chart. Example Chart 5 is of a man born August 23, 1884, progressed for his 26th year, August 23, 1920, to August 23, 1921. The progressed birth date is September 18, 1884. For information on tabulating and delineating progressed aspects, see: *The Progressed Aspects*, page 435, and *Interpreting the Progressed Aspects*, explained on page 485.

### 1. Lunar Progressed Aspects

12° ♍ -P☽ ☍ MC-R **August , 1910.** The Moon opposes the radical Midheaven from its place in the Third House, progressed. Worry and anxiety or discontent are likely to result in some discredit or setback in business. An unfavorable month in which to make any changes or attempts for promotion. The mother's health may be adversely affected. Sign no contracts, agreements, securities, etc., In fact, enter into no obligation in which there may be an element of risk or chance of failure, or where failure would mean loss of position and damage to the reputation. Do not travel.

**September, 1910.** As there are no aspects operating in September, the above aspect may have an influence in this month too.

**October, 1910.** No Aspects.

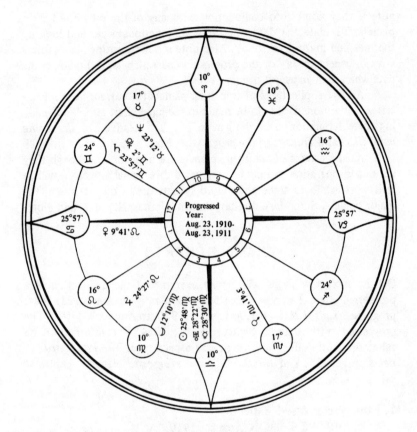

**Figure 36: Example Chart 5**

Notes:
+ Fire: ♃
- Earth: ♇ ☉ ♅ ☿ ☽
+ Air: ♀ ♄ ♂
- Water: ♀
own sign ♀
detriment ♄
natural house ☽

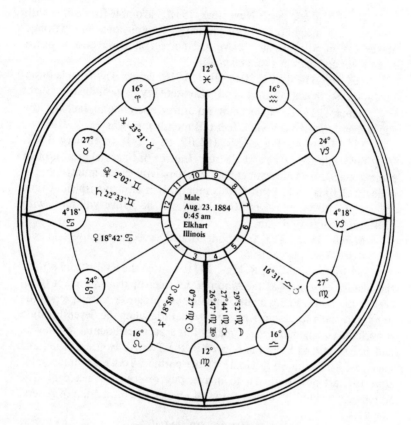

Figure 37: Progressed Chart.
Example 5

Notes:
+ Fire. ♀ ♃
- Earth: ♅ ☽ ☉ ♇ ☿
+ Air: ♀ ♄
- Water: ♂

natural house ☿
own sign ☿
own sign ♂

18° ♍ -P☽ Q AscR **November, 1910.** Favorable for dealing with brethren and neighbors, short journeys, commissions and writings. Makes the mind unusually active and correct in observations. Brings some favor and gain in a general way.

16° ♍ 31-P☽⊻♂R **December, 1910.** Brings new friends or acquaintances, much pleasure and also activiity and industry. Slight

**January, 1911.** There being no aspect operating in January, the above mentioned aspect will affect this month somewhat.

18° ♍ 42'-P ☽ ⚹ ♀ R; 18° ♍ 58'-P☽⊻♃R **February, 1911.** Very favorable for peace and pleasure. Chance of financial gain through some speculation or investment. If wife's nativity shows indications for children she may give birth in this month. It is also an auspicious time for a child to be conceived. On the whole the native will meet with pleasure, progress and gain.

**March, 1911.** The above mentioned aspect may affect March.

**April, 1911.** No aspects.

2° ♍ 33'-P☽ □ ♄ R **May, 1911.** Lowers the vitality and afflicts the health, especially as the Moon is the ruler of the Ascendant (Cancer) in the radix. Being in the Third House progressed, it depresses the mind and leads to gloom and anxiety. Saturn ruling the Seventh House (Capricorn) of the natal chart, makes this aspect detrimental to the wife and her health, as Saturn is posited in the Twelfth House of the natal chart, which is the Sixth House of the partner. This is an unfavorable time to start new business, to invest, buy or seek advancement. The watchword should be conservation of energy and protection of general interests.

23° ♍ 12'-P ☽△♅ P; 23° ♍ 21'-R☽ △ ♅ R **June, 1911.** This aspect relieves some of the adverse influence of the last aspect, but is not so strong as it might be, as Neptune was cadent (Eleventh House) at birth, and while the Moon is leaving the aspect of square to the natal Saturn (P ☽ sep. □♄R) it is forming a square to the progressed Saturn (P ☽□♄P) and therefore the indications for June are almost the same as for May.

24° ♍ 27'-P☽ ⊻ ♃P; 24°♍41'-P☽⊻♀ P **July, 1911.** The Moon semi-sextile Jupiter is slightly favorable in offsetting sickness and conducive to gain financially. The Moon semi-sextile Venus is slightly unfavorable for domestic affairs and dealings with friends and the opposite sex. This aspect will hardly be noticeable as the Moon was in slightly good aspect to Venus at birth (☽ Q ♀ ), and more especially as it is surpassed by the growing influence of the more powerful aspect of the Moon conjunct the progressed Sun, following.

25° ♍ 43'-P☽☌☉P **August, 1911.** This conjunction is not favorable for health and in this chart it occurs in the Third House, ruling the mind. As Uranus is also in close proximity (28°♍22') it will create intense mental activity, which will be a disturbing factor unless controlled. It causes danger of accidents on journeys and through railroads, electricity, etc. Otherwise it is conducive to enlightenment, progress and gain.

## 2. Progressed Mutual Aspects

P☉⚹AscP    The progressed Sun sextile the progressed Ascendand is conducive to the health of body, peace of mind, favor from those in authority, new friends, some elevation in rank according to the native's social position and in proportion to the Sun's power in the radix. In this chart the Sun occupies the Third House in Virgo in the natal chart and holds the same place in the progressed chart. The progressed Ascendant is still in the sign it held at birth, Cancer, but has progressed from 4° 18' to 25° 57', which brings a new influence into the life, namely that of the planet ruling this decanate of Cancer, Neptune, in addition to the influence of the Moon, significator of the natal (Cancer Ascendant).

P ☉☌♅P    The Sun is progressing through the Third House and is the ruler of the progressed Second House (Leo); natal Uranus is in the Fourth House, progressing to the Third House. Tends to domestic infelicity, trouble over property, change of residence, financial difficulties. Also inclines to journeying. Apt to disturb the health and produces nervous, excitable, radical, or rebellious states of mind.

P☿℞☌♅ P    Inclines to intense mental activity, which if rightly directed, may develop into clairvoyance. It will make the native keenly intuitive and he will know and understand things before they are spoken or before they happen. This activity must be rightly directed and controlled or it will cause mental disturbance. The native should carefully consider sudden ideas and plans before operating them.

## 3. Progressed Aspects to Radix

P☿℞☌♅R    (See P☿℞☌♅P above.)

P ☿ R ☌ ☿  R  When a planet progresses to an aspect of its own
radical place the tendency is to excite or set into motion its indications
in the birth chart, according to the nature of the aspect whether good
or adverse. The conjunction to its own place intensifies the activities of
a planet very similar to what might be considered a double influence of
that planet. In this case the progressed Mercury is retrograding towards
a conjunction with its radical place. Radical Mercury is in the Fourth
House while the progressed Mercury is in the progressed Third House,
thus intensifying conditions relating to the Fourth House and at the
same time activating the Third House influences.

P ♂ △  AscR  Mars progressed trine the Ascendant radix. As Mars
is in the progressed Fourth House this aspect will particularly affect
affairs ruled by that house, as well as those things which are designated
by the Ascendant. As Mars is the traditional ruler of the progressed
Fifth (Scorpio) House and rules the Tenth (Aries) Houses the matters
which are ruled by them will also be affected. As Mars is a very active
planet, the native will be actively concerned in affairs relating to his
parents in a beneficial manner. He is likely to make changes and
improvements in his home. As Mars is the traditional ruler of the Fifth
House this aspect will promote interest in sports and amusements. A
child may be conceived or born during this aspect. It may also incline
to gaming or speculation, or perhaps the purchase of property as the
Ascendant is in Cancer, a Fourth House sign (property). The native's
business will prosper through his own activities, and he will be accorded
some public credit or honors. (Mars, ruler of the Tenth House; the
Moon, ruler of himself and also a general ruler of the public.)

P ♅ ☌ ☾  R  You will notice that the progressed Uranus in 28° 22'
Virgo has moved to within 1° 30' of the radical Moon (29° ♍ 52').
These planets are in conjunction at birth and reference to the ephemeris
shows that it will require more than twelve days (years) movement
forward in the Zodiac before Uranus actually reaches 29° 52' Virgo at
which point the conjunction is partile. The effect of this progressed
aspect is to gradually increase the influence of the natal conjunction.

## 4. Parallel Aspects
P ♅ || ⊙ P all year. As both these planets are in the Third House
and rule the Eighth (Aquarius) and Second (Leo) Houses respectively it
will cause the mind to seek change and improvement, especially where

salary or finance is concerned. As Uranus usually acts prematurely, the native is cautioned not to make changes except after careful and deliberate judgment. This will be an excellent period for the native to study the Occult, Astrology, inventions and progressive matters generally. He will be very intuitive. Danger in travel.

P ☽ ∥ 10thHsP **September 23-October 23, 1910.** Some changes in his business will occur, necessitating short journeys and much correspondence. As the Moon is his ruler (Cancer Ascendant), it will prove beneficial and result in favor, popularity and advancement.

P ☽ ∥ ☿ P **February 23-March 23, 1911.** If the student will enter this at February 23, he will note that the Moon is at the same time making other favorable aspects to Venus (P ☽ ✱ ♀ R) and Jupiter (P ☽ ⊻ ♃ R), thereby designating this parallel of the Moon and progressed Mercury as a favorable influence.

P ☽ ∥ ♅ R **March 23-April 23, 1911.** Causes long journeys concerning railroads, inventions, or such things as Uranus rules. Very intuitive. Strange or prophetic dreams and intuitions. Danger in travel. Difficulty in domestic affairs. Changes concerning parents.

P ☽ ∥ ☉ P **March 23-April 23, 1911.** Favorable for advancement and popularity, short journeys, good for dealings with brethren, neighbors and matters of correspondence. Mental illumination. Good financial conditions.

P ☽ ∥ ♅ P **May 23-June 23, 1911.** Inclines to changes, investigation, interest in the Occult and all progressive matters. Makes the mind very alert, intuitive and inventive. Interest in affairs of brethren and neighbors. Danger in travel.

P ☽ ∥ ☽ R **May 23-June 23, 1911.** Tends to publicity, changes and advancement. Inclined to read and study. Domestic changes.

P ☽ ∥ ☿ R **May 23-June 23, 1911.** Conducive to business activity and to changes and removals, as Mercury was in the Fourth House in the natal chart. Inclines to interest in property.

## 5. Transits over Progressed Aspects to Radix

Note in *3. Progressed Aspects to Radix* that the progressed Mars is forming a trine to the radical Ascendant, P ♂ △ AscR. The effect of this aspect will be most noticeable when the aspect is supported or accentuated by transits of similar nature, that is, good aspects.

☉ ☌ ♃ R, ♂ ✱ (P ♂ △ AscR) Reference to the current ephemeris (1910) shows that the Sun is transiting the sign of Leo in August. The radix shows Jupiter at 18° 58' Leo. The Sun will transit this degree on August 12. The influence of the Sun conjunct Jupiter is very benefic. On August 12 there is also a favorable transit of Mars (4°♍) operating to the progressed Mars trine Ascendant radix, thus making the day doubly benign.

♂♂⊙R  Referring again to the ephemeris, it is observed that Mars enters Virgo on August 6 at which time it must transit over the place of natal Sun at 0° 29' Virgo. Mars crossing over the place of the Sun is very activating and disturbing. It inclines to feverishness and to accidents. As Mars will be in the Third House of the radix it will tend to excessive mental activity, haste, force, aggressiveness, contention, and accidents on short journeys.

☽ , ☿ ,♂ ♂ ⊙ R  Reference to the ephemeris again shows Mercury and the Moon also entering Virgo on August 6. This makes a combination of three planets all crossing the radical Sun on that day. The conjoined influence of all the Moon and Mercury is favorable but their conjunction with Mars is not. Hence, these mixed or contrary influences should produce a hectic day for this individual—a day in which he should exercise the utmost moderation, discrimination and tact, being extra cautious in writings, agreements, promises and short journeys.

☽ ✻ (P ♂ △ AscR)  On the same day a favorable transit occurs which will be helpful and tend to modify these indications somewhat. The Moon will be sextile to the progressed Mars trine the natal Ascendant aspect. Provided with this information, the native is enabled to act guardedly and thus avoid much of the difficulty indicated by the triple conjunction mentioned.

In similar manner the current ephemeris is checked against the progressed and natal charts, as well as the various aspects tabulated.

# Interpreting the Progressed Aspects

The following delineations have reference to all progressed aspects, whether formed to planets in the radix, in the progressed chart, or between one planet in the radix and the other in the progressed chart. The interpretations are general indications only and subject to modification and change according to the strength of the aspect (whether major or minor), the position of the aspected planets in the chart (whether angular, succedent or cadent), and the strength by dignity or weakness by debility according to the signs occupied.

In reading these aspects keep this fact constantly in mind, that by direction a planet can only bring to bear the influence it indicated in the radix, whether good or otherwise, and in proportion to its power by house, sign, aspect, etc. in the radix.

## LUNAR PROGRESSED ASPECTS

### The Moon in Good Aspect to Mercury

Makes the mind active, studious and creative. Inclines to success in journeys, writings, publishings, law, advertising or business, and general prosperity; changes and activity with inclination to read and study.

### The Moon Adverse to Mercury

Tends to anxiety, restlessness, nervous disorders and slander.

An adverse period for lawsuits, publishing, letter writing, signing of contracts, journeys and general business affairs. Friction with kindred or neighbors.

### The Moon in Good Aspect to Venus

A happy, peaceful, healthful, prosperous and fortunate period. The native inclines to the pleasures of Venus and it is strong testimony for courtship and marriage, especially the parallel or conjunction. With the married it indicates social and domestic pleasures, and the probable birth of a child, if such is indicated in the radix.

### The Moon Adverse to Venus

Losses, disappointment, bereavement among friends and sorrow in love and domestic affairs; extravagance, illicit relations, scandal or quarrels with the opposite sex, excesses according to the sign Venus is in; often indicates the loss of a child. To females, ill health and disappointments in all Venus affairs.

### The Moon in Conjunction or Parallel with Sun

Not good for health, especially in a woman's horoscope, producing an inert, lethargic, indifferent condition, resulting in feverish complaints and in ailments similar to an adverse aspect to Mars, which planet the Sun closely resembles in aspects. Otherwise the mind is free, generous and open. It brings changes, honor, gain in business, marriage and public favor for both males and females.

### The Moon Trine or in Other Good Aspect to Sun

Good for both sexes. Produces honors, popularity, promotion, influential friendships, gain through superiors and parents; good health; the mind is dignified, lofty, ambitious; good for speculation, marriage, fame and business. Success generally, especially in dealing with women and the common people, as well as with those in high office.

### The Moon Adverse to Sun

Unfortunate for all affairs of life. Denotes ill health, bereavement, loss of honor, fame, office, business, friends, support of superiors or parents and a very trying time generally. From water signs the native may take to drinking, and is inclined to company beneath his own station; from the Twelfth House, danger of imprisonment. With a female it affects the health particularly.

## The Moon in Good Aspect to Mars

Good for business, health, journies, new enterprises, and success generally. Shows gain through activity in Martian affairs; courage, generosity, a desire for active sports and exercise. Gain by military men, doctors, surgeons, etc., as denoted by Mars. Not so good with females, inclining to the society of the opposite sex; amorous and impulsive courtship and marriage, although good otherwise for activity and new projects.

## The Moon Adverse to Mars

Inclines the native to rashness, quarrels, extravagance, recklessness, disputes and litigation. He suffers discredit, slander and dishonor. Danger of fevers, smallpox and other Martian inflammatory disorders. Liable to wounds, bites, kicks, broken bones and accidents when traveling. If Mars is strong in the First, Second or Seventh House, he may lose by theft, fire or robbery. In fire signs, danger of high fevers, accidents by firearms, hurts by human hands; in earth signs, fall, hurts from animals, bites, etc.; water signs, scalds, danger of drowning, from drink, or excesses. This is a very critical period for women when under this aspect, as it signifies ill health, slander, discredit, attacks or trouble through moral indiscretions.

## The Moon in Good Aspect to Jupiter

An especially good direction for wealth, health and attachments. Conduces to gain, fame, honor and success generally; inclines to marriage, social advancement and voyages. Very good for health with women. A good period in which to start new business or make investments.

## The Moon Adverse to Jupiter

Bad for business. Trouble through law or the church. Losses in dealing with landlords, politicians, lawyers, magistrates, or in speculation, through poor judgment and miscalculation. The disposition is free, extravagant and profligate; the associates impose upon the generosity of the native, causing him to make bad loans and squander his money.

It disturbs the health by impurities of the blood, headaches, stomach and liver disorders.

## The Moon in Good Aspect to Saturn

Success in business, especially through elderly persons and Saturn things, popularity, new friends. The mind is active, patient, contemplative, serious, dignified and cares little for society but is attentive to business; deep and profound with good organizing ability. Good for matters relating to land, property, produce, mines. Also beneficial for things indicated by the house occupied by the Moon.

## The Moon Adverse to Saturn

Direful results; loss of friends, business, money, and danger of failure or bankruptcy, especially if either is posited in or ruler of the Second or Tenth House. Dishonor, losses, grief, disappointment and bereavement; morbid, melancholy, anxious state of mind; the health suffers from cold, lingering disorders; aches and pains according to the sign Saturn occupies. Unfavorable for the commencement of anything new. Very bad period for buying, investing or assuming heavy liabilities.

## The Moon in Good Aspect to Uranus

Produces pleasant journeys, advantageous removals and changes that are beneficial though sudden and unexpected, and according to the house in which the Moon is posited. Especially good for the above from First, Third and Ninth Houses. It sharpens the mental facilities and makes the mind curious, fanciful, eccentric, inventive and inclined to the investigation of the Occult; to research, exploration and travel. Brings new friends; correct intuition. The nature is romantic and fond of adventure. It inclines to society of the opposite sex.

## The Moon Adverse to Uranus

Causes sudden, unexpected, disastrous changes, journies and removals. Brings trouble through women, loss of credit or position, danger of accidents, slander, and disgrace; worry, anxiety and restlessness. The mind is sarcastic, bitter, obstinate, rebellious, hasty or irrational, and the actions indiscreet. Happening in the Seventh House, discord in marriage; in the Fifth House, illicit attractions, danger of loss in speculation; sorrow through children.

## The Moon in Good Aspect to Neptune

Gain through the mediumistic, inspirational and artistic faculties; also through schemes, secret alliances and secret orders. Rise through the influence of women. Enemies are subdued and existing evils brought to light that were designed to discredit the native. The mind is restless, emotional and given to pleasure. Prophetic impressions and premonitions. Favors matters relating to liquids, chemicals, oils, anesthetics, beverages and the sea.

## The Moon Adverse to Neptune

Produces secret enmities or intrigues against the native. Deception, fraud, plots and schemes which tend to bring him into disrepute. The mind is uneasy, worried and burdened with fear or strange forebodings. Seductive friends or associates. Bad for health, causing a negative physical condition; danger of ptomaine poisoning and danger on water. Confusion, indiscretions or complications.

## The Moon in Good Aspect to Its Own Radical Place

Changes, journies, gain by females, new friends, increase in business. Inclines to female society.

## The Moon in Adverse Aspect to Its Own Radix Place

Loss, disappointment, unfavorable changes, bereavement, unpopularity. To women it brings ill health.

## The Moon in Conjunction or Parallel with the Ascendant

Change of residence and travel by land or sea; social or business preferment if the Moon be fortunate by sign or aspects. Otherwise adversity, Lunar disease or accidents and danger by water. Increased interest in public and local affairs.

## The Moon in Sextile or Trine with the Ascendant

Active employment, friendship of ladies in authority or in social position; popularity, favorable publicity, general prosperity, marriage or birth of a daughter, according to the circumstances surrounding the native. Desire for change and travel.

### The Moon Adverse the Ascendant

Controversies, strife or disputes with women; conjugal misery, divorce, discord, jealousy, unpopularity, ill-health, intemperance, etc., according to the position of the Moon in the radix. An unfavorable period for traveling by land or sea.

### The Moon in Conjunction or Parallel with the Midheaven

If the Moon be strong and fortunate at birth: honor, renown, advantageous changes, traveling and popularity. Men usually marry under this influence. But if the Moon be weak and adversely configurated in the radix, losses and unproductive journies or voyages result, and the wife or mother suffers. Public disfavor.

### The Moon in Sextile or Trine with the Midheaven

Increase of substance, popularity, honors, gifts, favors from women. Active business and traveling are indicated, if from movable signs. To men it may mean marriage, or increase in business, improvement of position.

### The Moon Adverse the Midheaven

This bring unpopularity, scandals, quarrels with women, suffering wife or mother, public discredit and family disputes, according to the position of the Moon, whether in the Seventh, First or Fourth.


## THE PROGRESSED ASPECTS OF MERCURY

### Mercury in Good Aspect to Venus

Not of great importance, but increases interest in literature, music, dress and comforts. Pleasure in the fine arts, new friends and female acquaintances. Tends to refined society; adds a charm to the personality.

### Mercury Adverse to Venus

Reverse to the foregoing.

### Mercury in Good Aspect to the Sun

Excites the mind to great activity and gives an inclination for books, study, literature, writing and sometimes journies if either planet be in the Third or Ninth House. Honor and promotion through Mercurial affairs; increased business activity.

## Mercury Adverse to the Sun

Brings losses and annoyance through writings, publishings, letters, agreements and possibly journies, if either planet be posited in Third or Ninth House. Adverse criticism; loss of position.

## Mercury in Good Aspect to Mars

Increases the activity of both mind and body, thereby adding new stimulus to business and gain therein. Resourceful, industrious, mechanical, constructive, enterprising, confident, practical, executive and expressive.

## Mercury Adverse to Mars

Inclines to low company, loose morals. Acting upon the mind, it inclines to quarreling, thieving, forgery, scandal, etc.; a sarcastic, suspicious mental attitude; liable to engage in law and disputes and may commit violence on impulse. Worried, anxious states of mind, trouble in business or employment and with relatives.

## Mercury in Good Aspect to Jupiter

Strengthens the mind and gives good business judgment and foresight. Denotes popularity, promotion and success in things ruled by these planets according to their indications in the nativity; good for things ruled by houses occupied. Also for literary efforts, new studies, publishing, advertising and travel.

## Mercury Adverse to Jupiter

An unsettled mental condition. Losses through poor judgment and writings. If Mercury is not strong it inclines to trouble through forgery, libel, perjury, loans, misstatements, miscalculation, misplaced confidence, extravagance, excesses, legal violations and journies.

## Mercury in Good Aspect to Saturn

Gives a patient, persevering, systematic, studious, grave, dignified, practical mind; conduces to gain through discreet and prudent management of business affairs. If Mercury is in the First, Third or Ninth, it gives success in intellectual pursuits, writing, publishing, traveling, lecturing, teaching. Favors matters related to land, property, produce, mines, science, geology, etc.

### Mercury Adverse to Saturn

Trouble through slander, forged letters or documents and things ruled by Mercury. The mind is sarcastic, gloomy, bitter and given to much worry. Not good for health as it tends to poor circulation, indigestion, constipation and obstruction, and generous nervous derangement. Usually indicates trouble with landlords, tenants, employees, parents or other relatives. Loss by small animals, property, mines or lack of employment and illness. Hindrance, delays, disappointment and a trying time generally.

### Mercury in Good Aspect to Uranus

If from First, Third or Ninth House, or either planet the ruler thereof, inclines the mind to study and travel and gain thereby. Under this direction the mind is active, witty and original; gain through invention, electrical, aerial or transportation companies, publishing, advertising, writing, radio, electronics, research, exploration, risky ventures and such things as are ruled by these planets.

### Mercury Adverse to Uranus

Unsettled, sarcastic, impulsive, radical, rebellious, chaotic states of mind; difficulty with friends, kindred, civil service or municipal officers. Unsuccessful in literary pursuits; press criticism. Trouble through writings, either letters or documents. Great inclination to travel and sudden changes, or upheavel in plans and affairs. Danger on journies and through electrical contrivances, autos, engines, airplanes, etc.

### Mercury in Good Aspect to Neptune

If occurring in the Third or Ninth House, and the nativity so indicates, it strengthens the mental qualities and psychic nature, producing automatic writing, trance and inspirational speaking. Useful mental impressions and premonitions. Favors matters relating to food, hygiene, liquids, oil, beverages, the sea, and educational or healing institutions.

## Mercury Adverse to Neptune

Defective memory and tendency to mental confusion, nervousness, restlessness, over-sensitiveness, lack of self-control and liability to be led into dissolute habits. Deception and loss in business affairs and through things ruled by these planets. Misunderstanding, misstatements, concealment of facts, lack of proper information, perjury, forgery, anonymity are likely to lead to distress and trouble.

## Mercury in Conjunction or Parallel with the Ascendant

Change of residence, a journey, active business; a propensity for study, invention and writing, the results of which will be fortunate or unfortunate according to the indications of Mercury in radix.

If Mercury be very much afflicted at birth, an accident or serious sickness is threatened; many worries and annoyances. Trouble with neighbors or relatives.

## Mercury in Sextile or Trine with the Ascendant

Prosperity, active employment, traveling; gain by literary work, teaching or by speculating, if Mercury is in the Fifth House and well placed in Gemini or Virgo. May indicate birth of a child (nephew or niece), change of residence, new acquaintances.

## Mercury Adverse the Ascendant

This influence gives a disinclination for study, failure to pass examinations; mischief by writings, promises or agreements, or through the press; overwork; disease of the nature of Mercury and the planets with which it may be configurated; troubles with children and young persons, scandal, slander or discredit. To children this aspect often brings whooping-cough, bronchitis and convulsions, attended with danger.

## Mercury in Conjunction or Parallel with the Midheaven

If Mercury be strong, (in Gemini or Virgo, or in a cardinal house) gain by literary pursuits, traveling, teaching, etc.

If Mercury be afflicted, (in the progressed or radix) libel, legal difficulties, unfortunate trading, many business worries and annoyances.

### Mercury in Sextile or Trine with the Midheaven

Preferment, honor and increase of business, according to the strength and situation of Mercury in the radix.

Children are often first sent to school and young people to college or honorary degrees are granted under this influence. It usually produces a change of residence or travel in connection with business.

### Mercury Adverse the Midheaven

Troubles and losses are indicated, also danger of lawsuits, unjust sentences, libels and false accusations. Death of a child, cousin or neighbor frequently happens under this influence. Trouble through writings, promises or publishing.

## THE PROGRESSED ASPECTS OF VENUS

### Venus in Good Aspect to the Sun

Honor and preferment in a social way and much pleasure in refined amusements. Gain through business, profession, speculation, public occupation; it produces a generous, harmonious state of mind. Good for health; conducive to love affairs and marriage; indicates gifts, honors and promotion; inclines to the purchase of jewels, adornment, objects of art, furniture.

### Venus Adverse to the Sun

Causes extravagance or excess of pleasure; grief through the offspring; misfortune in love affairs and dealings with the opposite sex; an amorous nature and mutable in the affections. Loss through speculation. Social rebuffs; difficulty through matters related to beauty and adornment; lack of funds and ill health.

### Venus in Good Aspect to Mars

Inclines to the society of the opposite sex and general good time. Incites to love and marriage. The native is daring and free, delights in and gains through Venus affairs. Good for acquiring money through things ruled by these planets. Not good for morals, as no aspect between Mars and Venus tends to strict morality.

### Venus Adverse to Mars

Inclines to low company, loose morals, scandal, debauchery, loss through speculation and extravagance; trouble with partners or associates. Especially bad for women, and particularly so if Mars be in the Fifth, Seventh or Tenth House at birth, or in the progressed chart.

### Venus in Good Aspect to Jupiter

Good for the things governed by the houses occupied in progressed chart or in the nativity and also houses which they rule. Inclines to refined society and amusements and gain thereby; social activity, gain in business, finances, new adornments, furnishings; travel for pleasure, education or business.

### Venus Adverse to Jupiter

Losses through speculations and a tendency to extravagance through overdress, women and social amusements. Luxurious tastes, excessive pleasures, expensive undertakings. Liability to loss of money through loans, legal decisions or gaming.

### Venus in Good Aspect to Saturn

A modest, chaste, frugal, sincere state of mind; favors steady attachments in love and friendship. Gain by elders, superiors and solid business investment. Much good luck of a substantial quality. Favors matters of practical, artistic value, also land, property, mines.

### Venus Adverse to Saturn

Lax morals, bereavements, death of offspring, business losses, trouble in courtship and marriage, not good for speculation, investments, lands, mines, leasings, companies or banks. Tends to delay, disappointment, restriction, loss of business or employment and ill health.

### Venus in Good Aspect to Uranus

Gain in such things as are ruled by the planets in question. Inclines to the company of the opposite sex. Romance, new friends, increase in business, new facilities, improved methods, new and pleasant experiences.

## Venus Adverse to Uranus

Unfortunate for matters concerning the opposite sex. Extremely unconventional and indiscreet, liability to scandal and discredit thereby. Sudden and unexpected losses and estrangement from friends. Not good for speculation or risky ventures.

## Venus in Good Aspect to Neptune

Promotes success through speculation, shipping, liquids, oils and the Occult sciences; pleasure and benefit through friends, associations and acquaintances. Gain through secret organizations, by quiet, secluded efforts and things of artistic, pleasurable or comforting nature.

## Venus Adverse to Neptune

Financial loss through schemes, plots, theft and trouble through secret organizations, friends and associations; scandal and misrepresentation. Misunderstanding in love affairs, or financial loss from confusion, impractical procedure and vague, indefinite or involved ventures. Betrayed, fooled, duped, tricked or cheated.

## Venus in Good Aspect to the Ascendant

This aspect brings pleasure, gain, new friends, courtship, marriage, birth of children; purchase of articles of luxury, furniture, clothing, ornaments, etc., according to circumstances.

If Venus be afflicted (especially in a water sign) the conjunction may incline to dissipation or extravagance.

## Venus Adverse the Ascendant

Is not important unless Venus be very much afflicted, and then it will manifest according to the nature of the afflicting planet. It usually produces excess of pleasure, eating, drinking, etc., and ill health, accordingly; also extravagance and useless expenditure. To women it sometimes disturbs the generative system; to men danger of venereal diseases.

## Venus in Good Aspect to the Midheaven

This brings mirth, gaiety, pleasure-seeking, renewal of furniture, clothing, free expenditure, advancement in artistic pursuits, the birth of children and general prosperity. Love affairs commence and marriage often takes place under this influence. Indicates social distinction, honors and favorable publicity.

### Venus Adverse the Midheaven

Indicates scandal or annoyance on the part of women; loss of credit or reputation, extravagance, and, in some cases, dissipation. The mother, wife or sister suffers in health or other inconveniences; business and financial troubles.

## THE PROGRESSED ASPECTS OF THE SUN

### The Sun in Good Aspect to Mars

Denotes changes, activity, preferment, honor, health and strength. The mind is alert, quick in anger but soon appeased. The nature is frank, free, generous, candid, ambitious, progressive, venturesome, confident and aggressive. The native is inclined to active or strenuous sports; possesses constructive qualities and self-assurance; meets favor, promotion and success in Martian affairs; increased business activity and responsibilities. With women it conduces to marriage but usually of somewhat discordant nature.

### The Sun Adverse to Mars

Denotes sharp, acute attacks of sickness; accidents, cuts, burns, bites and danger from all inflammatory diseases and sicknesses, such as smallpox, fevers, cholera, fluxes, etc., according to the sign occupied by Mars. In a female horoscope, danger in childbirth. Under this direction one is liable to suffer loss by fire if either planet is in a fiery sign, inclined to fighting, anger, quarrels; danger of violence and robbery. A water sign conduces to drunkenness and excesses, if the nativity shows such.

### The Sun in Good Aspect to Jupiter

Exceedingly good for honor, wealth, health, fame, law and general success in all lines. If the radix indicates it, the native may expect advancement, preferment and honors through influential friends and gain according to the house in which Jupiter is posited. Very favorable for marriage, speculation, expansion, extension of interests and general prosperity.

### The Sun in Adverse Aspect to Jupiter

Very bad for money matters, law, speculation and health. It denotes liability to apoplexy, pleurisy, bursting blood vessels and general derangement of the system if the Sun is hyleg or Jupiter ruler of the Sixth House. Do not buy, loan, speculate or invest during this aspect. Loss through misplaced confidence, miscalculation or poor judgment.

### The Sun in Good Aspect to Saturn

Denotes substantial gain, public approval, honor, success in mines, lands and things of a Saturn nature; preferment and advancement through those in authority and also through the native's own efforts. The mind is dignified, lofty and austere, favored with concentration, confidence, good calculation, estimation and appraisal. The native is quiet, patient and persevering. A good period in which to make long-time investments, for building and buying.

### The Sun Adverse to Saturn

Very adverse for health, wealth and social standing. The native suffers loss of business, or credit and bankruptcy if the afflictions occur from the Second or Eighth House; sickness from the Sixth or Twelfth House, and possibly death from the Eighth House. The native incurs opposition, enmity and public disfavor. The mind may become unsympathetic, without regard for the feelings of others, selfish, calculating and pessimistic. It threatens the demise of the husband in a female horoscope. Very inauspicious time for new business, risky ventures, expansion, buying, investing, changing position or traveling.

### The Sun in Good Aspect to Uranus

Gain through the talents, inventions, public employ, popularity, fraternal societies and voyages. The mind is active and enterprising. Beneficial changes brought about suddenly and unexpectedly. Good for health and general welfare. Advancement in occult science. Journeys, if not in fixed signs. New interests, friends, undertakings and business improvements.

### The Sun Adverse to Uranus

Sudden and unexpected losses, calamities, accidents, enmities; loss of honor, public favor, friends and patrons. Uranus is separative in nature and causes trouble from any house in which it may be posited or may rule. Bad health, causing a disturbed, nervous, excitable, radical or rebellious state of mind; very unfavorable for marriage as it tends toward separation, estrangement, divorce or incompatibility.

### The Sun in Good Aspect to Neptune

The mind is sympathetic, kind and generous. Gain through the Occult and spiritual sciences; inclines to pleasure and benefit through the artistic faculties and traveling; by things of a hidden or secret nature and those of authority and government employ. Harmonious, constructive or enlightening impressions. Favors matters related to liquids, chemicals, drugs, oil, anesthetics, beverages, the sea and large institutions such as theatres, sanitariums, hospitals.

### The Sun Adverse to Neptune

Loss through fraud, scandal, schemes and intrigues. Loss of standing with those of authority. Disadvantageous changes and loss of occupation. Bad for health; annoying psychic conditions. Danger through drugs, narcotics, beverages or the sea.

### The Progressed Sun in Good Aspect to its own Radical Place

Honor, esteem, popularity, promotion, progress, success in business, general prosperity, improved health and many pleasures.

### The Progressed Sun in Adverse Aspect to its own Radical Place

Loss in matters mentioned above and a trying time generally.

### The Sun in Conjunction or Parallel with the Ascendant

If the Sun be strong and fortunate, in Aries, Leo or Sagittarius, and has no adverse aspects, gain by public favors from powerful people, advancement, employment, increase of reputation and credit; but at the same time liable to ill health through inflammatory complaints. To military men great preferment is indicated.

If the Sun be afflicted by the malefics, danger to life is threatened and trouble through the head, eyes and heart especially.

If the Sun be in conjunction with Mars, danger by fire or firearms and accidents of a Martian nature.

### The Sun in Sextile or Trine with the Ascendant

Health of body, peace of mind, favor from persons in authority, new friends, some elevation in rank, according to the native's social position. Women usually marry or have a son under this aspect, or receive social distinction.

### The Sun Adverse to the Ascendant

Disease according to the position of the Sun. Envy and enmity of persons in power; loss of employment and credit; danger to the father and in some cases danger of imprisonment, if Sun was heavily afflicted at birth. Traveling, changes, speculation, risky ventures, excitement and over-exertion should be avoided during this aspect.

### The Sun in Conjunction or Parallel with the Midheaven

Honors, advancement and increase of substance. To unmarried women it usually indicates marriage. But if the Sun is adversely configurated with the malefics, or in conjunction with fixed stars of a violent nature, it will bring disputes and possibly misfortune of a public nature; danger to the mother. Otherwise it denotes distinction.

### The Sun in Sextile or Trine with the Midheaven

This is an elevating influence, and if the nativity promises it, brings renown, great advancement, honors, popularity, credit.

It also benefits the native's parents. Public offices are often gained under this influence. To women it brings marriage or employment of a public nature, and social advancement.

### The Sun Adverse the Midheaven

This often brings loss of office or employment, bad trading, disgrace and sometimes bankruptcy and imprisonment. One of the parents suffers or may die.

## THE PROGRESSED ASPECTS OF MARS

### Mars in Good Aspect to Jupiter

Good for things indicated, according to the position of Jupiter in the nativity and by place of Jupiter in progressed chart. Tends to activity, determination and vim; gain through personal effort. Elevates the desires and aspirations, increases business interests; promotion, expansion, success through practical endeavor, good judgment and active execution.

### Mars Adverse to Jupiter

Indicates losses and trouble according to the nature of the two planets and their indications in the nativity according to the houses occupied; possibly through law, foreign travel, religion or competition, misplaced confidence or dishonesty. The subject may himself cause his own misfortune through hasty, impulsive action or extravagance, carelessness, hasty judgment, miscalculation or dissipation. Danger through fires if these planets are in fire sign. Subject to accidents, feverish complaints or strain.

### Mars in Good Aspect to Saturn

If one or both planets are prominent, denotes activity, steadfastness and credit through some courageous acts and well regulated business activity of practical, conservative nature. Good for building, repairing, improvements; constructive, mechanical or industrial activity; manufacturing, engineering, excavating, mining.

### Mars Adverse to Saturn

Especially unfavorable if from the First, Seventh or Tenth House. Inclines to quick, violent temper which leads to quarreling, fighting, jealousy and perhaps crime. Danger of accident and broken bones; loss in business or occupation; thefts; nervous apprehension and irritability; liable to sudden, sharp, serious attacks of illness.

### Mars in Good Aspect to Uranus

Quickens the mind and increases power; indicates gain through invention, engineering, construction, contracts, exploration, investigation, energetic activity, unique enterprise and extension of activities.

Since both are malefics, they usually produce no appreciable good, except through new, active methods or plans and aggressive business enterprise, personal industry and progressive business acumen.

### Mars Adverse to Uranus

From the First House, increase of temper, jealousy. From the Seventh House, intensifies and causes trouble with partners; divorce or separation.

From the Tenth House, unexpected and sudden calamities and disgrace. Municipal or political enmity.

Otherwise trouble through rash, hasty, forceful and erratic expressions, premature speech and action, sudden radical changes and accidents.

### Mars in Good Aspect to Neptune

Creates activity and enthusiasm in the investigation of occult subjects and secret missions and gain through matters connected with liquids, drugs, oils, beverages, chemistry, the sea or large institutions.

### Mars Adverse to Neptune

Danger from psychic conditions and phenomena. Tends to trouble by fraud, deception, scandal, bribery and mental disturbance; loss or accident on or by water, oils, liquids, poisons, drugs, thieves and habits. Avoid damp, unhealthy, foul or ill-smelling places where disease or noxious influences may lurk.

### Mars in Conjunction, Parallel, Square or Opposition with the Ascendant

Tends to over-positivity, rash, hot-headed, sarcastic combative attitudes.

Accidents or disease, according to the position of Mars. If Mars be in a fire sign, acute fevers or accidents by fire; in earth signs, danger of suffocation, especially if in bad aspect to Saturn in radix; in Taurus, small-pox or diphtheria; in the human signs, danger of homicide, or of being killed in a quarrel or battle; in a water sign, danger of a fall from a height, or acute fever. Women will be in danger through the opposite sex.

Of course, if Mars was well placed in the radix and had no bad aspects very little of the foregoing would transpire.

## Mars in Sextile or Trine with the Ascendant

This inclines the native to travel, sport, health exercises; to enter the army or navy, study medicine, surgery or chemistry or become an engineer, according to the radix. Women sometimes marry under this influence. Benefits the health, strengthens the constitution, increases the passions. The native assumes new responsibilities, enters into new projects. Very active.

## Mars in Conjunction, Parallel, Square or Opposition with the Midheaven

This is an adverse influence as it denotes quarrels, losses, fires, thefts and fraud. To military men and surgeons the conjunction brings advancement, but it is attended with some danger. The parents suffer in some respect.

Misfortunes are sure to result if changes and speculations be made while this Martian aspect is in operation.

## Mars in Sextile or Trine with the Midheaven

This signifies an active and prosperous period, especially for Martians. Busy, industrious, constructive.

# THE PROGRESSED ASPECTS OF JUPITER

## Jupiter in Good Aspect to Saturn

Good for legacy, gifts or promotion. Honors through science or law, gain through lawsuits and all things ruled by the planets and the houses they occupy, especially Jupiter. Substantial increase in general affairs, land, property, possessions, business, credit.

## Jupiter Adverse to Saturn

Loss through law, business, educational institutions, religious bodies and all things ruled by these planets. Loss of honor and credit, bad for health, peace of mind and business generally. Unfavorable for new or important undertakings or assumption of heavy liabilities.

## Jupiter in Good Aspect to Uranus

Gain through legacy, law, gifts of money, Uranian occupations, foreign travel, higher science, publishing, and religious or educational movements. Favors inventions, research, exploration, new studies, business expansion; interest in government and public welfare.

### Jupiter Adverse to Uranus

Tendency the same as the good aspect, but unattended by unexpected losses, obstacles and difficulties. Much annoyance and trouble over lawsuits, inheritance and financial affairs. Unfavorable for new undertakings or risky ventures.

### Jupiter in Good Aspect to Neptune

Favors traveling, dreams, visions, psychic conditions and honor through the investigation of religion from a scientific or occult standpoint; popularity and success in secret societies and through achievements in scientific research, medicine, chemistry, publishing, or large institutions.

### Jupiter Adverse to Neptune

Losses through speculation, fraud, imposture, cheating, treachery; discredit through religious matters, secret societies or foreign affairs. This aspect tends to disturb the health, necessitating care in diet, caution in use of stimulants, beverages, etc.

### Jupiter in Good Aspect to the Ascendant

Stimulates growth and increases size or weight of the body. This is fortunate for health and all affairs, prosperity, conviviality, new friends, advancement, favors, marriage, birth of children, inherited property, according to condition of the radix. Gives interest in travel, foreign affairs, education, philosophy and philanthropy.

### Jupiter Adverse the Ascendant

An indifferent state of health, often due to plethora. If Jupiter be afflicted by Mars, danger of measles, scarlatina, small-pox, pleurisy, etc. A bad time to deal with lawyers, bankers, brokers or speculators. Extravagant expenditure, carelessness, conviviality, misjudgment. Loss through loans, indebtedness, heavy liabilities or excessive overhead.

If the radical Jupiter was in conjunction with Ascendant, or afflicted, it may bring serious illness (but not necessarily fatal), arising from some disease of the lungs, liver, blood or hips.

## Jupiter in Good Aspect to the Midheaven

Preferment, honors, increase of wealth, benefits from persons in power, general happiness and prosperity. Social advancement, business expansion.

Single women usually marry under this aspect. To merchants it brings increase of trade; to the clergy, preferment; to lawyers, advancement and high repute. A good time to begin new undertakings if no other testimonies conflict.

## Jupiter Adverse the Midheaven

This chiefly brings heavy expenses and disputes with professional persons; nothing very adverse unless Jupiter be much afflicted in the radix, which gives tendency to loss through banks, speculation or risky enterprises. Not a good time to loan money or sign bail bonds.

## THE PROGRESSED ASPECTS OF SATURN

## Saturn in Good Aspect to Uranus

Quickens the mind and tends to a thoughtful, profound and penetrating attitude; success through determination and fixity of purpose in the investigation of the occult on a mental plane, such as telepathy, mental healing, suggestive therapeutics, etc.; also through inventions, vehicles of transportation, railroads, either electric or steam, and mining of lead, coal, platinum and aluminum. A great inclination for knowledge of the secrets of nature.

The aspects of these planets are more potent when occurring from the First, Third, Ninth or Tenth House. From the Tenth House are considered not so good since neither planet is entirely favorable in that house.

## Saturn Adverse to Uranus

Unfavorable generally; unexpected obstacles and disappointment. Accidents. This is one of those aspects which last over a long period and is felt when excited by transits of adverse nature, and usually affects the health.

From the Tenth House, loss of business, ill fame and disgrace.

## Saturn in Good Aspect to Neptune

Gives deep, clear, concentrated, inspirational thought and practical benefits through the psychical nature and the occult sciences generally; also benefit through elderly people, secret service organizations, investments, property, legacies and large institutions.

## Saturn Adverse to Neptune

Loss through plots, treachery, failures, speculation, and difficulty over legacies, business, etc. May suffer from psychic conditions. Health may be disturbed by improper diet, beverages, insufficient exercise or excessive nervousness, anxiety, fear and discontent.

## Saturn in Conjunction, Parallel, Square or Opposition with the Ascendant

If Saturn be Oriental (in the eastern half of the chart, between the cusp of the Tenth and Fourth Houses), a serious accident or a broken limb; if Occidental (the western half of chart between Midheaven and Nadir), danger of severe illness. In some cases this indicates a heavy cold with danger of fatal results; in others, melancholia and suicidal mania. Depression, restriction, delays, disappointment and many annoyances.

To women, dangerous internal diseases, possibility of disappointment or disgrace in love or matrimony.

## Saturn in Sextile or Trine with the Ascendant

Gain by elderly persons, legacies, mining, building, purchase or sale of lands, houses. Benefits the health, strengthens the constitution and produces many satisfactory conditions. Inclines to peace of mind, rest and feelings of security.

## Saturn in Conjunction, Parallel, Square or Opposition with the Midheaven

This indicates family troubles and losses or death of a parent or employer, loss of reputation and credit, theft, fraud and unpopularity; merchants and tradesmen lose heavily in speculative transactions and through general depression and limitations. May also indicate difficulties on the job or finding employment.

## Saturn in Sextile or Trine with the Midheaven

This shows pecuniary gain by farming, mining, building, legacies, favor and friendship of old people. Business and domestic conditions become more secure and favorable.

# THE PROGRESSED ASPECTS OF URANUS

## Uranus in Good Aspect to Neptune

Increases the intuition and psychic ability; inclines to journies, explorations, investigations, interest and gain in occult affairs, secret societies and progressive matters generally. Inspiration for writing, healing or social welfare.

## Uranus Adverse to Neptune

Gives intuition and the same interest in the Occult and mysterious, but investigation of such matters is accompanied by obstacles and difficulties; tendency to nervousness or vague apprehension.

## Uranus in Conjunction, Parallel, Square or Opposition with the Ascendant

This shows sudden losses (probably by railroads, airplanes, large corporations or inventions), disappointments, and if Uranus be afflicted, injuries; sudden journies (if in a cardinal or common sign), and changes of occupation. Estrangement and domestic difficulties. Strange feelings, thoughts and desires; rebellious, eccentric, radical, impulsive, spasmodic and given to sudden resolutions or changes in plans.

## Uranus in Sextile or Trine with the Ascendant

Gain of a totally unexpected nature; fortunate journies, removals, active business, also a desire to study or investigate Occult science. Increases the intuition and inventive faculty. Favors telepathy, clairvoyance and also new friendships; changes, reforms, improvements and new interests.

## Uranus in Conjunction, Parallel, Square or Opposition with the Midheaven

This is often attended by a sudden death in the family; pecuniary loss and troubles of a strange nature; disappointment in love and marriage; separation or estrangements. Peculiar mental condition and impulsiveness. Great desire for change, unexpected opposition, governmental interference, business changes, discredit.

### Uranus in Sextile or Trine with the Midheaven

Sudden and unexpected gain; sudden changes or traveling of an advantageous nature; favor and friendship of Uranian persons. Promotion and business advancement. Benefit by municipal or progressive affairs.

## THE PROGRESSED ASPECTS OF NEPTUNE

### Neptune in Conjunction or Parallel with the Ascendant

If adversely configurated in the radix, it now inclines to produce indescribable feelings and emotions, queer likes, dislikes, attractions and aversions. Interest in things of a mysterious or psychical nature. Desire to travel.

### Neptune in Sextile or Trine with the Ascendant

Pleasant and peaceful conditions. Interest in art, music, drama and psychical affairs. Correct premonitions, impressions or dreams. Gain by means of travel or liquids, oil, drugs, the cinema and things of a mysterious nature.

### Neptune in Square or Opposition with the Ascendant

Affects the health adversely and produces negative, lethargic states. Danger through liquids, drugs, anesthetics and psychical affairs. Liability to domestic complications, also to deception, misunderstanding or fraud.

### Neptune in Conjunction or Parallel with the Midheaven

If badly afflicted in the radix, it brings on peculiar difficulties, discredit, deception and business complications. But if well aspected in the radix, it will operate much the same as the sextile or trine.

### Neptune in Sextile or Trine with the Midheaven

Increase of trade, benefits through voyages, shipping, liquids, oils, drugs or psychical affairs. Credit and esteem through progressive or peculiar achievement.

## Neptune in Square or Opposition with the Midheaven

Danger of loss, discredit, business complications, scandal, misunderstanding, deception, fraud and treachery, especially in connection with things mentioned in the preceding paragraph.

# THE PROGRESSED ASPECTS OF PLUTO

Pluto moves so slowly through the Zodiac, that its progressed aspects will not be significantly different from its natal aspects.

# THE PROGRESSED ASPECTS OF THE PART OF FORTUNE

The position of the Part of Fortune in a progressed chart has no influence on the character or health, but is said to benefit any house in which it may be posited, by gain in things ruled by such house, subject to the quality of aspects it receives.

Benefic planets by progressed motion or by transit passing over or favorably aspecting the radical Part of Fortune are a favorable influence.

Malefic planets in like manner passing over or adversely aspecting it foreshadow loss.

# THE PROGRESSED ASPECTS OF THE MOON'S NODES

The Moon's North Node passing the place of, or forming a major aspect with the radical place of Jupiter, Venus, the Sun, the Moon, or Mercury indicates benefits to the native. Square or opposition to the benefics portends evil according to the house occupied by it and the nature of the planet afflicted.

The Moon's North Node passing in sextile or trine the radical Neptune, Uranus, Saturn and Mars is beneficial in nature. The square of opposition or conjunction to the malefics portends evil according to the houses occupied by it and the nature of the planet afflicted.

The Moon's South Node crossing over any planet is evil for the things ruled by the house occupied and the planet thus afflicted.

# Interpreting Transits

## THE TRANSITING MOON THROUGH THE HOUSES

The following delinations are the combined influences of the Moon and the house it is transiting through without consideration for any aspects which may be formed. An aspect would modify or accentuate the conditions as stated, according to whether it is favorable or adverse.

This section should be used as an example for deducing the influences. The same method or style should be employed when treating the house transit influence of the other planets, based on their delinations given in previous chapters. The influence of the planets by transit in houses is similar to the delineations given previously for the natal house positions.

### The Moon in the Ascendant, or First House

Affects the personality and brings matters of self into consideration. It brings desire for a change and overcomes conservatism by inclining to sociability or publicly. Increases action of moisture in head and face.

### In the Second House

Matters of finance will attract attention and it is a good time in which to plan methods, ways and means of increasing or conducting monetary considerations, especially those matters which involve dealings with the public or with commodities of a changeable nature.

509

Good for vocal exercise.

### In Third House

Inclines to short journies dealings with neighbors or kindred and correspondence. If you make up your mind about something when the Moon is in the Third House you are very apt to change it, especially if not in a fixed sign. Good for study of public affairs, matters of mental enlightenment and breathing exercises, as it affects the lungs; favorable for practice requiring dexterity of hands and fingers.

### In Fourth House

Arouses interest in the home, the place of abode and family or domestic affairs; also matters connected with land or property. This location of the Moon conduces to thoughts of change, if only to changing things about the house. It affects the breast and stomach and one should be careful in eating and drinking.

### In Fifth House

Gives a speculative tendency, an inclination to take changes, to favor romance, gaiety and the society of younger people. It conduces to happiness, mirth, a sense of freedom and increase of affections. Favorable for attending places of amusement.

### In Sixth House

Conduces to matters of employment, employees, labor, food, clothing, animals or sickness. It inclines to physical indisposition so that care should be given to hygienic methods. Overwork or over-indulgence in any way is likely to result in sickness affecting the stomach and bowels.

### In Seventh House

Awakens interest in matters connected with partners, associates, marriage, opponents and dealing with others. Unions, partnerships, etc., undertaken when the Moon is in the house are subject to changes and therefore care should be taken not to bestow too much confidence in the steadfastness of others, or continuity of deals transacted at this time for practice requiring dexterity of hands and fingers. A good time to read a new book.

## In Eighth House

With the majority of people the transit of Moon through their Eighth House is not very perceptible in effect, but it inclines to attention of monetary affairs or financial conditions of others, or the money of partner or associate, and causes the mind to revert to those who are deceased. But in others interest turns towards the occult or psychology. This is a good time to turn within for self-examination, or to watch one's actions for psychological and emotional intents. Thoughts of jealousy, vengeance or hatred should be released.

## In Ninth House

Turns the attention to higher channels of thought, matters of education, spiritual or psychical unfoldment and thoughts of journeys and reminiscence of distant scenes. Impressive dreams, when the Moon is in this house, are usually prophetic.

## In Tenth House

Inclines to business activity in a professional way or with professional people. It conduces to change in business methods or pursuits and brings up matters connected with honor, credit or advancement. Interest in mother's welfare and also that of the government or responsibilities. Use this period to reasess your goals and ambitions and your position in society.

## In Eleventh House

Usually brings one into contact with others in a social way, creates feelings of sociability and interest in friends. It usually produces new hopes and wishes and revives old ones.

## In Twelfth House

Gives interest in Occult affairs or matters of a secret or mysterious nature, and hospitals or other large institutions. It is apt to bring to the fore many restrictions or delays which annoy the native, but by withdrawing the mind from external things and silently communing with the inner self, while the Moon is here it is likely to shed light into the deeper recesses of the mind so that the way may be seen to extricate one's self from difficulty and find release from bondage.

# ASPECTS FORMED BY THE MOON'S TRANSIT

### The Moon in Trine or Sextile to the Natal Sun
Generally an indication of one of the best days in the month in a business way, provided at the same time the Moon does not form an adverse aspect with some other planet, and particularly with malefic planets in the radix.

### The Moon in Conjunction with the Natal Sun
Good also providing the Sun at birth was unafflicted. The conjunction is good for business, but not as good physically, as it sometimes tends to lower the vitality.

### The Moon in Adverse Aspect to the Natal Sun
The day is adverse for new undertakings or for dealings with people of high position, and is especially adverse for asking favors.

### The Moon in Good Aspect to Natal Jupiter
Next in power to the Moon's good aspects with the natal Sun. Including the conjunction and parallel, the good aspects to Jupiter are considered among the best which occur monthly. These aspects favor general business and social activity.

### The Moon in Adverse Aspect to Natal Jupiter
Not considered very malign, yet they incline to misjudgment, excess, extremes, extravagance, or over-estimation in business calculations or decisions.

### The Moon in Good Aspect to Natal Venus
Next in power, these include the conjunction and parallel. On the days when this aspect occurs, it makes one feel happier, more optimistic, more sociable, and more inclined to entertainment than usual. Very good for visits and dealings with women.

### The Moon in Adverse Aspect to Natal Venus
Not very important, but disfavors the things mentioned in the preceeding. In one with bad taste, this aspect can accentuate the problem to a noticeable degree.

## The Moon in Adverse Aspect to Natal Neptune, Uranus, Saturn, or Mars

All unfavorable indications, the worse one being the aspect with Saturn. No new business should be undertaken when the Moon is in adverse aspect with the place of Saturn at birth, if it can be avoided, for its tendency is to bring disappointments, loss, hindrance, delays, vexations, anxiety.

## The Moon in Good Aspect to Natal Neptune, Uranus, Saturn, or Mars

Tend to benefits through the things which they rule.

## The Moon Aspecting Natal Mercury, or Natal Moon

These are not very important however, when aspecting Mercury, it inclines the mind to excessive mental activity, and perhaps causes the native to be given more to talking and reading than usual. The aspects to the Moon incline to change and a desire to be on the move, especially if the Moon is in a movable sign (Gemini, Virgo, Sagittarius, Pisces).

## The Moon Aspecting the Natal Ruling Planets

The most important aspects of the monthly transit of the Moon are shown when it aspects the planet ruling the birth month sign, the planet ruling the ascending sign, or any planet which is in the Ascendant at the time of birth. When the transiting Moon favorably aspects a ruling planet it is a good time for matters or things indicated by that planet; on the other hand, it is unfavorable for those things when that same planet is afflicted by the Moon.

# THE INFLUENCE OF PLANETARY ASPECTS BY TRANSIT

## General Indications of the Good Aspects of Mercury

Correspond, look after accounts, write, study, attend to educational and literary matters, read, make speeches and attend lectures. Deal with commission and business men, also messenger, distributors, advertisers, publishers, editors, reporters, printers, book and stationery concerns, bookkeepers, architects, teachers, students, notaries, lawyers, scientists and young people.

When the planet is well aspected, it will be noticed that the mind is keen, alert, penetrating, ingenious, comprehensive, reasonable and versatile. The good aspects increase the intuition, imagination, mental sympathy, receptivity and adaptability. It stimulates the mental activity, gives read response to new ideas and gives clear perception, as it acts directly on the perceptive faculties. Makes one quick, active and businesslike. Things of a minor commercial character are accomplished with dispatch. Thoughts come clearly and speech or pen are fluent in expression. A good time in which to attend to educational matters, advertise, draw up contracts and seek information. Good for all affairs requiring a quick mind, fluent speech, nimbleness and dexterity in execution. Good for making minor changes, short journies, dealing with neighbors, kindred and business people generally. The mind is turned into an optimistic channel and finds pleasure and recreation in conversation, music, art, literature, novelty and change. Deal with books, manuscripts, lessons, etc.

### Adverse Aspects of Mercury

Keep from petty worries and over-anxiety, take no notice of trifling annoyances. Set a guard on the speech, act with prudence, write no letters, sign no contracts or agreements, make no important journies, changes or removals. Take no medicine. Avoid friction with brethren, cousins, neighbors or employees.

The adverse aspects to Mercury produce unfavorable conditions and tend to disturb the stomach, bowels and nervous system generally. The mental activity is intensified and one is unconsciously on a high tension leading to worry, anxiety, and turbulent or sarcastic states of mind.

It creates uncertainty, indecision and sensitiveness. One is apt to indulge in controversy and criticism or to say and do things which we do not really mean, and, in turn, we are likely to hear unpleasant news and meet with conditions which tend to disturb the mental equilibrium. During this aspect one had best not have anything to do with litigation or new business. Misunderstandings and annoyances are apt to appear. Special attention should be given to keeping in mental harmony and in a pleasant state of mind, for in that way much of the aspect is overcome; at least, that part of it which depends upon you for its manifestation.

## General Indications of the Good Aspects of Venus

A good time for all refined entertainment, pleasure and amusement, also for courtship, love, marriage, social and general prosperity and popularity. Buy and don new clothing (especially when the Moon is new). Cultivate new friendships with the opposite sex, seek the favor of ladies, visit friends, hold parties, musicales, etc. Deal with confectioners, hotelkeepers, housekeepers, restaurant managers, milliners, dressmakers, clothiers, tailors, artists, singers, actors, musicians, drapers, jewelers, decorators, florists and nurses. Make collections.

When this planet is in good aspect, it will be noticed that the mind strikes a lighter vein than usual, the feelings and emotions are easily aroused and the desire is to respond readily to affection with perfect sympathy. The aspect tends to elevate, improve and refine the mind, making it clear, bright, hopeful, cheerful, peaceful, gentle, kind and mirthful. The native is good-natured and genial and more than ever inclined to neatness in dress and good manners. Gives appreciation for the beautiful in nature, art or drama, and inclines to general public or business success through agreeable, attractive and engaging manners and sociability. Personal benefit and financial gain may be derived from dealing with things which please the public's taste for delicacies, amusement or adornment, and through people connected with those things; also through matters associated with houses, lands and fruits of the earth. One should strive to make the most of this planetary influence for improvements in all affairs in either business, social or domestic life.

## Adverse Aspects of Venus

Avoid the opposite sex. Be moderate and refrain from excesses of all kinds, but especially with regard to eating, drinking and amusement. Not a good time to obtain favorable results in matters of affection or pleasure, or in fact any of the things mentioned in the foregoing paragraph.

To women this aspect sometimes denotes physical indisposition. It tends to produce trouble through overindulgence or carelessness in habits and manners. It indicates a liability to disappointment or disagreement in matters of affection and the feelings or emotions generally. It is likely to upset and disarrange domestic conditions. Attachments and social affairs are apt to cause anxiety and also matters associated with the occupation, finances, property, possessions or partnership. The native is liable to be sensitive and easily wounded. During this aspect one had best not engage in social affairs or new undertakings (of the kind this planet rules as stated previously), nor will it be wise to cultivate new attractions. Quietly attend to present duties and associate with old and tried friends; shun speculation. In this way very much of the adverse nature of the aspect may be mitigated.

### General Indications of the Good Aspects of the Sun

Ask favors of those in good position and authority, also of those in government office. Seek employment; try for promotion; give presents; seek that which is lost; make public announcements and advance notices. A good aspect for spiritual unfoldment and for the society of sunny, optimistic and prosperous people.

The good aspects of the Sun promote loyalty, sincerity, ambition, energy, will power and adaptability; strengthen the constitution of both male and female. They tend to success, advancement, prosperity and assistance from powerful, influential or superior persons; also to popularity, progress, honor, esteem and friendship. Gain through enterprise and responsibility and through good-hearted, generous and radiant manners.

### Adverse Aspects of the Sun

Avoid persons of wealth, position and authority; also those in government office. Do nothing of importance; do not disclose your intentions; keep your own counsel. Begin only those things which are to be kept secret, private or obscure; avoid being overheated or becoming excited. The adverse aspects of the Sun tend to make one over-ambitious, venturesome, egotistical, irresolute, proud, haughty, yet sensitive, compelling, immoderate, over-confident, somewhat domineering and quick to take offense. Likelihood of difficulty in financial affairs through business or employment. The aspect also conduces to loss by speculation or through ill health and inferiors. Disappointment, misfortune or poor success with those of authority and high position.

### General Indications of the Good Aspects of Mars

Study, investigate or attend to business connected with chemistry, surgery, assaying, construction and mechanical affairs generally. Deal with animals by training, buying, selling or transportation. Conduct business matters associated with engineers, contractors, structural iron workers, sewer builders, scavengers, carpenters, lumbermen, machinists, smiths, barbers, hardware dealers, agents, police, soldiers, stockraisers, butchers, dentists and surgeons. Practice muscular development. Solicit, canvas.

The good aspects of Mars tend to make the native more than usually ambitious, energetic, firm, brave, ardent and resolute. It gives "tone" or strength to the whole system, muscular and circulatory; it increases the activity, force and vitality, and is a splendid aspect for work requiring great strength in occupations carried on out of doors. Its tendency also is towards success and promotion through resourcefulness and enterprise in business and personal affairs, or employments of responsibility that owe their existence mainly to push, pluck and perseverence, and in which results are largely accomplished through quick energetic, commonsense methods and hard work, which inspire confidence and trust from others.

## Adverse Aspects of Mars

The adverse aspects of Mars are troublesome influence, and unless exceeding care is exercised it is likely to lead to accidents and injuries on journies and difficulties or obstacles and much hard work in connection with changes and removals. While the aspect is in operation be temperate in affection and avoid excessive demonstrations; cultivate no new acquaintances and beware of contentions with friends; avoid all disputes and controversy. Utilize the mental and physical force equally, i.e., be careful not to overdo in muscular effort, conserve the energy, restrain the passions, avoid hasty, forceful actions and impulsive speech, beware of accidents, cuts, scalds, burns and bruises, be careful of the diet. Do not buy clothing, have no dental or surgical work performed. An unfavorable aspect for affairs connected with iron, steel, hardware, machinery or construction. Have no dealings with engineers, contractors, iron workers, surgeons, dentists, agents, police, etc., as mentioned in the foregoing.

The adverse aspects of Mars have a tendency to make one brave but headstrong, inclined to acts and words which are indiscreet or rash and likely to cause regret, humiliation or trouble. The temper is apt to be quick and the speech hasty, causing strife, difficulty or opposition from others. It tends to make one feel very self-confident, somewhat egotistic, domineering, daring and venturesome, but easily annoyed and irritated and apt to suffer from disregard of regulations or carelessness of consequences and through sex impulse or through scandal, criticism or enmity. It is an ill aspect for domestic happiness, and it often produces trouble in the dwelling place and also with regard to property.

### General Indications of the Good Aspects of Jupiter

The good aspects of Jupiter vibrate a fortunate or benefic influence, and during the aspect is a good time to open shops or places of business, begin new undertakings, ask favors, speculate, sell; providing however, that there is not on at the same time a malefic counteracting influence such as an adverse aspect of Mars, Saturn or Uranus. Take counsel or conduct matters associated with judges, lawyers, bankers, merchants, brokers, commercial men and physicians. Attend to affairs connected with education, colleges of law, business, science and medicine; also with matters related to philanthropic, charitable, religious or benevolent organizations. Make efforts for health or learning, study philosophy or healing. Conduct or attend important and formal social functions.

A good aspect of Jupiter conduces to clear, sound and usually correct judgment; inclines more than ever to honesty, truth, justice, benevolence, compassion, sympathy, friendliness and sociability. It increases the vitality and adds fertility and resourcefulness to the mental processes. It tends to make one jovial, generous, humane, hopeful and popular.

### Adverse Aspects of Jupiter

Avoid law or dealings with lawyers, judges, bankers, treasurers, cashiers, bondsmen, stock and sharesellers, speculators, brokers and woolen merchants. Have no dealings with philanthropic, charitable, religious or benevolent affairs. Shun speculation and investment. Sign no bonds, bails, guarantees or securities.

This is an unfortunate aspect for risky ventures or games of chance of any kind, as it is apt to lead to loss through misplaced confidence, dishonesty, excess and wrong judgment either in self or in others. The aspect tends to disturb the liver, and to women it is not good for the general health.

## General Indications of the Good Aspects of Saturn

Deal with plumbers, shoemakers, harnessmakers, hide and leather dealers, miners, masons, potters, excavators, gardeners, florists, farmers, agriculturists, landlords, coal and land dealers. Build, repair, dig and deal with land. Converse with and seek the favor of elderly people. Practice concentration, auto-suggestion and mental healing. Study organization and economics.

The good aspects to Saturn tend to produce a thoughtful, conservative, prudent, sober, contemplative and diplomatic mind, and help to make one provident, careful and attentive to business affairs generally. Increase of credit, popularity and esteem; gives self-reliance, systematizing and organizing ability, constructive execution; the aims of the native are advanced by subtlety, tact and method rather than by force. The aspect favors occupation and attainment to positions of trust and responsibility; the progress may be slow, but started under this aspect it is more secure and lasting. The good aspects to Saturn are favorable for matters connected with property, leasing, beginning a building, and other long-time projects. It tends to good, discriminative, conservative judgment in buying generally.

## Adverse Aspects of Saturn

The adverse aspect to Saturn is an unfortunate influence, therefore make no changes, removals or journies, start nothing new, ask no favors, seek not to gain; rest, avoid worry, do not let any discouragement or melancholy feelings gain possession, guard the speech. Do nothing of importance; it will pay to wait. One's judgment is apt to be aspect also operates to increase the activity of mind, making it restless, easily annoyed, romantic, venturesome, unconventional, daring, radical, rebellious of limitations and desirous of new scenes, and surroundings, and change of work.

## General Indications of the Good Aspects of Neptune

Attend to business affairs connected with shipping, chemicals, perfumes, brewing, deep-sea fish, oil, paints, mineral and charged waters, and liquids in general. Take journeys by water, take baths and oil rubs. Sit for psychic development, inspirational ideas, hold seances, visit psychics, practice psychometry. Attend secret orders.

The good aspects to Neptune incline to success and benefit through choice foodstuffs, canned goods, delicacies and things calculated to please the tastes of the public. They render active any latent emotions for romance and mystery and conduce to the reception of useful impressions and pleasant psychic influences.

## Adverse Aspects of Neptune

Guard against fraud and deception, beware of schemers, do not invest or buy. Observe well the psychic conditions and be careful regarding the cleanliness and purity of people and things you may contact; avoid hospitals, prisons and slaughter-houses. Be cautious with gas, ether, anesthetics, fetid odors and poisonous liquids; use extra caution with canned or bottled foods; keep away from the waters. Drink no oils, restrain the desires, shun psychic phenomena, hold no seances. Enter into no partnerships, associations, nor cultivate any new or doubtful friendships.

The adverse aspects of Neptune tend to produce seductive influences and confusion; likely to intensify any psychic emotions, bring subtle feelings and indefinable sensations. It leads to a desire for luxuries and to gratify exquisite tastes. Attractions to peculiar or mysterious people, to changeable colors and strange odors, sounds, etc. It leads to impressionability and psychic perception, but not of a desirable or satisfactory nature.

## General Indications of the Good Aspects of Pluto

Good aspects of Pluto make the native aware of subtle changes, psychic vibrations, ways people are influenced and manipulated. Pluto reacts mostly on a subconscious level so its vibrations may not be apparent to those with unrefined senses. Good aspects increase the sexual awareness, also.

## Adverse Aspects of Pluto

Natives tend to be more violent, hostile, destructive, lustful, and greedy during the adverse aspects. The desire for power and domination is increased. Restlessness and despondency may provoke change for change's sake without purpose or reason.

very poor or warped during this aspect. Deal carefully with elderly people; keep away from old buildings, dark cellars and gloomy districts; beward of falls, safeguard the health; guard against taking cold, seek optimistic and cheerful people, places and things. Eat lightly, abstain from flesh foods, take plenty of sleep. Do not invest, buy or exchange; have no dealings with landlords, builders, buildings, lands, mines, coal or lead.

This aspect interferes with good concentration and has an adverse bearing on the physical condition, so the native will do well to guard against exposure and also depression, doubt, fear, gloom or dissatisfied feelings. It is an exceedingly unfortunate aspect under which to be married. Any new undertakings commenced during its activity usually live long enough to cause regret, and eventually create a great deal of impatience through delays, hindrance, limitations, reversals, lack of suitable opportunities, and a train of other unfavorable circumstances; in fact, the fates seem to disfavor anything important set into operation at this time and especially those things which require quick consummation for their success.

## General Indications of the Good Aspects of Uranus

Other aspects permitting, this is a good influence for traveling in the interests of business or science, also good for making changes and removals. Keep the mind active, study new thought ideas, Astrology and inventions, as the vibrations of Uranus have affinity with things of that character. Investigate all things new, odd, unique, original, curious and mysterious; experiment; practice telepathy, suggestive healing, etc. Work for social reforms and humanitarian principles. Take electric and magnetic treatments. Deal with reformers, electricians, railroad people, aeronauts, chauffeurs, inventors, metaphysicians and experimental scientists. Take interest in Masonic, Occult and new thought affairs.

The good aspects of Uranus tend to make one active, firm, independent, enterprising and businesslike. This influence is conducive to fondness and friendship for the opposite sex, and also to gain through the occult and through advanced thought people. It tends to awaken the imaging faculties, quickens the thought and intuition and leads the mind into new, original lines of interest and investigation. It adds to the mesmeric and metaphysical faculty in a manner beneficial for healing and telepathy.

### Adverse Aspects of Uranus

This is not a good aspect in which to travel, change or move. Exercise extra caution in connection with engines, cars, airplanes, electric conveyances, electricity, machinery, inventions and explosives. Avoid the opposite sex, do not confide in strangers or in aged people, restrain impulse and hasty speech. Enter into no contracts or partnerships or associations; one is very likely to use strange, unusual or unexpected judgment during this aspect, change their ideas suddenly from what they had originally intended and afterwards wish they had not. Avoid electric, X-ray, radium or magnetic treatments under this aspect.

The adverse aspects of Uranus act as a separative or explosive quality and tend to the unexpected and to extremes. They often affect the health, interfering with the aura, the stomach and the digestive action, causing mental disturbance of different kinds, sudden or peculiar changes in the feelings or emotions; oppositions, aversions, repulsions and strange attractions. Unless restraint is practiced, the native will be impulsive, sarcastic, abrupt, peculiar, odd, eccentric, very independent and subject to separation, estrangement or misunderstanding.

# The Locality Chart

Moving from the original latitude of birth does not change or negate the indications shown in the natal, progressed, and transit charts, but a change of residence to another latitude may create other conditions which tend to accentuate or modify those which are denoted by the original birthplace latitude. We cannot evade the duly timed operations of nature which were cast or timed at birth to manifest at certain periods of life, but moving to a more suitable environment may help to improve our expression of the influence of aspects as they occur, so that one place may seem to be luckier or more fortunate than another.

### Transits and Change of Residence

A student having moved from his birthplace on the Atlantic coast to his present residence on the Pacific coast, wanted to know whether it will have any effect on the aspects of the transiting planets.

Although eastern time is three hours in advance (later in the day) than Pacific time, that makes practically no difference in the effects of transits. While the change of residence altered the clock time in its relation to that of the birthplace, it does not noticeably alter anything concerning an aspect itself, except that it appears to begin and to manifest at an earlier hour. However, the time of the beginning of an aspect is an intangible matter, and even if known exactly would be of little importance because the inception of its influence is so subtle, and gradual that some time must elapse before it produces any recognized or appreciable significant influence on either body or mind.

For instance, the Sun's apparent movement in the Zodiac is a transit of approximately 1° a day and it has an orb of influence of 12°, therefore, when approaching a planet in a nativity it begins the conjunction at some time on the twelfth day prior to its actual conjunction, regardless of where the native may then be residing. That beginning of the aspect is imperceptible, but day by day its influence grows in power and its expression becomes more noticeable until the day of its climax (partile), after which its influence rapidly diminishes.

When the Sun reaches the final degree constituting the conjunction it transits through it during the whole day, and in a nativity it would indeed be difficult to determine what time of that day the influence would be most strikingly manifest, although it would be but a simple problem in arithmetic to calculate the exact time of the conjunction, which of course would occur at a time that is three hours earlier on the Pacific coast than clocked in Eastern Standard Time.

While, as before stated, moving from one place to another does not alter the influence of a transit aspect, per se, there is a difference, but it is psychological rather than astrological. That difference is in the human response to the environment. In other words, a person's reaction to a planetary aspect when he is in Alaska will be quite different from his expression of the same aspect if he were residing in Florida, because environment determines much of the nature and quality of human activity. The channels for the manifestation of that aspect would be altered by the difference in climate, clothing, food, occupation, opportunities, personal contacts, mental attitudes, etc. Physicians often wisely suggest a change of climate to patients, but unless they understand Astrology are not always able to suggest the place best suited to the purpose.

## How to Find the Best Location

In the effort to choose a better location several charts should be made according to the following rule, each for a locality the native has reason to believe would be advantageous with regard to climate, chances for successful employment, etc, and from them choose the locality indicated by the best chart.

The locality chart changes the natal chart house cusps and house positions of the planets, but does not change the planets' signs and degrees, to conform to the amount of time difference and the new latitude. This provides a chart which shows the trend of changes to be experienced in the new place and the conditions to be met through the ability and characteristics with which the native was originally en-owed; that is, the racial planetary influences are expressed through different circumstances and environment.

For example: if Jupiter was originally in the Tenth House and moving took it into the Eleventh House, there would be tendency to carry on the profession more through social endeavors. If Jupiter were carried into the Ninth House, the tendency would be to change the profession to embrace publishing, foreign affairs, law, science, or religion.

One of the rules to be observed is to avoid taking your ruling planet into the twelfth or sixth houses; the former implies limitation; the latter, illness.

## CALCULATING THE LOCALITY CHART

The usual procedure for calculating the locality chart is as follows:
1. Find the Time of Locality Chart
2. Convert to Sidereal Time at New Locality
3. Correct for Longitude and Acceleration
4. Find the Ascendant, Midheaven, and House Cusps
5. Insert the Planets

The planets in the locality chart will be changed to new house positions. It is these house positions that are of particular significance in the new environment. As the houses show the direction in which the zodiacal tendencies and planetary influences manifest, the importance of the changed house positions is obvious.

### Locality Chart, Example Chart 5

As an example, suppose the native represented by Example Chart 5 (see Example Chart 5, page 475 and Figures 35 and 36) moved from the birthplace to Los Angeles, California. The new locality chart would be calculated as follows:

### 1. Find the Time of Locality Chart

Note the amount of time difference between the birth place and the new abode, by multiplying each degree of longitude difference by the time variable of four minutes. Adjust the standard time of birth by the time difference according to the rules:

**East of birthplace—add.** Add four minutes to clock time for every degree of longitude (one minute for each 15' of longitude) the new locality is situated east of the birthplace.

**West of birthplace—subtract.** Subtract four minutes from clock time for every degree of longitude (one minute for each 15' of longitude) the new locality is situated west of the birthplace.

This handy table can be used for looking up the time difference for each degree of longitude:

$1°$ longitude = 0h 04m time difference
$2°$ longitude = 0h 08m time difference
$3°$ longitude = 0h 12m time difference
$4°$ longitude = 0h 16m time difference
$5°$ longitude = 0h 20m time difference
$6°$ longitude = 0h 24m time difference
$7°$ longitude = 0h 28m time difference
$8°$ longitude = 0h 32m time difference
$9°$ longitude = 0h 36m time difference
$10°$ longitude = 0h 40m time difference
$11°$ longitude = 0h 44m time difference
$12°$ longitude = 0h 48m time difference
$13°$ longitude = 0h 52m time difference
$14°$ longitude = 0h 56m time difference
$15°$ longitude = 1h 00m time difference

**Table 20: Table for Changing Terrestrial
Longitude into Time**

**Note:** Observe caution in making the calculation for the amount of time difference when the move crosses the time meridian of Greenwich, that is, from east to west longitude or vice versa. For example, a move from $5°$ east longitude to $118°$ west is $123°$ difference ($5°$ + $118° = 123°$) or 8h 12m amount of time difference.

Remember to subtract one hour from the standard time of birth whenever Daylight Savings Time or War Time was in effect. After making this adjustment the resulting calculation is the time of the locality chart.

**Example 5. Person born August 23, 1885, 0:45 am, Elkhart, Ill.**
Elkhart, Illinois, the birthplace, has a longitude of 89° 30' west. The
new locality of Los Angeles, California, has a longitude of 118° west. A
time difference of 1 hr 54 min is subtracted from the standard time of
birth. No Daylight Savings Time or War Time was in effect.

| 118° | 00' | (new locality) |
|---|---|---|
| - 89 | 30' | (birthplace) |

| 28° | 30' | (longitudinal difference) |
|---|---|---|

| 28 | 30 | (longitudinal difference) |
|---|---|---|
| x4 | x4 | (correction per degree) |

112m  120 = 1 hr 54m    (correction for 28° 30')

| 0:45 am, August 23 = 12h | 45m | (pm, August 22) |
|---|---|---|
| − 1 | 54 | (correction) |
| 10h | 51m | (pm, August 22: new time of locality chart) |

## 2. Convert to Sidereal Time at New Locality

Add the new time of locality chart to the noon sidereal time for
afternoon times, subtract for morning times, just as when calculating a
natal chart (see Convert to Sidereal Time at Birth, page 77).

| 10h | 04m | 47s | (ST August 22, 1884) |
|---|---|---|---|
| + 10 | 51 | 00 | (new time of locality chart) |
| 20h | 55m | 47s | (ST at new locality) |

## 3. Correct for Longitude and Acceleration

Correct for longitude and acceleration just as when calculating a
natal chart (see Correct for Longitude and Acceleration, page 87, and
Table 7, page 88.

| 20h | 55m | 47s | (ST at new locality) |
|---|---|---|---|
| + | 1 | 49 | (acceleration for 10h 51m after noon) |
| | 1 | 19 | (longitudinal correction for 118° west: new locality) |
| 20h | 58m | 55s | (correct ST for new time of locality chart) |

## 4. Find the Ascendant, Midheaven and House Cusps

Look up the corrected sidereal time for the new time of locality chart in the Tables of Houses for the latitude of the new locality. The new house cusps are:

Ascendant–1° ♊ 08'               Seventh House–1° ♐ 08'
Second House–26° ♊ 06'        Eighth House–26° ♐ 06'
Third House–18° ♋ 18'          Ninth House–18° ♑ 18'
Midheaven–12° ♒                 Fourth House–12° ♌
Eleventh House–11° ♓ 24'      Fifth House–11° ♍ 24'
Twelfth House–19° ♈ 24'       Sixth House–19° ♎ 24'

## 5. Insert the Planets

Insert the planets in the same signs and degrees occupied at the original birth time. See Figure 38.

### Comparison of Locality and Natal Charts.

Comparing the locality chart for Example 5 (Figure 38) with the natal chart for Example 5 (Figure 36, page 476), it is readily seen that no particular advantage would be gained by such a move.

The beneficent Venus which occupied the important First House in the natal chart, is now reduced to a cadent position, which would certainly cramp his style.

Saturn affecting the First and Second Houses would cause concern over financial affairs.

Mars near the Sixth House cusp would cause trouble in employment, serious illness or surgical operations.

Jupiter and the Sun have left the natal Third House and entered the new Fourth House. This change of house position is neither advantageous nor detrimental.

Uranus, Mercury, and the Moon have departed the natal Fourth House and occupy the locality Fifth House, which might shift home

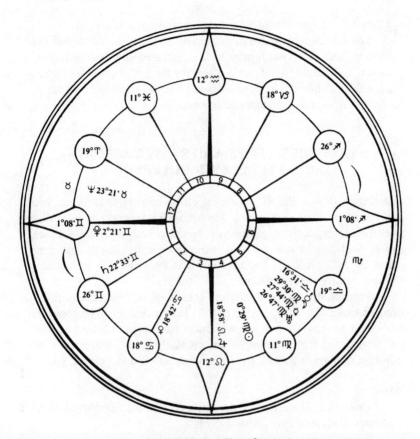

Figure 38: Locality Chart,
Example 5

and domestic interests to interests in sports and recreation.

The fact is, the native early moved to Chicago, which has Leo ascending, and as he has Jupiter in Leo, he fared very well in honors, position, and family life. After erecting the locality chart for determining the advisability of changing residence from Chicago to Los Angeles, he did not make the contemplated move.

## COUNTRIES, CITIES AND STATES ACCORDING TO THEIR SIGN RULERSHIPS

The following is a list of countries, cities, and states showing their sign rulerships. Note that some of the listings have more than one ruling sign. This information is useful in connection with ingresses, eclipses, and New Moons in relation to mundane events, helping to determine where the influences will be operative. It is also helpful in determining the best locality for an individual.

Suppose, for example, that an individual suffering severe afflictions was told to go away for his health. That person could be correctly advised to go some place which was under the benign influence of Jupiter, whereas otherwise, he might unfortunately go to a place under the influence of Mars or Saturn, and become worse off than before.

### Aries

Countries: Denmark, England, Faroe Islands, Germany, Iceland, Lebanon, Lithuania, Peru, Poland, Syria.

Cities: Birmingham (England), Brunswick, Capua, Cracow, Dallas, Florence, Leicester, Marseilles, Naples, Saragossa, Utrecht, Verona.

### Taurus

Countries: Australia, Austria, Cyprus, Greenland, Holland, Ireland, New Guinea, Iran, Poland, Tasmania, Israel.

Cities: Dublin, Leipzig, Palermo, Parma, Rhodes, St. Louis.

States: Florida, Georgia, Louisiana, Maryland, Minnesota.

### Gemini

Countries: Armenia, Belgium, Colombia, Ecuador, Egypt, Sardinia, Saudi Arabia, United Arab Republic, Venezuela, South Vietnam,

Wales.
Cities: Bruges, London, Melbourne, Metz, Nuremburg, Plymouth (England), Rio de Janeiro, San Francisco, Tripoli, Versailles.
States: Arkansas, Kentucky, Rhode Island, South Carolina, Tennessee, West Virginia, Wisconsin.

## Cancer
Countries: Canada, Holland, Iraq, New Zealand, Paraguay, Scotland, United States.
Cities: Algiers, Amsterdam, Berne, Cadiz, Genoa, Istanbul, Manchester, Milan, New York City, Pittsburg, Stockhom, Tunis, Venice, York.
States: Idaho, New Hampshire, New York, Wyoming.

## Leo
Countries: France, Italy, Madagascar, Sicily, the Vatican, Zanzibar.
Cities: Bath, Berlin, Bombay, Bristol, Chicago, Damascus, Detroit, Miami, Oklahoma City, Philadelphia, Portsmouth, Prague, Ravenna, Rome.
States: Alaska, California, Colorado, Hawaii, Missouri, Oregon, Washington.

## Virgo
Countries: Assyria, Brazil, Crete, Croatia, Greece, Rhodesia, Switzerland, Turkey, Uruguay, North Vietnam, Virgin Islands, West Indies.
Cities: Baghdad, Basel, Boston, Corinth, Heidelberg, Jerusalem, Los Angeles, Lyons, Moscow, Norwich, Padua, Toulouse.
States: Alaska, California, Hawaii, Virginia.

## Libra
Countries: Argentina, Burma, China, Egypt, Japan, Siberia, Tibet.
Cities: Antwerp, Charleston, Copenhagen, Frankfurt-am-Main, Johannesburg, Leeds, Lisbon, Vienna.

## Scorpio
Countries: Algeria, East Indies, Korea, Morocco, Norway, Paraguay, Philippines, Syria, Turkey, Soviet Union.

Cities: Baltimore, Cincinnati, Cleveland, Dover, Fez, Halifax, Hull, Liverpool, Milwaukee, New Orleans, Newcastle, Portland (Ore.), Tokyo, Washington D.C.

States: Montana, Nevada, North Carolina, North Dakota, Oklahoma, South Dakota.

## Sagittarius

Countries: Australia, Bolivia, Borneo, Chile, Czechoslovakia, Hungary, Madagascar, Pakistan, Spain, Yugoslavia.

Cities: Avignon, Budapest, Cologne, Naples, Nottingham, Provence, Seattle, Sheffield, Singapore, Toledo, Toronto.

States: Alabama, Delaware, Illinois, Indiana, Mississippi, New Jersey, Ohio, Pennsylvania.

## Capricorn

Countries: Afghanistan, Albania, Bulgaria, Greece, India, Lithuania, Mexico.

Cities: Brandenburg, Brussels, Port Said.

States: Connecticut, Iowa, New Mexico, Texas, Utah.

## Aquarius

Countries: Arabia, Abyssinia, Cyprus, Iran, Lithuania, Poland, Prussia, Russia, Sweden, Syria.

Cities: Bremen, Brighton, Detroit, Hamburg, Salzburg, Wichita.

States: Arizona, Kansas, Massachusetts, Michigan, Oregon.

## Pisces

Countries: Polynesia, Portugal, Samoa.

Cities: Alexandria (Egypt), Bournemouth, Lancaster, Seville, Worms.

States: Florida, Kansas, Maine, Nebraska, Vermont.

# The Estimate Chart

When a birth time is totally unknown, we must first work to get the right zodiacal sign on the Ascendant. To do this first draw up a chart for noon on the birth date. That is, enter the planets' positions as listed in the ephemeris for the date of birth. Then, turn the chart around and put each sign successively on the Ascendant. Study each sign carefully for one which best describes the native. Study this chart in connection with the kind of events furnished by the native as to sickness, accidents, etc., during the lifetime. Notice if the position of the chart then gives testimonies by planetary house positions which tally with the nature of the events as known.

Perhaps two or more signs ascending seem to fulfill the requirements, in which case further study of sign characteristics is necessary to determine which best fulfills all conditions. Naturally there is a chance here to err in judgment by attributing wrong virtues or influence to planets in the various houses, but a correct knowledge of the influences of each planet, together with the ability to combine the house and planet influences will do much to obviate the likelihood of mistakes.

## Example Chart 6

Example Chart 6 is of a man, born at Greenwich, England, April 5, 1863. Time of birth unknown. Make a chart for noon on the birth date. Turn the chart around from sign to sign and you will find that when Virgo rises it will nearly place the planets as desired.

533

Saturn ascending signifies the native's disposition, his deep and sensitive nature introspectively trying to fathom the mystery of life and improve natural qualities; attempting to ascend above the many limitations, restrictions, and delays encountered on the way. Therefore, look up 15° Virgo Ascendant under 52° latitude (Greenwich) in the Tables of Houses, and draw up the first estimate chart. See figure 39.

However, this places Uranus and Mars in the Tenth House, and that conjunction in the Ninth House would more closely describe the native's scientific and religious tendencies and also the accident which maimed his limbs in a foreign land. This conjunction in the Ninth House would signify accidents in lands foreign to that of birth, which would agree with limitations also signified by Saturn in the First House. These planets in the Ninth House would also endow the native with great zeal in the studies of the higher mind. Astrology etc., and would lead him far from the orthodox, conventional religions.

The sign of Gemini on the Midheaven would bestow Mercury proclivities and also incline to business life, thus more closely describing the native.

Mars and Uranus are in 16° and 17° Gemini, and to get them in the Ninth House, we must make the Tenth House cusp about 26° Gemini. Now look at the Table of Houses at the place where 26° Gemini is on the Midheaven. Draw up a second estimate chart using these house cusps. See Figure 40.

Note the Sidereal Time for the 26° Gemini Midheaven is 5h 42m 33s. The ST at noon on the birthday is 0h 53m 10s. The estimated birth ST is therefore some hours after noon, indicating an afternoon birth time. Subtract the noon ST from the estimated birth ST to get 4h 49m 23s. This is the estimated birth time—4:49:23 PM, April 5, 1863.

Note: If the result of subtracting is more than 12 hours, 12 hours would be subtracted from the result, and the answer would be an AM time of birth.

Now make a chart for the time thus derived, and call it the final estimate chart. See figure 41. Now this approximate time of birth can be further rectified by one of the following methods of calculation.

## Planetary Hour Method of Determining the Ascending Sign

One way to discover the Ascending Sign in order to draw up the estimate chart is by use of planetary hours. Take note of the time when a person asks for a personal horoscope or, if the request is by mail, the time the letter is written if it has been stated by the writer. If not, then the time the letter was received. Refer to the *Planetary Hour Book* and note which planet rules the hour in which the question is asked; a) it usually rules the sign ascending at birth; b) it is in a sign on the birth day which should ascend at the birth time.

When the planet ruling the hour is ruler of two zodiacal signs, a little careful study will show which of the two signs to choose as they give decidedly different descriptions.

Of course, this rule holds good only when the individual calls or asks in accordance with his own uninfluenced impressions.

## The First Aspected Planet in the Partner's Chart

Another rule which may often be applied to determining the estimate chart rising sign: Take the planet in a man's horoscope which the Moon first aspects after birth. That planet will almost invariably rule the sign rising in the wife's horoscope at her birth.

In a woman's horoscope take the planet which the Sun first aspects after birth, in the same way, and it will usually rule the husband's rising sign. If married more than once take the next planet aspected, as above, and so on according to the number of unions.

To make a chart for the partner, take about the middle of the sign answering the description which is ruled by this planet, and you will have a very close approximate chart with which to apply the rectification rules in order to determine the exact minute of birth.

## ARC OF EVENT RECTIFICATION METHOD

These rules are for rectifying a given or approximately known birth time by means of the timing of an important event in the life of the native, to find the exact zodiacal degree ascending in the natal chart and to obtain the correct birth time. It is assumed that the important event occurred when the planet was either conjunct or in an exact as-

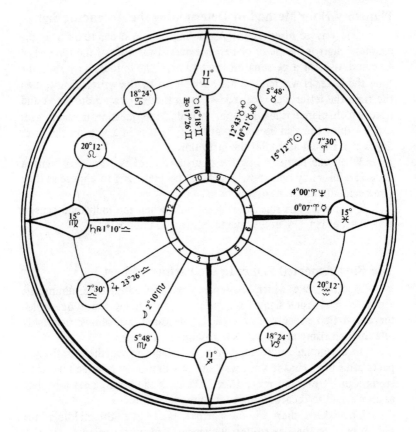

Figure 39: First Estimate,
Example Chart 6

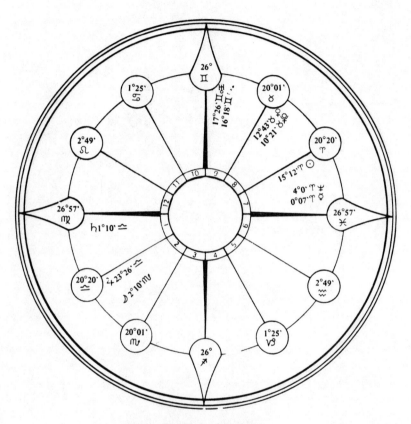

**Figure 40: Second Estimate,
Example Chart 6**

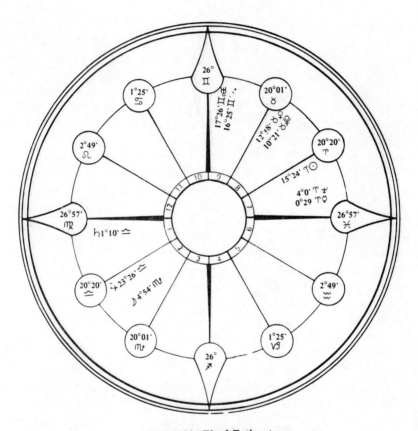

Figure 41: Final Estimate
Example Chart 6

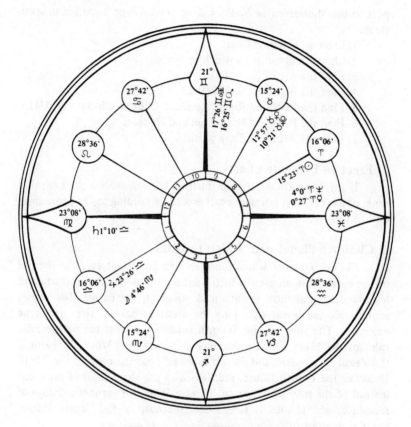

**Figure 42: Rectified Example,**
**Chart 6**

pect to the Midheaven or Nadir. This method will be discussed in seven steps:

1. Erect an Estimate Chart
2. Choose a Planet with which to Work
3. Find the Arc of Event (AE)
4. Find the Right Ascension (RA)
5. Find the Rectified Right Ascension of the Midheaven (RAM)
6. Find the Rectified Midheaven and House Cusps
7. Find the Rectified Time of Birth

## 1. Erect an Estimate Chart

If the approximate time of birth is known, erect a chart for that time, or use the final estimate chart erected according to the procedures outlined above.

## 2. Choose a Planet with which to Work

Choose a planet which represents an important event in the life of the native. Use an event which occurred before the age of thirty and has the first and most pronounced effect on the native. The planet should rule the house signifying the event or person. Here are some examples. The ruler of the Seventh House represents the partner; the ruler of the Sixth House represents an illness, etc. When the event is the death of a parent and Saturn is found near the cusp of the Tenth House or the Fourth House, use Saturn as the significator of the event instead of the ruler of the parent's house. When the event is a change of residence, and Uranus is found near the cusp of the Fourth House, try it as significator.

**Example Chart 6.** In our example, we choose as the event a long journey which took place on September 5, 1883, when the native was 20 years old. We therefore look to the ruler of the Ninth House, which is Venus, at 12° Taurus 58'.

## 3. Find the Arc of Event (AE)

From the year, month, and date of the event, subtract the date of birth. Convert the answer into degrees and minutes by allowing one degree for each year, five minutes for each month, and one minute for each six days over a month.

**Example Chart 6.**
1883 yr 9 mo 5 d (date of event)
1863 yr 4      5     (date of birth)
20 yr 5 mo 0 d 20 yr = 20° + (5 mo x 5 = 25') = 20° 25'
(Arc of Event)

## 4. Find the Right Ascension (RA)

Next, find the Right Ascension of the planet by referring to *Table 21: Table of Right Ascension and Sidereal Times.* The Right Ascension of a planet is its distance from the first degree of Aries measured along the equatorial circle.

**Example Chart 6.** The RA of Venus at 12° Taurus 57', is 40.32.8.

## 5. Find the Rectified Right Ascendant of the Midheaven (RAM)

If the planet in question is situated from the Midheaven or Nadir approximately an equal number of degrees to those constituting the AE, then work it to a conjunction with the Midheaven or Nadir.

If you find by the position of the planet in the estimate chart, that the event did not take place when the planet was conjunct the Midheaven or Nadir, but when in aspect to it, first find the Meridian Distance (MD). The Meridian Distance is the number of degrees the chosen planet is from the Midheaven. This is the same as the distance between the RA of the Midheaven and the RA of the planet in the estimate chart.

**Example Chart 6.**
85:38:5 (RA of the Midheaven 26° Gemini)
40.32:8 (RA of Venus 12° Taurus 57')
45:05:57 (Meridian Distance of Venus)

**A. Planet East of the Midheaven.** For planets between the Midheaven and the Second House cusp, on the left hand side of the chart.

When working by aspect, subtract the Arc of Event from the Meridian Distance. Then take the degree of an aspect nearest to the MD, and add them to the AE, to obtain a new AE.

**Note:** If the AE cannot be subtracted from the MD, work to a conjunction.

When working either to a conjunction or by aspect, proceed as follows: Subtract the AE from the RA of the planet, and the remainder will be the rectified Right Ascension of the Midheaven.

**Note:** If the RA of the planet is too small to be subtracted from, add 360 to it, then subtract the AE and use the remainder, which is the Rectified RAM.

**b. Planet West of the Midheaven.** For planets between the Sixth House cusp and the Midheaven, on the right hand side of the chart.

When working by aspect, add the AE to the MD. Choose an aspect nearest this figure. Subtract the AE from this chosen aspect to obtain a new AE.

When working to conjunction or by aspect, proceed as follows: Add the AE to the RA of the planet and the remainder will be the rectified RAM.

**Note:** If after adding the AE to the RA of the planet the sum comes to more than 360 (a complete circle), subtract 360 from it and use the remainder, which is the rectified RAM.

**Example Chart 6.**      20  25   (Arc of Event)

$\quad\quad\quad$ -+  45  06  (Meridian Distance)

$\quad\quad\quad\quad$ 65  31

The nearest aspect to 65° 31' is the sextile, 60°

$\quad\quad$ 60  00  (Sextile Aspect)

$\quad$ – 20  25  (Arc of Event)

$\quad\quad$ 39  35  (New AE)

$\quad\quad$ 39  35  (New AE)

$\quad$ + 40  32  (RA of Venus)

$\quad\quad$ 80  07  (Rectified RAM)

**C. Planet East of the Nadir.** For planets between the Second House cusp and the Nadir, on the left hand side of the chart, worked to a conjunction only.

Add the Arc of Event to the Right Ascension of the planet, then add 180 to that and the sum will be the rectified RAM.

**Note:** If after adding, the sum exceeds 360, then subtract 360 from it and use the remainder which will be the rectified RAM.

**D. Planet West of the Nadir.** For planets between the Nadir and the Sixth House cusps, on the right hand side of the chart, worked to a conjunction only.

Subtract the AE from the RA of the planet, then 180 to that and the sum will be the rectified RAM.

Note: If the RA of the planet is too small to be subtracted from, add 360 to it, then subtract the AE. To the remainder add 180 and if the sum exceeds 360, subtract 360 from it. The remainder is the rectified RAM.

When your work is complete to this stage, the Meridian Distance of the planet must be equal to the AE, regardless of whether the planet was east or west of the meridian. Find the difference between the RA of the planet and the rectified RAM and the remainder should be equal to the AE if the work has been done correctly.

**Example Chart 6.**

```
  80  07 (Rectified RAM)
- 40  32 (RA of Venus)
  ─────
  39  35  (AE)
```

## 6. Find the Rectified Midheaven and House Cusps

Find the rectified Right Ascension of the Midheaven in Table 21: *Table of Right Ascensions and Sidereal Times,* and note what zodiacal sign and degree it represents. Then enter a Tables of Houses, find that sign and degree on the Midheaven, and fill in the other cusps on the chart from the Tables for the correct latitude, in the usual manner.

**Example Chart 6.**

80.07 (Rectified RAM) = 21° Gemini.

Looking up 21° Gemini in the Tables of Houses, we find the following house cusps: Ascendant 23° Virgo 08'

Second House : 16° Libra 06'

Third House: 15° Scorpio 24'

Eleventh House: 27° Cancer 42'

Twelfth House: 28° Leo 36'

## 7. Find the Rectified Time of Birth

To find the rectified time of birth, note the Sidereal Time given in the Tables of Houses for the rectified Midheaven. This is the Sidereal Time at Birth.

From the Sidereal Time at Birth subtract the Sidereal Time given in the ephemeris for noon of the birth date, adding 24 to the ST at

| Deg. | Aries. | Taurus. | Gemini. | Cancer. | Leo. | Virgo. |
|---|---|---|---|---|---|---|
| 0...... | 0.00:00 | 1.51:38 | 3.51:16 | 6.00:00 | 8.08:44 | 10.08:22 |
|  | 0.00:00 | 27.54:5 | 57.48:9 | 90.00:0 | 122.11:1 | 152.05:5 |
| 1...... | 0.03:40 | 1.55:27 | 3.55:26 | 6.04:22 | 8.12:54 | 10.12:11 |
|  | 0.55:0 | 28.51:9 | 58.51:5 | 91.05:4 | 123.13:4 | 153.02:8 |
| 2...... | 0.07:20 | 1.59:18 | 3.59:37 | 6.08:43 | 8.17:03 | 10.16:00 |
|  | 1.50:1 | 29.49:4 | 59.54:2 | 92.10:8 | 124.15:6 | 153.59:9 |
| 3...... | 0.11:01 | 2.03:08 | 4.03:48 | 6.13:05 | 8.21:11 | 10.19:47 |
|  | 2.45:2 | 30.47:1 | 60.57:1 | 93.16:2 | 125.17:7 | 154.56:8 |
| 4...... | 0.14:41 | 2.07:00 | 4.08:01 | 6.17:27 | 8.25:18 | 10.23:35 |
|  | 3.40:2 | 31.44:9 | 61.00:1 | 94.21:5 | 126.19:5 | 155.53:7 |
| 5...... | 0.18:21 | 2.10:52 | 4.12:13 | 6.21:47 | 8.29:25 | 10.27:23 |
|  | 4.35:3 | 32.42:9 | 63.03:3 | 95.26:9 | 127.21:2 | 156.50:4 |
| 6...... | 0.22:02 | 2.14:44 | 4.16:27 | 6.26:09 | 8.33:31 | 10.31:08 |
|  | 5.30:4 | 33.41:0 | 64.06:7 | 96.32:2 | 128.22:7 | 157.47:0 |
| 7...... | 0.25:42 | 2.18:37 | 4.20:41 | 6.30:30 | 8.37:36 | 10.34:54 |
|  | 6.25:6 | 34.39:4 | 65.10:2 | 97.37:4 | 129.24:0 | 158.43:4 |
| 8...... | 0.29:23 | 2.22:31 | 4.24:55 | 6.34:50 | 8.41:41 | 10.38:39 |
|  | 7.20:8 | 35.37:8 | 66.13:8 | 98.42:6 | 130.25:2 | 159.39:8 |
| 9...... | 0.33:04 | 2.26:26 | 4.29:11 | 6.39:11 | 8.45:44 | 10.42:42 |
|  | 8.16:0 | 36.36:5 | 67.17:6 | 99.47:7 | 131.26:1 | 160.36:0 |
| 10...... | 0.36:45 | 2.30:21 | 4.33:26 | 6.43:31 | 8.49:48 | 10.46:09 |
|  | 9.11:3 | 37.35:3 | 68.21:6 | 100.52:3 | 132.26:9 | 161.32:2 |
| 11...... | 0.40:27 | 2.34:17 | 4.37:42 | 6.47:51 | 8.53:50 | 10.49:53 |
|  | 10.06:6 | 38.34:3 | 69.25:6 | 101.57:8 | 133.27:5 | 162.28:2 |
| 12...... | 0.44:08 | 2.38:14 | 4.41:59 | 6.52:11 | 8.57:52 | 10.53:37 |
|  | 11.02:0 | 39.33:4 | 70.29:8 | 103.02:7 | 134.27:9 | 163.42:1 |
| 13...... | 0.47:50 | 2.42:11 | 4.46:16 | 6.56:30 | 9.01:53 | 10.57:20 |
|  | 11.57:5 | 40.32:8 | 71.34:1 | 104.07:8 | 135.28:1 | 164.20:0 |
| 14...... | 0.51:32 | 2.46:09 | 4.50:34 | 7.00:49 | 9.05:53 | 11.01:03 |
|  | 12.53:0 | 41.32:3 | 72.38:5 | 105.12:3 | 136.28:2 | 165.15:7 |
| 15...... | 0.55:14 | 2.50:08 | 4.54:52 | 7.05:08 | 9.09:52 | 11.04:46 |
|  | 13.48:6 | 42.32:0 | 73.48:1 | 106.16:9 | 137.28:0 | 166.11:4 |

Table 21: Table of Right Ascension
and Sidereal Time

| Deg. | Aries. | Taurus. | Gemini. | Cancer. | Leo. | Virgo. |
|---|---|---|---|---|---|---|
| 16...... | 0.58:57 | 2.54:07 | 4.59:11 | 7.09:26 | 9.13:51 | 11.08:28 |
|  | 14.44:3 | 43.31:8 | 74.47:7 | 107.21:5 | 133.27:7 | 167.07:0 |
| 17...... | 1.02:40 | 2.58:07 | 5.03:30 | 7.13:44 | 9.17:49 | 11.12:10 |
|  | 15.40:0 | 44.31:9 | 75.52:5 | 108.25:9 | 139.27:2 | 168.02:5 |
| 18...... | 1.06:23 | 3.02:08 | 5.07:49 | 7.18:01 | 9.21:46 | 11.15:52 |
|  | 16.35:9 | 45.32:1 | 76.57:3 | 109.30:2 | 140.26:6 | 168.58:0 |
| 19...... | 1.10:07 | 3.06:10 | 5.12:09 | 7.22:18 | 9.25:43 | 11.19:33 |
|  | 17.31:8 | 46.32:5 | 78.02:2 | 110.34:4 | 141.25:7 | 169.53:4 |
| 20...... | 1.13:51 | 3.10:12 | 5.16:29 | 7.26:34 | 9.29:39 | 11.23:15 |
|  | 18.27:8 | 47.33:1 | 79.07:2 | 111.38:4 | 142.44:7 | 170.48:7 |
| 21...... | 1.17:36 | 3.14:16 | 5.20:49 | 7.30:49 | 9.33:34 | 11.26:56 |
|  | 19.24:0 | 48.33:9 | 80.12:3 | 112.42:4 | 143.23:5 | 171.44:0 |
| 22...... | 1.21:21 | 3.18:19 | 5.25:10 | 7.35:05 | 9.37:29 | 11.30:37 |
|  | 20.20:2 | 49.34:8 | 81.17:4 | 113.46:2 | 144.22:2 | 172.39:2 |
| 23...... | 1.25:06 | 3.22:24 | 5.29:30 | 7.39:19 | 9.41:23 | 11.34:18 |
|  | 21.16:6 | 50.36.0 | 82.22:6 | 114.49:8 | 145.20:6 | 173.34:4 |
| 24...... | 1.28:52 | 3.26:29 | 5.33:51 | 7.43:33 | 9.45:16 | 11.37:58 |
|  | 22.13:0 | 51.37:3 | 83.27.8 | 115.53:3 | 146.19:0 | 174.29:6 |
| 25...... | 1.32:38 | 3.30:35 | 5.38:12 | 7.47:47 | 9.49:08 | 11.41:39 |
|  | 23.09:6 | 52.38:8 | 84.33:1 | 116.56:7 | 147.17:1 | 175.24:7 |
| 26...... | 1.36:25 | 3.34:42 | 5.42:34 | 7.51:59 | 9.53:00 | 11.45:19 |
|  | 24.06:3 | 53.40:5 | 85.38:5 | 117.59:9 | 148.15:1 | 176.19:8 |
| 27...... | 1.40:12 | 3.38:49 | 5.46:55 | 7.56:12 | 9.56:52 | 11.48:59 |
|  | 25.03:2 | 54.42:3 | 86.43:8 | 119.02:9 | 149.12:9 | 177.14:5 |
| 28...... | 1.44:00 | 3.42:57 | 5.51:17 | 8.00:32 | 10.00:42 | 11.52:40 |
|  | 26.00:1 | 55.44:4 | 87.29:2 | 120.05:8 | 150.10:6 | 178.09:9 |
| 29...... | 1.47:49 | 3.47:06 | 5.55:38 | 8.04:34 | 10.04:33 | 11.56:20 |
|  | 26.57:2 | 56.46:6 | 88.45:6 | 121.08:5 | 151.08:1 | 179.05:0 |

30 degrees has the same R. A. and S. T. as 0 degrees of the succeeding signs.

## Explanation

The first column on the left designates the degrees of zodiacal signs. On the same line with the zodiacal degree in the six columns, will be found figures of sidereal time. Directly underneath the sidereal time are the figures of corresponding Right Ascension, or Arc, as it is sometimes called. The last figure in the R.A. refers to the tenths of a minute, i.e., 6 seconds of R.A. A planet in 2 degrees of the sign Taurus would have R.A. 29.49:04. When 2 degrees of the sign Taurus are culminating on M.C. the S.T. is 1.59:18.

0 degrees has the same R. A. and S. T. as 30° of the preceding sign.

| Deg. | Libra. | Scorpio. | Sagitt. | Capri. | Aquar. | Pisces. |
|---|---|---|---|---|---|---|
| 0..... | 12.00:00 | 13.51:38 | 15.51:16 | 18.00:00 | 20.08:44 | 22.08:22 |
|  | 180.00:0 | 207.54:5 | 237.48:9 | 270.00:0 | 302.11:1 | 332.05:5 |
| 1..... | 12.03:40 | 13.55:27 | 15.55:26 | 18.04:22 | 20.12:54 | 22.12:11 |
|  | 180.55:0 | 208.51:9 | 238.51:5 | 271.05:4 | 303.13:4 | 333.02:8 |
| 2..... | 12.07:20 | 13.59:18 | 15.59:37 | 18.08:43 | 20.17:03 | 22.16:00 |
|  | 181.50:1 | 209.49:4 | 239.54:2 | 272.10:8 | 304.15:6 | 333.59:9 |
| 3..... | 12.11:01 | 14.03:08 | 16.03:48 | 18.13:05 | 20.21:11 | 22.19:47 |
|  | 182.45:2 | 210.47:1 | 240.47:1 | 273.16:2 | 305.17:7 | 334.56:8 |
| 4..... | 12.14:41 | 14.07:00 | 16.08:00 | 18.17:26 | 20.25:18 | 22.23:35 |
|  | 183.40.2 | 211.44:9 | 242.00:1 | 274.21:5 | 306.19:5 | 335.53:7 |
| 5..... | 12.18:21 | 14.10:52 | 16.12:13 | 18.21:43 | 20.29:25 | 22.27:22 |
|  | 184.35:3 | 212.42:9 | 243.03:3 | 275.26:9 | 307.21:2 | 336.50:4 |
| 6..... | 12.22:02 | 14.14:44 | 16.16:27 | 18.26:09 | 20.33:31 | 22.31:08 |
|  | 185.30:4 | 213.41:0 | 244.06:7 | 276.32:2 | 308.22:7 | 337.47:0 |
| 7..... | 12.25:42 | 14.18:37 | 16.20:41 | 18.30:30 | 20.37:36 | 22.34:54 |
|  | 186.25:6 | 214.39:4 | 245.10:2 | 277.37:4 | 309.24:0 | 338.43:4 |
| 8..... | 12.29:23 | 14.22:31 | 16.24:55 | 18.34:50 | 20.41:41 | 22.38:39 |
|  | 187.20:8 | 215.37:8 | 246.13:8 | 278.42:6 | 310.25:2 | 339.39:8 |
| 9..... | 12.33:04 | 14.26:26 | 16.29:11 | 18.39:11 | 20.45:44 | 22.42:24 |
|  | 188.16:0 | 216.36:5 | 247.17:6 | 279.47:7 | 311.20:1 | 340.36:0 |
| 10..... | 12.36:45 | 14.30:21 | 16.33:26 | 18.43:31 | 20.49:48 | 22.46:09 |
|  | 189.11:3 | 217.35:3 | 248.21:6 | 280.52:8 | 312.26:9 | 341.32:2 |
| 11..... | 12.40:27 | 14.34:17 | 16.37:42 | 18.47:51 | 20.53:50 | 22.49:53 |
|  | 190.06:6 | 218.34:3 | 249.25:6 | 281.57:8 | 313.27:5 | 342.28:2 |
| 12..... | 12.44:08 | 14.38:14 | 16.41:59 | 18.52:11 | 20.57:52 | 22.53:37 |
|  | 191.02:0 | 219.33:4 | 250.29:8 | 283.02:7 | 314.27:9 | 343.24:1 |
| 13..... | 12.47:50 | 14.42:11 | 16.46:16 | 18.56:30 | 21.01:53 | 22.57:20 |
|  | 191.57:5 | 220.32:8 | 251.34:1 | 284.07:5 | 315.28:1 | 344.20:0 |
| 14..... | 12.51:32 | 14.46:09 | 16.50:34 | 19.00:49 | 21.05:53 | 23.01:03 |
|  | 192.53.0 | 221.32:3 | 252.38:5 | 285.12:3 | 316.28:2 | 345.15:7 |
| 15..... | 12.55:14 | 14.50:08 | 16.54:52 | 19.05:08 | 21.09:52 | 23.04:46 |
|  | 193.48:6 | 222.32:0 | 253.43:1 | 286.16:9 | 317.28:0 | 346.11:4 |

Table 21, continued: Table of Right Ascension
and Sidereal Time

| Deg. | Libra. | Scorpio. | Sagitt. | Capri. | Aquar. | Pisces. |
|---|---|---|---|---|---|---|
| 16..... | 12.58:57 | 14.54:07 | 16.59:11 | 19.09:26 | 21.13:51 | 23.08:28 |
|  | 194.44:3 | 223.31:8 | 254.47:7 | 287.21:5 | 318.27:7 | 347.07:0 |
| 17..... | 13.02:40 | 14.58:07 | 17.03:30 | 19.13:44 | 21.17:49 | 23.12:10 |
|  | 195.40:0 | 224.31:9 | 255.52:5 | 288.25:9 | 319.27:2 | 348.02:5 |
| 18..... | 13.06:23 | 15.02:08 | 17.07:49 | 19.18:01 | 21.21:46 | 23.15:52 |
|  | 196.35:9 | 225.32:1 | 256.57:3 | 289.30:2 | 320.26:6 | 348.58:0 |
| 19..... | 13.10:07 | 15.06:10 | 17.12:09 | 19.22:18 | 21.25:43 | 23.19:33 |
|  | 197.31:8 | 226.32:5 | 258.02:2 | 290.34:4 | 321.25:7 | 349.53:4 |
| 20..... | 13.13:51 | 15.10:12 | 17.16:29 | 19.26:34 | 21.29:39 | 23.23:15 |
|  | 198.27:8 | 227.33:1 | 259.07:2 | 291.38:4 | 322.24:7 | 350.48:7 |
| 21..... | 13.17:36 | 15.14:16 | 17.20:49 | 19.30:49 | 21.33:34 | 23.26:56 |
|  | 199.24:0 | 228.33:9 | 260.12:3 | 292.42:4 | 323.23:5 | 351.44:0 |
| 22.. . | 13.21:21 | 15.18:19 | 17.25:10 | 19.35:05 | 21.37:29 | 23.30:37 |
|  | 200.20:2 | 229.34:8 | 261.17:4 | 293.46:2 | 324.22:2 | 352.39:2 |
| 23.... | 13.25:06 | 15.22:24 | 17.29:30 | 19.39:19 | 21.41:23 | 23.34:18 |
|  | 201.16:6 | 230.36:0 | 262.22:6 | 294.49:8 | 325.20:6 | 353.34:4 |
| 24..... | 13.28:52 | 15.26:29 | 17.33:51 | 19.43:33 | 21.45:16 | 23.37:58 |
|  | 202.13:0 | 231.37:3 | 263.27:8 | 295.53:3 | 326.19:0 | 354.29:6 |
| 25..... | 13.32:38 | 15.30:35 | 17.38:13 | 19.47:47 | 21.49:08 | 23.41:39 |
|  | 203.09:6 | 232.38:8 | 264.33:1 | 296.56:7 | 327.17:1 | 355.24:7 |
| 26..... | 13.36:25 | 15.34:42 | 17.42:34 | 19.51:59 | 21.53:00 | 23.45:19 |
|  | 204.06:3 | 233.40:5 | 265.38:5 | 297.59:9 | 328.15:1 | 356.19:8 |
| 27..... | 13.40:13 | 15.38:49 | 17.46:55 | 19.56:12 | 21.56:52 | 23.48:59 |
|  | 205.03:2 | 234.42:3 | 266.43:8 | 299.02:9 | 329.12:9 | 357.14:8 |
| 28..... | 13.44:00 | 15.42:57 | 17.51:17 | 20.00:23 | 22.00:42 | 23.52:40 |
|  | 206.00:1 | 235.44:4 | 267.49:2 | 300.05:8 | 330.10:6 | 358.09:9 |
| 29..... | 13.47:49 | 15.47:06 | 17.55:38 | 20.04:34 | 22.04:33 | 23.56:20 |
|  | 206.57:2 | 236.46:6 | 268.54:6 | 301.08:5 | 331.08:1 | 359.05:0 |
| 30. ... | 13.51:38 | 15.51:16 | 18.00:00 | 20.08:44 | 22.08:22 | 24.00:00 |
|  | 207.54:5 | 237.48:9 | 270.00:0 | 302.11:1 | 332.05:5 | 360.00.0 |

Explanation

The first column on the left designates the degrees of zodiacal signs. On the same line with the zodiacal degree, in the six columns, will be found the figures of sidereal time. Directly underneath the sidereal time are the figures of corresponding Right Ascension, or Arc, as it is sometimes called. The last figure in the R.A. refers to tenths of a minute, i.e., 6 seconds of R.A. A planet in 2° of the sign Scorpio, would have R.A. 209.49:04. When 2° of the sign Scorpio culminate on M.C. the S.T. is 13.59:18.

birth if necessary. The answer will be the time of birth in the afternoon.

**Note.** If the answer is more than 12 hours, subtract 12 from it and the remainder is the time of birth in the morning.

Remember that the time of birth derived from the above method is mean local time, that is, real or Sun time, and not standard or clock time. There is a difference from one to thirty minutes between mean and standard time in the various time zones, as was shown in **Standard Time**, page 69.

**Example Chart 6.**

| | | | | | |
|---|---|---|---|---|---|
| 5 | h | 20 | m | 49 | s | (Rectified ST at birth) |
| − 0 | | 53 | | 10 | | (ST noon birthday) |
| 4 | h | 27 | m | 39 | s | (PM rectified birth time) |

## Supplementary Calculations:

1' of R.A. =   4s of S.T.
5' of R.A. =  20s of S.T.
10' of R.A. = 40s of S.T.
15' of R.A. = 1m  00s of S.T.
20' of R.A. = 1m  20s of S.T.
25' of R.A. = 1m  40s of S.T.
30' of R.A. = 2m  00s of S.T.
35' of R.A. = 2m  20s of S.T.
40' of R.A. = 2m  40s of S.T.
45' of R.A. = 3m  00s of S.T.
50' of R.A. = 3m  20s of S.T.
55' of R.A. = 3m  40s of S.T.
60' of R.A. = 4m  00s of S.T.

**Table 22: Relation of Right Ascension
to Sidereal Time**

The above table is used to interpolate the birth Sidereal Time when more exact work is desired, as shown in the example.

**Example Chart 6.**

80.12:3  (RA from Table 18 = 21° Gemini)
+ 80.07   (Rectified RAM)
5:3  (difference)

21° 00' 00"  (equivalent to 80.12:3 RA)
−       5 18  (equivalent to 5:3 RA difference)
        20° 54' 42"  (exact rectified Midheaven)

21° Gemini = 5h 20m 49s ST from Tables of Houses
5' 18" RA = 20 s of ST from Table 19

5h  20m  49s  (ST from Tables of Houses)
−          20  (equivalent difference)
5h  20m  29s  (exact rectified ST at birth)

5h  20m  29s  (exact rectified ST at birth)
−  0   53   10  (ST noon birthday)
4h  27m  19s  (PM exact rectified birth time)

**Note.** It is very seldom necessary to make such minute adjustments. The example is given so the student will be aware that such precision is possible.


# THE PRE-NATAL EPOCH RECTIFICATION METHOD

The laws pertaining to the pre-natal epoch are based on the observed relationship between the Moon and the Ascendant at birth. Since Ptolemy in the *Tetrabiblos* propounded the ancient doctrine which has become known as The Animodar of the *Tetrabiblos*, the subject has been dealt with by many eminent authors.

Originally its purpose was its use as a means of correcting given birth times; modern exponents apply it for that purpose and also for study of the pre-natal chart. The entire subject is rich in interest and possibilities for research. It is expecially valuable for correcting the horoscope of infants who are as yet too young to have had any striking events by which to rectify the time by the Arc of Event Rectification Method.

To rectify a given birth time by the pre-natal epoch method, make a horoscope for the given birth time, or the final estimate of the birth time, according to the preceding rules. By noting the position of the Moon and Ascendant, the length of the epoch, the Moon's sign and the Ascendant at conception can be determined, according to the following rules:

### Length of Epoch
1. When the Moon at birth is increasing in light and above the horizon the period is less than ten lunar months.
2. When the Moon at birth is decreasing in light and below the horizon the period is less than ten lunar months.
3. When the Moon at birth is increasing in light and below the horizon the period is more than ten lunar months.
4. When the Moon at birth is decreasing in light and above the horizon the period is more than ten lunar months.

## Moon's Sign at Conception
1. When the Moon is increasing at birth, it will be found on the epoch day in the ascending sign at birth.
2. When the Moon is decreasing at birth, it will be found on the epoch day in the sign which is setting at birth.

In other words, that day approximately ten lunar months previous to the birth date on which the Moon transits the exact degree of the natal Ascendant or Descendant is the day of the pre-natal epoch (conception).

## Ascendant at Conception
1. If the Moon is increasing at birth, its natal position will be the Ascendant in the pre-natal chart.
2. If the Moon is decreasing at birth, its natal position will be the Descendant in the pre-natal chart.

## To Find the Conception Date
Count ten lunar months or 273 days backward from the date of birth and note the date on which the Moon is in the sign it held at birth, or the sign opposite, according to the rules. Having found the lunar place, count forward or backward, as the case may require, until you come to the day when the Moon is in the sign ascending or descending at birth, according to the rules. Take that day on which it transits the exact degree on the horizon in the estimate birth chart. This is called the Epoch Day (conception date). In Llewellyn George's day this was referred to as the "Prenatal Epoch."

## To Find the Time of Conception

Ascertain where the mother of the native was residing at the time of conception, and refer to the Tables of Houses for the latitude of that place. In the Tables of Houses bring the Moon's longitude at birth to the Ascendant or Descendant, according to the rules, and note the Sidereal Time in hours, minutes, and seconds. This will be the Sidereal Time at epoch.

From the ephemeris take the ST at noon on the conception date. The difference between the ST at noon, and the ST at epoch will give the correct time before or after noon at which conception occurred. Therefore, subtract the ST at noon from the ST at epoch. If the answer is less than twelve hours, conception occurred after noon; at that time if the answer is more than twelve hours, conception occurred before noon. When the answer is more than twelve hours, subtract twelve from it for the morning time of conception.

Find the Moon's longitude for this derived time of conception, and it will represent the degree to be found on the Ascendant or Descendant at birth, according to the rules.

## To Find the True Time of Birth

When the ascending degree has been found, find that degree ascending in a Tables of Houses for the latitude of birth. Note the ST given for that degree; from it subtract the ST at noon on the birth date. The result will be the time of birth. Should these figures be less than twelve, it is the afternoon time of birth. If the answer is more than twelve, subtract twelve and the remainder is the morning time of birth.

# Astrological Dictionary

# Astrological Dictionary

**Accidental Dignity.** See *Dignity.*

**Affliction.** Unfavorably aspected. A debility. A planet is said to be afflicted when in square, conjunction, opposition, or quincunx to other planets or angular house cusps, or when in any aspect to Mars, Saturn, Uranus, or Pluto. An afflicted planet is said to be *impedited*, or *impeded.*

**Air Signs.** See *Elements.*

**Anareta.** Destroyer. Traditionally the planet which is believed to correspond with the termination of life. Usually an afflicted malefic planet, in conjunction or adverse aspect to the Hyleg.

**Angles.** The four points of the chart dividing it into quadrants. The angles are sensitive areas which lend emphasis to planets situated near them.

*The Ascendant,* eastern horizon, cusp of the First House, or Oriens.
*The Midheaven,* South Vertical, Zenith, cusp of the Tenth House, Meridian, or Medium Coeli (MC).
*The Descendant,* western horizon, cusp of the Seventh House, or Occidens.

*The North Vertical,* cusp of the Fourth House, or Immum Coeli (IC). Popularly called the *Nadir,* with which it sometimes corresponds.

**Angular Houses.** See *Houses.*

**Animoder of Tetrabiblos.** A method of birth time rectification presented by Ptolemy, now obsolete. Sometimes referred to as the *Sunrise Indicator.*

**Antipathy.** Inharmonious relations between planets, which rule or are exalted in opposite signs. Also, conflict between the natal horoscopes of two people corresponding with the aversion they feel for each other.

**Antiscia.** See *Parallel.*

**Aphelion.** See *Elongation.*

**Apheta.** See *Hyleg.*

**Apogee.** That place in a planet's orbit which is farthest from the earth. Opposite of *Perigee.*

**Apparent Motion.** Motion of the planets as seen from the earth, geocentrically measured, as opposed to the actual movement of the planets in their heliocentric, or Sun-centered, orbits.

**Application.** The approach of one planet to another planet, house, cusp, or exact aspect. The faster-moving planet *applies* to the aspect with the slower-moving planet. An applying aspect is considered stronger than a separating aspect. Opposite of *separation.*

**Arabian Parts.** Points which are usually the arithmetic combination of two planets and the Ascendant, sometimes involving eclipses and house cusps. The most commonly used of the Arabian Parts is the *Part of Fortune,* although the other parts provide additional interesting information as well.

**Arc.** Distance measured along a circle. In Astrology this refers to zodiacal longitude.

**Ascendant.** Rising Sign. Cusp of the First House. The Degree of the Zodiac on the eastern horizon at the time and place for which the horoscope is calculated. Each sign takes approximately two hours to rise above the horizon. Opposite of *descendant*.

An *ascending planet*, or *rising planet*, is one which is between 12° above and 20° below the Ascendant. A planet is strengthened by this position. More generally, any planet in the eastern hemisphere, between the Tenth House and Fourth House.

The *ruling planet* is the planet which rules the sign on the Ascendant.

**Ascension.** Due to the obliquity of the ecliptic, signs of long ascension require more time to rise above the horizon than do signs of short ascension.

Signs of *long ascension* in the northern hemisphere: Cancer, Leo, Virgo, Libra, Scorpio, Sagittarius.

Signs of *short ascension* in the northern hemisphere: Capricorn, Aquarius, Pisces, Aries, Taurus, Gemini. These are the signs most often intercepted in a horoscope.

**Aspect.** The angular relationship between planets, sensitive points, or house cusps in the horoscope. Lines drawn between the two points and the center of the chart, representing the earth, form the angle of the aspect, which is equivalent to the number of degrees of arc between the two points. Parallels and conjunctions are also termed aspects, though no angles are formed.

Major aspects: *conjunction*, 0°, a neutral aspect, its effect determined by the natures of the planets involved; *sextile*, 60°, a favorable aspect; *square*, quadrate, quartile, or tetragonous aspect, 90°, an adverse aspect; *trine*, 120°, a favorable aspect; and *opposition*, 180°, a neutral aspect, its effects determined by the natures of the planets involved.

Minor aspects: *semi-sextile*, 30°; *semi-square*, or semi-quadrate, 45°; *sesquiquadrate*, 135°; *quincunx*, inconjunct, disjunct, or quadra-sextile, 150°.

Seldom used aspects: *vigintile*, or semi-decile, 18°; *quindecile*, 24° *decile*, or semi-quintile, 36°; *quintile*, 72°; *tredecile*, 108°; and *bi-quintile*, 144°.

**Asteroid.** Planetoid. Numerous small celestial bodies whose orbits lie between those of Mars and Jupiter. The asteroids are not normally used in Astrology; yet, some attention is being paid to four of them: Ceres, Pallas, Juno, and Vesta. Another asteroid, *Lilith*, is used by some astrologers and its zodiacal longitude is recorded in an ephemeris.

**Astro-twins.** Two people with the same Sun Sign, Moon Sign, and Ascendant.

**Average Daily Motion.** See *Mean Motion*.

**Ayanama.** See *Precession of the Equinoxes*.

**Barren Signs.** See *Fertility*.

**Benefics.** Fortunes. Beneficial planets. Jupiter is traditionally called the *Greater Benefic*, while Venus is considered the *Lesser Benefic*.

**Birth Time.** The exact moment of the first indrawn breath of a baby.

**Cadent Houses.** See *Houses*.

**Celestial Equator.** The extension of the earth's equator out into space, perpendicular to the earth's axis of rotation. Distance measured along the celestial equator, eastward from the point of the Vernal Equinox, is called *Right Ascension* (RA), which corresponds to terrestial longitude. Right Ascension is measured in hours, 24 hours to the circle of 360°, 4 minutes of Right Ascension for each degree of arc.

The distance of a planet north or south of the celestial equator is measured in *Declination*, which corresponds to terrestial latitude. The maximum declination of the Sun is 23° 28' North at 0° Cancer, and 23° 28' South at 0° Capricorn. A planet situated on the celestial equator has no declination.

Measurement along the celestial equator between any point and the meridian (the line perpendicular to the equator passing through the Midheaven and Nadir), is called the *meridian distance,* expressed in hours and minutes.

**Collection of Light.** A planet which is in aspect to two others which are not in themselves in aspect to each other. The *collector of light* acts as an intermediary. Used in Horary Astrology.

**Comets.** Small luminous celestial bodies which circle the Sun on eccentric orbits. Comets often develop long fuzzy tails which point away from the Sun. Traditionally comets presage history-making events. The most famous comet is *Halley's Comet* which appears every 76 years.

**Combust.** Within 8° 30' of zodiacal longitude of the Sun. The nature of the combust planet is combined with that of the Sun; a weakening configuration. Mercury and Venus are the planets most often combust.

*An inferior conjunction* between Mercury or Venus and the Sun occurs when the planet comes between the earth and the Sun.

A *superior conjunction* between Mercury or Venus and the Sun occurs when the planet is on the opposite side of the Sun from the earth.

*Under the Sun's beams* is a traditional term used to indicate a planet that is within 17° of the Sun. Its influence is weakened, but not as much as if combust.

**Composite Chart.** See *Midpoint.*

**Conjunction.** See *Aspect.*

**Constellation.** Asterism. A group of stars named after a figure or pattern it is said to represent. Twelve constellations have the same names, but are no longer located in the same places, as the signs of the Zodiac. This group of twelve constellations is called the *Sidereal Zodiac,* Fixed Zodiac, or the Zodiac of the Constellations.

**Converse Directions.** A system of directions which employs the symbolic reverse motion of the planets, movement contrary to the natural course of the planets.

**Co-significator.** See *Significator.*

**Critical Degrees.** Mansions of the Moon. The subdivision of the Zodiac into 28 parts of 12 and 6/6° each, representing the Moon's average daily motion, beginning with 0° Aries, divided by sensitive points, the critical degrees, in the various signs.

Critical degrees of the cardinal signs, Aries, Cancer, Libra, Capricorn: 0°, 13°, 26°.

Critical degrees of the fixed signs, Taurus, Leo, Scorpio, Aquarius: 9°, 21°.

Critical degrees of the mutable signs, Gemini, Virgo, Sagittarius, Pisces: 4°, 17°.

**Culmination.** The arrival of a planet at the Midheaven, by progression, direction, or transit. Also, the completion of an aspect.

**Cusp.** See *Houses.*

**Cycle.** See *Revolution.*

**Daylight Savings Time.** DST. Summer Time. An artificial adjustment of clock time, one hour ahead. One hour must be subtracted from birth times recorded in Zone Standard when Daylight Savings Time is in effect, before the horoscope can be calculated.

During World War I (3/31–10/27, 1918, and 3/30–10/26, 1919) and World War II (2/9, 1942–9/30, 1945), Daylight Savings Time was in effect and was called *War Time.*

**Debility.** Positions and aspects which waken the nature of the planets. A planet is debilitated when adversely aspected, in a cadent house, or in the sign of its detriment or fall. Opposite of *dignity.*

**Decan.** Decanate. Divisions of each of the signs into three equal segments of 10° each.

**Declination.** See *Celestial Equator.*

**Decreasing in Light.** Waning. Third and Fourth Quarters of the Moon. A planet, particularly the Moon, during the half of its cycle from opposition with the Sun to the next conjunction with the Sun. Opposite of *Increasing in Light.*

**Degree.** Degree of Arc. One of 360 divisions of a circle. The circle of the Zodiac is divided into 12 signs of 30° each. Each degree is made up of 60' (minutes), and each minute is made up of 60" (seconds) of zodiacal longitude.

**Descendant.** Cusp of the Seventh House. The degree of the Zodiac on the western horizon at the time and place for which the horoscope is calculated. Opposite of *Ascendant.*

A *descending planet* is one which is generally between the Tenth House and the Fourth House in the western hemisphere.

**Detriment.** The sign in which a planet is unfavorably placed; the opposite sign of its own sign: The Sun in Aquarius; the Moon in Capricorn; Mercury in Sagittarius and Pisces; Venus in Aries and Scorpio; Mars in Libra and, traditionally, Taurus; Jupiter in Gemini and, traditionally, Virgo; Saturn in Cancer and, traditionally, Leo; Uranus in Leo; Neptune in Virgo; Pluto in Taurus.

**Dexter Aspect.** An aspect in which the faster-moving planet is ahead of, or has greater zodiacal longitude, than the aspected planet. This occurs when the aspecting planet is moving away from the slower-moving planet by direct motion, or toward it by retrograde motion. Also, loosely, a separating aspect. Opposite of *sinister aspect.*

**Dignity.** Positions and aspects which strengthen the nature of the planet. Opposite of *debility.*

*Accidental dignity* refers to the planet's position by house, aspect, or motion. A planet is accidentally dignified when it is near the Midheaven, in an angular house, in its natural house, favorably aspected, swift in motion, direct in motion, or increasing in light. The most important accidental dignity occurs when a planet is near the Ascendant or Midheaven.

*Essential dignity* refers to the planet's position by sign. A planet is essentially dignified when it is in the sign it rules, or in the sign of its exaltation.

*Domal dignity* occurs when a planet is in its own sign.

*Joy* is an obsolete term for a favorable position for a planet, though not technically a position of dignity.

**Direct Motion.** Proper Motion. Proceeding in the order of the signs, from Aries toward Taurus, etc. Denoted in the ephemeris by a "D". Opposite of *retrograde motion*.

**Directions.** The aspects between planets or house cusps in a progressed horoscope and those in the natal horoscope, or between transiting and natal planets or house cusps. Also, loosely, *progressions*.

*Primary directions* are aspects formed in a system of progressions which calculates one degree of forward movement for each of the planets in the natal horoscope, for each year of life.

**Dispositor.** The planet ruling the sign in which another planet is posited. A planet in its own sign has no dispositor. Used in Horary Astrology, and sometimes in progressed work.

**Diurnal.** Belonging to the day. Above the horizon, between the Ascendant and Descendant in the southern hemisphere of the chart. Opposite of *nocturnal*.

*Dirunal arc* refers to the portion of a planet's daily travel in which it is above the horizon. Opposite of *nocturnal arc*.

**Domal Dignity.** See *Dignity, Planetary Rulership*.

**Dragon's Head.** See *Nodes*.

**Dragon's Tail.** See *Nodes*.

**Dwadachamsha.** A subdivision of each sign into twelve equal parts of 2½° each. Used in Hindu Astrology.

**Earth.** Terra. The planet on which we live, represented by the center of the horoscope. The daily axial rotation of the earth from west to east, its diurnal movement, produces the appearance of the Sun, Moon, and planets rising in the east and setting in the west. The earth's annual revolution around the Sun produces the appearance of the Sun transiting through the signs. The earth appears to be in the opposite sign of the Sun.

The *terrestial equator* is a belt around the earth, halfway between the north and south poles.

*Geographical longitude* is a measurement east or west along the earth's equator beginning with the prime meridian at Greenwich, England, designated 0°, and proceeding east and west to 180° on the opposite side of the earth. Lines of longitude form circles perpendicular to the equator.

*Geographical latitude* is a measurement north or south of the earth's equator beginning with the equator itself which is designated 0°, and proceeding north and south to 90°. Lines of latitude form circles parallel with the equator.

**Earth Signs.** See *Elements.*

**Eclipse.** A phenomenon that involves the Sun, Moon, and the earth or occasionally other planets. There are usually two to six eclipses a year. The sign and degree of an eclipse is important, particularly in Mundane Astrology.

A *solar eclipse* is produced by the Moon passing between the Sun and the earth, cutting off the light of the Sun. This occurs when a New Moon, the conjunction of the Sun and Moon, takes place near a lunar node.

A *lunar eclipse* is produced by the earth passing between the Sun and Moon, casting its shadow on the Moon. This occurs when a Full Moon, the opposition of the Sun and Moon, takes place near a lunar node.

An *occultation* is an eclipse of a planet by the Moon.

*Immersion* is the beginning of an eclipse or occultation. *Emersion* is the ending when the planet comes out from under the Sun's rays.

**Ecliptic.** Via Solis. The Sun's apparent path around the earth, which is in actuality the earth's orbit extended out into space. So named because it is the path along which eclipses occur. The ecliptic forms the center of the Zodiac.

The *obliquity of the ecliptic* is the angle between the plane of the ecliptic and the plane of the celestial equator which varies according to the season.

**Electional Astrology.** The branch of Astrology dealing with the selection of an auspicious time for a particular purpose. Sometimes considered a branch of Horary Astrology.

**Elements.** Triplicities. Trigons. Four groups of three signs each symbolized by the four elements of the ancients: Fire, Earth, Air, Water.

*Fire Signs* are active and enthusiastic: Aries, Leo, Sagittarius.

*Earth Signs* are practical and cautious: Taurus, Virgo, Capricorn.

*Air Signs* are intellectual and sociable: Gemini, Libra, Aquarius.

*Water Signs* are emotional and sensitive: Cancer, Scorpio, Pisces.

**Elevation.** Altitude. The distance of a planet above the horizon. The most elevated position in a horoscope is at the cusp of the Tenth House. The higher the elevation, the more powerful the planet.

**Elongation.** The distance of a planet from the Sun, as viewed from the earth. The maximum elongation of the inferior planets is 28° for Mercury, and 48° for Venus. Mercury can therefore only form a conjunction and semi-sextile to the Sun; while Venus can only form a conjunction, semi-sextile, or semi-square to the Sun.

*Aphelion* is the maximum elongation of a planet; the point in its orbit in which it is farthest from the Sun.

*Perihelion* is the minimum elongation of a planet; the point in its orbit in which it is closest to the Sun.

**Ephemeris.** A listing of the Sun, Moon, and planets' places and related information for astrological purposes.

**Equator.** See *Celestial Equator, Earth.*

**Equinox.** Equal night. The point in the earth's orbit around the Sun at which the day and night are equal in length.

The *Vernal Equinox* occurs annually around March 21, when the

Sun enters Aries, and marks the beginning of the Zodiac. The ecliptic crosses the equator from south to north at the Vernal Equinox.

The *Autumnal Equinox* occurs annually around September 21, when the Sun enters Libra. The ecliptic crosses the equator from north to south at the Autumnal Equinox.

**Essential Dignity.** See *Dignity*.

**Esoteric Astrology.** Spiritual Astrology. The branch of Astrology dealing with the spiritual nature of the individual.

**Exaltation.** A sign in which a planet is favorably posited: The Sun in Aries; the Moon in Taurus; Mercury in Virgo; Venus in Pisces; Mars in Capricorn; Jupiter in Cancer; Saturn in Libra; Uranus in Scorpio; Neptune in Cancer; and Pluto in Pisces. Opposite of *fall*.

**Excitation.** The influence of a transiting planetary aspect bringing into effect a progressed aspect of similar nature.

**Extra-Saturnian Planets.** Modern Planets. Outer Planets. The three planets not visible to the naked eye, which lie outside the orbit of Saturn, and were discovered in recent times: Uranus, discovered in 1781; Neptune, discovered in 1846; Pluto, discovered in 1930.

Each of the extra-Saturnian planets is considered to be a *higher octave* of another planet: Uranus is a higher octave of Mercury; Neptune is a higher octave of Venus; Pluto is a higher octave of Mars.

**Face.** Divisions of each of the signs into six equal segments of 5° each. Not used by modern Astrologers.

**Fall.** The sign in which a planet is unfavorably placed; the sign opposite of its exaltation: The Sun in Libra; the Moon in Scorpio; Mercury in Pisces; Venus in Virgo; Mars in Cancer; Jupiter in Capricorn; Saturn in Aries; Uranus in Taurus; Neptune in Capricorn; Pluto in Virgo.

**Familiarity.** Any kind of aspect or reception between the planets.

**Fertile Signs.** See *Fertility*.

**Fertility**. Classification of sign according to productivity.

*Fertile* or fruitful signs: Cancer, Scorpio, Pisces. The fertile signs are good for planting when occupied by the Moon, and are indicators of offspring when occupying the cusps of the Fifth or Eleventh Houses.

*Semi-fruitful,* or moderately fruitful signs: Taurus, Libra, Capricorn.

*Barren* or sterile signs: Aries, Gemini, Leo, Virgo, Sagittarius, Aquarius. The barren signs are good for cultivation when occupied by the Moon, and are indicators of not having children when occupying the cusps of the Fifth or Eleventh Houses.

**Fire Signs**. See *Elements.*

**Fixed Signs**. See *Modes.*

**Fixed Stars**. The visible, seemingly immovable, stars as opposed to the Sun, Moon, and planets which are traditionally called the wandering stars. The fixed stars do not have a slight but measurable motion. Major visible stars in the northern himisphere are sometimes taken into account in astrological work.

**Focal Point**. A planet or aspect formation which is of primary importance within a horoscope.

**Fortunes**. Beneficial planets. Jupiter and Venus are always called the fortunes. The Sun and Moon, if favorably placed and aspected are also considered fortunate. Mercury and Neptune, being neutral, are fortunate when favorably placed and in favorable aspect to Venus or Jupiter.

**Frustration**. A term used in Horary Astrology when one planet is applying to an aspect of another, but before the aspect culminates, a third planet, by its swifter motion, interposes by completing an aspect of its own, thus deflecting the influence of the slower-moving planet.

**Genethliacal Astrology**. Natal Astrology. The branch of Astrology dealing with the individual. The horoscope cast for the birth time of the individual, showing his life potential, is called a *Natal Horoscope,* geniture, radix, or nativity. The individual under consideration is called the *native*.

**Geocentric.** Earth centerd.

**Great Circle.** Any circle, the plane of which passes through the center of the earth, such as the celestial equator, the meridian, the ecliptic, and the lines of terrestial longitude.

**Greenwich Mean Time.** GMT. Universal Time. The time at the prime meridian of 0° longitude. The standard for navigation, astronomy, international communications, and Astrology. Ephemerides are usually calculated for either noon or midnight Greenwich Mean Time.

**Heavy Planets.** The slower-moving planets whose influence is considered more serious than the other planets: Jupiter, Saturn, Uranus, Neptune, Pluto.

**Heliocentric.** Sun-centered.

**Hemisphere.** Half-circle. The division of the celestial vault into halves by the horizon and prime vertical. Also, the division of the horoscope into overlapping halves:

The *eastern hemisphere* from the Midheaven through the Ascendant to the IC; the Tenth through Third Houses.

The *northern hemisphere* from the Ascendant through the IC to the descendant; the First through Sixth Houses.

The *western hemisphere* from the IC through the descendant to the Midheaven; the Fourth through Ninth Houses.

The *southern hemisphere* from the descendant through the Midheaven to the Ascendant; the Seventh through Twelfth Houses.

**Horary Astrology.** The branch of Astrology in which a chart is calculated for the time a question is asked in order to ascertain the answer to that question.

**Horizon.** The circle which separates the visible and invisible world. The *rational* or *true horizon* is the great circle which surrounds the observer passing through the cardinal points. The poles of the rational horizon are defined by the Zenith overhead and the Nadir directly underneath the observer. A line between the Zenith and the Nadir would be perpendicular to the plane of the rational horizon.

The *celestial horizon* is the rational horizon extended infinitely out into space. The intersection of the eastern horizon and the ecliptic determines the Ascendant. This is the eastern point of the chart. The intersection of the western horizon and the ecliptic determines the descendant at the west point of the chart.

The *visible* or *apparent horizon* is the small amount of earth visible with the naked eye. It is parallel to the rational horizon.

**Horoscope.** Map. Chart. Figure. A diagram of the positions of the planets, including the Sun and Moon, calculated for a specific time and place.

A *natural chart* is a horoscope with Aries on the Ascendant and no intersected signs.

A *solar chart* is a horoscope in which the planets positions are calculated for noon Greenwich (taken from a noon ephemeris) but with the Sun's longitude on the Ascendant. Used when the birth time is unknown.

**Houses.** Mundane Houses. Division of the horoscope into twelve segments beginning with the Ascendant. The dividing line between the houses are called *house cusps*. Each house corresponds to certain aspects of daily living or earthly affairs. The houses are divided into three groups:

*Angular houses* are the strongest houses, corresponding to the cardinal signs: First, Fourth, Seventh, and Tenth Houses.

*Succedent Houses* are neutral houses, corresponding to the fixed signs: Second, Fifth, Eighth, and Eleventh Houses.

*Cadent houses* are the weakest houses, corresponding to the mutable signs: Third, Sixth, Ninth, and Twelfth Houses.

Houses above the horizon in the horoscope, the Seventh through Twelfth Houses are called the *day houses*. The First House through the Sixth House, below the horizon, are called the *night houses*.

**Hyleg.** Giver of Life. Particular zones in the horoscope concerned with longevity: 5° above to 25° below the Ascendant; 5° below to 25° above the descendant; 5° below the Ninth House cusp to 25° past the Eleventh House cusp. A planet that is hyleg is called the *Apheta* or the *Prorogator*.

**Immum Coeli.** I.C. Bottom of the Heavens. Cusp of the Fourth House. The lowest point on the ecliptic at which it intersects the meridian below the horizon. The northern point of the horoscope. Opposite the Midheaven. Also, loosely called the *Nadir*, which is opposite the Zenith.

**Increasing in Light.** Waxing. First and Second Quarters of the Moon. A planet, particularly the Moon, during the half of its cycle from conjunction to opposition with the Sun. Opposite of *decreasing in light*.

**Inferior Conjunction.** See *Combust*.

**Inferior Planets.** Those whose orbits are between the earth and the Sun: Mercury and Venus.

**Infortunes.** Malefic Planets. Mars, Saturn, and Uranus are always called the infortunes. Mercury and Neptune, being neutral, are infortunate when afflicted by position or aspect. Pluto is sometimes considered an infortunate planet.

**Ingress.** The entrance of any planet into any sign. Also, loosely applied to the Sun's entrance into the four cardinal signs at the solstices and equinoxes.

**Inner Planets.** The swifter-moving planets most active in the horoscope: Sun, Moon, Mercury, Venus, Mars.

**Intercepted.** A sign which is contained wholly within a house; it does not appear on any house cusp. Intercepted signs appear only in horoscopes; there are never any interecepted signs in the Zodiac.

In the northern hemisphere the signs most often intercepted are those of short ascension: Capricorn, Aquarius, Pisces, Aries, Taurus, Gemini. Intercepted signs appear more frequently in extreme north or south latitudes, and less frequently near the equator.

**Latitude.** See *Zodiac, Earth.*

**Lights.** See *Luminaries.*

**Lilith.** See *Asteroids.*

**Local Time.** Sun Time. True Local Time. Solar Time. The actual time at a location within a time zone, adjusted to compensate for the standardization of time throughout the zone. Noon local time is always when the Sun transits the meridian of that place.

**Logarithms.** Proportional logarithms. Tables of representational numbers which simplify the processes of multiplication and division into addition and subtraction. Used in horoscope calculation.

**Longitude.** See *Zodiac, Earth.*

**Luminaries.** Lights. The Sun and Moon, as distinguished from the planets. The Sun is the *Greater Light,* or *Greater Luminary;* the Moon is the *Lesser Light,* or *Lesser Luminary.*

**Lunar Phase.** The Moon's cycle from New Moon to New Moon is divided into four phases, each lasting about seven days.
*First Quarter.* From the conjunction (New Moon) to the square of the Sun and Moon. During the first half of this phase, when the Moon is between 0° and 45° ahead of the Sun, it is called the *Crescent Moon.* A waxing phase.
*Second Quarter.* From the square to the opposition (Full Moon) of the Sun and Moon. During the second half of this phase, when the Moon is between 135° and 180° ahead of the Sun, it is called the *Gibbous Moon.* A waxing phase.
*Third Quarter.* From the opposition (Full Moon) to the square of the Sun and Moon. During the last half of this phase, when the Moon is between 135° and 90° behind the Sun, the Moon is called the *Disseminating Moon.* A waning phase.
*Fourth Quarter.* From the square to the conjunction (New Moon)

of the Sun and Moon. During the last half of this phase, when the Moon is between 45° and 0° behind the Sun, the Moon is called the *Balsamic Moon*. A waning phase.

**Lunation.** Lunar period. New Moon. Synodical Lunation. The period from one New Moon, the conjunction of the Sun and Moon, until the next New Moon; 29 days, 12 hours, 44 minutes. Also, a chart drawn up for the time of the New Moon, used in Mundane Astrology. Also, loosely, the occurrence of the New Moon itself.

*Neomenium* is a traditional term for the New Moon, especially near the Vernal Equinox.

An *embolismic lunation* occurs each month when the Moon and Sun are in the same angular relationship, or lunar phase, as they were in the natal horoscope. The embolismic lunation coincides with a woman's fertile period and is the basis of astrological birth control.

**Malefics.** Evil planets. Saturn is traditionally called the *Greater Malefic*, while Mars is considered the *Lesser Malefic*.

**Mansions of the Moon.** See *Critical Degrees*.

**Matutine.** Stars or planets which rise before the Sun in the morning, particularly the Moon (Fourth Quarter), Mercury or Venus (oriental) when they appear in the morning. Opposite of *vespertine*.

**Mean Motion.** Average Daily Motion. Rate of Motion. The average motion of any planet during a 24-hour period: The Sun, 59' 08"; the Moon, 13° 10' 36"; Mercury, 1° 23'; Venus, 1° 12'; Mars, 33' 28"; Jupiter, 4' 59"; Saturn, 2' 01"; Uranus, 42"; Neptune, 24"; Pluto, 15". When traveling less than the average daily motion, a planet is *slow in motion*, or *slow in course;* when traveling more, it is *swift in motion.*

When a planet is moving faster than on the day previous, it is *increasing in motion*; when moving slower, it is *decreasing in motion*.

**Mean Time.** Mean Solar Time. Civil Time. The average day of 24 hours as measured by our clocks. Due to the uneven rotation of the earth, the day from noon to noon is slightly unequal depending on the season. Mean time refers to the agreed-upon average in standard use.

**Meridian.** The North-South Great Circle. A great circle which passes through the south point of the horizon, through the Zenith directly overhead, and through the north point of the horizon, and under the earth, through the Nadir. The Sun crosses the meridian at midday. The meridian corresponds to geographical longitude, and is at right angles to the prime vertical. Every point on earth has its own meridian. Also, in a horoscope, the line from the IC (see *Nadir*) to the Midheaven.

**Meridian Distance.** See *Celestial Equator.*

**Metonic Cycle.** A cycle of 19 years at the end of which the conjunctions of the Sun and Moon (New Moons) begin to occur successively in the same places in the Zodiac as during the previous cycle.

**Midheaven.** Medium Coeli. MC. Middle of the Heavens. Meridian. Cusp of the Tenth House. The highest point on the ecliptic at which it intersects the meridian which passes directly overhead of the place for which the horoscope is cast. The southern point of the horoscope. Opposite the *Immum Coeli.*

**Midnight Mark.** The mean local time at any place that is equivalent to midnight, Greenwich, England.

**Midpoint.** Half-sum. A point equally distant to two planets or house cusps. In the horoscope there are actually two midpoints for each pair of planets: one on the shorter arc, usually used in Astrology, and one on the longer arc, its opposite.
    A *composite chart* is a chart using the midpoints between pairs of planets in two or more natal horoscopes, interpreted as an indication of the relationship between the people involved.

**Modes.** Quadruplicities. Qualities. Three groups of four signs, one of each element.
    *Cardinal Signs* are active and powerful: Aries, Cancer Libra, Capricorn.
    *Fixed Signs* are organized and resistant to change: Taurus, Leo,

Scorpio, Aquarius.
*Mutable or Common Signs* are adaptable and resourceful: Gemini, Virgo, Sagittarius, Pisces.

**Mundane Astrology**. Political Astrology. Judicial Astrology. State Astrology. The branch of Astrology dealing with affairs of the world and collective activities of people.

**Mundane Parallel.** See *Parallel.*

**Mutable Signs**. See *Modes.*

**Mutual Reception**. See *Reception.*

**Nadir**. A point opposite the Zenith. Often incorrectly applied to the Immum Coeli. The IC, being on the ecliptic, is the point opposite the Midheaven.

**Natal Astrology**. See *Genethliacal Astrology.*

**Nativity**. See *Genethliacal Astrology.*

**Navamsas**. A subdivision of each sign into nine equal parts of 3 1/3° each. Used in Hindu Astrology.

**Nocturnal**. Belonging to the night. Below the horizon, between the descendant and Ascendant in the northern hemisphere of the chart. Opposite of *diurnal.*
*Nocturnal arc* refers to the portion of a planet's daily travel in which it is below the horizon. Opposite of *diurnal arc.*

**Nodes**. The points at which the orbit of the Moon or other planet crosses the ecliptic. The Sun has no nodes and its orbit defines the ecliptic. The planets' nodes change very slightly in a century. The Moon's nodes, however, retrograde along the ecliptic about 3' per day. The *ascending node* or north node occurs when the planet passes through the ecliptic from south to north latitude. The *descending node* occurs when the latidude changes from north to south.

*Dragon's Head.* Caput Draconis. Moon's North Node. The point at which the orbit of the Moon crosses the ecliptic from south to north latitude. A beneficial point. Opposite of the Dragon's Tail.

*Dragon's Tail.* Cauda Draconis. Moon's South Node. The point opposite the Moon's North Node. An unfavorable point.

**Nonagesimal.** The point 90° from the ascending point; the highest point on the ecliptic above the horizon.

**Noon Mark.** The mean local time at any place that is equivalent to noon at Greenwich, England.

**Occidental.** Western. A planet which rises and sets after the Sun. Also, the western hemisphere of the chart, from the Tenth House cusp through the descendant to the Fourth House cusp. Opposite of *oriental.*

Mercury is occidental during its *Epimethean Cycle* beginning with its superior conjunction with the Sun, moving direct until its maximum distance from the Sun, 28°, then moving retrograde until it reaches its inferior conjunction with the Sun.

Venus is occidental when it is *hesperus*, the *Evening Star*, beginning with its superior conjunction with the Sun, moving direct until its maximum distance from the Sun, 48°, then moving retrograde until it reaches its inferior conjunction with the Sun.

**Occultation.** See *Eclipse.*

**Opposition.** See *Aspect.*

**Orb.** The range of zodiacal longitude within which the influence of a planet or aspect operates, varying in size according to the specific planet and aspect. An aspect which is exact, has no orb, is called an exact aspect, or *partile aspect*. It has the strongest influence. An aspect which is not exact, yet still within the orb of influence, is called a wide aspect, or *platic aspect*. Its influence is weakened.

**Oriental.** Eastern. A planet which rises and sets before the Sun. Also, the eastern hemisphere of the chart, from the Fourth House cusp through the Ascendant to the Tenth House Cusp. Opposite of *occidental.*

Mercury is oriental during its *Promethean Cycle* beginning with its inferior conjunction with the Sun, moving retrograde until its maximum distance from the Sun, 28°, then moving direct until it reaches its superior conjunction with the Sun.

Venus is oriental when it is *Lucifer*, the *Morning Star*, beginning with its inferior conjunction with the Sun, moving retrograde until its maximum distance from the Sun, 48°, then moving direct until it reaches its superior conjunction with the Sun.

**Parallel**. Two planets which are equally distant from the celestial equator, having the same declination, either both north or both south, or one north and the other south. Similar in meaning to a conjunction.

A *mundane parallel* occurs when two planets are equally distant from any angle in the horoscope. The planets are then *antiscia*.

A *rapt parallel* occurs when two planets are equally distant from the meridian, at the point of the Midheaven.

**Part of Fortune**. Pars Fortuna. A point which is equally distant from the Ascendant as the Moon is from the Sun in longitude. An indicator of the lunar phase. The Part of Fortune is found by adding the longitude of the Moon to the longitude of the Ascendant and subtracting from the sum the longitude of the Sun. A mildly favorable point. The only commonly used of the many Arabian Parts.

If the Part of Fortune is conjunct the Ascendant, the native was born under a New Moon; if the Part of Fortune is conjunct the IC, the Moon was just beginning the Second Quarter. If the Part of Fortune is opposite the Ascendant, the native was born under the Full Moon; if the Part of Fortune is conjunct the Midheaven, the Moon was just beginning the Fourth Quarter.

**Perigee**. The place in a planet's orbit which is closest to the earth. Opposite of *Apogee*.

**Perigrine**. Foreign. The position of a planet in a sign in which it is neither dignified nor debilitated. No planet is peregrine if it is in mutual reception with another. Used in Horary Astrology.

**Perihelion**. See *Elongation*.

**Planet.** In Astrology this commonly refers to the Sun, the star at the center of our Solar System, the Moon, the earth's satellite, and the eight planets excluding the earth: Sun, Moon, Mercury, Venus, Mars, Jupiter, Saturn, Uranus, Neptune, Pluto.

**Planetary Hours.** A system in which the various hours of the day are ruled by the seven visible planets, beginning at sunrise with the planet which rules that day of the week: Sunday, the Sun; Monday, the Moon; Tuesday, Mars; Wednesday, Mercury; Thursday, Jupiter; Friday, Venus; Saturday, Saturn. The time between sunrise and sunset is divided into twelve equal segments. Since these times vary with the season, the length of a "planetary hour" is different from that of a normal hour.

**Planetary Rulership.** The sign in which a planet is most harmoniously placed: The Sun in Leo; the Moon in Cancer; Mercury in Gemini and Virgo; Venus in Taurus and Libra; Mars in Aries and, traditionally, Scorpio; Jupiter in Sagittarius and, traditionally, Pisces; Saturn in Capricorn and, traditionally, Aquarius; Uranus in Aquarius; Neptune in Pisces; and Pluto in Scorpio.

**Planetoid.** See *Asteroid*.

**Polarity.** The division of the signs and planets into positive, masculine, creative, dry, yang and its opposite, negative, feminine, receptive, moist, yin.

The *positive signs* are the fire and air signs: Aries, Gemini, Leo, Libra, Sagittarius, Aquarius. The *positive planets* are: The Sun, Mars, Jupiter, Saturn, Uranus, and Pluto.

The *negative signs* are the earth and water signs: Taurus, Cancer, Virgo, Scorpio, Capricorn, Pisces. The *negative planets* are: The Moon, Venus. Mercury and Neptune are *neutral* or *convertible planets* positive or negative depending on whether they are located in positive or negative signs.

*Gender emphasis* refers to the predominance of masculine or feminine elements in the horoscope.

**Political Astrology.** See *Mundane Astrology*.

**Ponderous Planets.** See *Superior Planets.*

**Precession of the Equinoxes.** The gradual movement of the Vernal Equinox Point, 0° Aries, which marks the beginning of the Tropical Zodiac, backward in relation to the constellations which define the Sidereal Zodiac, at the rate of approximately 50" per year, or one sign every 2,150 years, determining the *Astrological Ages*, or the *Great Months.*

The Equinox Point regressed into Pisces at the birth of Christ, the beginning of the Age of Pisces. The *Age of Aquarius* would then begin around 2150 AD.

The gap between the Tropical Zodiac and the Sidereal Zodiac is called the *Ayanamsa*, and was approximately 24° 25' in 1975.

**Prenatal Epoch.** The astrological moment of conception, about nine months before birth, but not necessarily coinciding with the actual time of biological conception. Used in rectification work.

**Primary Directions.** See *Directions.*

**Prime Vertical.** The East-West Great Circle. A great circle which passes through the east point of the horizon, through the Zenith overhead, through the west point of the horizon, and under the earth through the Nadir. It is perpendicular to the meridian.

**Progressions.** The symbolic movement of the planets after birth representing the future of the native. Usually refers to *Secondary Progressions.*

Secondary Progressions is the most popular system of progressions in which each day after birth represents the corresponding year in the life of the native.

**Promittor.** Promissor. A planet or configuration which signifies certain events. Used in Horary Astrology.

**Prorogator.** See *Hyleg.*

**Proper Motion.** See *Direct Motion.*

**Quadrants.** The four quarters of the chart. Also the four seasons of the year.

**Quadrature.** The Moon's dichotomes: changes, phases, or quarters. Also, a square aspect to the Sun, as occurs when the Moon is at the beginning of the Second Quarter or the beginning of the Fourth Quarter.

**Quadruplicities.** See *Modes*.

**Qualities.** See *Modes*.

**Rapt Motion.** The apparent diurnal motion of the Zodiac and planets from east to west caused by the earth's rotation in the opposite direction.

**Rate of Motion.** See *Mean Motion*.

**Reception.** A planet is received by the dispositor of the sign it occupies. Also, a planet receives an aspect by a faster-moving planet.
*Mutual reception* occurs when two planets occupy each other's signs, or more loosely, the signs of each other's exaltation.

**Rectification.** The process of correcting the given birth time by reference to known events or characteristics pertaining to the native.

**Refrantation.** A situation in which one of two planets applying to an aspect turns retrograde before the aspect is complete. The retrograde planet is said to *refrain*, signifying that the effect indicated by the approaching aspect will not materialize. Used in Horary Astrology.

**Relocation Chart.** Locality Chart. A horoscope cast for a change of residence by putting the natal positions of the planets into houses calculated for the new location.

**Retrograde Motion.** Apparent backward motion of a planet in the reverse order of the signs, from Aries toward Pisces, etc. Denoted in the ephemeris by a "R " Retrograde motion is an illusion caused by the relative motion of the earth and the other planets in their elliptical orbits. The Sun and Moon are never retrograde. Opposite of *direct motion.*

Mercury has a 20 - 24 day retrograde period; Venus, 40 - 43 day; Mars, 58 - 81 day; Jupiter, 120 day; Saturn, 140 day; Uranus, 155 day; Neptune, 157 day; Pluto, 160 day.

**Revolution.** Return. The return of the Sun, Moon or another planet to its natal place. Also, a chart erected for such an event. Used in progressed work. Also, loosely, any orbit or movement describing a circle.

The revolutions of the planets are measured in time taken to circle the Zodiac: the Sun, 1 year; the Moon, 28 days; Mercury, 1 year; Venus, 1 year; Mars, 2 years; Jupiter, 12 years; Saturn, 28 - 30 years; Uranus, 84 years; Neptune, 165 years; Pluto, 250 years.

**Right Ascension.** See *Celestial Equator.*

**Rising Sign.** See *Ascendant.*

**Ruling Planet.** See *Ascendant, Significator.*

**Satellite.** A planet or moon which revolves around another. The Moon is a satellite of the earth. Mercury and Venus have no moons; Mars has 2 moons; Jupiter has 12 moons; Saturn has 9 moons; Uranus has 5 moons; Neptune has 2 moons.

**Satellitium.** Stellium. A cluster or group of three or more planets in one sign or house. Often the focal point of the horoscope.

**Secondary Progressions.** See *Progressions.*

**Separation.** The movement of a planet away from another planet, house cusp or exact aspect. The faster-moving planet *separates* from the aspect with the slower-moving planet and is called the *separator.* A separating aspect is considered weaker than an applying aspect. In Horary Astrology a separating aspect corresponds to events just past. It is the opposite of *application* where a faster-moving planet *applies* to the aspect with a slower-moving planet. See also *application.*

Sextile. See *Aspect.*

Sidereal Time. Time based on the interval between two successive transits of 0° Aries over the upper meridian. One *Sidereal Day* equals 23 hours 56 minutes 4.09 seconds; which is divided into 24 sidereal hours of 60 sidereal minutes each. Sidereal time for noon or midnight for each day is given in the ephemeris and is four minutes later than the previous day.

Sidereal Zodiac. See *Constellations.*

Significator. Ruling Planet. Lord. The planet which rules the Ascendant. Also, the planet which rules the horoscope, section of a horoscope, mundane event, area of life, or question in Horary Astrology. Also, the planet which rules a sign.

The *co-significator,* or *co-ruler,* is a secondary or equal significator of a horoscope, section of a horoscope, mundane event, or area of life. Also, the traditional rulers of the signs now ruled by the extra-Saturnian planets: Mars is co-ruler of Scorpio together with Pluto; Jupiter is co-ruler of Pisces together with Neptune; Saturn is co-ruler of Aquarius together with Uranus.

Signs. The twelve 30° divisions of the Zodiac, beginning with the position of the Sun at the Vernal Equinox around March 21, 0° Aries: Aries, Taurus, Gemini, Cancer, Leo, Virgo, Libra, Scorpio, Sagittarius, Capricorn, Aquarius, Pisces.

Singleton. A planet standing alone in a quadrant or hemisphere or the horoscope. A singleton planet often acts as the focal point of the chart.

Sinister Aspect. An aspect in which the faster-moving planet is behind, or has lesser zodiacal longitude than, the aspected planet. This occurs when the aspecting planet is moving toward the slower-moving planet in direct motion, or moving away from it in retrograde motion. Also, loosely, an applying aspect. Opposite of a *dexter aspect.*

Solar System. The Sun with the group of celestial bodies which revolve around it. This group comprises nine planets, attended by 31 satellites, about 1200 asteroids which revolve in an orbit between that of Mars and Jupiter, and also comets and meteors. In order of increasing distance from the Sun: Mercury, Venus, the Earth and Moon, Mars and 2 moons, asteroids, Jupiter and 12 moons, Saturn and 9 moons, Uranus and 5 moons, Neptune and 2 moons, and Pluto.

**Solar Time.** See *Local Time.*

**Solstice.** Standing Still. The point in the earth's orbit around the Sun in which the ecliptic reaches its maximum obliquity.

The *Summer Solstice* occurs annually around June 22, when the Sun enters Cancer at 23½° N declination, highest overhead in the northern hemisphere. The longest day of the year.

The *Winter Solstice* occurs annually around December 22, when the Sun enters Capricorn at 23½° S declination, its lowest point in the northern hemisphere. The shortest day of the year.

**Speculum.** A table appended to a horoscope, containing the principal data concerning the horoscope, such as longitude, latitude, declination, right ascension, meridian distance, semi-arc and ascensional difference of the planets. Used in Primary Directions.

A *speculum of aspects* is a table made to show every degree in a horoscope that may be in aspect to the natal planetary positions. Used in transit work.

**Square.** See *Aspect.*

**Standard Time.** Clock Time. Zone Time. Agreed upon clock time consistent through the time zone. The *Standard Time Zones* are areas comprising 15° geographical longitude, 1 hour apart.

**Stationary.** A period in which a planet appears to be motionless just before turning retrograde or direct in motion. When the planet is in its *station.* The Sun and Moon are never stationary.

Mercury is stationary for 1 day before and after its retrograde periods; Venus for 2 days; Mars for 3 days; Jupiter for 5 days; Saturn for 5 days; Uranus for 6 days; Neptune for 7 days; Pluto for 7 days.

**Stellium.** See *Satellitium.*

**Succedent Houses.** See *Houses.*

**Sun Sign.** The sign of the Zodiac in which the Sun is located at any given time. The Sun Sign can be determined by knowing the day of the year, and is the basis for popular or newspaper Astrology.

**Superior Conjunction.** See *Combust.*

**Superior Planets.** Ponderous Planets. Those whose orbits are on the other side of the earth from the Sun: Mars, Jupiter, Saturn, Uranus, Neptune, and Pluto.

**Synastry.** The process of comparing two or more horoscopes interpreted in reference to the relationship between the people involved.

**Synodic.** The period between two successive conjunctions of two planets.

**Synodical Lunation.** See *Lunation.*

**Synthesis.** The art of combining the various and often contradictory influences seen in the horoscope. In order to give a balanced interpretation of the whole chart.

**Szygy.** Yoking Together. Three planets in a straight line, such as occurs between the Sun, Moon, and earth during the New Moon and Full Moon. Also, loosely, conjunctions and oppositions.

**Tables of Houses.** Tables giving the signs and degree for the cusps of houses in a horoscope appropriate to the latitude of birth, according to the Sidereal Time of Birth.

**Tables of Diurnal Planetary Motion.** Tables which give the distance a planet travels in a given period of time with reference to its daily motion.

**Tenancy.** The location of a planet in a sign or house.

**Terms.** Traditional subdivisions of the signs into five sections ruled by different planets, now largely in disuse.

**Testimony.** Indications seen in a horoscope. The synthesis of several testimonies or arguments constitutes a *judgment*.

**Transit.** The ephemeral, or on-going movement of the planets. The movement of a planet over or in aspect to a sensitive point, planet or house cusp in a horoscope.

**Translation of Light.** A situation in which one planet, separating but still within orb of aspect to another planet, applies to an aspect to a third planet, forming a chain in which the influence of the first aspected planet is passed on to the third planet.

**Trine.** See *Aspect*.

**Triplicity.** See *Elements*.

**Unknown Planets.** Hypothetical Planets. Eight symbolic indicators in Uranian Astrology: Cupido, Hades, Zeus, Kronos, Appolon, Admetos, Vulkanus, and Poseidon. Also, possible actual undiscovered planets, some of which have been hypothesized as Trans-Pluto, Persephone, Lilith, Vulcan and Arcturus or Psyche.

**Vespertine.** Stars or planets which set in the evening after the Sun, particularly the Moon (Third Quarter), Mercury or Venus (occidental) when they appear in the evening. Opposite of *matutine*.

**Void of Course.** A situation in which a planet will form no more major aspects before leaving the sign in which it is tenanted. Most often applied to the Moon in Horary Astrology.

**War Time.** See *Daylight Savings Time*.

**Water Signs.** See *Elements*.

**Zenith**. The point directly overhead. A line from any place to its Zenith would always be perpendicular to the plane of its horizon. Often incorrectly applied to the Midheaven. The Midheaven, being on the ecliptic, is south of the Zenith in the northern hemisphere. Opposite of *Nadir*.

**Zodiac**. Tropical Zodiac. Moving Zodiac. Circle of Animals. The circle or band following the path of the ecliptic, extending about 9° on either side of it. Distance along the Zodiac is measured in terms of *zodiacal longitude,* divided into 12 signs of 30° each beginning with the Vernal Equinox point at 0° Aries.

Distance perpendicular to the center of the Zodiac, the ecliptic, is measured in terms of *ecliptical* or *celestial latitude,* in degrees north or south of the ecliptic. The Sun has no latitude as its path defines the ecliptic.

# Index

in the signs, 268-270
progressed aspects of, 507
transits of, 520-521

Progressed Horoscope, (see Horoscope, progressed)

Progressions,
interpretation, 482
introduction, 435, 449

Quadratures, 32-33, 57

Quincunx, (see also Aspects, minor, 63

Quindecile, (see Aspects, minor)

Quintile, (see Aspects, minor)

Rectifications chart, (see Horoscope, estimate)

Retrograde motion, 72-74

Rising sign, (see Ascendant)

Ruling planets, (see Planetary Rulers)

Sagittarius,
ascending, 192-193
description, 31, 175-177

Saturn,
description, 37, 44, 212-214
dignified and debilitated, 54
in the houses, 275, 280, 283,

287-288, 291, 295-296, 300,
303, 307, 312-313, 316, 320
in the signs, 255-258
natal aspects of, 356-357
progressed aspects of, 503-505
transits of, 519

Scorpio,
ascending, 191-192
description, 31-32, 172-174

Second House,
description, 58
planets in, 278-281
ruler of, 363-365

Semi-sextile, (see Aspects, minor)

Semi-square, (see Aspects, minor)

Septile, (see Aspects, minor)

Sesqui-quadrate, (see Aspects, minor)

Seventh House, (Descendant)
description, 59
planets in, 298-301
ruler of, 371-72

Sextile, (see Aspects, minor)

Sidereal time, 68-69
how to find, 77-85

Significator, 54-55

## STAY IN TOUCH

On the following pages you will find listed, with their current prices, some of the books now available on related subjects. Your book dealer stocks most of these and will stock new titles in the Llewellyn series as they become available. We urge your patronage.

To obtain our full catalog, to keep informed about new titles as they are released and to benefit from informative articles and helpful news, you are invited to write for our bimonthly news magazine/catalog, *Llewellyn's New Worlds of Mind and Spirit*. A sample copy is free, and it will continue coming to you at no cost as long as you are an active mail customer. Or you may subscribe for just $10.00 in the U.S.A. and Canada ($20.00 overseas, first class mail). Many bookstores also have *New Worlds* available to their customers. Ask for it.

Stay in touch! In *New Worlds'* pages you will find news and features about new books, tapes and services, announcements of meetings and seminars, articles helpful to our readers, news of authors, products and services, special money-making opportunities, and much more.

*Llewellyn's New Worlds of Mind and Spirit*
**P.O. Box 64383-264, St. Paul, MN 55164-0383, U.S.A.**
* * *

## TO ORDER BOOKS AND TAPES

If your book dealer does not have the books described on the following pages readily available, you may order them directly from the publisher by sending full price in U.S. funds, plus $3.00 for postage and handling for orders *under* $10.00; $4.00 for orders *over* $10.00. There are no postage and handling charges for orders over $50.00. Postage and handling rates are subject to change. UPS Delivery: We ship UPS whenever possible. Delivery guaranteed. Provide your street address as UPS does not deliver to P.O. Boxes. Allow 4-6 weeks for delivery. UPS to Canada requires a $50.00 minimum order. Orders outside the U.S.A. and Canada: Airmail—add retail price of book; add $5.00 for each non-book item (tapes, etc.); add $1.00 per item for surface mail.

## FOR GROUP STUDY AND PURCHASE

Because there is a great deal of interest in group discussion and study of the subject matter of this book, we feel that we should encourage the adoption and use of this particular book by such groups by offering a special quantity price to group leaders or agents.

Our special quantity price for a minimum order of five copies of *The Book of Ogham* is $38.85 cash-with-order. This price includes postage and handling within the United States. Minnesota residents must add 6.5% sales tax. For additional quantities, please order in multiples of five. For Canadian and foreign orders, add postage and handling charges as above. Credit card (VISA, MasterCard, American Express) orders are accepted. Charge card orders only ($15.00 minimum order) may be phoned in free within the U.S.A. or Canada by dialing 1-800-THE-MOON. For customer service, call 1-612-291-1970. Mail orders to:

**LLEWELLYN PUBLICATIONS**
**P.O. Box 64383-264, St. Paul, MN 55164-0383, U.S.A.**

Prices subject to change without notice.

# THE LLEWELLYN ANNUALS

**Llewellyn's MOON SIGN BOOK:** Approximately 400 pages of valuable information on gardening, fishing, weather, stock market forecasts, personal horoscopes, good planting dates, and general instructions for finding the best date to do just about anything! Articles by prominent forecasters and writers in the fields of gardening, astrology, politics, economics and cycles. This special almanac, different from any other, has been published annually since 1906. It's fun, informative and has been a great help to millions in their daily planning. **State year $4.95**

**Llewellyn's SUN SIGN BOOK:** Your personal horoscope for the entire year! All 12 signs are included in one handy book. Also included are forecasts, special feature articles, and an action guide for each sign. Monthly horoscopes are written by Gloria Star, author of *Optimum Child*, for your personal Sun Sign and there are articles on a variety of subjects written by well-known astrologers from around the country. Much more than just a horoscope guide! Entertaining and fun the year around. **State year $4.95**

**Llewellyn's DAILY PLANETARY GUIDE:** Includes all of the major daily aspects plus their exact times in Eastern and Pacific time zones, lunar phases, signs and voids plus their times, planetary motion, a monthly ephemeris, sunrise and sunset tables, special articles on the planets, signs, aspects, a business guide, planetary hours, rulerships, and much more. Large 5-1/4 x 8 format for more writing space, spiral bound to lay flat, address and phone listings, time-zone conversion chart and blank horoscope chart. **State year $6.95**

**Llewellyn's ASTROLOGICAL CALENDAR:** Large wall calendar of 48 pages. Beautiful full-color cover and full-color paintings inside. Includes special feature articles by famous astrologers, and complete introductory information on astrology. It also contains a Lunar Gardening Guide, celestial phenomena, a blank horoscope chart, and monthly date pages which include aspects, Moon phases, signs and voids, planetary motion, an ephemeris, personal forecasts, lucky dates, planting and fishing dates, and more. 10 x 13 size. Set in Eastern time, with fold-down conversion table for other time zones worldwide. **State year $10.00**

**Llewellyn's MAGICAL ALMANAC:** This beautifully illustrated almanac explores traditional earth religions and folklore while focusing on magical myths. Each month is summarized in a two-page format with information that includes the phases of the moon, festivals and rites for the month, as well as detailed magical advice. This is an indispensable guide is for anyone who is interested in planning rituals, spells and other magical advice. It features writing by some of the most prominent authors in the field. **State year $6.95**

## HOW TO USE VOCATIONAL ASTROLOGY FOR SUCCESS IN THE WORKPLACE
**edited by Noel Tyl**

Announcing the most practical examination of Vocational Astrology in five decades! Improve your astrological skills with these revolutionary NEW tools for vocational and business analysis! Not since the work of Charles Luntz in 1942 has the subject of Vocational Astrology been so thoroughly explored. Now, in *How to Use Vocational Astrology for Success in the Workplace,* **edited by Noel Tyl,** seven respected astrologers provide their well-seasoned modern views on that great issue of personal life—work. Their expert advice will prepare you well for those tricky questions clients often ask: "Am I in the right job?" "Will I get promoted?" or "When is the best time to make a career move?"

With an introduction by Noel Tyl in which he discusses the startling research of the Gauquelins, this ninth volume in Llewellyn's New World Astrology Series features enlightening counsel from the following experts:

- **Jayj Jacobs:** The Transits of Experience/Career Cycles, Job Changes and Rewards
- **Gina Ceaglio:** Money Patterns in the Horoscope
- **Donna Cunningham:** Attitudes and Aptitudes in the Chart
- **Anthony Louis:** Void-of-Course Moon Strategies for Doing Business, Retrograde Planets, and Electional Astrology
- **Noel Tyl:** Special Measurements for Vocational Guidance, and How to Evaluate Personnel for Profit
- **Henry Weingarten:** 12 Principles of Modern Astro-Vocational Guidance, Planetary Rulership and Career Guidance, and The 21st Century Astrologer
- **Bob Mulligan:** How to Advance *Your Own* Career as a Professional Astrologer!

Read *How to Use Vocational Astrology* today, and add "Vocational Counselor" to *your* resume tomorrow! Includes the complete 1942 classic by Charles E. Luntz *Vocational Guidance by Astrology.*

**0-87542-387-6, 384 pgs., 6 x 9, illus., softcover**      **$14.95**

## YOUR PLANETARY PERSONALITY
### Everything You Need to Make Sense of Your Horoscope
### by Dennis Oakland

This book deepens the study of astrological interpretation for professional and beginning astrologers alike. Dennis Oakland's interpretations of the planets in the houses and signs are the result of years of study of psychology, sciences, symbolism, Eastern philosophy plus the study of birth charts from a psychotherapy group. Unlike the interpretations in other books, these emphasize the life processes involved and facilitate a greater understanding of the chart. Includes 100-year ephemeris.

Even if you now know *nothing* about astrology, Dennis Oakland's clear instructions will teach you how to construct a complete and accurate birth chart for anyone born between 1900 to 1999. After you have built your chart, he will lead you through the steps of reading it, giving you in-depth interpretations of each of your planets. When done, you will have the satisfaction that comes from increased self-awareness *and* from being your *own* astrologer!

This book is also an excellent exploration for psychologists and psychiatrists who use astrology in their practices.

**0-87542-594-1, 580 pgs., 7 x 10, softcover** $19.95

## HOW TO PERSONALIZE THE OUTER PLANETS
### The Astrology of Uranus, Neptune & Pluto
### Edited by Noel Tyl

Since their discoveries, the three outer planets have been symbols of the modern era. Representing great social change on a global scale, they also take us as individuals to higher levels of consciousness and new possibilities of experience. Explored individually, each outer planet offers tremendous promise for growth. But when taken as a group, as they are in *Personalizing the Outer Planets*, the potential exists to recognize *accelerated* development.

As never done before, the seven prominent astrologers in *Personalizing the Outer Planets* bring these revolutionary forces down to earth in practical ways.

- Jeff Jawer: Learn how the discoveries of the outer planets rocked the world
- Noel Tyl: Project into the future with outer planet Solar Arcs
- Jeff Green: See how the outer planets are tied to personal trauma
- Jeff Jawer: Give perspective to your inner spirit through outer planet symbolisms
- Jayj Jacobs: Explore interpersonal relationships and sex through the outer planets
- Mary E. Shea: Make the right choices using outer planet transits
- Joanne Wickenburg: Realize your unconscious drives and urges through the outer planets
- Capel N. McCutcheon: Personalize the incredible archetypal significance of outer planet aspects

**0-87542-389-2, 288 pgs., 6 x 9, illus., softcover** $12.00

## PREDICTION IN ASTROLOGY
### A Master Volume of Technique and Practice
### by Noel Tyl

No matter how much you know about astrology already, no matter how much experience you've had to date, you'll be fascinated by *Prediction in Astrology*, and you'll grow as an astrologer. Using the Solar Arc theory and methods he describes in this book, the author was able to accurately predict the Gulf War, including the actual date it would begin and the timetable of tactics, two months *before* it began. He also predicted the overturning of Communist rule in the Eastern bloc nations nine months in advance of its actual occurrence.

Tyl teaches through example. You learn by doing astrology, not just thinking about it. Tyl introduces Solar Arc theory in terms of "rapport" measurements, which you begin to do immediately, without paper, pencil, or computer, dials, or wheels. Just with your eyes! You will never look at a horoscope the same way again!

Tyl, in his well-known, very special way, also gets personal. He presents 30 Aphorisms, the keenest of maxims, the most practical of techniques, to create predictions from any horoscope. And as if this were not enough, Tyl then presents 20 Aphorisms for Counseling. Look for Tyl's "Quick-Glance" Transit Table, 1940-2040, to which you can refer more quickly than a computer. The busy astrologer will use this Appendix every day for many years to come.

**0-87542-814-2, 360 pgs., 6 x 9, softcover**                                    **$14.95**

## HEAVEN KNOWS WHAT
### by Grant Lewi

What better way to begin the study of astrology than to actually do it while you learn. *Heaven Knows What* contains everything you need to cast and interpret complete natal charts without memorizing any symbols, without confusing calculations, and without previous experience or training. The tear-out horoscope blanks and special "aspect wheel" make it amazingly easy.

The author explains the influence of every natal Sun and Moon combination, and describes the effects of every major planetary aspect in language designed for the modern reader. His readable and witty interpretations are so relevant that even long-practicing astrologers gain new psychological insight into the characteristics of the signs and meanings of the aspects.

Grant Lewi is sometimes called the father of "do-it-yourself" astrology, and is considered by many to have been astrology's forerunner to the computer.

**0-87542-444-9, 372 pgs., 6 x 9, tables, charts, softcover**                **$12.95**

**NAVIGATING BY THE STARS**
Astrology and the Art of Decision-Making
by Edith Hathaway
This book is chock full of convenient shortcuts to mapping out one's life. It presents the decision-maker's astrology, with the full range of astrological techniques.

No other one source presents all these cutting edge methods: Uranian astrology, the 90° dial, astro-mapping, Saturn quarters, hard aspects, angular relationships, the Meridian House System, secondary progressions, solar arc directions, eclipses, solstice and equinox charts, transiting lunation cycles, monthly kinetic mundascope graphs, among others.

To illustrate the immediate applications of the techniques, the author examines many charts in depth, focussing on study of character, destiny, timing cycles, and geographical location. She draws form 45 wide-ranging personal stories, including famous figures from history, politics, show business, the annals of crime, even corporations.
0-87542-366-3, 320 pgs., 6 x 9, softcover                                   $14.95

**PLANETS**
The Astrological Tools
Edited by Joan McEvers
This is the second in the astrological anthology series edited by respected astrologer Joan McEvers, who provides a brief factual overview of the planets. Then take off through the solar system with 10 professional astrologers as they bring their insights to the symbolism and influences of the planets.

- Toni Glover Sedgwick: The Sun as the life force and our ego
- Joanne Wickenburg: The Moon as our emotional signal to change
- Erin Sullivan-Seale: Mercury as the multifaceted god, followed with and in-depth explanation of its retrogradation
- Robert Glasscock: Venus as your inner value system and relationships
- Johanna Mitchell: Mars as your cooperative, energizing inner warrior
- Don Borkowski: Jupiter as expansion and preservation
- Gina Ceaglio: Saturn as a source of freedom through self-discipline
- Bil Tierney: Uranus as the original, growth-producing planet
- Karma Welch: Neptune as selfless giving and compassionate love
- Joan Negus: Pluto as a powerful personal force
0-87542-381-7, 384 pgs., 5-1/4 x 8, softcover                               $12.95

## ASTROLOGY FOR THE MILLIONS
**by Grant Lewi**
First published in 1940, this practical, do-it-yourself textbook has become a classic guide to computing accurate horoscopes quickly. Throughout the years, it has been improved upon since Grant Lewi's death by his astrological proteges and Llewellyn's expert editors. Grant Lewi is astrology's forerunner to the computer, a man who literally brought astrology to everyone. This, the first new edition since 1979, presents updated transits and new, user-friendly tables to the year 2050, including a new sun ephemeris of revolutionary simplicity. It's actually easier to use than a computer! Also added is new information on Pluto and rising signs, and a new foreword by Carl Llewellyn Weschcke and introduction by J. Gordon Melton.
**0-87542-438-4, 408 pgs., 6 x9, charts, softcover, $12.95**

## ASTROLOGICAL COUNSELING
**The Path to Self-Actualization**
**Edited by Joan McEvers**
This book explores the challenges for today's counselors and gives guidance to those interested in seeking an astrological counselor to help them win their own personal challenges. Includes articles by 10 well-known astrologers:
- David Pond: Astrological Counseling
- Maritha Pottenger: Potent, Personal Astrological Counseling
- Bill Herbst: Astrology and Psychotherapy: A Comparison for Astrologers
- Gray Keen: Plato Sat on a Rock
- Ginger Chalford, Ph.D.: Healing Wounded Spirits: An Astrological Counseling Guide to Releasing Life Issues
- Donald L. Weston, Ph.D.: Astrology and Therapy/Counseling
- Susan Dearborn Jackson: Reading the Body, Reading the Chart
- Doris A. Hebel: Business Counseling
- Donna Cunningham: The Adult Child Syndrome, Codependency, and Their Implications for Astrologers
- Eileen Nauman: Medical Astrology Counseling

**0-87542-385-X, 304 pgs., 5 1/4 x 8, charts, softcover       $14.95**